BEAU BRUMMELL

Also by Ian Kelly

Cooking For Kings:
The Life of Antonin Carême – The First Celebrity Chef

BEAU BRUMMELL

The Ultimate dandy

IAN KELLY

HODDER

First published in Great Britain in 2005 by Hodder and Stoughton
A division of Hodder Headline

The right of Ian Kelly to be identified as the Author of the Work
has been asserted by him in accordance with the Copyright,
Designs and Patents Act 1988.

A Hodder paperback

1

A CIP catalogue record for this title is available from the British Library

ISBN 0 340 83699 7

Typeset in Sabon by Hewer Text UK Ltd, Edinburgh
Printed and bound by Clays Ltd, St Ives plc

Hodder Headline's policy is to use papers that are natural, renewable
and recyclable products and made from wood grown in sustainable forests.
The logging and manufacturing processes are expected to conform to the
environmental regulations of the country of origin.

Hodder and Stoughton Ltd
A division of Hodder Headline
338 Euston Road
London NW1 3BH

For Oscar

Much more than the cult of the individual, Romanticism inaugurated the cult of the personality.

Albert Camus

Contents

Author's Note

The name Brummell exists with two widely recognised spellings: with one l and two. Because Brummell's first French biographer in the 1840s used a single l, this has been the form generally adopted in France and often in America. George Brummell himself, however, signed his name with two ls, and it is also the spelling in his baptismal record and is used therefore throughout this book. Spellings have generally been standardised. The Duke of Argyll, for instance, appears as 'Argyle' and even 'Argylle' in the writings of Harriette Wilson among others, but is 'Argyll' in this text. Similarly, the various marquesses known to Brummell are given their English spelling, 'marquess', rather than 'marquis', even though several used the French style in the early nineteenth century irrespective of the spelling used at the creation of their titles. It has also seemed least confusing to use the title by which a character was first known to Brummell, rather than any subsequently inherited.

Money conversions over time are notoriously unreliable. It is traditional to gain a working equivalent of an 1800 sum in the early twenty-first century by multiplying by between sixty and eighty. Brummell's £30,000 fortune on coming of age in 1799 may thus be calculated as equivalent to between £1.8 million and £2.4 million today. This calculation bears no relation – as instances – to house prices, staff wages or common foodstuffs, but can hold for some luxury goods. Brummell's house on Chesterfield Street recently went on the market at nearly £2 million, which would have eaten all Brummell's money by the usual calculation, but he *was* paying about a sixtieth of the current value of a Savile Row suit for his bespoke outfits. Meanwhile, Brummell's wealth is set against a period of economic boom-and-bust, periods of inflation and fluctuating exchange rates. An important undertow of Brummell's story is the effect of the French Revolution and the Napoleonic Wars on Anglo-French exchange rates, and the economic self-confidence of the burgeoning British Empire, which found a visual expression in one exportable art-form: men's fashion. At the same time Brummell's ability to support himself in France on a fraction of his London capital was predicated on the strength of the pound against a French currency shaken by the Revolution and the Napoleonic Wars.

The chapter-heading illustrations are taken from *Necklothitania*, or *Tietania, by One of the Cloth* and H. Le Blanc's *The Art of the Cravat*. Both guides were inspired by the dandy craze and by Brummell. The original explanations are given in an Appendix (see pages 561–66).

Prologue

Nothing was lacking. Lustres, candelabra, candles, masses of
flowers; and Brummell himself, in the blaze of all the lights,
stood in the centre, expectant.

Brummell's last soirée, Count d'Aurevilly

Room twenty-nine was at the top of the Hôtel d'Angleterre,
overlooking the slate roof-tops of Caen. Georgiana, Duchess of
Devonshire, *en route* to Paris with her daughter, was the first
guest to admire the view, and within minutes room twenty-nine
was pressed with Monsieur Brummell's other friends: the poet
Byron, the old playwright Sheridan, the Duke of Wellington and
Prince Frederick, Duke of York with Princess Frederica of Prussia.

Fichet, the French hotelier's son, was used to the metropolitan
glamour that still clung to the hotel's famous resident: it fell to
Fichet to attend Monsieur Brummell when he was holding one of
his soirées. Brummell had taught him how to announce royalty
and how much obeisance was expected by the victor of Waterloo;
and Monsieur Brummell had taught Fichet about clothes. It was
Fichet, also, who acted as valet to the hotel's celebrated dandy-
wit, helping him into his evening coat and handing him the
whitest of cravats with the reverance of a sacristan.

When it came, it came suddenly. One moment, Brummell held
out his arm to escort the Duchess of Devonshire across the room,
the next, his eyes were opened to the reality around him. The room
was empty. There was nothing in front of him but the candles, the
mirrors and the young Frenchman with pity in his eyes. Fichet
eventually became inured, he said, to the dark pantomime of
announcing Brummell's ghosts: the long-dead duchesses and

courtesans, the Regency celebrities who had been Monsieur's friends. But he dreaded the moment when Brummell woke from his masquerade and saw the reality around him; the ruination of his fame and fortune, and of his mind. 'Babylon in all its desolation,' as one friend of Brummell's said, 'was a sight less awful.'

The Frenchman would then blow out the candles, shut the windows and leave Beau Brummell – once the most sociable man in London – to the complete privacy, and the utter silence of his ruined mind.

~

June 1944. When the Allies took Caen after D-day landings, they entered a silent city. The ancient capital of Calvados and the stronghold of the 12th and 21st German Panzer Divisions had suffered a month of bombardment by British and Canadian heavy artillery and 2500 tons of RAF bombs. The eighteenth-century heart of the Île St Jean – the area leading up to the German HQ in the château – was destroyed. Canadian tanks ploughed straight from the pontoon-bridge over the river Orne and right through the ruins of the old town. 'Andy's Alley' – as the tank road to the château became known – flattened whatever had been left standing in its path: houses, shops, cafés and hotels.

Caen had been the jewel of the Normandy coast; a city built on a river island, with two royal abbeys and a wealth of bourgeois townhouses in honey-coloured stone. Its many English visitors said it reminded them of Oxford. Andy's Alley cut through Caen's destroyed centre, across the rue des Carmes, past the ruins of the Salon Littéraire and straight through the dining room of the bombed-out Hôtel d'Angleterre. Until then, in the hundred years since Beau Brummell had lived there, the hotel had hardly changed. An American soldier took a photograph of the building, blown open to the winds, which was later sold as a postcard souvenir to the GIs. As the tanks rolled by under three storeys of flayed hotel rooms, the wallpaper of room twenty-nine flapped in the breeze.

Most of the French population had left weeks before, when news had reached them of the landings on the Normandy beaches, and were sheltering on the outskirts of the city in an eighteenth-century asylum. The blind, deaf and confused who lived in the Hôpital du Bon Sauveur joined the city refugees in digging up the asylum's flower-beds as graves for Caen's war dead. Stray bombs fell as they worked, destroying some of the pavilions where insane gentlefolk had been incarcerated a century before. But the asylum, and its detailed archives of the mentally ill, miraculously survived.

INTRODUCTION: DANDI, DANDO, DANDUM

If John Bull turns around to look after you, you are not well dressed; but either too stiff, too tight, or too fashionable.

George Bryan (Beau) Brummell

Once it had decided to attach a blue plaque to the house in Mayfair where Beau Brummell once lived, the Greater London Council met a quandary over how to describe him. Londoners deemed worthy of this accolade have usually achieved fame through works or deeds: writers, scientists, soldiers and politicians. Although Brummell's name remained well known, the only accolade attached to it was considered also to be an insult: *dandy*.

In the end, the GLC committee opted for 'Leader of Fashion', though 'Leader of the Fashionable' might have been more precise, or simply 'Celebrity' – a word Brummell used and understood almost in its modern sense. 'Dandy', however, might have served them well. Beau Brummell was a dandy in several of the meanings of this most slippery of words. His contemporaries had also struggled to describe him. At school he was known as 'Buck'. But the soubriquet that stuck for George Bryan Brummell was 'Beau', the name he kept, used, and has been known by ever since.

Though George Brummell was a dandy, he would not have been pleased to be recognised as such in the sense the word is used today. For Brummell the aphorism that 'less is more' might have been invented. He was a disciplinarian – even an ascetic – in his sense of pared-down style. He never sought to be noticed in a crowd at any distance. He used almost exclusively three colours in his wardrobe: white, buff and blue-black, and wished to be recognised only by the simple perfection of what he wore by those who might note such details up close. His style, once created, he stuck to. This in itself could be said to have been a stance against fashion as currently understood. He was – to the modern mind – an anti-dandy. But the word 'dandy', like Brummell himself, has attracted many meanings over the years, and even within Brummell's own lifetime was a term used as compliment, insult, sexual slur or braggadocio. Dandies, like Brummell, are fascinating because they defy easy definition.

'Dandy', as used today, dates from the late eighteenth or early nineteenth century. The term has shifted in meaning from then till now, as words do. But notably the coinage of a word shifts when it has the power to fascinate as well as to insult. 'Dandy' has always had that power. The word first appeared on the Scottish borders as a mild insult at the end of the seventeenth century. As early as the 1770s the term resonated slightly differently in the revolutionary setting of North America in a rallying song, 'Yankee Doodle Dandy' – a dandy defined first by his fashion *faux-pas*:

> Yankee Doodle came to town
> Riding on a pony
> Stuck a feather in his hat
> And called it Macaroni!

Although remembered today as a folksy American anthem, the song was composed by the British troops – many of them Londoners – to poke fun at the American colonists and their 'variegated, ill-fitting and incomplete' uniforms. The British soldiers thought they were better dressed. The Macaroni style they sang about referred to a new, urbane and affected style in London, inspired by French and Italian fashions – the sort of metropolitan chic to which the colonists might never aspire. The London Macaronis, sometimes known as dandies, headed a craze that didn't last long. Nothing kills a fashion faster than ridicule, especially a fashion among men. The red high-heeled shoes, coloured wigs and make-up of the Macaronis, as worn by the youthful Charles James Fox, had the power to shock but not to endear or endure. The Macaronis soon disappeared, but one idea of the dandy remained: an urban peacock. 'Dandy', when used to describe the Macaronis, was quite near its current meaning as a term for a somewhat overdressed man.

The song 'Doodle Dandy' meanwhile, like the colonies, was lost by the British to the Americans, who took over the tune but rewrote the lyrics:

> Yankee Doodle keep it up,
> Yankee Doodle Dandy,
> Mind the music and the step
> And with the girls be handy.

'Dandy' shifted straight away in meaning to stand for approbation and approval, with overtones here of military style and heterosexual swagger, 'with the girls be handy'. 'Dandy' was a style that could also assert the wearer's manliness. Dandies flaunted themselves, which was always attractive to some. Dandies challenged the orthodoxy that put women, and their fashions, in the sphere of useless show, and men, and their clothes, in that of sober utility, and this radicalism was also potentially sexually attractive. The revolutionary songsters, having stolen the song, continued with their argument:

> And there was Captain Washington
> And gentlefolks about him,
> They say he's grown so tarnal proud
> He will not ride without 'em.

The first president was taking on kingly airs, had 'got him on his meeting clothes' and even had 'flaming ribbons in his hat'. He rode, separate from his troops, 'upon a slapping stallion', surrounded by gentlefolk. The meaning of 'dandy' was shifting yet again.

'Dandy', therefore, is introduced into the language in 'Yankee Doodle' – a song for men – with the three meanings it has carried since. First, it is used to ridicule provincialism and lack of strength, as revealed in clothes: Yankee Doodle Dandy has only a pony and thinks a feather in his hat turns him into a man-about-town. Then the idea is expanded to approve of dandies 'keeping it up' with the girls, and finally the idea of the dandy is used to mock the overdressed Washington; as a way to ridicule, but this time to ridicule the exclusive pretensions of an envied member of an upper class. 'Dandy' can be levied as compliment and insult to all the many vanities of men. Dandies are Macaronis, sexual adventurers, soldiers, chinless wonders, or all these things. Brummell's life described these various qualities also; to some he was Don Juan, to others a fop. He was briefly a soldier and always a poseur. Brummell himself saw one of the perennial shifts in the meaning of the word, from the positive to a term of derision. He was initially happy to be described as a dandy, just as he was to be called 'Buck' at school, and 'Beau' as a young man. But the dandy craze that followed in his wake, in London, then Paris and beyond, grew in his lifetime to such ridiculous proportions – men so tightly collared that they could not see their feet – that Brummell sought to distance himself from the term. His dandyism, moreover, invoked more than clothes: it was a way of being.

~

'Leader of Fashion' was, then, maybe not so poor a compromise for the Greater London Council. Brummell was a catalyst and a role model in a fashion revolution with an impact on the way we dress to this day. He was at the centre of what fashion historians have termed 'The Great Masculine Renunciation' when men turned their backs on highly decorative dress and took to nuances of cut, fit and proportion – in keeping with a revolutionary and neo-classical age, to express status, strength and sensitivity. From Brummell's time on, 'gentlemen would communicate with one another through the subtleties of tailoring, in a language that would seem not merely foreign but totally incomprehensible to those who were not gentlemen'. They would also, largely, wear blue, black and white. To put modern man into white shirt, clean linen, trousers and dark jacket might have been sufficient, as one recent writer remarked, to secure Brummell's fame, and his rules of dress have dominated male power-dressing ever since. Without Brummell there would be no suit, for men or, indeed, women, or tailoring in the Savile Row, Wall Street or, some have argued, in the Chanel sense. Modern fashion has one of its founding fathers in Brummell. The tailored look that has developed out of his style, however, he created in an unorthodox way – it has even been said in a very British way: he was a maverick who created rules. Where those rules, colours and ideas came from is one story in Brummell's life: the collage of Eton colours, military cloth, Hussar trousers, neo-classical aesthetics and the sexually flamboyant West End. It is a public story but also a very personal one. In this sense Brummell reveals himself to be in spirit an artist: his person attracted ideas and developing truths without his necessarily understanding or controlling them. He became a symbol for a new mode of urbane masculinity, while it was precisely his masculinity that was possibly the most complex, troubled and compelling aspect of his personality.

Brummell – the man and the name – has been a lodestar for paradoxes even before his defenders and detractors added layers of confusion. Even within his own lifetime, Brummell's name attracted stories and ideas that related more to his fame or notoriety than to the truth. It was commonly believed that he had brought the censure of the prince regent on his head by lounging on an ottoman in Carlton House and demanding of his royal host, 'Wales! Ring the bell!' It never happened. Brummell's attempts to deny the story were in vain. Like a modern celebrity, his image – the insouciant, audacious, stylish brat – had a power of its own that battled hopelessly with truth. He did not have a different tailor for each digit of his gloves, as some suggested, or wear fur coats to the opera, but the dandy craze took on its own

Gothic proportions after Brummell's demise and his name became a logo for a movement he no longer controlled.

One might have thought that there was scale enough in his elegant profligacy to render exaggeration obsolete. He did take hours to dress. He did change his linen with a regularity that shocked contemporaries, though it might not us. He did squander more money in a single night than most of his countrymen would earn in a lifetime. He did ask the prince regent's companion, 'Who's your fat friend?' and did declaim languorously when asked if he ate vegetables that he believed he 'may once have eaten a pea'. Like Oscar Wilde, who was celebrated enough to tour America long before he had had a single West End success, Brummell was renowned as a metropolitan wit before his personal style was copied by Londoners, Parisians and thence by urbane men the world over. His is also a story of fame, impure and simple, before it is an exploration of fashion.

Only partially did Brummell understand his celebrity. It was a new and an alarming construct in Regency London, a city with a hungry, irreverent press and a new leisured class opening a public discourse on how to spend their money. Even had he wished to marshal his fame to any higher good, there were personal tragedies – addiction and disease – that eclipsed Brummell's fame and his position, as Dr Johnson put it, as the 'arbiter elegantarium – the judge of propriety' in dress and manners. Brummell's was a rake's progress in the Hogarthian style, and many contemporaries saw in his decline into poverty and madness the necessary third act to youthful excess. We may judge less harshly today but his life unavoidably describes a tragic parabola that might make his end seem inevitable. Of course it was not.

Brummell's father probably saw a political career for his second son. His schoolfriends thought he would do well. One London season it looked as if he would marry an heiress. Some said he should have been a writer. What Brummell actually did, as Virginia Woolf once said, was perhaps less important than what he stood for, and came to stand for.

His life spans a transformation in fashion, but also in British society and in the history of London, and a crucial period in the making of modern manners and masculinity. The tragic arc of his life took him through a wide spectrum of society, not exactly coming from nowhere but certainly plumbing the depths as well as scratching the top-lights of existence. But he came to symbolise a new attitude in response to urban existence. He was indifferent to politics, above the vagaries of fashion, sought only to be envied and to make people laugh, and accrued around his person a cult based on his perceived personality. He was a celebrity in the first age when such a term was used. He has been cited as one of the models for Byron's *Don Juan*, not so much because he was sexually predatory – he was not – but rather because of his emotional detachment, his archness and a personal attractiveness cruelly mixed with misanthropy. His relationship to *Don Juan*'s and to Byron's style was also, notably, his wit. He had a stage-honed ear for comic cadence and the well-placed line. Brummell learned this at school, as a regular theatregoer and, quite possibly, as a participant at the family dining-table with his parents' theatrical associates, Richard Brinsley Sheridan and Thomas Harris. Contemporaries inevitably struggled to define and de-scribe the joy of an encounter with Brummell: the humour of a moment, the twinkle of manner that only occasionally married itself with verbal wit as fits the page. Nevertheless, they knew instinctively that this was the key to Brummell's personal allure, his appeal and power. In a self-doubting but wildly sociable milieu – the high society of a fast-changing world capital – Brummell's indefinable something was to be self-confident, and self-evidently great company.

~

There is no satisfactory portrait of Beau Brummell. Three mini-atures exist, one oil on ivory, the others reproduced in earlier works on Brummell, and there is one highly unflattering cartoon, one etching and some interesting family paintings from Brum-mell's boyhood. There was never a Thomas Lawrence portrait, a Romney or a Gainsborough; and the Joshua Reynolds picture in the Iveagh Collection was painted when Brummell was three.

That the most famous figure in London deliberately avoided portraiture in adult life is psychologically and culturally fascinating in itself. Brummell seems to have had some awareness that his fame outstripped his ability to live up to it in reproduced form, and that only the live event, the 'happening' – as Warhol might have said – of an encounter with Beau Brummell could match expectations. This leaves the writers in his wake with the dual problem of defining the man, and also the effect he had on others: his widely acknowledged but ill-defined 'presence', in the absence of a clear image. Fortunately the many records of Brummell in the memoirs of the period attempt, in lively detail, to record his physical presence as well as the effect of his charm. To meet Brummell was never to forget him. 'This man,' wrote one contemporary, 'possessed such a powerful intellect that he reigned even more by his presence than his words.' But his presence defied easy portraiture as surely as his visage: to some he was outrageous or ridiculous, to others a paragon of gentlemanly propriety. 'One of the dandy's main characteristics,' wrote the same contemporary, was 'never to do what [was] expected of him.' And Brummell must be applauded at least for his ability to surprise. But if he had charm, humour, style and wit, he was also unbearable to be with when the mood took him or the occasion brought his displeasure. He could be cruel, condescending and dismissive. Yet oddly few took against him for long: 'he displeased too generally not to be sought after'.

The search for the man behind the 'Beau' façade has therefore been entertaining as well as frequently frustrating. It has encompassed memoirs and diaries, country-house and royal archives, letters and tailors' accounts, wine merchants and snuff shops, fabric archives and an asylum. Brummell has been a beguiling companion on the journey: not the cold fish of legend, but warm, complex, evasive often, pretentious and annoying frequently, brilliantly witty with revivifying regularity and chillingly tragic. But never dull. His sardonic voice is audible in much of what he said and wrote, and in many of the anecdotes that collected around his name, and he has been, as a result, slippery.

He rarely said anything directly, or without taking the opportunity to make an elaborate comedic meander. He refused to take anything very seriously, including, which is enormously to his credit, himself. He was a poseur and a social-climber, but acknowledged that much about himself and about the cruel realities of his world. As he admitted to Lady Hester Stanhope, 'If the world is so silly as to admire my absurdities, you and I may know better, but what does that signify?' She paid him the compliment in return of describing him as the cleverest man in London. But if he was willing to dismiss his absurdities, a roll-call of writers and artists, as well as Lady Hester, line up to insist we should not. Lord Byron, William Thackeray, Thomas Carlyle, Benjamin Disraeli, Charles Baudelaire, Honoré de Balzac, Albert Camus, Edith Sitwell, Max Beerbohm, Oscar Wilde, J. B. Priestley and Virginia Woolf have all felt drawn to reference Brummell in their understanding of the modern mind and manners. As one more recent essayist insists:

If three things sum up our age they are science and technology, neo-liberal economics, and an infatuation with fashion and style. To understand the science [and economics] you must know . . . Darwin and . . . Adam Smith. To understand fully the importance of style and fashion and the instincts on which they rest, [an understanding of] Brummell is essential . . . The cult of celebrity, preoccupation with appearance, the new dandyism amongst men, the importance of 'attitude', the studied ironies of the post-modern era – all have their fore-echo in this astonishing [man].

But long before our time, indeed within a few years of Brummell's death, an amateur French philosopher was arguing that Brummell was instructive *not* in his achievements – as if fashion, manners and style were not in the realm of achievement – but rather he was instructive '*in his person*'.

The person of Brummell presents several paradoxes. Centrally intriguing is his sexuality. Even were it true – and it turns out it is very much *untrue* – that he was a sexless aesthete, 'cold, heartless and satirical', as one famous courtesan said – his image and legacy are intensely sexualised. They exist in the mirror of male sexual vanity: how we dress, act, present ourselves, and interact with women and other men. Brummell was the central figure, and the term is apposite, in a new London 'look' that drew on some of the more obviously sexual aspects of Augustan art but developed into the suit for modern city life. The way men began to dress because of Brummell was an arresting corollary to the sea-change in attitudes to masculinity, and the debate over gentlemanly behaviour that reverberates in the novels of Jane Austen as much as the politics of the Enlightenment. It was a challenging time for men, a time when manners and codes of conduct were changing. For some, especially in London, it was also a sexually licentious age, and the fashions for both women and men reflected this. Women flaunted their bodies and so did men. Brummell was intensely scrutinised by men and by women 'the most admired man of all the belles and beaux of Society' and his fame was closely allied with a re-imagining of masculinity. So it is hardly surprising that his love-life was a subject for prurient conjecture at the time and subsequently – as, indeed, would be the case for a modern celebrity.

I should allow an instinctive suspicion of the idea that anyone, even the most ascetically stylish, is asexual: a position held by a surprising number of fashion writers and by some contemporaries about Brummell. His pre-eminence in the memoirs of the courtesans of the period begins to belie this, but one startling discovery made early in the research for this book gave Brummell a human face that immediately made sense of much of his later life. He died of tertiary syphilis. The asylum in France where he died – still a working institution – keeps files that date back to the eighteenth century. The retired director of the asylum, Professor Pierre Morel, has had a lifetime's interest in the history of the hospital, and one hot afternoon in a modern prefab office there, he pushed across a Formica table to me a copy of Brummell's medical records and his death certificate. The originals are in disputed ownership, and have not been accessible to historians of the period before now. 'General paralysis of the insane', and 'general paresis' were used interchangeably at the period to signify dementia brought on by tertiary syphilis. The diagnosis was confirmed, in Professor Morel's opinion, by contemporary descriptions of Brummell. It is indeed bizarre that this diagnosis has never been conjectured before in any literature in English, but the Bon Sauveur medical records are unequivocal. The colour of Brummell's life shifted as a result of that discovery in Caen. If he was suffering from secondary, then tertiary syphilis through the 1820s and 1830s, then he contracted the disease at the height of his fame in London. Brummell's was indeed a rake's progress, but in a slightly more obvious, more human, more fallible and more libidinous way than previous writers have had access to imagine. At the same time, this is not a story of a disease, and Brummell has the right we all share not to be defined by his death, or to have the powerful image of an end foreshadowed in a sexual act overwhelm a life, on the whole, lightly lived.

~

Although there were tragedies and physical horrors to be revisited in the research for this biography, there have also been joyous riches. This is perforce the case for any writer on this period, and any writer on Brummell's life in London in particular. It was a voluble and literary age. His contemporaries wrote voluminously and also recorded lengthy conversations in their diaries and memoirs in the form of dramatic dialogues. People spoke in long, complex sentences, on and off stage, as is evident from the plays and novels as well as the diaries and memoirs of contemporaries. It is only fitting, then, to use sources in their original form to give the flavour of Brummell's world and the context within which he spoke and acted. He made impact through his presence, some mixture of insolence, charm and half-expressed sexuality, but he was also a man of words. He chose to write them down himself only in later life, from which period many of his letters survive. Fortunately, though he had neither time nor inclination at the height of his fame to write, many of his contemporaries recorded what he said, where and when. Brummell appears in the memoirs of the courtesans Harriette Wilson and Julia Johnstone, in the works of the diarists Thomas Raikes, Tom Moore, Lord William Pitt Lennox, Charles Macfarlane and Captain Gronow, and in the letters of Lord Byron, Harriet, Lady Granville, Princess Frederica, Duchess of York, Scrope Davies, Mrs Fitzherbert and the Prince Regent to name but a few.

Moreover, because the dandy in general, and Brummell in person, became a trope and type in fiction as well as in memoirs, his world of masculine manners and the man himself are recorded or referenced widely in fiction. He was re-created, in barely concealed fictionalised form, in novels that appeared within his lifetime and were considered by him – more or less reluctantly – to be true likenesses: *Pelham* by Lord Edward Bulwer Lytton, himself a dandy, and *Granby* by T. H. Lister. Brummell's world of London high society was also the backdrop for a whole school of fiction that used the clubs, gaming-houses and ballrooms of the fashionable West End as the setting for tales of love, triumph and ruin. These have all proved invaluable sources.

First among the fresh and vivid lights to be shed on Brummell must be from the courtesans, whose lives have been brilliantly researched and resurrected by recent scholars. Brummell's close association throughout his adult life with these women has been insufficiently acknowledged. They provide a unique perspective on London and the men of the West End whom they entertained, and also on Brummell. The London *demi-monde* presided over by the Three Graces – the three famous courtesans Harriette Wilson, her sister Amy Dubochet and Julia Johnstone – was also Brummell's world. His participation is hardly surprising as the *demi-monde* of courtesans overlapped the fashion-conscious, aristocratic and royal circles in which Brummell moved. Or, at least, it overlapped the male members of those circles. But he must have been surprised in later life to find himself vividly depicted – gossiping in opera boxes or gorging on late-night buffet suppers – by women whose existence had traditionally depended on discretion. Two whom he had known intimately went on to write detailed memoirs of their lives and loves.

The courtesans – variously known as demi-reps (representatives of the *demi-monde*) or Cyprians (votaries of the cult of Cypria or Venus) – were most descriptively titled the 'The Fashionable Impures'. They were a key feature of the lives of rich London men at the beginning of the nineteenth century. Within a generation they were gone, as the blanket of Victorian hypocrisy created a different economy of prostitution and more covert adultery – but an elegant veneer had existed over the West End sex trade through the later eighteenth century, one to which Brummell's family, it turns out, and Brummell himself were quite closely allied. Although the courtesans shared the same privileged world of theatre, opera, masquerade balls and racing carriages with high society, they were outside respectable society and the company of respectable women. (The popularity of masquerade balls was predicated on the understanding that they allowed all to mix freely: society ladies and gentlemen, and women deemed unrespectable or 'impure'.) As a result the courtesans had a privileged access to society, but also a sardonic perspective on its foibles that matched Brummell's own take on the world. One who was particularly well placed to understand this was the courtesan Harriette Wilson, who provides a major source of detail and speculation on the subject of Beau Brummell. Again, the fact that Brummell features prominently in Harriette's memoirs, as well as those of other courtesans and members of the *demi-monde*, is thrown into a slightly different light if he is reconsidered as a sexually active man. More pointedly, experienced venereal specialists at the time linked syphilis in London almost exclusively to professional sex-workers.

Harriette Wilson's Memoirs Written by Herself were the publishing sensation of 1825. Never before, and possibly not since, had someone in Harriette's position chosen to write about the many influential men with whom she had been intimately involved. Fortunately, unlike her friend Julia Johnstone who followed her into print, Harriette wrote rather well and had an ear for dramatic dialogue, honed, like Brummell, from a lifetime of theatregoing. Her memoirs are littered with verbatim accounts of conversations with the many society figures she had known – at the opera, private balls and parties. We hear Brummell's voice afresh and frequently in the account Harriette gives of it. Her publishers, Stockdale's, issued advance publicity of the men who would be mentioned in the forthcoming editions, bringing them instant notoriety and supposedly eliciting the advice from Wellington to 'Publish and be Damned.' In descending order of rank Harriette said she intended to expose the King (George IV), the Duke of York, Prince Coburg, the Dukes of Wellington, Devonshire, Argyll, Beaufort and Grafton; the Marquesses of Hertford, Headfort, Londonderry, Wellesley, Worcester and Tavistock; Lords Craven, Jersey, Melbourne, Charles and Frederick Bentinck, Byron, Proby, Burghersh, Alvanley, Dudley, Palmerston, Lowther, Ponsonby, Carysfort, Bessborough, Bathurst, Deerhurst and Bective. And this was before she got on to the mere commoner, Mr George Brummell – who knew them all. Many of the men mentioned, it was made clear, had been her lovers. They could buy their way out of her coming instalments (it was widely believed that the King paid up) and others may also have fallen for the ruse. Brummell was in no position to pay anything in 1825 so appears in later volumes of her memoirs, but in a largely unflattering light.

Yet despite her unusually intimate knowledge of the British peerage the 'supreme goddess in the temple of profligacy' declined to describe in any intimate fashion the core activity of her career. She mentions sex once, glancingly, saying she effected a reconciliation with the heir to the Duke of Argyll 'in the usual way, and on the spot'. Brummell's world may have been sexually licentious but the histories recorded of it, even the most candid, end at the bedroom door. Julia Johnstone also knew Brummell intimately. As teenagers they had even been neighbours. She followed Harriette swiftly on to the bookshelves with *Confessions of Julia Johnstone, written by Herself in Contradiction to the Fables of Harriette Wilson*. Between the two – Harriette and Julia – whatever their contradictions on the subject of Brummell, the courtesans draw a fresh and vivid portrait of the world in which Brummell moved: in their curricles in Hyde Park, the racy open-tops of their day, in their boxes at the opera, at supper parties, balls and masquerades and even as camp-followers of the 10th Light Dragoons at Brighton.

~

But for every moment of frustration that even candid Harriette Wilson draws a curtain over the secrets of her busy boudoir, there is the joy that Brummell's friends, acquaintances, acolytes and possible lovers wrote copiously about him and about the world in which they lived. It was a time of fast change, and they were aware of this. In the cases of Captain Gronow and Thomas Raikes, they became aware later that the world of their youth was a foreign land compared to the stricter morality and more staid times in which they wrote: mid-Victorian England.

Thomas Raikes, another ideally placed diarist and memoirist, had known Brummell since their first days at Eton. They remained friends throughout their lives and Raikes wrote about Brummell in his *France since 1830*, published in 1841, and in his lengthy *Journal*, published between 1856 and 1857. Son of a City banker who had been governor of the Bank of England, Raikes was known in the West End as Apollo. This was partly because of his looks (marred later in life by pockmarks: Count d'Orsay once asked cruelly if he used his nose to stamp the wax on his letter-seals) but mainly because Raikes was a City man who 'rose in the east and set in the west'. In later life he travelled widely, spending much time in Russia, where he knew Pushkin, and in Paris, whence he wrote his *Personal Reminiscences*. He also visited Brummell on several occasions in France. 'Amongst the dandies, no one was held in greater estimation, at least by himself, than Thomas Raikes,' wrote Lord William Pitt Lennox archly. He thought Raikes 'a gossip, flâneur and servile tuft-hunter . . . a Boswell never stumbling upon his Johnson' until, that is, he decided he would be 'satellite to the great [Brummell] and chronicler of [his] sayings and doings'. Raikes seems to have felt some envy towards his old schoolfriend in his glory-days and, though sympathetic to his plight in later life, felt obliged, in writing about Brummell, to turn his story into a Victorian morality tale, claiming that his friend had left a 'long list of ruin, desolation and suicide' in the wake of his 'creed [of] prodigality . . . gambling . . . and reckless indifference'.

Captain Rees-Howell Gronow was even less sympathetic to Brummell, but again left a wealth of anecdotes and period detail on Brummell's life and times in his *Reminiscences and Recollections*, published between 1861 and 1866. Son of a Welsh landowner, Gronow was another old Etonian, slightly younger than Brummell and a close friend of Shelley, the poet, whose Eton experience was so hellish. But Gronow shared with Brummell a working knowledge of life as a Hussar officer and of the masculine exclusivity of the London clubs. He also took the unusual step for his time of recording such society ephemera as the line-up for the first dance of the quadrille and the waltz in London. He wrote with nostalgia for a London that was fast disappearing. The captain's sartorial aspirations to dandyism, however, were mocked by the dandy clique around Brummell, as was his diminutive stature. They called him Captain No-grow. His *Recollections*, though fascinating and detailed, are often tinged, perhaps as a result, with a twist of bitterness.

Brummell himself was an accomplished writer. That his letters barely exist before his exile in France, and that even then he wrote in the style of comic whimsy he had learned as an Eton schoolboy and from the boxes of Drury Lane does nothing to reduce their impact. Comedy, as they say, is harder work, and he laboured to amuse his correspondents, which is as endearing as it is sometimes obscuring. Even as his world crumbled around him, Brummell's instinct as a writer was to hone sentences of elegant and lengthy density and to crack a joke. For all these reasons I make no apology for quoting at length from his and others' letters and poems and for letting George and the rest tell their story in their own words.

~

The voice that can never be ignored on Brummell is that of his first biographer, or more precisely chronicler, Captain William Jesse. He also collated and published nearly all the letters of

Brummell that form the core primary source for any biographer. Captain Jesse met Brummell in February 1832 in Caen. He must have known, or at least guessed, that Brummell was suffering from syphilis: Captain Jesse was only twenty-five but a worldly and well-travelled man. His writing and army careers had taken him to India, Turkistan and Sevastopol, and with Afghan caravans into Persia. His was an adventuresome and wandering mind and both qualities are amply on show in the seven-hundred-page *Life of George Brummell Esq. Commonly known as Beau Brummell*, which he wrote and published within a few years of Brummell's death. Jesse was a professional translator before he began to write his own works, and some of this background as a self-effacing reporter served him well as Brummell's chronicler. More than a third of the 1844 publication is taken up with Brummell's own writings, or those of his familiars. But Jesse chose to ignore completely, such was the gentlemanly code of the time, the salient issue of Brummell's illness.

Every subsequent writer on Brummell owes Jesse an immense debt of gratitude. His *Life of Brummell* was a truly monumental achievement, but also, in parts, arrestingly modern in its approach to reportage and celebrity. Jesse recorded verbatim conversations as recounted by Brummell's friends, and his mixture of prescience and prurience led him to 'interview' – by letter or in person – anyone and everyone he could think of whom he knew to have known Brummell and who might be willing to co-operate. He was indefatigable in searching for the sort of arcane detail that would doubtless have been lost without his efforts. Dozens of otherwise unavailable sources were collated while Brummell was still a living memory and as a result the thoughts of Brummell's schoolfriends are accessible to us, as are those of the asylum nurse and Anglican priest who attended his deathbed. Jesse thought of himself as a Boswell to Brummell's Johnson. He had been taken up by Caen society when he stayed there, recuperating from his Indian posting, and came to know Brummell well enough to be teased by the old Beau on his own attempts at dandyism. Brummell said he looked like a magpie.

Jesse's *Life* is the primary source for all subsequent works on Brummell, including this one. Fortunately much can be added or corroborated from other archives, as Brummell featured in so many areas of London life in the greatest age of diarists, memoirists and gossip-mongers. Jesse does not go into detail on the day-to-day life of a man-about-town, however, or the precise changes in men's tailoring at the time; neither does he have much to say about life in Brighton with the Hussars. He structured his *Life* around the letters and what he could find from contemporaries, for which reason the work is heavily weighted towards Brummell's post-lapsarian life in France.

Also down to Jesse is the survival of Brummell's extensive collection of poems (his own and others') in a collection dubbed by him 'The Album'. Captain Jesse appears to have acquired it in France after Brummell's death. This not only provides the sources for Brummell's own verses, but works especially composed for him, or in his company, by Sheridan, Byron, Lord Erskine and Georgiana, Duchess of Devonshire, among many others. They provide richly atmospheric detail on what filled Brummell's heart and mind as well as what made him laugh. More recently discovered is Brummell's own *Male and Female Costume*, a treatise on fashion. This, like Brummell's memoirs, he intended for publication, but, unlike his memoirs, he did not destroy. Jesse alludes to this treatise, but it turned up in its entirety only relatively recently. It forms the foundation to our understanding of Brummell's own philosophies on fashion.

If Jesse is an invaluable source, though, he is not always a completely reliable or straightforward one. He asked a lot of questions of Brummell's friends and acquaintances, but frequently not the right ones. It took a French writer of the same period to ask Jesse the salient simple question he had missed: was there one great love in Brummell's life? Many of those who contributed to Jesse's anthology of anecdotes did so either anonymously or were uncredited. Jesse was adamant that had he wished so to do, he could easily have served up 'a dish of scandal . . . so hot that it would have shrivelled up the ears of the most inveterate lovers of it'. But he chose not to. He alluded to the letters found after Brummell's death in a trunk in the Hôtel d'Angleterre, containing 'a great many locks of hair', but he drew a veil over much of Brummell's love-life, even obliterating names in the letters he did publish, as was the convention of the age. Some are decipherable, others are not.

Why, though, did Jesse never allude to the illness that cast a shadow over Brummell's later life? He had his own agenda, like any biographer, and was writing with a specific readership in mind. He was besotted with Brummell's legend and was an assiduous apologist for his hero, which was not an easy position for him, writing as he was in the 1840s. By 1844, and certainly by the time of the amended editions in 1854 and 1886, censure had been piled on the Regency, on the disreputable brothers of the prince regent, on their times, taste and mores. Queen Victoria had sold the Brighton Pavilion to Brighton Town Council for a knockdown price and turned up her nose at many of its luxurious furnishings. Aristocratic families like the Mannerses at Belvoir Castle – seat of the Dukes of Rutland – had destroyed records of the rake-helly lifestyle of their Regency uncles and in some cases even their portraits. The mid-Victorians were embarrassed by an older generation that had gambled away patrimonies built up over centuries, made dubious the paternity of several leading aristocratic families, seen the monarchy beset by sex scandals and the idea of a class of imperial stewards sullied by those who sought to define gentlemanliness by clothes, wit and snuff-boxes. Jesse began the de-sexing of Brummell as it seemed the appropriate thing to do, writing as he was just after an emblematic hero of the Regency had suffered an ignominious death from a venereal disease. Reviews of Jesse's book were few – even *Fraser's Magazine* ignored it. 'Folly will have its victims to the end of time,' intoned the *Athenaeum*. Only Thackeray dared to suggest that Brummell, despite his 'failings', would be 'the model for dandyhood for all time'.

Yet because Jesse chose in great part to let others speak for themselves about Brummell, and Brummell to speak for himself in his letters and poems, Jesse's *Life* is a treasure-trove of sources. It leads biographers a dance around and towards Brummell even if the last steps remain unguided and one's own.

~

At the same time that Jesse brought out his hefty *Life of Brummell* in 1844, on the other side of the Channel a French aristocrat had also become obsessed with Brummell and with dandyism. Count Jules Amédée Barbey d'Aurevilly, a Norman man of letters in the French philosophical tradition, had simultaneously embarked on a biography of Brummell. The English Dandy of Caen had become as famous in France as he was in Britain, and dandyism achieved a life of its own in France in the mid-nineteenth century, inspiring Frenchmen from Count d'Orsay to Napoleon III to, later, Marcel Proust. Count d'Aurevilly decided, after hearing of Jesse's monumental work, not to compete directly but to write as counterpoint an extended essay *Du Dandysme et de George Brummel* [*sic*]. At first it was circulated in Caen among those who had known Brummell, but later in 1845 it was published in Paris and exceptionally well received. D'Aurevilly had had access to many residents of Caen and Calais who knew Brummell – he had been a student there himself from 1829 to 1833 – and his description of Brummell's final descent into madness makes compelling and distressing reading. It is used today in the asylum where Brummell died as a textbook example of syphilitic dementia.

Thus were laid down the twin tracks of Brummell scholarship: the biographers following Jesse's lead and those dandyphilosophical essayists following in the spirit of d'Aurevilly. Because Brummell was never heard to express a philosophical position on anything more challenging than his shirt linen ('plenty of it, and country washing') the biographers have scoffed at the attempts to endow him and dandyism with portent. Conversely, because his achievements were unheroic, his style light-comedic and his love-life assumed to be bland, the essayists have poured scorn on him as a subject for serious biography. Which is all to look in the wrong place.

Beau Brummell has a story as both symbol and man. His position as *arbiter elegantarium* in the Age of Elegance, as pre-eminent figure in the culture of the first modern city and in the first Age of Surfaces (as his 'friend Sherry [Sheridan]' had it), and his role as fashion-plate at the birth of modern male fashion ought to secure his fame. His statue on Jermyn Street stands as testament to his position as founding father of London's tailoring reputation. His life also unlocks the turbulent, venal, fashion-and-celebrity-obsessed Regency age, but naturally turns a mirror on our own at the same time, with its familiar fascination with 'attitude', with fashion and with projections of sexual personae and celebrity. Dandyism is a quintessentially modernist pose, so to look anew at the ultimate and first dandy with fresh eyes and new evidence is timely. George Brummell, the man behind the Beau façade, tells his own story with little need for argument or embellishment: he was a man who claimed many hearts in his lifetime, made a unique and original impact and died more alone than is common. In the midst of the elegance and excess of his life and times is an utterly human story, with both high comedy and low tragedy, and the ever-changing panorama of London as its theatre. The 'eruption of caprice', as d'Aurevilly has it, that lends Brummell's life its singularity and dandyism its dazzle, was something the Frenchman thought peculiarly British. This may be so, but d'Aurevilly hovered more apparently to me when I read his admonition that only those who have never learned to smile disdain the dandy. Brummell can amuse and intrigue across the centuries, as he perhaps intended. 'So it was,' wrote d'Aurevilly, 'that Frivolity could show its head amongst a people with strict codes of behaviour and crude militaristic tendencies, as Imagination demanded its rights in the face of a morality too prescriptive to be true. Together they were translated into a science of manners and attitudes impossible elsewhere, of which Brummell was the finished expression and which will never be equalled again. We will now see why.'

PART I
1778–99

ASCENDANCY

The DANDY was got by *Vanity* out of *Affectation* – his dam . . .
Macaroni – his grandma, *Fribble* – his great-grandam, *Bronze* –
his great-great-grandam, *Coxcomb* – and his earliest ancestor,
FOP.

Pierce Egan, *Life in London*, 1820

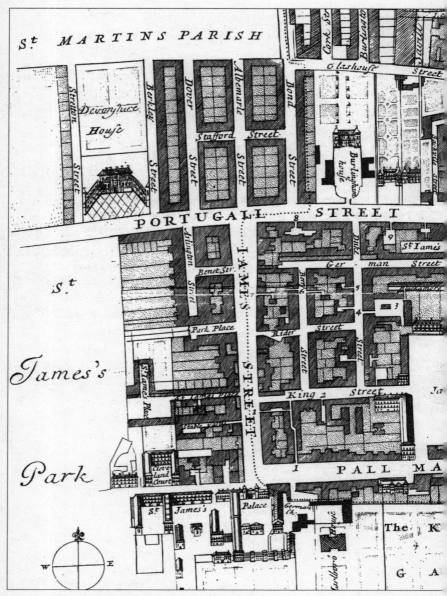

Part of the Parish of St James's, Westminster

ST. ANNS PARISH

Square

18

19 Street

Poultney

Brewer Street

Sherrard Street

Orchard St.

Richmond Street

25

24

Wind - mill

Rupert Street

26

Queen Street

32

31

Panton Yard

Castle Street

PICKADILLY 35

34 33

Coventry Street

Ger - man Street

36

Stable yard

Market Street

St. James's

37

HAY

Nortis St.

38

39

St. Albans

Market

40

Charles 47 Street

41

42

43

L 46 STREET 45

44

Charlton Ho:

KINGS

RDEN

Refferences
to the new Buildings

1 Benjamin Street
2 the Riding house
3 Taylor Street
4 Little Marlbr⁰. Street
5 S. James Gravel pitts
6 Little windmill Street
7 Gravil Lane
8 Little Silver Street
9 Little Peter Street
10 Kemps Court
11 Cock court
12 Hopkins Court
13 Husband Street
14 Maidenhead passage
15 Greens Lane
16 Prices Alley
17 Walkers Court
18 Red Lyon Yard

I

BLESSED ARE
THE PLACEMAKERS
1778–86

If you wish to have a just notion of the magnitude of [London]
. . . you must survey the little lanes and courts. It is not in the
showy evolution of building but in the multiplicity of human
habitations which are crowded together, that wonderful im-
mensity of London consists.

Dr Samuel Johnson, 1709–84

Walk in gentlemen, walk in; here they are – the family of the
Surfaces . . . Gad, I never knew till now that ancestors were
such valuable acquaintance.

Charles Surface in *The School for Scandal*, 1777

Three steps down from modern Piccadilly, at the original level
of the street, is the tablet marking the final resting-place of
Beau Brummell's grandparents. Their long but largely uneventful
lives had been spent almost entirely on the new pavements of
Piccadilly and within the boundaries of the parish named, like the
church in which they are buried, St James's. 'Here lies the body of
Mr William Brummell, who departed this life the 31st of March,
1770, aged 61 years. Also the remains of Mrs Jane Brummell, who
departed this life on the 27th July, 1788, aged 73 years.'

The Brummells were blessed with lives that were long by the
standards of the time. When the small family vault was reopened

in 1816 for its last resident, William Brummell's youngest son Benjamin, he had also surpassed his allotted three-score years and ten. William and Jane had had one more son, another William known as Billy. But he was to find a final resting-place in the grander crypt of St Martin-in-the-Fields. Billy Brummell's long life had taken him far beyond St James's and markedly up the social scale.

Old granddam Jane Brummell had once been a washerwoman and was possibly the daughter of a mere pastry cook. But she lived to see her son Billy Brummell made high sheriff of Berkshire, with apartments in Downing Street and Hampton Court Palace, and a fine country seat set in rolling parkland. And she lived to see Billy's own sons, a third William and his little brother George Bryan – an arrestingly beautiful and precocious child – painted by the society portraitist Sir Joshua Reynolds. George Bryan 'Beau' Brummell would stand as *chevalier d'honneur* at the wedding of the Prince and Princess of Wales in 1796 and become the most famous man in Regency England. The Brummell family's ascendancy through eighteenth-century London society had been fast and signal to the age.

~

By 1750 London was the largest city in the world, and by any definition the richest. In 1720 its population was estimated as 650,000 and as a million by the end of the century. London was double the size of the next largest city in the world, Paris. 'I have twice this spring been going to stop my coach in Piccadilly to inquire what is the matter,' wrote Horace Walpole in 1791, 'thinking there was a mob – not at all; it was only passengers [passers-by].' Visitors were overwhelmed by the spectacle of crowded humanity:

In the road itself chaise after chaise, coach after coach, cart after cart. Through all this din and clamour, and the noise of thousands of tongues and feet, you hear the bells from the church steeples, post-men's bells, the street-organs, fiddles and tambourines of itinerant musicians, and the cries of vendors of hot and cold food at the street corners . . . Before you are aware of it a young, well-dressed girl has seized your hand. 'Come, my lord, come along, let us drink a glass together,' or 'I'll go with you if you please.' [All this while] even in the wide streets all the world rushes headlong without looking, as if summoned to the bedside of the dying.

Three-quarters of Britain's trade went through London, but also much of Europe's. It was reasonable to suppose that the tobacco, coffee and rice gracing the dining rooms of Versailles, Vienna or the Vatican had come from the southern hemisphere via the port of London. The coffee-houses of the City of London, meanwhile, had developed into banking and insurance institutions to guarantee and profit by this trade, Lloyd's the prime example. The burgeoning wealth of the city led to a metropolitan population explosion, one fuelled by immigration from rural England much more than a rising birth-rate.

The London Beau Brummell's grandparents knew was bounded by Hyde Park Corner to the west, Tyburn Road to the north, the City and Port of London to the east, and the river itself to the south. Kensington and Chelsea were mere villages, Vauxhall was a pleasure garden of increasingly dubious repute, and Primrose Hill, Newington Green and even Euston – or Somers Town – were still considered sufficiently bucolic to be recommended to those suffering respiratory disorders as a result of the noxious sea-coal fumes. Further out, duellists met in the early-morning mists of Chalk Farm, Finsbury and Hampstead Heath, all considered so distant from either 'Town', the West End, or the 'City', old London, as to be virtually lawless.

The countryside could still be glimpsed by many of London's inhabitants about their daily business. This was perhaps a blessing as so many of them would have been, probably like the Brummells, first-generation city-dwellers. Open countryside lay south of the river, and also just north of Tyburn Road or Oxford Street, east of the City for those who travelled in that direction, while Hyde Park, with its sheep grazing up to the gates of Kensington Palace, brought the country almost into the West

End. The sounds of the country came into the noisy city: each morning the streets were alive with the songs of country traders: 'Sweet Lavender', 'Cherries Ripe', 'Milk Below Maids', 'Chairs to Mend'. There was a working dairy in Green Park, where the court ladies of St James's Palace could, in the style of Marie Antoinette, try their hands at milking cows. Livestock was a feature of this 'modern' capital. Cattle and sheep moved about the city on the hoof, fuelled by hay from the Haymarket. Milk came fresh from the cows stalled at the tea gardens at King's Cross and Pancras Wells. Geese and turkeys walked on foot to Smithfield Market, their feet tarred for the long journeys from the north and east. And every day many tons of dung had to be negotiated in the crowded streets of central London before, in the more fashionable areas, it was carted away. The city smelt like a badly run farm, made more 'pernicious [by] breathing the streams of endless putrefaction [and] the gross acid of sea-coal'. It was a dirty city, crowded and exceptionally noisy – the incessant fall of carriage wheels on cobbles was said to be 'like the fall of Niagara'. Yet one characteristic of London was set then that has remained: the grime and the dirt was flecked with green and with open spaces.

The beating heart of London – or 'Lonnon', as it was universally known by its inhabitants – was shifting as the city grew. Where other European capitals – Paris or Vienna – remained fashionable at their historic centre, London simply moved westwards, with servants like the Brummells in tow. Indigenous Londoners, or Cits, were harsh on the new West End servants who 'swarm up to London, deserting their dirt and drudgery, and in hopes of getting into service, where they can live luxuriously and wear fine clothes'. But it was becoming a well-trodden route to social ascendancy. The city, in moving westwards with its country-born servants, seemed almost to be in search of some green-edged ideal of London living, where pavements would be always in walking distance of verdant space and the mock-pastoral. The medieval City remained London's financial core, with close ties to the river and docks to the east. But the political life of the city stretched out westwards along the river, centred on the former royal palaces of Westminster and Whitehall, and – until the Hanoverians fell out of love with it – at Hampton Court Palace.

The residential heart of fashionable London followed politics west and north of the river. In part this was in tribute to the newer royal palace at Kensington, built upwind of the putrid capital. The West End, as it became known, smelt better by being on higher ground and also upwind of the City. To add to this were the parks that re-created rural England in safer, sanitised, garden form. Hyde Park, Kensington Gardens, St James's Park, Green Park: these became as much the nexus of social interaction for Londoners as the theatres, clubs, ball-rooms or the opera.

In moving westwards, London began to express the character that remains the city's to this day, of a city that sprawls over parks and gardens. And Londoners, despite an uncooperative climate, lived their lives a good deal out of doors. They were great walkers. It was a way to meet, gossip and compare social standing – as signified by one's companions, clothes and the complicated rituals of greeting and not greeting. Walking as a fashion was intrinsically associated with that most sociable of monarchs, Charles II – and Constitution Hill by Buckingham Palace is named after his constitutional walks, rather than anything so worthy as a political document.

Individual shops provided refuge for the walkers, places of resort for the fashionable where the price of entrance was the appearance of intention to buy. From the mid-eighteenth century, there was a confectioner's in Berkeley Square, Gunter's, which had a sitting room for exhausted walkers, serving ices and cakes. Berry Brothers, the wine merchants on St James's, offered a similar refuge, for men, who could pass the time in ordering wine, or having themselves weighed – an intriguing novelty – on vast scales imported for the purpose. The great purveyor of snuff, Fribourg and Treyer on the Haymarket, was also a meeting-point for walkers. All provided shelter from the rain, when the parks and gardens would suddenly empty (umbrellas being considered an insupportable affectation) and Londoners would pick their way across fast-flooding streets.

Londoners walked, they also shopped, but not just for the necessities of life. Increasingly going 'a-shopping' was perceived as another entertainment of the West End. Shops themselves became London landmarks, and signifiers of the movement of money from east to west. Emporia opened on the route west along Fleet Street: Bernard Lintot at No. 16, publisher of Pope's *Homer*, John Murray, later publisher to Lord Byron at No. 67 and Thomas Tompion, a watch and clockmaker on the corner of Whitefriars Street. But the further one ventured into the fashionable West End, the more luxurious the shopping became. On Piccadilly John Jackson's, trading since 1604, went into partnership with Richard Jackson, wax and tallow chandler at No. 190, to become Jackson's of Piccadilly. John Hatchard opened a bookseller's that was to become a meeting-point and enduring landmark. John Christie opened an auction house off Pall Mall in 1766 and William Asprey a shop specialising in *objets d'art* brought into the West End from his premises in Mitcham. It would later become a jeweller's. A German visitor in 1775 was awestruck:

On both sides tall houses with plate glass windows. The lower floors consist of shops and seem to be made entirely of glass: many thousands of candles light up silverware, engravings, books, clocks, glass, pewter, painting, women's finery, modish and otherwise, gold, precious stones, steel-work, and endless coffee rooms and lottery offices. The streets look as though they were illuminated for some festivity; the apothecaries and druggists display glasses filled with gay coloured spirits; the confectioners dazzle your eyes with their candelabra and tickle your nose.

One of these confectioners may well have been Jane Garret's father – but she, like her husband, found work in domestic service and later as a West End landlady. The westerly progress of the aristocracy and new money brought in its wake an ebb-tide of servants. The Duke of Bedford kept a staff of forty at his West

End mansion – for all he spent most of his time in the country – and even Mrs Clarke, setting up as mistress to the Duke of York late in the century, could not contemplate a household staff of less than twenty. To this class of West End servants belonged William Brummell and his young wife Jane Garret. Perhaps he came from the City, perhaps from rural England, perhaps even from an immigrant German family named Brüml. But by the early 1730s William and Jane were established Londoners, and West End Londoners at that. As parishioners of St James's, they were at the realigned centre of eighteenth-century London.

~

When William Brummell first enters written record in 1734, aged twenty-five, his employer was one Charles Monson, an MP, one of four brothers of a Hertfordshire family. Charles was not the eldest, and was consequently one of the better educated. He had been to Pembroke College, Cambridge, and was admitted to Gray's Inn with a view to a legal and parliamentary career. Aged thirty-eight, Monson exercised the prerogative of the younger sons of the Monson family – established in the seventeenth century when the family had lived in South Carlton, Lincolnshire – of entering Parliament as MP for Lincoln. Henceforth he lived partly at the family estate of Broxbourne, Hertfordshire, but bought a townhouse in the fashionable neighbourhood of Spring Gardens near the pleasure park of Vauxhall just south of the Thames and contracted a Londoner as his valet: William Brummell.

In 1737 Monson was appointed deputy paymaster of the forces and at the same time made note of a 'very excellent servant': Brummell. William Brummell's working days were split between Spring Gardens, Vauxhall, Westminster and a small house he bought in St James's: No. 10, Bury Street. This house rooted the family still deeper and for generations to come in the particular economy of their part of the West End because it was a business as well as a home. It had room for the growing family: William and Jane had three children – William, Benjamin and Mary. But there was also extra space in the house, which was let to young bachelors. William was kept so busy at Charles Monson's various places of work that he entrusted the running of this lodging-house at the corner of Bury Street and Jermyn Street to his wife, Jane. Later she was aided by her children.

Only once is William recorded as leaving London. Early in 1757 he was sent to Cambridge, to Trinity Hall, where Monson's youngest brother, Henry, was dying. Henry Monson had studied law at Cambridge, like his brother, at a college founded with precisely that discipline in mind, but had shown sufficient academic aptitude to be ending his days in the college he had first entered as an undergraduate as Regius Professor of Civil Law and university lecturer. Whatever the Monson family thought of academic life, they thought little of the domestic arrangements of a small and unfashionable college like Trinity Hall, and sent their trusted manservant, William Brummell, equipped with the latest London medicines, to nurse the ailing and unmarried Fellow. Henry Monson died nonetheless, aged sixty-one, on 15 February 1757; the dressing and accompanying of the body on its final journey back to the family seat at Broxbourne was entrusted to Brummell.

As a result of this infelicitous nursing trip, one personal letter survives from William, a rare example of a servant's family life entering the written record. It is a note to his master with mention of Brummell's son 'Billy': the first record of Beau Brummell's father. William Brummell writes in search of an invalid's feeding vessel that he has left in London and needs at Trinity Hall for his patient. 'If not in Spring Gardens,' Brummell explains to his master, 'it may be found in Bury Street. It was used when Billy was ill.'

Billy was then twelve years old.

Charles Monson retired from Parliament and the house in Bury Street was increasingly the centre of the Brummells' world. William Brummell retired completely as a valet after Charles Monson died in 1764, and lived off his savings and the comfortable income, arranged by his wife, of the rooms that they let.

They had bought wisely. The approach to St James's Palace from the north, St James's Street, had been an important thoroughfare since the seventeenth century, but the extension of the city westwards, and of Piccadilly in particular, had made St James's Street immensely fashionable. But only for men. 'I hate your St James's Street,' wrote a new secretary at the French Embassy. 'One only ever sees men there!' Quite when St James's Street became entirely a masculine preserve is not clearly defined. The coffee-houses that predated the gaming clubs of St James's were largely but not exclusively male, but gradually respectable women ceased to walk this particular part of town. It may have been that the windows of the clubs that superseded the coffee-houses encouraged a sort of institutionalised voyeurism to develop. Certainly, by the 1790s the novelist and playwright Fanny Burney is able to place an ingénue inadvertently in St James's and have her fiancé desperate for her not to be *seen* there: simply being recognised on St James's Street could instantly destroy a woman's reputation.

This is not to say that no women were to be seen on St James's Street. They were. And they were conspicuously dressed in the latest fashions, and very likely riding in a curricle. But these fashionable ladies were not ladies of quality or respectable, for all that they were famous and admired. They were courtesans, among the most influential and inspirational women of their time, and a signal new feature of the area in which the Brummell family were based. St James's was at the centre of the West End's *demi-monde*, a world presided over by courtesans. The world of the 'demi-reps', or Fashionable Impures, encompassed the theatres, ballrooms and high-class brothels of the area. It was a world to which men of fashion had access, but women of fashion did not. The Brummell family home straddled these worlds, actual and physical: its occupants lived, worked and acted as landlords on the fringes of the *demi-monde* and of respectability. In this sense, the Brummells were at the precise epicentre of eighteenth-century life, on the moral and physical fault-line that typified the age: the West End.

Bury Street was laid out in 1670 parallel to the larger St James's Street. It was the house on the eastern corner of Bury Street and

Jermyn Street that William and Jane Brummell first leased from the Crown and then bought. It was an area well known for a particular style of rental accommodation. William Pitt had lodged on Jermyn (sometimes German) Street in 1763, the celebrated actor David Garrick had taken rooms there before moving nearer to Covent Garden, and the young rake William Hickey had rented nearby. The young men who chose to live there through the eighteenth century were variously serviced by the local economy. There were two chandlers, a stocking-maker and a peruke (wig) maker on the next street to Bury: Duke Street. A Mr Mason had a yard nearby bearing his name, before he went into partnership with a Mr Fortnum and opened a store on Piccadilly. Juan Famenio Floris had set up a perfumier's in 1730, the only Jermyn Street shop from this period still trading there today and still run as a family business. Paxton and Whitfield opened a cheese shop nearby in 1740, which took up residence on Jermyn Street a little later and remains. Shirtmakers, bootmakers and hatters were also just beginning to make their mark.

But another vital part of St James's parish economy was shaped all around the Brummells' Bury Street home. Just to the south, Bury Street led into the alleys and courtyards off King Street – notably King's Place – which serviced this resolutely masculine part of town with brothels. Some of these were bagnios, or bathhouses, where, Casanova had noted, a gentleman could get board, bath and bedmate for six guineas: 'a magnificent debauch'. Most were houses owned by madams in the traditional manner. Nos. 11–13 Bury Street, opposite the Brummells at No. 10, were high-class whorehouses as were numbers 24–30. Handily for novice men-about-town or strangers to London, there were various metropolitan guides. One even provided an exhaustive listing of the West End prostitutes, with reviews, allowing an intimate appreciation of the Brummells' neighbours' talents. One, Miss W—is 'advertised' in this guide, *Harris's List of Cyprians*, as a 'very musical lass, . . . she performs all her paces in a pleasing manner, and keeps exact time to every motion . . . always urging encores'. Another, 'a good pretty Scotch lass . . . with extraordinary good teeth', was said to be 'always to be seen at the parlour window; her price is one pound one [shilling], but, she will rather accept of half a guinea, than her friend should return home with his burthen'. For reason of these celebrated neighbours, it was said that no woman other than a courtesan, a demi-rep or out-and-out prostitute would be seen south of Bury Street. When the courtesan Harriette Wilson first threw herself into the arms and protection of Frederick Lamb, he knew exactly where to go to find furnished rooms at hourly and nightly rates: Jermyn Street at the corner of Bury Street. Jane Brummell, presumably, always turned right out of her front door towards Jermyn Street rather than left towards King's Place, but she can hardly have been ignorant of the trade all around her.

But if young women took lodgings on King's Place and lower Bury Street with the intention, as Harriette Wilson wrote, of a life 'free from constraint', many young men also sought lodgings in the area to be near them. Bury Street was perfectly placed between the clubs of St James's and the aristocratic salons of Piccadilly and is only fifteen minutes' walk from Westminster. Although much of the area was redeveloped in the later nineteenth century, the louche spirit of these Georgian back-streets can be sniffed today in the surviving alleys, Crown Passage and Angel Court. The area suited young men who wanted to be part of the *demi-monde*, to live in the new social centre of London, or who wanted 'bachelor' apartments near their work. It was an area that rarely accommodated married couples like William and Jane. For their children, Billy, Benjamin and Mary, it was a worldly environment in which to grow up. On the way to weekly worship at St James's Church, they would have passed Floris the perfumier's and Mason's provisions yard, but also crunched over the discarded clay pipes outside the Golden Lion pub and seen the last of the drunken rakes slouching home from a night at Mrs Fisher's on King's Place.

Quite possibly the Brummell family would have remained on this rung of the new West End economy and on the outer fringes of respectability, had it not been for a chance encounter in 1761. One of the young men who came knocking at Mrs Brummell's door was Charles Jenkinson. He was a new Member of Parliament. Billy Brummell, then a teenager, had penned a notice for his mother, 'Apartments to Let', presumably after the departure of a recent lodger. Charles Jenkinson was impressed by the rooms and, so he later claimed, by the handwriting of young Billy Brummell. He moved in, and offered work to his landlord's teenage son in his office at Westminster.

Charles Jenkinson, later Lord Liverpool, was only thirty-four years old at the time, unmarried and new to London. It was not considered worthy of remark that a young politician on the make should rent rooms next door to some of the busiest brothels in the country. Quite to the contrary: in political circles Jenkinson was considered a safe pair of hands. As a young man he had inherited an estate in Oxfordshire, Burford Lawn Lodge in the forest of Wychwood. By 1756 he had achieved some fame as the author of 'Verses on the Death of Frederick, Prince of Wales' and for writing more sober pieces on the need for standing armies. He had even penned election songs for the MP Edward Turner in his campaign for a parliamentary seat at Oxford. This catholic approach to political writing had brought him to the attention of Lord Bute, whose private secretary he became. Bute later appointed Jenkinson as an under-secretary of state, which position required him to be a Member of Parliament. A seat was duly found for him at Cockermouth, Cumberland, to which he was elected in 1761. It was this that necessitated his acquisition of London lodgings near Westminster, and his response to Billy Brummell's handwritten advertisement placed in the window of 10 Bury Street.

The new lodger was already on his journey towards political fortune, on a road William Brummell senior would have recognised from his days working for Charles Monson. Like Monson, Jenkinson was a serial collector of sinecures. He purchased the valuable patent-issuing position of clerk of the Pells in Ireland, and under the wing of Lord Bute, *de facto* prime minister in the early years of the reign of George III, he rose to be joint secretary of the Treasury. When, shortly afterwards, Bute retired, Jenkinson became leader of the King's Friends – a political party of sorts in the House of Commons.

In 1763, Jenkinson used his burgeoning influence at Westminster to have his office-boy, Billy Brummell, taken on in a clerkship at the Treasury. Billy Brummell's rise to fortune had begun in earnest.

In February 1765 William Brummell senior, a 'Gentleman, being sick of body but of sound mind, memory and understanding', made his last will and testament leaving Bury Street and its contents to his wife, Jane Garret. She was also to receive an annuity of sixty pounds a year. The profitable lodging-house and all monies were eventually to be passed on to his three children in equal parts, thus setting a tradition in the Brummell family of opposition to primogeniture that would have unexpected effects in the next generation. Charles Jenkinson was appointed as executor, with '20 guineas for his trouble'. William Brummell was five years premature in worrying about his will, but Jenkinson proved himself a friend to the family nonetheless, for when he lost his office at the Treasury in 1764 he made sure that Billy Brummell did not lose his. Billy was raised to the grade of underclerk at the Treasury at a hundred pounds a year. Jenkinson also gave his former landlord's son a shining testimonial: 'I cannot conclude this letter,' he wrote to Charles Townshend, Chancellor of the Exchequer in the new government, 'without returning you thanks for having taken under your protection Mr Brummell [Billy]. He acted under me as a clark [sic] for many years with great diligence, skill and fidelity, and I am persuaded that you will have the same reasons to be satisfied with him.'

Presumably Townshend was satisfied, because when he in turn left office, feet first, in 1767, Billy Brummell was immediately taken on by his successor, the Tory Lord North. When, three years later, Lord North was appointed first lord of the Treasury (prime minister), Brummell was in place as his private secretary. It was a position he held as long as North held his, and it was as a civil servant sitting on the right hand of 'The God of Emoluments [Lord North]' that Billy Brummell was to acquire both influence and unforeseen riches. In 1770 he, with Lord North, moved into the newly renovated property on Downing Street where they would live for the next dozen years.

North had been in Parliament since 1754, representing the family seat of Banbury. Like Jenkinson, he was a member of the King's Friends in the House of Commons. This position he took seriously and literally, once denying that there was even such a post as prime minister in the British Constitution and believing his position under God, Parliament and the King involved primarily serving the best wishes of the latter. He took a hard line against the American colonists, believing this rightly to be the King's wish. 'North had a great contempt for popularity,' a contemporary wrote, 'and in a review of his own political career . . . stated that he has never voted for any one of the popular measures in the last seven years.' It was his aristocratic disregard for popularity and Parliament that irritated the press and public, and some of this seems to have rubbed off on Brummell. North's term in office saw the successful negotiations with Spain and France for control of the Falkland Islands in 1771, the 1772 Royal Marriage Act that sought, unsuccessfully as it soon turned out, to keep the throne free from scandal and popishness. 1773 saw the Boston Tea Party and by 1775 the American colonies were in open rebellion. On the first of many occasions, North offered his resignation to George III only to have it refused. By 1782, the American war was lost and Parliament voted not to continue its prosecution.

Billy Brummell was right-hand man to a politician who was blessed neither in his professional nor in his personal life. North was said to have a tongue too large for his mouth, causing a sort of speech impediment, and an embarrassingly close resemblance to the King, George III. This led to the commonly held belief that his mother had had an affair with the King's father, Frederick, Prince of Wales. In Lord North's case, these Hanoverian features, whatever their origins, arranged themselves into what was described as a head-turning ugliness, only exceeded by that of his immediate family at Downing Street. There is an anecdote of a man turning to Lord North at No. 10 and asking, 'Who is that frightful woman?' only for the prime minister to reply, 'That, sir, is my wife.' In an attempt to dig himself out of a hole, the man rejoined, 'No, I didn't mean *her*, I meant the monster next to her.' 'Oh, *that* monster, Sir,' replied the prime minister, '*that* monster is my daughter.' (Frederick Robinson, prime minister from 1847–53, used to enjoy telling this story over dinner at No. 10, until Lady Charlotte Lindsay, a guest, leaned over to him and said, 'I know. I am Lord North's daughter.')

North lived in the official residence in Downing Street from 1770 until at least 1782. Brummell, his secretary, was given apartments there also – possibly in what is now No. 11 Downing Street, more often the residence through the twentieth century of the chancellor of the exchequer. He may have had accommodation in the old servants' attic of the house, now a private flat for the resident prime minister or chancellor. Most of the iconic features of Downing Street were created just as North came to power, some even ordered by Billy Brummell. The prime minister occupies the house on Downing Street in his (or her) capacity as first lord of the Treasury and so it was that the Treasury had decreed in 1766 that a 'Great Repair' be enacted upon the site. This work on the 1730s house, and the connected property behind – once home to one of Charles II's illegitimate daughters – was far from complete as North, and Brummell, stepped through the door. The house, or rather connected houses, were at that stage called No. 5 Downing Street. The modern Downing Street numbering system was created under North and Brummell in 1779. Yet North was the first prime minister to have the iconic black oak door with a lion's-head knocker opened for him – by Brummell. The brass letterbox, imprinted 'First Lord of the Treasury', and the elegant wrought-iron archway, surmounted by a lantern, were ordered for North, quite possibly by Billy Brummell. They also laid a new floor in the entrance hall at No.

10, the chequered pattern of black and white marble over which visitors first step into the corridors of power to this day. The 'awkward' house proved a little cramped for the growing North and Brummell families, along with the other staff, so in 1771 North applied successfully to the King to be given the keys to the Crown property of Ranger's House in Bushey Park to the south-west of London. As a mark of gratitude to his secretary and to have him nearer this residence, in March 1772 Billy Brummell was granted a grace-and-favour apartment in Hampton Court Palace. He had already come a long way from the bagnios of Bury Street.

The Tudor palace at Hampton had fallen out of royal favour. It was said that George III had unhappy memories of the time he had spent there as a child, and Cardinal Wolsey's sixteenth-century buildings were hopelessly out of date and unfashionable by the late 1700s. Courtiers, politicians and men like Brummell – who would, these days, be termed civil servants – were colonising the former palace, granted suites of rooms in it by the King or the lord chamberlain as a mark of political favour, or for their retirement. Some treated this royal largesse, like any other court privilege, as an opportunity for profit, and sub-let the apartments for personal gain. When George III found out about it he objected passionately, and began to pay great attention to petitions for accommodation and to the housekeeper's reports on what went on in the palace grounds. Dr Johnson lobbied unsuccessfully for accommodation – the decline of his application a sign of dis-pleasure on the part of the King or the lord chamberlain. Billy Brummell, on the other hand, at North's insistence, was granted Suite XVII on the second floor on the east side of Clock Court, part of a gallery known as Gold Staff. The accommodation and impressive address, however, came at a price: George III, with fifteen children as proof of his attachment to the higher ideals of matrimony, insisted Billy Brummell marry his mistress.

Miss Richardson was one of the great beauties of her age. She was also the daughter of the keeper of the Lottery Office, a lucrative government post in the process of drawing funds for new bridges over the Thames at Westminster and Blackfriars. Her family, long renowned for their looks and wit, had a reputation also as peculators. Young Miss Richardson was descended from Sir Thomas Richardson, chief justice in the reign of James VI of Scotland, who, when once pelted by a criminal, stooped to avoid the sharp missile and said, 'You see now, if I had been an *upright* judge I had been slain.' His descendant inherited some of his cynical spirit, and perhaps some Celtic colouring, boasting a great deal of fair, even ginger, hair, which is piled up as a Marie Antoinette beehive in the one surviving painting of her originally titled simply 'Miss Richardson'. Her first name is recorded only in the Westminster baptismal records of her later children: Maria, William and George Bryan Brummell. She was called Mary.

Where, when and how Mary first met Billy Brummell is unknown, but the relationship was arrestingly unconventional. Miss Mary Richardson – in possession of good looks and some means, descended from a man with a monument in Westminster Abbey – was mistress to Lord North's private secretary by 1772. He was the son of a valet. The existence of this apparently mismatched relationship, begun some time in the early 1770s, begins to sketch the shape of two otherwise shadowy characters in the history of Beau Brummell: his parents. Mary Richardson, an enigmatic figure recalled mainly for her beauty as a result of one admired painting, was willing to marry 'beneath' herself, for love or money. But more than this, she had been willing to risk her reputation: the scandal and censure of living openly as the mistress of Lord North's secretary. She was either a passionate romantic, a radical or both. Alternatively, Mary Richardson, like so many women who would later befriend her son and like the women around Bury Street so familiar to her husband, was a more 'professional' mistress. She may already have lost her reputation, in circumstances we will never know (it was not an uncommon situation, even for the well-to-do) and must have felt indebted to the King for finding herself in that rare, though not unique position, of becoming a married courtesan.

Her young husband, meanwhile, was clearly rising fast under

Lord North's wing, and living fast with it. Questions were raised over the apparent upstart. He was mentioned in the papers, wrongly described as the son of 'a footman to Mr Pelham and . . . an industrious washerwoman – the late Charles Townsend gave him the run of the kitchen and after that be became an under commis at the treasury through that gentleman's interest'. Some of the details were correct, if not the names. Billy, it would seem, had that dubious early distinction of minor celebrity: being miscredited in the press. But people were beginning to take notice of Lord North's secretary. Even the fact that Billy Brummell was known to the King sufficiently for George III to be aware of his domestic arrangements already proved how far he had risen from Bury Street. He was becoming a very well connected and a very wealthy man.

The North administration was financially corrupt. This did not shock or alarm contemporaries, and was not cause for censure from the opposition within Parliament, which would have operated in a similar way were it in office instead. (The second edition of the Geneva Bible, published in the eighteenth century, was popularly known as the 'Whig Bible' because of its misprint 'Blessed are the placemakers'.) The buying and selling of government appointments, like army commissions, was accepted practice. So, too, was the buying and selling of votes. Members of Parliament were most often elected with votes bought from the 'forty-shilling freeholders', who made up less than four per cent of the population but were the only men polled in an election. Men bought their way into Parliament and expected to make money out of it while insisting that the public interest was best served this way, as well as the interests of wealth production.

A treasurer and paymaster of the Ordnance in 1763 later explained how the House of Commons was 'bought': 'I was myself the channel through which the money passed. With my own hands I secured above one hundred and twenty votes [in favour of the Treaty of Paris]. Eighty thousand pounds were set aside for the purpose. Forty members of the House of Commons received from me a thousand pounds each. To eighty others I paid five hundred pounds apiece.'

The man who recorded this unashamed confession in 1790, Sir William Wraxall, added that 'the same system certainly continued during the period of the American Revolutionary War when John Robinson [junior secretary to the Treasury] and under him Brummell, were its Agents.'

Billy Brummell would probably not have considered himself corrupt, or an embezzler as such. In the prime minister's gift, and eventually in Brummell's gift, were a large number of posts and sinecures, and to him fell the duties also of paying for House votes with money, privileges or posts. So it is not surprising in a system that equated rights with wealth that a man like Brummell, given the right to be immensely influential, felt justified in arrogating to himself commensurate wealth.

'Dear Brummell,' begged the man who had once been his parents' lodger, Charles Jenkinson, 'if you can be of any use to the poor man who is the bearer of this, I shall always be obliged to you. I have always pitied his case, yet have no means of making any provision for him.' Brummell was in a position to make 'provision' for such cases. He found the bearer of the letter, the poet Richard Tickell, a post as commissioner of stamps. He was also able to secure for him free and prestigious apartments near his own in Hampton Court Palace by a warrant dated 28 September 1782. Tickell was brother-in-law of the lord of the Treasury, Billy Brummell's new friend Richard Brinsley Sheridan. Brummell, Sheridan and Jenkinson all rallied round to support Tickell, but their efforts proved ineffective. Tickell's 'pitiable case' was that of manic depression and he committed suicide by throwing himself off the top of the palace. 'The fall was so violent,' wrote Horace Walpole, 'that there was a hole a foot deep made by his head in the gravel walk.'

The ability of Billy Brummell to try, at least, to ease the life of others brought him influential friends. More than this, his post also allowed him to make direct personal profit. The Treasury's station-ery bill, as one example, amounted to around £5000 annually during North's term of office. All the contracts were approved by Brummell, all the stationery had to be approved by him, and many of the suppliers paid him back-handers. He also acquired sinecures and paid posts: as joint receiver of the duties on uninhabited houses in London and Middlesex, comptroller of the Hawkers and Pedlars Office, agent and paymaster to the Out-Pensioners of Chelsea Hospital, agent to the Navy and agent for the Horse Grenadiers, which the King gave him in person when his son, the Duke of York, became colonel. By the late 1780s these posts alone netted Billy Brummell over £2500 a year on top of his salary, which itself was generous, set at nearly £1000 per annum, a sum sufficient to put its recipient above suspicion of corruption – or so it was argued, apparently without irony. Billy Brummell's income from these three sources: government pay, officially sanctioned sinecures and officially acknowledged back-handers, added up to over £3500 per year: some quarter of a million pounds in today's money. To this should be added unknown sums accrued through the dividends from his investments in government stock, to which information he had privileged access, and other investments in the West Indies. He also had close dealings with the reorganisation of the East India Company. 'See Mr Brummell as soon as you can,' urged Warren Hastings, the governor-general of the East India Company, 'for he is active and intelligent, and has more influence than any man with Lord North.' This 'influence' cost those who sought to direct it. Brummell's combined incomes – many known, some only surmised – put him into the top drawer of London society in monetary terms, with perhaps fewer capital assets than many of the aristocracy, but with an expendable income, by 1778, surpassed by no more than six hundred people in the entire kingdom. The years from 1770 to 1782 of the North administration saw the accretion of the Brummell family fortune, allowing the next generation of the family an entrée into London society as independent gentlefolk.

With Billy's wealth and position came a new circle of friends. Charles James Fox, the Whig politician, fell out with North in

1774 but remained on friendly terms with Brummell. The play-wright and politician Richard Brinsley Sheridan worked in the same government department through which Brummell had risen, the Treasury, and they became close associates. The American-born painter Benjamin West (the historical painter to the King) became a friend as did the president of the Royal Academy, Joshua Reynolds. 'Breakfast with me tomorrow,' writes Brummell, to the well-connected Caleb Whitefoord from Downing Street in 1781, 'after which I shall be happy to accompany you to Sir Joshua Reynolds' and Mr West's.' Even in introducing painter-friends to potential clients, Billy Brummell was a fixer.

The men of his immediate political circle were largely self-made like himself, or in one case self-ruined. Charles James Fox was a great-great-grandson of Charles II, but his father's side were commoners, his politics were radical and his fortune was largely lost at gambling before he entered Parliament, aged nineteen. He had been in his time 'a prodigious dandy', the very 'egregious coxcomb' of overdressed mid-eighteenth-century Macaroni style. It was said his buttonhole was once larger than his head. But by the time Billy Brummell knew him at Westminster, Fox's style was a good deal less colourful, though no less shocking: he dressed in buff, blue and hunting boots, and with no particular attention to personal hygiene. This was taken to show his political sympathy with the American revolutionaries.

Richard Brinsley Sheridan, in contrast to Fox, was, like Brummell, from an unconventional background. In Sheridan's case this was Smock Alley, Dublin, where his father ran a theatre. Sheridan used his success as a playwright in the highly profitable London theatre scene to support a political career, and by the time Billy and Mary Brummell were accepting invitations from Sheridan to Covent Garden and Drury Lane, it was because their new friend co-owned the theatres.

The two men most closely associated with Billy Brummell, privately and professionally, in the years of the North administration were dazzling, irresolute, hardened and dissolute. Fox and Sheridan worked and played hard, gambled, drank but also lived, loved and argued with animal appetites, as was expected in a much more colourful parliamentary age. Fox once walked from Oxford to London in a day; Sheridan wrote *The Rivals* in a week. Billy Brummell spent twelve years 'in habits of intimacy with perhaps the most delightful of companions . . . possessed of more *bonhomie* and powers of pleasing . . . than any other of the great public men of [the] time', and naturally a good deal of the Fox, Sheridan and North styles rubbed off on him. It is to his credit that he remained on friendly terms with all of them, despite their various political fallings-out; but it was Fox and Sheridan who appeared most frequently as later house-guests of the Brummells, and they who most clearly defined the worldly London political milieu in which Billy and Mary Brummell now moved.

On 7 June 1778 a fair-haired boy was born in Downing Street. He was given the name George Bryan and his birth completed the family of three children born to Mr and Mrs Brummell in quick succession. His mother almost certainly endured her confinements at the apartments above No. 10 or No. 11 Downing Street, as George was baptised on 2 July at St Margaret's, Westminster, the parish church of the House of Commons. The Brummells were still living in Downing Street two years later. The inclusion of 'Bryan' as the middle name for their third child, an unusual name for the period, and the Irish spelling, is unaccounted for. There is no other record of 'Bryan' used as a Christian name in the entire weighty vellum tome in Westminster Abbey in which George's baptism is recorded. However, the name features once as a surname: in May 1772 a John Bryan was baptised, a son to one Joseph Bryan. This was the same year that Billy and Mary Brummell married. Joseph Bryan may well have been a Westminster civil servant, a colleague of Billy. George's elder sister, Maria, is not entered; neither, indeed, is there any record of their parents' marriage. George's elder brother, born on 30 January 1777, does appear in the register. He was christened, by family tradition, William. Maria, William and George Bryan shared a nursery at Downing Street with the children of Lord North – only a few hundred yards from Bury Street, but in every social sense an enormously long way from the class of new London immigrants to which their grandmother belonged.

In 1778 London was gripped by a mania for a new novel written anonymously by a young lady concerning the adventures of a country ingénue, new to the big city. The eponymous heroine was called Evelina, and the novelist was soon discovered to be the shy daughter of a court musician, Dr Burney, who called herself Frances or Fanny. Fanny Burney was a West End girl, a friend of Dr Johnson and of Garrick the actor. The unexpected fame that followed the publication of *Evelina* brought her a court appointment under Queen Charlotte, further widening her experience of Georgian society as it suffered the paroxysms of the first Regency crisis. Unlike her heroine, Fanny knew London well – its manners and mores.

As depicted in *Evelina*, the London into which George Bryan Brummell was born in 1778 was full of entertainments of every variety, but great perils as well for those who put a foot wrong in public, as elaborate codes of conduct became ever more divisive. To a large degree *Evelina*, the character and the novel, concern themselves with what it is, in a changing world, to be a gentleman – or woman – a person of substance and honour. London was changing fast as a result of the population explosion and new money. It was, for the first time in its history, a properly anonymous city, more like the modern notion of a metropolis. Evelina is typical of a new type of self-invented character, someone almost without a real name or background at the start of the novel, who is able to create her own worth through her good nature and abhorrence of both pretension and mean-spiritedness. It helped, of course, that she turned out to be the daughter of a baronet, and that the man she finally decides is the perfect gentleman also happens to be a lord. But if class distinctions remained, it was proving possible to challenge and to break through them.

Seventeen seventy-eight also saw *The School for Scandal* run into its second sell-out year at Drury Lane. The Brummells had seen it when it opened. If Billy went to celebrate the birth of his son with his friend Sheridan backstage, as was their habit, it was to the accompaniment, as David Garrick put it, of the 'bursts of laughter and an uncommon Agitation of Spirit in the Audience' that punctuated Sheridan's greatest success. *The School for Scandal* had held a mirror to its audience that recognised its own face instantly, with laughter and some alarm. Hypocritical, sardonic and blithe by turns, the Surface brothers, Charles and Joseph, were true modern Londoners. Nothing was quite what it seemed any more – reputation and reality were changing fast in the new West End where the old, intimate moral certainties were gone for ever. But the explosive impact of *The School for Scandal* was as joyous as it was shocking. It was a liberating thought for young Londoners that they could create themselves, and rejoice in their escape from 'moral rigorism'.

There was much to celebrate and laugh at in the anonymous metropolis. And for Billy and Mary Brummell too, and for their three small children, London in 1778 was becoming a city where they could reinvent themselves. No one seems to have commented that the new tenant of an expanded suite of rooms at Hampton Court Palace was the son of a valet from a dubious part of town, or that his wife had been his mistress. The Billy Brummells and their three children had youth, looks and the patronage of the highest in the land in a city brimming with optimism and new money. And in the baptismal records for George Bryan Brummell at Westminster Abbey, a Brummell is recorded for the first time as 'Esquire': a gentleman. They had arrived.

George Bryan's earliest childhood was spent mainly at his parents' apartments in Downing Street and at his grandmother and Aunt Mary's in Bury Street. He was taken to the collective bosom of a close-knit circle of women. His mother had three sisters living in London. His father's sister and mother lived and worked on Bury Street, and as the youngest grandchild on both sides, it can be assumed he was petted and adored.

It was, however, no easy thing to be a small child in London in the 1780s: the necessary fear was that a baby might not survive. The burial records of the period have long columns of C for 'child' against a high proportion of the names. The deaths-in-childhood rise to a full third of all burials in the winter months, and in one inner-city parish of the period, three-quarters of those juvenile deaths are for under-fives, and half for babies of less than a year old. Only if you survived until your sixth birthday did you have a decent chance of living into middle age.

Recent excavations and crypt exhumations at inner-city parishes such as St Bride's in the City, Christchurch, Spitalfields and St Marylebone have unearthed yet sadder truths about George's contemporaries. Nearly 15 per cent of London children, rich and poor, were suffering from rickets, a result of under-nourishment but also of the Stygian fug that hid the sun from London children. It was said that each morning Westminster was 'cover'd by a cloud of Smoak, most people being employed in lighting fires' and that rainwater was often 'black' with pollution. Only on the clearest spring days was it possible to see the top of St Paul's Cathedral which was otherwise 'always enveloped in cloud of smoke'. Bandy-legged children would have been a relatively common sight. In response to the fear of rickets, children were encouraged to walk young, encased in 'trotters', like circular stabilisers. George, happily, was a large and robust baby, whose appetite bordered on greedy – a trait upon which his aunts felt compelled to comment. His aunt Brawne informed Captain Jesse that her main memory of George in early childhood was of a boy so determined to eat damson tart that he screamed with frustration when he was too full to continue – a recognisable, healthy toddler.

Though some of the vagaries of London life at the time must have been unavoidable, even for those in the Downing Street nursery, Brummell's was set to be a safe and privileged city upbringing. This was interrupted however, by the political unrest that surrounded his father's employer. On 7 June 1780, George Bryan's second birthday, the family home was besieged by a violent mob. London was quite precisely alight with anti-popery, fuelled by Lord North's attempts at making concessions to Roman Catholics in Britain, and 'mad' Lord Gordon's hysterical anti-Catholic rhetoric in response. Seven major fires were visible from the roof of Downing Street, mainly the houses of prominent Catholics and the Catholic chapels of foreign embassies. Fifty thousand people marched on Westminster and, late in the day, a mob moved on the prime minister's residence. Lord North was having dinner with friends, including Brummell and Sir John Macpherson, later governor-general of India, who left this account:

We sat down at table, and dinner had scarcely been removed, when Downing Square [now Street], through which there is no outlet, became thronged with people, who manifested a disposition, or rather a determination, to proceed to acts of outrage . . . Mr Brummell, Lord North's private secretary, who lived likewise [there] was in attendance, but did not make the company. With his habitual good humour, the Prime Minister asked what was being done to defend No. 10. There were, he was told, 'twenty more grenadiers, well armed, stationed above stairs . . . ready on the first order to fire on the mob'. He gave instructions that 'two or three persons' should be sent out to the mob to warn them there were troops in the house ready to fire if there was 'any outrage'. The populace continued to fill the little square, and became very noisy, but they never attempted to force the street door . . . By degrees, as the evening advanced, the people . . . began to cool. We then sat down again quietly at the table and finished our wine.

Night was coming on . . . and the capital presenting a scene of tumult and conflagration in many quarters, Lord North, accompanied by us all, mounted to the top of the house, where we beheld London blazing in seven places, and could hear the platoons firing regularly in several directions.

George Bryan's father, interrupted from family birthday celebrations to attend a political dinner below, would have been understandably alarmed to have troops stationed in the family apartment, and mob violence overwhelming Westminster. After this the boys and their sister spent more and more time out at Hampton with their mother.

On 28 September 1782 the Brummells extended their small empire at Hampton Court Palace for the last time. They were granted the suite of apartments adjacent to suite XXX, Silver Staff Gallery: suite XXIX on the top floor on the north side of Fountain Court. They commissioned their friend Joshua Reynolds to paint their sons as if in the grounds of the palace; the result was exhibited to great acclaim at the Royal Academy Exhibition in 1783. Both George and his brother William wear dresses in the picture, as was customary for young boys at the time, and frolic in the manner that was so admired of Reynolds's child portraits: at ease with nature and their innocent place in it. The artist spent hours playing with his young sitters to catch this fluid, easy and apparently unaffected moment. Then he sent the children away and dressed wooden dolls in their clothes in his London studio in Leicester Fields, now Leicester Square, where he could more easily work at re-creating the 'moment' without the distraction of being in it. Reynolds's pupil, James Northcote, recalled the 'grand rackets there used to be at Sir Joshua's when the children were with him! He used to romp, and play with them, and talk to them in their own way; and whilst all this was going on, he actually snatched these exquisite touches of expression which make his portraits of children so captivating.' George and William had thirteen appointments with their father's artist friend, for sittings always at eleven a.m. while they were still playful and awake, all between 27 December 1781 and 26 February 1782. Their mother visited the studio on 22 March 1782 to see the completed portrait. The Brummells also commissioned a picture from Thomas Gainsborough of their daughter Maria, sitting alone, again as if in the grounds of Hampton Court.

These two paintings were, in a sense, the first entrance into society of the Brummell heirs. The Reynolds studio was in itself an entrée into society, a place where the great and the good – and the up-and-coming – all met. One visitor to Reynolds's studio never forgot meeting the precocious youngest Brummell boy. She, too, was sitting for a portrait, a more studied occupation for her, as she was the actress and writer Mary Robinson, known to history and to her lover the Prince of Wales as 'Perdita'. Her day at Reynolds's studio proved the inspiration for her first major poem. It marks the first literary appearance of Beau Brummell, aged nearly four, as Perdita Robinson's 'infant cherub'.

Ainsi va le Monde

Reynolds, 'tis thine with magic skill to trace
The perfect semblance of exterior grace;
Thy hand, by Nature guided, marks the line
That stamps perfection on the form divine.
'Tis thine to tint the lip with rosy dye,
To paint the softness of the melting eye;
With auburn curls luxuriantly displayed . . .
The task is thine, with cunning hand to throw
The veil transparent on the breast of snow:
The Statesman's thought, the Infant's cherub mien,
The Poet's fire, the Matron's eye serene . . .
Nations unborn shall celebrate thy name
And waft thy mem'ry on the wings of Fame.

The slightly androgynous quality of Reynolds's portraits of children, so admired at the time, was precisely reiterated by the wearing of dresses, irrespective of the sitter's sex. Boys did not get into 'long trousers' until as late as their seventh birthday, though in practice it often made sense to put them into soft leather trousers as young as four. These were worn by boys only, and not by men: a sort of inversion of later practice, as it was knee breeches and stockings that young men adopted once they entered adolescence. George Brummell is shown in this first portrait quite typical of a boy of his time and class; it is not, as has been suggested, some harbinger of later sartorial unorthodoxy. The wide-set, playful pale eyes of the grown man are recognisable in this first portrait, as well as the slightly petulant turn of the mouth which helped so much, later writers claimed, with his comic delivery. George's colouring, like his siblings, favoured his mother. His hair went darker in adulthood – it is variously described as red, dark brown or sandy – but as a small child he was almost strawberry-blond.

A watercolour in the map collection of the British Library has recently come to light, which features Hampton Court in the 1780s. There are two boys in the foreground with, apparently, their mother. They are dressed almost identically to the Brummell boys in Reynolds's painting. Although they are accompanied, it should be allowed, by a very different-looking dog from either canine featured in the Reynolds' work – a large wolfhound as might suit the Tudor palace – it is likely that the boys are the Brummells. At least one of the dogs in Reynolds's painting, the spaniel that tugs at George's sash, appears in other Reynolds's works, and was therefore most likely the painter's. The other dog probably belonged to George Bryan and William. It is a feature of George Brummell's life that dogs are frequently mentioned almost as family friends. It was one of the passions he shared with Princess Frederica, the Duchess of York, and dogs filled a large part of his lonely later life in exile. By the evidence of these two paintings, one definitively of the Brummell boys, the other a new find, George was a dog-lover, in the style considered abroad so typical of the British gent, from a tender age.

In the years before George could have been much aware of it, his father was regularly called away from Hampton Court on vital political business. Through the early 1780s Billy Brummell made desperate attempts to help North cling to power with the support of his friends Fox and Sheridan. The three politicians were not easy bedfellows, no matter how hard Brummell tried to manoeuvre them into a coalition. Sheridan was radically opposed to almost all of North's policies and the King's, and Caleb Whitefoord preserved a letter, almost certainly written by Fox when drunk, that is blue with vitriol at the North government:

a weak, stupid, fat-headed mule of a **** of an administration without spirit of regard for the honour or prosperity of their country, and a drowsy indolent Premier, whose only talent lies in fucking with a most indecent shameless haggess . . . You laugh at the disgraces of your country while you are dividing its spoils among yourselves.

Nevertheless, amazingly, Brummell mediated between the three and arranged meetings, on one occasion in the unlikely neutral setting of the stage wings of the Haymarket Theatre, to which Sheridan had privileged access. The argument became so heated, according to one witness, that shots rang out, convincing some that the politicians were involved in a duel. Fox swore to Sheridan that the coalition with North could be as 'fixed as the Hanover succession'. Nonetheless, unsurprisingly, it lasted only a few months.

In late 1783 the administration collapsed and North resigned his office. So disheartened was he with politics that when Billy Brummell informed him that officers had arrived to collect the ancient seals of office, North opted to stay in bed, Lady North with him, as they were collected from his bedside table. He was not to vacate Downing Street with the alacrity that has typified later changes of government. The new prime minister, William Pitt the Younger, was only twenty-four, and showed no immediate desire to move into a house he later described as 'vast and awkward'. The Norths loitered at No. 10, but the Brummells moved out faster. They bought a house in Abingdon Street, Westminster, which they used as a London address until at least 1786.

Billy Brummell had profited enormously from his time in Downing Street. Though still only in his fifties, he decided to quit the civil service and, in large part, London. In the style of many other *nouveaux riches* of the age, he decided to put his money into property and land and duly bought a country estate that came on to the market that year, sixty miles west of London.

~

The country house William Brummell bought on his retirement from politics in 1783 was at the very height of architectural fashion, and the perfect family home for his young family. Donnington Grove in Berkshire was a new house, built only twenty years before in pink-grey grizzle brick in the radically modish style that came to be known as 'Strawberry Hill Gothic'. Its architect, John Chute of the Vyne, had been a member of Horace Walpole's Committee of Taste, men who had sought to fuse with neo-classicism a whimsical and imagined style of olde England they called 'Gothick'. Consequently Donnington Grove had imitation battlements and mullioned windows, Gothic arches supporting high Georgian door-frames and a medieval-style 'cloister' that led off to the children's bedrooms, suspended below a glass skylight thirty feet above the hall. The house was and is exquisitely pretty – a remarkable early example of Georgian Gothic, designed for urbane owners expecting the most modern comfort and decorated in a style that felt romantically ancient. Of course it was all fake.

Donnington Grove nestled in its own landscaped valley above the tiny river Lambourn near Newbury and boasted a real four-teenth-century castle in the grounds, associated with Geoffrey Chaucer and Richard II. However, the view of the ruined castle from the upper bedrooms had been achieved only by flattening trees and some of the hill. There was a hermitage down by the river, built in rustic flint just before the Brummells' arrival, and still in want of an occupant. The upper floor cloister-balcony was suspended in imitation of a cathedral whispering-gallery but constructed in the latest manner from wrought iron. In every sense Donnington Grove was an up-to-the-minute fashion acces-sory: an artificial ancient country seat. The house looks a little bleak and isolated in the 1772 painting of the estate that remains in the property, and the style, though attractive by day, speaks also at night of the 'gloomth' – the term invented by Horace Walpole of Strawberry Hill for picturesque warmth and Gothic gloom – that appealed so much to fashion-conscious urbanites like Mr and Mrs William Brummell.

In December 1772 *Gentleman's Magazine*, which prided itself on defining all that a fashionable gentleman should know, think or feel, wrote about the house:

Donnington Grove . . . is built in the Gothick style, and the grounds about it are ornamented with much taste. The situation is on a rising ground, backed by a hill crowned with wood, out of which rises Donnington Castle . . . There is a winding gravel walk through both groves on the banks of the river, which opens to several retired and pleasing scenes; at one spot is a pretty rustic Gothick temple, built of flint, near a cascade, which the river forms by falling over a natural ridge of stone. The whole place is laid out with great taste.

The 'great taste' notwithstanding, the Brummell children – Maria, William and five-year-old George Bryan – are more likely to have been impressed by the walnut herringbone banister, all sixty smooth feet of it, which winds around the stairwell and the forty-seven steps to their bedrooms. Gloomthy Donnington Grove was to be George Brummell's country home, when not at school or in London, for much of the next ten years.

As soon as the Brummells had acquired the property they set about making additions and improvements. The previous owner and the man who built Donnington Grove, Sir Joseph Pettit Andrews, an antiquarian and lawyer, had been forced to sell. He had overspent on his Gothick pile, and, as his fortune declined still further, found himself obliged also to sell to the Brummells the neighbouring manors of Church Speen and Chieveley. With this extra land – nearly 800 acres in total – Billy Brummell set about major landscaping of the gardens, realigning the old Bagnor and Lambourn roads and diverting the river to form that most necessary of eighteenth-century garden features: a reflecting lake. Next the Brummells began to worry about the style of entertainment possible at their new country seat.

Donnington Grove still bears the marks of the Brummells' social ambitions. Like all fashion-conscious Georgian landowners, they wanted to create an Arcadia without visible signs of the economy that supported their luxury. They had a paper-mill demolished – it spoiled the view – and replaced it with a medieval-style fishing pavilion. The lower Gothic windows were replaced with modern sashes such that the view of nature so artfully arranged might not be interrupted, and guests could step straight from the lower-floor rooms into Arcadia. The entrance of the house was remodelled, with the importation of a 'Chippendale Gothic' porch, and finally the original symmetry of the house was destroyed by the addition of two dining rooms. One, later a drawing room, was built in perfect classical proportions, but sticking out to the side of the Gothic house. The second was a dining pavilion, quite near the house but commanding sunset views of the park and designed for summer entertaining, for the withdrawal of ladies, or for the most private political soirées. In their two new dining rooms – the one attached to the house also doubling on occasion as a ballroom – the Brummells set about playing host to their London friends and to the local gentry.

The little parish of Shaw-cum-Donnington had not seen anything quite like it. Charles James Fox, living in a scandalous ménage with his mistress Mrs Armistead relatively nearby, became a regular visitor. So, too, did Richard Brinsley Sheridan. Both Fox and Sheridan were major stars in the new political firmament now that North had been eclipsed. Sheridan in turn introduced Brummell to the theatre manager Thomas Harris, who had staged many of his most successful runs, including the première of *The School for Scandal*, when it was said the roof of Drury Lane appeared likely to collapse from the roar of 'applause and laughter'. The theatrical and literary-political crowd brought their own brand of high jinks down to the country. Other weekend visitors included one Mr Joseph White, with his unmarried sister, Sarah. Sheridan convinced Miss White that Thomas Harris was secretly in love with her and, given the romantic setting and his theatrical turn of mind, only needed Miss White to present herself in a suitably stage-romantic style to declare his intentions. Miss White duly 'dressed herself in the costume of one of those pastoral beauties immortalized in Chelsea china and, attired in a stiff dress of primrose brocade and a gipsy hat, with pale blue ribbons, sat by the side of the pond in the grounds with a fishing rod in her hand, the best part of a broiling summer's day'. Eventually the miscast shepherdess realised she was the butt of one of Sheridan's famously cruel practical jokes, flounced back to her room and left Donnington, never to return.

Sheridan also introduced the Brummell boys to his own son, Tom. Tom Sheridan was older than George and William, and as bad an example as any parent might fear for their sons. Tom's schoolmaster described him as having 'wit and humour, but not a particle of knowledge'. The wit doubtless impressed young George as it did all of Tom's schoolfellows. When his father later told Tom to take a wife, Tom replied, 'Yes, sir, but whose?' When his father, in an interchange worthy of Captain and Jack Absolute in *The Rivals*, told Tom that he would cut him off with just a penny to his name, Tom asked if he might have the penny straight away. It was through Tom Sheridan that George Brummell would later be introduced to London's most famous courtesan, Harriette Wilson, who once said she could not trust herself alone in a hackney coach with the playwright's playboy son.

There was shooting and riding for visitors like Sheridan and his son Tom, and evidence that the Brummells employed liveried servants to help with shoots and serving guests in the park. George learned to ride from the stable block his father had built, to hunt, shoot, and swim – a useful skill, as it turned out, at school – in the invitingly clear, slow waters of the Lambourn. There were some local playmates as the other large house of the neighbourhood, confusingly called Donnington Priory, had children of the same age as George, and the Brummells entertained families from the wider area, once George's father sought to inveigle himself in local politics (he was made high sheriff of Berkshire in 1788).

Yet the house, for all its extensions and pretensions, was not a large country seat. There were only eight principal bedrooms, so that, with the children in residence, house parties were necessarily intimate. It is easy to imagine George, William and Maria at the low iron railings of the upper cloister, watching the comings and goings of their parents' glamorous friends from their vantage-point high above the hall: three pairs of dazzled eyes. The house and its guests affected the children in different ways.

George's sister Maria never really left Donnington. Typical of her class and sex, she was not sent away to school, met, very young, a Captain George Blackshaw of a local family and married him. She settled on the captain her generous inheritance and with it he bought a nearby cottage in which they lived, off her money, bringing up two daughters who in their turn married well. She and her young brother George were never close, but they were brought up, in effect, separately. George and William were soon to be sent away to school. Maria's move from London to landed gentility came to define her life as though she were a Jane Austen heroine and accordingly her marriage brought her obscurity. George chose the city.

It has become part of the legend of the house that the two boys, unlike Maria, were occasionally invited to join the adult party, and that George's early introductions to the Devonshire House set in London, presided over by the ageless Georgiana, Duchess of Devonshire, came as a result of his easy relationship with the avuncular figures of Sheridan and Fox. The scale of Donnington Grove makes this plausible. There is even a revealing story of how George Brummell, back from school, first heard of the French Revolution in the flint hermitage by the weir at Donnington and from none other than Charles James Fox. An image more appropriate to the age and characters could not easily be invented: the boy who would eschew politics in favour of fashion was told of the French Revolution in the setting of an artificial hermitage, itself a sort of foppery of English landscape design. That he should be delivered the news straight from a key player in the world of London politics, a former Macaroni but by 1789 a dress-down Whig, links so many strands of Brummell's early life that one is tempted to assume the story apocryphal.

But undoubtedly Donnington Grove made its impression upon young George Brummell. It could not fail to engage the imagin-ation, and was built to appeal to those whose image of the countryside and of English history is formed more by literature than by reality. George learned the essential country skills of a gentleman at Donnington: hunting, shooting, fishing, swimming, perhaps also the landscape architecture and drawing he used in later life. But unlike his sister he never chose to live in the country again. Donnington had allowed him to mix easily and comfortably with some of the greatest, and wittiest, minds in England and to be groomed in the skills of what it was to be a gentleman in a manner his father, whose adolescence was shaped on Bury Street, must have envied.

Likewise it is tempting to see the louche metropolitan figure of Charles James Fox as a model by which George would begin to define and redefine what it was to be a gentleman. Fox, a former poseur, instinctively political, romantically and sexually dissolute, was also a great wit: the foremost epigrammatist of his day. And it was broadly these qualities that brought young George Brummell to the attention of his schoolfellows, at Eton College, where Fox himself had been a schoolboy twenty-five years earlier.

2

THESE ARE NOT CHILDISH THINGS

ETON 1786–93

Would you your son be sot or dunce?
Lascivious, headstrong, or all at once?
Train him in Public with a mob of boys
Childish in mischief only, and in noise,
Else of mannish growth, and five in ten
In infidelity and lewdness, men.
There shall he learn, ere sixteen winters old,
That authors are most useful pawned or sold,
That pedantry is all that schools impart,
But taverns teach the knowledge of the heart.
There waiter Dick with Bacchanalian lays
Shall win his heart, and have his drunken praise,
His counsellor and bosom-friend shall prove
And some street-pacing harlot his first love.

Thomas Cowper, 1731–1800

Three times a year the courtyard of the Swan With Two
Necks pub – between Bishopsgate Street and Lad Lane in the
City of London – became crowded with schoolboys returning to
Eton after the holidays. Some were suffering the last of their
schooldays before taking up army commissions or places at
Cambridge or Oxford. Some were as young as seven or eight
and leaving home for the first time. English public schools in the

eighteenth century had no set age of admission or graduation. School communities could encompass orphans of six and lunks of twenty, though the main body of Eton College was composed of nine- to sixteen-year-olds. Coaches from the firms of Thumwood and Moody were booked each term, *en* caravan, to take the London Etonians back to school. Parents could buy their sons a ticket for inside or outside the coach. Consequently, before the boys even started on their journey to school, the class divide that would define much of their lives during an Eton term was already in place.

The poorer scholarship boys called 'Collegers' or 'King's Scholars', whose places were assured according to the medieval statutes of the college, rode outside. At school they would sleep in one enormous dormitory, the infamous Long Chamber, and be fed on mutton and bread. The 'Oppidans' or fee-paying boys, who were the sons of the aristocracy, the Church and the well-connected, would live in private boarding-houses and could buy oysters and apricots, beer and pork griskings from the grocers and publicans of Eton high street. Oppidans sat inside the coach. One such boy, in January 1786, was George Bryan Brummell, aged seven and a half, sitting between his elder brother William and the nine-year-old son of Lord North. It was Lord North who had nominated all three boys for entrance to Eton. A thin boy opposite, the son of a City merchant, introduced himself as Tom Raikes. He had already spent a year at Eton, but he was not much older than George. The two became friends for life.

For George, William and young North, this coach journey marked the beginning of their Eton schooldays. They would all be entered in the same form at Eton, the first or lowest. Their coach passed under Temple Bar with the rest of the caravan, drove along Piccadilly and through the toll gates at Hyde Park Corner, then headed almost immediately into bleak open countryside.

The winter of 1785–6, one of the century's harshest, had seen the Thames freeze over under old London Bridge. The roads to Windsor provided easier passage when frosted and Thumwood and Moody could expect their coaches back by late evening after the fifty-one-mile round trip to Windsor – minus their noisy cargo of schoolboys.

In 1786 Eton College already spilled across both sides of the small street that extends from Windsor Old Bridge. The chapel roof and the Tudor school buildings – newly extended – dominated the skyline of the little town and were visible from Windsor Castle and from the water-meadows for miles around. The high street that linked Windsor to the college was lined with the shops that supported the school community: Pote's the bookseller, Miller's the tailor, Egelstone's the hatter and Atkins's the shoemaker. There were three coffee-houses: Jones's, Ramlet's and Layton's, which sold, among other provisions, large quantities of oysters – the cheap fast-food of eighteenth-century youths. There was a haberdasher's too, Charter's, that sold, as a sideline, toothbrushes, 'Spence's tooth powder' and soap to those adolescent boys who had advanced ideas of personal hygiene.

There was also an inn, the Christopher, of somewhat ill-repute, where older boys drank. It was just opposite the school's main gate. The masters had it shut down a little after Brummell's time at Eton, as soon as they could acquire the freehold from the Crown, and suspiciously soon after a bastardy writ was issued from a barmaid there, against one Lord Hinchingbrooke, an Eton sixth-former. He was given ten strokes of the cane for his misdemeanour – fewer than the punishment for a missed 'absence' call at school.

The chapel and ancient buildings of the school were on the right as one crosses the river, the boarding-houses, largely, on the left. The lives of the Eton boys, then as now, straddled two worlds: Eton itself – insular, gossipy as any academic institution, constipated with arcane traditions – and the real world of provincial England. They studied classics in the mornings, and bet on horses and brawled with bargemen in the afternoons; their education would encompass Greek tragedy in the original, but also the bawdy low-comedy of the Christopher inn and its rumoured brothel. They would grow from small, unworldly boys into classical scholars and seasoned drinkers. It was an education well suited to the age.

George Brummell's new school had been founded by King Henry VI, 346 years beforehand, in honour of the patron saint of children, St Nicholas, and for the education of poor boys. But by 1786 Eton had already grown well beyond its founding principles. Although the King's Scholars – up to seventy of them but often fewer – remained central to the life of the school, the *raison d'être* of Eton, from the point of view of most of the other three hundred boys and their parents, was more social than educational. At the end of the eighteenth century, Eton had already established itself as the leading English boarding-school. If not the oldest, it was certainly the most socially advantageous. Of the boys in Brummell's year, two had already inherited marquessates, one was a lord, one a baronet, and another eleven had courtesy titles as sons or grandsons of peers.

William Brummell, George's father, was far from blind to the social cachet of an Eton education. Old Etonians abounded within his immediate political circle. Charles James Fox had been sent there from 1758–64, with an interruption for the 'extravagant vulgar indulgence' of a Grand Tour of Europe from which he returned to the sixth form a confirmed continental-style Macaroni. Nevertheless Fox counted his education in classics at the college as the keystone to his oratorical skill at Westminster. Lord North was also an Old Etonian. Both he and Fox have Greek and Latin verses from their schooldays preserved in the college archives, a marker of erudition, application and approval from High Table. If Lord North had had Brummell's sons put down for Eton in the hope of the same approbation, he would have been disappointed. Neither boy appears in the record of first-class work that was 'sent up' and preserved. But both boys benefited from their schooldays. Another contemporary Etonian, the Duke of Wellington, supposedly remarked that the history of Waterloo had been prefigured on the playing-fields of Eton in this period. George's later history was also strongly coloured by Eton, and a style – linguistically elegant, socially adept, sartorially aware and, some might claim, sexually ambiguous – forged at and by the school in the years that he spent there.

What first greeted the Brummell boys as they trundled up Eton high street was a scene of confusion and, for the little ones like George, some alarm. A near contemporary, another of the 'lags of the school' describes the arrival for a boy like George:

We went first straight to our Dame's [boarding-house] and from there were sent to College to collect sheets and bedding. On entering [the Long Chamber] a scene of indescribable confusion greeted me. It was nearly dark, and there were no lights except a few tallow candles carried about here and there by the boys. The floor was covered with bedding, each bundle being wrapped in a coarse horse-rug, far inferior to what would now be used in a gentleman's stable. The noise and hooting of nearly fifty boys each trying to identify his scanty stock of bedding, combined with the shouts of the other elder boys calling for their fags, gave me a foretaste of my future lot.

George would then have returned to his boarding-house with his allocated bedding: two horsehair blankets, some sheets and one bolster pillow. Collecting bedding at the beginning of term was one of the few ways in which the boarding-houses were directly connected with the school. Otherwise the dames' houses operated almost autonomously, which was just one small part of the anomalous world George was entering.

School fees were not paid directly to Eton College by parents. Instead monies to individual masters – George's tutor and the headmaster – were listed as part of the expenses in a dames' end-of-term bill and made up a rather small part of the expense of sending a boy to Eton. The fabric of the college itself was supported independently by lands granted to the establishment at its foundation in 1440. The feeding and clothing of a boy like George was not considered the school's responsibility so these expenses appeared either on his dame's bill, or as termly accounts from the shopkeepers of Eton. George's habit of living off credit – a common trait of his class in this period – was formed at Eton.

The college dominated the school day, naturally enough, but the dames' houses provided the context in which Eton Oppidan boys slept, ate, socialised and shopped. As a result their lives were much more closely tied to the small towns of Eton and Windsor than was the case for the Collegers, locked up in the Long Chamber from dusk till dawn and fed and clothed by the college.

George and William were sent to board with Dame Yonge at No. 7 Jourdelay's Place. Mrs Yonge, a boarding dame since 1751 and most likely a widow, had two daughters and a son who was a King's Scholar at Eton. Along with these, she looked after forty Oppidan boarders. The house, purpose-built in 1722, remains an Eton boarding-house to this day but in Mrs Yonge's time it housed the forty boys in a score of rooms, two to four boys to a bedchamber. Brothers often slept together in one bed. George's domestic life was henceforth centred on No. 7 Jourdelay's Place, three minutes' walk from the back of College Chapel, via Eton high street and the manifold later temptations of the Christopher inn. No matter how self-possessed and precocious he may have been as a child, it is unlikely he settled down to sleep easily that first bitterly cold night, knowing, at seven and a half, that he was at the bottom of a strange and abrasive new social order. The next morning the boys would be woken before daylight to scurry across the high street to be assigned a tutor. In George's case this was one Mr Hawtrey.

George and William appear on the school lists for later in 1786 in seventh and ninth places respectively in a class of ten. The roll-call of Eton boys was fitfully recorded, but eventually published in the 'Eton Lists' and sold for three shillings in the bookstore, Pote's, on the high street. As the boys' names are recorded neither alphabetically nor in order of class status (though titles and even relationship to title is made apparent), it is often assumed that the lists are a guide to academic standing. This is only partly true. Over the years different masters used different systems, and status within the school – the leader of the school parade, for instance – could gain ascendancy in the class lists, probably irrespective of academic worth. However, when George Bryan Brummell was entered in the Eton Lists on Election Day 1786, 29 July, simply as Brummell *mi* (minor) he is second from bottom in the entire school of 341 boys. As this is the school's first-form list, the placing is almost certainly by age. The only younger boy, marked as Mr King because he was the grandson of the 1st Earl of Kingston, was only six.

George and William remained in the same class together. There was less than two years between them in age, but even less of a gap in academic ability. By tradition, sons of the same family entered and left Eton in the same years, be they two, three or more years apart in age. It made for easier accounting and travel arrangements and the younger siblings were expected, where possible, to keep up academically. George managed to do so. This may explain why he is variously described as an excellent scholar, and a mediocre one. He did brilliantly at keeping up with his elder brother, but only once rose to the top of the class. The Brummell boys stayed together through the second form in 1787, through Lower Greek in 1788, and – as a revolution gripped France – Brummell minor rose above his brother in Upper Greek. While the reign of Robespierre came and went in Paris, the fourth and fifth forms were passed through by both Brummell boys, never more than five places apart in the class listings.

Deus pro sua infinita clementia, Ecclesiae suae concordiam, et unitatem concedat Regem nostrum Georgium, ut pupillam oculi sui conservet, et pacem huic regno universo, aliisque Christianis omnibus largiatur, per Christum Dominum nostrum. Amen*

The Eton morning prayer was the first George heard of Eton Latin – pronounced, it was said, after the Hanoverian fashion, with *v* sounded as *w*. It would have been largely unintelligible to him, as to his new classmates, but Latin was the first, indeed only,

---

* May God by virtue of his infinite clemency grant concord and unity to his Church, and protect our King George as the pupil of his eye and bestow peace on this whole Kingdom and on all Christians, through Christ our Lord, Amen.

subject for the new boys, so they would learn soon enough. These boys, whom George first met that January morning in the schoolyard, were almost exclusively his social superiors. New classmates came and went over the years, but the Eton first form as recorded in 1786 provides a telling glimpse of how the Brummells' social sphere had shifted: 'Eliot, Braddyll, Coxe, Estridge mi, North, Sewel, Brummell ma, Russell, Brummell mi and Mr W. King'. Later they were joined by little Lord Tullibardine.

Of these boys, Braddyll came from Cumberland, of a landed family, and went on to become a lieutenant colonel in the Coldstream Guards and high sheriff of Lancaster. Estridge minor, who had a brother four years ahead at Eton, was far from his birthplace of St Kitts, but stayed in Britain and is to be found, ten years after his boyhood encounter with George Brummell, a captain in the 1st Dragoons. North, the prime minister's son, went on to St John's College, Cambridge, but thence to a relatively undistinguished career once his father left office. Russell, too, had travelled from London with the Brummell boys: he was the son of a rich City merchant. Lord Tullibardine inherited the duchy of Atholl in 1830 despite years of mental instability that began at Eton. He was first declared 'of unsound mind' as early as 1798. Little King, the earl's grandson and the only boy in the school younger than George, was always sickly. In 1797 he went up to Trinity College, Cambridge, but died aged only eighteen 'in consequence of a violent cold caught by his getting overheated and then wet at a . . . party'.

Such were the expectations, great or unforeseen, of the boys whose names were called along with George Bryan's in the schoolyard. Thence Mr Hawtrey, their tutor, took them down to the lower school for their first lesson.

Quid est vestrum nomen?
(What is your name and surname?)
Quam vetus estis vos?
(How old are you?)

Qua operor vos adveho ex?
(From what village or town do you come?)
Ex quod duco operor vos adveho?
(From which county do you come?)

Each boy was asked in turn and in Latin the questions posed as part of the entry 'examination' for the King's Scholars. Some basic knowledge of the classics was expected, but not assumed, of the first-form boys, but what they did not know would soon be drummed into them. Their first two years were devoted entirely to Latin. The third and fourth forms were named Lower Greek and Upper Greek in a fashion as unimaginative as the syllabus itself. After that, Latin and Greek took equal space within the syllabus. But before George could grasp any of this, there were the language and traditions of the school itself, also ancient and arcane, to assimilate.

A 1766 document on the Eton daily schedule, annotated up to 1771, and seemingly designed as a guide for heads of other schools, provides an unusually clear idea of the Brummell boys' routine. George prepared his lessons at Dame Yonge's, unsupervised except by older boys, while teaching took place in vast classes, where repetition, rote learning and strict discipline were the order of the day. Several classes, of up to sixty boys each, were often taught simultaneously in different corners of the barn-like upper rooms. There were lessons even for the smallest boys from eight to nine a.m., from eleven to twelve midday, and from three to four and five till six p.m. On a regular week, only Monday, Wednesday and Friday were full days. Tuesday was a complete day off, Thursday was a half-day – the actual hour at which school ended being in the gift of the masters and dependent on good work – and Saturday a 'play at four'. Sunday was a holiday of sorts also. On Friday afternoon there was an extended two to three thirty p.m. period. Friday's business was considered 'very material' and not to be interrupted by special events, wherever possible.

On Tuesday and Saturday there was a proper lie-in, with the morning roll-call in the schoolyard delayed till nine o'clock. On Sundays there was an earlier roll-call and attendance in school was obligatory until chapel at eleven. Thence the whole school repaired to the upper school where a member of the fifth form read aloud to the boys, usually pages of the improving *The Whole Duty of Man*, before they all returned to chapel at three.

The Thursday half-day was in the gift of the provost, and was requested by a boy, usually a sixth-former, who had done good work. The boy was 'sent up to play' – a term still in use at the school – and was allowed to absent himself from eleven o'clock on the Thursday to copy out on gilt-edged paper the exercise, which he then presented to the provost at noon. It is these special papers, along with verses in exquisite copperplate hand, that are preserved as examples of the best college work. A fifth-form praeposter or prefect read evening prayers after the lesson, which ended at four o'clock, once the provost had approved the work 'sent up', and this was a signal to the whole school that play might begin: 'I give thee most humble and hearty Thanks, O most merciful Father, for our Founder King Henry VI and all our other Benefactors, by whose Benefits we are in this college brought up in Godliness and good learning.'

The boys were thenceforward free, to wander the town, to play games, but to be back in their boarding-houses by dusk. In winter they shut at six o'clock and the assistant masters did rounds, calling names at seven and again at eight. In the summer, the days ended later, but lock-up came invariably by eight. Only the Collegers were literally locked in – unsupervised. The Oppidans' boarding-houses observed varying degrees of laxity in keeping boys in their beds, and the older ones were often to be found in the Christopher inn. The vital thing was to attend to 'absence' calls and prayers in the schoolyard and chapel.

These were the written rhythms and rituals of George's new life at Eton. The reality, however, was that things were much more complicated. Routine was rare at Eton. Religious festivals, but also Founder's Day and Court Days – the anniversaries of the King's Coronation, and of the births and marriages of senior members of the Royal Family – all interrupted school life. Unless these holidays, which were observed by Eton, as both a religious and a royal foundation, fell on the regular full holidays of Sunday or Tuesday, the whole school day was changed to accommodate the boys' attendance in chapel or lining the streets of Windsor to cheer military bandsmen or the Royal Family. Missed lessons had to be fitted in elsewhere.

Breakfast could be changed by an hour – usually it was after the end of the first class, but it could be rushed through before eight o'clock to add a bleary-eyed lesson as necessary. The evening meal, traditionally mutton – exclusively so for the King's Scholars – was served at any time from five to seven, again to add lessons. Also to be considered were the commitments the boys made outside the strict school curriculum to masters who appear on the school bills. Again, these lessons had to be timetabled with regard to the religious and royal calendar for all they were taught and paid for privately. George was taught French, out of school hours, by Messieurs Lemoine and Porny. If either found an apt pupil in Brummell minor at Eton, they would have been disappointed to learn that by the time he came to live in France thirty years later he was claiming he had never been taught to *speak* a word of French. Mr Dore had more success as George's dancing master, though Brummell's later 'cool' manner and tight-fitting clothes limited his attendance on the dance floor – and in this he has been taken as one of Jane Austen's inspirations in having her starchy hero Mr Darcy eschew country dancing. George had a fencing master, Henry Angelo, and took up a lifelong passion for drawing under the tutelage of Mr Cooper and Mr John Robert Cozens, a grandson of Tsar Peter the Great who taught Eton boys water-colour technique, before suffering a mental breakdown in 1794.

George was expected to read extensively in the long hours shut up at Dame Yonge's, though the reading list shows little appreciation of any literature more modern than Alexander Pope, and Shakespeare is absent from the Eton syllabus, despite the recent successes of actor-manager Garrick in revivifying the reputation of the 'Bard of Stratford'. George became a passionate and dedicated reader, writing and conversing on the latest novels in later life, but at school he was restricted to only the most improving works. The 1766 treatise on the Eton curriculum states that boys 'are supposed to read at their leisure hours, Dr Middleton's *Cicero*, Tully's *Offices*, Ovid's long and short verses, *Spectator*, etc, Milton, Pope, Roman History, Graecian History, Potte's *Antiquities*, and Kennet's and all other books necessary towards making a compleat scholar'.

The syllabus proper at Eton College, then, was rigorously classical. It was not, however, always unimaginatively so. After 1766, Eton offered an education that encouraged performance of classical texts and creative and expressive writing, albeit in the styles of the ancient world. As the boys' skills in Latin and Greek increased, they were encouraged from Upper Greek onwards (around thirteen years of age, though it should be noted George was top of the class aged eleven) to specialise in imitation of classical verse and rhetoric – in performance and even in comic writing. Desperately dry by modern standards – every Monday in Upper Greek George had to recite twenty verses of Greek Testament by heart – there was the prospect of lighter relief as the years passed. The polish and wit for which Brummell was later lauded can be traced to his teenage years, spent construing, writing and performing in the style of classical Athens and Rome.

The headmaster's division of fifth-form boys, for instance – about 120 of them, taught *en masse* – had seventeen lessons in a regular week. Ten were spent purely on construing, with the further seven given over to 'repetition' of rote-learned Latin and Greek texts. A week's worth of work for these seven lessons by the end of George's time at Eton would include:

Homer, twice, 35 lines each time
Lucian, twice, 40 lines each time
Virgil, twice, 30 lines each time
Scriptores Romani, twice, 40 lines each time
Poetae Graeci, 30 lines
Horace (hexameters) 60 lines.

The tempos and rhythms, the intellectual and aural balance that define classical verse were drummed into Etonians as if they were to be a schoolboy chorus in an antique tragedy. But as they progressed through the school they began to take centre-stage themselves, and increasingly were encouraged to exercise their imaginations.

The boys had 'saying lessons' from *Selecta Ovidio*, Tibullo, and Propertio in the fifth form. In the summer, from 'Whitsuntide to electiontide the *Odes of Horace* [were construed] instead of Lucian', which one classicist describes as akin to turning from military history to light verse, and these were spoken aloud as well as studied on the page. When the novelist Fanny Burney, then a lady-in-waiting to Queen Charlotte at Windsor, visited Eton with the King and Queen in 1791 she was 'entertained', with the royal party, by Eton boys declaiming odes in Greek and Latin.

As young Etonians' voices broke, they were expected to take part in more and more speech-making, drama and performance. 'We have likewise Speeches which are spoken before the school,' the 1766 syllabus treatise confirms, 'with the emphasis and proper stress on particular words. These speeches . . . no doubt learn the boys to read with propriety. The sixth form boys only speak and declame and they [are] suffered to skip a whole week's exercises if they have a Declamation to make, or speech to get [up].'

The last few weeks of term before the summer and winter holidays were entirely set aside for the study and performance of Greek plays. The main parts were taken by older boys, and occasionally a master. Indeed, the upper school was tutored all year in extracts from classical drama as part of the Monday and Saturday morning routines. George became familiar with the less gory and sensual passages from *Oedipus Tyrannus*, *Oedipus Coloneus*, *Antigone*, *Phoenissae*, and *Septem contra Thebas*. Four plays by Euripedes were performed regularly in their unexpurgated form: *Hecuba*, *Orestes*, *Phoenissae* and *Alcestis*.

As well as the end-of-term Greek plays it seems that the academic study of Greek and Roman drama inspired extracurricular amateur theatricals in the long hours in which boys were cooped up together, either in the Long Chamber or in their boarding-houses. A watercolour from Brummell's time preserved in the school archives depicts a performance at one end of the riotous Long Chamber, with boys perched on beds and boxes forming an audience, all with the authentic air of a modern school play. One Etonian play of the period in English does survive, titled *Out of the Frying Pan and Into the Fire*. Its author later claimed, however, that even the diversion of classical or vernacular comedy could not improve on the Etonians' favourite winter pastime: rat-hunting in the infested older buildings. The skins were nailed up as trophies. To the skill of a rat-catcher and the ear of the classical poet, then, the Etonian was expected to add the polish of an actor.

Like Fox and North before him, and George Canning his contemporary, Brummell learned at Eton to be a confident public speaker, in Latin, Greek, and later English, and his physical poise and confidence on the stage of London life also owed much to an Etonian fascination with classical drama and amateur theatricals.

The style of humour for which Brummell later became famous also dates from his time at Eton. The monastic erudition of the Eton boys was put to more unexpected use than just the performance of Greek plays. A late-eighteenth-century Etonian was expected to be a poet, an actor – but also a wit.

Each fifth- and sixth-former was expected every week to compose at least five or six original stanzas, sometimes in Latin, sometimes in Greek iambics, but with stress on the reduction of an argument to an epigram. Here is a lesson from Brummell's Fifth Form syllabus.

If the week be regular, the Master sets an extempore theme at three o'clock (on Monday) and the boys are to make four long and four short verses in the manner of Martial like this one:

> *Otiosus*
> *Occurris quocunque loco mihi, Posthume, clamas*
> *Protinus, et prima est haec tua vox, 'quid agis?'*

Hoc, si me decies una conveneris hora,
Dicis: habes puto tu, Posthume, nil quid agas.

Brevitas
*Si placet Brevitas, hoc breve Carmen habe.**

If boys are not able to cut a joke on the theme, they ought by no means to be punished.

In other words, Etonians were schooled, from the late eighteenth century onwards, to emulate a manner of witty adumbration, the style of the classical Roman epigrammatists, and to excel in the reduction of an argument or idea into a pithy closing comment, or, as the 1766 treatise has it, a 'joke'. George Brummell, who carried on writing classically scanned verse into old age, was clearly inspired to polish the sheen of his classical education by relishing wit and brevity more than grandiose rhetoric or even verse-writing. This trait, which sometimes played out as the incisive 'put-down' but just as often figured as the casually warm and witty aside, was one of the signal traits of his personality, one remarked upon, copied and admired. It was a style, it should be noted, that typified the high comedy of the period – also classically inspired: the apparently frothy comedies of Sheridan and Garrick, of Colley Cibber, George Coleman or Fanny Burney that allowed the language of the Augustan age a comic life. It was a style that stayed with Brummell into old age, and even beyond the departure of his reason.

～

* Tedious/dull.
Wherever you meet me, Posthumus, you holler
At once, and these are your first words: 'How do you do?'
This is what you say, even if you meet me ten times within the hour.
I think, Posthumus, that you don't have enough to do.

Concisely/with wit.
So why don't you just let brevity be the soul of your wit (tune/epitaph)?

In Brummell's day Eton College had no uniform as such. In this it was typical of schools of the period. There was no need to create an artificial homogeneity as there was much less range of either cloth or colour available for children's clothes in the late eighteenth century. The youngest boys arrived at the Swan With Two Necks pub *en route* to Eton dressed more or less alike, and more or less like their fathers, without any admonition from the college to do so. The college felt no call to give a further corporate identity to their pupil body around Eton and Windsor. Etonians were conspicuous enough, even the Collegers, by being dressed as 'gentlemen'. They were relatively clean and their clothes, breeches, stockings, shoes and jacket, looked sober and Sunday-best all week.

However, the range of fabrics – and colours – on sale at Pitt's and March, the drapers on Eton high street, was expanding rapidly. This was also the case across the country, thanks largely to the East India Company. And Eton Oppidans, with some disposable income and some competitive swagger, took advantage of the new possibilities. George's specific expenditure on clothes as a schoolboy is unknown. However, an unexpected cache of documents was rediscovered only relatively recently, shedding new light on the sartorial education of Eton schoolboys of Brummell's generation. Scrope Davies, fellow Etonian, near contemporary and acolyte of Brummell, left England in some haste in later life. He entrusted before his flight a miscellany of papers, personal and financial, to his bankers. When a fiscal descendant of the bank, Barclays, was moving its West End premises in 1976 this long forgotten depository was opened in the presence of Davies family members and bank archivists. Because Scrope had gone on from Eton to become a close associate of Lord Byron, there was excited interest in the letters and the financial records revealed. (It was Lord Byron who had suggested that Scrope improve his ways by marrying and 'begetting some Scrooples'.) What has not received attention was that Scrope had also been on intimate terms with Brummell. George's last missive written in England, an appeal for a quick loan, was sent to Scrope. (The request was declined.) Both Scrope and George had patronised Eton high street as schoolboys, and the Scrope Davies accounts as they relate to Eton are revelatory on this subject. Scrope, like George, came from a relatively modest background compared to his schoolfriends and, like George, he left Eton a dedicated dandy.

One term's accounts sent in two instalments from the draper on Eton high street are typical. On 26 November 1799 and 27 February 1800 John March the draper enclosed accounts for payment to Scrope's parents. In the last Eton term of the eighteenth century, Scrope had ordered six yards of huckaback at eleven shillings a yard. This was a stout linen with a rough surface and was used for towels by the Eton schoolboys. (Scrope was ahead of his time, like Brummell, in maintaining modern standards of personal cleanliness. He ordered soap from Charter's on 15 September, 10 October and 16 November, at a shilling a bar, and repeatedly bought their sixpenny toothbrushes.) The rest of the term's drapery accounts are given over entirely to luxury fabrics. One yard of blue and buff toilinett – a fine woollen used almost exclusively for waistcoats in the 1790s – and five yards of silk binding and silk at a guinea per yard. Also one yard of India dimity, a cotton fabric, woven with raised stripes or figures, again a luxury fabric for waistcoats. Thence the teenager took his haul to the tailors to have his clothes made up. James Miller, the Eton tailor, submitted a bill for thirteen guineas for this same period, via Scrope's dame, Mrs Harrington. Miller lists forty-one different items, some repairs but also five waistcoats, four coats, six pairs of breeches and two academic gowns. This term's accounts were not unusual for Scrope and do not amount to evidence therefore of a growth spurt but rather regular spending for an upper boy at Eton with an interest in clothes in the 1790s. In total that term Scrope Davies, by no means an unusually wealthy Eton schoolboy, spent thirty-five pounds one shilling and sixpence at the various Eton high street purveyors who submitted accounts to his dame, a sum amounting to well over £5000 in today's money, and the majority of this was on the fabric and construction of his wardrobe. It would be fair to assume that George, nicknamed 'Buck Brummell' at Eton, bought and ordered in this same manner and made his first forays into fashion as an Eton school-boy. Crucially also, the trouser, as yet an anathema for grown men, was assumed by boys and youths from the 1760s, and Eton boys ordered their own from the high street before they pro-gressed to knee breeches and stockings. The man who would later introduce the modern trouser to London fashion first ordered his cut and made on Eton high street as early as the late 1780s.

As Eton boys progressed through the school, they became regulars at the local drapery and tailor's, ordering their own bespoke clothes – even trousers – in some of the latest fabrics. This facet of the Eton education was almost unique: the boys were far enough from home to be obliged to clothe themselves accord-ing to their own taste but near enough to the fashionable world and the court for the Oppidans to be encouraged in a competitive dandyism as the new fabric economy allowed. They also formed, courtesy of Eton, the ruinous habit of shopping on account – at their parents' expense.

~

'Buck' Brummell would have been bemused to hear himself described as a dandy or, for that matter, a beau. The term 'Beau' was not used for George at school and was not in regular coinage. Although it had some currency as part of the French lexicon that peppered eighteenth-century letters and conversation, it was not yet the aspirational title Brummell's own fame would lend the word. Beau Nash had not completed his re-imagining of Bath. Beau Montrond was a minor player in the convoluted politics of France. Brummell took to the nickname 'Buck' at school either on account of his clothes – he was described even as an adolescent as taking more than common care with his sports kit on a rainy day – or his personality and background. The term is used in a 1782 poem 'The Bawd' to describe sexually licentious Londoners. Bucks were men-about-town, men of the world, West End boys. They came top of the list in the poem's catalogue of 'Bucks, Bloods, Choice Spirits and Demy Reps of the Present Age' in

London's *demi-monde*. Less dashing than blades, but without a hint of the effeminacy of fops, bucks were fashion-conscious to some extent, but with a cosmopolitan swagger and just a hint of sexual danger. His schoolboy nickname therefore begs further questions about Brummell's reputation at school, and his mien for surviving Eton.

Schools teach much more than is on the curriculum, and pupils pick up more from their contemporaries and outside the classroom than many teachers would be happy to acknowledge. Less is documented, necessarily, of the life of an eighteenth-century Eton schoolboy *outside* the classroom, yet we know a surprising amount about George's lifestyle and habits at school. An unusual series of documents from the period have survived in the Eton archive, collected together as *Nugae Etonenses*, that sought to expand an understanding of the entire Eton community, already by the late eighteenth century a subject of some curiosity, and not a little ridicule. Moreover, such was the sea-change in attitudes to education over the next generation, and the growth in the number of public schools, that many Victorian Old Etonians put pen to paper to praise or defame their schooldays in England's most famous educational establishment. Several even wrote about 'Buck' Brummell. Old Etonians rarely recalled what they learned of the classics at school. They remembered instead the games, the flogging, the fagging and Montem.

When I went to Eton [reminisced one old boy of the late eighteenth century], 'Cocky' Keate [Dr John Keate] ruled the lower regions. There was too much tendency to favouritism: either from rank or ability; some had the lion's share of being called up. The fairest chance a boy had was in his papers, his copy of verses, his theme, and his personal stock that no one could touch.

Captain Gronow also remembered Dr Keate from Eton, and blamed his temper on his 'diminutive stature', called him the 'little autocrat', and said he 'avenged himself upon the persons of delinquent boys'.

Lord Chatham later wrote that he 'scarce observed a boy who

was not cowed for life at Eton: that a public school might suit a boy of turbulent forward disposition, but would not do where there was any gentleness'.

The poet Percy Shelley was to suffer a lifetime of nightmares after the trauma of his Eton schooldays: a catalogue of official and unofficial psychological torture. There was a prevailing atmosphere of actual or repressed violence, much later described as akin to a royal court of the *ancien régime* – an atmosphere, Cyril Connolly later opined, where self-preservation was assured by wit, humour and the guarding of one's 'personal stock that no one could touch'. How then did George Brummell pilot himself through an Eton adolescence? How and why did the wide-eyed innocent painted by Sir Joshua Reynolds transform himself into 'Buck' Brummell?

When George Brummell entered Eton the headmaster was Jonathan Davies – a man noted for the loudness of his voice and his preference for life in London rather than Eton. In his absence, the school was run by a lower master, William Langford, who also held Court appointments as canon of Windsor and chaplain to the King. For this reason, Langford had schoolboy malefactors marched *en masse* up the hill to Windsor Castle for group floggings. Davies was succeeded as headmaster in George's time by one Dr Heath, known as 'Ascot Heath' – perhaps for his wild and uncompromising manner. He once caught a boy at cards, took out his birch and said, 'You shuffle and I'll cut.' On another occasion he flogged seventy boys in one session and 'was laid up with aches and pains for more than a week'. 'Boys, you should always be pure of heart,' Brummell's teacher Dr Keate is quoted as saying, 'and if you are not pure in heart, I'll flog you.'

A Regency Etonian who had suffered at his hands wrote with icy equanimity about the prevailing ethos:

Boys will stand flogging, and have no absurd notions of injured personal honour on that score, whatever modern theorists may hold. It is anything like interference with recognised privileges, right or wrong, which they resent as an indignity. Their notions of the liberty of the subject are as strongly defined, however absurd the definition may sometimes be, as those of any independent Englishman of riper years: and no head master will rule a public school successfully, who has not tact enough to understand and recognise this claim. Either he will spoil the honesty and manliness of his boys, or he will ruin the interests of his school.

It was an age that saw only good in the beating of children – especially boys. Their social class was no deterrent. One of George III's daughters, Princess Sophia, recalled the Prince of Wales and Duke of York as children at Windsor being 'held by their arms and flogged like dogs with a long whip'. The violent lifestyle of a later generation of 'Regency bucks' (and their apparent interest in *le vice anglais* as catered to by the brothel madams of St James's) may perhaps be attributed to the late-eighteenth-century reliance on the whip as the fundamental tool of schooling.

Eton life was portrayed by the masters as a constant battle with the boys. There had been and would be again several full rebellions when the entire college descended into anarchy. Such had been the case in 1768 and there would be full-scale revolts in 1810 and 1818. When the schoolboys rose up, there was little the masters could do about it. There were insufficient staff and the buildings were hopelessly overcrowded but, more than this, it was a violent age, one that saw nothing strange in the unsupervised imprisonment of adolescent boys and the threat of maiming violence as the main tool in their discipline. Whatever slack was given to them therefore tended only to confirm their masters' worst fears. There were tandem races around Eton (small racing carriages, not bicycles) by those older boys with access to such or the money to hire. There was cockfighting at Bedford's Yard and bull-baiting at the appropriately named Bachelors' Acre, just the other side of the Thames. The river itself provided the most dangerous sports. Boys dived off Windsor Old Bridge when the river was backed up by the sluice, fights broke out frequently with the Thames waterboatmen, and there were notorious drownings, including that of the young Earl of Waldegrave in 1794.

The Etonians were constantly at loggerheads with the 'cads': the Eton town youths of similar age who sought to fleece them of their pocket money by fairish means or foul. The 'cads' were eventually banned from the college precincts. George himself only narrowly avoided getting involved in one violent escapade on the river, and then only with recourse to the age-old armour of comedy. A boatman-cad who had found himself in some altercation with the schoolboys was on the point of being thrown over the bridge into the low waters of the Thames by a mob of over a hundred Etonians. Buck Brummell – perhaps fourteen at the time – caught the attention and laughter of the Etonian and cad hooligans alike by shouting: 'My dear fellows, don't send him into the river. The man is evidently in a state of perspiration, and it almost amounts to a certainty that he will catch cold.' Brummell was rewarded with guffaws, perhaps some bemusement in the face of such paradoxical whimsy – typical of his later style – and the bargeman was released.

Not all violent encounters could be so easily defused, or abuse avoided. The masters relied heavily on floggings to assert control, but also, famously, a system of devolved power known as 'fagging'. Younger boys acted as servants to older boys, in return for which privilege older boys ruled the boarding-houses in the place of adults. At night in particular, there was no proper adult supervision from dames, 'domines' (the few masters who ran boarding-houses) or the college itself. The potential for abuse – of every variety – became notorious through the next century and a half. Those boys, like Shelley, who disobeyed or disappointed their fag-master could be flogged by the head-of-house – an older schoolboy – though in practice he often allowed other senior boys to flog their fags if they so chose.

I was appointed to fag for a member of the Sixth Form [writes one boy from this period], the condition of life was very hard indeed. The practice of fagging had become an organized system of brutality and cruelty. I was frequently kept up until one or two o'clock in the morning waiting on my masters at supper, and undergoing every sort of bullying at their hands. I have been beaten on the palms with the back of a brush, or struck on both sides of my face, because I had not closed the shutter near my master's bed tight enough, or because in making his bed I had left the seam of the lower sheet uppermost . . . and I had *inter alia* to count his linen, to make lists for the laundress, and to fetch water for his basin from the outdoor pump. When I wished to obtain water for my own use, I was told that . . . any ablutions of mine must take place at my dame's. On arriving there I found a room of the barest description with a sanded floor . . . which was set apart for such as required it. In this room I had my breakfast which consisted of a couple of rolls, some butter and a cup of milk . . . When I was kept fagging late at night, I had to look forward to the probability of a flogging on the next day for not knowing my lessons. I say nothing of the minor discomforts of having the tassel of one's nightcap set on fire in the night, and having one's bed turned up on end and finding one's heels in the air.

It took two fifth- or sixth-form praeposters to hold down a boy to be flogged across the flogging-stool – a little like library bookcase steps – an example of which remains in the college museum. 'Praeposters or monitors are chosen for their purpose,' is the chilling phrase used in the *Nugae Etonenses*.

Some boys ran away, others wrote pitiful letters to their parents begging to be brought home. 'Dear Papa,' wrote one, 'Eton is a very bad place and I should be glad to leave it. Besides I lead a very unhappy life for I am forced to wait upon the Big Boys while they eat supper and to goe down for every thing they want and if I do not do it directly they beate me very much and I dare not tell. I and two other boys wait upon them as a Servant . . . I assure you Papa I will not keep company with bad boys but indeed there is very few good ones in the Place.'

But the rewards for those who stayed the course were considerable, and their years of torment were quickly forgotten in the years of privilege or of being, in turn, the tormentor. 'Whatever might be the success in after life,' wrote Stratford Canning of his time at Eton as a near contemporary of Brummell, 'whatever gratification of ambition might be realised, whatever triumph might be achieved, no one is ever again so great a man as when he was a Sixth Form Boy at Eton.' In typically terse form, George III, a regular visitor at Eton, made the same point. When Canning met the King and replied to his royal interrogator that he was in his final year at Eton, the King told the adolescent that this rendered him 'a greater man than I can ever make you'.

For George Brummell, as both fag and later fag-master, 'fagging' was the structure of his schooldays and the social context within which he learned his first lessons about power and charm. He seems to have made a fast study of these early and harsh truths in serving and being served. He acquitted himself tellingly well, at least in the eyes of some: 'I knew him well, Sir,' wrote one classmate, years later, 'he was never flogged; and a man, Sir, is not worth a damn who was never flogged through school.' Some insight into how and why George Brummell, quite untypical of the time, survived Eton physically unscathed is given by his fag-master, the older boy to whom George was assigned on his first day at school.

All these three most happy years George was my fag. He was a far livelier lad than his . . . brother, William: indeed no one at the school was so full of animation, fun and wit. He was a general favourite. Our dame [Mrs Yonge] his tutor [Hawtrey] and my tutor . . . and Dr Goodall, all petted him. You ask me whether he was pugnacious; I do not remember that he ever fought or quarrelled with any one; indeed it was impossible for anyone to be more good-natured than he was. With George, afterwards General Leigh, and Lord Lake and Jack Musters, who were all in the same house with us, and Berkeley Craven . . . and with all his other intimate companions, I never heard of his having a single disagreement. Like them he was not in the least studious, but a very *clever* and a very *idle* boy, and very *frank*; and then, whatever he became afterwards, not in the least conceited, though Nature seemed to have supplied him with a quadruple portion of amusing repartee . . . I recollect nothing about his fondness for athletic exercises, boating, cricket etc., but I really believe that no Etonian was ever more popular with all his companions than George Brummell.

It is an affectionate testimonial, written a lifetime after the impressions were first made. George was funny and self-confident enough to engage in 'witty repartee' even with much older boys. He had little need to be pugnacious. Despite the absence of great wealth, status or supreme academic ability, he could begin to negotiate the perilous world of Eton by deploying 'fun and wit'. It was a signal lesson. George's fag-master goes on to relate that his greatest talent was in the making of cheese on toast, of which the head boy in the house was entitled to a triple portion. This was no insignificant skill on George's part in the eighteenth century – the Duke of Bedford was scarred for life by his ineptitude at the same, and the famous Londonderry ambassadorial silver service created for the great gourmet Lord Charles Stewart featured centrally a dish for toasted cheese. Brummell had a genius for achieving excellence in apparently trivial acts, this first one within the rigid class structure of school. Brummell avoided the birches and whips of schoolmasters and senior boys by the unique force of his personality. As he grew, though, he added another skill to aid him through Eton.

The account of Brummell's fag-master contradicts the evidence elsewhere in this one regard: Brummell became, some years *after* his time as a junior fag, an accomplished sportsman. He played cricket for Eton in the first eleven in the summer of 1793, scoring 0 out and 12 runs, and making three catches in his opponents' second innings in a match against Oldfield Club of Berkshire. He swam, and was on the river in the summer more than the playing-fields. He also played football. Old Etonian Captain Gronow later insisted that Brummell 'distinguished himself at Eton as the best scholar, the best boatman and the best cricketer; and, more than all, he [possessed] the comprehensive excellences that are represented by the familiar term "good fellow"'.

This breeziness of character is also described by another, younger boy:

I knew Brummell at Eton, he was in the Fifth Form, and I in the Lower School, but I well remember his appearance – he had a fair, florid complexion, and a quantity of light curly hair, which it was the fashion in those days to wear long enough to hang upon the shoulders. He was a strong, muscular boy . . . and I can even now recollect seeing him, with thick shoes and striped worsted stockings drawn over his knees (quite clean and tight) going to play foot-ball – in summer he used to be on the river, not at cricket in the playing fields.

This was the Eton his father had intended for him, the one, as envisaged in a contemporary novel, where a son might be 'roughed about among boys, [and thereby] learn to be a man'. Billy Brummell was closely allied to a government that saw the most humiliating defeat in British military history: the American War of Independence. It had a direct effect on schooling at the time, especially at Eton. Many had queried the competence of the British military and ruling élite and 'whether some miscarriages on the naval and military departments have not been indirectly caused by the selection of fine gentlemen, of men of levity of appearance . . . to command armaments'. George's education was designed to make him seem, and ideally be, a paragon of English gentle*manliness*. Eton rose to the challenge in Brummell's time, such that, by the beginning of the new century, a professor of modern history could happily assert that Britain's greatness came 'from hardy sports [and] from manly schools' like Eton.

For 'Buck' Brummell then, life at Eton was not all classics, flogging and fagging. His 'personal stock' as a 'good fellow' full of 'witty repartee' as well as an ease on the sportsfield combined to smooth his passage through school, and possibly to find him the nickname 'Buck'. And there was fun to be had, most of it involving balls, the Thames or, in the spirit of the age, the persecution of animals. There was swimming in the summer at Sandy Hole, Pope's Hole, and South Hope – deep and slow meanders in the Thames. There were three river-skiffs used by the boys, *Piper's Green*, *Snake* and *My Guinea's Lion*, which could be raced from Datchet to Windsor Bridge. Alarmingly, boys had access to six guns for shooting swallows and swifts, and although the tradition of chasing a ram down the high street to be stoned to death had fallen into desuetude by Brummell's time, there was cat- and duck-hunting and regular badger-baiting on Eton Common. Brummell would later hunt, unenthusiastically, with the Belvoir, and owned shooting pistols against the possibility of a duel. There was a real-tennis court and even billiards, with private matches at a 'billiard table keeper' in Windsor called Lawson, Sibson & Russell. Further afield, if the boys could get there, there was ample opportunity for betting on horses at Datchet, Chalvey, Sunninghill, Gerrards Cross, Cranford Bridge, Maidenhead Bridge, and even Ascot. The college employed a 'Pursuivant of Runaways' with four thuggish assistants to round up the boys from the surrounding area during race meets, to be back in school for lock-up. It was the great age of betting and Eton schoolboys were no exception: they bet on horses, pugilists, dogs, badgers and tandems. And when the boys were kept within the school grounds they would bet on anything else they could think of. *Nugae Etonenses* provides a remarkable list of the games played in or around Eton in Brummell's time with both betting and fun in mind.

Cricket, Fives, Shirking Walls, Scrambling Walls, Bally Cally, Peg-Top, Peg in the Ring, Goals, Hopscotch, Headimy, Conquering Lobs, Hoops, Marbles, Trap-Ball, Stealbaggage, Puss in the Corner, Cat Gallows, Kites, Cloyster and Flyer Gigs, Tops, Humming-tops, Hunt the Hare, Hunt the Dark Lanthorn, Chuck, Sinks, Starecaps, Hustle-cap, Football, Slides in the School, Leaping Poles, Slide Down the Sides of the Stairs from Cloysters to College Kitchen.

Cricket at Eton is mentioned by Horace Walpole as early as 1734. 'Eton Fives', as the game has become known, was played between the buttresses on the north side of the chapel until 1848 – involving, by Eton logic, only four players. It is considered to be one of the ancestors of squash. 'Shirking Walls', it seems, was a variety of fives; 'Conquering Lobs' a sort of conkers with marbles. Hoops was the London import of rolling iron hoops, either specially made or stolen from carters, hit with a birch stick and raced against an opponent. There seemed no end to the inventiveness of the boys. But it should be pointed out that Brummell's schooldays slightly predate the sports mania that came to dominate the public-school ethos a generation later. None of these games, even cricket, was on the school timetable as such.

Eton College created and helped promulgate several games that have become part of the British experience of school. Eton, moreover, was the model for new boarding-schools catering to the growing and socially ambitious middle class. Yet in key respects the effect of Eton on Brummell and his coterie was not viewed in a comprehensively positive light by the generation that followed. Increasingly, the rake-helly, libidinous lifestyle of the Regency generation typified by Brummell was blamed on a schooling that allowed their sexuality to run amok, insufficiently sublimated – a later term but a Victorian idea – at school. The reputation of Eton in the period Brummell was there became the catalyst in the exploding sports mania. Sports, it was soon argued, had a moral imperative *within* the curriculum, allowing young men to be schooled together *without* fostering addictions to gambling, drinking and worse. It is ironic that the young jock, Buck Brummell, would come to symbolise in later life a generation that seemed to have insufficient time for participatory sport and too much for urbane fashion, wine, gambling and sex. Sport, on the periphery of Brummell's school experience, became the idealised sublimation of adolescent male sexual energy and central to the school experience for generations of British men. If, as Victorian educationalists believed, Brummell's Eton had provided insufficient sublimation to the sex-drive of 350 adolescent boys, what did they get up to instead?

'What nasty indecent tricks do they not also learn from each other,' wrote Mary Wollstonecraft of life in English public schools in 1792, 'when a number of them pig together in the same bedchamber, not to speak of the vices which render the body weak?'

The late eighteenth century saw three different aftershocks of the Enlightenment disrupt the bedrooms of adolescents; a troubling collision for boys like George Brummell. There had been a marked slackening in traditional sexual morality, notably among the aristocracy, certainly in London. The Enlightenment's emphasis on personal expression – at its most extreme in the philosophy of 'libertinism' – and the parallel attacks on the traditional teachings of the Church figure prominently as causes. Concurrently, and again associated with Enlightenment thinking, there had been a sharp rise in the production of pornography. This was a result of a loosening of censorship, increased literacy and the wider printing boom. Brummell's generation also saw what one might term the first great age of *British* pornography, as opposed to the French, imported, and more expensively illicit variety – partly due to the blockades of the French revolutionary wars. But the Enlightenment had also, perhaps perversely, spawned a growing body of 'scientific' literature expressing extreme paranoia about the dangers of masturbation.

Quite when Buck Brummell grew aware of any of this is conjecture. There is some argument over the possible falling age of puberty in boys in this period. Anecdotally it is worth noting that near contemporaries William Hickey and Lord Byron had their first sexual experiences, more or less consensually, aged thirteen and nine respectively. Certainly there was a widening gap between the age of sexual maturity and the age of marriage, which was part of what fuelled rising bastardy rates and the sex trade in London, and doubtless the wave of pornography. Much of this new erotica would have been familiar and accessible to Eton boys. It was masked in the language and imagery of the classical world they knew so well – *An Account of the Remains of the Worship of Priapus, Lately Existing at Iserna, in the Kingdom of Naples* (1786) is typical of the 'classical' porn that flooded the market after the rediscovery of the Pompeiian frescos in 1763. The sexually explicit political satires of Hogarth, Gillray and Rowlandson should also be seen in this light. All three artists liberally interwove classical themes and allusions, biting satire and sexually explicit and scatological material. All three also catered to the demand for porn as was sold from Pote's in Fleet Street and therefore, indubitably, from Pote's on Eton High Street.

Contemporary with this, the second half of the eighteenth century saw an anxious rise in treatises on masturbation. The 1710 tract on the Heinous Sin of Self Pollution, *Onania*, by Balthazar Beckers, remained forced reading for many schoolboys and their masters throughout the eighteenth century. This book expanded exponentially over the years in proportion to the growing hysteria about masturbation, from sixty pages to 194 by its sixteenth edition, so that by Brummell's adolescence it ran to 300 pages. Meanwhile Dr Tissot's 1764 treatise *L'Onanisme*, immediately translated into English, promised all the horrors that became catechistic over the next generations: 'lassitude, epilepsy, convulsions, boils, disorders of the digestive, respiratory or nervous systems, and even death'. The only recommended remedy for George's generation: daily exercise, low diet and regular bowel movements. The 1793 Eton prayer book, issued for the use of Brummell and his schoolfellows, would have raised eyebrows but not alarm by suggesting private devotions in response to 'Involuntary Morning Ejaculations at Waking, or Rising'.

O do away, as the Night, so my Trangressions, scatter my Sins as these Morning Clouds.

Lord forgive whatever thou hast seen amiss in me this Night.

Lord deliver me from Sloth and Idleness; from youthful Lusts and ill Company, from all dangers bodily and ghostly.

In a sense this rise in anxiety about adolescent wet dreams and masturbation seems at odds with an age of general adult permissiveness and a pornography boom. But Eton was known to hold particular temptations and these register as the concerns addressed in the prayer book issued to parents and boys. The Collegers were known to suffer abuses in the unsupervised communal fug of Long Chamber, the least of which was using the smaller boys as floorcloths to polish the boards. The fee-paying boys were considered also to be at risk, as they shared private rooms, and in some cases beds. Eton's founding statutes intriguingly forbade bed-sharing after fourteen. Yet a rival school found it worthwhile to advertise in 1786 that the boys might share a room but 'each will have a bed to himself'. A Harrow parent wrote in 1774 that 'wherever [my son] goes I insist upon his constantly sleeping alone . . . for reasons that will increase with his years'. Clearly it was a matter of concern that boys would 'pollute' themselves, and each other by example, and that masturbation and mutual masturbation would weaken the boy and ruin the man. It was a psychologically fraught position for boys like Brummell, in the years now acknowledged to include most men's sexual peak. Despite the easy tolerance society showed towards the sexual practice of Etonians' parents and elder brothers, the boys knew that society was overwhelmingly condemnatory of their own likely sexual practice – masturbation. There have been theories that this paradox relates to the rise of the Evangelical Church, or even the equation of unproductive 'spending' with poor economic management. The most plausible argument, so far as schoolboys were concerned, was that the Enlightenment that had freed adult sexuality had, conversely, accorded too important a role for the innocent, individualised child to allow for any corruption in youth. Quite when this age of innocence was set to end, and libertinism take over, must have been a disquieting issue for George Brummell in particular: painted by Reynolds as a sexless nymph in 1782 and expected to be a rounded libertine on taking up his army commission in 1794, a dozen short years later.

Homosexuality, by contrast with masturbation, was viewed with ambivalence. Though illegal and in theory punishable by death since 1533, buggery or sodomy, as homosexual practice was variously termed, was an acknowledged fact of the London *demi-monde*. At boarding-schools, including Eton, it is less clear what behaviour was acceptable to masters, dames or, indeed, fellow pupils. The literature suggests, for adolescents, there might well have been much more guilt associated with masturbation than with homosexual acts. Homosexuality among adolescent boys was viewed in the late eighteenth century, in that time-honoured term, as a 'phase'. 'I have in my mind's eye a list . . . of those who at my school were conspicuous . . . in this particular manner [homosexuality],' wrote one Old Etonian of Brummell's school-fellows. 'Those very boys have become Cabinet Ministers, states-men, officers, clergymen, country gentlemen et cetera . . . they are nearly all of them fathers of thriving families, respected and prosperous.' Homosexuality in boarding-schools was not to be addressed directly for an entire century, when a brave headmaster of Clifton College set the cat among the pigeons by publicly suggesting sodomy was a signal trait of Victorian boarding-schools. At that time those schools, Eton as the prime example, with a tradition of private bedrooms rather than dormitories, were viewed as particularly susceptible.

Brummell never alluded to or admitted to any homosexual experience at Eton or subsequently. His supposed 'abstemious-ness' in matters sexual (largely an invention of his Victorian biographers as a way to disassociate him from his coterie, men whose indiscretion and sexual licence had become legendary) in conjunction with Brummell's place in the history of fashion have led some to assume him a closet homosexual. The evidence points in the other direction. Yet there is undoubtedly an aesthetic to the Brummell myth and manner that today would be labelled at the very least 'metrosexual'. Eton holds some keys in decoding this developing sexual persona. One Eton master writing later in the nineteenth century asks the reasonable question, 'Isn't it really rather dangerous to let boys read Plato if one desires that they should accept conventional moralities?' and the image of Eton well into the twentieth century is, of course, profoundly homo-eroticised. Of the 1790s things are less clear-cut. As stated, the cult of sport that had as its founding principle the sublimation of male sexual desire (ironic though that may seem) grew out of a belief that the Regency rakes had been 'spoiled' at school by a lack of organised sport, and too much free access to gambling, loose barmaids or each other. 'Our sons should be Spartans in their persons and habits,' thundered one educationalist, before adding, apparently without irony, 'and Athenians in their literature.' But this same Regency generation seemed unusually untroubled by sex, in all its forms, as compared to their repressed or hypocritical grandchildren. A more modern writer has summed up the situation Brummell found himself in at Eton like this:

The inbuilt forces that made for this last tendency [homosexuality] may thus be briefly summarised. First and most fundamental the single sex character of the institution and the age of its inmates. Second the cult of games, [later] promoted by masters, which added a touch of the numinous and more than a touch of the romantic to the physical beauty, the grace of movement and elegance of form so common in young athletes . . . [lastly] applying only to those who could read Greek authors easily or were curious enough to read them in translation, the ethos of Athens in the fifth century BC.

In almost every regard this holds true for Brummell's Eton. The cult of games may have been less expanded in the 1790s compared to a generation later, but the classics were almost the entirety of the curriculum in Brummell's day, precisely when an eroticised neo-classicism was inspiring the Royal Academicians, not to mention the pornographers whose work sold in Fleet Street and Eton. It was a heady atmosphere, undoubtedly.

Brummell emerged from Eton typical of his class and contemporaries, possessed, no doubt, of a morbid horror of masturbation (arguably psychologically damaging in itself), largely tolerant of homosexuality but, more especially, highly sensitised to homosexual situations and very likely to homo-eroticised art. The memoirs about Brummell at school fail to address the issue of sex directly, which is hardly surprising given the period or the class of the men responding to fellow-Etonian Captain Jesse's appeal for anecdotes. But Brummell's old schoolfellows do, in their way, write about love. George was 'handsome'; 'manly'; 'muscular'; 'lively'; a 'good fellow'; 'full of animation, fun and wit. A general favourite'; 'No young Etonian was ever more popular.' Brummell was, from his schooldays, the *object* of male admiration or even desire. However, from these first years of sexual maturity he professed himself to be heterosexually predatory. The key story at Eton involves the headmaster's daughter, the Montem parade and, typically of the later man, clothes.

~

Montem was a holiday of misrule and fancy dress at Eton. The origins of this ritual called Montem, or Ad Montem (To the Hill!) are lost in time but clearly predate the college. The fancy-dress festival was described as an 'ancient tradition' in 1561. It involved a procession of the entire school to nearby Salt Hill on the first Tuesday after Whitsun. Every boy was involved, all assigned titles, duties and ranks in a military-style parade. The 'Captain of Montem', a 'blooming youth' called Harris in Brummell's last Montem in 1793, had flowers thrown at him by Windsor shop girls and odes composed in his honour by local songwriters. Harris found himself the Lord of Misrule for a day, which could also earn him substantial sums. The rest of the school was ranked as mareschals, ensigns, colonels, lieutenants, stewards, sergeants, corporals and saltbearers, with the other boys titled 'polemen'. Each rank tried to outdo the ones below in the flamboyance of their dress, which by Brummell's time was hired from theatres as far away as London and included costumes of 'Turks, Albanians, courtiers of Charles II and George I, Highlanders and hidalgos'. Coaches came out from London filled with the boys' families, and locals gathered to watch the spectacle in the manner of the 4 June celebrations at Eton today (which marks King George III's birthday and is the festival that has taken over as the high point of the Eton year). The boys would leave school early in the morning, and the march was both musical and high-spirited. The violence that became associated with Montem was a result partly of drinking, but mainly of the 'trick-or-treat' extortion that also defined the day. Eton boys in bizarre fancy dress were posted on the main highways and waterways near Eton and Windsor, and demanded a toll on Montem day, shouting, '*Salt, salt*', or '*Mos pro Lege*' (custom before law). All the monies went to the captain, to help him with his university career, though to him also fell the expenses of the day, which could be great. Young 'Captain' Dyson spent £205 on his Montem in 1784 against a taking of £451. Even royal spectators were not exempt from this schoolboy toll. It is said that William III's Dutch guards were so alarmed by a direct demand for money on the way to Windsor that they came near to killing several schoolboys, who were only saved by the ridiculousness of their garb. Brummell's schoolfellows found themselves handed fifty guineas each by King George and Queen Charlotte in 1793 and 'blooming' Captain Harris netted £1000 from his Montem.

Some years things got out of hand. Salt festivals generally have an ancient lineage, and are often associated with springtime, fertility rituals and children, but also with an element of enacted violence. Eton College seems to have colonised this local salt-rite in the late Middle Ages, and assigned to it its own brand of colourful militarism and more than a dash of sadism. Eventually Queen Charlotte put an end to the whipping of the 'dirtiest boy' all the way down Salt Hill by the entire school, but as a result of the chaos caused by the attendant toll extortions, Montem became, by Brummell's time, a triennial event and the festival was eventually banned by Prince Albert in the 1840s.

According to the college archives, Brummell took part in three Montems. They are worth noting, as stated, with regard to an event involving a local girl in 1793, but also as Montem relates to an understanding of Eton costume, Brummell and fashion. Montem provided an occasion for the renewal of Eton garb, just as it did for a restocking of crockery in the Lower Hall – one of the captain's expenses. The boys were expected to dress up for Montem, even if they were not appointed officers in the parade. In portraits of George and William Brummell from this period, owned by descendants of the family, the boys have been wrongly described as wearing 'Eton uniform': in fact they are in the habit of the Montem 'polemen' or 'musician polemen', the positions they held in the Montem parades in 1787 and 1790. Indeed, this was the look of the majority of the school at Montem: a dark blue jacket, with two rows of brass buttons, allowing a view of a white stock at the neck, and paired with paler breeches. In contrast, the older boys dressed in parody of courtiers and looked, deliberately, overdressed and ridiculous.

The Montem polemen's garb is a fascinating precursor to what became, twenty years later, part of the London dress-style that Brummell made famous. It was in effect a uniform: quasi-militaristic, flattering to the chest and shoulders but softened round the neck, featuring a palette of dark blue, buff and white. If, as seems possible, Brummell first saw the Prince of Wales – the most overdressed man in Europe – at the Montem of 1790 or 1793, he might well have been struck by the parallels between what then passed for high male fashion, and the ridiculousness of the Montem officers' fancy-dress. He, in contrast, spent most of his Montems, and much of his time at Eton, in a sober uniform that counterpointed *outré* excess.

The 1793 Montem was the occasion of Brummell's first recorded attempt at seduction – fuelled to what degree by alcohol, schoolboy bravado or hormonal high spirits we cannot know. He was spotted, later in the day after Eton had descended into a sort of good-humoured anarchy, using his Montem musical instrument to unorthodox ends: serenading the headmaster's daughter.

This first time I saw him is thoroughly impressed upon my recollection. I was returning at night . . . along the lane [and] I heard music, and on clearing the end of the house, which was then Harrington's, since then Holt's, I saw three boys dressed in fantastic dress, making a mock serenade under the window of Miss Susan Heath, the eldest daughter of the headmaster. The instruments which thus interpreted their feelings for this lady were a hurdy-gurdy, a triangle, and a French horn – the last being played by Brummell mi[nor]. Who held the other two, I do not remember, but the scene was so infinitely amusing, that I could never forget it. I did not know his name, but I soon learned it; afterwards I was often fagged by him, and his gaiety and good nature to lower boys were felt and acknowledged.

Key elements of the Brummell legend are already in place: details of his dress, his humour and a sort of play-acted sexuality, a sexuality enacted within the arena of other men, which in modern terms would be seen as typical teenage behaviour. At Eton his world may have been highly sensitised to homosexuality, with masturbation roundly condemned, and sexual acts most often sublimated in favour of hopeless love. But in this scenario Brummell is painted simply as the object of male gaze, and in his actions, if anything, a conventional teenage boy. His sexuality, at school as in later life, is best understood within terms that have subsequently been described as homosocial. His was a world of men – or boys – from his formative years, which had a strong element of acknowledged desire. Social historians have argued that such homosocial structures are unrelated to homosexuality in so far as a strong element of homophobia may be a part of homosocial 'male bonding'. But in Brummell's case, at Eton and beyond, his place within the world of men was markedly body-conscious, and was in that sense sexualised with or without any element of homosexual desire.

George wrote a short poem about Susan Heath, which he added years later to his collection of verses. It places his ardour within this slightly competitive mien, though the competition is not so much generally with his contemporaries – for whom he was clearly showing off – as with his elder brother William. It is the only occasion George ever alluded to pique at being the younger brother. There is, as it happens, no record of Susan and William, then or subsequently, forming any sort of relationship.

> The Younger Brother's Claim
>
> Whene'er in rapturous praise I speak,
> Of Susan's eye, of Susan's cheek,
> And own my ardent flame;
> They tell me that I praise in vain,
> For Susan proudly will disdain
> A younger brother's claim.
>
> Yet my fond heart will not resign
> The hope it form'd to call her mine
> When first my eyes beheld her
> Is still believe my Bible true,
> For there 'tis clearly proved that you,
> Susannah, hate an Elder.

Possibly it was written as a joke for his friends with nothing more heartfelt at the end than a deft scriptural allusion.

~

Buck Brummell would have been remembered from his school-days even if he had not gone on to be the most famous man in England. His fag-master, his fag, and other contemporaries write lovingly of him from the far side of fifty years and the Victorian cultural revolution. He used his formidable wit and good looks to become the most popular boy at school, never succeeding too conspicuously in his schoolwork to threaten such a position, and avoiding through eight years of a potentially brutalising establish-ment a flogging at the hands of either schoolmasters or fellow pupils. In all of this he was, before he even left Eton in late 1793 or 1794, recognisably the later man and well *en route* to being the very mould of fashion. But his poise and repartee hid a profound sense of personal unworthiness that was more than a reflection of his lowly background. For one thing, he was already developing traits of fastidiousness that would in time become legendary and may speak partly of an uncomfortable relationship with his body. This may be attributed to his position in the male gaze at Eton, a supremely homosexualised environment. It may also be related to growing up in a highly sexualised society that was at the same time violently antipathetic to any direct outlet of adolescent male sexual energy. Worse still, as this final anecdote suggests, though George Brummell was in every point the Man of Feeling of his age and the idol of his schoolfellows, in his father's eyes he remained a failure, a wastrel, and a second-best second son:

About [this time] his father, having been informed of some peccadillo he [George] had committed [possibly the incident with the head-master's daughter], sent his butler from Donnington with a paternal letter to his eldest son, which began, 'My dear William,' and another to the Beau, commencing 'George'. George's letter was in other respects a most disagreeable one intimating as it did the order for his immediate return, with all his clothes, his father having determined not to allow him to return again to Eton. Hearing of his trouble I went to his room and found him with the two letters before him: they were wet with tears: – such a stream of tears I never saw, and have never seen since.

'George,' said I, 'what's the matter?' He could not speak: but, sobbing, pointed first to – 'My dear William,' and then to the monosyllable 'George'. I give you this anecdote as a trait of his being possessed . . . of a warm heart. His father relented also, for after the next holidays George reappeared amongst his companions, the most manly boy of them all.

The last phrase was pointed. Jesse's anonymous contributor to the collection of Brummell-at-school sour‹ ‹s recalled not just George's warm heart, but his return to Eton 'the most manly boy of them all'. Had his father's antipathy hardened him in some recognisable way? Was this purely a physical description, one of the several that sketch an object of schoolboy hero-worship? Or did Brummell boast, or did his schoolfriend merely sense, that something momentous had happened that holiday from Eton back at the family apartments in Hampton Court Palace? For where Susan Heath, the headmaster's daughter, had merely laughed at his musical wooing, at home 'Buck' Brummell had experienced both the romance, and trauma, of the adult sexual world. Next door to his father's apartments he had found a kindred spirit, a girl destined to be one of the most famous courtesans of their age, but then only sixteen, not yet 'fallen' and quite possibly for the first time in love. Her name was Julia Johnstone.

3

THE WORLD IS VERY
UNCHARITABLE

1793–4

[A young man] may commit an hundred deviations from the
path of rectitude, yet he can still return, every one invites him; in
sober truth he gains an *éclat* by his failings, that establish him in
The Ton, and make him envied, instead of pitied or despised.
But woman, when she makes one false step . . . becomes a mark
for the slow moving finger of scorn . . . The world is very
uncharitable.

Julia Johnstone, née Storer

Unhappy child of indiscretion,
Poor slumberer on a breast forlorn!
Pledge and reproof of past transgression,
Dear, though unwelcome to be born.

George Bryan Brummell,
on the birth of Julia's love-child

Julia Storer was a year older than George Brummell, a year
that makes an appreciable difference between a fifteen-year-
old boy and a sixteen-year-old girl. Her parents had apartments in
Hampton Court Palace that overlooked the Brummells' from the
opposite side of Fountain Court. The families shared privileged
access to the palace grounds but had little else in common.
George's parents came from a line of hard-working servants
and civil servants, their wealth founded on officially sanctioned

peculation and rental property in the West End. Julia's antecedents, on the other hand, were aristocrats. Her mother was the Honourable Elizabeth Proby, daughter of Lord Carysfort, and maid-of-honour to Queen Charlotte. It was because of her mother's Court appointment that the family had grace-and-favour apartments in the palace, used by the Hon. Mrs Proby when the Queen did not require her attendance in London. Julia's father was Thomas Storer of Belle Isle, Jamaica, and Golden Square, London. He had married well with his money – based on the West Indian slave trade – acquiring a whole set of aristocratic in-laws. Julia started her seventeenth year as a well-connected débutante, but ended it a 'fallen woman', pregnant and disgraced. She was never accepted back into society and barely spoke again to any female members of her family. Harriette Wilson – who lived with Julia in adult life when they were both professional courtesans – later claimed Julia's 'fall' began uncomfortably on a stone staircase, next door to the Brummell family apartments at Hampton Court Palace. She further claimed that Julia and George had been in love.

Julia's father died in 1792. That year she was presented at Court. She had been expensively educated abroad to the most polished standard. But Julia quickly decided on a more independent course than the one her widowed mother or old Queen Charlotte had in mind for her. 'What a fortune is my mother's! – said I, such a one will never do for me; I am for freedom and independence.' She gave up on her German lessons – the Queen had said she would help her make a solid German match – and decided to take a more adventurous path. Julia was free-spirited from the first, her heart 'so very, very mad', according to Tom Sheridan, 'a woman of very violent passions', according to Harriette, but 'combined with an extremely shy and reserved disposition'. She was also unusual in her looks: not a classic beauty of her age or any other, she had great strength of features. She was dark, with large, piercing eyes, and hair that fell in long ringlets, after natural or artificial means. She was a tomboy of sorts, like her friend Harriette Wilson, with a certain masculinity of manner – as it was described at the time – that allowed her to hold her own in a world dominated by men. George Brummell's first love was from a mould that would cast many to come: an unconventional beauty, a strong, independent-minded woman. And somewhat older than he was.

The story of Julia, and of George, was described by Harriette Wilson and Julia. Their versions differ wildly.

It was much later in life that Julia came to write her *Confessions* just as her former friend Harriette Wilson had done. But Julia wrote 'in contradiction to the fables of Harriette Wilson'. Their memoirs often contradict directly, and if they do not, they offer very different slants on actions and consequences. This much both memoirs had in common: George Brummell, and a desire to paint as sympathetically as possible their own initial 'fall from grace' that prefigures the whole of the rest of the story. The thread of George's role – at exactly this point in Julia's narrative – can be woven only by splicing together these two conflicting strands.

Julia's own account of her 'fall', a scene set in her own record and all others at Hampton Court Palace, is at odds with Harriette's in key respects. Julia insists she ran away from home, taking an unpaid position as a companion to one Mrs Cotton, whose husband, a dragoon captain, happened to have apartments at Hampton Court Palace where he duly seduced her. 'At the early age of sixteen I fell victim to my own inexperience,' she wrote. 'I was handed out of the carriage [at Hampton Court] by a military officer: the sight inspired me with unusual pleasure.' In truth this was not quite how it happened, and Julia was not quite the ingénue she paints herself.

Colonel Cotton cut something of a dash around Hampton Court Palace. He was in the 10th Light Dragoons, the country's most fashionable regiment. Julia, like George, first saw the modish uniform around the formal gardens of Hampton Court and its ancient barracks. But Julia was lying in saying she first saw the uniform or the man when she was an unguarded female at large in the world. Julia started an affair with Cotton and, it has been suggested, with her young neighbour George Brummell, some time around her sixteenth birthday when her whole family were at Hampton Court. It suited her later purposes to draw herself as a friendless, orphaned lady's companion, 'abandoned to the care of strangers at the most critical period of a young girl's existence' and undone by her master and her own 'inexperience'. The truth was a little more complicated.

Harriette Wilson meanwhile insisted Brummell was in love with Julia Storer at Hampton Court in 1792 and 1793 when they were fifteen and sixteen respectively. The Brummell family had moved from Suite XVII in the Gold Staff Gallery on the South Front to the even more prestigious set of connected suites in Fountain Court, Nos. XXIX and XXX in the Silver Staff Gallery. The Cottons were near neighbours, in Suite XXI, a floor above. The Storers were just opposite, almost underneath the Cottons. The picture Harriette Wilson draws of the Hampton Court Julia and George knew was entirely accurate in key physical details. A Hampton Court Palace address sounded gracious; the reality was often less so. The palace apartments ranged from palatial to single rooms in the former galleries. Some were made by jerry-building extra floors in the great Tudor kitchens, and others had been created by completely re-structuring the early Georgian kitchen buildings as a private house. Each grace-and-favour apartment found a way to improvise a cooking space out of fireplaces or former closets after the royal kitchens had ceased to exist. The Storers, for instance, cooked in what had previously been the royal Chocolate Room on the 'Coffee Room Staircase'. Practically and architecturally the palace was being turned into a rabbit-warren. Some addresses referred to apartments so tiny that they had been created from former galleries simply by curtaining off 'cubicles' from the immediate neighbours. The division walls that were put in – a very few remain – were thin. Harriette Wilson's version takes this into account and, though partisan, has a clearer ring of truth to it than Julia's own.

This is Harriette's version of Julia's story, the one she swore Julia had told her. Sixteen-year-old Julia Storer was overcome with boredom at the 'starchied and stately . . . old Anglo-

Germanic' Court, and alarmed at the prospect of an arranged marriage into the German nobility. Yet the palace suited her imaginative nature, and she found there two alternative prospects of adventure and romance. One, a cocky Eton schoolboy, her neighbour George Brummell, 'violently in love with her', the other, a thirty-year-old married man, Colonel Cotton.

The colonel was described by both Julia and Harriette as one of the handsomest men in England. His wife had recently given birth to their ninth child and was suffering from some malaise – possibly post-natal depression – and for this reason, or simply as a means of birth control, she had made her intention clear never to share a bed with the colonel again. Who seduced whom then is unclear: the priapic dragoon or the rebellious schoolgirl. Their first sexual encounter took place 'on a stone staircase' probably off Fountain Court, or the unused kitchen staircase to the Great Hall. Later trysts took place in Julia's own bedroom, with only a curtain partition between the lovers and the sixteen-year-old girl's mother, the Hon. Mrs Storer. The palace was fulfilling its potential for Julia, for romance, intrigue and adventure and living up to its subsequent reputation as a hotbed of sexual intrigue in confined spaces. Once she hid the colonel under her bed. The lovers' joke backfired on Julia, to her eternal embarrassment, as the naked soldier was treated not only to the sight of her sister undressing (Julia's room was also the family dressing room) but to a private conversation between teenage sisters about their pimples. George, meanwhile, was left out in the cold. 'He is an old flame of mine,' Julia was later heard to remark, 'who was violently in love with me, when I was a girl, at Hampton Court.' After she started sleeping with Cotton, she said, she never saw him again, till they bumped into each other years later at the opera. Brummell, ever the gentleman, greeted her 'with surprise, joy and astonishment at meeting with her'. They later rekindled their affair. With Cotton, George was less sanguine. 'No man in England stinks like Cotton,' he later averred, making him the one exception for his general rule against perfumes: Cotton, he spat, could do with 'a little Eau de Portugal'.

In choosing Cotton and not Brummell, Julia changed her life for ever. Where a teenage romance, even consummated, might have been hushed up and forgiven, an affair with an older married man put Julia on the path to her later notoriety. Within a few months of losing her virginity on a back staircase of Fountain Court, Julia realised she was pregnant. Like many an unwanted teenage pregnancy, its very fact was denied by those most immediately associated with it – even Julia – until the last possible moment. The hidden pregnancy was eventually revealed when Julia's waters broke in the middle of one of Queen Charlotte's interminable, standing, audiences. The consequent scandal nearly ruined the family. Julia's brother challenged Cotton to a duel, Julia was thrown out of both the Storer and Cotton apartments, and, alone and unattended, suffered five hours of labour in an unused room at Hampton Court Palace before delivering her baby boy herself. George was sent back to school, both shaken and moved by Julia's plight and that of her baby son.

As Julia well knew, the punishment for her was to be much harsher than anything a man might suffer for a similar 'indiscretion'. She was never received in respectable society again. She and the colonel went on to have five children together, and a marriage of sorts based in a little cottage in Primrose Hill. This was only possible because Julia had some financial means independent of her family or lover – a highly unusual situation for a Georgian woman. She called herself 'Mrs Johnstone' and the colonel kept up a double, quasi-bigamous life, known as 'Mr Johnstone' in Primrose Hill with his children and 'wife' and Colonel Cotton by his regiment and in town. But by the time Brummell met Julia again, some time in 1804 or 1805, she had been deserted by Cotton and was living with Harriette, leading members both of the 'Cyprians', who had such wealth and fame as courtesans that they could throw balls attended by all the greatest figures of the day, many of them their lovers. Julia was comprehensively 'fallen' and a seasoned, professional mistress.

> For never handsome gypsy drew in
> A man so soon to shame and ruin . . .

wrote Henry Luttrell of the professional love-life of his fictionalised Julia. George and she resumed their affair, however half-
heartedly, and George went on to introduce her to a number of
her later 'protectors'.

'I never had the honour to refuse his hand in marriage,' Julia
wrote of Brummell, 'because he never offered it to me.' She
counter-claimed that it was Harriette who was in love with
George: 'I verily believe . . . Harriette would most gladly have
taken him,' but this is typical of her step-by-step contradiction of
everything Harriette wrote. George himself was evasive on the
subject: 'Julia and I,' said Brummell, 'are very old friends you
know.' If he held Julia's affair with Cotton against her – in terms
of sexual morality or pure sexual jealousy – it didn't prevent him
making 'strong love' to her later in life, perhaps in the manner of
an affair born of a school reunion. But for a first affair, his tryst
with Julia certainly had a dramatic and sobering conclusion. If
there was anything more to what went on at Hampton Court, any
sexual content to their teenage romance, he did not follow the
example of Harriette and Julia in publishing. But it is intriguing to
note that Julia is insistent she lost her virginity to 'the impassioned solicitations of . . . one of the handsomest and most
accomplished [men] of the age'. Brummell is a hovering presence
in both courtesans' memoirs: not rich enough to warrant their
threat of scandal-mongering, still famous enough to be worth
mentioning. Perhaps Julia did indeed have two lovers, both
Cotton and the schoolboy 'violently in love with her'. Such would
be typical of her later behaviour. Certainly Colonel Cotton
himself is never described elsewhere as either 'accomplished' or
'passionate', so she might have been alluding to a truth that she
could not admit as it contradicted her position as an ingénue
fallen prey to an older man: namely that she had been Brummell's
lover. She held a special place in his heart, as in Tom Sheridan's,
and the poems George chose to keep about this episode in his life
are melancholy and tinged with regret. This one was written by
Tom Sheridan for Brummell to keep in his album.

To Julia

Since you will needs my heart possess
Julia, 'tis just I first confess
The faults to which 'tis given.
It is much more to change inclined
Than restless seas or raging wind,
Or aught that's under Heaven.

Nor will I hide from you the truth,
It has been from its very youth
A most egregious ranger:
And, since from me it oft has fled,
With whom it was both born and bred,
'T will scarce stay with a stranger.

So now, if you dare to be so bold,
After the truths that I have told
To like this arrant rover,
Be not displeased, if I confess
I think the heart within *your* breast
Will prove just such another.

Sheridan's poem 'To Julia' reflects a worldly acknowledgement that hearts like theirs are too gadfly to be won by anyone for ever. He was writing about George Brummell's heart as well as his own and Julia's. George's companion poem on Julia Storer expands this theme into a valediction at the birth of a child born of such compromised love:

Unhappy child of indiscretion,
Poor slumberer on a breast forlorn!
Pledge and reproof of past transgression,
Dear, though unwelcome to be born.

Yet, spite of these, my mind unshaken,
In parent duty turns to thee;
Though long repented, ne'er forsaken
Thy days loved and guarded be!

And though to rank and place a stranger
Thy life an humble course must run
Still shalt thou learn to fly the danger
Which I, too late, have learned to shun.

And lest the injurious world upbraid thee
For mine, or for thy mother's ill,
A nameless father still shall aid thee
A Hand unseen protect thee still.

Meanwhile, in these sequester'd valleys
Still shalt thou rest in calm content;
For innocence may smile at malice,
And thou – oh! Thou art innocent!

The second and fourth stanzas give the impression that George felt himself implicated in the birth, but they were written many years later, and may even allude to another affair entirely. Almost certainly the child was Cotton's. George's love was more akin to the hopeless crush many teenage boys experience for the more sexually mature girls of their own age, but as a first lesson in adult love it was certainly harsh and scarring. It rang chords with him throughout his adult life, surrounded as he was by unwanted pregnancies, by inconstant love affairs and adulterous liaisons and later still when he was living with the reminder of 'past transgression': his own degenerative venereal disease.

Cotton, as Julia wrote, came out of the affair neither 'pitied' nor 'despised' but only 'envied'. This did not go unnoticed by his rival in love. George Bryan Brummell, rejected by Julia in favour of an older man in uniform, set his heart on winning a commission with the Colonel's own regiment, the 10th Light Dragoons. As Julia said, 'A hussar's cap and feather gives such a fillip to the spirits of a young miss, you don't know.'

~

In early March 1793, George's mother died. She was buried on 16 March in a new family vault in the crypt of St Martin-in-the-Fields. The boys came back to London for the funeral, but were at

Eton through the following summer term, their last but one. Though George clearly resembled his mother in his looks, he makes no mention ever of an affinity of character or a particular closeness. His world had become almost entirely masculine in his time at Eton, and quite possibly the death of Mary Brummell, following fast on his bruising affair with Julia Johnstone, pushed him further into a world in which the feminine was, essentially, foreign. Like his later friend, the Prince of Wales, George Brummell had a series of relationships with rather older women. This may articulate some of the loss he felt when his mother, a virtual stranger to him through his later childhood, was taken from him completely.

George, William and Maria were about to face a still harsher test, which had far more dramatic repercussions on their young lives. In early March 1794 news came from Donnington Grove that their father had also died. The siblings again gathered in London to see their father taken down the steps to the crypt of St Martin's, a year and a day exactly after their mother. None of the three teenage Brummells could take control of the finances, as stated in the terms of their father's will, due to their legal minority. The estate, valued at around £60,000, nearly £5 million in today's money, was to be administered by the executors – first among them the former Charles Jenkinson MP, by then Lord Liverpool – and Donnington Grove sold.

Old Mr Billy Brummell had stayed in London after his wife's funeral in 1793 and instructed the completion of a new will. Possibly he had been ill for some time, and certainly the death of his wife had alerted him, just in time as it happened, to his own mortality. The will's unusual stipulation that the family estate be sold and the proceeds split equally between the children was in the new fashion of land tenure pioneered in France. It was also the same principle followed by Billy's own father, William. Charles James Fox would have approved of this undermining of primo-geniture. The thoughts of George's elder brother, William, on the matter are not recorded. George therefore, although a 'younger son', faced none of the usual social impediments of that position.

He would be as rich, on coming of age, as his brother or, for that matter, as his sister's husband. But as minors the three bereaved Brummells had no say in what immediately happened.

Billy Brummell's will left the old family house in Bury Street to his sister Mary Tombs. Annuities of fifty pounds and a one-off hundred-guinea gift were willed to each of his wife's sisters, who had married an actor and a Welshman respectively. To the unmarried Richardson sister, Grace, he left two hundred pounds, which he doubled to four hundred in a codicil shortly before his death. To three of his colleagues in the Chelsea Agent's Office, and the Navy Agent's Office, who had helped him administer the Chelsea Hospital and naval sinecures (and possibly in payment for their collusion), a hundred pounds each 'for the trouble they will respectively have in settling my office accounts after my decease'. They had helped administer the harvesting of funds that had created the Brummell fortune. Similarly the substantial sum of a thousand pounds was gifted to one William Francis Johnston, an extra clerk in the secretary of state's office who had somehow warranted Billy Brummell's special approbation. The will rewarded his colleagues and safeguarded against the prying eyes of press or public by ensuring everyone involved in the creation of the Brummell fortune was simultaneously rewarded and potentially inculpated. There was therefore never a whisper from anyone that there was anything untoward about a government official who had entered office as a secretary and was leaving a fortune to his children, one surpassed by no more than a few hundred in the land.

To his daughter Maria, he left 'all my Jewells, Watch and Diamonds and Trinkets now in the Possession of Messrs Drummond [the Charing Cross bankers] which I hope she will wear in Memory of her ever to be lamented and never to be forgotten Mother'. The jewels of a metropolitan beauty and society hostess like Mrs Mary Brummell cannot have had much opportunity of further airing in the country soirées attended by a captain's wife in rural Berkshire, but they formed part of a substantial dowry Maria brought to Blackshaw, and were passed on in turn to her daughters' aristocratic husbands. Billy gave fifty pounds each to all of his servants and mourning rings to his old theatre friends, Thomas Harris and Richard Brinsley Sheridan. There were fifty guineas each for the executors of the will. After a few other gifts, the residue was left to the three children: nearly twenty thousand pounds each, or around £1.6 million today.

Billy Brummell's will, according to the *Gentleman's Magazine*, was 'just and generous' with 'the same liberality which characterised his life'. His fortune, the magazine wrote, had been acquired due to 'unremitting attention to business, the strictest integrity, and an amiable disposition'. The magazine had further been informed that Mr Brummell had left bequests to local Berkshire charities before his demise, despite the imminent sale of Donnington Grove. 'His private virtues were to be distinguished in the neighbourhood of Donnington, particularly on behalf of infant poor, many of whom by his benevolent exertions have been saved from impending destruction and must now severely feel and truly lament his loss.' The will, however, makes no mention of such charities.

George was still only fifteen, and he had lost the glamorous but distant figure of his mother and his disapproving father. Shortly after their father's death he and William were both removed from the world they knew best, Eton, neither of them yet in the sixth form, and sent to Oxford. Sir John Macpherson and the lawyer Mr White of Lincoln's Inn, the old family friend who had so often been a visitor at Donnington, stood as guardians. They might have been acting in accordance with the last wishes of Billy Brummell, an understandably anxious father. He seems to have felt that the boys' best interests after his death would be served away from school in the less exalted, more hardworking crowd at Oriel. Oxford was the next rung on the ladder of political success, should either boy be inspired to follow in their father's profession. (Cambridge tended to serve better for aspiring churchmen and lawyers.) Doubtless old Billy Brummell had tired of George's school reports that came thick, fast and complaining during his final illness, and had necessitated sending his butler from

Donnington with letters of such severity that George was reduced to tears. The bitter loneliness of this period of his life when he lost both parents fast on the trauma of his abortive first love affair began to shape, out of the cocky Eton schoolboy, the emotionally reticent adult man.

In May 1794, after the Easter holidays in which they had buried their father, William and George Brummell arrived as commoner undergraduates at Oriel College, Oxford. There is little record of George's involvement in college or university life. Some buttery receipts are all that attest to his undergraduate career. A later fellow of the college, writing in the 1880s, fails to make any mention of either Brummell in the alumni of the late eighteenth century. He is keen to point out, however, that Oriel was in the vanguard of the new academic meritocracy of Oxford, and understandably cites Thomas Arnold as the main example of this (elected fellow in 1815) rather than Brummell or his contemporary the Marquess of Worcester, who left endowments to the college for scholarships from the West Country. In 1794 Oriel contrasted little with Eton in terms of dull religious routine, glorious architecture and bad food. But as an Oxford undergraduate, for the few months George could count himself such, Oxford offered a much freer lifestyle than Eton had. 'I spent fourteen months at Magdalen College,' wrote the historian Gibbon, of Oxford in Brummell's day. 'They proved to be the fourteen months the most idle and unprofitable of my whole life.' Lord Malmesbury, similarly, who had been at Oxford before George, wrote that 'the discipline of the university happened to be so lax that a gentleman commoner was under no restraint and never called upon to attend either lectures or chapel or hall . . . The set of men with whom I lived were very pleasant but very idle fellows. Our life was an imitation of high life in London.' Nor should it be assumed that George Brummell was unusually young in going up to Oxford before his sixteenth birthday. The lifestyle, as hard-drinking as has been the case for more modern undergraduates, was enjoyed by students as young as fourteen.

The only picture of Brummell as an undergraduate is fictionalised, but nevertheless has the stamp of Brummell's own approval and is quoted at length as a result by Captain Jesse with the recollections of the Beau. It is a description of a fictional character called Vincent Trebeck in the novel *Granby* by Thomas Henry Lister published in 1826. Vincent Trebeck was widely accepted at the time as having been based on George. It is on the whole a sympathetically drawn character, so it is not surprising perhaps that George later agreed it was a reasonably accurate one. At Oxford, according to the vision of Brummell in *Granby*, George

consumed a considerable quantity of midnight oil, but very little of it over his books; and it was not so much from a meritorious motive as a wish to do something that nobody thought he could or would do that he wrote for the Newdigate Prize. It is true that he was not successful, but his copy was considered the second best, and he contrived to make people believe that he would have been [first] if he had taken sufficient pains, for his friends asserted that his failure was mainly owing to his indolence in having neglected to count his verses.

Like George, Vincent had been an Etonian, and 'never did anyone glide with more ease and rapidity from the blunt un-ceremonious "hail-fellow-well-met" manner of the schoolboy into the formal nonchalance and measured cordiality of the manly collegian'. Vincent/George 'was more celebrated, however, for his systematic violation of college rules than for his stanzas; he always ordered his horse at hall-time, was the author of half the squibs that appeared on the screen, turned a tame jackdaw, with a pair of bands on, into the quadrangle, to parody the master, and treated all proctors' and other penalties with con-tempt'.

This character is therefore recognisable from Eton: Brummell the joker, Brummell the flouter of rules and regulations, Brum-mell the writer of squibs. The Brummell who puts himself in for the Newdigate Prize has either not learned his later style of effortless superiority or is entirely a fiction. Even so elements of this description, even the detail of the Newdigate Prize, are mistakenly attributed to Brummell himself in later biographies –

eliding fiction and fact in a manner the man himself might have admired. Brummell wrote lengthily and constantly, but never risked coming 'second best' at anything.

He rapidly progressed in the exclusive habits to which he had found himself predisposed, the little that remained of the schoolboy frankness was quickly thrown aside in his violent desire to be perfectly correct; and, to gratify this taste, he cut one of his brother Etonians, because he entered a junior college, and discontinued visiting another, because he had invited him to meet two men of . . . Hall. The plan which he acted upon was to make intimacies with men of high rank and connexions: he was a consummate tuft hunter; and to the preservations of an embryo baronet or earl, he fancied it necessary to sacrifice a friend a term.

This is again only partially an accurate picture of Brummell at Oxford. Aside from the fact that this scheme of 'cutting friends' hardly made sense of a student who only stayed a few months, Jesse goes out of his way to refute the whole image: 'It does not at all accord with the character given him by . . . those contemporaries at Oriel with whom I am acquainted.' He writes, 'this college sketch [is constructed only] to correspond with the habits and disposition of Trebeck in after life'.

At Oxford Brummell's character was unalloyed with the snobbery or hauteur that would affect him in later life. It was his easy charm that allowed his social progress at school and university. He had been popular at Eton, and would have been popular at Oxford if he had deigned to stay there. But his Oxford career lasted only a few months. George was at Oriel through the Easter term only of 1794. He was expected back after the summer vacation, but only William showed up. Instead, George had approached Sir John Macpherson, the chief executor of his father's will, with a proposition. He suggested a small part of his inheritance be used to buy an army commission.

In the years when all boys disassociate themselves from their parents, with greater or lesser animosity but with necessary effect for their later psycho-sexual health, George Brummell lost both of his to the crypt of St Martin's. Studies on any childhood bereavement make for dark reading, but the loss of parents during adolescence can be particularly damaging, often more so than loss at an earlier age. It can leave an adolescent confused, angry and self-doubting – unable to enact the subtle distancing of leaving home because home ceases to exist. The bereaved themselves later talk of the concomitant feelings of anxiety and of guilt – as if the parent's death is the adolescent's fault. At the same time that George Brummell lost his parents he lost also his first 'violent' love, Julia Storer (Johnstone) to an older man. These were trying times for Brummell, for all that his contemporaries described him as on the brink of manhood and a picture, even in Trebeck's fiction, of insouciant breeziness. It was an act. Brummell was, and remained, a lonely figure and a bleakly misanthropic comic. The 'much admired drawing' he hung over his mantelpiece in adult life was titled *The Angry Child*.

Whether or not George Brummell and his friend George Byron discussed Julia or their similar experiences of first love is unknown, but the poem Lord Byron wrote after they talked some years later has uncanny echoes of Brummell's torment over Julia and the imprint of the same experience of rejection. It was preserved in Brummell's album.

> Go—! Triumph securely – the treacherous vow
> Thou hast broken, I keep but too painfully now;
> But never again shalt thou be to my heart
> What thou wert – what I fear for a moment thou art:
> To see thee – to love thee – what heart could do more?
> To love – to lose thee, 'twere vain to deplore!
> Ashamed of my weakness, however beguiled,
> I shall bear like a man what I feel as a child.
> If a frown cloud my brow, yet it lours not on thee;
> If my heart should seem heavy, at least it is free:
> But thou, in the pride of new conquest elate,
> Alas! E'en envy shall feel for thy fate.—
> For the first step of error none e'er could recall,

And the woman once fallen for ever must fall;
Pursue to the last the career she begun,
And be false unto many, as faithless to one
And they who have loved thee will leave thee to mourn,
And they who have hated will laugh thee to scorn;
And he who adored thee – must weep to foretell
The pangs which will punish thy falsehood too well.

George ran away from Oxford to join the army – an artificial family of men. The regiment was the same one in which his former rival Colonel Cotton served. It was the most fashionable in the country, and the Prince of Wales had recently been appointed its colonel-in-chief. Quite how a seventeen-year-old came to take up a commission in the glamorous 10th Light Dragoons is the next question in the unprecedented ascendancy of Beau Brummell.

4
THE
PRINCE'S OWN

1794–9

You all no doubt have heard
What has lately occurred
In the celebrated Troop of the Hussars
Where if you like to pay
A Cornetcy you may
Now purchase and avoid those ugly scars!
Song, 'The 10th Hussars'

George Bryan Brummell met George Augustus Frederick, Prince of Wales, in 1793 or 1794. The heir to the throne was in his early thirties but nevertheless a friendship developed between him and the teenage Oxford undergraduate. The passion they shared was for clothes.

As early as 1782 the Duchess of Devonshire, friend to both the prince, and later Brummell, described George III's eldest son as 'fond of dress even to a tawdry degree' and that 'his person, his dress and the admiration he has met . . . from women take up his thoughts chiefly'. Although *Gentleman's Magazine* and *Bon Ton Magazine* wrote of the prince as 'always the best dressed man at court' he had come of age in the last great epoch of the peacock-male and was frequently overly – not to say ridiculously – dressed. Thirty years after George IV's death, William Thackeray recalled that as Prince of Wales he had dressed up in every kind of uniform, and every possible court dress – in long fair hair, with powder, with and without a pigtail – in every conceivable cocked-hat – in dragoon [hussar] uniform – in Windsor uniform – in a field marshal's clothes – in a Scotch kilt and tartans, with dirk and claymore (a stupendous figure) – in a frogged frock-coat with a fur collar and tight breeches and silk stockings – in wigs of every colour, fair, brown, and black.

The first opportunity Buck Brummell at Eton had of seeing the fashion disaster that was the Prince of Wales was in July 1791. The prince visited the college in the company of his parents during the celebrations for the King's fifty-third birthday. There was singing and dancing, as well as the more formal classical oration at which the schoolboys excelled. The prince wore

a bottle green and claret-coloured striped silk coat and breeches and silver tissue waistcoat, very richly embroidered in silver and stones, and coloured silks in curious devices and bouquets of flowers. The coat and waistcoat embroidered down the seams and spangled all over the body. The coat cuffs the same as the waistcoat. The breeches likewise covered with spangles. Diamond buttons to the coat, waistcoat and breeches, which, with his brilliant diamond epaulette and sword, made the whole dress form a most magnificent appearance.

Such was the height of fashion in 1791. There was a rival style developing, a simplified line and palette adopted by the American and French revolutionaries. It was based, ironically, on an idea of an English country gentleman: a dark coat, usually blue, a buff waistcoat, riding breeches and riding boots. It was a style Buck Brummell knew well as he had seen it frequently at Donnington Grove. It was the style adopted by Charles James Fox – in particularly slovenly form – as an allusion to his political philosophy, and worn at least once by the prince himself to annoy his father. But more often the prince still dressed like an aristocrat at Versailles.

The Duchess of Devonshire had been of the opinion since the Prince of Wales's youth that he would run to fat early in life and that his large frame and imposing bearing would lose its battle with his expanding weight. She was right. By 1799, Thomas Farington the artist was aware of the added attention to dress his bulk demanded, and that the prince 'dresses surrounded by 3 glasses in which he can see his person'. His stomach had to be corseted in a 'Bastille of Whalebone' – euphemistically titled a 'belt' by his tailors – and he had begun, when he met Brummell, to pioneer a fashion for the highest of collars, bound with a stiff 'stock' that helped push his ruffle of chins into the semblance of a jawline. The Thomas Lawrence paintings from the turn of the century featuring this high collar, a sort of neck corset, allow an appreciation of how far fashion and art can go in flattering royalty.

Hiding the truth of his corpulence was one sartorial obsession for the prince. The other was military uniforms. George III had not allowed his eldest son any role in the military, despite ever more pressing demands from the prince that he, like his younger brothers, be given something to do. More than doing was the appearance of doing, and the prince was determined to be able to wear a uniform. When his brother, the Duke of York, visited Berlin in 1791 the Prince of Wales demanded of him a catalogue of details on continental uniforms. He wanted his brother to buy for him 'the compleat uniforms, accoutrements, saddle, bridle, &c, of one of the Zieten's Hussars . . . as well as one of the Officers compleat uniforms, cloathing, sword, cap, saddle, bridle, chabrack, pistols, in short, everything compleat'. He then studied what was brought back, and began designing and ordering his own version. As Caroline, Princess of Wales, observed cattily, 'My husband understands how a shoe should be made or a coat cut . . . and would have made an excellent tailor, or shoemaker or hairdresser; – but nothing else.'

For a man obsessed with the image of royalty, the military uniform assumed a key significance. The principle icon of monarchy that the age allowed was that of the 'soldier-prince' in the mould of Frederick the Great of Prussia, and all the Hanoverian princes were schooled to admire the look and manner of martinet

Teutonic royalty. Even without the heroic drama of the Bonaparte on the other side of the Channel, the prince would have
sought for himself the image of a military leader. Such was the
issue's importance in his mind that he wrote directly to Sir Henry
Dundas, secretary for war, threatening that if he was not granted
the rank and uniform of major-general 'it must lead to a total
separation between the King and [myself]'. He put it more
eloquently to his father: 'I have no option but to lead a life
which must to the public eye wear the colour of an idleness . . .
and which, from the sense of its so appearing, must sit irksomely
upon me.' A uniform would make him appear properly royal – a
soldier-prince leading his people. In letters to his father he likened
himself to the Black Prince, and in the portraits he commissioned
he posed himself as man of action, a military prince. Seeking in
adult life the approbation he had never received from his parents,
he often appeared to be trying to impress with clothes: an actor in
search of a role. In the end the military costume was all he got.

The prince wanted to head a regiment of his own, which he
could both command and dress as he pleased. In 1783 his wish
was, in part, granted. The new 10th Regiment of Light Dragoons
was 'honoured' by the King with the title 'The Prince of Wales's
Own'. The prince became colonel-in-chief only in 1793, when
Britain declared war on revolutionary France and royalty in the
military suddenly seemed like a useful rallying call. The prince's
new military title was backdated to November 1782 so he would
not be deemed a novice colonel in army orders of precedence –
most importantly, relative to his brothers. But it was made clear
that he would never serve in battle or abroad, and it was therefore
unlikely that the 10th would see harsh service. Because they were
reserved for occasions when looking good was important – when
not in Brighton they acted as royal escorts in Windsor and
London – and were treated with delicacy by military command,
the regiment became known as the 'China 10th'. As a result it
began to attract officers intent on a non-combatant military
career in close proximity to the courts of the Prince of Wales
at Carlton House and the Royal Pavilion at Brighton. In these

regards a commission in the 10th became at once both a sort of draft-dodge and entrée to high society. It also furnished its officers and men with an excuse to wear by far the most up-to-date and flattering of uniforms.

How, then, was George Brummell, who had in no sense completed his education at either Eton or Oxford, and was, no matter how mature his demeanour, aged only sixteen, granted such a prize as a commission in the Prince's Own? It was widely assumed he had been selected for his cornetcy – the first rank of commissioned officer in a British cavalry troop – by none other than the new colonel-in-chief himself. Within a few years three stories were in circulation explaining how the Prince of Wales and the schoolboy had come to know each other. In two versions they had met in London; in the other, at Windsor. Conflicting tales were cited in different editions of the *Reminiscences and Recollections* of Captain Gronow. None of these stories reflects very well on George Brummell, as a social climber, or on Prince George, as an abuser of his position.

One version of the story quoted by Gronow, among others, had young George first meeting the commander of his future regiment in Green Park. This picturesque anecdote cast George's aunt Searle – his mother's sister – as leading lady. She worked in Green Park as a milkmaid at the ornamental dairy, just near Clarges Street where there was at that time a small duckpond. Mrs Searle claimed that she was looking after her nephew there in the summer of 1792 when the dairy was honoured by a visit from the Marchioness of Salisbury, accompanied by the Prince of Wales. The prince struck up conversation with the schoolboy and asked him, in the recognisable manner of royals in conversation with schoolchildren, what he intended to do when he left school. George replied that he wanted to be an officer in the prince's own regiment. This combination of cheek and ambition gives this story some credibility. The prince laughed and said George should write to him when he left Eton. Mrs Searle, in a believable aside in Gronow's version, added that she saw little of Brummell as 'soon as he began to mix in society with the Prince, and his visits to me became less and less frequent and now he hardly ever calls to see his old aunt', but that he had, in his youth, had 'nice manners'. The true story is probably more prosaic.

George, by his own telling, first encountered the Prince of Wales at Eton and Windsor. This was inevitably the case, as the Royal Family were frequent visitors to the school, being both patrons and near neighbours when in residence at Windsor Castle. Whether the prince and schoolboy actually spoke is less clear. Brummell said they did, on the terrace at Windsor Castle, and that even then each recognised in the other a fascination with what they were wearing, and what it was to present oneself in public as a gentleman, and that in this respect Brummell 'acquitted himself to the Prince's satisfaction'. It seems the prince was struck not so much by Brummell's attire – most likely the blue, buff and white of the Montem polemen – than by his confident self-assurance, always the more arresting in the very young. 'He . . . displayed there all that the Prince of Wales most esteemed of human things: a splendid youth enhanced by the aplomb of the man who has judged life and can dominate it, the subtlest and most audacious mingling of impertinence and respect, and finally a genius for dress and deportment protected by a gift for perpetually witty repartee.'

A third possibility remains that George was slightly known in the prince's circle even before this as a result of an early introduction at Devonshire House in Mayfair. His father's friends Sheridan and Charles James Fox were on easy terms with the Duchess of Devonshire, who in turn was the sort of hostess who sought out new, glamorous and young additions to her London guest lists. This places Brummell's first introduction to Georgiana, Duchess of Devonshire, in late 1793, fast on the heels of her return from a scandalous exile in which she had given birth to an illegitimate child. This at least was Tom Raikes's later account of the connection that got young Buck Brummell from Eton into the flashest regiment in town.

All this said, the application to the regiment probably went by the usual route. The prince had the opportunity to blackball candidates, and he certainly made Brummell's life regally easy once he was in the regiment, but to begin with Brummell probably had strings pulled for him by one of his guardians. Sir John Macpherson, a close associate of Brummell in the North administration and frequent Donnington guest, was the first named of the several guardians appointed for Maria, William and George by the terms of their father's will. He was also one of several figures at Westminster who regularly placed names on lists of applicants to suitable regiments. It seems that George wrote from Oriel to Sir John Macpherson, bypassing Mr Joseph White at Lincoln's Inn, who was supposedly in charge of the Brummell sons' education, requesting that money be released from the estate to buy a cornetcy in the 10th Light Dragoons. It would cost him £735. Thence, he knew, he would be in much closer proximity to his friendly acquaintance, the Prince of Wales, and *en route* to a much more exciting life than Oriel could offer.

The first thing George needed to do, which occupied his interest as much as it had for his colonel-in-chief, was to order a uniform. The 10th Light Dragoons' uniform was dark blue, with pale yellow facings and silver-thread braiding. It was also alarmingly expensive. There was a blue sleeveless 'upper jacket' or 'shell' with braided epaulettes, cut long on the body and worn over a sleeved under-jacket. Both items were 'frogged and looped' or embroidered with horizontal braidings in white satin, and were further decorated with real silver tassels and 'Elliot' balls. The entire body was lined with white silk. The headdress was a large 'Tarleton' helmet – named after a hero of the American War of Independence, Colonel Banastre Tarleton: 'a perfect model of manly strength and vigour', who loved to gamble, could tame a wild stallion and was a well-known womaniser. The outlandish helmet he made fashionable was formed of a peaked leather skull, bound round with a leopardskin turban, fastened on the left with a silver clasp; the 10th Light Dragoons' was in the style of the Prince of Wales's feathers. To cap it all there was a high black fur crest, in antique Roman style, from front to back.

A singular feature of the 10th were their riding breeches. They were white, tight, trouser-length and worn uncomfortably, considering they were a cavalry regiment, without underwear. They were themselves a sort of fashion item. In part this was because British riding-wear was being adopted in post-revolutionary France, which saw in riding breeches and boots an egalitarian corollary to the politics of the Enlightenment: a look for Everyman. Partly this was an unexpected echo, in the design of military uniforms, of neo-classicism. The cavalry officers doubtless thought of their breeches as a practical solution to controlling a horse in the English manner, which is to say with their legs rather than the horse's bridle, and in this they were right: the design was functional in allowing close contact between horse and rider. Fashion became wedded to functionality, however, in the pale and form-fitting breeches, which echoed classical statuary: the marble-coloured wool, woven on stocking looms, gave the rider's legs the appearance of nakedness.

Moreover the 10th, uniquely, had breeches that in some cases reached their feet – trousers in effect – held in place with instep stirrups, over which riding boots could be worn, or shoes at night. Brummell first tried on this military hybrid, pantaloons – for all they had the appearance most often of knee-length breeches – in the early summer of 1794. It would eventually be the style he made fashionable for a new generation, one that became, ultimately, modern trousers.

A young officer like Brummell was expected to buy his own uniform. In May 1794 he made his first trip, financed by the trust fund set up for the Brummell children, to Schweitzer and Davidson's at 12 Cork Street. They made all the prince's uniforms, and all the uniforms for his officers at this time. An infantry officer could expect to pay up to forty pounds for his uniform – more than a working man's annual wage. A Light Dragoon or heavy-cavalry officer, meanwhile, was expected to pay around £150. The regiments that came to relish the name 'Hussars', however, had uniforms and accoutrements costing up to £300. Records for one officer of the 10th Light Dragoons show a single uniform bill of £399 7s. 6d., and the prince's uniforms, only slightly more elaborate than the other officers', regularly cost over £344 each. Once cornetcy and uniform were paid for, George had little change out of a thousand pounds from his inheritance.

There was no standard-issue cloak for the Light Dragoons; instead they pioneered a continental fashion for the *pelisse*, an off-the-shoulder fur throw. It was the most expensive part of their uniform: one belonging to the prince cost a hundred pounds; another, hardly less expensive, was described as an 'Extra superfine blue cloth Polony Peless [*pelisse*] richly trimmed with silver, the borders and edges of rich silver work, rich silver bullion fringes for the hips, silver tassels on the skirts . . . fur trimming, silk lining and pockets, extra double plated buttons, [with] lambs wool interlining and materials compleat.' In wearing fur *pelisses* the dragoons were signalling their desire – and the prince's – that they should be regarded as 'Hussars', a title unknown in the British Army until they were granted this soubriquet in 1806. The term was Hungarian in origin, a corruption of the Magyar *husz ara*, the price of twenty, alluding to the conscription of every twentieth man, or a man from every twentieth household. Brummell later referred to his time in the 'Hussars' and it was to have a profound influence on his sartorial style and, as a result, that of Regency London. But in point of fact the regiment he joined in 1794 called themselves Light Dragoons and continued so to do for all his time there. However, they thought of themselves as Hussars, behaved like Hussars, and dressed like them accordingly.

The Hussar regiments in continental Europe had grown a reputation in the eighteenth century for wild living, military prowess, and for dazzling, flattering uniforms that veered towards the outlandish. Consequently the Hussar look had been a commonplace masquerade costume in the late eighteenth century in London, and this was how the Prince of Wales first wore it. The *pelisse* harked back to the original 'Hussars' in medieval Hungary who hunted wolves on horseback, and flung the pelts over their shoulders. The fur *pelisse* as a fashion statement in early-nineteenth-century Europe was a distant echo of this wild-man soldiering.

The Hussar title, and the Hussar style of frogged, braided and fur-trimmed uniform, had stirred the imagination of the Prince of Wales since his youth. In this, he was heavily influenced by three expatriate and disreputable Frenchmen, all ex-Hussars. One was the Duc d'Orléans, Bourbon prince but later regicide, who loaned the prince vast sums of money, never to be repaid. Another was the Duc de Lauzun, whose French Hussars had been instrumental in the British defeat at Yorktown. He was, nonetheless, well known and well regarded in London. The third Hussar in the prince's background was the Marquis de Conflans, who set new standards of debauchery in his Hussar messes, once downing in one a bootful of claret for a bet. Some standards were maintained, however: he used his own boot.

There were Hussars working as mercenaries and horse trainers in the British Army as early as 1745, fighting both for and against Bonnie Prince Charlie. For the 10th Light Dragoons therefore – a relatively young regiment of light cavalry – the eventual step to being Hussars was a sartorial rather than a military one. They were already a cavalry regiment of skilled horsemen. It gave, as Julia Johnstone had said, and Lydia Bennet in *Pride and Prejudice* clearly felt, such 'a fillip to the spirits of a young miss, you don't know'.

Kitted out in the blue, white and silver of the 10th, Brummell set off for Brighton. The coaches left from the White Horse cellar at the western end of Piccadilly, with tickets for sale from Davies and Co. in the sanded-floor undercroft waiting room. The coach ran via East Grinstead and Lewes and took twelve hours to get to Brighton. Only four passengers could ride inside.

From June of each year, the 10th Light Dragoons camped at Brighton at 'a delightful spot near to the sea-side' to the west of Brighton itself, towards Shoreham. Wells had been dug in 1793 to better equip the campsite. The prince, according to *The Times*, liked to 'dine at the mess every day and be in actual service in all respects'. 'Actual service' for the Prince of Wales, however, involved the construction of a large marquee equipped with a suite of rooms and a 'spacious kitchen' with 'all sorts of conveniences attached'. The chairs for the royal marquee alone were said to have cost a thousand pounds, and the whole campsite was laid out with 'corresponding elegance'. The panorama – the young Hussars and their mock-medieval tented city – was thought sufficiently picturesque to inspire several painters. The prince spent all that summer of 1794 'manoeuvring his regiment'. The country was at war in earnest, but the prince had been informed he could not 'with propriety go through the ranks of General Officers' but must content himself as 'Colonel at the Head of a Regiment [the 10th]'. He threw himself more and more into life with his regiment in a toy-soldier pantomime that prefigured his later delusions of himself as the 'victor of Waterloo'. It was during the course of this hot Brighton summer that he and Brummell first got to know each other well.

It was an easy atmosphere in which to mingle with royalty and with the well connected – an atmosphere, royalty aside, not unlike the Eton sixth form of the day, but a good deal more raucous. The prince was not above engineering the election of young officers, like Brummell, to maintain the party atmosphere at Brighton. When a vacancy occurred, the prince took an interest. The regiment had already attracted the sons of the Duke of Rutland, Lords Charles and Robert Manners, who became close friends of Brummell. It also boasted among its number Lord Charles Stanhope (later Petersham), who remained friends with Brummell for the next twenty years, Lord Charles Kerr, son of the Duke of Roxburghe, Lord Bligh, son of the Earl of Darnley, Lord Lumley, son of the Earl of Scarborough and Lord Edward Somerset, son of the Duke of Beaufort, as well as Frederick Ponsonby, Lord Bessborough's son, and the only man Harriette Wilson said she had truly loved.

In the case of Ponsonby, the prince even lobbied the young man's father on behalf of the regiment. 'By various exchanges that have lately taken place in my regiment,' he wrote to Lord Bessborough, a commission would be available for Ponsonby. The prince went on to point out that even higher ranks would soon fall vacant and be available for sale for as little as '£650' and that in mere weeks Ponsonby would 'probably become . . . a Lieutenant'.

I need not, I trust, add, that in coming into my regiment, every attention will be shewn to your son, but that it is also no detriment to know, that he is coming into a regiment, supposed to be one of the first in the service, and of which the Corps of Officers is entirely composed of Men of Fashion and Gentlemen, and the most regular and orderly Corps of young men that exists.

The 10th were many things, but regular and orderly they were not. Jack Slade, who joined the regiment a little before Brummell, recalled the hard drinking in the mess. The officers of the 10th had wine glasses specially made with no stems, so that they could be replaced on the table only after they had been emptied. The prince, when once asked to sing, replied that all the best songs he knew were 'two-bottle songs', and proceeded to down such – and sing. Those who could not keep up with the pace quietly emptied their glasses under the table. But most drank. It was a mixed crowd, in so far as they were not all noblemen, but they were all considered worthy of the prince's company in terms of being, as the prince put it, 'men of Fashion and Gentlemen'. It was an enclosed world of men in which wit was relished but in the barrack-room manner – a convivial but knockabout atmosphere, recalled by a veteran thirty years later with rueful nostalgia:

The officers of those days [were] . . . thrown headlong into a vicious school . . . where at times they were expected to act as if in reality they were thinking beings, and at others chastised for merely thinking. [The officers] were suffered to get drunk, swear, gamble, seduce, and run into debt at pleasure; that such a school produced many scamps, many incorrigible, bad characters is but little surprising; it is indeed, truly wonderful that it produced anything else.

Life as a dragoon officer in the late eighteenth century was a school for scandalous behaviour:

The reputation of being what in slang phraseology of the day was called 'a three bottle man', 'a devil of a fellow for the ladies', 'a wild and extravagant dog' was at this time far from being injurious to [an officer's] professional reputation, and was quite likely to get him an appointment as that of an Aide de Camp, whose principal duty in those days was to fill the decanters and see that they were emptied before they left the table.

Consequently Brummell's particular brand of rhetorical whimsy, honed at Eton and Oxford, was redirected in the army into a darker comic inversion, where everything that the outside world deemed bad was good – and funny. Brummell was 'the life and soul of the mess with his regiment, for his original wit and collection of good stories were inexhaustible; and at the dinner table he always kept his brother officers in roars of laughter'. 'Every regiment in those days had a practised and privileged jester . . . whose province it was to put an immediate stop to serious conversation by a pun or joke' and restore 'that hilarity which usually pervades military society.' Black humour was evidently prized; lewdness and scatology were reserved for occasions exclusive of respectable women, which most, of course, were. Brummell's gift of mimicry was honed in the course of all this barracks badinage, a gift he shared with the prince. The only man whose range of impersonations was acknowledged to be wider than Brummell's was the prince himself, whose 'powers of mimicry were so extraordinary', said Brummell, 'that if his lot had fallen that way, he would have been the best comic actor in Europe'.

The raucous regiment became notorious in Brummell's time as 'the most expensive, the most impertinent, the best dressed, the worst moralled regiment in the British Army'. For a young man without parental guidance in the world, he was running with a wild crowd. 'Its officers, many of them titled' were derided as 'all more or less distinguished in the trying campaigns of the London season . . . all intimates of the Prince-Colonel.' The 10th responded to the prince's example by drinking heavily, living loosely, riding well and dressing superbly when the occasion demanded. They could certainly put on a good show. On 10 August 1794 they were reviewed on the Sussex Downs with the Royal Horse Artillery by General Bruce and commended on their 'soldierly appearance and the exact manner in which they went through their military evolutions'.

George Brummell had learned some horsemanship at Donnington Grove, so in this respect he was well suited to life with the 10th. They took great pride both in their riding and in their horses – officers were expected to provide their own – and Brummell's pre-eminent task as a cornet was to look good on horseback while bearing the guidon (standard). There was no formal provision of basic training for an officer in the army until 1801, but there were guidebooks that young cavalrymen like Brummell were encouraged to keep always in the pockets of their jackets – the guides of Bland and Simes. These explained how to perform the manual and platoon exercises of the firelock and carbine rifles. Constant study of these and the regimental orderly and records books constituted officer instruction. Training with the lower ranks in the company of more experienced officers was, in theory, meant to allow every newly commissioned man to learn by example 'and inform themselves of every article of their Duty . . . by asking Questions of their superiors'.

There was a drill sergeant who attacked the ears of the new recruits and officers, memorably recorded by one of the 10th 'girls' woken from her slumbers by the daily eight a.m. harangue:

'Tik nuttis!! The wurd "dror" is oney a carshun. A t'wurd "suards" ye drors um hout, tekin a farm un possitif grip o'th'hilt! Sem time, throwing th'shith smartly backords, thus! "DROR SUARDS!!"'

Senior officers, in turn, were 'to teach their Subalterns their duty and see they do it by fair means, and tell them their faults and omissions . . . and let them know they are not to have their Pay to be Idle'. For the officers it was a clubby atmosphere of enthusiastic amateurism, quite at odds with the brutal realities of the war raging across the Channel.

Brummell addressed the regimen he was set with an air he was developing even as a teenager: of amused indifference. Quite soon after his gazetting in the summer of 1794 a loose charger was seen galloping down the ranks of the regiment as it stood in formation on parade. This exchange was considered worthy of record by a military memoirist:

'WHOSE HORSE IS THAT?' bawled the Colonel. 'Mr Brummell's sir!' came the reply. 'Send him here!' Brummell duly came. 'What have you to say?' demanded the Colonel [the story is recorded with the note that the colonel used additional military expletives].

'The fact is, Colonel,' [dead-panned the young cornet] 'my horse is a very fine animal and wanted to show off his paces, so I let him go.'

'A reply,' [noted the old soldier] 'which merely added fuel to the fire.'

Army training had its costs, however, even for a cavalryman like Brummell, set on avoiding all appearance of effort or anxiety. Some time early in his military career, Brummell took a bad fall from his horse. He met with an uncooperative cobblestone, which smashed his nose to the left. The bridge was set, but crooked to the side. To some, this added character and a rougher edge to a face that had looked soft and somewhat haughty beforehand. To others, Julia Johnstone in particular, Brummell's broken nose for ever ruined his looks. He was no longer the perfect boy.

Brummell rode with aplomb, and played his part to the hilt as one of the Falstaffian drinking partners to the Prince of Wales's Prince Hal. But it can have been of no surprise to his family or Eton friends that he turned out not to be a born soldier.

The best-known anecdote in military circles became the story of how Brummell recognised the men under his command. At parade each day, he made it his habit to arrive late and get in line quickly on his mount by the expedient of riding to the front of one particular trooper with a drinker's bloodshot nose. It was the sort of thing Cornet Brummell noticed. The troop, inevitably, was rearranged pending the enrolment of some new recruits, and Brummell's blue-nosed marking point was moved.

Brummell galloped into place.

'How now, Mr Brummell?' cried the sorely tried colonel. 'You are with the wrong troop!'

Brummell swivelled in his saddle to check that he was in front of the bloodshot nose, which, indeed, he was, although not in front of any other of his men. 'No, no, sir, you are quite wrong. A pretty thing indeed, if I did not know my own troop!'

The story that evening was added to Brummell's repertoire of self-deprecating mess-room anecdotes at a dinner with the prince, and a small piece of the mosaic of his legend fell into place: Brummell, too insouciant to know or care who his men were. Brummell, the disengaged, witty amateur. Waggish and indifferent. His prince-colonel laughed. The style of gentlemanly behaviour Brummell was developing meant never looking as if you cared too much, or worked too hard. Except, perhaps, at play.

For a well-dressed young dragoon officer around Brighton, there was plenty to amuse. Within a few months of his gazetting in 1794 the dragoons were given a central role in Brighton's annual celebrations of the prince's birthday. There was music and fireworks, 'a transparent painting of His Royal Highness's coronet and crest adorned with red roses, a garter star decorated with woodbine and lilies and HRH's initials beautifully written in flowers'; the decorations were further embellished with 'a wreath of laurel, the whole encircled with the British oak and acorns and the motto 'Brighton's Support' in honour of the prince who was quite simply that.

The *Public Advertiser* claimed nothing could outshine the prince-colonel's 'principal amusement', which was 'in manoeuvring his regiment' and so on 30 August a still larger grand field day and sham battle was staged on the downs with the prince-colonel commanding and charging with his men. 'All the beauty and fashion of the neighbourhood attended the field.'

According to *The Times* the young blades of the 10th kept a schedule that summer in accordance with Brighton high life: 'Most of them keep their own blood-horses and their girls. At one o'clock they appear on parade to hear the word of command given to the subaltern guard; afterwards they toss off their *goes* of brandy, dine about five, and come about eight to the theatre.' It was a fine life, a metropolitan life. Brighton's population might hover around five thousand out of season, almost a village, but when the prince and the dragoons were in town – seven thousand assorted troops under the command of officers like Brummell – the whole tone of Brighton changed.

In 1794 Brighton was already Mayfair-by-the-sea. The architecture, even the clotted-cream paint on the stucco, was indistinguishable from the most fashionable parts of London, and the inhabitants in many cases were the same people. Henry Holland had designed an elegant neo-classical 'Marine Pavilion' for the prince, which dominated the Steine – Brighton's main promenade route perpendicular to the seafront. The Brighton that Cornet Brummell knew looked like London and was, in style, everything the later Regency period came to epitomise: restrained, elegant, classical. This hid a very different style of living for the coterie around the young Prince of Wales. For them, Brighton was relaxed and indulgent, much freer than London – especially in terms of sexual morality. The young officers of the 10th were all out of sight of their parents, the moral guardians of the previous generation, and were setting the rules themselves, rules that, come the Regency, would be the orthodoxy of London society too.

The new wife of Sir John Lade, Letitia, Lady Lade, was typical of Brighton society in Brummell's time. She had previously served the Duke of York, in a non-military position, and also Mr Rann, a notorious highwayman. She was said to act as procuress for the prince, soliciting on his behalf the virgin daughters of genteel Brighton families. She was also conspicuous around Brighton driving her own carriages at breakneck speed. There was also the Marquess of Queensberry, an ageing roué nicknamed 'Old Tick' by the 10th Light Dragoons. The prince had spotted him at the Brighton theatre with Mrs Harris, the fruit-woman, and asked her if she was not afraid of the consequences of flirting with the rake. 'No, Your Highness,' she rejoined, 'for alas, His Grace is like an old clock: he can tick but he can't strike.'

Many of the dragoons kept common-law wives in Brighton, their 'girls', who were set up in styles strictly in accordance to the rank of their lover. It was unusual for a dragoon officer to be married. When the Marquess of Worcester took a commission in the 10th, Harriette Wilson came with him; he arrived ahead of her to set up a household for her on Marine Parade as if she were his marchioness.

As colonel-in-chief, the prince occasionally had cause to explain a type of battle fatigue particular to the 10th on manoeuvres in Brighton: 'A very serious venereal attack,' he wrote to the army commander-in-chief, his brother, the Duke of York on 15 September 1795, was laying up one Captain Fuller of the 10th and putting him outside active duty for the immediate future. 'Nothing fresh but an old business which has hitherto only been patched up,' the worldly prince explained, 'but which [the doctor] assures him now with perseverance he will completely get rid of.' He enclosed a medical note.

Brummell kept no particular 'girl' in Brighton but was exposed for the first time in his adult life to the frequent company of women – most of whom, it should be allowed, were far from respectable. Although Harriette Wilson was in Brighton a little after Brummell, her memoirs are a vivid reminder that the world Elizabeth Bennet dreaded for her sister Lydia was very real, very brazen and based all around the 10th Light Dragoons' officers' mess. The 10th took their 'girls' to the Brighton theatre, and even to the Marine Pavilion. They openly cohabited with them, and invited them to wild nights in the barracks dining room. In leaving Oxford and joining the dragoons at Brighton, Brummell conformed to a family pattern his father had tried to break: he was once again in the *demi-monde*, among prostitutes and courtesans just as if he had been back at Bury Street. Sexual licence was all around him. He was nineteen. If, as seems most probable, he contracted the venereal disease that eventually killed him from a whore, it would have been at Brighton that he formed the habit, typical of his class and era, of frequenting prostitutes. 'These great [army] depots,' wrote one contemporary, 'are the fertile hotbeds where syphilitic disease is sown broadcast amongst the young soldiers.'

The most highly regarded of the kept women of Brighton was the secret wife of the prince-colonel himself, Mrs Fitzherbert. Hers was the grandest house on the Steine apart from the prince's own, and she was held in good regard by the people of Brighton, and by the 10th Light Dragoons. She even attended military parades to watch her 'husband', the prince, dressed in her own version of the Light Dragoons uniform, Prince of Wales feathers in her hair.

The widowed Maria Fitzherbert had married the Prince of Wales in December 1785. This marriage was illegal in the eyes of the law but not in the eyes of the Roman Catholic Church, to which she claimed devotion, and allowed her to accept the prince's attentions and money. She may have known he would not and could not stay faithful to her, but seemingly, she loved him. At the same time she enjoyed the status and privileges of royalty – especially in Brighton. In Brighton she was 'treated as a queen' and when she dined out she was 'led out to dinner before princesses'.

Mrs Fitzherbert organised entertainments for the 10th Light Dragoons officers, perhaps in an attempt to lure them away from drink. There was music, a passion of the prince, but also amateur dramatics at which George Brummell excelled. There were cricket matches, fencing competitions, dinner parties and dances. She also attended with them the race meetings – and she and the prince even had a run of good luck on the horses.

Mrs Fitzherbert was thirty-seven when she and Brummell first met in the summer of 1794, and coming to the end of her second reign of influence. She had already lost the Prince of Wales more than once to other mistresses, and the fact of her marriage had been denied twice in the House of Commons, on the direct authority of the prince. But they had reunited in 1791, and maintained a brief period of domestic contentment and relative financial rectitude until things began to wrong again in 1793.

One of the least attractive qualities of the man Maria Fitzherbert called her husband was his inconstancy. Few friends, no family members and none of his many lovers remained close to the prince throughout his life: he was always falling out of friendships and falling in love. This trait had disastrous consequences for his young *protégé*, George Brummell, and in 1794, in a different manner, a grave effect on the prince's relationship with Maria. By the time George Brummell came to know them, the prince's attentions had moved away – again temporarily – from Mrs Fitzherbert, who found herself in the distressing position of being two-timed by a husband who was being leaned on by Parliament and the King to take a legitimate, royal, Protestant bride. As with all the trials of her long life, she took these latest blows – the prince's intended marriage and his simultaneous affair with an overweight grand-mother nine years his senior – with a grace that impressed many, including the new young cornet in her husband's regiment, George Brummell. To complicate matters, Mrs Fitzherbert may also have been pregnant, although the evidence for this is not conclusive, with the first of three 'secret' daughters fathered by the prince. Two of these supposed daughters, Mary Anne Smyth and Minney Seymour, were later 'adopted' by Mrs Fitzherbert as her nieces and referred to by the prince (by then George IV) as his 'daughters'. Brummell's close association with the prince during the years in which he may have fathered a secret family, as well as a legitimate one, was part of what made the potential of his memoirs in later life so explosive.

The newer, older woman in the prince's life in 1794, however, was the redoubtable Countess of Jersey, a confidante of his mother, Queen Charlotte, and a formidable rival to Mrs Fitz-herbert. Frances, Lady Jersey was described as 'clever, unprin-cipled, but a beautiful and fascinating woman, though with scarcely any retrieving really good quality'. In a scurrilous rating of the attributes of leading London ladies by the *Morning Post* she had scored nought out of twenty for both principles and sense. In London society she was known as 'Lucretia'. Maria Fitzherbert later allowed that her split with the Prince of Wales in 1794 was as a direct result of 'the twofold influence of the pressure of his debts on the mind of the Prince, and a wish on the part of Lady Jersey to enlarge the Royal Establishment in which she was to have an important situation'. Or, as *Bon Ton Magazine* put it, 'the union between this fashionable pair, the prince and Mrs F . . . has at length been resolved. The lady retires to Switzerland . . . and a settlement of £6000 per annum. The gentleman visits Jersey.'

Lady Jersey, unlike Mrs Fitzherbert, had some interest in pushing the prince towards the legal marriage he had long been avoiding. Queen Charlotte may have encouraged her to suggest to him that he could resolve his debts and his unpopularity if he were to take a legal wife and beget an heir. He seems not to have needed too much convincing. William Pitt reluctantly agreed that the country would increase his Civil List income from £60,000 to £100,000 a year, and there was also his income from the Duchy of Cornwall. William Cobbett, writing in 1830, pointed out bitterly that the original sum already represented enough to support '3000 labouring families for a year'. Parliament also allowed him more than £20,000 towards a royal wedding. The prince agreed, and immediately spent £54,000 on jewels for his nuptials.

It shows some considerable success on the part of George Brummell, in terms of his social ascendancy and his budding friendship with the prince, that less than a year after joining the regiment and still only in his teens he found himself standing as *chevalier d'honneur* at the ensuing wedding of George, Prince of Wales, to Princess Caroline of Brunswick.

The choice of bride was another effect of Lady Jersey's influence. Of all the many eligible Protestant princesses of Europe, Princess Caroline Amelia Elizabeth of Brunswick-Wolfenbüttel was perhaps the least suited to be sacrificed on the altar of dynastic obligations to a man like the Prince of Wales, sensitive, insecure and fastidious as he was. Lady Jersey knew this: she intended the young bride to be no real rival to her. Princess Caroline had been brought up in a small German court far from the cosmopolitan sophistication of London. She was six years younger than the prince, utterly inexperienced in the world, and given to girlish fits of pique (that much they had in common) but also crass and vulgar jokes. She was said to eat raw onions, a German fashion of the day, and wash rarely. Wellington said it was self-evident that Lady Jersey had chosen Caroline to be Princess of Wales for her 'indelicate manners, indifferent character, and not very inviting appearance from the hope that disgust for the wife would secure constancy to the mistress'. If so, she was to be disappointed, but the marriage nevertheless proved a disaster.

George Brummell fell headlong for the romance of a royal wedding, and blithely described the princess as 'a very handsome and desirable looking woman'.

Once the marriage settlement had been arranged between the courts of St James's and Brunswick-Wolfenbüttel, with no more than an exchange of portraits between the couple themselves, the princess was readied to be shipped off from Germany in the company of Lord Malmesbury. His round trip to collect her took him nearly five months, partly due to inclement weather during the winter of 1794/5 and the advance, despite this, of Napoleon in the Netherlands, but also to Malmesbury's deliberate delay as he endeavoured to polish Caroline's manners. It was a hopeless task. She lacked, he wrote 'character and tact . . . she has no governing powers . . . with a steady man she would do vastly well, but with one of different description there are great risks'. Caroline, with Malmesbury, arrived at Greenwich on 5 April 1795.

The escort sent to greet her was from the Prince's Own 10th Light Dragoons, and was headed by Lord Edward Somerset and Cornet Brummell. Somerset and Brummell were late. It was a Sunday morning, and they had been carousing on the Saturday night in London with a disconsolate prince. They and the carriage for the princess, drawn by six horses, galloped up to the quayside, with an annoyed and flustered Lady Jersey inside. She had been appointed lady of the bedchamber to the new bride, an act of astonishing tactlessness and cruelty even on the part of a prince famous for both – and her first responsibility had been to meet the princess. She greeted her, criticised her dress, then told the princess that she would not sit facing backwards, as it made her feel sick. Lord Malmesbury was forced to point out that, were that the case, she should never have accepted the post.

The dragoons thence escorted the bride-to-be and the piqued mistress of the bridegroom to St James's Palace. Brummell, as his rank befitted, flew the guidon of the regiment, along with the princess's standard.

On meeting Caroline for the first time, the Prince of Wales took one look at her and turned to Lord Malmesbury to mutter ungallantly, 'Harris, I am not well; pray get me a glass of brandy.' Then he left the room. Brummell, Malmesbury, Lord Edward Somerset and Lord Moira stared at the floor as the benighted princess exclaimed, in French, 'Does the prince always behave like this? I think he's very fat, and he's nothing like as handsome as his portrait.'

It was an unimpressive insight for seventeen-year-old Brummell not only into the character of his new friend and princely 'patron' but also into the unique pressures of palace life.

Brummell, like many of his contemporaries, was broadly sympathetic to the plight of a young woman who, whatever her personal shortcomings, was hopelessly out of her depth in her marriage to the Prince of Wales. The prince's actions continued to reflect extremely badly on him, though Brummell tended to put the best possible gloss on things. For a young man just eighteen months out of school, these were heady days. 'Never,' wrote *Bon Ton Magazine*, 'was public as well as private solicitude wound up to such a high pitch.' But public and press were determined that this was to be a fairy-tale wedding and poured compliments on the diminutive German princess 'whose virtues no less than her personal charms give her a lawful claim to love and esteem as to the admiration of the British nation in general'.

The royal couple were given no time to reflect on the mistake they might be making, and were due to be married a few days later, on the Wednesday night. The King did not see that this was fit reason to withdraw the prince's unmarried brothers from their military duties, so Lord Moira and George Brummell stood in as 'best men' along with the Dukes of Bedford and Roxburghe.

Cornet Brummell was becoming part of the inner royal sanctum, taken to the warm heart of the prince – a place, however, where it was not always comfortable to be.

It must have been exciting and alarming in fairly equal measure, exposed both to the glamour of royalty and the tawdry personal politics of the House of Hanover. On their way to the ceremony the prince confessed to Moira and Brummell his eternal love for Mrs Fitzherbert. At the wedding – in Inigo Jones's Queen's Chapel by St James's Palace, acting as Chapel Royal at the time, swagged in crimson velvet and silver tissue – the groom was conspicuously drunk. He, Moira and Brummell had been drinking the prince's favourite brandy, marasquin or maraschino, in an attempt to improve the prince's mood and his breath. To the strains of Handel's wedding anthem, 'he hiccoughed out his vows of fidelity' while making eyes at his mistress, Lady Jersey, placed nearby in the choir pews. When the Archbishop of Canterbury asked if anyone knew of any impediment why the prince might not be married, Brummell and Moira fixed their eyes on the floor and the prince burst into tears. The 'happy' couple retired almost immediately to bed (the wedding had been inexpediently timed for eight p.m., precisely when the prince and his cronies would usually be drunk) and the bride said the groom was so inebriated he 'passed the greatest part of his bridal night under the [fire] grate, where he fell'.

The next day Brummell accompanied the newlyweds to Windsor, and thence to Kempshott. He was one of the party whom Caroline later claimed ruined her honeymoon by partying with the prince and lying about the castle 'constantly drunk, sleeping and snoring in boots on the sofas . . . & the whole resembling a bad brothel much more than a palace'. Rather than making love to his wife, the prince seems to have decided to act up to his coterie of young male friends, playing partly for sympathy and partly in the traditional spirit of drunken male braggadocio. After his wedding night, Brummell was the first person he saw, and he bragged through his hangover that 'nothing could [have gone off] better', and winked that although 'her manners were not those of a novice', on seeing him naked she had gasped like a heroine of erotica, '*Mon dieu, qu'il est gros!*'* He seems not to have taken this as a double-edged compliment.

Yet at the same time he complained viciously at the simple dynastic imperative of impregnation, claiming that she had eschewed Malmesbury's advice to try washing all over and that she 'showed . . . such marks of filth both in the fore and hind part of her . . . that she turned my stomach and from that moment I made a vow never to touch her again'. In the three nights they spent together, however, they conceived a child – Princess Charlotte of Wales, born nine months later. But it was an ugly start to an ugly marriage, and one in which Brummell felt ever more torn between his loyalties to the prince and his instinctive kind-heartedness towards the princess. His is a lone voice from this period in their marriage, one that puts an unusually positive glow on what was largely reported as a disaster. His singularity in this, as the one close witness who claimed, briefly, there was some good feeling between the royal couple, may be the nostalgia for his own youth and first taste of royal glamour, or equally a small truth remembered by one who had little more to do with the princess beyond her honeymoon. '[They] then appeared very satisfied with each other,' he later said, 'and it was only when the intrigues of [Lady Jersey] began to take effect that any disagreement between them became apparent.' Or so it seemed to Cornet Brummell. The new Prince and Princess of Wales moved to their new, separate, apartments at Carlton House, and Brummell returned to his regiment.

Brummell's late teens were spent on the regular progress with the 10th light Dragoons, with occasional elevations to the highest society. It must have been a disturbingly schizophrenic existence. Long summers in Brighton with the regiment meant days in the mess tents and on horseback, and evenings at the Marine Pavilion with the Prince of Wales. October generally saw a decamp inland. Next the 10th went to 'Croydon and the places of the neighbour-

* 'My God it's huge!' or 'My God he's so fat!'

hood', and then on 'King's Duty' at Windsor or as ceremonial guards at the empty royal palace at Hampton Court. Brummell found himself each autumn back in his childhood home, but this time staying in the barracks by the palace, not within it, with the ghosts all around of his family and the heartbreak of Julia.

There would often be a return to Brighton around Christmas, and in the spring another round of mock battles and a larger camp. Some years the troops around Brighton numbered over ten thousand. The 1794 and 1795 camps, high above Brighton's Race Hill, served also as lookouts into the Channel and the expected French invasion. On a clear day messages could be sent to Shoreham and Seaford or passed to ships off the coast. Panic broke out one morning when troops rallied on Brighton beach after a signal was misread at the camp. Townsfolk heard the rumour of invasion, took to the beach with their own weapons and started a fight with the British soldiers whom they mistook for French.

The Light Dragoons saw action in Brighton only once, against smugglers. In October 1794 they impounded five hundred 'tubs' of contraband gin, leaving two of their number to guard them while the others went to Shoreham to alert the Customs office there. On returning, they found that the two officers left in charge had decided to open the gin, in the true spirit of the times and of the regiment, and started an impromptu party on the beach.

Life with the 10th was not all drunken raillery. In 1795, Brummell was close witness to a mutiny, and the ensuing harsh justice of the British military. The actual revolt was not in his regiment, but in the Royal Oxford Militia, camped nearby at East Blatchington near Newhaven. There was a tradition of professionally exploited gambling in this, as in many other regiments at camp, and great hardship in the ranks as result. Specifically, some soldiers of the Oxford had raided a flour mill and also a grain ship at harbour with the intention of improving rations in the ranks. They had also sold their spoils around the immediate area, to help clear their gambling debts. There had been a series of poor harvests in the 1790s, and bread prices were high so there was, understandably, some local sympathy for the men of the militia who had been undercutting local grain prices. Nevertheless several militiamen were singled out to be punished for this 'mutiny', a civil crime committed while serving in the army. Six of the men were sentenced to a thousand lashes each – practically a death sentence – and one to be transported to Botany Bay. But two of the ringleaders, Sergeant Cooke and Private Parish, were to be used as an example to the local troops and populace, and were sentenced to death by firing squad. The local anger was such, and the sympathy within the Royal Oxford Militia, that it was decided the sentence should be carried out not by the men's own regiment but by the nearby 10th Light Dragoons. On 13 June 1795 both regiments gathered in the natural amphitheatre of Goldstone Bottom. The lashings were halted at three hundred each on the advice of a dragoon surgeon, but Cooke and Parish were instructed to kneel inside their open coffins and a dragoon officer – Brummell or one of his comrades in arms – gave the order to fire. The scene was considered so exceptional in its cruelty that the regimental chaplain fainted, never to recover consciousness, and the bloodied grass became a place of local pilgrimage.

Brummell rose in the ranks to lieutenant in 1795 and then, in 1796, to captain. This gave him extra duties, which he would not have appreciated, and cost him dear: £997 10s. for the lieutenancy and £2782 10s. to be a captain. But the prize was worth it in one regard: the uniform kept getting better.

As a captain Brummell had the right to wear yellow facings on his jacket and have a red busby-bag and red cloth facing to the sabretache that supported his sword. The swords were curved like scimitars with a plain cross-bar over the 'Mameluke' hilt, which had no knuckle bow or any protection for the fingers. It was designed to terrify the enemy in battle, to cut falling silk – an unlikely necessity in combat – but its delicacy of line and real lack of weight exposed its owner's knuckles to serious injury. It was all about the look: it was, as the Marquess of Worcester put it, 'the square thing'.

Officers had grey fur for their *pelisse* and for their busby, real silver lace on the jacket, with three loops of silver at the cuff, as a reference to the Prince of Wales's feathers. All this ate into Brummell's inheritance. He was expected to 'keep up [repair] his expensive uniform and horse appointments, to purchase his own chargers and barrack furniture'. He was also obliged to 'pay 8*s*. 5*d*. a day for the forage of each of his horses and to subscribe considerable sums to the mess and band fund, to pay his own groom and servant and to pay [their] income tax'. An officer's pay was slightly less than the price his commission would have gained him if invested as an annuity: officers were meant to lose money in the army. It was argued that this was what guaranteed they were gentlemen, not mercenaries, and 'gave them an interest in the country which they defended'.

All this was less a point of contention for Brummell and his fellow officers, however, than their hair. In the 10th they wore it long, in a queue, or tied pigtail, and powdered, which Brammell abhorred. In civilian life all those possessed of a fine head of hair, and with the inclination to show it off, had eschewed the fashion for powder and wigs for several years. William Pitt's tax on hair powder in 1795, levied to help pay for the war with France, proved the death knell to the fashion. By the late 1790s men of fashion wore their hair short and brushed forward in the style that brought to mind marble Roman emperors, and, ironically, Napoleon. In September 1795 there had even been a ritual cropping and washing of hair in the former powder room of the fashion-conscious household of the Duke of Bedford at Woburn Abbey. But in the army the style of queues and powder persisted, the one element of 10th Light Dragoon dress that was considered less than stylish.

It was unkindly suggested that the reason Brummell quit the army in the late 1790s was due to hair fashion. It was typical of the sort of jibe levied against him, but he had probably initiated it himself as a self-deprecatory aside – making consequence out of inconsequence as was increasingly his style. His real reasons for handing in his commission were to do with timing and his disinclination to face a long-term military career. In 1799 he would come of age and, meanwhile, the 10th Light Dragoons were about to be sent to the North.

The 1795 Brighton 'mutiny' had been a foretaste for Brummell of the new political realities of wartime Britain. Poor harvests, heavy taxation and the upheavals of the industrial revolution conspired to spoil the fun of the 10th Light Dragoons. Their ability to handle a mutinous crowd in Sussex had been noted, and they were due to be sent to the north of England, not for any specific duties so much as to provide a show of strength in troubled times, and to help assert the rule of law. In early 1798 they were due to be transferred to Manchester and Brummell took this as his signal to act on an idea that had been brewing since the Prince of Wales's wedding. Of the two sides of his army life that he had experienced – the glamour of being an officer escort of the Prince of Wales at his wedding, and the institutionalised brutality that typified his military role in Brighton – it was clear which one better suited his personality. Brummell had decided to quit the army some time before he did so, but the prospect of a freer rein with his inheritance, and the prospect of being outside the royal circle, precipitated a decision. It wasn't so much that a tour of duty in the North threatened harsh duties without the excitement of battle – although it did – so much as the inevitability that the Prince of Wales would not accompany them that convinced Brummell Manchester was not for him. The story he told, naturally, put a slightly more glib spin on things: 'The fact is, Your Royal Highness,' began Captain Brummell, interrupting the prince at his toilette at the Marine Pavilion, Brighton, 'I have heard that we are ordered to Manchester. Now you must be aware how disagreeable this would be to me. I could really not go: think, Your Royal Highness, *Manchester*!'

The joke was for a moment lost on the prince, so Brummell was obliged to carry on: 'Besides, *you* would not be there. I have, therefore, with Your Royal Highness's permission, determined to sell out.'

If he had worried that this might offend his friend and colonel-in-chief he was mistaken: 'Oh, by all means, Brummell,' said the prince, 'do as you please.'

Brummell left the regiment in late 1798. He was followed soon afterwards by some of the officers who had made his life and the prince's such fun: Lords Charles and Robert Manners and Lord Edward Somerset. The regiment continued to attract the second sons of the aristocracy and those who imagined Brighton exactly as Lydia Bennet in *Pride and Prejudice*: a vista of tents, officers and girls chasing men in uniform. But the prince's love for his 10th Light Dragoons waned, as it was wont to do with all his passions. He kept the uniform, naturally, constantly let out to fit his bulk, for suitable occasions and military portraits. Appropriately enough therefore it was the regiment's impact on fashion that was of far greater import than anything it might have effected on the battlefield:

Hussar dress – outlandish, outrageous and foreign – was an ideal vehicle for the expression of [the Prince of Wales's] opposition to his royal father. The 'hussar craze' became the military manifestation of the same desire for 'exclusivity' that pervaded the upper realms of London society . . . and was responsible for the rise of the 'Dandy'; in fact, the two were inextricably bound up, as many of the leading dandies had, at one time or another, been hussar officers.

Prince among them, of course, was Brummell.

In the months before his twenty-first birthday in June 1799 Brummell continued to spend time with the officers of the regiment. His immediate expectations, his portion of the inheritance, which had grown under Macpherson's care, allowed him to set up the lifestyle for which he would become famous. He furnished himself with a racing curricle, horses and staff. None of this was remarkable for a young man in his position, but the style with which he flaunted his wealth was. His friends were amused. As Jesse wrote,

One of his brother officers humorously told me that he attended to his [military] duty far better after he had left the regiment than he did when he belonged to it; for he seldom passed within twenty miles of their quarters without turning out of his road and paying them a visit. On one of these itinerant calls he drove into the barracks yard in his carriage, with four posters [post-horses]. 'Halloo, George!' said a friend from the mess-room window, 'when did you take to four horses?' 'Only since my valet gave me warning for making him travel with a pair.'

The friendship founded in the regiment between the prince and Captain Brummell was singular. 'The future George IV,' wrote Count d'Aurevilly, 'recognised in Brummell a portion of himself, a portion which had remained healthy and 'ι minous; and this is the secret of the favour he showed him.'

It cannot be ignored that from the first there was a subtext to the 'violent intimacy' between Brummell and the Prince of Wales that bordered on the homoerotic. Indeed, one biographer of the prince regent has gone so far as to suggest that a friendship played out around a mutual fascination with clothes and fashion went some way to suggesting that both men were bisexual. Within a few years, certainly, the prince would be attending Brummell's half-naked toilette, rather than the other way round, as if it were a royal levee and he a loyal valet. But there was no direct sexual content in their relationship: it was more complex and intriguing than that. At the start of the friendship the prince was in the position of power, not only as Brummell's – indeed almost everyone's – social superior, but also as commander of the regiment. Absent from most accounts is the further simple fact that he was twice Brummell's age. The wedding to Caroline of Brunswick, which placed Brummell for the first time at the centre of royal life, saw him standing shoulder to shoulder with the Earl Moira and the Dukes of Bedford and Roxburghe; all men in their early middle years, like the prince. Brummell's place in the regiment was that of a joker: it was this that was noted rather than, necessarily, the clothes he had in common with everyone else. It was a world of men in which he had learned to excel, different from Eton only in the added spice of disreputable women, extra freedom, cash, and the shared irresponsibility of the mess-room, which always mitigates against the formation of separate, romantic bonds. It was part of the prolonged adolescence that was the prince's world, and by extension the world of many over-privileged men of the time.

His schoolfriend Thomas Raikes noted Brummell's ease in the presence of royalty, and the unflappable good-humour that characterises those who can swim in the immediate wake of the famous. 'He was liberal, friendly . . . always living with the highest in the land on terms of intimacy but without *bassesse* or truckling . . . it is only justice to say that he was not only good-natured, but thoroughly good tempered. I never remember to have seen him out of humour . . . He also had a peculiar talent for ridicule (not ill-natured) . . . which enabled him to laugh people out of bad habits.'

Brummell's place at the royal wedding was assured by neither age nor privilege: quite simply, he must have been enormously liked. His interest in uniforms, the first shared passion with the Prince of Wales, can hardly have accounted for this, any more than a sexual frisson would have done even had there been one.

Brummell's good looks and assured bearing must have helped his entrée into the adult world – but one other key factor, especially on that tense and unpleasant wedding day at St James's Palace, was the signal trait of Brummell's character, and the most elusive: he made people laugh.

PART II
1799–1816

'A DAY IN THE HIGH LIFE'

I will attempt to sketch the day of a young man of fashion; and of such a one a single day describes his whole life.

He thinks of rising about eleven in the morning and, having taken a slight breakfast, puts on his riding coat and repairs to . . . all the fashionable streets off Hyde Park . . . visits the most noted shops and . . . After bespeaking something there, he . . . drives from one exhibition to the other, stops at the caricature shops and, about three, drives to a fashionable hotel. Here he takes his lunch, reads the papers, arranges his parties for the evening and at five strolls home. His toilet he finds prepared and his valet waiting for him . . . by seven he is dressed and goes to dinner . . . At nine he goes to the play. Not to see it . . . but to flirt from box to box, to look at ladies whom he knows and to show himself to others whom he does not . . . he then proceeds to a rout, a ball, or the faro-bank of some lady of distinction . . . about four in the morning, exhausted with fatigue he returns home; to recommence, the next morning, the follies of the past day.

'A Day in the Life of a Young Man of Fashion',
The Stranger in England, Christian Goede, 1807

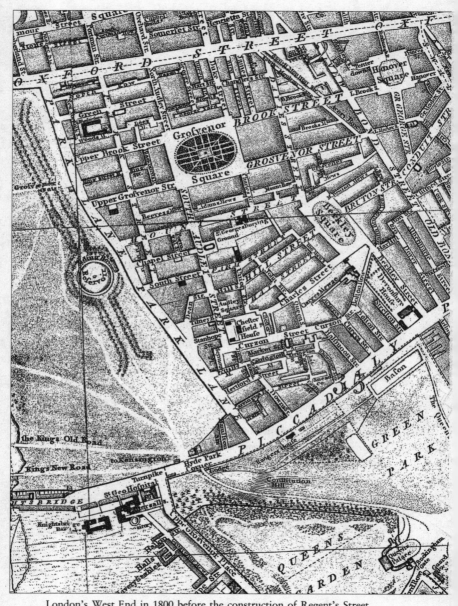

London's West End in 1800 before the construction of Regent's Street.
Bottom left, Rotten Row (The Route du Roi or King's Road).

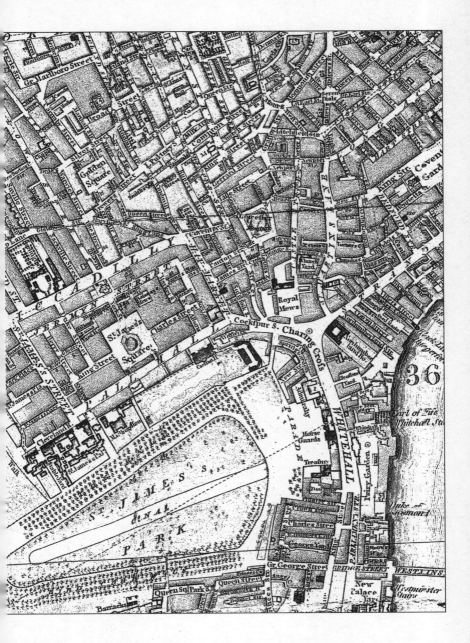

MORNING

5

DANDIACAL
BODY

A Dandy is heroically consecrated in this one object; the
wearing of clothes wisely and well, so that as others dress to
live, he lives to dress.

Thomas Carlyle, 'The Dandiacal Body'
in *Sartor Resartus*, 1833

Amongst the curious freaks of fortune there is none more
remarkable in my memory than the sudden appearance, in
the highest and best society in London, of a young man whose
antecedents warranted a much less conspicuous career . . . there
are comparatively few examples of men obtaining a similarly
elevated position simply from their attractive personal appearance and fascinating manners.

Captain Gronow, *Reminiscences*, 1862

'In London,' Casanova said, 'everything is easy to him who has
money and is not afraid of spending it.' It was an aphorism by
which twenty-one-year-old George Brummell set about his assault on London society. On his coming-of-age in 1799 a third of
the family estate was released to him. *Gentleman's Magazine*
estimated this fortune to be £20,000, Brummell later claimed it
was between £40,000 and £50,000 and Thomas Raikes struck at a
middle figure of £30,000, or nearly £2.5 million in today's money.

His brother William bought an estate at Wivenhoe near

Colchester with his third of the inheritance and lived the life of a country squire. His sister Maria's money was given over by law to her husband Captain Blackshaw and eventually it allowed their daughters to marry into continental nobility. George Bryan Brummell, however – the youngest of the three and in the usual run of things the one who should have had no 'expectations' and been forced into a career – spent his inheritance rather differently. His first acquisitions were the finest wardrobe the West End could offer, and a suitably fashionable address in which to wear it.

The house he moved into in 1799, 4 Chesterfield Street, still stands. It has barely been altered in the intervening centuries, save for the addition of Victorian bay windows at the back – over-looking the current Saudi Embassy – and the removal of a hidden servants' staircase. It is a tall, thin house with only two rooms, front and back, on each of the three main floors, either side of the central staircase. There is a kitchen-basement below and servants' attic above. The fan window above the front door and the wrought-iron lamp-arch through which one enters the house could have been designed to replicate those Brummell would have remembered from his childhood home in Downing Street. It was a modish house, but a modest one – at any event by the standards of Mayfair – yet it was perfectly placed for George Brummell to make his entrance into society. Chesterfield Street was ten minutes' walk from Hyde Park Corner and only yards from the back of Devonshire House (since demolished), the epicentre of the Whig aristocracy. It was at the precise mid-point of that 'parallelogram between Oxford Street, Piccadilly, Regent Street and Hyde Park', which Sydney Smith said, at the time, 'enclose[d] more intelligence and human ability, to say nothing of wealth and beauty, than the world has ever collected in such a space before'. George Selwyn, the wit and politician, had lived on the same street, and the Duke of Clarence, later William IV, took the house at the north end with his mistress, the celebrated comedy actress Mrs Jordan. The Prince of Wales became a regular visitor to Brummell's bachelor townhouse and the men who became known as the 'Dandiacal Body' crowded into the small front room each morning in the hope of being invited upstairs to see Brummell.

Quite soon after Brummell's acquisition of No. 4 this upper room became, bizarrely, as important a focus of London society for fashionable young men as Ranelagh or Vauxhall Gardens, Drury Lane or the Oxford Street Pantheon had been to their parents. The front dressing room at No. 4 Chesterfield Street was the inner sanctum where Brummell's levee took place, and this became a sophisticated diversion in its own right. Brummell's coterie, many of them former dragoon officers, launching their London careers in politics, the arts or society, were attracted to Chesterfield Street to watch how he dressed. They included the Dukes of Bedford, Argyll and Rutland, Lords Charles and Robert Manners and the Marquess of Worcester. Lord Alvanley was a constant member along with Lord Frederick Bentinck, Henry Pierrepoint, 'Poodle' Byng, Thomas Raikes, Tom Sheridan, Scrope Davies and, later, the young Lord Byron. (No respectable woman, of course, could visit an unmarried young man like Brummell, with the possible exception of his sister, who never came to London.)

Brummell's wealth, among such a body of men, was not considered extraordinary. Nor had he displayed any particular talents, except for witty repartee and good humour. But the way he dressed, in an age when the rules of attire were changing, was considered so remarkable that men *en route* to Tattershall's to see their horses, to Carlton House to see the Prince or to Berry Brothers to order port-wine and have themselves weighed, first called in on Chesterfield Street, to see how they should dress; to be considered – from all angles – gentlemen.

Brummell's new household was small. There was a man-servant, and a cook (also a man) and this 'small but *recherché ménage*' was completed by two horses – one of which was a fine Arab stallion named Stiletto, looked after by a groom, James Ell, for Brummell to ride in Hyde Park in the afternoons. He took particular interest in the hiring of valets. His first, Robinson, like his successors, stayed with him for more than a decade. This must attest to reasonable working conditions in the Brummell household, despite the exactitudes of the wardrobe care and dressing routines, although Brummell did not pay his valets particularly well. Perhaps he considered the advantages of the job – a fashionable address and employer, some cast-off clothes and minimal dinner-service duties, as sufficient perquisites. He tried to hire one particularly sought-after valet soon after he arrived at Chesterfield Street. The man had found himself out of work when his master Colonel Kelly, 'the vainest man in London', burned to death trying to rescue his favourite boots. The valet asked for two hundred pounds a year. 'Make it two hundred guineas,' said Brummell, 'and I'll work for *you*.'

Brummell furnished his home with the latest fashions, Buhl furniture and Sèvres porcelain. The small library, at the back on the ground floor, 'was stored with . . . works [showing] the same good taste'. Brummell became an avid collector of books and poetry so that eventually his library expanded to include 'the best works of the best authors of every period and every country'. 'Amongst the books were some good historical works, the standard poets, two editions of Shakespeare, his friend Ellis's Specimens of Early English Metrical Romances, bound curiously in raised calf, the Quarterly and Edinburgh [Reviews], the Memoirs of de Grammont, Chesterfield's Letters, Berrington's Abelard and Eloise and a large collection of novels.' He spent little on paintings, for fear, perhaps, that they might distract from the main artwork he intended his guests to admire: himself. But he was not considered extravagant in anything he did, even in his clothes. Some of his inheritance he even spent wisely on annuities, which were paid to him until his death. He would have been well advised to put more of his capital into 'the funds' and certainly to have done the same with his later substantial gambling wins. But he was not wise with money. The gaming book at White's Club, which he joined that year, records that he lost a bet that he would be married before the end of the century. Perhaps he thought he would marry a fortune so did not have to hold on to his own. Or perhaps he did not think about the future – after all, he was twenty-one.

There is limited wine-cellar space at No. 4 but an unexpectedly large coal-cellar for such a modest house, which extends under Chesterfield Street. Sea-coal fuelled London and, more specifically, Brummell's addiction to bathing. He was not in the vanguard of fashion in this area: an earlier gentleman's house in Bristol was built with a stone plunge-pool and, of course, the Prince of Wales and his set honoured the custom of sea-bathing in Brighton, if 'more on the beach' as one contemporary had it, 'than in the observance'. But Brummell bathed in hot water, and this was considered remarkable. Almost as remarkable as the fact that he bathed every day 'and every part of his body'.

Although he kept eau-de-Cologne as part of his 'comestibles' his most famous early dictum on personal style was so unusual it was recorded by several diarists: 'No perfumes, he used to say, but very fine linen, plenty of it, and country washing.' Captain Jesse noted this, and Harriette Wilson used the same words in her *Memoirs*, which predated Jesse's. The fields of Islington were hung with the shirts of men like Brummell, not just to infuse them with the neutral smell of country air, but to avoid the soot-spotting that marked city-dried whites. The clothes were to be clean and so, Brummell reasoned, should be the body underneath, rather than masked with perfume. The musk, civet, pomatum and geranium scents with which the previous generation had sought to disguise their lack of personal hygiene were banished, like wigs and lace. Bathing was the foundation of Brummell's Spartan aesthetic: his dandiacal body was to face the world unalloyed with perfumes or powders, 'trinkets or gew-gaws', as natural as the classical statues his style would emulate.

Those visitors who were allowed upstairs into Brummell's dressing room were presented with an unexpected sight. Brummell kept the door to his bedroom ajar so that he could carry on a conversation while he washed, shaved and dressed. For some or all of this he was totally or partially naked, 'in the buffs, *in naturalibis*', as he put it, which was part of the reason, no doubt, that his physique was noted in so many memoirs. He exfoliated his body all over with a coarse-hair brush and later in life, as guard against a recurrent skin complaint, he took to bathing in milk first and then water. An attitude to his own body, which was at once both exhibitionist and, in practice, ascetic and self-punishing, may have been a hangover of his Etonian education. He was also quite clever enough to enjoy the ridiculousness and despise the shallowness of his own sudden fame.

Rather than trusting Robinson the valet, Brummell shaved himself. 'Kings by birth were shaved by others,' as Napoleon said to Talleyrand, 'but he who has made himself *Roi*, shaves himself.' The Dandiacal Body bought cakes of shaving soap (1*s*. 6*d*.), badger brushes (5*s*. 6*d*.) and razors (sixpence a sharpening) from Renard's of St James's, along with toothbrushes, nail-brushes, combs and soap. Brummell used a series of miniature cut-throat razors, then applied himself to 'stray hairs' with the aid of tweezers and a dentist's magnifying mirror. Such scrupulous attention to detail was revered: his 'ablutions', it was said, 'would have gained him a reputation for sanctity in a Mahomedan country'. He later bought a complete shaving set including a spitting bowl – spitting being considered a vital morning ablution – made out of best silver, on the soundly Brummellesque principle that 'it is impossible to spit into *clay*'.

One modern barber has suggested this tortuous shaving regime – the numerous blades and the painful recourse to tweezers – may relate to the fashion Brummell and the Prince of Wales pioneered for high neckcloths. For the prince's part, this fashion hid his fatness. For Brummell it either hid, or created and then exacerbated, razor rash. The width and curve of some hairs – black and red are the thickest – tend to work against the razor, and can push individual hairs back under the skin, causing unsightly 'razor bumps' or 'razor rash', especially if the ingrown hairs are further irritated by the friction of a high starched collar and neckcloth. In any event, Brummell struggled to keep his beard as he desired it, before he moved on to the great feat that may have created his shaving problem in the first place: the perfect necktie.

Brummell, it was said, 'was the first who revived and improved
the taste for dress [among gentlemen] and his first great innovation was effected upon neckcloths'. The prince's fashion was not
working well for most men. The 'neckcloths . . . were then worn
without stiffening of any kind, and bagged out in front, rucking
up to the chin in a roll'. Either that, or they were so highly
starched that men could only 'test their fitness for use by raising
three parts of their length by one corner without [the neckcloth]
bending'. Brummell found a discreet compromise that was difficult and time-consuming to effect, but which came to be considered the acme of understated style.

First Robinson handed his master a plain shirt, lightly starched,
with a collar attached 'so large that, before being folded down it
completely hid his head and face,' and did up the tiny Dorset
buttons at the neck and cuffs. The collars on Brummell's shirts
were high, but there was a dart of fabric removed at the back that
allowed freer movement. 'The first *coup d'archet* was made with
the shirt collar which Brummell folded down to its proper size', in
other words so that the collar fold almost touched the ears. Next
Brummell was presented with a triangle of fine Irish muslin, cut
diagonally from a square yard and plainly seamed. This was
folded twice over at its widest point and wrapped carefully round
the neck. Brummell stood in front of a mirror keeping his chin in
the air – before he tied the tail ends in one of several manners that
became signifiers themselves of allegiance and taste. An extensive
pseudo-political treatise was later published on the subject,
Necklothitania, stating as a well-understood axiom that 'it must
be a great desideratum to every gentleman to persuade the rest of
the world that he is one: as, however, he cannot employ the same
means to prove it to them as he would to his intimates, he
necessarily must accomplish it by his dress, for 'The [neckcloth]
oft bespeaks the man.'

The initial tying of the neckcloth was only the first manoeuvre.
The Dandiacal Body who gathered to watch were more interested
in Brummell's next move. Slowly he lowered his chin in a series of
small 'declensions' that rucked down the necktie. Ideally it held

the contours of the neck rather than bulging out or folding inwards. It was this moment of self-sculpting that men came to study and emulate, because it was this that framed the face as well as dictating the angle of head. Once the starched cloth was pressed into place, and the whole rubbed with an older shirt to preserve the pleats, it would stand the rigours of the day. 'If the cravat was not properly tied at the first effort it was always rejected.' Often the shirts, too, would have to come off: perfection cost in laundering as well as in time. Wealth and style were no longer to be flaunted with lace and spangles but in a perfection of line that the cognoscenti would recognise, and cost the wearer in other ways. So the theatricality of understated chic became signal, with Brummell casting himself – even in this first adornment of the day – as both protagonist and *metteur-en-scène*.

Not all of Brummell's morning guests were honoured with a personal audience. Many waited downstairs. However, they were not altogether denied an element of the theatrical experience enacted in the dressing room. Robinson the valet made a point of passing the downstairs room with 'a quantity of tumbled neckcloths under one arm' and, naturally, this was noted by the gentlemen. On being interrogated, Robinson would solemnly reply, 'Oh, these sir? These are our failures.' Certainly something of Brummell's deadpan style had rubbed of on the valet. More tellingly, the arrangement of No. 4 Chesterfield Street makes it apparent that Robinson had to go out of his way to pass the first-floor rooms. The 'tumbled neckcloths' were part of Brummell's stagecraft.

Tying a neckcloth in the Brummell manner was the first of Brummell's sartorial gifts to a small coterie of young but influential men. It became the badge of dandyism and evolved slowly into the starched collar and tie that descended to the modern day. It was, for Brummell, the beginnings of his anti-style style: a simple perfection of line that took attention and know-how (and Brummell to set the fashion) but did not, *per se*, require wealth. As one dandy wrote

> My neckcloth, of course, forms my principal care,
> For by that we criterions of elegance swear
> And cost me each morning some hours of flurry
> To make it appear to be tied in a hurry.

Lord Byron was an assiduous disciple of the style, adding, later, a twist of Romantic dishabille and leaving his collar and neck-cloth a little undone. Several of his early portraits were later overpainted to replace a Brummell neckcloth with a Byronic open shirt. In his dandy youth, Byron followed Brummell's style to the letter.

Linen, like all other items of clothing, was not bought ready-to-use in Brummell's day. Bedsheets, towels and tablecloths, as well as shirts and undergarments, were bought as fabric-lengths and made up, often within the household, as required. Because they needed most frequent washing or repair they fell outside the usual realms of interest for the fashionable: a valet would shop for linen for his employer and it fell to Robinson, initially, to keep up a constant supply of white linen at Chesterfield Street. One German prince visiting London remarked on the expense of laundering and linen-buying:

As a sample of the necessities of a London dandy, I send to you the following statement by my fashionable washerwoman, who is employed by some of the most distinguished 'elegan[t]s', and is the only person who can make cravats of the right stiffness, and fold the breasts of shirts with plaits of the right size. An elegant then requires per week, twenty shirts, twenty-four pocket handkerchiefs, nine or ten pairs of 'summer trousers', thirty neck handkerchiefs (unless he wears black ones), a dozen waistcoats, and stockings *à discretion*. I see your housewifely soul aghast. But such a dandy cannot get on without dressing three or four times a day, the affair is *tout simple*, for he must appear: 1st Breakfast toilette; a chintz dressing gown and Turkish slippers: 2nd Morning riding dress; a frock coat, boots and spurs; 3rd Dinner dress; dress coat and shoes; 4th Ball dress, with 'pumps', a word signifying shoes as thin as paper, and with each [fresh linen].

One early effect of Brummell and his followers was to make neckties, shirts and their scrupulous whiteness desiderata of gentlemanly fashion. So tailors began to take a specialist interest in linen for their clients, and some of their bills survive. There is a fascinating document in the collection kept by John Murray of Lord Byron's complex financial arrangements showing just how wide-ranging the linen requirements of a young follower of Brummell were becoming. In April and May 1805 the young Lord Byron required over seventy-five yards of fine Irish linen, for shirts and bedsheets, costing more than fifteen pounds, and four and three-eighths yards and half a nail of expensive French cambric, at eighteen shillings a yard, for shirt fronts, which were often of separate material from the rest of the garment: finest Irish muslin or cambric. Russia-towelling was ordered for bath towels, and diaper towelling (damask linen) for nightshirts. Lord Byron also required six nightcaps, considered so essential to good health that they remained on the lists of requirements at some Oxbridge colleges and at Eton into the late nineteenth century.

Like Brummell, and all young men of fashion, it appears that Byron wore underwear rarely or not at all. A study of Scrope Davies's accounts reveals a similar absence, and Prince Pückler-Muskau's mention of the number of 'summer trousers' a gentleman needed refers to the same issue. The older generation kept with older ways; some of the very rare examples of male undergarments surviving from the period belonged to Thomas Jefferson and Thomas Coutts, the banker, but in their dotage. The younger set aspired to a different aesthetic, and the line of the trouser was not to be interrupted by rucked shirt-tails or underwear. It was a style inspired by neo-classicism, revolutionary ideals, cavalry-chic and cockiness. But the young followers of Brummell were flaunting, primarily, their wealth.

The fashion for the whitest clothes – trousers and waistcoats as well as shirts and neckties – that was pioneered by Brummell gave subtle expression to a disinterest in the cost of linen and laundering. The accounts of Brummell's dandy friend Scrope Davies allude to frequent and expensive repairs and replacements of pale

pantaloons and breeches, and shirts are reordered (and mono-
grammed) with expensive regularity. Small triangles of fabric,
gores or gussets, were sewn into underarms for ease of movement,
but also to be replaced, in an age before anti-perspirant, once
irredeemably sweat-stained. Even so, it was an expensive business. Shirt cuffs, likewise, were worn long, more than an inch
beyond the arm of the jacket, in order to establish the unaccept-
ability of getting one's hands dirty. The semiotics of peacockery
were changing. Instead of flamboyance, Brummell and his followers chose a style that discreetly asserted their wealth. As the
author of *Necklothitania*, who called himself 'A Man of the
Cloth' explained, it was a complicated business to flaunt your
wealth in the age of Equality:

It can hardly be imagined how political events should, even in the
remotest way, influence or affect the thermometer of fashion; but it is
nevertheless perfectly true, that both the American and French Revolutions have totally changed it – a change, no doubt, very dis-
advantageous to the man of the *Haut Ton*, inasmuch as it has
completely obliterated all distinction between the Occidental (West
End) nobleman and the oriental (City) shoppy; the master from his
servant, &c. by instilling into the minds of the plebeians an idea that
they were equal in point of rights, to their superiors, by birth – what a
monstrous and unnatural supposition! – and consequently producing
in their low and grovelling minds a wish to appear as such.

. . . yet that custom [of aristocratic overdressing] possessed enormous advantages, forming, by the furious expense necessarily incurred
to support it, an impassable barrier, and insurmountable obstacle, to
the aping attempts of the lower orders and shabby genteels, to appear
accoutred as their superiors. Now, alas! Fashion has made it quite
otherwise; a tradesman can have his coat made short-waisted, the tops
of his boots shallow, his waistcoats cut as they ought to be, and many
other similar things, equally as well as the higher ranks, and even in
many instances better.

Pure, clean lines and fabrics appeared classically egalitarian but
to the trained eye the new classical wardrobe also signified

wealth, status and style. Less, for the first time, was more. For this same reason the fashion for trouser stirrups Brummell imported into London from the military came to have a dual meaning. Leather straps that did up under the instep kept the line of the trouser in place – stretched from braces to feet. This was entirely within a neo-classical precept: 'The character of the classical body is established . . . through an emphasis on continuity of surface, line, form and contour . . . the qualities to be demanded of . . . figures are those of unity, simplicity and a continuously flowing movement from one part of the body to the next.' At the same time, trouser stirrups could only be done up with the aid of servants. Brummell's wardrobe might hint at idealised lines and statue-like simplicity, but it took staff and money to maintain, and at every occasion of dressing and undressing throughout the day, Robinson was indispensable.

'He was tall, well made, and a very good figure,' wrote Thomas Raikes of Brummell's own dandiacal body. 'Nature had indeed been most liberal to him,' wrote Jesse. It was a singular facet of his sudden fame that one element of it was explained in very physical terms, and Jesse went into extreme detail:

He was about the same height as Apollo [the Apollo Belvedere was newly exhibited in London] and the just proportions of his form were remarkable; his hand was particularly well-shaped; and, had he been inclined to earn his livelihood . . . he would readily have found an engagement as a life sitter to an artist, or got paid to perambulate . . . from fair to fair, to personate the statues of the ancients.

This arrestingly allusive description was in keeping with Jesse's own hero-worship of Brummell, but also with a new fascination for the physical form of man. Not unlike our own age, Brummell's had seen a reappraisal of male physicality that alarmed the older generation as much as it defined the younger. The pugilist clubs that opened in the West End could even be understood as forerunners of modern gyms in so far as fashionable gentlemen were forced to consider their physical well-being from the point of view of how they looked.

Brummell's early celebrity rested on the role he assumed as poster-boy for a new version of metropolitan masculinity: restrained, muscular, unfoppish, anything but the 'dandy' of folklore. His rapidly established status as the leader of fashion, quite separate from his reputation as a wit, was built on a 'look' that perfectly mirrored the age.

In large part Brummell's place in the history of fashion can be attributed to some simple facts: he possessed naturally a neoclassical body and was in a position to be noted for it on account of his celebrated wit and his friendship with the prince. Brummell's physique was mentioned by contemporaries from his schooldays onwards. The 1790s indeed was probably the first period when such a thing as 'proportion' might be discussed openly as part of a gentleman's attributes.

For centuries, educated Europe had picked at the remains of the ancient world for artistic inspiration and a validation of current ideals. And Greek and Roman depictions of the strength, naturalness and perfection of the (naked) form suited the ethos of urban Europe as Brummell came of age – just as the idea of mathematical proportion appealed anew in the building of Georgian London. The revolutions in France and America may seem now the most obvious fruits of the Enlightenment but at the time, in London, the philosophical confidence of the new urban élite became incarnate in the way men and women dressed and behaved. Cynicism was some part of the new urbane ethos. So, too, was a hybrid of authoritarianism on the one side and a revolutionary celebration of excess and (sexual) licence on the other. Many of the ideas that fed into this were foreign in origin: French philosophy, American Utopianism, Greek and Roman art. But as it played out in the remodelling of male fashion, neoclassicism found its new centre in the West End and a 'hero in wool' in Beau Brummell.

A cast of the Apollo Belvedere from Rome had been exhibited in London in 1753, and versions of it – engravings and plaster casts – became the foci for a wide-ranging debate on manners, masculinity, effeminacy, form and dress. By taking Apollo as his chosen simile Jesse makes a case for Brummell's 'manly' attributes, which his readers would have immediately understood. Most often the Apollo was counterpoised with the Farnese Hercules and the epicene Antinous. These statues appear in Hogarth's satirical engraving *The Analysis of Beauty* and reproductions were often on view at John Cheere's statuary yard on Hyde Park Corner, where the gentry went to order nudes for their gardens. The perfect proportions and apparently effortless superiority of the Apollo Belvedere became the measure of man in late-eighteenth-century London. His is not an overworked musculature – by contemporary standards certainly – but almost as much as his supposed bodily perfection, it was the bearing and expression of the statue that was commented upon: 'He has shot his arrow,' wrote one observer, 'and knows its success.'

The same writer goes on to describe the set of Apollo's mouth and face in almost exactly the same words Jesse later uses of Brummell: 'His is indeed a strong expression of indignation, which opens his lips; distends his nostrils, and contracts his brows, but it is the indignation of a superior being, who . . . scorns the efforts of his enemy.'

The fact that Brummell was likened to the Apollo placed him squarely in the corner of strength and honest 'manliness' as opposed to dancerly poise. It also suggests that his arrogant bearing – disliked by some – was part of a conscious or unconscious aping of the Apollo and of classical attitude as it was then understood. Most importantly, unlike the balletic Antinous, the Apollo Belvedere was never accused of looking effeminate – indeed, quite the opposite: 'If I was a woman,' travel writer Lancelot Temple wrote, 'I should be more in love with the APOLLO than as a man I am with the VENUS.'

The modern body might feel restricted by the clothes of the period but the tailored and close-fitting style Brummell pioneered was in direct response to the fascination he and his contemporaries felt for new ideas of freedom and Greek aesthetics. Men were displaying the lines of their bodies every bit as much as the 'nymphs' of Kensington Gardens in their gauze drapes. In a sense men's fashions were more naked. The Greek and Roman statuary on display in London depicted draped female figures, but the highest ideals of antique art were expressed, by men, in the nude. Ladies who aspired to the Empress Josephine look might, according to legend, have dampened their muslin dresses to make them cling to their bodies. Men's fashion, for which Brummell played catalyst, found another route.

Matte fabrics – especially wool, and tailoring that either held the body or sculpted it – replaced draped silk, glitter and swathing. A radical restriction of colour to white, skin tones, blue, grey and black no longer signified humility or even sobriety. Instead the sculptural strength of form and line was reiterated, in the manner understood latterly by black-and-white photographers. This may or may not have been a misunderstanding of actual antiquity – many statues originally were brightly coloured – but as classical forms were understood and valued in Brummell's day, classical male nudity could be suggested in cloth.

Men's coats were the most sculpted garments – displaying the craft of London's tailors rather more than the torso muscles of the wearer, but both aspiring to the same classical ideal. As one fashion historian has claimed, 'Dressed form became an abstraction of nude form, a new ideal naked man expressed not in marble but in natural wool, linen, leather . . . The perfect man, as conceived by English tailors, was part English gentleman, part innocent natural Adam, and part naked Apollo . . . a combination with an enduring appeal in other countries and other centuries.'

Many visitors to the statuary depository or the Royal Academy were uncomfortable with any context in which the male body was gazed at, as being both weakening to the male sex or even perverse (the Royal Academy and the British Museum routinely removed male genitals and replaced them with carved fig-leaves). Brummell, as a leader of body-conscious fashions, was likewise in danger of censure. He might not exhibit himself naked, even if Jesse suggested he could have made a living in so doing, yet his style drew a mixed response parallel to that for the male nudes at

Cheere's statuary yard. As counterpoint, Brummell took inspiration from a quite separate aesthetic: English country horsemanship. This contextualised in a sporty and military milieu the arrestingly body-formed clothing. It also equated masculine corporality with horse-flesh (which could be more openly admired than the male body): 'I have heard sensible people say that a man has nothing to do with beauty – That a man is handsome enough if he does not frighten his Horse. But is beauty confined to one sex? If you have a handsome mare, does it signify nothing what an awkward clumsey [sic] beast your horse be? Beauty most certainly belongs to both sexes.' The equestrian portrait and equestrian statue – sometimes with semi-naked rider – lent martial masculinity to Napoleon, the Prince of Wales and Tsar Alexander I among others. The bravura physicality – both equine and human – of the Elgin marbles, exhibited in 1806, gave further authenticity and acceptability to the look; it was the ideal visual corollary of Empire: noble, muscular, self-evidently aspirational, utterly uneffeminate. The clothes that seem so restrictive to us were the casual sportswear of their day – Hessian riding boots, riding breeches and cutaway riding jackets – so that even West End 'loungers', who had no intention of riding anywhere, could give the appearance of readiness to mount a horse and gallop towards revolution.

The perfect man – as conceived by English tailors and the hybrid of neo-classical aesthetics and sporty cavalry chic – turned out to be George Brummell. He might have ruined the perfect aquiline symmetry of his face in the 10th Light Dragoons, but as a clothes-horse he was unrivalled, and his physicality accordingly noted and admired as it might be of a modern celebrity. His ascendancy as a leader of fashion was predicated on creating and modelling a London look that came to dominate men's fashion. The strength, the vitality, and some of the self-doubt of the age was expressed in its fashions and their relationship to ideals of manhood and gentlemanliness. The age, similarly, is naked to the eye in its interest in the male body; in fashion and art, and in the case specifically of George Brummell's.

Brummell's physique was considered a more salient feature even than his height, which was telling in itself once it is established that he was, for the age, remarkably tall. Thanks to the descriptions of Brummell, and his known weight, recorded assiduously by his wine merchants, Berry Brothers of St James's, it is possible to deduce his height with reasonable precision. Brummell was first weighed on Berry Brothers' coffee scales, as was the habit of the loungers of St James's, on 23 January 1798. The records are still kept at the shop, detailing the fluctuating girths of all Brummell's contemporaries including the royal dukes and displaced French royalty. After four years of almost constant riding Brummell weighed twelve stone nine pounds (179 pounds or 81 kilograms) in 1799 in his wooden-heeled Hessian boots. Boots like these in a private collection in London weigh precisely two pounds (one kilogram), and taking into consideration the ensemble without greatcoat – which he wore in later weighings but not on these first occasions – Brummell's weight falls to around twelve stone six pounds (176 pounds or 80 kilos). It was a weight he maintained, with brief fluctuations, until he suddenly gained bulk around his thirtieth birthday – when he was appointed perpetual president of a new club, Watier's, said to serve the best dinners in London. The constant references to his slimness, or the perfection of his proportions in his twenties, however, when taken in conjunction with the currently accepted scale of ideal weight, would put a man of this weight at between six feet and six feet two inches, or 183 and 190 centimetres in height – a full six inches (fifteen centimetres) taller than the average in 1799. Even so, it was the manner in which he bore himself that caused greater interest, as well as his tailors' skills in turning his physique, the 'turn of his leg', into a feature of his fame.

The clothing, then, of this perfect dandiacal body forged Brummell's initial fame. The style was in strict accord with the same classical principles of sculptured proportion that were noted in his naked self, applied to his clothes. It is a paradox that discussion of Beau Brummell and dandyism should have become synonymous with one another, when one considers that Brummell's simplicity in dress was inimical to the modern understanding of the word 'dandy'. It was revolutionary primarily in its simplicity.

'The look' was described by Jesse, Byron, Raikes, Gronow and Harriette Wilson among others; it was that of 'having well-fashioned the character of a gentleman'. Over his white shirt and perfect neckcloth, Brummell wore a pale or white waistcoat – or 'vest' in the parlance of tailors of the period and in modern American usage. The waistcoat hid a small addition to a gentleman's wardrobe that is often forgotten in the annals of fashion history, and Brummell's place in it: braces or suspenders. These are absent from the wardrobes of the previous generation, but make up a regular feature in the surviving tailors' bills of Brummell's friends Scrope Davies and Lord Byron. Without them, the severe line along the thighs and lower legs was impossible, and belts were both inimical to the style and unflattering to the majority. Brummell wore breeches or tight pantaloons in the morning, in soft stocking-woven fabric or often soft leather. All this pale and white palette was thrown into sharp relief with two items in dark colours. A dark jacket – always deep blue – was cut away at the front to form tails, for ease on horseback but also to increase the apparent length of the wearer's legs. Black Hessian boots – from Hesse in Germany – completed the ensemble. These were riding and walking boots with a tassel at the front that served to distinguish them from turn-top riding boots, which briefly had about them the taint of Napoleon. The perfection of the cut and sculptural strength of the style were communicated with even greater clarity and seriousness by the sober palette. The specific colours of white, buff and dark blue owed a good deal to the Montem polemen dress at Eton, which was in itself a version of a military cadet's attire. Brummell's ensemble appeared a little like a military uniform for urban, civilian man.

Surviving examples of all the items that made up the Brummell look are held in the collections of the Museum of London and the National Costume Museum in Bath. First, all these clothes attest to the skill of the tailors and the high expectations of dandy consumers like Brummell. The craftsmanship is still apparent from the individually sewn buttons, loops and buttonholes, to the one concession to military dash: hand-turned brass coat buttons. In construction terms Brummell's clothes did not vary enormously from the embroidered silk coats and breeches that his father wore. But when unbuttoned and examined, they reveal the tailor's art, and a new importance the dandies felt in their individual corporality as well as a unified, urbane chic. The colours were muted and uniform, but the coats are padded out between the lining and the outer fabric, especially across the shoulders and chest, to define, expose or create the appearance of the individual's musculature. The real art of bespoke tailoring was born from this need to redefine each body according to a perceived ideal, rather than swathe a body generically in fabric suited to his class. These coats, as one fashion historian has attested, were 'designed to fit a body trained in the rules of deportment, a wearer well used to framing his identity as public spectacle through posture and a discerning attitude to dress'. The backs all have three seams running from the arms and centrally, sculpting the coat into the back and almost obliging the wearer to improve his posture.

Surviving breeches and pantaloons extend this sense of a restrained, idealised form. They are never in bright colours or patterned fabrics. The tyranny of monochrome was descending on men's city wear. They were cut to fit tight to the body, even to the extent of a central back seam and corset-lacing at the small of the back, to pull the trousers in and up like a saddle. Likewise, buttons that fastened below the knee kept breeches taut down the upper leg, with braces or suspenders pulling in the opposite direction. The buff-leather day breeches of the period were so well crafted that some are still loaned out by London costumiers. Evening breeches, by contrast, were of sheer and delicate black silk-jersey. The shirts were of one piece, collar and all, with often a yoke of fabric across the shoulders before pleated arms that allowed free movement under the silk linings of the coat. The cuffs and collar tips were exquisitely hand-sewn, but then so were the tiny monograms that grace the plexus, to be seen by no one but the dandy, his laundress and his lover.

Descriptions of the items in terms of colour, construction and feel can only sketch their meaning to Brummell and his Dandiacal Body. The effect of the limited palette was, and has remained, to underscore the sculptural qualities of the 'suit', and to prioritise cut and tailoring. The point of Brummell's clothes was that they fitted him perfectly. It was not a showy or a colourful look. It was exceptionally well modelled on him, but it came to suit, quite literally, everybody. It was a small thing to be famous for, but of unexpected consequence for Brummell and London.

The style made immediate impact. This was not so much because Brummell had been an innovator – although in small part he had. His impact came because the style required a re-education of many men – notably Brummell's friend the Prince of Wales. The prince became a devotee of this pared-down style, and is depicted dressed in exact imitation of Brummell as late as 1821. No style could easily flatter the ever-widening prince, but the skill of the tailors Brummell and he shared reshaped him. The austerity and simplicity of the style was at first inimical to the creator of the Brighton Pavilion, but he, like the rest of London, was in thrall by the turn of the century to neo-classical tailoring and the rules of dress dictated by a young commoner with an intuitive under-standing of restrained elegance and some natural gifts with which to deploy it.

In this revivification of London men's fashion, Brummell was easily cast as priest and prophet. Once his friend the Prince of Wales adopted both the style and the habit of attending the Chesterfield Street levees, Brummell's position in fashion history became assured. He had both the required arrogance, poise and connections, but also understood that the rules were intimidating to many. Brummell's fictionalised *alter ego* in the novel *Pelham* even issued a code of instruction for the Dandiacal Body; a mantra for recitation when shaving and dressing:

—Keep your mind free from all violent affections at the hours of the toilet. A philosophical severity is perfectly necessary to success.

—Dress contains two codes of morality – private and public. Attention is the duty we owe to others – cleanliness that which we owe to ourselves.

—Always remember that you dress to fascinate others, not yourself.

—The handsome may be showy in dress, the plain should study to be unexceptionable; just as in great men we look for something to admire – in ordinary men we ask for nothing to forgive.

—A man must be a profound calculator to be a consummate dresser . . . there is no diplomacy more subtle than dress.

—There may be more pathos in the fall of a collar, or a curl of a lock, than the shallow think for.

—The most graceful principle of dress is neatness.

—Dress so that it may never be said of you, 'what a well-dressed man,' but 'what a *gentlemanlike* man!'

—To *win* the affection of your mistress, appear negligent in your costume, to *preserve* it, assiduous: the first is a sign of the passion of love, the second of its respect.

—Avoid many colours and seek by one prevalent and quiet tint to sober down the others.

—Nothing is superficial to a deep observer! It is in trifles that the mind betrays itself.

—Inventions in dressing should resemble Addison's definition of fine writing, and consist of 'refinements which are natural, without being obvious'.

—He who esteems trifles for themselves is a trifler – he who esteems them for the conclusions to be drawn from them, or the advantage to which they can be put, is a philosopher.

'The Father of Modern Costume', as Max Beerbohm titled Brummell, had a style that was uniquely his, but perfect to the spirit of the age; 'quiet . . . reasonable, and beautiful: free from folly or affection, yet susceptible to exquisite ordering; plastic, austere, economical'. It appeared post-revolutionary, neo-classical, ordered and Enlightened and in this it did indeed seem democratic.

It did not shout wealth or privilege, it quietly insisted the point. It celebrated, not least in the sheer time it took to achieve the look, wealth, privilege and elegant indolence. Brummell's revolutionary fetishising of detail was later described by Baudelaire as defining 'the man who is rich and idle, and who . . . has no other occupation than the perpetual pursuit of happiness . . . whose solitary vice is elegance'.

This apparently democratic style was at first taken up only by the richest young men of London's West End. The Bucks, Beaux and Pinks of the Ton, the West End Loungers and Regency Rakes were the makers of new masculine manners, because the rules were changing. They accepted Brummell's orthodoxy in fashion, but set about writing in their own hands various versions of masculine bad behaviour. The Dandiacal Body of men who gathered at Chesterfield Street achieved a homogeneity in their attire, but their ideals of gentlemanly behaviour varied wildly.

Lord Alvanley became Brummell's closest friend and ally. His title was not ancient – in fact, his antecedents came from the middle classes like Brummell's. He was said to look like a butcher, but was regarded as the most warm-hearted of the dandies, and one of the funniest, 'combining brilliant wit and repartee with the most perfect good nature'. He lived nearby on Park Street and was at this time an officer in the Coldstream Guards. He was also a noted athlete, having run a mile in under six minutes along the Edgware Road for a bet of fifty guineas. The courtesans loved him, so did society hostesses, and he and Brummell remained in contact all their lives.

Unlike Brummell, Alvanley thought a knowledge of gastronomy as important as sartorial elegance in the accomplishments of a modern gentleman. He gave the best dinners of any bachelor in the West End, and once challenged the club he shared with Brummell, White's, to concoct the most expensive meal they could dream up. Thirteen different species of rare game birds were used for one *fricassée*, the ingredients alone costing £108 5s.

Alvanley also perfected the dandy drawl in speech, affecting indifference to any calamity. Perhaps his wit was a shade less

1. The Brummell Children by Joshua Reynolds: George Bryan 'Beau' Brummell aged three and a half (with dog) and his elder brother William, aged five. Exhibited at the Royal Academy in 1783, this painting marked the Brummell family's new status in London society.

2. and 3. William (*left*) and George (*right*) in 1790 in the uniform of the Eton Montem polemen. At Eton, George was known as 'Buck Brummell'.

4. Eton Montem, or Ad Montem ('to the hill!'). This ancient festival grew so riotous that Prince Albert eventually banned it.

5. The Montem pole-men uniform was remarkably sober. Although Montem involved misrule and fancy-dress, the pole-men dressed in sober quasi-militaristic 'suits'. This democratic and pared-down style seems to have struck Brummell as more flattering and more masculine than the prevalent male fash-ions of the period.

6. Theatricals in Eton's Long Chamber. Though the curriculum at Eton adhered strictly to the classics, it was expected also that boys would excel in oratory, performance and at honing pithy aphorisms (in Greek and Latin).

7. An illustration, finished by Brummell and from Brummell's own Male and Female Costume (1822). 'A Greek Warrior in His Travelling Dress.' Brummell believed men's fashions should follow classical lines and flatter the body.

8. This dandy wears pantaloons that mimic nude Greek statuary, though their tailoring is inspired more directly by Hussar riding breeches. He is also wearing Hessian boots, made fashionable by Brummell.

9. London became renowned for the finest men's tailoring in the world, working on principles of classical proportion. This tailor is taking the key measurement from the scye or 'shoulder's eye'.

10. Meyer (later Meyer & Mortimer) pioneered with Brummell the modern trouser, often with instep straps in the style of military overalls. They still trade on Sackville Street.

11. 'I, Brummell, put the modern man into pants, dark coat, white shirt and clean linen. I dare say that will be sufficient to secure my fame.' An early-nineteenth-century coat with gilt metal buttons, velvet collar and plain waistcoat and breeches.

12. and 13. Brummell bought his hats from Lock & Co, hatters on St. James's Street which is also still in business. Their records include one 1808 order from Brummell for two new hats with the intriguing note that they be delivered to Brummell's steam-baths: the 'New Hummums' (hammams), 'a place where people get themselves cupped'.

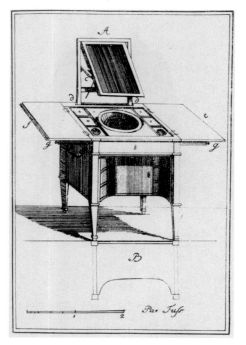

14. 'His ablutions would have gained him a reputation for sanctity in a Mahomedan country.' A dandy's dressing-table, after Chippendale. Brummell took several hours to shave and dress and an invitation to his levee became highly prized amongst London's fashion-conscious élite.

15. Silver and glass ointment or pill box with Brummell's crest. Similar boxes were inserted into the Chippendale shaving table above.

16. 'Brummell's snuff-boxes', from a collection owned by descendants of the Brummell family. Brummell's tobacconists sold out of any snuff brand to which he lent his name.

The DANDY CLUB.

Drawn Etch.
by Richd Dighton.

Dec. 29. 181

17. and 18. Though eminently suitable for satire, the extremes of the dandy movement were eschewed by most men. Brummell's simple, elegant lines and attention to detail and to tailoring evolved quietly into the Savile Row suit; possibly Britain's most enduring contribution to the art of dress.

DANDI   DANDUM.

DANDO.

The Dandies Coat of Arms.

19-22. Despite being celebrated for his looks and style, George Bryan (Beau) Brummell never sat for a full-length portrait. In his late teens he broke his nose badly after a fall from his horse, which may account for the different renderings of his features in the four portraits – miniatures and etchings – attributed as him.

sharp than Brummell's, but his delivery was said to be priceless. When once challenged to a duel on Wimbledon Common, he insisted on giving his jarvey (cabbie) a hefty tip, pressing it into his hand with the words: 'I give it to you not for taking me, but for bringing me back.' He survived.

Some of the set came to literary prominence, notably Matthew 'Monk' Lewis and, of course, Lord Byron. Lewis's *The Monk* was considered so 'revoltingly licentious' that Charles James Fox crossed the floor of the House of Commons to congratulate the young author, a fellow MP, and the book became a bestseller. He followed this with a minor poetic triumph, *Alonzo the Brave and the Fair Imogene*, but he never repeated his early commercial success. He remained part of the dandiacal set, however, and Brummell added both Lewis and the Monk's eccentric black butler to his growing repertoire of impersonations. It is unrecorded if Byron's was also a voice Brummell could impersonate, but it was widely held at the time that aspects of Byron's *Don Juan* were based closely on Brummell and the Dandiacal Body. 'I liked the Dandies,' wrote Byron, of the high-living friends he made through his Cambridge contemporary Scrope Davies. 'I had more than a touch of dandyism in [my] minority . . . enough of it to conciliate the great ones at four and twenty . . . [the dandies] were always very civil to me, though in general they disliked literary people.'

This philistinism would certainly be true of the Manners brothers, Lords Charles and Robert, and their elder brother the Duke of Rutland. Their model of gentlemanliness was more 'Corinthian' or sporting. They hunted to hounds, formed their own Rutland Militia, based at the family seat Belvoir Castle, giving Brummell the courtesy rank of major, and boxed with Gentleman John Jackson who had a pugilists' club at 13 Bond Street – also frequented by Byron. The Mannerses possessed that indifference to physical danger that is so often the gift of great wealth or great stupidity, and recklessly drove racing curricles around the circuit made up by St James's Street, Piccadilly, the Haymarket and Pall Mall. They often crashed.

Others of the Dandiacal Body, while perfectly dressed, behaved even more eccentrically. Lord Petersham, the 'maddest of all the mad Englishmen', according to Princess Lieven, went into mourning for a lost love called Mrs Browne by dressing head to foot in brown and having his coach dyed the same colour, along with his servants' livery. He also created a snuff mix in her honour, and with Brummell developed a passion for snuff and collecting snuff-boxes. These clubbable men had suitably schoolboyish nicknames for each other. Brummell's City-born schoolfriend Thomas Raikes became 'Apollo', not so much because he was good-looking as because he rose in the East End and set in the West. 'Kangaroo' Cooke was so called as he let loose a court of circus kangaroos for a dare. The enormously tall 'Teapot' Crawford was, depending which story one follows, either cracked, tea-obsessed, or possessed of some notable physical trait noted 'far back in his Eton days' and never forgotten. The Marquess of Hertford – a serial rake with a miscellany of illegitimate children and one model for Thackeray's Marquess of Steyne in *Vanity Fair* – became known as 'Red Herring' on account of his ginger whiskers and redheaded progeny. 'Poodle' Byng lost his Christian name on account of his (apparently natural) tightly curling blond hair, prompting Brummell to remark when he saw him in a carriage with a real poodle, 'Ah, Byng – a family vehicle I see!' Lord Barrymore limped, so was known as 'Cripplegate'; his two disreputable brothers were known as 'Hellgate' and 'Newgate' – so their unfortunate sister was dubbed 'Billingsgate' for reasons necessarily ungallant and fortunately unrecorded.

On the fringes of the Dandiacal Body were hopeless social adventurers like 'Romeo' Coates and 'Golden Ball' Hughes. Golden Ball's fortune was one of the largest in the country: he bought the Duke of York's entire country estate when it was sold. But whereas 'Brummell set the fashion, Ball Hughes merely followed it'. And not always very well. His social climbing was considered too obvious, and his money too lavishly spent. Worse still, 'He looked as if he walked on stilts, and had swallowed the kitchen poker.' 'Romeo' Coates, meanwhile, became a laughing stock for spending a large proportion of his fortune in launching himself on a stage career. The production of *Romeo and Juliet*, in which he invested and cast himself in the lead, was a commercial triumph, but only because the audience treated Coates's performance as pure comedy, so that the lovers' death scene had to be replayed several times for encores. His greater *faux-pas*, however, was considered his dress sense. He began to eschew Brummell's advice by wearing eye-catching diamond buttons and eventually gave up altogether on the restrained chic of the dandies, designing himself instead a coach in the shape of a conch, surmounted by a large golden cock and the legend, 'While I live, I'll crow.'

Some others also tried to outdo Brummell, in terms of apparent vanity or drawling wit. Apollo Raikes once refused a duel on the principle that it would be unfair, his opponent being 'so ugly that a bullet could make little difference', whereas he, Raikes, being so beautiful, had much more to lose. Lord Westmorland, meanwhile, chose to emulate Brummell's laconic delivery as well as his dress sense, and expressed the dandiacal disinterest in politics by refusing to stand for the exiled Louis XVIII of France. '*Je wouldrai si je couldrai*,' he explained, '*mais je ne cannais pas.*' As Raikes wrote,

The manners of the Dandies were themselves a charm. Their speech was pleasant, their language thoroughbred. Many among them were highly gifted, doing all that they did well – a school of gentlemen, liberal and open-handed, ephemeral as youth and spirits, yet marked with that endearing quality, that they remained, with few exceptions, true and loyal friends, tested through years of later adversity.

The friend who did not stay constant was, nevertheless, at the centre of the original Dandiacal Body: the Prince of Wales. Without him, Brummell's fame and influence were unthinkable. He was a decade or more older than most of the others who gathered at Chesterfield Street, but he seemed determined to live at least some of the time as if he were still a playboy prince, not a married father within reach of the throne. He was as flattered to be included with a set of new-thinking young men as they were to bask in the refulgence of royalty. The prince also expected that the high jinks of the Brighton 10th Light Dragoons would be replayed at Chesterfield Street, and in this he was correct: the royal visits to No. 4 did generally end in a 'deep potation'. But the prince's interests were sartorial as well as social. Brummell was fun to be around; he was also instructive, on the arts, poetry and gossip, but especially on the new fashions. The prince, who had always prided himself on being the First Gentleman of Europe, faced the new century trying to relearn the rules of how a man-about-town should dress. Brummell's effect upon the prince's dressing and shopping habits is outlined in the accounts still held in the Royal Archives. By early in the nineteenth century, the prince had moved away from the 'bespangled' glamour of his own teens and twenties and was ordering plain white waistcoats by the dozen, buff and black pantaloons, and repeatedly altering, mending, relining and repairing his elegant new white and off-white pantaloons.

~

Brummell's rules of dress and manner were spread by the immediate dandy set around him, so that soon the style was seen all over fashion-conscious London. Foreigners noted the increasing homogeneity of men's attire in London, and, largely, this was viewed admiringly.

The physiognomy of both sexes in London is prepossessing, though the men are better formed than the women [wrote one]. Yet in England, it is scarcely possible to know a lord from a tradesman, a man of letters from a mechanic; and this seems to arise from the sovereignty of fashion in the metropolis. The [men's] fashions . . . are simple and harmonious . . . the colour is invariably becoming, and the tout-ensemble agreeable . . . as the coat is cut, so must the waistcoat and breeches correspond; nor would this suffice, unless the shape of the hat, and exact measure of the boot, were in perfect unison; every reform therefore must be radical. [Foreigners who] will not attend to these minutiae must thank themselves if they find they are stared at, or ridiculed, as they walk the streets.

Max Beerbohm later dated the birth of the suit itself to 'that bright morning when Mr Brummell, at his mirror, conceived the notion of trousers and simple coats'.

The sobriquet 'Beau' stuck to Brummell some time around the turn of century. Just as the meaning of 'dandy' is skewed to the modern ear when taken in the context of Brummell's Dandiacal Body – men of deliberately understated chic, not *outré* dress – so the term 'Beau' came to be read differently in the light of Beau Brummell. It was universally accepted as his name or title soon after his first season in London in 1799. At its simplest, it was merely a description: Brummell was good-looking, and women as well as men noted this. 'He was,' said Lady Hester Stanhope, 'envied and admired by both beaux and belles of all ranks of society.' Previously, the style 'Beau' had had overtones of affectation and controlling social ambition. Beau Brummell, however, rewrote the rules. Like the codes of dress themselves, he remoulded the idea of being Beau to suit himself. If people expected flamboyance because he was 'Beau' and he was a dandy they would be disappointed, just as Caroline Jermyn was at first when she met his fictional *alter ego* in *Granby*. She had expected

to view in him an excess of all the peculiarities of that tribe [the dandies].

She saw, therefore, with surprise, that he wore a dress in no respect distinguishable from that of ten thousand others; that he had neither rings nor chains, that his head was not fixed at any particular angle, and that the quiet and almost careless tie of his cravat, plainly showed that . . . he had not believed the axiom that 'Starch makes the man.' Then there was nothing supercilious or affected in the manner . . . but an air of intelligence and subdued satire, and an intuitive quickness in his eye, in the short glance which he bestowed upon her, which rather restored him to her estimation.

Brummell was not conspicuously dressed – that was not the meaning of being Beau. Another observer wrote that when he first saw the celebrated young Beau Brummell he was 'struck by the misapplication of this title [Beau] . . . he was dressed as plain as any man in the field, and the manly expression of his countenance ill accorded with the implication the sobriquet conveyed'.

As it turned out London society granted him a sort of immortality by christening him 'Beau' but it was a double-edged compliment. Like 'Perdita' Robinson or 'Gentleman' Lewis – actors and adventurers also – Beau was admired but also lightly scorned: his fame, like theirs, was fascinating because it spoke of the evanescence of things, of the surfaces, which, Sheridan said, were the trait of the age.

To some of the Dandiacal Body, Beau Brummell's dressing ritual at Chesterfield Street had the appearance of a knight preparing for battle or a matador for a bullfight. By 1800 he was well on his way to building the carapace that would protect him in the social and sexual warfare waged in the salons and on the streets of London. As bulwark against this he had his clothes and his manner: a character called Beau. Because his style was intimidating, in its precision and austerity, and because his wit was developing the harshness of the professional cynic, few became close with him, for all that he was wildly sociable. For some, the emotional unavailability of 'The Beau' added to his attractiveness. But he maintained only a few close friends – notably his former dragoon-officer friends the Manners brothers, and Thomas Raikes, whom he had known at Eton. And, of course, he had no family to speak of. But at twenty-one, with wealth, health and London at his feet, it is hardly surprising that he gave little consideration to either past or future and lived for his moment in the high life.

By late morning Brummell was dressed and ready for London. His outfit was described as 'similar to that of every other gentleman: – Hessians [boots] and pantaloons, or top-boots and buckskins, with a blue coat, and a light or buff-coloured waistcoat; of course fitting to admiration on the best figure in England'. He donned off-white or pale yellow kid gloves in the hallway and stepped out into Chesterfield Street. He turned left, towards Curzon Street, and faced London with the insouciant confidence of one who knows he is young, envied and perfectly, but not over, dressed.

6

SIC ITUR AD ASTRA:
BESPEAKING THE WEST END

Turning the corner of a lane I came upon a Signpost, whereon
stood written that such-and-such a one was 'Breeches Maker to
His Majesty,' and stood painted effigies of a Pair of Leather
Breeches, and between the knees, these memorable words SIC
ITUR AD ASTRA [This is the way to the Stars].

> Thomas Carlyle, *Sartor Resartus*
> (The Tailor Retailored), 1833

That's the fashion, father, that's modern ease. A young fellow is
nothing now, not without the Bond Street roll: a toothpick
between his teeth, his knuckles crammed into his coat-pocket.
Then away you go, lounging lazily along!

> George Coleman the Younger,
> *The Heir-at-Law*, 1797

By the time Brummell left Chesterfield Street each day it
was gone twelve. In wet weather it was his habit to have
Robinson order a sedan chair – the umbrella being a novelty
that never met his approval – but more often he walked. At the
turn of the nineteenth century men strolled arm in arm in
London as a matter of habit and routine, and it came to be
considered a mark of particularly high social standing in the
West End to be seen walking with Beau Brummell, and notably

to be part of the coterie seen leaving Chesterfield Street with him.

Brummell collected walking-sticks, some topped in the fashion of the time with shapes that revealed themselves as caricatures of famous friends only once their shadow was cast across a wall. Accessories were part of the London look. Walking-sticks, fob-watches, snuff-boxes, gloves and hats: these were vital desiderata in the creation of the perfect dandy, and their acquisition was part of Brummell's daily round of London pleasures. As well as the canes (there were many in the later sale of his effects), Brummell allowed a few links of a watch-chain to show across his waist-coat, wore occasionally one plain ring, and claimed eventually to have a different snuff-box for every day of the year. And single-handedly he began the decimation of the beaver population of North America after he was seen out with a glossy, beaver-skin top hat. New gloves, always in the palest leather, had to be bought frequently as they could not easily be cleaned and soon showed dirt. But the choice of accessories was not the primary interest of those who turned to look at Brummell. Harriette Wilson recorded how men in the West End 'made it a rule to copy the cut of [Brummell's] coat, the shape of his hat, or the tie of his neckcloth', so that he was pointed out in the street as he walked.

Because his sartorial choices were admired and copied, the character of the emerging West End began to be shaped by his shopping habits. The new tailors and accoutrements shops open-ing north of Piccadilly, on the redeveloped Burlington Estate, soon realised the potential benefits of young Captain Brummell's custom. Not only might it bring the Prince of Wales to them as well, and his fashion expenditure was legendary – in 1803 he spent £681 14s. 9d. at one tailors alone – but many male customers 'made it a rule to copy the cut of his [Brummell's] coat'. Those most anxiously on the lookout for young Beau Brummell there-fore were the shopkeepers who needed the imprimatur of his custom. And, from the start, they extended their credit to him.

Five streets in particular formed Brummell's shopping constituency, establishing themselves as magnets for male shoppers for decades if not centuries to come: Bond Street, Savile Street (later Row), Jermyn Street, St James's Street, and later parts of the new Regent Street. The all-male preserve of St James's Street was in effect extended north of Piccadilly as a result of Brummell and his coterie, establishing a whole area of the new West End as the site for satisfying masculine desire. And although there were pugilist clubs and pornographic print shops on Bond Street, and tobacconists and wine merchants on St James's Street, increasingly the desire this part of London met in men was for clothes.

By far the busiest street on Brummell's early-afternoon circuit was Bond Street. There were three famous hotels on it: the Clarendon, which sold outrageously expensive French meals; Stephen's, where former officers like Brummell ate and where by early afternoon it 'was not uncommon to see thirty or forty saddle horses and tilburies waiting'; and Long's, a former coaching inn. The one public house, the Black Horse, had beer cellars so extensive they now form the storerooms of Sotheby's. The first bookstore on the street, Brindley's, had opened in 1728 and Bond Street, initially, was famous for its circulating libraries and stationers.

By the time Brummell came to shop there at the end of the eighteenth century Bond Street had many diversions beyond its hotels and bookstores. One could buy boots, walking-sticks, snuff-boxes, toiletries, theatre and boxing-match tickets. And, before the construction of Regent Street, Bond Street was the major north–south thoroughfare in the West End – often grid-locked by the press of carriages. The main reason for this was that it was the prime site in which to be seen in early afternoon:

At one [o'clock] the streets begin to fill with carriages and saddle-horses; and now the people of fashion begin to move about. The ladies form parties to go shopping; the gentlemen [are] accompanied by single grooms . . . the squares fill with ladies in their morning dress, presenting lovely groups to the observation of the passenger. Carriages then crowd Bond Street, making it almost impassable; and the frequent stoppages at the different shops abounding in every article of taste and luxury, create much confusion . . . the gentlemen pass . . . up and down the street, to see and be seen; and the foot pavement is so perfectly covered with elegantly dressed people as to make it difficult to move.

In the wake of the dandy craze, tailors also set up all along Bond Street. The most famous was soon Weston's at No. 34 Old Bond Street (they later moved to No. 37), there was also Walker's at No. 5, Saunderson's at No. 19, Allen's, Guthrie's and Richardson's, and a specialist breeches maker, Tossell's, at No. 29. Brummell's Hessian boots came from Bond Street. Mr Hoby, the bootmaker, had an outlet there, as well as on the corner of St James's and Piccadilly, and employed three hundred cobblers between the two. He died worth £120,000. Brummell also bought there a version of 'top boots' or riding boots with white turn-downs. These were utterly impractical for riding, but were very much in keeping with his strict monochrome, while alluding to the British cavalry-wear. There were army braid-makers, and army accoutrements sellers, hatters, glovers, hosiers and shirt-makers. Asprey's – on 'The Bond Street Straits' where the street narrows – sold fitted dressing-cases. The one auctioned among Brummell's effects may well have been bought from there.

Brummell could get his hair cut at Brewster's at No. 48, order guns from Grierson's at No. 10 – he owned several – or buy opera-glasses, pens or whisker-dye from the crowded emporia that lined the street. He could check in his horses at Mavor's, the veterinary surgeons, at No. 40, or buy his opera-box subscription at No. 33 – assuming he was in possession of a voucher from one of the lady patronesses who restricted access to the best seats at the opera. And gentlemen could even have a bath and shave at Dr Culverwell's bathing establishment at No. 23. Anything from coaches to country estates, from Persian carpets to the latest teas and coffees could be bought on Bond Street, along with sheet music, caricatures, political pamphlets and erotica from the dozens of print shops and booksellers. Brummell was also able, through most of 1799, to view 'The real embalmed head of Oliver Cromwell (where the rattlesnake was shown last year) at No. 5 Mead Court, Old Bond Street', along with a 'Mummy of Cleopatra', the 'Jewels of the Queen of Sheba' and 'Julius Caesar's sword'. The Cromwell head, as it happens, may have been real.

The richness and variety of shops and amusements on Bond Street, wrote one French expatriate in London, 'dazzled my eyes and distracted my attention'. Bond Street became, as a result of the hotels, amusements, lending libraries and, most importantly, its vast array of new shops, a sort of open-air salon. As the young hero of the successful comedy *The Heir-at-Law* explained to his father, a young man was nothing until he'd learned how to 'lounge lazily' along Bond Street, window-shopping with a 'toothpick between his teeth'. Byron met Walter Scott there, Lord Nelson could been seen walking from his lodgings at No. 141 to Lady Hamilton's at No. 130, and a new, celebrated leader of fashion, a young dragoon officer and confidant of the Prince of Wales, Beau Brummell, became himself one of the attractions of an afternoon's shopping.

Brummell was a great connoisseur of fabric. He had learned a certain amount on Eton high street, in ordering and having his Eton clothes made up, but in London he developed a passion for cloth, and what could be done with it. As he walked further east from Bond Street he came to the alleys of the redeveloped Burlington Estate, which merged seamlessly into Soho before the construction of Regent Street. Here, between Piccadilly to the south and Berkeley Square and Conduit Street to the north, a new fabric economy was forming on Cork Street, Glasshouse Street and a small cut-through called Savile (sometimes Saville) Row. It was familiar terrain for Brummell even before 1799 as his avuncular family friend Mr Sheridan had set up home there with his young wife, Hecca.

The range of fabrics, lacings, leathers and buttons available around Savile Row rose with the twin forces of empire and industrialisation. Merinos, jersey weaves and doeskins were bought to make day clothes, while evening-dress pantaloons and trousers were made from cashmere, keysermere or cassimir and stretchy silk-stockinette imported from India but often worked and woven in Macclesfield. In summer, Brummell also bought drill, a stout linen, and nankeen, a heavy twilled cotton. Velvet and pure silk, so far as men were concerned, were employed only for collar turns and linings respectively. Even in high summer, coats were most often made of wool, always with the smoothest of matte surfaces. Brummell popularised 'super-fine' broadcloth, keysermere and a mix of the two: 'Bath coating'. These felt-like fabrics were not the easiest with which to work, as they held their own line unless skilfully cut and 'sculpted' with paddings made of layers of linen, cotton, buckram and wool. One tailor, Mr Schweitzer of Schweitzer and Davidson, was considered the master at working these fabrics, and he began to quote Brummell to other customers as an authority on what would work best: 'The Prince wears superfine and Mr Brummell the Bath coating; but it is immaterial which you choose, Sir, you must be right . . . Suppose sir we say the Bath coating – I think Mr Brummell has a trifle the preference.'

Tailors stocked their own fabrics also and could take samples to clients less interested in 'a-shopping', but the fabric emporia continued to have a grip on the market. Material, tailoring and cut – along with posture and body-consciousness – became necessary considerations for the male London élite. For many, the expression of an interest in fabric, like an appreciation of Greek statuary, was simply one more signifier of the cultured gentleman. As so often in commodity culture, however, there was some erotic context to this new arena of expenditure. Tailoring was an exclusively male preserve, but fabric shops, like milliners and hat-makers, were staffed by women. They were some of the few young women in this predominantly male part of town who were not sex-workers, so naturally enough lines became blurred. By the time the Burlington Arcade opened a few years later the millinery girls were immediately associated with prostitution. The glazed, oil-lit windows provided the perfect shop-front for 'professional beauties' as well as for fabric and hats.

Nor did the elision of the old West End sex trade into new West End tailoring end there. Some tailors were known to provide the space, facilities and alibis necessary for illicit liaisons. It could be one reason for the numerous fittings: 'it was a gentleman's world, a gentleman's club. So they had twenty fittings at their tailors . . . and in the back, round the corner, there would be something else . . .' The West End thereby extended north of Piccadilly its long tradition of sex trade, but Brummell and his coterie grafted on to this something much more respectable, exportable and long-lasting. They added a new, though allied, desire for the finest outfits, and gave a newly sexualised and masculine context to an activity that had been traditionally outside the preserve of establishment men: clothes-shopping.

In his early years in London Brummell patronised primarily three tailors. The first, Schweitzer and Davidson on Cork Street, between Bond Street and Savile Row, was also popular with the Prince of Wales. Schweitzer became famous for the cut of his coats. Davidson made a small fortune simply from the trade in alterations on the coats made for the prince. Second, there was John Weston's at No. 34 Old Bond Street, which made waistcoats, breeches and shirts and became, as result of Brummell's patronage, a favourite of the prince and later Lord Byron. The third was Jonathan Meyer's on Conduit Street, a little further north, which had made Brummell's later Hussar uniforms and with whom he pioneered the forerunner of modern trousers. Although Captain Gronow wrote that Brummell favoured most frequently 'that superior genius Mr Weston, tailor, of Old Bond Street', his was not a singular loyalty. He also shopped at Stultz, Staub, Delacroix, Nugée and others, variously on Savile Row, Glasshouse Street, Bond Street and Jermyn Street. He purchased fabrics independently as the London leisured classes could, on Bond Street, Jermyn Street and, after 1813, Regent Street. He bought his hats on St James's Street, his boots on Bond Street and Piccadilly and called in frequently, according to their accounts, to buy his snuff-tobacco at Fribourg and Treyer, which remained, until quite recently, at the top of the Haymarket.

Towards the end of the eighteenth century London tailors began to assume a reputation throughout Europe and the New World as fashion leaders. It helped that they were at the centre of the world's richest city just when male fashions were changing, but specifically they had sought-after skills based on their working knowledge of heavier wool-based fabrics. This in turn was consequent to their long experience in fine cloth – as opposed to silks; a result of climatic need to fashion layers of clothes of varying functions and work with wool. Some of the businesses Brummell frequented, however, were not British. Several of the key names in the birth of Savile Row tailoring were German and Bourbon French, for all they relied on British craftsmen in their cellars and attics: Schweitzer, Meyer, Nugée and Stultz were all refugees who had fled the advance of Napoleon's armies. Their skills had been honed on continental uniforms, themselves often versions of British cavalry-wear in heavy military broadcloths, using water-resistant fabrics to make strong, sculptural impressions.

The Napoleonic wars had enormously increased demand for uniforms in early-nineteenth-century Europe, and, just as medical knowledge advances tenfold on the battlefield, so men's tailoring, it might seem, was advanced by Napoleon's cannon. These continental military tailors had also, necessarily, honed their skills only on men. In Theodore Hook's early-nineteenth-century *The Man of Many Friends*, when Colonel Arden is setting up home in London he is advised to have clothes made at one of Brummell's tailors, Nugée's. '[This] tailor was of course a foreigner, like the proposed cook; it being an established axiom in this country that its natives are incompetent to the dressing either of dinner or dandies.' Nugée later retired to Brighton with 'a small fortune invested in some superb houses in Kemp Town'. Brummell's tailors may have come to London as refugees but they could retire on £100,000 or more, if they had been fortunate enough to have their craftsmanship recognised and publicised by the Beau.

In order for this to happen, the new tailors of the West End tended to specialise in particular items of the wardrobe. In one satire on the West End from 1806 the hero is astonished by the range of specialised tailors on Bond Street alone:

When he stopped to be measured for a suit of clothes, what was his surprise to learn that Mr Larolle made only coats, and they had a dozen doors further to drive before they reached 'the first hand in the world at waistcoats, braces and inexpressibles'. The same 'artist' who excelled at fitting a dress shoe, would have been intolerable as the manufacturer of a pair of boots and though Mr Flint the hatter assured us that for round walking hats there was not a superior shop in London; yet he would confess that for an *opera hat* Mr Breach did certainly 'cut the trade'.

Schweitzer and Davidson on Cork Street specialised in coats. They began experimenting on new cuts and seams both with, and on, Brummell through the first decade of the nineteenth century. The system of 'darting' the back of men's coats to shape the cloth into the body was pioneered in London at this time, as well as the 'fish dart' that added a seam at the side. The three-seam kite-back of the previous century worked well on the flat-cloths that came into fashion: together they helped mould the coat inwards from the widest point at the shoulders, following the line of an idealised torso, which might or might not be represented in reality underneath. Soft domette padding was sewn over form-holding but coarse horsehair cloth called lappet-cloth. Wool and buckram layers were oversewn with thousands of individual stitches, in patterns like corn rows. Slowly the layers of the upper torso and shoulders were built up before the cut flat-cloth was moulded over the top. And always, in hand-sewing, Schweitzer and his assistants pulled the cloth in the direction it would eventually hold. A bespoke collar or lapel could only ever turn in the direction the tailor intended; a thousand of his stitches insinuated every contour. A first 'baiste' fitting for the baisters or finishers assured Brummell that the garment was progressing as he intended. A second and third fitting was customary. Collar, cuffs and blind button-holes were achieved last. Pockets were relegated by Brummell to the back of the coat, so as not to spoil the line, hidden in the folds of the tails. So precisely could the new tailors mould the fabric to the body, while subtly flattering or improving where necessary, that Lord Byron was moved to remark of a Schweitzer coat on Brummell that 'you might almost say the body thought'.

Contemporaries noted the revolutionary new style, and Brummell's pre-eminence in having it adopted:

The shape of the coat, which had varied [in the 1790s] from a sort of Newmarket cut-away to a short-waisted thing with tails descending to the ankles, à la Robespierre, now received a great deal of attention. A young man of no family pretensions . . . became the oracle of fashion. The dandies of the day regarded him as their king; even the Prince of Wales, who aspired to the character of being the best dressed man in his royal father's dominions, was content to take the pattern of his garments for this influential person: Mr George Brummell.

Brummell also ordered surtouts or greatcoats from Schweitzer and Davidson for winter wear. These were significantly heavier garments, so much so that they were noted in the weighing books at Berry Brothers. Made out of even heavier worsteds and 'Norwich stuff' – another felt-like beaten wool – they were still exquisitely cut and moulded. An example from 1803 survived unworn and unblemished in a bank vault in the City. Though the cut is fuller, and the coat billows almost into a skirt below the waist, the lines of the upper torso are strongly cut and assume a martial bearing in the wearer. Small references to military chic were another part of the appeal of Schweitzer's coats and surtouts. The shoulder padding was in imitation of epaulettes and also restructured the torso to the V shape of classical statuary. The buttons, meanwhile, as with uniforms of the period, were not all strictly functional. They alluded to the pips of military rank, and have remained on jacket cuffs into modern times with similar disregard for utility. The placing and number of buttons and blind button-holes developed their own arcane semiotics, as is still the case. Then: velvet cuffs and cuff buttons for Tories, none for

Whigs; metal stud-buttons for daywear, never in the evening – except for staff in livery.

Shapes and styles of men's tailoring that have become almost invisible through their ubiquity can be dated to this time, and in part to Brummell. In order to sculpt the heavy fabrics into the neck and shoulder of demanding clients like Brummell, the collar came eventually to be formed from two pieces. The lapels were turned out as if from the lining of the coat. The collar itself, however, was cut from a different piece of fabric, with the warp and weft of the cloth in line with the vertical muscles of the neck. This separate collar stood round the back of the neck and lifted the fabric up and into the nape and hairline, and was joined to the lapels, which then lay flat across the pectoral muscles. In keeping with the sculptural aesthetic, the face, neck and shoulder would never be draped, but always framed, and the cloth would repeat the structure of the muscles underneath. Between these two parts of the new, sculptural coat-collar, a signature of West End tailoring was born: the W cut that sits either side of all suit and jacket lapels and has endured, in varying dimensions, to this day.

The intimate relationship Brummell developed with his tailors was a product of this attention to detail. Theirs was a partnership of sorts in that they both benefited from each other, but more than that, there was a physical and creative intimacy woven into their joint projects. One such encounter between Brummell and his tailor was immortalised in this extract from the 'Brummell' novel *Pelham* in which Schweitzer also made an appearance as 'Mr Schneider', the somewhat sycophantic tailor of Cork Street:

'Good morning Sir; happy to see you returned. Do I disturb you too early? Shall I wait on you [later]?'

'No, you may renew your measure.'

'We are a very good figure, sir, very good figure,' replied Mr Schneider surveying me from head to foot, while he was preparing his measure. 'We want a little assistance though; we must be padded well here, we must have our chest thrown out, and have an additional inch across the shoulder . . . all the Gentlemen in the Life Guards are padded there sir, we must live for effect in this world, sir. A *leetle* tighter round the waist eh?'

The tape-measure itself as a tool central to tailoring can also be dated to Brummell's era in London. Measuring came to be standardised, and the tape-measure brought into regular use where beforehand tailors had used 'strings' and cut on the body and on tailors' dummies. In order to express the homogeneity and classical proportions that Brummell made the central feature of men's dress, individual measurements, ironically, assumed a greater importance. Tailors' guides explained the need, as did Pelham's tailor, to pad, cut and sculpt to remodel the male form into something closer to a classical ideal of strength and proportion. In the absence of colour and dazzle, this would be noticed as never before. Although radical expedients such as corsets (known as belts) and calf-muscle stocking-implants were not unknown, the new look was achieved mainly in the subtle remoulding of the body achieved by cutters, tailors and effects like the sculpted W collar. These neo-classical tailors learned to conform to principles long understood in art, but based on Greek mathematical aesthetics. Like Michelangelo and Albrecht Dürer before them, tailors split the man into eight equal parts, or head-lengths. According to these classical proportions, the frontal measure from head-tip to chin should be equal to one-eighth of an adult man's full height, or one-quarter of the distance from chin to fingertips. By the same token, the nipple line falls two-eighths of the way down the full height of a man. If it didn't, the tailor could still give the impression that it did. More specifically, the tails of Brummell's coats were cut precisely two-thirds of the way down the seven-eighths of his height that made up his body – this was considered the best-proportioned look. In Brummell's case, therefore, Schweitzer cut tails forty-two and a half inches from nape to tail-tip. Men come in many different shapes, but the eight head-lengths of classically proportioned tailoring theorised that more men could be made to appear of perfect Brummellesque proportions if the rules were followed.

Brummell expected to be measured with all his clothes on, bar his coat. The tailor began from behind, taking measurements of width of the shoulders and the distance from the nape of the neck to the small of the back, and to the crease below the buttocks. He measured Brummell next by draping the tape round the neck, then taking it under the arms to the back. This established the fall of the armhole and also the depth of scye – the 'shoulder's eye' – that point on the back below the neck and parallel with the underarms. From this point, the tailor would measure out and down, while noting any curvature of the spine and, in particular, the extent, and asymmetry, of the shoulder slope. These 'defects' could be hidden in the cut of the coat. Next, for form's sake, he measured the circumference of the hips at crotch level, but from behind, then the thighs and calves (the latter would not survive as a measurement necessary for modern tailoring, but was important in the cut of pantaloons and trousers, if not knee-breeches).

Brummell was next asked to raise his arm and crook it as if eating at table, so that the tailor could measure from shoulder to wrist, via a bent elbow. A sign of a good tailor was that he measured *both* arms, such that he might create the illusion of perfect symmetry whether or not it existed in reality. Fine measurement of wrists, neck, biceps, chest, waist and hips followed, as well as measurements down the outside of the leg from waist and hips to knee and floor, and along the top and across the front of the shoulders. This would allow the perfect cut and padding of the collar, shoulders and upper coat, so that the jacket fell open elegantly, never creasing inwards from under the arms. Next the tailor took measurements from waist to knee, and knee to ankle, and measured the inside leg.

Complete measurements of the entire body were taken by each tailor, irrespective of the commission; the length of the coat related, in the new schema of classical proportions, as much to the length of the legs as to the length of the torso. Discreet note-taking was as important as measurement. Did the gentleman stoop or hold his chest too far forward? Was the waistline a reality still, or a fictive projection of the tailor? How rounded was the seat? To all these questions, small enciphered marks could be made against a sketched 'tailor's doll' to re-order the man according to the new ideals of masculine perfection. This was all a prologue to the series of scenes that would mark the creation of a particular garment. Five or six fittings were not uncommon and, after his tutelage with Beau Brummell, the Prince of Wales once took seventeen before one coat finally met his approval.

In 1796 a 'Society of Adepts in the Profession' published *The Taylor's Complete Guide or A Comprehensive Analysis of Beauty and Elegance in Dress*. The guide insisted that the tailor's job was not fashion, *per se*, so much as to be timeless and classical. Tailors did not encourage their patrons to be overly concerned with fashion, so much as with strength in orthodoxy. 'It is but of little consequence to a complete taylor [*sic*] what the fashions are; his business is to fit the body, that no constriction or unnatural compression may be felt in any part.' The truest signifier of a fine tailor, the hallmark that came to define Bond Street and Savile Row tailoring, was the ability of the tailor to hide a multitude of sins – sloping shoulders, concave chest, excess weight – and create instead, or enhance, an idealised male form. When urbane Tom takes his rustic friend Jerry to the fashionable tailor's Dicky Primefit in the hit Regency comedy *Life in London* their purpose is

> The art sublime, ineffable
> Of making middling men look well.

One of the next shops to benefit from Brummell's custom and his sudden celebrity was Jonathan Meyer's on Conduit Street. Where Schweitzer and Davidson made Brummell's coats, Meyer's made Brummell's breeches and trousers. Before the age of the suit, this was considered a quite separate job. Trousers, breeches and pantaloons made for complicated tailoring. There were darts and corset-lacings cut into the lower back, a defining seam on some between the buttocks and a 'fall' of between five and eight inches wide, buttoned at the side, instead of flies. Behind this flap were small pockets, usually one on each side, for small change. Some trousers had side pockets as well. There were matching brace-buttons on some and attached stays, strings and internal linings behind the flap – all frequently replaced. The whole was expected to be a figure-perfect fit. Brummell eschewed the wide pantaloon, favoured in Brighton perhaps in imitation of sailors, as he did the similarly baggy Cossack fashion that followed Tsar Alexander I to London in 1814. He wore slim-cut trousers or 'pantaloons' that flattered his famously long-legged frame. For daywear these were made of leather, mercerised cotton or nankeen and plain cotton in summer. Evening wear necessitated black, according to the new aesthetic, and Brummell wore sheer black silk jersey, made up as breeches for Carlton House or the theatre, and as pantaloons for the clubs. He defused accusations that he was vain about his legs by typically absurd whimsy: when he was spotted limping on Bond Street with an injured leg, he explained the true tragedy of the circumstance: 'I know, it's a deuced bore, but the worst of it is, that it is my *favourite* leg.'

In trouser design he had some immediate impact and also long-term effect. The fashion magazine *Le Beau Monde* (1808) de-scribed his trousers as 'stocking breeches and stockings all in one piece . . . [a] longitudinal pantaloon'. They were not always stocking-woven, however. Brummell and Jonathan Meyer the tailor pioneered an alternative style that attempted to replicate in fabric or leather the three-dimensional form-fitting style of stock-ings and silk-jersey stockinette. Brummell's pantaloons and trou-sers therefore had only one seam on each leg, running down the outside. Sometimes it was discreetly embroidered, as was also the case with the 'clocks' or embroidered panels that ran up the outer side of men's and women's stockings. This practice is lightly alluded to still in the braiding that runs down dinner-jacket and military trousers. Moreover it was at Meyer's, one morning in 1799 or 1800, that Brummell suggested attaching a strap to the bottom cuff of new trousers. The trousers would not wrinkle irrespective of whether boots were worn or not, or in the move from sitting to standing or in and out of carriages. It also lengthened the appearance of the leg. The fashion survived into

the early twentieth century in civilian wear and is still a commonplace of formal military uniforms, where they are known as
'overalls'.

At Meyer's, Brummell's list of requirements grew with each
season. Knee breeches were being replaced by (usually wide)
trousers or (usually narrow) pantaloons, but not entirely.
Brummell retained breeches as part of his summer wardrobe,
and for his occasional visits to the country. They were also
required formal-wear when attending the prince at Carlton
House. Brummell had them made of light materials such as
nankeen (a hardy cotton fabric, closely woven and often in the
Whig buff or white) and knitted silk stockinette. He often wore
leather breeches for informal daywear, which suggested sports-
manlike intent among the leisured classes whether or not they
truly intended to ride in Hyde Park. These were more durable
than the other materials used, but also highly sensuous garments
made of doeskin or chamois leather, which cut well and again
suggested the classical nudity that impressed the age. Meyers'
presumably employed a specialist leather-worker as they were
difficult garments to get right. Harriette Wilson wrote of
Brummell's discriminating eye:

I found my very constant and steady admirer Lord Frederick Bentinck
waiting for me.

'I have got on a new pair of leather breeches, today, and I want
[you] to see how they fit,' [said Lord Fred.]

Brummell at this moment, was announced.

'How very *a propos* you are arrived,' I remarked. 'Lord Frederick
wants your opinion of his new leather breeches.'

'Come here, Fred!' said Brummell. 'There is only one man on earth
[at Meyer's] who can make leather breeches!'

'Mine were made by a man in the Haymarket,' Bentinck observed,
looking down at them with much pride.

'My dear fellow, take them off directly,' said Brummell.

'I beg he may do no such thing,' said I, hastily, 'else, where would he
go to, I wonder, without even his small clothes?'

'They only came home this morning,' proceeded Fred, 'and I thought they were rather neat.'

'Bad knees, my dear fellow, bad knees!' said Brummell, shrugging his shoulders.

Brummell went on to advise his friend both to moderate his passion for the expensive courtesan Miss Wilson and to burn his new leather breeches.

Later, Harriette was party to a separate discussion between Brummell the leather connoisseur and his bluff chum Lord Robert Manners:

'Those leather breeches are not bad; who made them?' asked George Brummell, of his lordship.

'Why,' said Bob Manners, speaking very slow, 'the breeches maker.'

Harriette Wilson was exactly the sort of person young men visited to show off their new breeches. The lightness of colour, the use of stocking silk and brushed leather, the framing of the thighs with boots and cut-away jackets was not lost on her any more than on other contemporaries. Brummell may have thought of this perfect tailoring and use of pale colours and sensuous materials as the subtlest echoing of classical lines, but others raised eyebrows. Often his style of trouser, copied all over London and by the Prince of Wales himself, courted censure.

Recent fashion theorists Anne Hollander and Aileen Ribiero have pointed out what is apparent from many paintings of the period: that tight pale breeches, such as those pioneered by George Brummell, accented the crotch exactly as do the poses of antique statuary. It was the first time since the codpieces of the Tudor and Jacobean court that fashion had made a central feature of the male sex. But if the fashion framed the genital area, it did not lend any support to the occasion – and in polite society, as a result, Brummell's style of trousers were sometimes referred to as 'inexpressibles'. One Persian ambassador to the Court of St James was moved to write that he found the Brummell style of trousers 'immodest and unflattering to the figure . . . [they] look just like under-drawers – could they be designed to appeal to the ladies?' A more sympathetic or aroused observer noted that they were 'extremely handsome and very fit to expose a muscular Thigh', and society hostesses were later said to regret the passing of the fashion because 'one could always tell what a young man was thinking'. Some have even suggested that phrase 'the turn of the leg', signalling female approval of men in novels and plays of the period, was understood euphemistically. *The Taylor's Complete Guide* suggested the simple expedient of lining tight trousers – especially if made for light summer wear and depending on the wearer's interest in modesty or revealing his thoughts – either with swanskin (flannel) or cotton.

Meyer and Brummell thereby forced an issue of intimate interest to fashion historians and Savile Row satirists. The fashionable legwear of late Georgian London accentuated the genitals by pushing them down one trouser leg – an inversion, ironically, of the fig-leaf modesty as practised upon the classical statues that had inspired the fashion in the first place. Consequently the choice in men's tailoring of which side one dresses – and on which leg the trouser-seam is uppermost – dates exactly from this period and style. Although most subsequent styles have been significantly more modest, tailors have kept the inside leg high on one side rather than bifurcating the trousers with a low crotch. Of course, this may miss the point from a horse-rider's point of view, and Brummell had helped import the style specifically from a cavalry regiment. The 10th Light Dragoon breeches were recognisable riding garments, akin to modern jodhpurs, and in some instances leather-underlined. They also obliged the wearer to dress to one side. It is a choice forced by riding garments and the ancestry of the trouser in late-eighteenth-century British cavalry-wear – specifically Brummell's 10th Light Dragoons – is signalled in the evolution of this modest tailoring issue. The consequence has been bespoke tailors discreetly making an encoded mark in their fitting notes and cutting extra cloth in one leg accordingly.

The third of Brummell's favoured tailors was 'the superior

genius' John Weston on Old Bond Street. He was an exception to Brummell's usual choice of tailor in that he was British. He is credited by Captain Gronow with having an overview of Brummell's attire, but specifically he also made his waistcoats. These were either white, black or buff. The front of Brummell's waistcoats was, of course, the most conspicuous part of his clothing and was therefore remarkable for its austerity and simplicity. The back of the waistcoats, meanwhile, though never seen in public, was a testament to Weston's art. Seams in cruciform curved the fabric into the back, and there were lacings down the lower vertebrae – two or three strings – that pulled the diaphragm slightly in and encouraged a flat-stomached posture while forcing the chest out. Often, for ease of movement, these back panels were made of silk, which moved more freely against the same material lining the coat. The waistcoats had ten to twelve buttons running down the cotton-twill front, and a repetition at the neckline of the W cut detail used in the coats. The waistcoats had pockets either side and, if the surviving examples are to be trusted, were ruthlessly starched. Though Brummell insisted that necks should remain quite stiffly held in starched collar and neckcloths, and arms could not articulate very freely at the shoulder, there was nevertheless a good deal of freedom possible in every other regard. The legs and lower torso were the freest part of the body when fully dressed, for ease of horse-riding and dancing. This was one more echo of classical statuary: expressing nobility and strength of purpose in a pose held stiffly above the waist, and freedom, as well as sexuality, in a fluid lower body.

The dandiacal connoisseurs were expected to recognise true quality in the clothes they wore. The tailor who was sure of his work, therefore, only needed his goods on the right back. Indeed, the tradesmen of the area around Savile Row found it expedient, as the dandy craze grew, to eschew advertising altogether and did not even put anything in their shop-window or a nameplate on the door. It was a question of exclusivity and the nuances of class: exactly what the English had long excelled at but defined in cloth. Tailors looked instead to the appeal generated by Brummell. This was why they extended their credit to him, and why, over the years, they began to come to Brummell, rather than the other way round. The shaping of the old Burlington Estate into the centre of men's tailoring, as it has remained, was achieved through Brummell's corralling of the country's wealthiest men, who all lived or had residences nearby, into the tailors' shops around Savile Row. It could never have been done by advertising, or without key characteristics of the area and of London society that Brummell well understood. The West End had never known such affluence but also had an established history of catering to masculine desire. The same clubbability of the men on the one side, and exclusivity of the institutions on the other, which supported the St James's Street gaming houses and the King's Place bagnios, granted clientele, prestige and fame to the new tailors of Savile Row – especially those who found their clothes worn publicly by Brummell.

Brummell's promiscuous shopping habits, however, meant that no one tailor could claim he was responsible for the Brummell look. As Jesse said, '[it is unclear whether Meyer] or Brummell . . . first invented the trouser foot loop. The Beau at any rate was the first who wore them, and they immediately became quite the fashion.' Meyer benefited from the innovation, but presumably not exclusively. Other tailors caught on to the idea via Brummell, such that the tailor could in no way eclipse Brummell's fame. 'Give me the man who makes the tailor, not the tailor who makes the man,' as the Brummell character in the novel *Pelham* exclaims. 'You can tell a Stultz coat anywhere, which is quite enough to damn it; the moment a man's known by an invariable cut [and tailor's name] it ought to be all over with him.' Likewise, Brummell's other fictional characterisation in *Granby* fulminated that he 'scorned to share his fame with his tailor, and was, moreover, seriously disgusted at seeing a well-fancied waistcoat, almost unique, before the expiration of its "honeymoon" adorning the person of a natty apprentice'.

Brummell further guarded his pre-eminence as *arbiter elegantiarum* by refusing to offer serious advice on the subject. Instead he developed a detached and ironic attitude to fashion, quite as polished as his coat buttons. Whether this was a deliberate ploy, or simply a result of his instinct for comedy is unclear, but the effect was that he deflected direct enquiry into his style or his shopping choices by deft use of the ridiculous or the barbed. When asked how he kept his boots so brilliantly black, he coolly advised the use of best champagne froth for polishing. When asked by the Duke of Bedford for a direct opinion on a coat he replied, 'Coat? You call that a coat?' Then there was his positively proto-Wildean instruction that men should never 'ride in ladies' gloves, particularly, he said, with leather breeches.

Like many with an intuitive understanding of a style or art, he was not particularly interested in talking or writing about it, and though he later essayed a treatise on male fashion, his heart was not in it. He was for the wearing of it, not the discussing it. Being a dandy, more to the point, was never going to be just about clothes for Brummell. It was a pose with which to fascinate and intrigue, and he would have been a good deal less fascinating about style if he had chosen to talk about it more – or more seriously.

Brummell's fame and recognition of his personal style went hand in hand and developed, according to one satirist, into an absolute mania. There were 'Dandy Lawyers, Dandy Parsons, Dandy Physicians, Dandy Shopkeepers, Dandy Clerks, Dandy Authors, Dandy Beggars, and Dandy Pickpockets', according to the author of *Dandymania*, who called himself Jackey Dandy.

According to T. H. Lister, Brummell soon wearied of this cultish aspect of his fame. He 'sickened of giving names to cloaks, hats, and pantaloons, and panted for a higher pedestal than . . . a tailor's shop board . . . As it was his ambition to be inimitable, he found it much better to shun any outward peculiarities, and trust alone to "the nameless grace of polished ease" which he really possessed in a remarkable degree'.

He never gave the impression of being bored with clothes or shopping, but it would be unfair to consider him a devotee of fashion. He helped create a style, then stuck with it as if it were an immutable orthodoxy. The higher pedestal to which he aspired was not the high office his creditors must have wished for him. Rather, his clothes were the first signifier of the dandy pose, 'the polished ease' that impressed society much more than what he wore and which appeared to some a higher calling in itself.

'Dandyism,' wrote Count Barbey d'Aurevilly, of his hero Beau Brummell, 'plays with the regulations, but at the same time pays them due respect.' It is the perfect insider's revolt, and Brummell seems to have known the essential ridiculousness of being radically fashionable. 'It is folly that is the making of me,' he told one of the few women he felt understood him. When she asked him why he did not devote himself to a higher calling or use his cleverness to greater purpose than fashion, he rejoined that he knew human nature well enough to realise such was his best and fastest route 'to separate himself from the ordinary herd of men'.

'Eccentricity [is the] fruit of English soil. [It is] the revolt of the individual against the established order,' explained d'Aurevilly, from the perspective of a Frenchman, and 'Dandyism . . . is the force of English originality when applied to human vanity.'

Beau Brummell needed the oxygen of society: he was rarely alone from waking to sleeping through all his days in the high life. But he felt himself unique in a way he seems to have found unforgiving. Though his impact on the history of men's tailoring and the West End economy was far reaching, he was no tailor's dummy. His style was aped, but he was increasingly a man apart, dissecting with his own sardonic wit the style to which he gave his name and counterpointing high fashion with an accretion of affectations that began to alienate as much as they fascinated. How else, as d'Aurevilly remarked, but by comic affectation, to establish himself in his highly affected society?

Before the end of his first season in London Brummell's debts began to mount. Most tailors would not expect to be paid for at least six months, and some only submitted annual accounts. In this it should be allowed that their stock outgoings were covered to some extent by gentlefolk supplying their own fabrics. Even so, many tailors operated almost like banks, with more prestigious clients offered better overdraft terms: Harriette Wilson described Stultz the tailor as a money-lender in exactly this context, and Lord Byron's tailors were still asking for payment for his servant's mourning liveries four years after the death of his mother. Lock's, Brummell's hatter at No. 6 St James's Street, gave a shilling reduction on all items for cash payment, but this was a rare incentive. It was quite common for credit to be extended for two or three years at a time and the gentry took ample advantage of this.

Brummell, however, was encouraged to shop even further beyond his means. The supposition of the tailors was partly commercial – his custom worked for them as ideal advertising – and partly pragmatic: Brummell appeared to be headed for great high office as one of the favourites of the heir to the throne. His ability to maintain a line of credit relied therefore on his maintaining his position in fashion and society, and both, in effect, were reliant on the prince.

AFTERNOON

7
A RIDE ON
ROTTEN ROW

Civility, my good fellow, may truly be said to cost nothing: if it
does not meet with a due return, it at least leaves you in the
most creditable position.

George Bryan Brummell

As for love – I conceive it a mere empty bubble
And the fruits of success never worth half the trouble;
Yet as Fashion decrees it, I bear the fatigue
That the world may suppose me a 'man of intrigue.'
'The Fine Man or Buck of the First
Set', *The Pursuits of Fashion*, 1810

According to Lord Byron, the list of the great men of the age
that included himself and Napoleon began with George
Brummell. He made this remark, eyebrow-raising even at the
time, once they were all in exile, and Brummell's inclusion in the
list was, to some extent, a whimsical comment on the evanescence
of fame, a 'summit' that he said was 'lost in vapour'. However,
within the tight confines of the world as defined by London's high
society, Byron had barely exaggerated Brummell's previous celebrity and influence. 'That congregated mass of folly, that busy
fretful turmoil of conflicting littlenesses which is called "Society"' took Brummell to its collective heart, and for that society,

Brummell's ascendancy, as if from nowhere, was seen as quite comparable to Napoleon's. Both were 'curious freaks of fortune', in the words of Captain Gronow. Entirely separately Byron had also remarked that he would rather have been Brummell than Emperor of France and 'always pronounced the name of Brummell with a mingled emotion of respect and jealousy'.

Brummell, too, took delight in the parallel, coincidental, chronologies of his career and Napoleon's. It appealed to his inverted sense of seriousness that his lightweight career should ever be linked with the world stage, and his conquests to those of the Bonaparte. Of course they had little in common. Brummell's conquests were social, and occasionally romantic or sexual. Napoleon, it need hardly be said, was in the process of changing the map of Europe. It is a feature of Brummell's life and times that he, like his contemporary Jane Austen, made barely any mention of the political cataclysms on the continent or the constant fear of invasion that formed the undertow of English political and social life at the time. Brummell's and Austen's worlds – London high society and the respectable gentility of provincial England – existed in parallel to, but utterly removed from, the horrors of war and political turmoil of the early nineteenth century. Nevertheless, the same years in which Bonaparte rose as first consul and then emperor of the French also saw Brummell achieve a sort of supremacy over London society.

London society operated in Brummell's day like a series of concentric circles. High society was exclusive by its very nature, but what typifies Regency society through the glory-days of Brummell's reign was the systematic way in which it went about excluding others. Exclusion was one of the key *raisons d'être* of the gentlemen's clubs, but also of the etiquette of greeting and dressing. The signal peculiarity of Brummell's career was that he came from outside the immediate spheres that had formed society but came to dictate the language of exclusion from an apparently unassailable position at the centre.

A whole language was developing for expressing the subtleties of exclusivity. Chateaubriand, the French writer and diplomat, noted that the vocabulary of Brummell's associates seemed to change in London 'almost as often as each session of Parliament . . . the fashions for words, the affectations of language and pronunciation change in High Society so often that a man who thought he knew English finds six months later that he does not'. They even changed the words for themselves, as listed by the writer of a novel on *The Exclusives*:

The Society of the Ton; the dynasty of the Ton; the court of the ton; the empire of the ton; devotees of ton; the elite of the ton; the polished ultra of the Ton; ultra-tonism; The Ton; the World of Fashion; the fashionable multitude; the *canaille* of the fashionable world; a *société choisie*; a society *distinguée*; a select coterie; a race apart; young men *de la première volée*; a *haut grade* in society; the corps elite; The Elite.

In London, this system of exclusivity was nowhere so conspicuously played out as in the West End's premier park: Hyde Park.

> The Park! That magnet of the town
> That idol to which all bow down!

wrote Henry Luttrell, his tongue firmly in his cheek,

> See how the universal throng
> Borne in one swelling tide along
> Crowds to its turf-clad altars, there
> To beg the blessing of fresh air!
> Can Europe or the world produce
> Alike for ornament or use
> Such specimens of order, dress
> Health, comfort, in-bred cleanliness?

In the afternoon, especially in good weather, Brummell took to riding in the park, which extended then as now from Tyburn Lane (Park Lane) to Kensington Palace: three hundred and fifty acres of city parkland. He was an accomplished horseman but this was not a sport of the physical variety. Rather Hyde Park – notably the horse-and-carriage avenue called Rotten Row – functioned as a sort of outdoor salon, where the rituals of greeting and not greeting, doffing hats in acknowledgement or 'cutting' those out of favour were enacted with the rigour of a military inspection. 'Where the fashionable fair,' as Lord Byron put it, 'can form a slight acquaintance with fresh air.'

One fictionalised account from the period describing a Brummell 'cut' gives a clear, and unattractive, impression of the man in action on Rotten Row: 'In the art of cutting he shone unrivalled: he knew the "when", the "where" and the "how". Without affecting useless short-sightedness, he could assume that calm but wandering gaze, which veers, as if unconsciously, round the proscribed individual.' This was Brummell's world: distance was preserved, anyone could be escaped, all was show and banter. The callous snobbery involved in his self-appointed position as one of the regulators of who was 'in' and who was 'out' at the park is distinctly unappealing to the modern ear and eye. To Brummell's contemporaries all this was mitigated by his wit. 'Have you ever endured so poor a summer?' shouted one friend in passing.

'Yes,' he replied, 'last winter!'

It was in Hyde Park he was asked by another dandy where he got his boots blacked and announced to all who might hear, 'My blacking positively ruins me; it is made with the finest champagne!' A talent to amuse remained a signal part of his attraction to the wider world: an ability to enliven the inherent tedium of society rituals with well-placed impertinences and pronouncements designed to make people laugh.

Though accessible from Piccadilly and Oxford Street, Hyde Park remained largely rural in Brummell's day, with tethered cows, roaming sheep and wild deer. In this mock-sylvan setting Brummell rode in the company of women as well as men. Men would ride singly or accompanied by a groom – Brummell stabled his horses on the edge of Hyde Park – while women rode in a *vis-à-vis* for two, furnished with 'powdered footmen in smart liveries, and a coachman who assumed all the gaiety and appearance of a wigged archbishop'.

Coachmen notwithstanding, it was an easy-going and attractive environment in which to exercise, socialise and flirt.

In the age of the Romantic poets everyone acknowledged that in Hyde Park the landscape was tame:

> None view it awestruck or surprised
> But still, 'tis smart and civilized.

Brummell saw the comedic possibilities of the false pastoralism of the park and of Romanticism itself. It was the age when the Romantic landscape was being discovered, or created, in art and gardens. Brummell went to elaborate lengths of satire when faced in Hyde Park with a rider extolling the virtues of the rugged lakeland landscape and asking Brummell which lake he most admired (he never ventured so far north).

'Robinson,' he said, turning to his valet who sometimes accompanied him in the park.

'Sir?'

'Which of the lakes do I admire?'

'Windermere, sir.'

'Ah, yes, Windermere, so it is.'

The exchange would be worthy of Jeeves and Wooster or the plays of Oscar Wilde. It also made a point in a subtly Brummell-esque manner: few pretensions are as ridiculous as the urban fashion for the countryside. Hyde Park, for fashion-conscious Londoners like Brummell, was quite rural enough.

Brummell rode in through the Apsley Gate, which led straight to the main axis of social intercourse: Rotten Row. 'Is there a more gay and graceful spectacle in the world?' wrote Disraeli of Rotten Row. 'Where can one see such beautiful women, such gallant cavaliers, such fine horses, and such brilliant equipages?' It provided more than the opportunity for Brummell to show off his riding, his horses and his ability to quip. It was also one of the few environments in which men and women 'of rank and fashion' could mix easily with each other in large numbers. Unlike Vauxhall Gardens, where the fashionable ran the risk of a rather too intimate proximity with those outside their charmed sphere,

Rotten Row remained the preserve of the highest echelons of society. 'In those days,' Captain Gronow pointed out, only the cream of society 'would have dared to show themselves . . . nor did you see any of the lower or middle classes of London intruding themselves in the regions [of Hyde Park] which, with a sort of tacit understanding, were given up exclusively to persons of rank and of fashion.' Why this should have been so when there was no charge for admission or porter at the gate beggars easy understanding.

The fortunes of Ranelagh, Vauxhall and the Pantheon on Oxford Street had all waned over the precise issue of too easy an access for the 'exclusives' to feel comfortable. Prices had gone up accordingly, but the Regency, and snobs like Brummell, were discovering a more insidious system of social filtration and nowhere was this easier than in the open air, and on horseback. The *Bon Ton* self-selected those who were to be included – the fashionable and well-connected – and the cost of maintaining a horse, equipage and the related costumes excluded all but the very rich. Anyone on Rotten Row therefore was rich and fashionable. Consequently mothers and chaperones were a little less watchful of their daughters and companions: everyone was deemed eligible company. There was more gossip and exchange of news and views between the sexes than was possible at any other time of day except a late-night ball at Almack's. It was in Hyde Park therefore, necessarily, that Brummell's acquaintance with women grew exponentially. And his popularity, humour and easy club-bability with men should not be read as an inability to enjoy the company of women, or for women to enjoy his. Quite the contrary:

Never was there such a man [wrote Tom Raikes] who during his career had such unbounded influence and what is seldom the case, such general popularity in society. Without being a man of intrigue . . . he was the idol of the women . . . Not only because he was a host of amusement in himself, with his jokes and his jeers, but because he was such a favourite with the *men*, that *all* were anxious then to join the party [of women] . . . Brummell was as great an oracle among the women of the highest rank in London, and his society much courted and followed, as amongst his male associates.

The attributes that had allowed Brummell an entrée into the world of London fashion as a style leader for men were attractive to many women. Two descriptions from the period, one of Brummell and one inspired by him, picture him as he was first seen on Rotten Row, and explain some of his unique fascination.

His face was rather long, and the complexion fair; his whiskers inclined to sandy and his hair light brown. His head was well-shaped. The forehead being unusually high. His countenance indicated that he possessed considerable intelligence, and his mouth betrayed a strong disposition to indulge in sardonic humour; this was predominate in every feature. His eyebrows were equally expressive with his mouth, and while the latter was giving utterance to something very good-humoured or polite, the former, and the eyes themselves, which were gray and full of oddity, could assume an expression that made the sincerity of his words very doubtful. His voice was [however] very pleasing.

Brummell never read this description, but the next one he did, and when he had, he asserted he was convinced the author had talked to many who had known him in his prime:

[Brummell] had great powers of entertainment, and a keen and lively turn for satire; and could talk down his superiors, whether in rank or talent, with very imposing confidence. He saw the advantages of being formidable, and . . . had sounded the gullibility of the world; knew the precise current value of pretension and soon found himself the acknowledged umpire, the last appeal of many followers.

He seldom committed himself by praise or recommendation, but rather left his example and adoption to work its way. As for censure, he had both ample and witty store; but here too he often husbanded his remarks, and where it was needless or dangerous to define a fault, could check admiration by an incredulous smile, and depress pretensions of a season's standing by the raising of an eyebrow. He had a quick perception of the foibles of others, and keen relish for bantering and exposing them. He could ingeniously cause the unconscious subject to place his own absurdities in the best point of view, and would cloak his derision under the blandest cajolery.

Imitators he loved much; but to baffle them – more. He loved to turn upon the luckless adopters of his last folly, and see them precipitately back out of the scrape into which he himself had led them.

Originality was his idol. He wished to astonish, even if he did not amuse; and had rather say a silly thing than a commonplace one. He was led by this sometimes even to approach the verge of rudeness and vulgarity; but he had considerable tact, and a happy hardihood, which generally carried him through the difficulties into which his fearless love of originality brought him. Indeed, he well knew that what would, in the present condition of his reputation, be scouted in anybody else, would pass current with the world in him.

Such was the far-famed and redoubtable [Mr Brummell].

A fearless love of originality and disdain for cant might win many friends, but this seems not to have been Brummell's purpose so much as a happy side effect. Brummell's dandy pose held the world in satirical contempt just as much as it held tailoring to be the supreme art, while a subversive and sardonic manner, then as now, begot a crowd. Beyond this Brummell's personable warmth and his wit – often lost in the retelling of those jokes that closely equate snobbery with humour – brought him many admirers. The women who were drawn to him and whom he chose in friendships or love affairs are especially revealing of the man, his mind and manner. He met them first, and most frequently, in Hyde Park.

~

The women with whom Brummell shared the most enduring and intense relationships over his years in London and who rode with him on Rotten Row, were strong, intelligent – and usually titled. Although he had many sexual trysts with women – and possibly with men – and with professional courtesans, they were shallow affairs compared with the profound friendships that structured his days in London and his later letter-writing from France. These longer-term friendships remained just that, and the sexual frisson that undoubtedly underpinned them was not acted upon – with one likely exception. The four women to whom he was most closely linked in London, and for some time afterwards, were Georgiana, Duchess of Devonshire; Princess Frederica, Duchess of York; the society beauty Elizabeth, Duchess of Rutland; and the eccentric bluestocking Lady Hester Stanhope.

There was an obvious pattern to these connections. All four women were of high social rank, and the Duchesses of York and Devonshire and Lady Hester were more than a decade older than Brummell. But they were all strong, independent, wilful and artistic – women who could offer Brummell support in his social advancement and access to the best that London had to offer, but who also found a complicity of mind and taste with the young dragoon who had had such a sudden impact on London, and who seems to have made them laugh.

～

All her life, Lady Hester Stanhope, like Brummell, refused to sit for a portrait. As with Brummell, this signified an unwillingness to be easily placed or pigeonholed (the choice of portraitist immediately signalled status and artistic taste) while at the same time, also like Brummell, Lady Hester had a keen interest in her own image. She was considered something of a beauty in her youth but at thirty-three, when Brummell first knew her, she was thought, by the rules of the day, a confirmed spinster. Why this should have been so when, as well as looks, she had remarkable connections and kept house from 1803 for her uncle William Pitt at Downing Street, was explained by her singular character and independence.

Hester Stanhope spoke freely, openly and had strong political opinions. It was rumoured that she took lovers. She knew she was beautiful, and of commanding presence – she was nearly six feet tall – but set little or no store by the life of society in comparison with that of the mind. 'I was never what you call handsome, but brilliant,' she wrote. 'My teeth were brilliant, my complexion brilliant, my language – ah!'

She wrote, travelled and pressed her political opinions in Downing Street whether or not she was asked for them. But she was not without personal vanity. According to her own account, she kept her skin a pearlescent white all her life, such that at five paces' distance the sharpest eye could not distinguish the pearls at her neck. The style of her relationship with Brummell was set when he teased her in public about this: he removed her earrings and said, 'For God's sake take [them] off, and let's see what's beneath them!'

They seem to have struck up a friendship as early as 1801, when Lady Hester was semi-ostracised by her immediate family for her radical ways and refusal of a chaperone. They were probably introduced by her cousin, another maverick in the Stanhope family, the dandy Lord Petersham, who had been in the dragoons with Brummell in Brighton. By the time Lady Hester became chatelaine of Downing Street, Brummell had an easy entrée back to one of his childhood homes, and when she left it in 1807, on Pitt's death, and set up home with her two younger brothers she saw even more of Brummell. 'She was excellent at mimicry [like Brummell] and she had more wit and repartee,' wrote her doctor, 'than falls to the lot of many women.'

She was, like Brummell, at once alone in the world and also a 'darling of society'. She had a marked style all of her own – once attending the State Opening of Parliament to represent her uncle in 'black and green velvet ornamented with gold and studded with rubies'. Queen Charlotte was moved to comment on the dramatic effect. She struck poses, and was admired by many but, like Brummell, her romantic affairs were deemed inconclusive. She was quick to fall in love but found most men wanting, not least intellectually. She had at least one affair with a man significantly her junior and her cross-dressing in later life signalled to others that she was a lesbian. Prince Pückler-Muskau announced that she had taken an Arab lover when she ran away to the Lebanon in 1811. 'The Arabs,' she countered, 'have never looked upon me in the light either of man or woman but as *un être à par* [a being apart].' As such, she and Brummell were a pair.

By 1803 she was writing Brummell long, flirtatious letters, whose intimacy suggests a deep friendship and already some shared history. She had just engaged Brummell's former groom after a tour of the Continent, and wrote in part for a reference. Brummell's reply does not survive.

Cheltenham Spa
30 August 1803

If you are as conceited as formerly, I shall stand accused of taking your groom [just] to give me an opportunity of writing to you for his character. All the inquiry I wish to make upon the subject, is to be informed whether you were as well satisfied with James Ell when you parted with him, as when he had Stiletto under his care. If so, I shall dispatch him at the end of next week, with my new purchases to Walmer, where I am going shortly. You may imagine I am not a little happy in having it in my power to scamper upon British ground, although I was extremely pleased with my tour, and charmed with Italy.

I saw a good deal of your friend Capel at Naples: if he fights the battles of his country by sea as well as he fights yours by land, he certainly is one of our first commanders. But of him you must have heard so full an account from Lord Althorp, for they were inseparable, that I will only add he was as yet unsuccessful in the important research after a perfect snuff box when I left Italy. Should [these researches] prove successful, Capel, on his return, will of course be made Admiral of the White, for the signal services he has rendered to coxcombality.

I met with a rival of yours in affectation upon the Continent, William Hill! I fear it will be long ere this country will again witness his airs, as he is now a prisoner: this, perhaps, you are glad of, as his society of statues and pictures has infinitely

improved him in this wonted qualification, and therefore rendered him a still more formidable competitor.

Hester L. Stanhope.

The tone is teasing, even sisterly, and yet there is acknowledgement both of her intimate understanding of Brummell's
foibles and also the potential of a 'rival in affectation'. She
addresses him, as he did her, as an equal. Captain Jesse was
sufficiently intrigued by this letter and by rumours still extant in
society – even after Brummell and Lady Hester had both long left
the country – of an affair between the prime minister's niece and
Beau Brummell that he sent a friend of his, already in the Middle
East, in search of her. Lady Hester had left England before
Brummell, in 1811, and at first it was assumed that she was
travelling again on a Grand Tour of the continent. But this time,
she headed for the Middle East and immersed herself in the
culture of the Levant – modern-day Syria and Lebanon – and
never returned to England. Some said she had never recovered
from the death of her uncle, William Pitt, others that she had
decided to distract herself from a heart broken by John Moore,
or, Jesse suggested, Brummell himself, with travel. The bluestocking aristocrat who had once hosted dinners at Downing
Street took to living with Bedouins and wearing the dress of an
Arab man.

Naturally enough, when reports of this came back to London,
Regency society was scandalised. Conversely, though, no one was
particularly shocked: anything was possible of Lady Hester
Stanhope. She wrote discursive memoirs with her physician,
and when Captain Jesse's informant found her, she was living
in a hermitage atop Mount Elias, surrounded by Albanians,
Turks and Lebanese in the ruins of a Syrian convent. She ruled
the locals with a mixture of tyranny and British bravura, but no
money: her pension from Parliament, granted for services as
official hostess at Downing Street, was paid erratically. When
the Englishman found her, the news she wanted from London was
of two men: Wellington, and Beau Brummell.

Her conversation was more than ordinarily eloquent, though tinctured with somewhat of the strangeness that pervaded her whole life and character. [Brummell] appeared to have been an especial favourite of hers; and although I am unable to repeat the description she gave it, I can, even now, fancy that I see him riding up to her in the Park to give her a stick of perfume of his own manufacture; a peculiar mark of favour, granted on condition that she promised faithfully not to give a morsel to the Prince, who was dying to get some. I hinted at Brummell's eccentricities; but she replied that he was an exceedingly clever man, always suiting his conversation to his hearers, and that he almost always paid her the compliment of talking very sensibly. She added she had once rebuked him for some folly or other, and inquired why so clever a person as he was did not devote himself to a higher purpose than he did? To which Brummell replied that he knew human nature too well, and that he had adopted the only course which could place him in a prominent light, and enable him to separate himself from the ordinary herd of men.

Such was Lady Hester's verdict on Brummell from the perspective of old age and a distance both geographical and cultural. She had forgotten the ways of London sufficient to eat sitting on the floor, using her hand. But Brummell remained vivid in her imagination. She allows his cleverness, but, like any true politician, cannot see much beyond the flat horizons of seriousness and was frustrated by Brummell as she was by most of mankind.

Jesse's informant, passing Lady Hester's on the road to Damascus, was singularly intrigued by Brummell's sexuality, as was Jesse: this is one interpretation of the 'eccentricities' hinted at in the hope of Lady Hester's elucidation. She was having none of it. Theirs was a meeting of minds and wits, nothing more, but her fascination with him remained even though she had long before, and without regret, given up London society. We see from Hester Stanhope Brummell's appeal as one who treated women seriously, and in the same regard his particular appeal and skill is evidenced: he made people feel special, well treated and individually regarded. For a woman of the period, from a man, this probably felt dramatically unusual. Had he been so minded, and used his political acumen to engage Lady Hester on the subject she felt worthy of attention, he might have gone much further with their friendship. She was patently intrigued by him, but saw through his carapace: she was familiar with so many of its supportive structures. She could do high style, when demanded, she was accounted a wit and brilliant mind, she was an outsider who had conquered London. If he could tease and pique her to the extent of removing her earrings in public – an intimate action and a brave one on any man's part – she was capable of coming back at him where it hurt. As he chatted to her in Hyde Park – she in her carriage, he on horseback – she commented on a passing officer, another 'rival' in her affections.

'Yes, but who ever heard of his father?' said Brummell, with the dismissive air of the habitual snob he had become.

'And who ever heard of *yours*?' countered Lady Hester. This was especially pointed, given her position at Downing Street, where Brummell's father had been a sort of political servant. Brummell reflected for a moment, then stated his credo for Hyde Park: an intimacy that perhaps he could have shared only with Hester Stanhope, who had the position and the intellect to understand.

'Ah, my dear Lady Hester, who indeed ever heard of my father, and who would have heard of me, if I had been anything but what I am? It is my folly that is the making of me. If I did not impertinently stare duchesses out of countenance and nod over my shoulder to a prince, I should be forgotten within a week: and if the world is so silly as to admire my absurdities, you and I may know better, but what does that signify?'

He smiled and rode on.

~

Georgiana, Duchess of Devonshire, fast-living doyenne of London society and the most celebrated political hostess of the previous generation, was twenty-one years older than Brummell and had known him since he was a schoolboy. He had been introduced to Devonshire House on Piccadilly by Fox and Sheridan when he was still at Eton and his initial exposure to the circle surrounding the Prince of Wales in the late 1790s was attributable to the rapprochement then between Georgiana and the prince. Georgiana was forty-three in 1800 when she and Brummell first came to see more of each other in the close world of the Whig aristocracy, in Hyde Park and at Georgiana's parties.

The duchess was facing the twin problems of reintroducing herself to London after several years' exile abroad – since the birth of her illegitimate baby, Eliza, by Earl Grey – while simultaneously launching her legitimate daughter, 'Little G' (Georgiana), on London society. Devonshire House – the Cavendishes' main London residence, a veritable palace on the north side of Green Park – had been undergoing major renovation, but was ready by June 1799, according to the *Morning Post*, 'for the reception of its noble owners'. The balls and parties in honour of Little G at Devonshire House and Chiswick, where the duchess also entertained, marked the beginning of the new phase in Georgiana's life also: reacceptance by society, by the Prince of Wales and even by Mrs Fitzherbert, with whom she had clashed violently in the past. The same parties were also young Brummell's earliest forays into her world.

Described in her youth by Horace Walpole as a 'phenomenon' and by the *Morning Post* as the 'Most Envied Woman of the Day', Georgiana was more pitied than envied by 1800. Her unorthodox but spectacular looks were lost: she had suffered a tumour behind her right eye, which, after the invasive techniques of eighteenth-century medicine – leeches, 'flushing', blisterings and caustics – had left her scarred and half blind. She had exhausted her restive spirits on politics and politicians and was also deep in debt – to the tune of £200,000.

Georgiana had not only seen her place as a great beauty and leader of fashion eroded. Before her illness she had been used to a radical degree of independence, such that her physical disability (the eye tumour left her with chronic headaches) depressed her even more than it attacked her vanity. She remained able to write, however, and poured much of her energies into letters and verse, and encouraging the same in others. She wrote one poem to the woman who had shared much of her life, and indeed had shared her husband, in the age's most scandalous *ménage à trois*, Lady Elizabeth Foster – who married her lover, the Duke of Devonshire, after Georgiana's death. The poem expresses the softening heart of a woman who had learned some of the comfort of surrendering independence to the arm of another. George Brummell, her new young friend, also received a copy, slightly extended, its sense changed in the context of an experienced older woman writing to a young man. He kept it, in her handwriting, in his album.

> I've Known all the Blessings of Sight
> By the Duchess of Devonshire
>
> I've known all the blessings of sight,
> The beauties that nature displays,
> And traced in the splendour of light
> The glories that streamed in the blaze.
> Yet though darkness its sorrow has spread,
> I grudge not the pleasures I've known,
> Since, reclining, I thus lay my head
> On a breast that I know is my own.
>
> I've valued the charms of the rose,
> As I pluck'd it all fresh from the tree;
> I have kiss'd it, and bid it disclose
> Its sweets, for I meant it for thee.
> But memory still has its bliss,
> Though no longer I gaze on thee now;
> More sweet than the rose is thy kiss
> And more fresh and more lovely art thou.
>
> The life of roebuck was mine,
> As I bounded o'er valley and lawn,
> I watch'd the grey twilight decline
> And worshipp'd the day-breaking dawn.
> I regret not the freedom of will,

Or sigh as uncertain I tread:
I am freer and happier still
When by thee I am carefully led.

Ere my sight I was doom'd to resign,
My heart I surrender'd to thee,
Not a thought or an action was mine,
But I saw as thou bads't me to see,
Thy watchful affection I wait,
And hang with delight on thy voice;
And dependence is soften'd by fate,
Since dependence on thee was my choice.

The poem's inclusion in the collection Brummell kept of verses written to or for him goes unmentioned in works on Georgiana, but if it was written or extended with him in mind, it makes an impressively moving case for a hopeless infatuation on the duchess's part. The first three stanzas do not appear in the version she wrote to Lady Elizabeth (Bess) Foster. These additional stanzas in Brummell's version define a breast to lean on as well as regret, on the author's part, that she is no longer seeing or able to see her 'lover'. Brummell's famously delightful voice is referenced, and he plays the part of the worshipped dawn to the cold light of (Lord) grey. Georgiana knew all about the life of the roebuck that was Brummell's, and no longer hers, but there is more than the affectionate counsel of an old family friend on offer: she mentions his tender kiss.

Poems are not evidence, and love poems are more slippery than most. Nevertheless, as related by more than this poem, there grew between Brummell and Georgiana a complicity, as past and present darlings of society. He knew his advancement was aided by her place in the *Haut Ton*, just as she knew that the success of the Devonshire House balls in launching her gauche daughter on London was heightened by Brummell's presence. The poem, in the context of the anecdotes that surrounded Georgiana and George, and Brummell's later writings after the duchess's untimely death, suggest their friendship had a profoundly felt core and that he had a special place in her affections as her star was fading, and his rising.

Brummell's album came to be littered with the poetic effusions of Georgiana, and their mutual friends. In this respect theirs was a literary relationship and it may well have been that Georgiana, like Hester Stanhope, felt the need to suggest to Brummell he *do* something with his fame and talents. She had offered protection and encouragement to artists and writers in the past – even accommodating the novelist Charlotte Smith at Devonshire House. Together she and Brummell read in French and Italian, and she translated verses to be inscribed into the album. Though the archive at Chatsworth yields no evidence that Brummell was invited there, he claimed he was and there is little reason to doubt him based on the intimacy on show in their writings. He called her 'beautiful and enthusiastic' and cited as a particular family trait the 'generous natures' of the Devonshires. Their literary flirtation started off innocently enough, and in keeping with the age's accepted intercourse between the sexes. When Brummell had his hair cut, the ageing coquette wrote that she would

> Here in the bower of beauty, newly shorn,
> Let fancy sit and sing how love was born.

Their friends knew of their literary sport and joined in. When the duchess's favourite spaniel, Faddle, died, Charles James Fox penned some verses for Brummell to put into his album: 'On the Death of Faddle . . . an early victim to love'. When they were all together, at Devonshire House we assume but cannot know, the duchess read a poem she had written about Fox's friend James Hare: 'a loved companion and a friend sincere'. She next wrote a long mock-heroic saga in verse, 'Borino the Brave', almost certainly for performance, and one must imagine them laughing together as she describes a 'Bedlamite Duchess' who 'with gesture uncouth' aims her arms and her heart 'straight at the Youth'. How much was meant by any of this is unclear: on the one hand it was a parlour game played by talented amateurs with time and ink on their hands. On the other, it was a literary flirtation between two arch flirts, which may or may not have exhausted itself on the page. Within the playful rules of their poetical soirées almost anything could be said, but Brummell chose to keep a series of poems that are remarkable for their frank depiction of an older woman revivified by the attention of a younger man. It is tempting to take quite seriously the intention behind such lines as

> My cherished hope, my fondest dream
> Still dearest rests on thee,
> [which she wrote to him, again undated, but which he kept]
> A blank without thee all would seem
> And life would lifeless be.
>
> The place thy presence glads to seek
> Is where I'm ever best,
> And when I hear thee kindly speak,
> And speak to me, I'm blest.
>
> But should hard fate command it so,
> Still dearest I'm resigned,
> And if from me thou'rt bent to go,
> Or alter'd or unkind –
>
> Unfelt by thee, my silent care
> Shall never claim relief,
> And still I'll wish thou mayst not share
> My solitary grief.

If these poems are taken at face value, Georgiana and Brummell were playing a dangerous game with each other's affections, even if their reputations were untouched. Only once does she hint that she, for one, lusted for something more from the recipient of her verse:

> O'er her white breast he spread his purple wing,
> On kisses fed, and silver drops of dew,
> The little wanton into Cupid grew,
> Then armed his head with glittering sparks of fire
> And tipp'd his shining arrows with desire.

This classically inspired heavy-breathing aside, the roles Georgiana and Brummell take on in their writings (mainly hers to him) place their relationship in the long tradition of courtly love. It was the obvious model for a friendship, played out in poetry, of an older, high-status woman and a romantic young man. There is one Jesse anecdote on Brummell that can reasonably be attached to his 'affair' with Georgiana and, if correctly so, the implication is inevitable that their literary love affair did get a little too close for comfort. The story is of Brummell's dismissal from a country-seat house-party. The style of the scene as it was related around London bears much similarity to the drama of the period, but that in no way undermines its authenticity. Brummell had learned his manners and his wit from the theatre and from theatre practitioners. So, too, it might be added, had the 'duke'. The scene, as relayed by Jesse, took place at Chatsworth, Hardwick or Chiswick, one of the Devonshires' country retreats:

'It is related of [Brummell] that he came one morning into the library of a noble friend, at whose house he was frequently a visitor, and told him, with much warmth and sincerity of manner, that he was very sorry, very sorry indeed but he must positively leave.

'Why, you were not to go till next month!' said the hospitable peer.

'True, true,' replied Brummell anxiously, 'but I must be off.'

'But what for?'

'Why the fact is – I am in love with your duchess.'

'Well, my dear fellow, never mind that, so was I twenty years ago – is she in love with you?'

The Beau hesitated, and after for a few seconds staring at the white sheep-skin rug, said faintly, 'I – believe she is.'

'Oh! That alters the case entirely,' replied the peer, 'I will send for your post horse immediately.'

Jesse's anecdote, like so many in his collection, is deliberately vague about persons, place and dates, but there is every reason to believe this story was current in London as a minor comic scandal involving the Duchess of Devonshire. If so, it places Brummell in an idealised light as *chevalier d'honneur* in their poetic tale of courtly love: knowing precisely when to bow out once his sentiments, out of keeping with the tradition, are returned in kind by his lady.

In 1806 Georgiana died unexpectedly, and in great pain, from an abscess on the liver. Brummell was as shocked and moved as the many who had found her the most vivacious and exciting woman in London. William Roscoe had recently had some success with a poem meant for children but taken up by many, called *The Butterfly's Ball*. In memory of Georgiana, Brummell himself wrote a companion piece, *The Butterfly's Funeral*. Such poems, he later wrote, 'were in vogue with all the world in London' and because Georgiana Spencer had been the sort of celebrity whose death – like that of her distant kinswoman, Diana Spencer – was treated as an occasion for public mourning, Brummell briefly found an alternative and unexpected fame himself, as the people's poet:

The Butterfly's Funeral

Oh ye! Who so lately were blythesome and gay,
At the Butterfly's banquet carousing away;
Your feasts and your revels of pleasure are fled,
For the soul of the banquet, the Butterfly's dead!

No longer the Flies and the Emmets advance,
To join with the friends in the Grasshopper dance;
For see his thin form o'er the favourite bed,
And the Grasshopper mourns for the loss of his friend.

And here shall the daisy and violet blow,
And the lily discover her bosom of snow;
While under the leaf, in the evenings of spring,
Still mourning his friend shall the Grasshopper sing.

What is one to make of such whimsy? Brummell was right to proscribe the poem in years to come with the explanation that it was the fashion of the time, and it should be read also with the usual allowances for the recently bereaved. *The Butterfly's*

Funeral, however, was an unexpected commercial success (Brummell's only one and, like most society poets of the period, he did not benefit financially by a single penny). It sold three thousand copies as soon as it came out, and its publisher, John Wallis, went on to sell more. It also set Brummell in the public mind as the Grasshopper, and it described, in a sense accurately, the false, childlike world in which he, Georgiana and their friends lived. To the rest of the world, fascinated though they might be by the scandalous liaisons and gargantuan debts of Georgiana, she, like Brummell, lived an unreal existence, as light as quicksilver and as insubstantial as grass.

More perplexing, however, is what to make of an 'affair' conducted over several years by two of the leading celebrities of the age that has left in its wake no letters, no gossip and little evidence beyond sentimental verse. Doubtless, had the infatuation moved towards anything worthy of gossip there would be a record, so it is fair to assume that the two social gadflies from different generations held a mutual fascination for each other more thrilling for them than romance. In any event he was, in the time-honoured phrase, young enough to be her son.

A touching coda on the affair is presented by Georgiana's daughter, Lady Harriet Cavendish. She also met Brummell in Hyde Park and around London after she was presented to society in 1802, but was unimpressed with many of her mother's more glittering friends. 'Mr Brummell,' she later wrote, 'keeps us waiting rather than wishing for him. I feel it a matter of perfect indifference whether he arrives at any moment or not at all.' He was due at a house party she was holding at Tixall Hall in Staffordshire, an event all but buried in the emotional fall-out of her mother's generation's sexual roundelays. For one thing, Harriet had been married off to Lord Granville Leveson Gower, even though he had two illegitimate children with Georgiana's sister Lady Bessborough. Lady Bessborough was also among the guests, as both aunt-in-law and mistress of the host, along with her married daughter, Lady Caroline Lamb, who was deranged with love for Brummell's friend Lord Byron and 'alternating in tearing spirits and in tears'. Perhaps Brummell was meant to lighten the occasion. He and Harriet took refuge from the emotional dramas around them in memories of her mother. He sketched for her a copy of the famous Joshua Reynolds painting of Harriet's mother and sister at play. She gave him a poem she had written about her mother that she thought he might understand: 'The Voice of Praise'. It concludes:

> The lover lulls his rankling wound
> By hanging on his fair one's name!
> The mother listens for the sound
> Of her young warrior's growing fame.
> Thy voice can soothe the mourning dame
> Of her soul's wedded partner riven,
> Who cherishes the hallow'd flame
> Parted on Earth, to meet in Heaven!
>
> That voice can quiet passion's mood,
> Can humble merit raise on high,
> And from the wise, and from the good
> It breathes of immortality!
> There is a lip, there is an eye
> Where most I love to see it shine,
> To hear it speak, to feel it sigh,
> My Mother! Need I say 'tis thine?

In losing Georgiana, in 1806, Brummell had not lost a great love, but in its way the removal of the Voice of Praise was as damaging to him as if he had. Not only would the death of this glamorous mother-figure have reopened the wounds of his own mother's death, but had she lived, Georgiana might have been the ideal voice of admonition: she had known all the beauties of society; she had also known all the dangers of gambling.

❧

Lady Elizabeth Howard, who had grown up at Castle Howard as the daughter of the 5th Earl of Carlisle, was, unlike Georgiana, a contemporary of Brummell. Born in 1780, she came out in London society at the same time as Brummell, but almost immediately became engaged to the twenty-one-year-old Duke of Rutland. She was nineteen. The duke, who had inherited the ancient title and the estates and castles that went with it as a nine-year-old boy, was not a close friend of Brummell. His wilder younger brothers, however – Lords Charles and Robert Manners – were, and it was through these two fellow dragoons that Brummell met the duchess at the duke's lavish coming-of-age party at Belvoir Castle in the winter of 1799. Brummell had been invited as a friend of the younger Manners brothers as well as of the principal guest, the Prince of Wales.

1798–99 was one of the bitter winters that pitted the last decades of the eighteenth century, and there was skating on the lake near the castle. A bullock was roasted in honour of the twenty-first birthday, and was said to be frozen on the side that wasn't cooked. There were fireworks and dances for the noble visitors and the local populace. Brummell put noses slightly out of joint, first for skating in an *outré* fur *pelisse*, rather too well and too early in the morning, such that locals came to applaud him in the mistaken belief that he *was* the Prince of Wales. Then his actions led to a full fire alert at the castle, with alarums ringing into the night, when he pulled the fire-bell rope that hung near his bedroom. As pandemonium raged through the castle, which was crowded with visitors for the festivities, young Mr Brummell stuck his head out of his window and apologised loudly for 'having disturbed you, but the fact was my valet forgot to bring my hot water'.

Lady Elizabeth Howard, another guest, married the party's host within a few months. Brummell became a firm favourite with the new young duchess, as he was with her brothers-in-law, but seemingly never hit it off with the duke. Elizabeth and he shared a passion for sketching and watercolours – she later published sketches from her tours of France and the West Country – and, although he stabled horses at the nearby Peacock Inn, he generally avoided the hunting that was a feature of Belvoir hospitality in favour of spending time with her. If his relationship with Georgiana was literary, it was painterly with Elizabeth, Duchess of Rutland. She executed views of the estate in watercolours, and used her specialist interest in landscape to begin remodelling the gardens at Belvoir. Early in her marriage she began planning renovations to the ancient castle, that, with the architect James Wyatt, would eventually inspire the prince regent's similar reinvention of a Gothic castle at Windsor. Brummell, meanwhile, sketched from life and from other painters, and at least once painted Elizabeth herself. Captain Gronow noted an attentive Brummell at Almack's Club in London, talking 'earnestly to the charming Duchess of Rutland', and Brummell himself later admitted that the duchess and he 'were great friends in those days'.

She seems to have relished the more sympathetic company of Brummell to the boorish, boyish crowd enjoyed by her husband and his brothers, the 'Bad Manners'. When she presented her husband with the longed-for heir, a full fourteen years after their marriage, Brummell appeared to have expectations of being appointed a godfather. He wrote from Oatlands Park, Surrey, in August 1813:

> My dear Duke
> I must beg to offer my most sincere congratulations upon the birth of your son, an event which I am sensible the Duchess and yourself will hail with every satisfaction – and may his future years be as permanent in 'bloom' as his first appearance promises . . . As to young Granby I will answer for his welfare, at least till the age of eighteen when he is sure to be ruined by the Turf from the natural propensity to it which he is certain to imbibe from his Father and the place of his nativity [Cheveley, near Newmarket Races].
> Yrs without a guinea
> George Brummell

His cheeky suggestion that he stand as guardian or godfather to the much-titled tot was not taken up – and over the years the Manners family found Brummell to be a particularly bad example to its younger members.

This letter was written towards the end of his friendship with the duchess: over the years their happy companionship cooled markedly. The closeness they found during hours sketching and talking together declined at some point late in Brummell's London career. Bulwer Lytton put forward the explanation that: '[A noblewoman] easily consoles herself for the loss of a [dandy] lover – she converts him into a friend and thinks herself, nor is she much deceived, benefited by the exchange.' Yet Elizabeth had never thought of Brummell as a lover so much as a complicit companion in the struggle to maintain metropolitan manners in a household that Jesse typifies as full of 'greasy galloping farmers'. Her loyalties were to her class and her husband (and the family money).

Brummell inveigled the younger Manners brothers into ever more hazardous financial affairs, but worse than that, from Elizabeth's perspective, he presumed too much on the friendship built up at Belvoir when he was in the harsher light of London society. He came near to insulting the duchess's sister, Lady Catherine Howard, at one London ball in an exchange that seems to reveal Brummell a little the worse for drink: having 'cruised around the room asking everyone where he could find a partner who would not throw him into a perspiration, [he] at last cried out "Ah, there she is! – yes, Catherine will do: I think I may venture with her."'

And London was also shocked when Mr Brummell presumed publicly to give the Duchess of Rutland – his contemporary but still one of the highest-ranking noblewomen in the land – advice on fashion: 'In heaven's name, my dear Duchess, what is the meaning of that extraordinary back of yours? I declare I must put you on a backboard and positively walk out of the room backwards, that I mayn't see it.' If Brummell considered this a witty impertinence, the deeply offended duchess and others in the room certainly did not.

He remained a regular guest at Cheveley, the Mannerses' estate near Newmarket (it was said a room was kept permanently in readiness for him) and he was so well known at Belvoir that one of his horses remained stabled there in the care of a groom called Fryatt, but it must be assumed Brummell's invitations came increasingly from the Manners brothers and not from the duchess. Nevertheless, when she died in 1825, Brummell was moved to break the silence of decades between himself and the duke to express his sorrow:

Dec 3 1825

My Lord,

You will no doubt at the present distressing moment be surprised if not offended at my taking the liberty to address you. Years have passed away since I had the honour to be numbered amongst those who shared your early friendship . . . the remembrance of former times, the happiest in my life, when during many months of the year I was received in your Grace's family almost as an inmate, presses deeply upon my heart at an instant like this . . .

~

The woman whose friendship endured the longest, and who has the strongest claim to have been the love of Brummell's life was a royal duchess: Princess Frederica Charlotte Ulrica Catherine, Princess Royal of Prussia and Duchess of York and Albany. She was twelve years his senior. Princess Frederica had grown up in the court of King William II of Prussia, spoke English with a strong German accent and corresponded invariably in French, signing herself 'Frederique'. Brummell wrote back in English. She and Brummell first met in 1800 through her husband, the Prince of Wales's bluff brother Frederick, Duke of York and Albany. The royal couple were already nearly a decade into their childless marriage and nearly as long into an informal though amicable separation. The duke lived in London at his house in Piccadilly, later converted into apartments and named after his second title, Albany, or he lived with his regiments. The duchess occupied Oatlands Park, near Weybridge in Surrey. The Yorks had bought Oatlands on their marriage in 1791 with the impressive allowances of £18,000 from the Civil List, £7000 from Ireland and a full

£45,000 a year from the duke's holdings as Prince-Bishop of Osnabruck. Prince Fred visited 'Princess Fred' at weekends, but kept a mistress, Mrs Clarke, in town.

Thomas Raikes was certain of the issue between Princess Fred and Beau Brummell: to begin with she was the most useful stepping-stone in his social ascendancy. 'The Duchess [of York] was very partial to Brummell, and, as she has great finesse and was a very nice discriminator of good breeding and manner the approbation of such a woman must be highly creditable to the individual himself.' She was kind and cultured but possibly rather bored with the Hanoverian court. London's fashion-conscious *Bon Ton Magazine* implied criticism when it wrote that 'The Duchess resides entirely at Oatlands and sees no one but the royal family.'

She shared with Brummell a love of animals, of sketching and of house-party frolics. Brummell's acceptance in society was enormously bolstered by his popularity in the affable alternative 'court' at Oatlands. His power base widened from the Prince of Wales and the Duke of York's louche and pseudo-military circle of loud men, to one in which he was equally at home: a house-party set only hours from London.

I have several times stayed at Oatlands with the Duke and Duchess of York – both of them most amiable and agreeable persons [wrote one regular house guest], we were generally a company of about fifteen, and our being invited to remain there 'another day' sometimes depended on the ability of our royal host and hostess to raise sufficient money for our entertainment. [Despite their impressive income, the Yorks were constantly in debt.] We used to have all sorts of ridiculous fun. The Duchess kept, beside a number of dogs for which there was a regular burial-place, a collection of monkeys. Lord Alvanley and Monk Lewis [were] great favourites at Oatlands along with Beau Brummell.

Oatlands, by virtue of having a legitimate regal chatelaine who was also considered a charming hostess, was unique among the royal palaces, and it had a special place in the memories of those who were invited there as a result. 'Oatlands might be deemed a court,' wrote Raikes, 'in which the affability on one side and the respectful attention on the other were equally remarkable . . . [it was] the only existing retreat of correct manners and high breeding.' The stamp of character upon the place was Princess Frederica's, and Oatlands came to represent an attractive hybrid of aristocratic respectability and distinct eccentricity. Princess Frederica kept many animals, mainly dogs but also monkeys, parrots, a llama and a kangaroo, and was said to have been distraught when Oatlands had a major fire – not by the damage it caused so much as the upset to her animals. Their elaborate mausoleums are the only legacy at Oatlands of this characterful and popular hostess.

In truth Frederica was not greatly suited to the Hanoverian British court at the beginning of the nineteenth century. It was not that she was an intellectual, but she was more keenly interested in her immediate domestic sphere and friends and, unfashionably, the welfare of animals, than with the court or high society. '*Mein Gott*,' she was quoted saying, as imitated by Monk Lewis, 'dey are so dependent on us for kindness and protection, I t'ink we ought to love dem, if only to wake the better part of our nature; dey are sincere; dey are honest.' A Newfoundland dog walked obediently in her funeral cortège some years later, from Oatlands to Weybridge church. In this somewhat suburban, dog-loving mien she might be seen as the precursor to modern British royal ladies. 'The Duchess of York is a pattern for others to emulate,' wrote *Bon Ton Magazine*, but could find little more exhilarating to say about her than that 'she pays her tradesmen's bills regularly, and writes her own drafts on her banker'. These were enclosed with her trademark pink notepaper, heavily embossed with flowers and lyres.

She was somewhat ahead of her time in seeing part of the role of royal consort as charitable, and put her name to innocuous local causes. Barely a year after her marriage her support was solicited in a much more political campaign: slavery abolition in the West Indies. 'It has been mentioned,' intoned the obsequious writer of *An Address to HRH the Dutchess* [sic] *of York Against the Use of Sugar*, 'that you were the friend of the poor and that your acts of beneficence were such as required exertion.' She did not or could not lend her name to the abolitionist cause but it was supposed she talked to the duke about it. She was briefly then the focus for that mixture of gallantry, prurience and politicking that surrounded a new member of the royal family, but it did not survive her seclusion at Oatlands. Public attention soon moved on, forgot that she had briefly inspired a fashion for tiny tight shoes, and she was left in peace.

She was not, however, unattached to the capital. She made dutiful appearances at court and at the opera, but chose to stay twenty miles to the south-west with her pets, and receive weekly gossip and updates on the metropolis from the crowd around Brummell she asked down for weekends.

A chaise was booked every Friday to leave St James's Street at five o'clock with the Duke of York and any of his party to go to Oatlands. The initial invitation to Brummell was certainly on the assumption that he would be an entertaining house guest for the duke and would help keep him, to some extent, away from the card tables. But Frederica enjoyed the attentions lavished on her by her husband's young friend. She had 'a very superior mind', according to one Oatlands visitor, 'highly cultivated by books . . . she was able to take the lead on any subject . . . she had very refined taste and great knowledge.' She was a county lady who knew all about the world, but had decided to withdraw from the city in favour of her garden, dogs and – in her case – shell-decked 'grottoes'. Oatlands was the ideal weekend retreat from the hurly-burly of the West End and Brummell came to treasure it – and Frederica.

Oddly enough the Yorks' marriage was known as one of 'the most unvarying steadfast affection' and she and the duke ended their days on good terms. The early years of their marriage, however, before and during her friendship with Brummell, were typified by structured and consensual separations, despite the intense pressure on them both to provide further heirs (the duke was second in line to the throne when they married). This distance may be explained by some sexual misalliance. The princess was fastidious and sensitive. The duke was 'big, burly, loud and cursing'. He became embroiled in so disastrous a sex-scandal – his mistress sold military commissions and was arraigned in front of the House of Lords – that he was forced to resign as army commander-in-chief. Some claimed the Yorks had an open marriage, and there was some likelihood of this once it became widely known from her less-than-discreet doctor that medical opinion considered her incapable of producing an heir. If she did take lovers, Brummell was a prime candidate. 'Believe me that no one can feel the loss of your society more keenly than I do,' she wrote coyly in French. 'I will never forget the tender moments that I have had because of you, and the only thing that can compensate me would be the certainty of your welfare.' She sent him lavish presents and also tenderly home-wrought items including hand-sewn cushions. They once bought a lottery ticket together, with what future spending in mind one can only speculate.

He gave her a dog – which they immediately christened 'Fidelité'. 'No one could be more sensible than I to your kind thoughts on my birthday,' she wrote to him. 'Please accept my most sincere thanks for this handsome little dog, that, I like to flatter myself, can be a symbol of faithfulness in our ongoing friendship, to which I can assure you I attach the highest value.' He even once essayed that most reckless of gifts from a man to a woman: a dress. It was made entirely of Brussels lace and he thought it would suit her. It cost him 150 guineas.

At least one rather lavish gift is recorded in return: for Christmas 1815, Princess Frederica ordered for Brummell a tortoiseshell and gold-inlay snuff-box. It was one of the more expensive items on the shopping list she gave her lady-in-waiting, but, at ten pounds, cost rather less than he had spent on her. Brummell's Christmases and New Year's Eves were almost invariably spent at Oatlands. The princess imported German Christmas traditions to England a full generation before Prince

Albert effected a similar change in royal and British yuletide festivities. The first Christmas tree in Britain – loaded with oranges and sweetmeats – was probably the one displayed at Oatlands Christmases early in the nineteenth century, and Princess Frederica converted the whole ballroom at Oatlands into a traditional German Christmas fair, with greenery, gingerbread and candles. Richard Sheridan, beset by debts but still the 'best company in England', was often a member of the Oatlands party. He wrote a long poetic dialogue about the revels there for Lord Erskine and himself to perform in the guise of local rustics, 'swains not exactly in the bloom of youth'. Brummell kept a copy in his album. Lord Erskine 'replied' the next Christmas with a verse of his own, also kept by Brummell, praising the 'elegant form' of the princess. Where Sheridan is quite at ease creating stage doggerel for the purposes of a house party, the former chancellor, Lord Erskine, reveals a heavy talent for obsequious flattery of his hosts. However, in describing the company around the table at New Year's Eve he comes to Brummell, 'one in gay circles well known':

> Yet, who see him in rounds of amusement alone
> Know little about him – they see him at ease,
> A high man of fashion, with talents to please;
> But believe me, in London to rise to the top
> Like Brummell (since London discarded the fop)
> You must know all that's known to the highest in place,
> And possess the rare gift to give knowledge a grace.

Was there anything more to Brummell's long and close relationship with the princess? Almost certainly. For one thing, when Brummell's creditors were pushing him to publish his memoirs, in the style of Harriette Wilson or Julia Johnstone, and secure his retirement by selling stories from his day in the high life, he refused because Princess Frederica had made him promise, he said, that as long as any of the royal brothers lived, he would not reveal anything from their shared past. This may conceivably have been out of extreme loyalty to her husband, who had heaped scandal on the Royal Family already. Frederica may, as a royal princess, have felt a strong loyalty to the tarnished Crown and the benighted person of the regent and simply wanted to preserve him from further revelations about their wilder youth. But these seem insufficient claims on her or Brummell's indulgence. Probably there was something more specific she wanted kept secret . . . an affair to which Brummell could allude only by mentioning her name whenever he was asked why he would not publish his memoirs. To some this looked like either extreme gallantry or extreme foolishness. Others guessed that his gentlemanly code of honour kept one card close to his heart.

According to one report, the duke once caught the duchess *in flagrante delicto* when he returned to Oatlands unexpectedly. With whom, it is not known. But when Brummell died, one of the few possessions he had kept from his days in the high life was a miniature of a woman's eye. An odd keepsake – but one that in its day was given as a token between lovers. The prince regent kept a miniature in exactly the same style of Mrs Fitzherbert, the love of his life; it was buried with him. Brummell's miniature was of the left eye of Princess Frederica.

8

THE
DANDY CLUBS

No tender love-suits in their thoughts could he trace,
The suits of the Tailor had taken their place,
For beauty's soft chains that the true lover feels,
They had only brass chains, dangling over their heels,
He could read in the hearts of those dashing young Friskers
Only curricles, Overalls, Boots and Large Whiskers.
Haut Ton or Cupid in Bond Street, c. 1806

White's and Brooks's, the St James's Street gentlemen's clubs, both elected Brummell as a new member when he first moved to London in 1799, and he later became a founding member of Watier's club and its president for life. His late afternoons were spent in the elegant fug of these clubs, from which women were barred, and two of which, White's and Brooks's, remain today much as they were when he knew them.

The most important of the Regency clubs, because of the difficulty of entry, was White's. Founded in 1693, originally as White's Chocolate House on the site that is now Boodle's on St James's Street, the club was considered practically an alternative House of Lords by the time Brummell was elected at the end of the eighteenth century. 'To be admitted a member of that body gave a young man a "cachet" such as nothing else could give.' For Brummell, known initially only to the Prince of Wales's set, these clubs were an entrée to the wider world of establishment men. Though Watier's became briefly a rival in terms of exclusivity, membership of White's was such a supreme form of distinction within London society that Disraeli was moved to compare acceptance as an accolade outranking the Order of the Garter.

White's had been established as a refuge for Tory grandees, but by 1800 its politics were subordinate to its social pre-eminence to the extent that Brummell, a notional Whig, could become a leading member. He revived the club's reputation among the young and fashionable, rather than simply among the aristocratic and distinguished, thereby helping to blur the lines between the Old Club and the Young Club. As a side-effect, White's finances improved steadily during Brummell's time as a member, as young men stayed later and spent more. The Rules of the Club, dating from 1781, laid down the ten guineas annual membership, procedures for terminating subscriptions and for 'blackballing' aspiring candidates. The Rules also stipulated that the 300 strong membership was to be renewed every time it fell to 280, by twenty new members chosen by a committee. The nineteen others who joined with Brummell in 1799 were nearly all in their twenties, and members already of his unofficial Dandiacal Body.

The façade of White's clubhouse – formerly the home of the Countess of Northumberland – was remodelled during the second half of the eighteenth century, and a little later a bay window was added over a former doorway that became a landmark on St James's Street. Here Brummell held court in the afternoons, in a bow window that became known as the Beau Window. The men of the Dandiacal Body re-formed several hours after they had gone their separate ways from Chesterfield Street, 'mustered in force' around Brummell's chair in the Beau Window, watching the world go by and telling jokes. It was said that 'an ordinary frequenter of White's would as soon have thought of taking his seat on the throne in the House of Lords as of appropriating one of the chairs in the bow window'. Lord William Pitt Lennox was one of their number and described Brummell 'holding his own, in [his] quiet manner, above the brilliant sestette', but struggled to define the comic moment: 'The conversation upon the topics and the scandal of the day . . . wild humour has its instant, its supreme moment for real enjoyment, and that pleasantry which has kept a company in a roar of laughter at the right time is vapid when revived.'

Some of Brummell's uglier *bons mots* can be placed to the chair in the Beau Window – even when they cannot be dated. When asked if he had seen his brother in town, Brummell replied to his friends that he had ordered his rustic relative 'to walk the back-streets' until he had visited a decent tailor. When asked what he had thought of a weekend in the country, he said he had had to return to town, as he had found a cobweb in his chamber-pot. Grantley Berkeley, Coldstream Guards officer and son of Earl Berkeley by his mistress Mary Cole, recorded one particularly inane conversation among the dandies, at the expense of one less well dressed:

'My dear fellow,' said Brummell, 'where did you pick up that extraordinary affair you have put on your back? I protest I have never seen anything so singular.'

'Most singular indeed,' said Lord Yarmouth.

'Maybe it's an heirloom?' Lord Fife suggested.

'Coeval with Alfred the Great, at least,' observed Lord Alvanley.

'Exactly!' said Lord Wilton.

'It is not your fault, mine goot sir,' said Prince Esterhazy, 'you shall be not to blame because a devoid-of-conscience-influencing tradesman deceived you when you him the honour do to purchase of his delusive fabrics.'

'*Is there anything the matter with my coat?*'

'Coat?' exclaimed Brummell. 'Coat?' cried the others in chorus. 'For heaven's sake my dear fellow, don't misapply names so abominably! It is no more like a coat than it is to a cauliflower – if it is, I'll be damned!'

Such was the style that passed for repartee among the fashionistas of White's Beau Window.

The world of White's was tight, exclusive and, some claimed, bitchy. 'Damn the fellows,' retorted a notoriously bad-tempered member of the Guards' Club opposite, who had been denied membership of White's, 'they're upstarts, fit only for the society of tailors.' The Beau Window serves as a perfect image for the *Haut Ton*, the society Brummell conquered: insular, indolent, looking out on the world and down on it. It also encouraged men of fashion in an age before mass-media to hone their skills as fashion commentators or, given the inability of passers-by to respond, as voyeurs. The members of Brummell's Beau Window set were, in a sense, the first 'fashion police'. When the Beau Window was enlarged in 1811, Henry Luttrell thought the fact worthy of record, which inspired him to satirical verse:

> Shot from yon *Heavenly Bow* at White's,
> A critic arrow now alights
> On some unconscious passer-by,
> Whose cape's an inch too low or high;
> Whose doctrines are unsound in hat,
> In boots, in trousers, in cravat.
> On him who braves the shame and guilt
> Of gig or Tilbury ill-built;
> Sports a barouche with panels darker
> Than the last shade turned out by Barker,
> Or canters with an awkward seat
> And badly mounted, up the street.

However, the comment, censure and wit of the Beau Window was not all fashion-conscious, fatuous or ill-considered. Sir William Fraser in his *Words on Wellington* wrote later that 'within that sacred semi-circle . . . there was more shrewdness, good sense and knowledge of things, to be found than in any other space of the same size on the face of the globe'. Brummell passed judgements not just on dress from his chair in White's window, but also on gentlemanly behaviour. The Duke of Wellington was not a man to be impressed by clothes, yet Sir William Fraser, who knew him well, claimed he 'had a high opinion of that mysterious and terrible tribunal, "White's Bow Window"'. The duke said that the Guards were the most troublesome people in the army when there was nothing to do, but when active operations began, they were the best soldiers. None of them misbehaved when there was duty to be done. 'White's Window would not permit it.'

~

Slightly less fashionable than White's, but joined by Brummell nonetheless, was Brooks's. This was and is just across the street from White's, slightly nearer St James's Palace. It had been founded only twenty years before by the former manager of another club, Almack's, called William Brooks, and initially it was the most political of the clubs – 'the most famous political club that will ever have existed in London'. While the Church of England received the discourtesy title of the 'Tory Party at Prayer', Brooks's became known as the 'Whig Party at Dinner'. Brummell later expressed the opinion that 'the Whigs kept the best company' in London.

Brooks's was arguably the most elegant of the London clubs in architectural terms. Henry Holland, son-in-law of Capability Brown and architect to the Prince of Wales, had created in the Great Subscription Room one of the finest interiors in London. Restrained, neo-classical, the style of Brooks's was the style its members exported to their country seats and civic buildings all over Britain and beyond. The walls in Brummell's day were greenish grey and the curtains red damask. There were painted allegories over the doors, appropriately Bacchus, Venus and Cupid, and one of the largest barrel vaults in the capital, festooned with gilt swags, crowned the famous Subscription Room. The effect, however, was cool and patrician. The Eating Room, just right beyond the Venetian Window, was even painted in the buff colours of the Whig Party, the same muted colours Brummell chose for his pantaloons and waistcoat, setting the fashion for all Brooks's members to do the same.

Brummell was invited to join by his father's Westminster drinking partners, Charles James Fox and Richard Sheridan, and Brooks's, by 1800, had acquired a good deal of their louche and high-spending reputation. The club had entered its years as a

gambling den, where family fortunes accumulated over generations were lost on the roll of a die or turn of a card. But if
fortunes were lost, others were made. One founder member, Mr
Thynne, 'having won only £12,000 during the last two months
[from fellow members] . . . retired in disgust'. On the other hand
Lord Cholmondeley and Mr Thompson of Grosvenor Square
made nearly £400,000 between them at the Brooks's tables from
other club members.

When Brummell joined, the club was populated by a slightly
more raucous, though older, crowd than White's. Garrick, the
ageing theatre star, was a member. So, too, was the Duke of York,
who had once become so intoxicated at the club with some older
cronies that he and they wrecked all the furniture and were
persuaded off the premises only at the open end of a blunderbuss.
Brooks's members had also included the more sedate Sir Joshua
Reynolds, the slavery abolitionist William Wilberforce, the historians and philosophers David Hume and Edward Gibbon, the
prime minister William Pitt, and Thomas Greville, whose book
collection was one nexus of the British Museum. It was a
mixed crowd. Brummell joined with his friends Poodle Byng
and Thomas 'Apollo' Raikes and encouraged, as at White's, a
return to the roaring days of the clubs' and members' youth. The
tone at Brooks's, therefore, changed somewhat between day and
night, as the older men, generally, left the club to the gambling
and drinking of a younger, more aristocratic crowd, unencum-
bered by families, scruples or political careers.

Brooks's was open, in effect, twenty-four hours a day. Of the
fifteen dukes who were members at the end of the eighteenth
century, the Duke of Devonshire was perhaps the most habitual
all-night attendee. He so frequently avoided Georgiana's parties
at Devonshire House by staying through the night at Brooks's,
dining alone on 'broiled blade-bone of mutton', that he and the
shoeshine boy who worked outside were practically on first-name
terms. Over the years a night at Brooks's ended for many with a
trip to a usurer or money-lender – often in the City – to secure a
loan to pay the gambling debts accrued in the club. One of the

first rooms Brummell passed, therefore, on entering Brooks's during the afternoon, the Strangers' Room, became known as 'the Jerusalem Chamber' as it was so often crowded with Jewish money-lenders during the day, attempting to accost members and retrieve their money.

On the whole the serious card and dice gambling of Brooks's and White's was left to the evening. Daytime gambling was of a different hue. Brummell and his friends ended arguments and disputes by entering abstruse bets in the leatherbound Betting Books that are still owned by Brooks's and White's. Members bet on horses and prize-fighters as one might expect. They also bet on the sex of their own children, or of other people's children or of their mistresses'. They bet with macabre frequency on the imminent deaths of friends and enemies and on each other's illnesses, and on the tragic degeneration of the old king's mental state. They bet through the French Revolution on the heads of France's aristocracy, and as battles loomed in the revolutionary and Napoleonic wars, they bet on who would win and how. Brummell, however, most often made political and military wagers. 'Mr Brummell bets Mr Irby one hundred guineas to ten that Buonaparte returns to Paris (Decr 12th 1812)'; 'Mr Brummell bets Mr Methuen 200 gs to 20 g that Buonaparte returns alive to Paris [from Moscow], Decr 12th 1812.' Brummell won. Similarly he entered bets on which of his friends would win by-elections and on the likely majorities in the House of Commons. No one would argue with Brummell on a matter of taste or elegance, but about politics he was forced to defend his corner and bet accordingly. His father's political intentions for his second son in sending him to Eton and Oxford paid off at least in Brummell's ability to wager and win on Westminster by-elections.

Money changed hands daily, often very large sums. No matter how much a man like Brummell might be in debt to his 'duns' – the shopkeepers, tailors and servants who supported his lifestyle – it was anathema to renege on a gambling debt for all that it was unenforceable in law. It was a debt of honour between gentlemen, taken with enormous seriousness, even though, or perhaps because, the wagers often expressed the refusal of high society to take life seriously.

White's Betting Book dates from 1743. At first the bets were recorded by a club servant but by Brummell's time they were registered by members. When they took over the responsibility one wag scribbled in the margin, 'About this time it is supposed the nobility of England began to learn to write.' The bets were meant to amuse as well as to end or defuse arguments, but they also provide a sample of the rarefied and ridiculous world in which Brummell flourished. For the gentlemen of Brooks's, White's and Watier's, the Napoleonic wars were treated with the same casual amusement as the sex of the Duke of Clarence's latest illegitimate offspring. But the bets provide a tragi-comic footnote to the world of Brummell. He and his friends described the divinity that shaped their lives with recourse to financially incontinent wagers, some of which, ultimately, provided endings in themselves.

~

The domestic arrangements of clubs like White's and Brooks's were strictly ordered, and some had already been in place for more than a generation when Brummell joined. It suited the men to keep strict regimens when it came to mealtimes and even to menus:

The dinner to be always upon the Table at a quarter past four o'clock. The Bill to be always called for at half past the Hour after Six, Supper Quarter before Eleven, Bill half an hour past twelve. Any person in the room after Dinner or Supper is upon the Table or before the time appointed in the Rules for the Bill being called for [will] pay his share of the Bill . . .

The foreign News papers of The Hague, Amsterdam, Brussels, Faulkners Dublin Paper, the Caledonian Mercury of Edinburgh besides all the London News papers must be taken . . . Tho the Prices of Dinner & Supper are fixed & [the Club] orders them without any direction from anybody, yet any Member may speak for any Dish cheap or dear but he must pay for it and it must be a

Separate Article from the Bill for that Person. NO HEALTHS DRUNK
AND NO TOASTS.

The latter instruction, presumably, was to avoid arguments,
political or personal, as much as drunken speeches. 'The menu
of a [club] dinner', according to Captain Gronow, followed a set
pattern irrespective of the establishment 'and was thus composed:
Mulligatawny and turtle soup were the dishes first placed in front
of you, a little lower the eye met with the familiar salmon at one
end of the table and turbot, surrounded by smelts, at the other.
The first course was sure to be followed by saddle of mutton, or a
piece of roast beef, and then you could take your oath that fowls,
tongue and ham would follow as assuredly as darkness follows
day.' Such were the dinners at White's and Brooks's – with
dessert, ordered by both clubs from Messrs Granges, the confectioners in Bond Street, costing as many pounds as there were
guests.

Brummell ate at his clubs. He moved twice in his time in
London, from Chesterfield Street to South Audley Street and then
to 13 Chapel Street (now Alford Street) – these houses are now
demolished – but he stayed within walking distance of his clubs.
As well as all the formal meals, when Parliament was in session
food was always laid out for *ad hoc* dining: 'cold meats, oysters
etc at 4s malt liquor only included . . . or biscuits, oranges, apples
and olives at 10s 6d'. Although there was no gaming or betting in
the Eating Rooms, there was, conversely, eating at the gaming
tables. Pulled chicken (chicken 'pulled' into shreds) was a club
favourite and also 'cold fowl, fruit, bisquits [*sic*] with to drink,
tea, coffee, cyder [*sic*] and spruce beer' (a dark molasses beer
flavoured with spruce twigs).

Brummell's clubs, Brooks's and White's, also pioneered the
meal that need not interrupt conversation or gaming, the 'sand-
wich', named after the eponymous gambling-addict earl. One of
the earliest uses of the word is to be found in the journal of
Edward Gibbon, a Brooks's member. The clubs encouraged day-
long eating and drinking for those with an appetite for either, but

the food, despite White's statutes inviting members to contribute an annual extra guinea 'towards having a good cook', was poor. Brummell turned out to be fashion-conscious about more than his clothes, and to have more in common with the gourmet Prince of Wales than an interest in tailoring: he became the leader of a small group of dissenters within clubland that sought to import finer – French – food and cooking styles. Ultimately, this led to the foundation of a new and rival club.

Captain Gronow recalled a dinner at Carlton House in 1814 attended by Brummell and other members of both White's and Brooks's when the prince asked for everyone's opinion of clubland food. Sir Thomas Stepney spoke for all the men present in describing 'the eternal joints, or beef-steaks, the boiled fowl with oyster sauce, and an apple tart – this is what we have, sir, at our clubs, and very monotonous fare it is'.

Sir Thomas – according to Thomas Raikes an 'epicurean Croesus' – was inspired to improve the situation along with Brummell and the prince. There and then the prince suggested that they found a club together aspiring to the higher ideals of the novel French cult of 'gastronomy'. Brummell was to be appointed perpetual president and the prince summoned his personal chef for advice on the kitchens. Jean Baptiste Watier – until the arrival in 1817 of the French star chef Antonin Carême, the leading authority on food in Regency England – was duly sent for from the cavernous kitchens of Carlton House. The new club, it was decided, would be named in his honour. Watier declined to cook at the club, or the prince declined on his behalf, but the chef suggested another royal cook, Labourie, to run the kitchen in his stead and Madison, a royal page, to manage it. It was soon said that 'Labourie's dinners were exquisite; the best Parisian cooks could not beat Labourie.' At first the club was billed as a musical society and singing club – there were several in London at the time – but its key selling point was the higher ideals of French gastronomy espoused by Labourie and the achingly fashionable sensibilities of its founding members. As intended, the twin attractions of the finest food in London and the famous wit and dandy Beau Brummell as perpetual president soon attracted 'all the young men of fashion and fortune'. Thomas Raikes recorded in his journal that 'the dinners were so recherché and so much talked of in town that . . . the catches and glees [the singing clubs] were superseded by card and dice and most luxurious dinners were furnished at any price, as the deep play rendered all [meal] charges a matter of indifference'. The club, at 81 Piccadilly, on the corner of Bolton Street, was a runaway success – at least, as far as the reputation of its food and its social sophistication were concerned. Unfortunately Brummell made no money from it.

Brummell's taste in food had begun typical of his class and age; Harriette Wilson described him as a dedicated carnivore. But the occasion of dining provided, for Brummell, another stage on which to shine, and he became more interested in food through his twenties and as a result of his presidency of Watier's. His famously slim and athletic figure, unsurprisingly, suffered and his weight grew steadily, especially after the opening of Watier's, from twelve stone nine (177 pounds or 81 kilos) at the start of his London career to thirteen stone ten (192 pounds or 93 kilos) a decade later. Like his young friend Byron – who took to an eccentric diet consisting of vinegar and bread – Brummell suffered from the conflicting fashions of the time: sophisticated gastronomy on the one hand and tight clothes on the other. Neither poet nor dandy maintained the figure that London society and tailors had first admired.

Watier's did not last long by clubland standards. It closed in 1817, a result of the exile of its president, Brummell, and the near ruin of most of its members. However, it set a pattern that has persisted in clubland: great chefs, trained in royal or restaurant kitchens, are headhunted by clubs to attract members. The most food-centred of the London clubs, Crockford's, which arose from the ashes of Watier's in 1828, appointed as chefs first Louis Eustache Ude and then Francatelli, pupil of Antonin Carême. Consequently Brummell played a part in introducing French *haute cuisine* to clubland. Watier's and Labourie set a pattern followed subsequently by many London clubs in quietly educating English gentlemen about fine French food and wines.

Drinking was heavy during club meals and beyond. 'There were then four- and even five-bottle men,' according to Captain Gronow, only kept from alcohol poisoning by the slow progress of their inebriation: they were 'drinking very slowly' on account of the 'very small glasses'. Even so three dandies were known as six-bottle men: Lords Panmure, Dufferin and Blayney were regularly so drunk that they were 'reduced to a state after dinner [that anyone half sober] would pronounce them fit for nothing but bed'. Despite the wars with France, claret, burgundy and champagne were still consumed, along with port, sherry, Madeira and Marsala. It had been the custom of Tories and Jacobites to drink French wines, in deference to 'the King over the water' (the Stuart Pretender) while Whigs drank the more politically neutral port. But by 1800 lines had blurred. Pitt remained a confirmed port drinker, but the Peninsular Wars gave the British Army a taste again for claret – supplied out of Bordeaux – and the London clubs restocked it after the Anglo-Russian occupations of Paris in 1814 and 1815. Brummell favoured champagne, which was then weaker, sweeter and less fizzy than its modern counterpart, though some of the suppliers' names are recognisable: Moët and Dom Pérignon. Brummell himself drank with greater moderation during his high life in London than he had during his days with the dragoons, although, from time to time, he was described as drunk by Harriette Wilson and by the Duke of York among others.

At the clubs, snuff had ousted smoking as the tobacco-vice of choice. By 1773, Dr Johnson had noted that 'smoking has quite gone out' but it took Brummell and the dandies to put an end, temporarily as it turned out, to pipes and cigars in fashionable London circles. Snuff – the ground, often moist stems of the tobacco plant – was very expensive. Spanish Stuff, the Prince of Wales's favourite, cost three pounds a pound. Brummell bought snuff for the prince as early as 1799: a pound of Bureau and Canister as a thank-you token for we know not what, priced at seven shillings and sixpence. Between 1810 and 1824, of the ten regimental messes with accounts at the snuff purveyors Fribourg and Treyer, only two bought cigars as well as snuff, and White's accounts concur that snuff was what gentlemen, in Brummell's time, preferred. Brummell bought Martinique, twenty to thirty pounds at a time as it arrived fresh from the London docks, with an occasional jar or two of Marino or Macouba – the latter scented with attar of roses.

Brummell was the supreme dictator at his clubs, but especially at Watier's, of the manner in which snuff was to be taken. It was a habit defined by its paraphernalia as much as the addictive pleasure of tobacco. The small hinged boxes were kept in the hidden pockets of tail coats, or, if they were slim, in the side pockets of waistcoats. Brummell maintained that snuff-boxes should be opened and the snuff taken from box to nostril with the use of only one hand. This required dexterity and concentration. Of course, the ideal was to effect the whole operation mid-sentence without appearing even to glance at the expensive commodity or its more expensive container. Brummell flicked open the lid of the snuff-box with the thumb of his right hand, which had the effect of presenting the lid, usually highly decorated or even jewelled, to the onlooker. Then the same thumb was used to convey a small amount of snuff in the indentation by the thumbnail to the nose, the box meanwhile held at the chin. A small nicotine 'hit' was thereby delivered via the septum as powdered cocaine was taken in the jazz age. The haughty angle of the head that became a feature of dandy caricatures, and is the pose taken by Brummell in one miniature, may have been a tilt adopted by habitual snuff-takers to avoid unsightly brown drips. This appears, parenthetically, to be the etymology of the terms 'toffee-nosed' and by extension 'toff'. 'Sniff [the snuff] with precision,' one 1800 dandy manual advises, 'with both nostrils, and without any grimace.'

Brummell's collection of elaborate boxes was sold off after his exile, but many from the period survive and the descendants who own the Brummell family portraits have also inherited a large collection of snuff-boxes, some of which are likely to have been Beau's. The snuff-box lid miniatures express political or amorous affiliations or depict pets, houses, children or classical or erotic scenes. One popular design was in the shape of a woman's lower leg and shoe. One of Brummell's had an invisible hinge, called a 'Lawrence Kirk', which caused much amusement at Carlton House when the prince failed to find a way in. Lord Liverpool, the prime minister (son of the Brummell family lodger, Charles Jenkinson), tried to open it with a knife, prompting Brummell to cry out, 'My Lord! Allow me to observe that's not an oyster but a snuff-box!'

Brummell's habit of collecting snuff-boxes was copied by the Prince of Wales and the Duke of York. The latter did not even like snuff, but was given so many boxes for his collection he decided eventually to have them melted down and made into a silver-gilt salver with the names of all the donors on the side.

Brummell was not above using his influence to his own financial ends – at least to the extent of making a joke of the situation. When the snuff purveyors Fribourg and Treyer had a new consignment or 'hogshead' of snuff due to be opened, they invited Brummell to take the first sniff in the hope he would spread the fashion for a new brand as he might a new cut of waistcoat.

The hogshead was duly opened in the presence of the arbiter [Brummell] who, after taking a few pinches, gravely pronounced it a detestable compound and not at all the style of thing that any man, with the slightest pretensions to correct taste could possibly patronize. This . . . petrified the purveyors, and the companions of [Brummell] left him to discuss the matter with the proprietors. No sooner had they gone than Brummell said 'By some oversight I did not put my name down on your Martinique list . . . since the Hogshead has been condemned you won't object to my having three jars full of it.' Messrs Fribourg gladly yielded [according to Jesse at least], for in a few days it having become known [that Brummell was taking the new snuff] not a grain was left.

It was Byron who dubbed Watier's the Dandy Club. He cited four dandies as the prime movers in the club, Brummell, Alvanley, Henry Mildmay and Henry Pierrepoint. They were also members of Brooks's and White's, like most of the members of Watier's. But where White's and Brooks's had other affiliations, as political party headquarters and gambling dens and also had long-established membership, Watier's relied entirely on the dandy set. The evanescence of the club was ordained in its foundation; Brummell was the club's key player and its fate was linked to his.

Brummell initially had 'the good sense to eschew [the] deep potations, blade-bones of mutton and the music of the dice box' at Watier's, wrote Captain Jesse. ' 'Tis true he dropped in occasionally on their orgies . . . to enjoy the jokes, but not to steep his own intellects in wine.'

This was all to change after his relationship with the Prince of Wales went into decline. At Watier's, Brummell had sown the seeds of his downfall – or, at least, the financial aspect of it. He developed there what would now be termed a gambling addiction. So long as the gambling was restricted to the inanities of the Betting Book he and his fortune were relatively safe: he could return to Chesterfield Street with cash in his pocket or the promise of it, where Robinson awaited him with a more formal change of clothes for the evening. Later in the day, however, the gaming got much more serious at the clubs, and at Watier's in particular. As perpetual president of a club that became as notorious for gambling as for gastronomy, Brummell's dangerous addiction was fed and encouraged daily, to the despair of his friends and of his growing number of creditors.

EVENING

9
THEATRE ROYAL

Not a nod, not a curtsey that was not the result of art; nor a look nor a smile that was not designed for murder; all affected indifference and ease, while their hearts at the same time burned for conquest.

Oliver Goldsmith at the theatre

Many a beau turned his head wishfully towards our box, anxiously waiting to observe a vacancy . . . Beau Brummell, Fred Bentinck, Lord Fife, the Duc de Berri and a great many more were visitors [but] when the performance had concluded, we always remained late in the rooms, amusing ourselves with George Brummell.

Harriette Wilson, *Memoirs*

After nightfall the most dazzlingly illuminated spaces in London were the theatres. Just two had Royal Patents to perform plays – the Theatre Royal, Drury Lane, and Covent Garden. The King's Theatre (confusingly, later Her Majesty's) was the primary opera house and there was a fourth drama venue opposite the King's on the Haymarket, called the Little Theatre, though its licence to perform plays extended through the summer season only. The Lyceum on the Strand achieved popularity after the Drury Lane company decamped there in 1809 (while the

Theatre Royal was being rebuilt). After that it returned to staging musical dramas. There were smaller music venues, but these five West End houses – Drury Lane, Covent Garden, the King's Theatre, the Little Theatre and the Lyceum – were the ones frequented by society. Between them, by the beginning of the nineteenth century, with a London population that numbered nearly a million, they sold twelve thousand seats a week. And for those, like Brummell, who might consider themselves fashionable or cultured it was unthinkable not to be a regular theatregoer.

The Theatres Royal waxed and waned in popularity. Drury Lane was run by Sheridan – past his most prolific years as a playwright by 1800 but still a successful producer – and Covent Garden by Thomas Harris. Both managers were family friends of Brummell, who referred to Sheridan as 'my friend Sherry'. The King's Theatre in the Haymarket – larger and grander than La Scala in Milan – achieved pre-eminence in fashionable circles over both Covent Garden and Drury Lane, once it dedicated itself exclusively to opera.

All five theatres, however, were crowded, noisy and – throughout the evening and on both sides of the footlights – brilliantly lit: so much so that it was suggested a Persian arriving unschooled in European ways would be hard pushed to distinguish who was on stage and who was watching. One reason for this was that the theatres had no practical means of dimming lights even had they wanted to, so the audience was as illuminated to itself as to the actors on stage. But the audience had no inclination to sit in the dark. Whereas those in the galleries had perhaps more real interest in the play, Brummell and his friends in the boxes and pit – as the stalls were then called – came just as much 'to furnish out a part of the entertainment themselves [as if] acting a part in a dumb show'. The *Haut Ton* seemed 'to assemble only to see and be seen'. The London theatres provided the opening act of Brummell's evening play, but for him, like everyone else on and off stage, going to the theatre was a performance in itself.

The plays were as familiar to Brummell as to the rest of the audience because the repertoire on offer was small and frequently repeated. There were constant revivals of Shakespeare's tragedies in the early nineteenth century, largely thanks to David Garrick. *Macbeth* was rarely out of repertoire – Mrs Siddons performed the Thane's wife at Covent Garden intermittently from the late 1780s to 1812. *The Merchant of Venice* was especially popular after 1814 when Edmund Kean electrified audiences with his naturalism in the role of Shylock, and *Romeo and Juliet* (in which Perdita Robinson made her début) remained a favourite. Sheridan's reworking of Vanbrugh's *The Relapse* as *A Trip to Scarborough*, and his previous hits *The Rivals* and *The School for Scandal*, were frequently revived, as were the comedies of James Townley, Colley Cibber and George Coleman (the Elder and the Younger) such as the ever popular *Clandestine Marriage*, *The Heir-at-Law* and *High Life Below Stairs*. In 1800 the celebrated comedy actress Dora Jordan – Brummell's neighbour on Chesterfield Street – was still playing the lead role in *The Country Wife* fifteen years after her initial success in the part. Such was the theatrical recycling culture of the times that Brummell found himself watching the same productions at Drury Lane and Covent Garden – in some cases probably in the same costumes – with which his parents would have been familiar in the 1780s. For Brummell and his crowd, this familiarity had some practical benefit. The constantly revolving but rarely changing repertoire of plays formed the background of the evening's entertainment, but they frequently missed the opening acts. 'The nobility,' noted one stranger in town, 'seldom arrive till between ten and eleven o'clock, when the piece is more than half over.'

Robinson, Brummell's valet, was sent to bag a seat, unless Brummell had arranged to hire or loan a box (Robinson must have had a bizarre and frustrating experience of English drama), and Brummell arrived after eating at one of his clubs. 'As for the First [Act],' explained one regular theatregoer, 'one would not be thought so *outré* as to witness it – the attempt would require a sacrifice of the dessert and Madeira and completely revolutionize the regularity of [one's] dinner arrangement.' The *Haut Ton* came, generally, after dinner, and expected a rousing last act or two, possibly followed by a farce, or a musical 'Afterpiece'. One particularly popular late-night show at the time was a comic ballet called *Pitcairn Island*, based on the story of the *Bounty* mutineers. Only an opening-night performance or a special benefit night – for the personal profit of one actor – received the courtesy of being seen in its entirety.

The arrival of Brummell and the *Haut Ton* more than half-way through the evening's entertainment coincided with a separate commotion. After the second interval, theatres sold off all empty upper and lower gallery seats at half price. What with the arrival of Brummell and his crowd in the boxes and the noise of the extra seats being filled, the performers and middle-class theatregoers faced a good deal of disruption. But this was only one of the many distractions of the theatre and opera-going experience. The hundreds of candles that lit both the auditorium and the stage were tended assiduously and nervously by candle-trimmers and snuffers. If they trimmed too soon they risked knocking lit candles down and starting fires – both Covent Garden and Drury Lane burned to the ground in 1808–9 – but if they trimmed too late, theatregoers complained of hot wax dripping on them from above. Fruit sellers plied their trade throughout the performances, and some plied other trades on the side; business transactions took place between members of the audience and those in the boxes, and theatre staff, personal messengers and footmen carried around the theatre items of gossip, orders for carriages, money, love notes and bills of exchange. And many more people were packed in than would be considered comfortable or safe in generations to come. Sheridan for one employed a large front-of-house staff at Drury Lane to cope with the mêlée: there were individual box-keepers, box-inspectors (against the worst excesses of the upper classes in dark corners), also four lobby-keepers, fourteen door-keepers, four messengers and seven box-office staff.

There was hustle, distraction and excitement. In an age when Londoners were patently self-regarding and referred without irony to their city as 'The World', the theatre was the one place when everyone was on show together. Passions were high, even before the music struck up or the first lines were spoken, and so were the stakes – for the performers both on and off stage. Like the society of which it was a perfect cross-section, the theatre seemed almost ungovernable. As a crowd it felt, like society, always on the point of revolution, which was part of the thrill. It hissed and applauded, shouted, laughed and cried, always in full view of its own image. As a crowd it could be entertained or enthralled, amused, amazed or appalled, but was never predictable. The theatre was the place were the *demi-monde* and real world, the factual and the imaginary, the political and the artistic, the sexual and mercenary all met together. Decorous and highly decorated on the surface – the King's Theatre auditorium was even considered worth seeing in its own right – the theatres were also riotous, sexually heightened arenas in which passions of every variety were stirred and the crowd could never be ruled.

When prices rose in 1809 after the theatre fires, the Covent Garden audience rioted for sixty-seven nights in a row. When in 1805 the tailors of London found that Brummell's exacting standards – which had brought them such commercial success – were to be parodied in a comedy called *The Tailors, or a Tragedy in Warm Weather*, they organised a boycott, sent death-threats to the lead actor and threw scissors and cutting-shears at him when he made his first entrance on the opening night. The ensuing riot spilled out into the Haymarket and was only broken up by a platoon of Life Guards called from duty at Carlton House. The play closed.

Brummell arrived almost nightly by sedan chair or carriage. He was reputed to ask his chair carriers to take him several paces into the theatre so that he could step straight from the quilted swansdown interior to the plush inside of the opera foyer. This was probably an exaggeration, but evening wear for Brummell and his followers was much lighter than daywear, so some worry over the cold was perhaps understandable. The theatre was not ticketed at each entrance, and entry to the boxes and the pit was by token – made of silver or ivory in the case of the King's Theatre – or by recognition. The Duke of Bedford, for instance, had granted Brummell free entrée to his box by himself (No. 38) but declined to lend it to him so that he could invite a party. 'I make it a rule never to lend my box, but you have the *entrée libre* whenever you wish to go there, as I informed the box-keeper last year.' After working his way through the crush and the darkness of the corridors and candlelit staircases, Brummell entered the theatre itself and his gilded box, awash with light and 'all fitted up with crimson velvet'. 'The lighting [of a theatre box] is better adapted for being seen than for seeing,' wrote Prince Pückler-Muskau; 'in front of every box hangs a chandelier which dazzles one and throws the actors into shade.' Brummell's box was, of course, a stage in its own right.

One's appearance in a particular box at the theatre signalled the shifting allegiances and relative status within society. It announced one's presence in London and participation in its life. How one was received and acknowledged, whom one invited in, or to which boxes one was invited, all served to illustrate the changing web of alliances: financial, sexual or political. The Princess of Wales was roundly applauded at the theatre when her treatment by the prince became public knowledge. The re-entry of Georgiana, Duchess of Devonshire, into society was also acknowledged at the opera, as was her rapprochement with Mrs Fitzherbert. The Marquess of Worcester 'ran up three times to the opera' to see if Harriette Wilson was back in London, but lamented to the Duke of Leinster 'she did not make her appearance'. When Brummell needed his creditors to know he was in London and in confident rude health, he showed himself at the opera.

As well as presenting a spectacle of aristocratic power-play, boxes, like the stage, were the site of more prurient voyeurism. Just as the elision between the skid-alley careers of actresses and prostitutes was well established and understood, so too theatre boxes offered a stage on which to perform rituals of sexual display and availability. The owners of boxes might want only to strut and fret for the purposes of personal vanity, but the boxes also shop-fronted flirtations with romantic or mercenary intent. And, generally, the nearer the stage, the more exhibitionist the occupants of the boxes were thought to be, like the two rakes Bulwer Lytton describes 'seated in the box nearest the stage [indulging] in debauchery as if it were an attribute of manliness and esteemed it, as long as it were hearty and English, rather a virtue to boast of than a vice to disown'. Walter Scott harrumphed against these same front boxes where 'one half come to prosecute their debaucheries so openly that it would degrade a bagnio'.

Brummell's friend Harriette Wilson took her regular box in this theatrical and exhibitionist spirit. Like all of the most celebrated courtesans she rented boxes near the stage for the season. She took a box at the opera every Tuesday and Sunday night, and at the theatre from Thursday to Saturday. These boxes were showcases in which she could flaunt her attractions but also from which she could solicit and meet potential 'protectors'. 'Many a beau,' she wrote, 'turned his head wishfully towards our box, anxiously waiting to observe a vacancy for one.' A young man's reputation could be made, in a certain sense, from being seen next to Harriette, Julia or one of the other 'Fashionable Impures'. 'Beau Brummell, Fred Bentinck, Lord Fife, the Duc de Berri, Berkeley Craven and a great many more were visitors,' wrote Harriette. The box at the theatre provided Harriette and her later readers with a chance to view Brummell as the theatre crowd saw him, making his entrance:

The celebrated beau, George Brummell, who had been presented to Amy [Harriette's sister] by Julia, in the Round Room at the opera [a notorious pick-up venue at the King's Theatre], now entered our box and put poor Julia in high spirits. Brummell, as Julia always declared, was, when in the 10th Dragoons, a very handsome young man. However that might have been, nobody could mistake him for any thing like handsome at the moment she presented him to us. Julia assured me that he had, by some accident, broken the bridge of his nose and which said broken nose had lost him a lady and a fortune of twenty thousand pounds. This, from the extreme flatness of it, of his nose I mean, not the fortune, appeared probable.

He was extremely fair, and the expression of his countenance far from disagreeable. His person, too, was rather good. Besides this, he was neither uneducated nor deficient. He possessed, also, a sort of quaint, dry humour [so] it became the fashion to court Brummell's society, which was enough to make many seek it, who cared not for it: and many more wished to be well with him, through fear, for all knew him to be cold, heartless, and satirical.

Harriette's harsh verdict on his character and looks notwithstanding, she later admits that 'when the performance had concluded, we always remained late in the rooms, amusing ourselves with George Brummell, Tom Raikes, and various others . . . Tom Raikes . . . is a mimic [as well as Brummell] and he can take off Brummell very tolerably, as well as the manners of the *vieille cour France beaux* [*sic*] but I never discovered that he could do anything else. Brummell often dined with him.' Raikes remembered those times fondly and stated categorically that 'happy was she in whose opera box Brummell would pass an hour' while neglecting to mention that in his youth he, too, had been part of the jolly party with Harriette and the other 'Impures'. Such was the crush of beaux attempting to spend time with the courtesans, and with Brummell, and be seen in their company, that a row erupted over the numbers allowed entry into boxes. Sheridan and the theatre managers eventually set a rule that the main boxes 'were meant for no more than six'.

By spending so much time at the theatre in the company of courtesans Brummell was expressing the clear double standard of his age. He, as a single man, could move freely from the boxes of the courtesans to those taken by members of high society. No woman could move so easily between the different spheres of *demi-monde* and real world that overlapped at the theatre – and a married man was offering a direct insult to his wife if he publicly consorted with courtesans in her presence. Brummell, on the other hand, was always drawn to glamour. Harriette, her sister

Amy and his childhood friend Julia allied him with the decadent world of the Cyprians – and allowed him the semi-public performance of a flirtation that was not just sexual but dangerous. These women relied even more on image and on presentation than did Brummell but he had no need to acknowledge them as publicly as Harriette would have us believe he did. Something in him drew him to Harriette and Julia and to the rituals of sexualised social intercourse. This may have been a performance to vie with the one on stage, yet Harriette positions Brummell as an insider at her court, sufficient for her to lose patience with his 'absurdities' or grow jealous of his fame.

The world of the Georgian theatre had infused Brummell's understanding of life from his earliest years. He had sat at table with Richard Brinsley Sheridan and Thomas Harris at Donnington Grove and played in classical roles at Eton. But the theatre in London offered a new mirror to his understanding of his place in the world, and his wit and style seem to have been heightened by an appreciation of theatricality learned on site. The drama of the time, like the drama of Brummell's life, played constantly on themes of class, rank, social mobility and manners. The class reversals or Cinderella transformations wrought in the classic comedies of the era would have had special interest to Brummell, arguably the first commoner to dominate London high society. *She Stoops to Conquer*, *The Devil to Pay* (Mrs Jordan's most successful comedy, the *Pygmalion* of its day) or *The Heir-at-Law*, which Tom Bertram is so keen to perform in Austen's *Mansfield Park*, are all comedies of class confusion and social mobility. The opposition between 'high' and 'low' – in manners, in comedy, of class – became a constant theme in London drama at this time.

Playwrights and actors sought desperately – and often successfully – to engage simultaneously the voluble and mercurial crowd out front, from the footmen in the gallery to the lords and ladies in their boxes. The satirical edge and acute sensitivity to the nuances of class as a target for comedy found its way across the footlights and into the writings of Jane Austen, Fanny Burney and

Lord Byron to name but three theatre-loving writers. Similarly, theatre comedy closely informed Brummell's style of humour. His stage-honed style was evident to Jesse either from meeting him or from the many descriptions he solicited from those who would have known Brummell from the theatre:

[His] flexibility of feature enabled Brummell to give additional point to his humorous or satirical remarks, his whole physiognomy giving the idea that, had he devoted himself to dramatic composition he would have written in a tone . . . resembling *The School for Scandal*.

Gronow, Raikes, Moore and Wilson all make reference to Brummell's sardonic smile, his love of the perfectly turned phrase and readiness to poke fun at pretension, the legacy of his years in West End theatre boxes and at the dinner table with Sheridan.

But unlike Sheridan, Fanny Burney (who wrote plays as well as novels, unperformed in her lifetime) and, of course, Jane Austen, Brummell's stage-learned wit was not always warm or evenly balanced. His audience, unlike theirs, did not include the servants in the galleries: his pronouncements were designed to appeal to the class he dominated. In this, he can sound as archly snobbish as the *ancien régime* harridans who are the butts of Austen's, Burney's or Sheridan's satire: gargoyles like Lady Catherine de Burgh or Lady Wilhemina Tilney. However, stage humour is apparent in Brummell's acute awareness of the ridiculousness of class pretension, which he attacked instead from the inside. When he complained about catching a cold through being left in a room with a 'damp stranger', or that he could never love a woman who ate cabbage, or when he assured a lady, shocked and honoured by the favour of his company, that he could talk to her because 'no one is watching', he seemed to stake his place in a stage tradition, certainly as one begetter of arch camp but also as a child of Georgian high comedy.

The theatre that exposed him to high comedy also exposed him to low life and to the crush of the crowd. His inability to muster the right words in such a situation provided more comic opportunity, but this time at his expense. Harriette Wilson, like Brummell, knew her comedy from the stage and from theatre-inspired comic novels. She relates one story about Brummell almost as a parody of the scene in Fanny Burney's 1778 novel *Evelina* in which the eponymous heroine finds herself in a mortifying encounter at the opera with *nouveaux riches*. Harriette sets the scene during high summer when 'Thirty Guineas were I know refused for a box on the upper tier', and the King's Theatre is full to overflowing:

I now observed a very corpulent gentleman sailing towards us. He had a lady leaning on his right arm, and two ugly daughters.

'La! Papa, don't pull so,' said the eldest daughter. 'Somebody has shoved the comb out of my head, I declare, and I have torn my dress.'

Beau Brummell at this moment passed between Lord Petersham and this interesting party. As the pressure prevented the possibility of advancing, the corpulent gentleman after taking out his pocket hand-kerchief, and wiping his head and face, seemed about to address Beau Brummell, and I promised myself not a little amusement from observing the very essence of vulgarity in close contact with the finest man in town.

'Warm work this, sir,' said the corpulent gentleman to Brummell, who merely answered, by a look of dismay.

'Brummell! Brummell!' (mistaking [him] for some acquaintance of his own I believe) 'Sir,' addressing the beau smirkingly, 'I fancy, Sir, I have had the pleasure of meeting you before? I am sure I have. You are the gentleman as sung such a good song at our club.'

The well taut muscles of Lord Petersham's face were nearly giving way . . . at the idea of Brummell singing a good song, at Mr Smith's Club but Lord Alvanley whispered, gravely, in Smith's ear, that he had no doubt it was the very same person, adding that Mr Brummell did sing a remarkably good song, but was always shy, at receiving compliments in public.

'Sir,' said Smith, bowing to Brummell, 'I shall be most happy to see you, at my snug box at Clapham. All my family are fond of a good English song, and I will venture to say, I can give you as good a bottle of port wine, as any in England.'

The crush of the theatre also posed problems of etiquette in the presence of royalty and Brummell was once caught in the lobby of the opera among a tide of theatregoers as the prince was trying to leave. It says something extraordinary about their relative standing in society that the unpopular prince could be 'stared out of countenance' by a mere commoner, and Thomas Raikes's shock was only tempered by his admiration in recording the encounter:

Brummell came out, talking eagerly to some friends, and, not seeing the Prince or his party, took up a position near the check-taker's bar [to retrieve his hat]. As the crowd flowed out, Brummell was gradually pressed backwards until he was almost driven against the Regent, who distinctly saw him but who of course would not move. In order to stop him therefore, and prevent actual collision, one of the Prince's suite tapped [Brummell] on the back, when Brummell immediately turned sharply round, and saw that there was not much more than a foot between his nose and the Prince of Wales's. I watched him with intense curiosity and observed that his countenance did not change in the slightest degree, nor did his head move; they looked straight into each other's eyes. The Prince was evidently amazed and annoyed. Brummell, however, did not quail or show the least embarrassment. He receded quite quietly, and backed slowly step by step till the crowd closed between them, never once taking his eyes off the Prince. It was impossible to describe the impression made by this scene on the bystanders; there was nothing insolent in his manner, nothing offensive; by retiring with his face to the Regent he recognised his rank, but he offered no apology for his inadvertence (as a mere stranger would have done); as man to man, his bearing was adverse and uncompromising.

The theatre was the site for public displays of affection, loyalty, attraction or allegiance. It could also be the site for petty skirmishes in long-term friendships or, it seems, the rival posturings of two arrogant and fêted celebrities.

~

The presence of Harriette Wilson, Julia Johnstone and their 'Impure' associates at the theatre made some society ladies uncomfortable. The managers of the Italian Opera House on the Haymarket saw an opportunity. In 1804 they suggested that the opera employ the same system as the clubs: only those deemed fashionable *and* respectable might be allocated tickets for the pit and boxes. Opera was already more expensive than the theatre: prices started at a guinea for a seat in the gallery, as opposed to a shilling in the theatre. Opera boxes could cost from a hundred to as much as a thousand guineas for the season. 'The opera may be called the exclusive property of the affluent, who take boxes by the year,' wrote one German traveller, 'the pit [also] has been added to the accommodation of the nobility, and in order to exclude improper company, the admission was raised to half-a-guinea [and] the dress is the same as the boxes.'

This new exclusivity was considered absolutely necessary once the King's Theatre extended the entertainment on offer from just an opera to supper and a ball afterwards. 'Let the theatre be got up upon the same exclusive system [as the clubs],' wrote one critic, 'and you shall have . . . the most gorgeous audience.' The most gorgeous audience duly arrived, once, after 1805, 'no one could obtain a box or a ticket for the pit without a voucher from one of the lady patronesses', namely the Duchesses of Marlborough, Devonshire and Bedford, and Lady Carlisle, the Duchess of Rutland's mother. This was a pivotal moment in the evolution of the modern West End as it stamped opera, as compared to plays, an aristocratic art-form. Not only did the men dress according to Brummell's strict dicta, but on evenings following Royal 'Drawing Rooms' (the official receptions for ambassadors at royal residences, for instance) Brummell and his cronies would attend the opera 'in full court dress'. The opera might be even more 'stamped with aristocratic elegance' than the theatre, but the audience still arrived late, and noisily. There were more boxes at the King's Theatre and many bought exclusively for the season. The ruse failed, however, in terms of keeping the likes of Harriette Wilson from the opera: she had her lovers book in their names, and so the game continued. At one point she even kept a box, bought in the name of her young lover the Marquess of Worcester, just opposite that taken by his mother, the Duchess of Beaufort. They stared daggers at each other for an entire season. It suited Harriette's purposes to be in more select company and to have her coquettish games and elegant solicitations accompanied by the music of Italian opera.

Between acts and after the final performance the King's Theatre opera furnished a further luxurious locale for sophisticated flirtation. This was the Round Room. The chamber was a 'circular vestibule, almost lined with looking glass, and furnished with sophas [sic] in which female loveliness is not only seen but reflected'. So central was this room to the linked love-life and career of Harriette Wilson that she intended originally to title her memoirs 'Sketches from the Round Room of the Opera House'. For men like Brummell, the life after the opera, or even during intermissions, was both in the Round Room and also the Green Room (dressing room) of the King's Theatre. Here, dancers and actresses were used to entertaining their sponsors and protectors and, in some cases, making extra money by allowing them to watch them undress.

The two great divas of the age were known to Brummell as they moved in the same circles. Madame Grassini, who made her first appearance in 1803 in *La Vergine del Sole* by Mayer, was the only rival to Mrs Billington as London prima donna. 'Not only was she [Grassini] rapturously applauded in public, but she was taken up by the first society, fêtée, caressed, and introduced as a regular guest in the most fashionable assemblies.' In March 1805, Mrs Billington's star came back into the ascendant when she scored a huge success in Bach's *La Clemenza di Scipione*. However, she was best known for her roles in Mozart's *La Clemenza di Tito* – initially the most popular of Mozart's operatic works in England. In Brummell's time, both divas were succeeded by Madame Catalani, who 'introduced to the London stage Mozart's *Marriage of Figaro*, in which she acted the part of Susanna admirably'. True to archetype for a Latin prima donna, her histrionic manner alienated the rest of the King's Theatre singers who quit *en masse* and set up a rival company at the Pantheon, the assembly venue on Oxford Street, rather past its best. Catalani put about a rumour that the building was unsafe and the new company's licence only allowed them one-act operas and no ballets. For both reasons sales were poor, Brummell and the *Haut Ton* never attended, so the singers were forced to reapply for their jobs in the Haymarket and the Pantheon fell yet further into desuetude.

Intriguing to relate, Brummell, often credited as one of the models for Byron's *Don Juan*, was almost certainly in the audience at the London première of *Don Giovanni* at the King's Theatre in 1816 in which all three divas sang. Its sexually licentious themes had been considered too shocking for it to be performed in any of the thirty years since its first production in Prague in 1787. When the London première finally took place, elements of Giuseppe Gazzaniga's alternative score were interpolated along with new words by the librettist Lorenzo da Ponte, then working in London. But it proved a huge success at the King's, where the audience were well attuned to the nuances of seduction and betrayal. It struck many as having direct parallels with the new men-about-town, with their sardonic, indifferent posturing and the sexually sophisticated mores – and some would have noted, too, the parallels between the heartless Don and the social adventurer in Harriette Wilson's box, whom she described as 'cold, heartless and satirical'. Three years later, Byron published *Don Juan*.

~

After the theatre, or instead of it, Brummell repaired to the company of the Prince of Wales, later prince regent, at Carlton House. This was the scene of Brummell's anointing as a member of the prince's immediate circle – it was one thing to have been on familiar terms with him in the environments of the dragoons barracks and the Brighton Pavilion, but quite another to have ease of admission to an official royal residence, built, precociously, with its own Throne Room. But Carlton House was also the site both of Brummell's Bacchanalian partying with the prince and of their bitter rows. It was a suitably dramatic backdrop.

Alterations on the house had begun in 1783 under the direction of the prince's favoured architect, Henry Holland. From under Holland's Ionic columns (one of the few elements of the palace to survive later demolition) Brummell stepped late at night into a palace unrivalled in England and across the marble flagstones of a forty-four-by-twenty-nine-foot vestibule supporting a domed roof on Siena marble pillars. From this his eye could turn, via a Pompeiian green and red octagonal hallway, lit entirely by gaslight, into apartments displaying every style and taste that had titillated the prince. There was a Red Satin Drawing Room, a Blue Velvet Drawing Room and a Golden Drawing Room. There were Doric and Corinthian columns, Grecian busts, Roman mosaics and French Gothic fan vaulting. It was not, it must be safely assumed, the taste that Brummell himself might have enjoyed, but it had been built to impress and it did. The stairway that connected these apartments to the prince's private suites above was lit by a stained-glass dome (illuminated from behind at night, again by gas) painted in imitation of Raphaels, and at the foot of this staircase stood guard a monumentally tall hall porter.

The prince liked tall servants – footmen were recruited from the army and from France, and paid on a scale that favoured the tall to encourage tall young men to apply. The porter who could 'see over the gates', however, was also grossly overweight, and was dubbed as a result, possibly by Brummell, Big Ben. It was a joke he came to regret.

This nickname predates the famous bell and its tower on the new Palace of Westminster – built after the fire of 1834. It also predates the infamous prize-fighter, Big Ben Caunt, a celebrity at the time, after whom the bell was named. It may just be, then, that the boxer who lent his nickname to the clock-tower bell and who came from near Byron's home at Newstead in Nottinghamshire was, in turn, nicknamed Big Ben as a reference to the bulky porter so well known to the dandies of London.

All the visitors to Carlton House passed Big Ben on their way in, and he and his nickname were established long before Brummell made the mistake of using the same name to tease the similarly hefty Prince of Wales. He compounded this misfired joke by applying the name, by extension, to Mrs Fitzherbert, also caricatured by this period (1810 onwards) as greatly overweight. He called her 'Benina'. These were the first of a series of Carlton House *faux-pas* that began to strain Brummell's relationship with the prince. Perhaps familiarity at the prince's, even his mistress's, expense might have been acceptable in the Brighton barracks of the 10th Light Dragoons. Now, though, they were all a good deal older, and perhaps also Brummell was less secure in the prince's affections. Or he cared less about the prince's approbation.

Because Brummell was permitted the Privilege of Entrée – into the royal presence – he was shown by footmen not into the lesser West Ante Room but into the Circular Room. It was at the time the largest circular room in the country after the Chelsea rotunda at Ranelagh Gardens. There was Roman tent drapery around the walls, and a domed ceiling painted in representation of the sky from which hung a chandelier of cut glass representing an inverted fountain. The whole was reflected in giant mirrors between porphyry columns. There were blue-silk-covered settees lining the circumference, on which Brummell awaited the prince.

In the absence of ladies, the prince generally met his friends in the connecting Blue Velvet Drawing Room and Blue Velvet Closet, which was hung with some of the prince's favourite paintings: Van Dyck's *Charles I* and landscapes of the Flemish school. These two rooms connected with the inner sanctum for the prince: more drawing rooms in gold and red, a 'Bow' room, a library and a Gothic dining room. For larger banquets, this opened out into the exuberant Gothic Conservatory Dining Room – but Brummell ate more frequently with the prince under the eight mock-medieval chandeliers of the small dining room with its Garter Knights' motto on the ceiling, '*Honi soit qui mal y pense*', picked out in gold leaf and ormolu.

The prince's intimate friends would gather regularly under the new gas chandeliers. Musicians often played in an adjacent room and the wine flowed freely. Unsurprisingly, in this atmosphere of luxury and easy familiarity, the prince was at his most relaxed.

His guests, however, forgot at their peril their host's position, and Brummell trod a thin line between behaviour that was amusing, and that which was considered rude.

During one drinking session at Carlton House, a comment of Brummell's so enraged the prince that he threw a glass of wine into Brummell's face. Brummell, sitting on his right, picked up his own glass and threw its contents into the face of the person on *his* right with the loud instruction, 'The Prince's Toast: pass it round!' This much was greeted with laughter.

Brummell did, however, misread the prince's loyalties to his various mistresses and very possibly once ordered '*Mistress* Fitzherbert's carriage' – a double insult as it misapplied both Maria's class and her marital status, as she understood it, *vis-à-vis* the prince. At the time the prince was in the hands of Lady Jersey, but he returned, repeatedly, to the forgiving Mrs Fitzherbert, who decided not to forgive Brummell.

The deterioration of the friendship between Brummell and the prince was signalled by small fissures that grew – to many imperceptibly – into a rift. When Brummell put down his snuff-box on a sideboard in front of Mrs Fitzherbert (women had only recently taken to snuff) the prince snapped, 'Mr Brummell, the place for your box is in your pocket, not the table.'

When the prince saw a snuff-box of Brummell's he particularly liked, he asked if he might have it, then said, 'Go to Gray's [the jewellers on Bond Street] and order any box you like in lieu of it.' Brummell asked diplomatically to be allowed one with the prince's miniature on it, studded with gems, to which the prince agreed. The snuff-box was duly commissioned, only for Brummell to find, when he called for it, that the prince had expressly cancelled the order. He also refused to return Brummell's original. 'It was this more than anything else,' according to one who knew them both, 'which induced Brummell to bear himself with such unbending hostility towards the Prince of Wales. He felt that he had treated him unworthily and, from this moment, he indulged himself by saying the bitterest of things.'

There was, then, no clear falling-out. Brummell had witnessed the prince's inconstancy in friendship and in love, and as he himself grew in status and experience he seems to have considered the prince's behaviour merely immature. At first he addressed the issue by making a joke of it. One of his dandy friends, Colonel McMahon, asked him what he thought of the prince's displeasure and Brummell responded, 'I made him what he is, and I can unmake him.' It was a classic comic inversion of the plain facts, which in its Wildean way stated a small truth: by 1811 Brummell was more fashionable than the prince. This in turn led Tom Moore to pen a short satire of a (forged) letter that had been printed from the prince to the Duke of York in 1812. The author is in theory the prince.

> Neither have I resentments, nor wish there should come ill
> To mortal, except, now I think on't, Beau Brummell;
> Who threatened last year, in a superfine passion,
> To cut me, and bring the old King into fashion.

Nevertheless, Brummell was included on the guest list for those invited to Carlton House in June 1811 for the celebratory ball marking the accession of the Prince of Wales as prince regent. Because of the tragic circumstance that had led to the prince's assumption of monarchical prerogatives – the madness of his father George III – there were mixed responses to his eager desire to celebrate the occasion. Old Queen Charlotte boycotted the festivity, and insisted her five surviving daughters do the same. Both the Princess of Wales and 'the other wife', Mrs Fitzherbert, stayed at home, the first uninvited, the second invited but refusing to attend unless granted the 'Rank given her by yourself [the regent] above that of any other person'. Nothing, however, could dampen the spirits of the new regent, who broke all Brummell's codes of elegant dress, returning to the diamonds, the aigrettes and red velvet ensemble of his youth 'of not very good taste or very well made'. Three thousand guests were invited and two thousand entertained to dinner, most of them in the Gothic Conservatory Dining Room; £2585 had been spent on the 'fittings' – decorations – but this paled in comparison with the

£61,340 gold dinner service off which Brummell and the guests ate. 'Nothing was ever half so magnificent,' wrote Tom Moore, 'it was in reality all that they try to imitate in the gorgeous scenery of the theatre; and I really sat for three quarters of an hour in the Prince's room after supper, silently looking at the spectacle, and feeding my eyes with the assemblage of beauty, splendour, and profuse magnificence which it presented.'

Three days after the fête the gates of the palace were thrown open to the public and thousands flocked in to see the famous interiors that had been a backdrop for so many years to Brummell and the prince's revels and rows. On 25 June 1811 thirty thousand visitors traipsed through to gawk. The regent vowed never to let it happen again, and his affection for the palace began to wane just as it had for so many of his lovers and friends. His inconstancy was legend, so far as women were concerned, but two betrayals caused a different sort of comment and bewilderment, among friends and in the press, as they seemed so inexplicable. One was his abandonment of his friendship with Brummell and the other was his abandonment of Carlton House, which he ordered pulled down in 1826. For Brummell, the evening of 19 June 1811 at Carlton House was his last view of the inside of that or any other royal palace.

10

SEVENTH HEAVEN OF THE FASHIONABLE WORLD

To that Most Distinguished and Despotic
CONCLAVE
Composed of their High Mightinesses
Of
ALMACK'S
The Rulers of Fashion, the Arbiters of Taste,
The Leaders of Ton, and the Makers of Manners,
Whose sovereign sway over 'the world' of London has
Long been established on the firmest basis,
Whose Decrees are Laws,
and from whose judgement there is no appeal

Miss Stanhope, dedication in the novel *Almack's*, 1827

On Wednesday nights, the epicentre of the World as understood by Brummell was neither Carlton House nor the theatre but Almack's Assembly Rooms on King Street, St James's. Unlike the clubs of St James's Street, Almack's was attended by women as well as men and was only open at night. The club's years of success as *the* assembly rooms for the *Haut Ton* were precisely contemporary with Brummell's own glory-days, a time when, as Lord William Pitt Lennox said, 'happy was the young lady and young gentleman who basked in the sunshine of [Almacks]', a club Captain Gronow described simply as 'The Seventh Heaven of the Fashionable World'.

The Assembly Rooms had been opened by a Scot called Mac-Call or Macall (who decided some anagram of his name might sound more aristocratic) in 1764 in order to create a 'most magnificent suite of rooms' as a safe haven for high society. One prerequisite of entry was the correct attire, and this came to be in Brummell's gift. By 1801 the Brummell look was required uniform for Almack's – which meant his evening costume, consisting of white cravat and waistcoat, dark blue or black tail coat and black knee breeches and stockings or tight black pantaloons. A 'solemn proclamation' went out from the club to the effect that only 'silk stockings, thin shoes, and white neckcloths [were to be] invariably worn'. Wider trousers, or any addition of colour, were unacceptable. Brummell's rules for men's attire at Almack's began to pare down men's evening wear to the formal black and white that has remained, evolving by the end of the nineteenth century into the even more structured 'White Tie and Tails'.

Admission itself was by ticket only – called a voucher of admission and made of cardboard – on sale, in theory, on Bond Street. They could only be bought, however, by those on the List. The List was compiled – in the manner espoused by Wilde's Lady Bracknell – on lines of respectability, genealogy and fashionability: two out of three might suffice. This was 'selection with a vengeance', wrote Lady Clementia Davies, 'the very quintessence of aristocracy'. The arbitrators were known as the Lady Patronesses. In Brummell's day they were Lady Castlereagh, Lady Jersey (Sarah Sophia, the 5th Countess), Lady Cowper (later Lady Palmerston), Lady Sefton, Mrs Drummond Burrell (later Lady Gwydyr and later still Lady Willoughby de Eresby), and the ambassadresses, the Austrian Princess Esterhazy and Russian Countess Lieven. Between them, it was supposed, all European gentry and nobility might be scrutinised and found acceptable . . . or wanting. Wealth would not guarantee entry, but neither, automatically, would birth. 'Into this sanctum sanctorum of course the sons of commerce never think of entering on a Wednesday night [but also] three fourths of the nobility knock in vain.' Good looks or talent might help, but what the Lady Patronesses scrutinised was '*ton*'. Dandies had a good chance: Tom Moore was admitted and noted proudly in his diary, 'Went to Almack's (the regular Assembly) and stayed till three in the morning. Lord Morpeth said to me: You and I *live* at Almack's.' Many were refused entry: of the three hundred officers of the prestigious Foot Guards, Captain Gronow reckoned 'not more than half a dozen were honoured with vouchers of admission'. Almack's was, he said, 'a temple of the *beau monde*'.

Brummell had not the slightest problem getting on to the patronesses' List, but began to wield power himself as one of the arbiters of whom to include and whom to strike off. The Lady Patronesses looked to him for acknowledgement that the party was as it should be, and it was because of this that the story circulated that a duchess had insisted her daughter court favour with Mr Brummell before anyone else in the room. As Henry Luttrell explained:

> All on that magic List depends;
> Fame, fortune, fashion, lover, friends,
> 'Tis that which gratifies or vexes
> All ranks, all ages and both sexes.
> If once to Almack's you belong,
> Like monarchs you can do no wrong.
> But banished thence on Wednesday night,
> By Jove, you can do nothing right.
>
> Here is the only coalition
> 'Twixt Government and Opposition,
> Here parties, dropping hostile notions
> Make, on their legs, the self-same motions,
> Beauty each angry passion quenches,
> And seats them on the self same benches,
> There to uphold, without a schism
> The Patronesses' despotism.

Lady Louisa Lennox, daughter of the Duchess of Richmond, was reminded in no uncertain terms that she must solicit Brummell's good favour as well as that of the Lady Patronesses. 'Do you see that gentleman near the door?' the duchess was reported by Jesse to have said to her daughter, 'whom she had brought for the first time into the arena of Almack's'.

'He is now speaking to Lord [Alvanley?]'

'Yes I see him,' replied the light-hearted, as yet unsophisticated girl; 'Who is he?'

'A person, my dear, who will probably come a speak to us; and if he enters into conversation, be careful to give him a favourable impression of you, for,' and she sunk her voice to a whisper, 'he is the celebrated Mr Brummell.'

At the time this story was considered remarkable. Possibly never before had a commoner wielded such influence in the arena of high society; the triumph of celebrity over aristocracy was both novel and alarming, but, Jesse insists 'this is no fiction': he knew the lady.

Brummell helped to advise the Lady Patronesses primarily on the acceptability of other gentlemen. 'The rules of admission', according to the travel writer Major Chambre, were detailed, structured, and as 'incomprehensible' as any of the rituals he encountered in Amazonia.

No lady or gentleman's name could continue on the list of the same patroness for more than one set of balls. No gentleman's tickets could be transferred; nor could ladies procure them for their female friends, nor gentlemen for gentlemen. A mother might give hers to a daughter, or one unmarried sister to another. Subscribers who were prevented coming, were requested to give notice to the lady patronesses on the day of the ball by two o'clock, at [Almack's] that the vacancies might be filled up.

And so on. The constant, vigilant interest of the Lady Patronesses, guided in some instances by Brummell, kept everyone in check, and in their thrall.

What greeted those dubbed by Brummell and the Lady Patronesses worthy of entry was, on the one hand, rather unimpressive.

Though the Almack's ballroom was over ninety feet long, high and well lit, there was little else to recommend it. At 'the upper end, on a raised seat or throne, sat the Lady Patronesses', nodding acknowledgement as the invitees arrived. There was a weekly ball, on Wednesday, with a small band, but the décor was modest and the food deliberately mediocre. Weak lemonade was served, dry biscuits and brown bread and butter. This ostentatious simplicity doubtless appealed to Brummell as much as the garish opulence of Carlton House must have set his teeth on edge. It was part of the same Regency aesthetic of rigorous simplicity that he espoused in dress, but taken to somewhat parsimonious ends. 'There shall be no ostentation of wealth, no suppers,' says a patroness of Almack's in Edward Bulwer's 'dandy' novel *Godolphin*. 'It will be everything if these entertainments [are] perfectly distinct from those of rich bankers, rich bankers cannot afford to vie with us.' The point of Almack's rather was to dance and to be seen. It was the most elegant and exclusive of cattle-markets and the site of brokered deals that were as often illicit as licit and matrimonial. Where the core activity of the St James's Street clubs was gambling, the core issue at Almack's was sex and marriage. 'We go to these assemblies [at Almack's] to sell our daughters and to corrupt our neighbours' wives,' wrote one habitué. 'A ballroom is nothing more or less than a great market-place of beauty.'

The charge, both erotic and mercenary, was fuelled by music and drink. Although alcohol was not served on the premises, many arrived late from the theatre or elsewhere already quite drunk. Added to this nightclub atmosphere was the particular delight of people who believed they had gained entry to a gathering of an élite, which amounted to a frenzy, according to Lord Melbourne: 'You, who know Almack's, know that this is one of the strongest, if not the very strongest passions of the human mind.' Of the Regency mind, and Brummell's, Lord Melbourne's assertion would certainly hold.

Most nights the assemblies remained relatively staid, but on Wednesdays the dancing went on well into Thursday morning. Even so, no one was admitted after eleven p.m. The Duke of

Wellington himself was once refused entry by Lady Jersey 'such that hereafter no one can complain of the application of the rule of exclusion'. Perhaps because of the potential for 'frenzy' the ladies attempted to control the dancing as they did the entry. Gentlemen who could dance well were shown particular favour in coming seasons and this was some of Brummell's appeal to the Lady Patronesses in the early years of his time in London. He danced for a few seasons, then took to scrutinising from the sidelines, helping the patronesses adjudicate on those who could and could not dance. The latter might find themselves off the List. Captain Gronow tells of one Guards officer who found himself included and his wife excluded on those grounds and challenged Lady Jersey's husband to a duel on this account.

In this fraught but sexually heightened atmosphere, the latest dances were introduced into London society. The quadrille, a new French 'square' dance that gained enormous popularity, was first seen at Almack's, but only after Lady Jersey had mastered it. The waltz meanwhile – a continental prospect of almost as much imaginative erotic charge in London as Napoleon himself – was only accepted under the personal patronage of the much admired Countess Lieven.

For those not wishing to be seen waltzing at Almack's before sufficient rehearsal, the Duke of Devonshire allowed classes at Devonshire House. 'No event ever produced so great a sensation in English Society as . . . the German waltz,' wrote Thomas Raikes, 'in London fashion is – or was then – *everything* [so] old and young returned to school, and the mornings which had been dedicated to lounging in the Parks, were now absorbed at home in . . . whirling a chair around a room to learn the step and measure of the German waltz.' It is unclear if Brummell took to waltzing, though it is tempting to suggest there was some new exercise in his indolent lifestyle: the Berry Brothers records show that he lost the weight he had gained in the early years of Watier's gastronomy club soon after the waltz craze hit London.

The same year, 1813, that brought the waltz also brought Parisian socialite and writer Madame de Staël to London, with her daughter in tow. They threw themselves into London society with gusto, made a beeline for Almack's and were sufficiently informed on all matters English to know that they should endeavour to make a good impression on Mr Brummell. Byron observed them in action and was unsurprised when Brummell and Alvanley, among others, 'took an invincible dislike to the de Staëls, both mother and daughter'. 'Despite all her talents and attractions', Captain Gronow claimed, London thought her 'somewhat of a toady'. Brummell, according to Byron, 'was her aversion and she his . . . they [the dandies] persecuted and mystified Mme de Staël most damnably'.

Germaine de Staël had got on the wrong side of many people she had determined to charm in the past, as Byron well knew. Napoleon went so far as to exile her from France. She was said to lack a sense of humour, which may well have been the worst trait in Brummell's mind, but in any event he and Alvanley played an elaborate practical joke on her and her pushy daughter, Albertine, who Brummell nicknamed 'Libertine', for the amusement of themselves and those in on the joke. Brummell whispered to Madame de Staël at Almack's that his friend Alvanley, the stocky bachelor, was worth a full £100,000, in want of a wife, and more than usually vain about his looks (it was acknowledged generally that he had none). One of Alvanley's favourite stories for years afterwards was how, dancing the new waltz with 'Libertine' at Almack's, he saw Lord Jersey enter and said to Albertine, 'What a handsome man Jersey is!' soliciting the response from his eager French escort, 'He shall not be so pretty than you, milord.'

Brummell kept a watercolour sketch of himself at Almack's by Dighton, which was bought by a friend of Captain Gronow after Brummell's flight and later used in his book to illustrate, with Gronow's explanation, those 'well worthy of notice from the position they held in the fashionable world'. It gives a surprisingly cosmopolitan account of the guests at a Wednesday night at Almack's, which included French, German and Italian nobility as well as the 'habitual Princess Esterhazy, so long Ambassadress of Austria in London'. Prominently in the foreground, however, is

The Great George Brummell [standing] in a dégagé attitude, with his fingers in his waistcoat pocket. His neckcloth is inimitable, it must have cost him much time and trouble to arrive at such perfection. He is talking earnestly to the charming Duchess of Rutland.

~

Almack's was not the only club that threw balls in the evening. White's also did on occasions considered worthy of committee members' attentions. The Prince of Wales had come near to handing in his membership when White's threw a ball celebrating the recovery of his father from one of his bouts of illness, but when Napoleon was defeated in 1814 Brummell and the rest of the club were rightly convinced that the prince would approve of a grand celebration. King Louis XVIII of France visited London in May, and in June 'Napoleon's Vanquishers' came to London: the Tsar of Russia and the King of Prussia. Balls were thrown in their honour all through the summer and one of the earliest and grandest was organised by White's.

The club has kept details of the planning for the fête, held on 21 June 1814, for which Brummell was one of the committee. On 25 April 1814, it was 'Resolved that the Club at Whites will give a ball in celebration of the late glorious events and that a subscription be opened for this purpose, not exceeding twenty guineas per member.' By 1814 there were 500 members, but even so they struggled to find the £10,000 cost of the ball they threw. The new Duke of Devonshire, Georgiana's son, lent them Burlington House for the occasion, which suffered a crush of nearly four thousand people, including the visiting Tsar of Russia and King of Prussia. White's spent £800 on candles, £900 on wine and £2,575 on the dinner; £200 worth of china was broken.

Watier's was not to be outdone, and in the frenzied summer of festivities the club decided to throw a ball, which was set for the week following White's, on 1 July. There had already been 'illuminations and fireworks, a fair in Hyde Park, frigates on the Serpentine and going in State to the theatres and great dinners without end and great parties and balls for the great people'. John

Cam Hobhouse wrote that this round of celebrations left 'no repose either of body or mind'. So Brummell and his club members at Watier's set on reviving jaded socialites by adding a touch of sex to the metropolitan glamour. They invited everyone in masquerade, and along with their society lady friends, included the courtesans. Harriette Wilson left a long account in her memoirs. The demi-reps finally stormed the barricades of respectable society, dressing as boys and shepherdesses (Julia Johnstone and Harriette respectively) and waltzing with the Tsar of All the Russias. They queued in their carriages from 'five in the afternoon as, by so doing, we should stand a chance of arriving between nine and ten o'clock'. The men were either in full dress uniform or in fancy dress but they were all masked. Only the members of Watier's were distinguishable, and dressed as light blue dominoes.

They [the Watier's men] were unmasked [Harriette wrote]. No one else was admitted but in character. The members of Watier's Club were as attentive to us as though they had all been valets, and bred up to their situations, like George Brummell, who, by the bye was the only exception. Instead of parading behind our chairs, to enquire what we wanted, he sat teasing a lady, with a wax mask, declaring that he would not leave her, till he had seen her face.

~

Dancing and socialising might command much of his time, but as his day in the high life wore into late evening, Brummell moved to the gaming tables. They provided both excitement and success for Brummell, who certainly had his fair share of thrilling wins. He was estimated one season to have won over £30,000 on horses and another £26,000 during one sitting at cards. Jesse claimed he once won £60,000, three times the amount of his original patrimony, but failed to put it into annuities and lost it all again within the week. Although his inheritance had furnished him with more ready cash than most men of fortune could expect in their early twenties, there was no land or investments to back up the style of high-stakes gambling that had become *de rigueur* at the London clubs. At night they were, as one commentator explained, little more than gambling dens:

> How easy is [their] only rule!
> Buy toys – make love, laugh, eat and drink,
> Not often sleep, and never think.
> From joy to joy, unquestioned, ramble:
> But chiefly, O my pupils, *gamble*.

Faro, or pharoah, had been popular in England in Stuart times, possibly introduced from France by Charles II's mistress Louise de Kerouaille. It was fitting then that her, and his, descendant, Charles James Fox, should help repopularise the game at Brooks's in the later eighteenth century. It made him a fortune, which he promptly lost again. It is a game played between a dealer, who keeps bank, and the rest of the company. Fox and his friend Richard Fitzpatrick kept the bank for Brooks's, and Fox later told George Selwyn, the writer and politician, that he had made £30,000 in the first year. 'Charles and Richard's d. . . . d faro bank,' wrote Selwyn, 'swallows up everybody's cash who comes into Brooks's.' The game was still running when Brummell joined the club a generation later, with several families already ruined, but other fortunes secured for generations. Lord Robert Spencer, for instance, won £100,000 and never played again.

The point about faro was that it favoured the house or bank, like roulette. Georgiana, Duchess of Devonshire, optimistically tried to set up her own faro bank as a means of making money to pay off previous gambling debts, and for every horror story there was one on whom Fate had more than smiled. 'I never saw such a transition from distress to opulence,' wrote Selwyn, about one of Fox's winning streaks, 'from dirt to cleanliness. He is in high spirits and cash.' Brummell hit a particularly purple patch after the false victories over Napoleon in 1814. Although Europe would be at war again within a year, after Napoleon's escape from Elba, the brief peace saw London thronged with battle-weary officers whose brush with mortality had sharpened their optimism, if not their skills, on the gaming tables. In the true spirit of an addict,

Brummell also found a good-luck talisman, the loss of which he later blamed for his financial ruin. It was a crooked sixpence, a symbol of Christmas good fortune, that he picked up one dawn in Mayfair.

It was five o'clock one summer's morning [wrote Thomas Raikes], when Brummell was walking home with me through Berkeley Street and was bitterly lamenting his misfortune; he suddenly stopped on seeing something glittering in the [gutter]; he stooped down and picked up a crooked sixpence. His countenance immediately brightened. This, said he, is the harbinger of good luck. He took it home, and before he went to bed, drilled a hole in it and fastened it to his watch-chain. The spell was good (this was I think in 1813) during more than two years he was a constant winner at play or the turf, and I believe realized nearly £30,000.

The losses that might be sustained during a winning streak were more problematic for Brummell if they continued for any length of time as, by his mid-twenties, his capital was already dwindling. His response at first was histrionic, and he play-acted a sort of fey desperation – as he might have done in the face of being made to ride in wet weather at the risk of splashing his white boot-tops. When he lost a particularly large sum at table, for instance, he called for the waiter to fetch him some pistols so that he might shoot himself. At this, another club member, a Mr Hythe, supposedly mad but not so mad as to miss the opportunity of a joke at Brummell's expense, offered him his own pistols with the words: 'Mr Brummell, if you wish to put an end to your existence, I am extremely happy to offer you the means without troubling the waiter.' Thomas Raikes recorded that the primary effect of this offer, after laughter, was alarm around the club that their maddest member should be in possession of loaded pistols.

Life as a professional gambler beckoned as Brummell moved into his thirties. Play was hard and fast at Watier's and while he won there was sustenance from its sport. The main game here, unlike Brooks's or White's, was macao. This was a variant on twist or *vingt-et-un* – which required only nerve and an ability to dissemble, qualities Brummell had acquired early in life. Raikes recalled Brummell coming in one night to Watier's from the opera to find the tables crowded and the play particularly high. All places were taken, so he joined Tom Sheridan, his old friend from Donnington. Sheridan was ill, in debt, and fighting a legal action in Scotland for 'assault and trespass', i.e., adultery, served against him by his lover's husband. The 'damages' were set at a thousand pounds.

Tom Sheridan was never in the habit of play but, having dined freely, had dropped into the club and was trying to catch the smiles of fortune by risking a few pounds which he could ill afford to lose . . . Brummell proposed to him to give up his place and go shares in his deal; and, adding to the £10 in counters which Tom had before him £200 himself, took the cards. He dealt with his usual success, and in less than ten minutes won £1500. He then stopped, made a fair division and, giving £750 to Sheridan, said to him, 'There, Tom, go home and give your wife and brats supper and never play again.

As Raikes said, the gesture was 'characteristic of the times, the set, and of the spirit of liberality in Brummell which was shown towards an old friend in a way that left no pretext for refusal'.
Brummell played with panache, nerve and great success but, like his much wealthier friend Georgiana, Duchess of Devonshire, he did not know when to stop. Either that, or his nihilistic gambling was parallel to a darker strain in his character. Raikes claimed his glittering personality could turn black and morose and in this his gambling was both cause and effect.

The life which Brummell led at last plunged him into difficulties. He had lived constantly beyond his means, was deeply in debt, and the notorious usurers Howard and Gibbs refused further supplies unless furnished with the securities of friends. Here his popularity supplied a source which was fatal to the purse of many of our friends in the sequel. At this period Watier's Club, which had been originally established for harmonic meetings, became the resort of all the fine gentlemen of the day; the dinners were superlative and high play at macao was gradually introduced. The first effort of the beau was unsuccessful, and, as he was then addicted to games of chance, his depression became very great indeed.

Lord Byron, who knew Brummell well during his years as president of Watier's, was equivocal about the joys and horrors of gambling. For him, like Brummell, gambling was another sensory sport with which to distract attention from the world – indeed, Byron compared it explicitly to sex. He might have been describing Brummell on the precipice of his fall when he wrote:

I have a notion that Gamblers are as happy as most people, being always *excited*. Women, wine, fame, the table, even Ambition, *sate* now and then: but every turn of the card, and cast of the dice, keeps the Gamester alive: besides one can Game ten times longer than one can do anything else . . . I have thrown as many as fourteen *mains* running, and carried off all the cash upon the table occasionally: but I had no coolness or judgement or calculation. It was the *delight* of the thing that pleased me.

Brummell's notorious 'coolness' allowed his early formidable success as a gambler. What, then, changed his fortune? Perhaps simply the roll of the dice: there is a certain providence in the fall of the cards that gamblers acknowledge means a true winner must know when to quit. It may be that Brummell found a new excitement, a new, desperate means of feeling alive in the luxuriant tedium of London society, by risking more than he knew he should. In this, he may also have been expressing the self-destructive impulse that was beginning to exhibit itself in his personal behaviour. As Thomas de Quincey, 'the English Opium Eater', observed, 'the true impulse in obstinate incorrigible gamesters . . . is not faith, unconquerable faith, in their luck; it is the very opposite principle – a despair of their own luck; rage and hatred in consequence as at the blind enemy working in the dark.'

When Brummell was in one of his winning patches he decided to throw a masked ball. Several other members of the Dandiacal Body, Lord Alvanley, Henry Pierrepoint and Henry Mildmay, were also doing well at the tables so the four set about hosting an evening at the Argyle Rooms, which, it was decided, should be another masquerade. It suited them well, perhaps especially the actor in Brummell, to produce an event of the innate theatricality of a masked ball. It also allowed them to include their wide circle of friends on both sides of the divide of social respectability. The Argyle, meanwhile, on what became Regent Street, was associated with parties 'emanating from the leading ladies of the *demi-monde*', according to Lord William Pitt Lennox, where 'balls and fancy-balls were constantly got up . . . where nothing could exceed the entertainment and the mirth was . . . uproarious'. On Brummell's insistence, however, no invitation was sent to the prince regent. He and Brummell were in the middle of one of the periodic spats that appeared to be punctuating the decline in their mutual affection. They still moved in similar circles, but were not, that month, talking to each other. Whether Brummell would have maintained this unusual stance, of not inviting the prince, is unlikely. His interest in throwing a well-received party might have won out over his interest in piquing the prince. The regent, however, simply announced from Carlton House his intention of attending a much-talked-of party so the dandies were obliged to send an invitation, signed by all four of them.

On the evening of the masquerade the hosts lined up at the doors of the Argyle Rooms to greet their guests. The masked guests came in full military regalia or fancy dress, the women in elaborate costumes. The hosts, however, dressed as bewigged footmen of the seventeenth century and greeted their guests holding multi-branched candelabra.

The prince arrived, and bowed first to Henry Pierrepoint. Next in line was Brummell, but the prince ignored him and moved on to Alvanley and then on into the room. Many witnessed the event: the four dandies and the guests both behind and in front of the royal party. There was a slight shocked silence at this 'cut': Brummell was, after all, one of the hosts. Then Brummell's classically trained voice enunciated loudly to his neighbour: 'Alvanley, who's your fat friend?'

Pierrepoint later wrote that in the eyes of London society, if not the prince, in those days '[Brummell] could do no wrong', and it must be assumed that Brummell thought his words would be taken – like so many other of his precisely wrought impertinences – as 'a witty retort to a provocation, rather than an unmannerly insult'. Those further into the room, however, could see the prince's face and were immediately aware that the remark, which has since gone down in the annals of British comedy, had 'cut to the quick' the hefty heir to the throne 'by the aptness of the satire'.

Had Brummell lost his knack of the perfectly judged comic line? Or was his attack on his first protector another example of a man suffering a breakdown – financial, possibly physical and certainly, as it transpired, social?

It was not the end of the evening – which was accounted by many a great success – nor was it the end of Brummell's reign in London, as some writers later suggested. The remark, as with so many stories surrounding Brummell, was recounted frequently and with different supporting characters and locations (Lord Moira and St James's Street, for instance). But the effect was the same, no matter the details of the incident, an effect more slowly corrosive than explosive. Brummell found himself finally, unintentionally perhaps, but decidedly and categorically *outside* the royal circle. This left him much more vulnerable to his creditors, who, as his gambling addiction worsened, turned into a clamorous horde.

NO MORE A-ROVING SO
LATE INTO THE NIGHT

So, we'll go no more a-roving
So late into the night
Though the heart be still as loving,
And the moon be still as bright.

For the sword outwears its sheath,
And the soul wears out the breast,
And the heart must pause to breathe,
And love itself have rest.

Lord Byron, 1816

In Society, stay as long as you need to make an impression, and
as soon as you have made it, move on.

George Brummell

Late in his day in London, like so many promiscuous men of
his generation, Brummell contracted a sexually transmitted
disease. 'Dates,' as Harriette Wilson aptly put it, 'make ladies
nervous and stories dry,' and the exact occasion of Brummell's
infection can only be surmised by analysis of his later symptoms.
He might have noticed a tiny, painless chancre on or near the
glans of his penis about three weeks after the sexual act that
passed on to him the disease-carrying spirochetes. He might not.

But five to twelve weeks after the sexual encounter, he developed a severe fever, accompanied by a strange copper-coloured rash, which would not have itched, on his soles and palms. For a fastidious man like Brummell, this would have been unsettling, yet not nearly so unsettling as what happened next. Small, lightly suppurating patches appeared on his mouth and gums, followed by a patchy loss of body hair, aching bones, loss of appetite, insomnia, a terribly sore throat and headaches that, cruelly and punctually, racked him at set times of the day. Brummell, a man of the world and former dragoon officer, a man who offered advice on sex to professional courtesans, cannot have been ignorant for long that he had contracted syphilis.

Like any dragoon officer or London rake, he knew exactly what to do. He went to an establishment like Mrs Philip's Warehouse on Half Moon Street, 'seven doors up from The Strand, on the left', which sold sheep-gut condoms – in three useful sizes – to the cognoscenti, but also mercury, arsenic and iodine pills, and soothing almond oils. In less than a fortnight, he would have hidden the symptoms of the pox – which abated after treatment with these strong poisons and unguents – and thought himself cured.

On the one hand it is hardly shocking to discover, quite simply written in Brummell's medical records in France, that he suffered for many years from syphilis – 'the clap' or 'pox', as he would have called it. (The two were thought to be differing stages of the same disease, and often gonorrhoea, the clap, and syphilis, the pox, were indeed contracted at the same time.) Only a little later in the century it was estimated that 15 per cent of the population of Paris and London had them both, but the proportion was higher in the circles in which Brummell moved. The long-ignored fact of his syphilis, however, puts much of Brummell's later life in a radically different context. It also colours an understanding of his sexuality and how he spent the end of his days in London's high society, as well as what compounded the trauma of his leaving it.

Theories on Brummell's sex-life abound. The fascination

originated in his personal attractiveness, noted by his contemporaries, that was, in part, sexual. It relates also to his place in the history of fashion, for vanity and style-consciousness in men have, for whatever reasons, traditionally been linked to the sexually proactive or deviant. Moreover, Brummell himself has been described by cultural historians as a symbol, not unlike Byron, of a sort of New Man, of 'overstated manliness' and 'unambiguous masculinity' but who was also clearly in touch with his feminine side. This, in juxtaposition to his apparent indifference to sex, intrigued even the writers who knew him personally – Jesse, Raikes, Gronow and Wilson – who found that his sexuality presented some sort of enigma they felt drawn to address. These contemporaries, like the later biographers, covered all the possibilities and fall accordingly into four overlapping camps, arguing that Brummell was either asexual, homosexual, heterosexual or bisexual.

Brummell as an asexual has had particular appeal to the ascetically stylish, who hold that dandyism is incompatible with conventional sexuality. It was the position held, in effect, by Jesse: 'The organ of love in his cranium was only faintly developed. Independently of his deficiency in warmth, he had too much *self-love* ever to be really *in love* . . . he was a thorough flirt but his love was as light and as elegant as everything about him.' He reconciled Brummell's unmarried state to a sexual persona that was self-involved and emotionally unavailable. Even so, Jesse went on to catalogue a series of love-letters written by Brummell and to entitle one passage of his book 'The Beau in Love', as if to cover any accusation of effeminacy on Brummell's part but leave him untouched by sex.

Jesse's position on the subject of Brummell's sexuality is at best evasive and at worst deliberately obscurantist. His primary interest appeared to be to protect Brummell's name and, by extension, his own work. It would have been evident to many as a distinct possibility that a man with Brummell's later symptoms was dying of syphilis, but this would only have compounded a role Jesse knew Brummell was fulfilling in the early-Victorian imagination: that of a justly ruined profligate. So textbook-perfect were Brummell's later syphilitic symptoms that Jesse would have been at pains to whitewash his hero and put readers off the scent of sexual degeneracy.

Beyond this it should also be pointed out that the image of Brummell as an asexual, utterly uninterested in sex, was also refuted by his schoolfriends, some of them even in Jesse's own account. And then there is the undeniable evidence of his attending doctors in France, Dr Edouard Vastel and Dr John Kelly, who were in a position by 1840 to realise the clear link between Brummell's symptoms and an ancient syphilitic infection. This puts paid for good to the image of Brummell as the virgin saint of fashion.

Though in theory it is possible to catch syphilis from any sexual encounter and, in unlikely circumstances, by kissing, in practice syphilis was spread by armies on the move, by professional sex-workers, and by those who consorted frequently with either. Brummell may have been supremely unlucky, as he became at cards and dice, but it is unlikely that his syphilis points to anything other than a fairly active, though ill-considered, sex-life.

By one particularly cruel twist of fate, the aftershock of the battles of the Napoleonic wars may have had a double impact on Brummell's decline, with regard to both his gambling debts and his syphilis. The victorious British Army affected both. The rush to the tables of officers fresh from continental battles, playing hard and raising stakes, was a much-noted aspect of the years 1814–16. Brummell was not the only man ruined financially (debts compounded Byron's need to leave England and necessitated Scrope Davies's flight). But those same officers imported a different fever from the continent, and rushed from the gaming tables to the brothels of the West End with a virulent new strain of syphilis that spread quickly through the officer classes, the bagnios and brothels of London and thence, in turn, to their other habitués. It was a common effect of troop movements at the time, as one later writer memorably warned: 'there is a splendid [new] pox in town, as pure as the time of Francis I. The entire army has been laid up with it, boils are exploding in groins like shells, and purulent jets of clap vie with the fountains.'

Asexuality therefore provides an unsatisfactory explanation of Brummell's sexually 'cool' persona, which must have developed in response to a more complex sexual psyche. There is nothing in his syphilitic infection, however, to negate the theory that he was gay. The potential for his being homosexual may be inferred perhaps from the absence of heterosexual opportunism expressed by Thomas Raikes's 'he was not a man of intrigue'; from Hester Stanhope's interrogator who asked about his 'eccentricities'; and from countless writers since who have described him unjustly as 'mincing', 'camp' or even as a 'bitchy queen'. However tempting this conflation of the perceived style of the man and his apparent distance from women, the weight of opinion at the time, and the weight of evidence since, points strongly against his being exclusively homosexual. His schoolfriends thought him strongly heterosexual – although admittedly this posture is not uncommon among adolescent boys regardless of their eventual sexual orientation. But those who wrote about him soon after his death were adamant in asserting his heterosexuality, as if rumours of something then considered 'a monstrous sin against nature' had already been added to the catalogue of his sins that justified, in some popular morality tale, his demise in France.

Was Brummell, then, despite his apparently advanced feminine side, quite simply an emotionally unavailable heterosexual? It might seem the simplest answer, for all one would expect him in that case to have left in his wake, as that other celebrity dandy Lord Byron did, a trail of emotionally short-changed women. His affairs, as compared to his passionate friendships, seem tepid, yet they yielded some finely wrought love-letters from a man more used to high style than high romance: 'It was scarcely possible,' admitted Jesse, 'for him to be constantly in the society of the most beautiful girls in Europe . . . without having a preference for one of them, or perhaps half a dozen: and this was the case.' As evidence, Jesse cited the numerous letters Brummell had kept, containing 'silken tresses and delicate distresses' that he destroyed later in life. Barbey d'Aurevilly concurred that 'With such success, such command over society's opinion, such extreme youth to enhance his fame, and his air of charm and cruelty that women both revile and adore, there is no doubt that he inspired many conflicting passions.' How serious Brummell was in his conventionally romantic dalliances is a matter of conjecture, but it seems doubtful that they ever had his whole attention, let alone his heart. His appearance on the London stage as a young rake-about-town was a role he played to the hilt, with the expectation, like the hero of any stage or novel romance of the period, that closure would come with matrimony. Not only did he bet a friend that he would marry as early as the winter of 1799–1800, he also wrote a long letter early in the new century with all the cocksure flamboyance of a young blade who had made a decisive play for a young woman's hand. He was told, probably not for the first time, and in the time-honoured fashion, that the lady would rather be friends:

Dear Miss ——
When I wrote to you a century ago, in plaintive strains . . . you told me, with pen dipped in oblivion's ink from Lethe's stream, that I must desist from my vagaries, because I was trespassing on consecrated ground; but you offered me instead, your *friendship*, as a relic – by way of a bone to pick, among all my refined and elegant sensibilities! I then, by way of initiating myself to penance, inscribed you a missive, in appropriate terms of mortification, presuming too, that it was the privilege, not the duty of my vocation, to mortify you also, as a votary, with a little congenial castigation. I dare say I wrote to you in a most absurd and recriminating manner, for I was excited by the pious enthusiasm of my recent apostasy; and I was anxious to impress upon your more favourable opinion, the exemplary and salutary progress I had made in my new school. You are, it seems, displeased at it, though my heresy from my first delightful faith was your own work. I know not now where to turn for another belief.

The letter then appears to shift tone, as if it had been left and returned to when Brummell was in a more forthright or sober frame of mind:

> I will tell you in plain unmystical language, for I have not yet learned to renounce *that*, I was irritated because I thought you had cut me dead in the morning; and when I was *tête-à-tête* with my solitary lamp in the evening, a thousand threatening phantoms assailed me. I imagined that you had abandoned me; in short, a cohort of blue devils got the better of me, and I am now all compunction and anguish. Pray be once more an amiable and compassionate being, and do not contract your lovely eyebrows any more (I wish to heaven I could see them this instant!) in sullenness at all my numberless incongruities and sins. Be the same Samaritan saint you have already been to me: you shall never more repent it. Whatever I may have said in a frenical [*sic*] moment of exasperation was *unsaid* and *unthought* an hour afterwards, when I sought my couch, and proffered my honest prayers for forgiveness from above, and profanely from you who are upon earth. I am more than conscious of all my derelictions – of all my faults, but indeed they shall be in future corrected, if you are still a friend to me. I had vaunted, in the vanity of chivalrous spirit, that I had at length proved one in myself, but it was empty ostentation, for I find that I cannot exist but in amity with you.
>
> Your unfortunate supplicant
> George Brummell

Brummell's vagaries, incongruities and derelictions make it all too clear why Miss X must have wearied of his confusing alternating passion and distance, only to try to settle for a friendship that looked as though it would be just as infuriating. However, Brummell's good nature, not to mention a stage-honed sensitivity to the verbosity of eighteenth-century sentiment and its potential for humour, rescued him at least from dullness. If the nineteenth century was so young that he had last written to Miss X in 1799 then he, too, should be allowed his youth: he was only twenty-two.

Less easy to forgive, however, are his repeated 'engagements' to young women in London, played as tricks for his own vanity, the amusement of his friends, or out of a misplaced sense of courtesy. 'He never attained any degree of intimacy with a pretty young woman that he did not make her an offer,' wrote Jesse, meaning an offer of marriage, 'not with the idea of being accepted, but because he thought it was paying the lady a compliment and procured her an unusual degree of *éclat* in the fashionable world.' The ladies in question may have felt differently about the *éclat* of being proposed to and, in effect, jilted by London's most famous bachelor all within the space of an evening. 'The most favourable opportunity that presented itself for [proposing] was at a ball in the neighbourhood of Grosvenor Square, but his measures on the occasion were so badly taken that he and the intended Mrs Brummell were caught in the corner of the next street, a servant having turned mother's evidence.'

If this last point is true, it deserves more pause than Jesse gives it. Brummell was set to elope but was thwarted by a lady's maid on the corner of Grosvenor Square? It is the stuff of Lydia Languish's less improving bedside reading and scarcely attributable to Brummell, unless, of course, he had no intention of more than a play-acted elopement. It sounds as disingenuous as his intention to marry 'Lady Mary', which didn't work out, he told a friend, because he discovered the lady in question 'ate cabbage'.

His 'affairs' in adult life bear the same hallmarks as his early attempts at seduction as an Eton schoolboy, serenading the headmaster's daughter under her window. They were light-hearted dramas with Brummell casting himself as the juvenile lead: humorous, elegant and enacted as if with an audience in mind or in sight, a romantic suit to be tried on and discarded as ill-fitting. All of which would be understandable of a young man schooled in the ways of 'Gentleman' Lewis, the romantic-comedy leading man at Drury Lane, and humorous in the context of a sixteen-year-old. But in the context of the harshly commercial Georgian marriage market, where the loss of a woman's reputation could cost her a lifetime of unhappiness, Brummell seems to have been carelessly cruel.

The other letter to which Jesse had access is also from the end of an affair, a little later in Brummell's adult London life.

The Lady Jane ————, Harley Street

My Dear Lady Jane,

With the miniature it seems I am not to be trusted, even for two pitiful hours; my own memory must be, then, my only disconsolate expedient to obtain a resemblance.

As I am unwilling to merit the imputation of committing myself, by too flagrant a liberty, in retaining your glove, which you charitably sent at my head yesterday, as you would have extended an eleemosynary sixpence to the supplicating hat of a mendicant, I restore it to you; and allow me to assure you, that I have too much regard and respect for you, and too little practical vanity myself (whatever appearances may be against me) to have entertained, for one treacherous instant, the impertinent intention to defraud you of it. You are angry, perhaps irreparably incensed against me for this petty-larceny. I have no defence to offer in mitigation, but that of frenzy. But we know that you are an angel visiting these sublunary spheres, and therefore your first quality should be that of mercy; yet you are sometimes wayward and volatile in your seraphic disposition – though you have wings, still you have weapons, and these are, resentment and estrangement from me. With sentiments of the deepest compunction,

I am always

Yours miserable slave

George Brummell

Again Brummell references his frenzy and the celestial provenance of the lady he addresses. He mixes liberally stage rhetoric, frivolity, mock-theology and vague appeals for amicable forgiveness. In affairs of the heart, Brummell was infuriating. He presumes upon an affection sufficient to tease Lady Jane about the glove 'which you charitably sent at my head yesterday', but he has been asked for an immediate return of the miniature – a significant token of regard at the time – which could only mean Jane was already fearful for her reputation. The inference is that Brummell might use the miniature as evidence of an attachment in which Lady Jane did not feel secure. His play-acting at romance also presumed an audience, just as it had when he was a school-boy, of the men who later fed these stories around town and years later to Jesse.

Brummell played at affection, was adept at flattery, was evidently attractive and amusing and knew it, but in addition to this he chose deliberately to send out a differing signal. He was also unavailable. He had been 'cut dead' by Miss X but only after she had been forced to get angry with him for 'trespassing on consecrated ground' (the idea of marriage, or perhaps she was already engaged). He is desperate, in the conclusion of these amatory skirmishes, to be seen in the best light: to remain friends and to avoid hurt – but it is apparent that damage was done. Miss X and Lady Jane were left with eloquent and elegant letters (not so attached to them that they were unavailable to Jesse twenty years later: perhaps they had been sent back to Brummell who then kept them), but little else.

Brummell's heart was with his older women friends, with Princess Frederica in particular, and his character had been set quite early as a brittle confection. His dalliances, epistolary and we may assume actual, were flirtations with the idea of romance and marriage but little more. They were hurtful to the women involved, but they were never, as Brummell himself later con-fessed, 'that unaffected and fervent homage which [is] a heart's life blood'. He did not know what it was like to be in love until many years later and too late in the day to do anything about it.

His elusiveness in love and the offence it caused is also apparent in the number of times he was 'called out' to duel. This was the only acceptable closure for a love affair in which the woman felt her honour, and by extension that of her family, was called into question: 'If a gentleman detract from another gentleman, the resource that is prescribed . . . [is a duel],' wrote the authors of *The Laws of Honour and the Character of Gentleman*, stating that the most common grievance between gentlemen was their conduct *vis-à-vis* unmarried women. Brummell was challenged frequently to account for his conduct, but opted to treat even this as a joke. When he was challenged to offer 'satisfaction or an apology' by the protector of one lady and given five minutes to make up his mind which he would choose, Brummell replied, 'In five minutes, sir! In five seconds or less if you prefer!' He joked that he was 'not naturally of an heroic turn' and turned the one duel he did fight, at Chalk Farm, into an extended self-deprecatory monologue casting himself as world-weary coward: ' "You have taken a load off my mind!" he said to his second [his opponent had failed to show up]. "Let us go *immediately*!" '

In respect of these letters and putative love affairs, there is a different possibility of their context: they may not have been written to 'respectable' women at all but to courtesans. Their play-acted, stylised sentiment, and the emotional thrust and parry of gloves thrown and men 'cut dead' is precisely the manner in which the professional courtesans and actresses traditionally negotiated the early stages of an affair. This is not the light in which Jesse presents them, but it is possible that Brummell was adhering to the family tradition of allying himself very closely with the *demi-monde*, and even contemplating marriage with ladies who played a game he enjoyed.

If through fifteen years in the high life Brummell never formed a conventional sexual relationship or, despite the financial and societal pressures to marry, only once found himself in a half-hearted and aborted elopement, was he, perhaps, a closet homo-sexual? Or given his recorded affairs with women, was he bisexual?

The strongest case for a Brummell affair with another man is weak, but tempting to consider, as the other party in the story is the bisexual Lord Byron. Brummell kept two poems that Byron had given him in his album. One, quoted previously, was on the subject of fallen women in general, Lady Caroline Lamb and Julia

Johnstone, seemingly, in particular. The other poem Byron gave directly to Brummell:

> To one who promised on a lock of hair
> By Lord Byron
>
> Vow not at all, but if thou must,
> Oh! Be it by some slender token;
> Since pious pledge, and plighted trust,
> And holiest ties, too oft are broken
> Then by this dearest trifle swear,
> And if thou lov'st as I would have thee,
> This votive ringlet's tenderest hair
> Will bind thy heart to that I gave thee.

The poem had its first publication, undated, in Jesse's *Life of George Brummell*, and was not published in Byron collections for over a century. It bears comparison with some of Byron's earliest known poems, 'A Woman's Hair' and 'To a Lady Who presented the Author with the Velvet Band which Bound Her Tresses' (both 1806) and has been dated by some Byron scholars to this period. However, it is more likely, recent Byron scholars claim, to have been written in 1814 when Byron was twenty-six and Brummell thirty-six. It might have formed a 'companion piece' to the other poem in Brummell's collection, which Byron wrote between 1812 and 1814. Both were shown to Lady Melbourne, but it seems Byron gave 'To One Who Promised' to Brummell. It is a winning piece, and 'if thou lov'st as I would have thee' presses an urgent suit indeed if it is written by one bisexual young man to another. But there is nothing more. The letters Brummell had in his possession from Byron, which he claimed 'would produce more than sufficient to pay my debts', he destroyed. It was the Age of Sentiment: it might have been another parlour game – the poem might even have been written about Lady Caroline Lamb and given to Brummell in some spirit of bonded machismo. Byron's sexual predilection seems to have been for late-adolescent boys, and having his mistresses, Caroline Lamb for one, dress as pages. There is no record of his sexual interest in any older man.

On the other hand, there was an ill-defined bond between Byron and Brummell, a mutual fascination that had more than a frisson of pure attraction. Byron, after all, had said he would rather be Brummell than Napoleon, and his personal style, his 'Byronic' manner, was inspired in part by Brummell, as previously discussed. His poetry also became marked by the dandy pose, 'the characteristic rapidity of movement from absurdity to serious-ness', as one Byron scholar noted, that typifies Brummell's letters, the move from sentiment to satire, and the ability to encompass every tone 'from the tender to the devastatingly dismissive which we associate with the best satiric poetry'. In this sense, too, Brummell is closely caught up in the style that informed Byron's sexually athletic hero Don Juan. The epic poem, published after Brummell and Byron's respective flights from London, tells the story of the mythic womaniser, but sets his tale in part in the world that both dandies knew well: London's high society. Brummell is mentioned by name, along with many other members of the *Haut Ton*, and Don Juan was taken largely, and rightly, as a Byronic self-portrait. Others were less sure, and in the 1819 *Don Juan Unmasked, being a key to the mystery attending that remarkable publication*, the author suggests the other person-alities who have informed the poetic creation:

He abounds in sublime thought and love of humour, in dignified feeling and malignant passion, in elegant wit and obsolete conceit. [He] alternately presents us with the gaiety of the ballroom and the gloom of the scaffold, leading us among the airy pleasantries of fashionable assemblage and suddenly conducting us to haunts of depraved and disgusting sensuality . . . [he] turns decorum into jest, and bids defiance to the established decencies of life.

To those who knew any of the dandies, but especially Brum-mell, this amounted to an espousal of the entire dandy code. Don Juan turned the world upside down: the ridiculous was serious, passion was met with indifference, decorum was turned into jest.

But Don Juan, like Byron, knew well the haunts of 'disgusting sensuality'. Did Brummell also bid defiance to the established decencies of life as Byron had? If he did not have an affair with Byron – and it is flimsy evidence on which to base the claim – is there evidence for his bisexuality anywhere else?

Jesse, again, was keen to put readers off the idea, which may be read as a clear signal that he knew or suspected more than he let on. Conversely it might have meant there was nothing to know. The very term 'sexuality' dates from Brummell's period and it is worth recalling that our modern nomenclature for sexual tastes would have bemused men of Brummell's generation, linguistically and practically. There had been no such thing as a 'homosexual' in Brummell's schooldays, only people who committed 'sodomitical acts'; neither in his adulthood was there general acceptance of the idea of bisexuality. People were as they practised, and in Brummell's circle there was a wide-ranging definition of sexual morality. Any hint of sodomy as a sexual practice, however, between parties of whichever sex and no matter whether consensual, was so abhorrent that the very possibility was enough to compound Byron's need to flee the country.

Brummell's practice we cannot know, any more than Harriette Wilson's – and she wrote about a lifetime as a professional courtesan yet mentioned only a single sexual act. Brummell's *personality*, on the other hand, was considered deviant in sexual terms, through his disinterest in attaching himself to one declared mistress and his conspicuous 'self-love' (homosexuality in the classical sense). Moreover, although his schooldays and their period, in the late eighteenth century, were typified by a *laissez-faire* attitude to acts that today would be termed homosexual, attitudes in London were shifting fast in his early adulthood towards the supposed moral high ground of the Victorians. Although the age was yet to turn against the rakish heterosexual behaviour of Brummell's friends, it was already turning strongly against homosexuals. Economic turmoil and the war played their parts doubtless, as did the shifting ideals of masculinity in which Brummell had played a key role. But London was sent into paroxysms over the case of the Vere Street (male) brothel in 1810. 'The existence of this club,' thundered *The Times*, was 'detestable and repugnant to the common feelings of nature', and the twenty-three men who were apprehended in the White Swan pub, variously dressed as brides and bridesmaids, were submitted to the 'fury of the mob' bent on 'universal expression of execration'. They were put in the stocks outside the Haymarket theatre and pummelled to unconsciousness with 'offal, dung . . . and remains of diverse dogs and cats'. Attitudes had changed a good deal since the 1790s.

If he was bisexual, Brummell would have been wise to keep a mask over the issue, as his later acolyte Jesse would over the whole area of his sex-life. As for his syphilis, if anything this may count slightly against his being bisexual. At the time, it was widely held by many doctors that syphilis could not be caught through acts 'of sodomies and bestialities'. In strictly clinical terms they were wrong but in early-nineteenth-century epidemiological terms the doctors knew what they saw: syphilis was almost unheard of among Regency homosexual men. Dr Swediaur, the leading authority at the time, wrote of one particularly baffling case: 'after a voyage of four months a violent [syphilitic attack] broke out before [the man, an East India Company official] went ashore, though he could have received no infection during the voyage, *as there was not a woman onboard*.' It simply did not occur to doctor or patient that syphilis could be caught other than by heterosexual sex. Clearly, in this instance, *en route* to India, there were infected sailors who infected others (and there were East India Company officials who were less than honest with their doctors) but homosexual infection was so rare as to be unthinkable to a physician like Dr Swediaur after a lifetime's experience.

It is worth noting that later in the nineteenth century, in France, it became apparent to doctors that syphilis could be passed on through homosexual sex. Likewise earlier in the eighteenth century one London doctor had believed that 'any Friction or rubbing of the Yard' could transmit 'the Pocky contagious

Miasms' thought to spread the disease. This doctor, John Marten, specifically included contagion via 'one Man's conversing with, or having Carnal use of another Man's body, viz b . . . . . y [buggery] or by . . . a Man's putting his erected Penis into another Person (*Man* or Woman's) mouth'. Yet by the early 1800s the assumption and bias in London was that syphilis occurred only as a result of missionary-position intercourse, and was caught most often from professional sex-workers. Syphilitic husbands, consequently, assumed they could avoid infecting their wives if they resorted temporarily to anal intercourse. Brummell's syphilis is inconclusive in absolute terms as it relates to his sexuality, but at the time – simply by virtue of experience and empiricism – it would have been taken as further evidence of his heterosexuality.

It must also be acknowledged that the apparent enigma of Brummell's sexuality was possibly itself a construct of a deliberately beguiling man. Brummell refused to be pinned down. Just as he refused to sit for a full-length portrait, he knew that he would be less powerful in society if his status was clearly attached to one person: wife, lover or courtesan. He knew, like Byron, that the lowliest 'end of Fame' was merely 'to have, when the original is dust/A name, a wretched picture, and worse bust'. His was the most famous image of Regency masculinity, and yet there is no adequate record of how he looked or dressed. He knew that an element of his renown needed to be ill-defined, uncaptured. To this extent, those who have argued that a true dandy can never marry are right.

One last speculation remains, bolstered by the likelihood that Brummell's syphilis developed before, possibly long before, he left England. By 1816 he was already exhibiting symptoms – reckless behaviour, the self-loathing concomitant to gambling addiction, lethargy and sexual lassitude – that may be symptoms of a well-established syphilitic infection. No date, no person and no sex can be attached absolutely to his infection. However, the fact of his infection, in conjunction with his known circle in London, makes it likely that Brummell, though romantically elusive, was sexually active in the West End brothels that had been local fixtures for the

Brummell family for several generations. He may have had a public persona of emotional unavailability and sexual ambiguity, but in private it appears likely he had sexual liaisons within the circle of the professional courtesans he knew so well. Recent scholars have achieved detailed resuscitations of the life of the *demi-mondaine* Harriette Wilson, and it is in juxtaposition to her unconventional career trajectory, and that of Julia Johnstone, that Brummell, the syphilitic, is probably best understood.

After the opera, the theatre or Carlton House, and invariably on a Saturday night, the place for men like Brummell to repair was the champagne supper hosted by the Three Graces – Harriette Wilson, Julia Johnstone, and Harriette's sister Amy Dubochet – at York Place. The house was owned by General Madden, Amy's lover. He spent a good deal of time out of London or attending the Margravine of Anspach, formerly Lady Craven, at Brandenburg House and in his absence, Amy, Julia and Harriette entertained. Amy's champagne and cold-chicken parties were sociable, fashionable and planned almost exclusively for men. Alcohol flowed freely, men vied for the attention of the few women there, and there was food late into the night, dismissed airily by Harriette as 'merely a tray-supper'.

'In one corner of the drawing room,' she wrote, 'with plenty of champagne and claret [was] Brummell', who made a beeline first for the food, according to Harriette, 'in his zeal for cold chicken'. The rooms soon became a crush of men: Amy's lovers William Ponsonby and the MP Hart Davies – who paid money just to pat her arm – and Harriette's, the Marquess of Lorne and the Duke of Wellington. The suppers became a focal point of 'half the fashionable men of the town', Harriette wrote, and Julia recalled how 'the beaux all crowded in'. It is unclear whether there were many other women present at all, but often there were – none of them respectable, none of them true competition for Harriette, Julia or Amy, and these women were more sexually available to Brummell than the expensive Three Graces.

Under the pseudonym of Bernard Blackmantle, one habitué of these evenings later published a scandalous *roman à clef*, *The*

English Spy, with a chapter and verses on life with the courtesans. The Cyprians, as the courtesans were invariably called, threw wild parties:

In the supper room . . . spread forth a banquet every way worthy of the occasion . . . the rich juice of the grape and the inviting richness of the dessert were only equalled by the voluptuous votaries who surrounded the repast . . . Ceremony and cold restraint of well regulated society was banished in the free circulation of the glass. The eye of love shone forth the electric flash which animated the heart of young desire, lip met lip and soft cheek of violet beauty pressed the stubble down of manliness. Then, while the snowy orbs of nature undisguised heaved like old ocean with a circling swell, the amorous lover palmed the melting fair, and led her forth to . . . penetrate the mysteries of Cytherea.

Frequently in her memoirs, Harriette mentions Brummell's presence at these soirées, and his conspiratorial affection for the courtesans is remarkable. She narrates one scene, in her favoured manner of a dramatic dialogue, that sets the tone of Brummell's familial ease in Cyprian company. Harriette describes first how she was looking for an excuse to thin out the oppressive crush of men:

'I vote for cutting all the grocers and valets who intrude themselves into good society,' [I said].

'My father was a very superior valet,' Brummell quickly observed, 'he kept his place all his life, and that is more than Palmerston will do,' he continued, observing Lord Palmerston, who was in the act of making his bow to Amy, having just looked in on her from Lady Castlereagh's.

'I don't want any of Lady Castlereagh's men,' said Amy. 'Let all those who prefer her Saturday night to mine, stay with her.'

'Why Brummell went there, for an hour, before he came here,' said Alvanley.

'Mr Brummell had better go and pass a second hour with her ladyship,' retorted Amy, 'for we are really too full here.'

Seemingly Brummell started to make his exit, for Harriette met him on the doorstep just as she was leaving the party early for an assignation with the Marquess of Lorne. Brummell handed her into 'one of the Russian's carriages' that she was borrowing to take her to the Argyll townhouse. '"To Argyll House, I suppose?" said Brummell, then whispered in my ear, "You will be Duchess of Argyll, Harriette."'

It was not long before Brummell decided, according to Harriette, to throw his hat into the ring as well, in competition, as it were, with the great men of the age who had been her lovers:

My reflections were interrupted by my servant, who brought me a letter from George Brummell, full of nonsensical vows and professions.

'When, beautiful Harriette, will you admit me into your house? Why so obstinately refuse my visits? Tell me, I do entreat you, when I may throw myself at your feet, without fear of derision from a public homage on the pavement, or dislocation from the passing hackney coaches!'

'The rest,' Harriette claimed breezily, 'I have forgotten.'

There seems little doubt, however, judging by the style of a man who threatens to be dislocated by passing hackney cabs, that this was Brummell in the full flow of his dramatic muse. But again the seriousness of his romantic intent is unclear. Harriette ultimately said she found him 'cold', but nevertheless sought his company and even his advice on how to deal with men who did not want to stay after sex: 'The man does not want you to pass the night with him?' said Brummell, 'so e'en put your head on the pillow and read Peter Pindar, or fancy yourself in the steam-boat, while they are pumping.'

Julia Johnstone claimed Harriette wanted Brummell as a sexual trophy, while Harriette claimed Julia and Brummell were more than just old friends. It would be almost inconceivable for Harriette and Brummell to have launched on a full-blown affair because he could not afford her and she knew it. She ran hot and cold with him if her *Memoirs* are to be believed, often amused, sometimes flattered, always intrigued and occasionally irritated. Her writing managed both to 'conceal passion [for Brummell] and reveal it', according to Barbey d'Aurevilly, and Jesse claimed she was affected by '*la jalousie d'une femme*' for 'a woman can hardly be expected to forgive a man for being more elegant than herself'. Nevertheless, Brummell came near to fighting a duel over her, quite possibly challenged by her lover, the Duke of Wellington, but he opted instead to chase 'the man of war' out of his house with a red-hot poker.

Brummell was a fairly constant presence in the lives of Harriette and Julia: he lived his late evenings in the *demi-monde* as, in a sense, his family always had. He and Julia had a deeper and long-established understanding. They re-met at the opera, more than a decade after the teenage fumblings in the corridors of Hampton Court Palace. He said they were 'very old friends'; she said he had been 'violently in love with her'. Harriette inferred that they took up where they had left off, as lovers, which Julia denied, but Brummell, by virtue of being the subject of their argument, was tied ever more tightly to the courtesan world. Even Fanny, another of Harriette's sisters, informed Harriette that Brummell and Julia had been 'making strong love lately . . . Oh the shocking deceiver!' 'Tell Julia,' said Harriette, knowingly, 'not to believe one word he says.' The truth will never be known. It is unlikely Brummell ever slept with Harriette, who was a little too commercially inclined for all they had an affinity of independent-mindedness. It is likely, however, he resumed his affair with Julia at some stage, but it should be noted that despite her notoriety she had slept with few men. Had anything else happened within their clique to explain how Brummell caught a virulent dose of the pox and put himself into a tailspin of nihilistic depression and reckless gambling?

One symptom of primary syphilis is a cruelly erratic libido: one minute, the thought of sex is almost repugnant, the next, the sufferer is gripped with what Guy de Maupassant, another syphilitic, memorably described as 'the majestic pox! Alleluia! I screw the street whores and trollops, and afterwards I say to them, "I've got the pox," and I just laugh.' In the throes of his syphilitic euphoria he once coupled with six prostitutes within an hour (with witnesses). If Brummell was infected early with the pox, in his twenties even, it might have determined his whole adult sexual persona – 'cool' alternating with a more desperate neediness, and the possibility of more reckless couplings. Of course, this does not explain his initial infection. It is likely, though, that he caught syphilis late in his day in London. For one thing, although it killed him, he lived as long in exile as he had in the high life. For another, his self-immolating behaviour followed by a slow decline into physical disability and eventual madness expresses the full pathology of primary, secondary and tertiary syphilis played out over the years from around 1814.

Charlotte Hayes, a famous 'abbess' or madam who been in the West End sex trade long enough to feature in *Harris's List* (of West End prostitutes) in the early 1780s, finally met her end in 1811, mad with syphilis. Her story is instructive, as she was typical of the women Brummell had known all his adult life; her various establishments around St James's were frequented by all the male crowd around the Prince of Wales, including the prince himself. By the time Brummell knew her, she had become Mrs O'Kelley, having married an Irish conman Dennis O'Kelley and set up to live on the horizontal earning power of a 'Protestant nunnery' of high-class prostitutes. *Town and Country Magazine* agreed that the series of 'nunneries' the O'Kelleys came to operate around King's Place, St James's, 'administered Absolution in the most desperate cases', and called her a 'Living Saint' because she rendered miracles such as 'liquefying any amount of Golden Guineas into Champaign and Burgundy, [could] cure the Evil of Love and broken hearted Swains by the Touch'. They extended credit to their gentleman customers, in the manner of the local tailors and wine merchants – the young rake William Hickey got into trouble with them for introducing one Scottish captain who spent a fortune on 'wine, women, bed and bawd' and skipped town without paying.

Similarly there is a cartoon in the collection at the British

Museum entitled *A Meeting of Creditors* depicting the Prince of Wales beset by West End madams demanding payment for long and exotic lists of sexual favours enjoyed on account. Black Moll, the only Black brothel owner at the time, demands payment for her 'Count' and services from 'purl rods' [*sic*] to 'tipping the velvet'. Mrs O'Kelley's establishments, all within yards of the gentlemen's clubs of St James's, looked like respectable town-houses, with servants, lights and even musicians and card rooms. Only at the very end of the evening did the party split into couples – sometimes larger groups – and retire to bedrooms on the upper floors. A West End visitor, Baron Johann Wilhelm von Arch-enholz, described

the many noted Houses in . . . St James's kept for People of Fashion. A little street called King's Place is inhabited by Nuns of this Order who live under the direction of rich Abbesses. You may see them superbly clothed at Public Places . . . each of these Convents has a Carriage and servants-at-livery . . . the price of admission to these Temples is so exorbitant that the Mob are entirely excluded . . . only a few can aspire to the Favours of these Venal Divinities . . . the bagnios are magnificent buildings . . . the Furniture not unworthy of the Palace of a Prince. They can produce everything to enrapture the senses . . . the Women are instantly brought in Sedan chairs and only those cele-brated for their Fashion, Elegance and Charms have the honour of being admitted.

Without such women, the baron went on to say, 'the theatres would be empty' for the men of fashion flocked to see the wares in the boxes as much as the play itself.

These were the circumstances, on balance of evidence, in which Brummell most likely contracted syphilis. The high price on maidenheads was one clear effect of the general anxiety over venereal disease at the King's Place 'nunneries'. Mrs O'Kelley's one surviving 'tariff' – possibly fictional – puts a twenty-guinea price tag on 'Nelly Blossom, aged 19 who has had no one for four days and is a *Virgin*'. But 'Saint' Charlotte O'Kelley admitted to friends that 'a Maidenhead was as easily made as a Pudding'. One of her girls, Miss Shirley, went through 'twenty-three editions of virginity in a week, [but] being a bookseller's daughter,' said Mrs O'Kelley, 'she knew the value of repeated First Editions'.

Cynicism aside, Mrs O'Kelley was aware of the dangers of venereal disease for her girls and for trade, and like many West End madams sold condoms on the premises. It must be assumed that there was a general reluctance to use them, and the added diminution of their efficacy as prophylactics because they were washed and reused. It should be allowed that there is no record of Brummell ever entering such an establishment, only the likelihood, given his known companions and his later illness, that he did. Mrs O'Kelley herself was ancient by the time Brummell hit town, but her establishments continued to flourish under her successor 'abbesses' Mrs Matthews and Mrs Dubery, well into the nineteenth century.

There were other ways, too, in which it is reasonable to speculate he may have become infected. Brummell was a central figure in a crowd of men who frequently courted as a group the attentions of a single woman – a leading lady in society like Princess Frederica or more often a courtesan. Harriette Wilson once admitted to being in a large gathering of men all of whom she had known sexually. It was part of the *demi-monde* scene that was also Brummell's. 'The amorous beaux,' wrote the author of *The English Spy*, 'naturally inflame the ardour of each other's desires by their admiration for the general object of excitement [a courtesan or prostitute] until the possessing of such a treasure becomes a matter of heroism.' Sexual conquest in this scenario becomes 'a prize for which the young and gay will perform the most unaccountable prodigies, sacrifice health . . . and eventually life, to bear away in triumph the fair conqueror of hearts'.

It could be argued that this behaviour exhibits an extension of the 'unnatural' world of public schools like Eton, where sexuality is first understood in the context of an all-male world. It must also be said that this particular style of promiscuity, reminiscent of the activities of modern sports teams or, for that matter, Russian ballet stars, where the *esprit de corps* of a group of men is expressed in competitive courting, or even group sexual activity with a single woman, speaks of a barely suppressed homosexual bond. It was beyond doubt the sexual practice of the generation of libertines that preceded Brummell's: the Hellfire Club and Monks of Medenham who held orgies liberally intermingling 'taste, luxury, debauchery and vice'.

The Cyprians' balls were in a tradition of entertainment for men that had as its premise and ultimate goal a much more erotic intent than dancing. Perhaps the most famous was the Grand Bal de Mort, held by the courtesan Elizabeth Mitchell but attended by many aristocratic ladies of fallen reputation. The invitees wore fig leaves, in the biblical tradition, but over their faces, and were otherwise naked. The evening, inevitably, declined into an orgy. Masquerades, such as the one organised by Brummell in 1813 at the Argyle Rooms, were barely concealed imitations of this Cyprian practice. Masqueraders could flirt without fear of recognition, but were also likely to be more aware of their body language. The theatricality of the Cyprian fêtes went to its extremes for the re-enactment, staged by Mrs O'Kelley, of the 'Tahitian Feast of Venus' – a spurious tribute to the anthropological researches of Captain Cook. The masqueraders were entertained by live sex acts performed by South Sea islanders (Mrs O'Kelley's latest girls), 'all spotless virgins', and 'a dozen well-endowed athletic youths . . . each holding a dildo-shaped object wreathed in flowers'. Twenty-three gentlemen 'of the highest breeding', including five Members of Parliament, turned up to watch and participate. The nature of the entertainment on offer at the Cyprians' balls was altogether more sedate, but the purpose was identical. The Cyprians found theatrical means to drum up support for their particular endeavour: Harriette, Julia and Amy sold sex.

The tight world of the Cyprians, where only gentlemen of the *Ton* were admitted, expressed masculine exclusivity in terms Brummell would have well understood. Sex was part of the group experience. If Brummell's supposedly semi-hidden sexuality and projection of a 'cool' sexual persona was symptomatic not of asexuality but of a highly sexual if troubled bisexuality – might such an experience after a Cyprians' fête explain his syphilis? Even his earliest encounters with Susan Heath, the headmaster's daughter, or Julia Johnstone, may be seen as setting a pattern that was continued, disastrously, in adult life. Brummell chased women in the company of men: his sexual development was arrested at this adolescent stage. In this he was far from atypical of his class, time, and a means of sexual relation that has been described as homosocial, but with Brummell the effect was possibly underlined as a consequence of his mother's death.

He was attractive to both women and men and was himself clearly able to discern attractions in both. There is nothing but surmise, based on his position as sexually 'other', to point towards his homosexuality or even bisexuality, though neither can be easily discounted. He may have caught syphilis from sexual contact with any number of the conquering heroes of Waterloo. On the other hand the balance of probability, given his syphilitic condition and the amount of time he spent in the company of courtesans – now understood as a wildly promiscuous rather than a merely scandalous world – was that he was sexually involved with one or more of them, within the context, however intimate, of their shared 'ownership' by his coterie of men. The picture of the Cyprians' ball in *The English Spy*, and its description from Bernard Blackmantle, make it clear that there were many more sexually available women present than just the Three Graces. One of these may well have been the sexual partner, shared with others present at different times, who passed on the infection to Brummell.

By 1816 it must have been obvious to Brummell, and to his friends, that he had syphilis. It was unlikely to have been talked about: gentlemen didn't. The advertisements for the cures that appeared at the time in French and English periodicals make it clear that this prevalent disease was dealt with quietly, privately and, to a surprising degree, effectively. Doctors were known to treat ladies infected by their husbands without either party within the marriage being aware of the diagnosis. The mercury administered as pills and as ointments did rid the patient of the more obvious symptoms of infection: the chancre disappeared; the rash subsided. But men like Brummell were tragically in error when they thought they were cured and could resume their lives and sexual practice. And the horror that awaited many was not so much the return of the disease, but that their infection would be passed on, even to unborn children. And then there was the depression. Brummell wrote frequently about his 'blue devils', which would have been exacerbated by his syphilis and by the mercury poisons. This, as much as the alternating effect on his libido of the disease, was what caused his growing isolation and his self-destructive behaviour. The man, the disease and its effect were known well to Bulwer Lytton when he created his fictionalised Brummell in *Pelham*:

It was a strange thing to see a man with costly taste, luxurious habits, great talents peculiarly calculated for display, courted by the highest members of the state, admired for his beauty and genius by half the women in London, yet living in the most ascetic seclusion from his kind, and indulging in the darkest and most morbid despondency. No female was seen to win even his momentary glance of admiration. All the senses appeared to have lost for him, their customary allurements.

Those who knew Brummell, and who recognised what was happening to him, had good cause to be anxious for his welfare and for the future.

THE END OF THE DAY

12

PLAY HAS BEEN
THE RUIN OF US ALL

'Play,' he said, 'has been the ruin of all.'
'Who do you include in your all?'
He told me there had been a rot, in White's Club.
Harriette Wilson quotes Beau Brummell

May 1816 was one of the bleakest on record. Unknown to Londoners, the Indonesian volcano of Tambora had erupted the previous year and sulphur clouds were playing havoc with the world's weather. The winter had been more than usually harsh in England, with a road opened down the frozen Thames and thousands dying of cold; the trees in Green Park, which Brummell had known since he was a boy, did not come into leaf until late in the spring. It became known as 'the year without a summer'.

It was also a year of unremitting gloom for Brummell. He was suffering the fitful depressions and physical malaise associated with syphilis and its mercury therapy, but to compound this he was also approaching financial crisis. From 1811 to 1815 he had bought into a series of annuity schemes allowing him to be advanced large cash sums by City bankers on the promise of long-term – indeed, lifetime – repayments. In so doing he had been obliged to find co-lenders of obviously aristocratic and monied backgrounds, with clear expectations of inheritance. He turned to his old friends Lords Robert and Charles Manners.

Brummell's own expectations of advancement were decreasing and money-lenders in the City made it their business to be aware of the rising and falling hopes of the *Haut Ton*. The ball at the Argyle Rooms had marked publicly the deterioration in his relationship with the regent. He was becoming less able to service his debts, and the acknowledgement of his credit-unworthiness is evidenced in his need to borrow money from as far outside the City as Ripley in Yorkshire. The Manners brothers, like Brummell, were gambling heavily, but they had large allowances from their elder brother, the Duke of Rutland, and until 1813 they were presumed heirs to the dukedom. Their names stood well in Brummell's favour, and the cash, borrowed in the three names jointly, was nearly all for their impecunious friend.

The state of Brummell's financial affairs is best delineated in the Muniment Room at Belvoir Castle – the Duke of Rutland's family archive. It contains a number of detailed accounts of the debts Brummell accrued in collusion with Lords Charles and Robert Manners. Like any modern credit-card abuser, Brummell and the Manners brothers went back time and again to different money-lenders to mine lines of credit that they had little prospect of repaying. There are two annuity covenants, as examples, from May 1811, one of which runs:

Covenant between George Bryan Brummell, Esq., and Lord Robert Manners and William Walker of South Lambeth, County of Surrey, for the purchase of an annuity of £100 during the lives of George Brummell and Lord Robert Manners for the sum of £600 to be paid by the said William Walker to George Brummell and Lord Robert Manners.

In other words, William Walker 'invested' £600 for the satisfying return of £100 a year up to the death of the last of the two rakes. The second covenant from the same month was for a much larger sum, £1080, paid by a Mr George Jackson of Ripley against the annual repayment for life of £180, again by Brummell and Lord Robert. Three years later, in 1814, Brummell again sought cash with the Mannerses as co-guarantors, but this time with

Lord Charles as signatory. The six annuities detailed in the Belvoir archive harvested total cash sums of £6496 in the years 1811–14, against a repayment of £1024 due annually from the three of them for the term of their natural lives. There is every reason to believe that by 1816 Brummell had bought into more of these schemes elsewhere. Financially, it was madness. All three men were in their early thirties, and would pay off the whole sum within six years. If they lived and honoured their debt, the annuitants – William Walker and George Jackson – stood to make a killing. Meanwhile the borrowers would have had to be very desperate indeed to secure cash on such terms.

Only the recklessness of gambling addicts or the self-destructive impulses associated with syphilitic or liminal crisis makes any sense of these actions. The Belvoir archive points to the crux of the issue for Brummell: his smaller debts could be ignored for years, but gambling debts needed immediate payment. Brummell could not maintain his position in society otherwise. In 1814 several annuities were bought on the same day: 14 October. Brummell had some desperate need for cash that could only have been a gambling debt. The hope, as with any gambler, was that Lady Luck would return, whereupon the annuities might be bought back – at great expense. But Brummell must have known that his financial redemption was falling below the horizon of possibility. He had sold his life into the hands of unscrupulous money-lenders and into an unsustainable future.

Then in early May 1816 Brummell joined Lord Alvanley and the Marquess of Worcester – Harriette Wilson's former lover – in raising yet another loan. Though not as badly in debt as Brummell, Alvanley had exhausted his regular lines of credit: after a lifetime of applying to Jewish money-lenders in the City, he joked with dinner guests in March 1815 that he needed to find a lost tribe of Israel, as he and Brummell had 'exhausted the other two'. Most likely a large proportion of the money was meant to cover Alvanley and Brummell's existing annuity payments. According to Julia Johnstone, this 1816 loan was for the sum of £3000, but Harriette Wilson said she had heard – and she was in a better position to know – that it amounted to £30,000. If it was the latter figure, Brummell was probably hoping to buy back some of his more expensive annuities, but his good intentions did not last long. With the recklessness of a gambling addict and a depressive, Brummell took his share of the money straight to the card tables. He lost again, heavily. He had not even dared to show his chit at Watier's but had gambled instead at a club with an even harsher house banker: Gordon's on Jermyn Street. He stayed on, late into the night, until he had lost over five thousand pounds. He went back to Watier's, found Worcester, and confessed what he had done with the money. He would be unable to meet his share of the repayments on the loan secured to pay off previous ones. Worcester then did something foolish or angry or both: he told Richard Meyler, who was one of Brummell's many minor creditors. It was Meyler, armed with this information, who became known, in Harriette Wilson's much-quoted phrase, as 'the dandykiller'.

Richard Meyler had arrived later on the London scene with the dandies and courtesans who surrounded Brummell, and he had been regarded at first with some suspicion. He was an Etonian contemporary of Brummell's younger friend the Marquess of Worcester but was, like Brummell, an orphan who had come into an equivalently large inheritance (£30,000) before he was of age. They had therefore a certain amount in common and might perhaps have been friends, but Meyler developed a loathing for Brummell, a poisonous mix of envy, jealousy, disdain and class-consciousness. This might have been a result of Brummell's snobbery, which was reaching Gothic proportions – Meyler's money was new, from the Bristol sugar trade, and Alvanley referred to him as 'that damned methodistical little grocer'. The mutual disdain was more directly a result of Meyler's infatuation with Harriette Wilson and his suspicion – correct as it happened – that Brummell made fun of him to her from their opposing boxes at the King's Theatre. Meyler sat with his friend the Duchess of Beaufort, 'who was known to encourage a very motherly kindness towards young men, particularly if they were well-looking', while Brummell sat, laughing, with Harriette. Harriette was considering moving on from her protector, the Duchess's son the Marquess of Worcester, who had been sent abroad by the family to cool his ardour. Harriette's warnings about Meyler, from Brummell among others, only made him more attractive to her. 'No woman can do anything with [him],' she was told, 'for Meyler really don't know what sentiments means . . . [He] is a mere animal, a very handsome one, it is true, and there is much natural shrewdness about him.' He was considered a little unhinged, dangerous, even, especially sexually: 'His countenance is so peculiarly voluptuous that, when he looks at women, after dinner, though his manner is perfectly respectful, they are often observed to blush deeply, and hang down their heads, they really cannot tell why or wherefore.'

This apparent animal magnetism and Meyler's position as a sudden favourite with Worcester's mother, seems to have made him irresistible to Harriette. They began a passionate affair, conducted often at the home of Julia Johnstone, for fear, initially, of Worcester finding out. But when Worcester, Brummell and the rest of society became conscious of the affair, Meyler was painted as the wrongdoer much more than Harriette, and Harriette encouraged him to believe that Brummell had poisoned society against him. Harriette set up with Meyler as her protector – ironically in the same house that Worcester had rented for her at the height of their affair, on Lisson Grove near the new Regent's Park – and they began several years of violent disagreements followed by passionate reconciliations. She described him as 'one of the worst tempered men in England'; he called her 'a very tyrant . . . who neither esteemed nor trusted [me]'. By 1816 the affair was over, and Meyler and Worcester, in the way of men who had Harriette in common, became friends. But Brummell's name was linked for ever in Meyler's mind with the emotional stress of life with Harriette and the humiliations heaped upon him by Brummell's coterie at the outset of his liaison with her.

So, when Worcester told Meyler that Brummell was comprehensively going to renege on a debt, Meyler decided to act.

The next day, Wednesday, 15 May 1816, he went to the club he shared with Brummell on St James's Street: White's.

Harriette Wilson soon heard the news, and her *schadenfreude* at the time can be guessed from the relish with which she later narrated the unfolding drama:

The story was this. Brummell, Alvanley and Worcester agreed to raise thirty thousand pounds, on their joint securities. Brummell, having made Worcester believe that he was, at least, competent to pay the interest of the debt, the money was raised, and the weight of the debt was expected to fall on the Duke of Beaufort [Worcester's father], who, after strict enquiry, partly ascertained that Brummell was deeply involved without even the most remote prospect of ever possessing a single guinea. When Meyler heard of this he became furious, both on Worcester's account, and his own, declaring that Brummell had borrowed £7000 from him which he had lent, in the fullest conviction that Brummell was a man of honour.

I asked Meyler how he could be so very stupid as to have been deceived even for an instant, about Brummell?

'I would forgive him the £7000 he has robbed me of,' [said Meyler], 'but on Worcester's account, I shall expose him tomorrow at White's.'

'Why not let Worcester fight his own battles?'

'That is just what, for the Duchess of Beaufort's [his mother's] sake, I wish to prevent . . . Brummell, I will certainly expose: because he has basely obtained a sum of money . . . I hold it my duty, as an independent gentleman, never to give my countenance, nor society, to a man who has done a dishonourable action . . .'

[He] kept his promise of exposing Mr Brummell at White's Club, where he placed himself, the following morning, for the sole purpose of saying to every man, who entered, that Mr Brummell's late conduct, both towards the Marquess of Worcester and himself had been such as rendered him a disgrace to society and most unfit to remain a member of that club. Tom Raikes it was, I believe, who acquainted Brummell of this glowing panegyric on his character.

The impact of this on Brummell's position in London society cannot easily be overstated. Meyler was 'asking him out', or threatening him to a duel, if he chose to defend his name. If he did not, if he accepted the truth of what was said and Meyler's right to say it, he would put himself outside society. Meyler was only stating what was widely known to be the case, but to state it drew a line under Brummell's career: his name as a gentleman had been impugned, and his options were fight, flight or pay up.

Brummell addressed a few lines to Meyler [Harriette continued] begging him to be informed if such had, really and truly been the expressions made use of? Meyler answered that, not only he had used the expression, but, that he further proposed returning to the club, on the following day, for the sole purpose of repeating them, between the hours of two and four, to any body who might happen to be present, and if Mr Brummell had any thing to say to him in return he would be sure to find him at White's during that particular time.

The inevitability of what was happening would not have lessened the gnawing ignominy of facing it. Brummell made no reply and spent the rest of the day alone. He made one insouciant purchase at his snuff purveyors, Fribourg and Treyer on the Haymarket, of a two-and-a-half-pound jar of Martinique, and went home. Harriette claimed he went round 'about a dozen' of his acquaintance begging fifty-pound notes, but this was an unlikely preparation for the subterfuge that followed. He did, however, write to one friend, Scrope Davies, who happened to be at dinner with Lord Byron in Charles Street, Pall Mall. Captain Gronow recorded the letter and its reply partly for their distinct dandy panache in the face of tragedy, partly because Scrope's inability to help nailed Brummell's fate as surely as it pointed to his own.

Whilst [Byron] was dining with a few friends, a letter was delivered to Scrope Davis, which required an immediate answer. Scrope, after reading its contents, handed it to Byron. It was thus worded:–

My dear Scrope,
Lend me £500 for a few days; the funds are shut for the dividends, or I would not have made this request.
G Brummell

The reply was: –
My dear Brummell
Tis very unfortunate, but all my money is locked up in the three per cents.
Scrope Davis

The next day, Thursday, 16 May 1816, there was an air of celebration in London in what had otherwise been a dismal year. The heir to the throne, Princess Charlotte of Wales, had announced her engagement to Prince Leopold of Saxe-Coburg-Saalfeld and crowds gathered at the Queen's House – later remodelled as Buckingham Palace – to offer congratulations. There was such a crush that ladies's court trains were ripped and men lost their hats, only to recover them, somewhat dented, on tables lining the exit, and the cartoonist Cruikshank scored another commercial success caricaturing the ridiculous rich squeezing through a palace doorway.

For Brummell the day was no laughing matter. He stayed quietly at home and wrote some letters, made plans, and dined alone on cold capon and a bottle of claret that he ordered in from Watier's.

Then he dressed. He wore his usual evening attire of sheer black pantaloons, black coat and waistcoat, white shirt and cravat. Nothing was unusual in his manner or appearance. It has always been related that he attended the opera that night as usual to acknowledge a few acquaintances, but he cannot have done. There must have been a last-minute change of plan as *The Times* records that the second benefit performance for the tenor Mr Braham of the opera *La Cosa Rara* at the King's was cancelled at short notice. Presumably Brummell went instead to Covent Garden, as he was seen in public in a theatre box, and saw the last act of a play there. The title must have given him pause for thought: it was *Love, Law and Physic*. There were acquaintances at Covent Garden to whom he could nod recognition, but he slipped out before the curtain-call into the cold spring night.

A coach was waiting for him, but not his own. It drove him

across old Westminster Bridge to Clapham Common, two miles south of the river, where his own carriage was waiting in a place where no one was likely to recognise it. He had slipped out of London as suddenly as he had arrived seventeen years before, and by the time theatre-goers were looking for him in the lobby of Covent Garden, in the Great Subscription Room at Brooks's or the supper parties of the courtesans, he was galloping through Kent heading south to the coast. He travelled through the night the seventy turnpike miles via Dartford, Rochester, Sittingbourne and Canterbury to Dover where he chartered a small boat that slipped its moorings before dawn to take him to France. He never set foot in England again.

'He did quite right to be off,' quipped his boon companion, Lord Alvanley, who was one of the very few to know of the plan. 'It was Solomans's Judgement.'

PART III
1816–40

A MAN OF FASHION, GONE TO THE CONTINENT

A Catalogue
of
A very choice and valuable assemblage
of
Specimens of the rare old Sèvres Porcelaine
Articles of Buhl Manufacture
Curiously chased Plate
Library of Books
Chiefly of French, Italian, and English Literature, the best
Editions and in fine Condition
The Admired Drawing of *The Angry Child*, and others
Exquisitely Finished by Holmes, Christall de Windt
and Stephanoff
Three capital double-barrelled Fowling Pieces
by Manton
Ten Dozen of capital Old Port, sixteen dozen of Claret (Beauvais)
Burgundy, Claret, and Still Champagne;
The whole of which have been nine years in bottle in the
Cellar of the Proprietor
also, an
Assortment of Table and Other Linen, and some Articles of
Neat Furniture
The genuine Property of
A MAN OF FASHION
Gone to the Continent
which
by order of the Sheriff of Middlesex
will be Sold by Auction
by M. Christie
on the Premises, No 13 Chapel Street, Park Lane
on Wednesday, May 22nd and following Day.

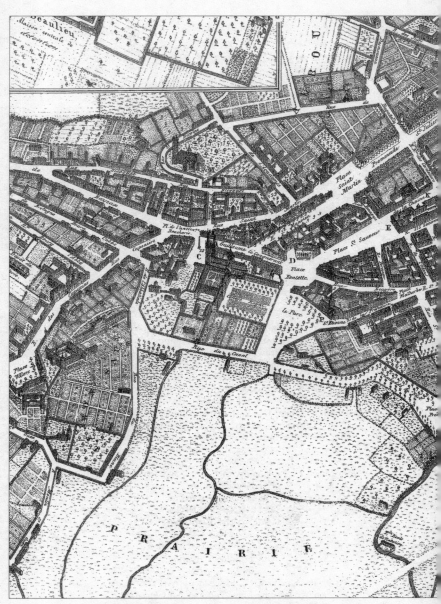

Caen, 1840, where Brummell lived after he left Calais until his death in the year this map was drawn. The prison is visible off the Place Fontette and the asylum of Bon Sauveur is on the far left.

13

ROI DE CALAIS

1816–21

Calais is peopled with English slight sinners and heavy debtors,
the needy and the greedy [it is] a sort of purgatory for half-
condemned souls.

Harriet 'Harryo' Cavendish,
later Lady Granville Leveson Gower,
daughter of Georgiana, Duchess of Devonshire

Early in the afternoon of Saturday, 18 May 1816, the boat
Brummell had hired to take him across the Channel docked
in Calais. The ancient city presented a grey and unappealing
prospect, being a semi-fortified staging-post rather than a town
such as Brummell had ever known before. But it represented
freedom of a sort. Had Brummell stayed in England he would
have faced the censure of society but also the living death of
debtors' prison without any realistic prospects of paying back
the money he owed. Any of the dozens of London tradesmen to
whom he owed money could, in theory, have had him incarcerated. In practice, the arrest warrants were expensive, so
several would have had to club together to issue a writ for
debt, but this was far from uncommon once word of ruin was
out. When the stock market crashed in 1825, 101,000 writs for
debt-arrest were issued, and at any given time during the
Regency there were upwards of a thousand gentlemen im-

prisoned in London for debt – most often in the notorious King's Bench prison in Southwark.

The continent provided the only answer, and one that was, for men and women in Brummell's position, both traditional and commonplace. But debtors stayed in Calais if they had been forced to flee without preparation. An Englishman was beyond English law in Calais, but could only proceed further into France with a passport, and a passport would not have been granted to anyone thought likely to be fleeing the law.

The place to stay in Calais for debtors on the run and English travellers was Dessin's Hotel just off the Place des Armes. It was run by a Gascon family who had long profited from English gentry on the first or last leg of Grand Tours, and from distressed gentlefolk like George Brummell who beached themselves first, and often permanently, in Calais.

Dessin's – or Dessein's – Hotel offered guests a large courtyard and garden, 'commodious baths', a small theatre, and even the novel concept of a 'restaurant'; unheard-of in London in 1816. It was sufficiently regal – and suitably well-placed next to the Hôtel de Ville – for it to have been used by the returning Bourbon monarch three years earlier for his first address as King Louis XVIII on French soil. As a result it was known as 'L'Auberge des rois'. But Dessin's was almost as famous among the British for having been the home of Lawrence Sterne, the author of *Tristram Shandy*. Brummell settled himself in, with his mind entirely on the English side of the Channel, and began what would be a long and voluminous epistolary relationship with his former London friends.

His first letter – of apology appropriately enough – was to Robert and Charles Manners. They had been left to shoulder large debts without him, which they could only hope to cover by going cap in hand to their brother, the Duke of Rutland. Brummell wrote to them from Dessin's on the day he arrived.

Calais, May 18, 1816

Dear Lords Charles and Robert,
Persecuted to the worst extent by those to whom I was indebted,

without resource or the hope to evade or protract the execution of those menaces which, I was well assured, would have been instantly enforced against my personal liberty, I have been driven to the only alternative yet left me upon earth – that of quitting my country for ever. I am indeed most sensible, acutely so, of the heavy wrongs which such a step must inflict upon those who from their former friendly regard for me were induced to impose upon themselves a future charge for my immediate assistance . . . I have not extenuation to advance beyond the desire to retain the only blessing, if such it can be called, still within my reach, which is personal freedom and even that I would have voluntarily yielded could I have felt assured its surrender might in any way have exonerated you from the trust in which you have been involved on my account. The responsibility would still have existed the same on your parts had I forfeited myself to a gaol.

In acknowledging my obligations to you – for great they are – and in lamenting my inability to repay them, I still feel anxious in the wish to realise the promised power of future remuneration . . . It was pressure of circumstance which compelled me to adopt so precipitate, and I will say so disgraceful, a measure at the exigence [*sic*] of the moment.

I abandon my country a beggar and I can look forward to no means of subsistence beyond the year – yet I feel some remote satisfaction in the idea that the slight reparation I am offering is everything that is left to your former friend.

His characteristic interweaving of the self-dramatising, the self-pitying and the truly heartfelt was only remarkable for the uncharacteristic absence of humour. There was little to joke about. Brummell's state of mind was, for him, fairly honestly exposed and his feelings of guilt were unguarded along with his desperate anxiety. His sensation of intense loneliness can only have been exacerbated by his strange new surroundings and the suddenness of the change. He had moved from the largest city in the world – where he had been a celebrated figure for fifteen years in a sociable, voluble and cosseted circle – to a provincial port with few social amenities, surrounded by working people who spoke a language in which he was far from fluent. It is hardly surprising his mind was reflective and backward-looking. And there was much to repine.

Lord Charles and Lord Robert's elder brother, the Duke of Rutland, bought back all the annuities for sums considerably larger than the original amounts paid out to their friend Brummell, sums Brummell had speedily lost at the tables of Watier's, Gordon's, Brooks's and White's. How many tradesmen Brummell left in his wake to regret their trust in him is unknown, but he left thousands, maybe tens of thousand of pounds of debts, which could not possibly be covered even by the sale of the lavish contents of his London home. He did not own the house on Chapel Street. 'The cry of indignation that was raised at his departure,' Thomas Raikes wrote, in response to the reasonable annoyance of the Manners brothers, was nothing compared to the real suffering Brummell's flight inflicted on small tradesmen. Raikes was a City man as well as a dandy and had a better grasp on who paid the price in cases of spectacular bankruptcy like Brummell's. 'What a long list of ruin, desolation, and suicide could I now trace,' he wrote, 'to this very source [Brummell's flight].'

The sale intended to recoup some of these debts for Brummell's creditors took place within days of his flight, on Wednesday 22 May. While Brummell sat scratching out apologetic letters in Dessin's Hotel in Calais, in Mayfair, 13 Chapel Street became choked with excited buyers – the curious-minded as well as bargain-hunters – waiting for Mr Christie to start the bidding. News had spread fast of Brummell's disappearance and there were wild rumours about the money he owed, and about the amount he had run away with. One gossip reported inaccurately that 'the fraternity of [the] high life is thrown into a state of extreme consternation by the disappearance of Beau Brummell . . . with £40,000, the whole of which he is said to have fraudulently obtained.' A few days later the same scandalmonger repeated a story that 'Brummell's private debts are very considerable . . . Lord Wellesley says he is in Picardy.' On 20 May Sir Robert Peel wrote to Lord Whitworth that 'Mr Brummell has decamped to the confusion of his collaterals and his creditors . . . and has conferred the benefit of his countenance upon the Continent . . . I believe some public good as far as the rising generation is concerned, will result from the downfall of such heroes as Mr Brummell.' *The Times* meanwhile started running daily advertisements for the Christie's sale: 'Rare old Sève [*sic*] Porcelain, Buhl, Cabinets, books, Drawings, Plate and Wines etc. Tomorrow and the following day, punctually at one. THE very elegant EFFECTS of a MAN of FASHION GONE to the CONTINENT, at his late residence, 13 Chapel Street, Park Lane.' The sale was set for the Wednesday and Thursday, but in the event, everything was sold within a few hours on the Wednesday. The Duke and Duchess of York sent a representative, Lords Bessborough and Yarmouth were there to bid, with Lady Warburton and Sir Henry Smith. But also present was Brummell's creditor John Mills, in the company of one Colonel Cotton – Brummell's rival for the affections of Julia Johnstone twenty years before.

The sale amounted to almost everything Brummell had ever owned. It included his mahogany sliding cheval dressing mirror, and the ebony-framed mirror that once graced the mantelpiece in his drawing rooms at his Chesterfield Street and Chapel Street homes. His medicine box was sold, emptied of its expensive mercury and arsenic pills, and so, too, was the watercolours box that had been his companion on many restful hours with the Duchess of Rutland. A full dinner service was notable only for its large number of breakfast plates; breakfast was the meal Brummell was most likely to host for his dandiacal friends. There were sixteen pairs of best linen sheets, and forty huckaback towels. A single cup and cover of Sèvres china fetched eighteen pounds, a ewer and basin twenty-six, a silver tea-kettle forty-seven, and one drawing, Holmes's *A Family Party at Dinner*, went for eighty-five guineas. Paintings of Lord North, the Duke of Rutland, Nelson, Pitt and the King (George III) fetched lower prices, but the competition for 'knick-knacks' was great. One snuff-box, on being opened, was found to contain a note from Brummell. It was one he had intended to give the prince, if the prince had not demanded another and never paid for it: 'This snuffbox was intended for the Prince Regent,' Brummell had scribbled on the small piece of paper inside, 'if he had conducted himself with more propriety towards me.' Over £1100 was raised by the sale and handed over to the presiding Middlesex bailiff for division among those of Brummell's creditors who could prove his debt. First in line, it must be assumed, were the many tailors who had been extending credit for over a decade.

One aspect of the sale that has gone unremarked is that the prices bid were well above the usual market rate for what was, mainly, upmarket bric-à-brac. Those who bought his books and table linen, his glasses and Manton guns, not to mention his claret and Still Champagne clearly wanted items touched by celebrity and notoriety, much as might be the case today. Yet barely a single piece is known to have come on to the auction market, with the name still attached, in the years since. Brummell's fame has endured, but the generation that came immediately after him was unwilling to use his name to burnish heirlooms or help sell their parents' art. The artefacts lost their association and the story of their unusual provenance.

~

In France, Brummell may have lost his old knick-knacks but was not for long without his friends. Dessin's was busy that summer. Prince Esterhazy stayed on his way back to London and was therefore one of the first of Brummell's many visitors in exile. Lord Glenbervie came a short while later. He had married one of the daughters of Lord North whom Brummell had known as a boy. Lord Glenbervie wrote to his son 'how Brummell had changed since we saw him at Brighton on his first joining the Tenth Dragoons – handsome, ingenuous and clever . . . Brummell, who has now been twenty-two or twenty-three years on the town, and has been nicknamed [in Calais] The Dowager Dandy.' But Dessin's Hotel proved either too expensive or too public for Brummell, or both. 'The hotel', according to a contemporary travel writer, was 'frequented by none but persons of rank and fashion, the charges, therefore, are proportionately high'.

Brummell had left England not quite as destitute as he claimed to the Manners brothers, but even so he maintained he had 'means of subsistence' for just six months. Wisely he had remained in possession of his carriage. He had paid to load it on board the boat that he had chartered at Dover (three guineas extra for haulage). One of his early practical actions in France was to sell it to the owner of Dessin's, Monsieur Quillac, which freed up some much-needed capital. Brummell had also managed to smuggle out of Chapel Street at least one trunk of precious clothes, and also some small items of Buhl furniture and even china. These he kept for the time being, and started looking for lodgings.

By law, Brummell could only consider accommodation within the ancient city walls of Calais. Fortunately there was plenty of rental accommodation on offer, and the rooms he chose were conveniently close to the entertainments of Dessin's, in a former hotel that had been converted into apartments and a bookstore. The former Hôtel d'Angleterre overlooked the rue Royale, which ran from the Place d'Armes to the rue Française, where Emma Hamilton had died in 1815. The artificial grandeur and high-ceilinged dimensions of a hotel once the haunt of travelling aristocrats was perfect for Brummell's idea of himself in exile. The building had been abandoned during the Revolution, then bought in the mid-1790s by a Monsieur Leleux who had done well out of the years of the Terror. Listed as a joiner when he signed up to the revolutionary Garde Nationale in 1789 he had made so much money fighting in the Americas under General Miranda that he had returned to Calais, bought up the ransacked hotel and remodelled the ground floor as a bookshop, soon said to be the best in Calais. But the building was too large for his needs, so he let the upper floors to lodgers. At this grand but distressed building, under the blank ovals that had once framed busts of King George II and his consort, before their images were torn down by a revolutionary mob, Brummell set up home.

He had two large rooms overlooking the busy rue Royale – its name newly restored along with the Bourbon monarchy. He also had a small bedchamber at the rear, connected to the other two rooms by a corridor. His resilience of spirit was remarkable. He furnished the rooms with the few things he had brought from London, then set about spending the money from the sale of his carriage, buying the accoutrements he would need to set himself up as a Gentleman of Fashion, living elegantly, as Lord Stuart de Rothsay and Brummell himself later quipped, 'between London and Paris'.

For many months, cash appeared not to be a problem. Monsieur Leleux rented him a small garden under the ramparts of the old city walls, and granted him permission to redecorate his rooms, even to the extent of laying a chequered marble floor in an unused corridor and staircase that connected his apartments to the street, thus fashioning for Brummell a private entrance. The flooring was of the same design Brummell must have remembered from the entrance hall at Downing Street. Next he papered the dining room with expensive crimson wallpaper and ordered furniture from Paris, so much, over the years, that Jesse heard the supplier had made thirty thousand francs' profit on the transactions. He re-created a London salon in the ruins of this former Calais hotel, with floor-to-ceiling prints and drawings, matching suites of Buhl and ormolu furniture in the Louis XIV style favoured by the British regent, bronzes, japanned screens and 'a large cabinet with brass wire doors' for his new collection of 'extremely beautiful Sèvres china'. For a man who claimed he was destitute, Brummell cut a regal figure around Calais. Where did all the money come from? One story went round that an anonymous benefactor had made a large deposit into a Calais bank in his name; another that the Duchess of York had bought an annuity scheme for him, which was paid until her death in 1820. It seems likely that both stories were true, as Brummell lived relatively well for several years, and it was widely allowed that Captain Samuel Marshall, Calais's British consul, was paying over sums to him. Brummell also knew that an appearance of wealth would extend credit to him when he needed it. And soon enough he did.

Meanwhile, he entertained in his apartments. The European peace – brokered at the Congress of Vienna in 1815 and after the battle of Waterloo – meant that Calais was once again bustling with visitors on their way to or from Britain. The quayside was rebuilt, a lighthouse constructed for night crossings to England, and between 1816 and 1818 there were upwards of four hundred departures a month. Many of these were explained by continuing repatriations of British troops – twelve thousand men along with some three hundred horses per month in 1816. With them came many officers, some known to Brummell, and in their wake many more aristocratic visitors. Talleyrand's comrade in amours, Beau Montrond, passed by *en route* to London and gave Brummell a Siena marble ink-blotter that had once been Napoleon's. The Dukes of Wellington, Richmond, Beaufort and Bedford all visited. Lord Yarmouth was back and forth, buying French art and antiques towards what would become the Wallace Collection. Lords Sefton, Jersey, Willoughby d'Eresby, and Stuart de Rothsay all climbed the stairs from the chequered hallway to pay court – as if, as Harriette Wilson said, Brummell were some 'lion at a zoo'. 'Every bird of passage from the fashionable world,' wrote Prince Pückler-Muskau, 'pays the former patriarch the tribute of a visit.' Fellow Etonian Berkeley Craven was soon in exile too, bringing news that their schoolfriend Thomas Raikes would also visit on his way back from Paris. Brummell immediately wrote to Raikes asking him to buy snuff: '2lb of Façon de Paris [best Paris snuff] . . . I have not a pinch remaining to befriend my sluggish evenings.' It wasn't long also before Brummell saw Lord Alvanley again and Lady Granville wrote to her sister later that first year of his exile to say, 'Mr Brummell is the happiest of men, lives chiefly with the natives and enters into all the little gossip and tittle-tattle of the place with exactly the same zest as he was wont to do in England.'

Calais turned out to be an excellent venue for Brummell, a European crossroads where everyone was forced to wait for the tide, and pay court to the Beau in exile. When Harriette Wilson, *en route* to Paris, decided to pay a call she noted immediately that

nothing much had changed in the world since she had last seen
Brummell carousing in Mayfair. She littered her description with
dialogue, as ever, much of it in her eccentric rendition of French:

Curiosity induced me to enquire about him as I passed through Calais
. . . I made the beau a hasty visit, just as the horses were being put to
my carriage. My enquiry, *si Monsieur Brummell etoit visible?'* was
answered, by his valet, just such a valet as one would have given the
beau, in the acme of his glory, *bien poudre, bien ceremonieux, et bien
mis, 'que Monsieur fesoit sa barbe. Pardon,'* added the valet, seeing me
about to leave my card, *'mais Monsieur recoit, en fesant la barbe,
toujours. Monsieur est à sa seconde toilette actuellement.'*

I found the beau en robe de chambre, 'de Florence', and if one might
judge from his increased embonpoint and freshness his disgrace had
not seriously affected him. He touched lightly on this subject in the
course of our conversation, *fesant toujours la barbe, avec une grâce
toute particulière, et le moindre petit rasoir que je n'eut jamais vu.*

'I have heard all about your late tricks, in London,' said I. Brummell
laughed, and told me that, in Calais, he sought only after French
society, because it was his decided opinion that nothing could be more
ridiculous than the idea of a man going to the Continent, whether
from necessity or choice, merely to associate with Englishmen. I asked
him if he did not find Calais a very melancholy residence?

'No,' answered Brummell, 'not at all. I draw, read, study and . . .'
then turning to me [he said] 'There are some very pretty French
actresses . . . I had such a sweet, green shoe, here, just now. In short, I
have never been, in any place, in my life, where I could not amuse
myself.'

There had, however, been one stunning change in Brummell's
appearance. When he arrived in France he shaved off all his hair.
This was noted without alarm by Harriette and others, and
Brummell even mentioned it to his friend Tom Raikes, but to
those in the know it was another sign that he was not well. The
stress or a mismanagement of his mercury regime had led to the
recurrence of a syphilitic symptom: alopecia. Undaunted, he
shaved off the hair that remained, the better, it was acknowledged

at the time, to apply the mercury unguents that kept the skin complaints at bay, and commissioned a smart brown wig, that was, according to Harriette, 'nature itself', and passed himself off as twenty-five 'at a little distance'.

He wrote a defiant if melancholy missive to Thomas Raikes later in the summer:

As to the alteration in my looks, you will laugh when I tell you your own head of hair is but a scanty possession in comparison with that which now crowns my pristine baldness; a convenient, comely scalp, that has divested me of my former respectability of appearance (for what right have I now to such an outward sign?) and [with my new wig] I should certainly pass at a little distance for *five and twenty*. And so, let me whisper to you, seems to think Madame la Baronne de Borno the wife of a Russian officer who is now in England, and in his absence resident in this house [Leleux's]. Approving and inviting are her frequent smiles and she looks into my window from the garden-walk; but I have neither the spirits nor inclination to improve such flattering overtures.

Entertaining actresses in his Florentine dressing-robe and smiling from his window at Madame la Baronne, Brummell wiled away his days, with no particular 'spirits nor inclination' to take advantage of his position as a local celebrity to seduce anyone. His syphilis, intermittently, would have precluded such an idea. It was wrongly assumed at the time that syphilis was non-communicable when the symptoms were in abeyance, and generally people preferred to believe themselves cured but, unsurprisingly, syphilis and its mercury treatment could cause impotence and general loss of libido.

He was further held back in his sociability by the poor standard of his spoken French and this he sought to rectify. He engaged a former *abbé* who charged him three francs an hour for French lessons – his first since leaving Eton. Scrope Davies cruelly joked to Byron that he had heard their old friend Brummell was struggling with French grammar, and had 'been stopped, like Buonaparte in Russia, by the *elements*'. Byron stole the joke to use in his poem *Beppo*:

Crushed was Napoleon . . .
Stopped by the Elements – like a Whaler – or
A blundering novice in new French grammar.

The poet had the decency to acknowledge his plagiarism and said,
with regard to Davies, that 'fair exchange [is] no robbery' as
Davies had 'made his fortune' telling Byron stories at dinner. In
any event, it was all an unfair joke at Brummell's expense. His
written French had always been adequate – he had been reading
letters from Princess Frederica in French all through their
relationship – but in France it was the spoken word he struggled
at first to master. Eventually his language master pronounced that
he had *un ton parfait*, and expressed surprise that he had never
learned to speak the French language in England.

Monsieur Leleux appreciated his efforts. He spoke of him with
enormous admiration and affection several decades later, describing him as *si amusant, si amusant qu'on ne pourrait rien lui
refuser!** 'Sir,' he continued, 'I would have kept him for nothing if
he would have stayed: ah! He certainly was a very droll fellow.'
An ability to amuse suggests Brummell's lessons paid off, and he
was able to communicate with his trademark panache, in French,
within his first year in Calais. 'We used to call him *le roi de
Calais*,' the town tobacconist's wife recalled to Jesse, 'he was a
truly fine man, very elegant, and [to start with] he always paid his
bills and was very good to the poor.'

In order to maintain his lifestyle, he hoped to be appointed
British consul in place of Captain Marshall. Unfortunately for
him, consular positions in France were often held for life and
Marshall was in conspicuously good health. To complicate
matters, Brummell came to be on very friendly terms with
Marshall and 'all his family'; they even had a running schoolboy
joke about their bad French. His alternative hope was that
Marshall might be promoted to another post, and Brummell
appointed as consul in his stead. This could only be effected at
a fairly exalted level in the Foreign Office, so Brummell assidu-

* 'So amusing that we could refuse him nothing!'

ously buttonholed his high-placed friends as they passed through Calais to lobby on his behalf. He lived his life as he always had: on expectations of future advancement and on his charm.

His life in Calais soon settled into a routine, punctuated by the arrival of the ships from England and the possibility of visitors. He described to Raikes how

surprised [you would be] to find the sudden change and transfigura-
tion . . . accomplished in my way of life and *propria persona*. I am punctually off the pillow at half past seven in the morning. My first object – melancholy it may be in its nature – is to walk to the pier head and take my distant look at England . . . The rest of my day is filled up with strolling an hour or two round the ramparts of the dismal town, in reading, and the study of that language which must hereafter be my own, for never more shall I set foot in my own country.

He took to the French taste for *café au lait*, and read the *Morning Chronicle*, at Dessin's, despatched from England. 'I dine at five, and my evening [is] occupied in writing letters. The English I have seen here – and many of them known to me – I have cautiously avoided . . . Prince Esterhazy was here yesterday, and came into my room unexpectedly without my knowing he had arrived. So much for my life hitherto on this side of the water.'

Brummell became so punctual in his routine that Calais work-
men recalled to Jesse setting their lunch-hour by his hour of dressing for the afternoon (they would see him move from his parlour overlooking the street to the back): '*Ah, voilà Monsieur Brummell; c'est midi.*'

He contracted a valet, Sélègue, within weeks of arriving in Calais. Brummell's levees were soon open to visitors as they had always been: Harriette Wilson was specifically invited in at this hour. He was attended regularly, however, only by his dog, Vick, and by his parrot. The parrot was not housetrained, and was meant to live in a garden cage, but joined Brummell often to be fed on 'wine and biscuit'. It had, it was said, a marked similarity in feature, and in habit of repetition, to Byron's close friend John

Cam Hobhouse who visited Brummell soon after his arrival in Calais. 'I could hardly believe [my] eyes,' he said condescendingly, 'seeing Brummell in a great coat drinking punch in [his] little room.' As revenge, Brummell named his voluble parrot after Byron's companion and introduced it to all his visitors as 'my Hobhouse'.

Vick was a terrier bitch, who became so grossly obese on the diet of titbits fed her by Brummell and his visitors that she slowed down the progress of her master's walks around the ramparts of Calais. After many months of this regime of over-indulgence she died. 'Brummell, in great distress standing at her side,' said, in typically self-dramatising vein, that he had 'lost the only friend he had had in the world'. Vick was buried in the gardens of Dessin's Hotel and Brummell refused to see visitors for three days.

As the months dragged on, Brummell's routine became ever more fixed, and his obsessive love of his dogs the more marked. Like Princess Frederica in her unofficial retirement at Oatlands, he settled into a prematurely aged pattern of life, but the burghers of Calais thought of him as a harmless and amusing English eccentric, strolling with his dogs and talking to them as friends. He had a series of poodles after Vick including one, Atous, who was trained by a soldier of the Calais garrison to take hot muffins from the fire and offer them round to Brummell's English tea guests. Whether they accepted them from the dog's mouth is unrecorded. 'Like a true cynic,' wrote Jesse, Brummell ceased to be affected by the stories brought to him by his friends from London of the sufferings or joys of people he had once known, 'though a flood of tears was always ready when a dog died'.

Brummell's afternoons were spent with his dogs and looking out to sea. He cut a melancholy figure. The cliffs of Dover were sometimes visible from the ramparts – and he was often visible to incoming vessels. At five he returned to Leleux's to dress for dinner, which he took, almost every day, at Dessin's Hotel at six. It was noted that he favoured imported Dorchester Ale to any of the French wines on offer, and although he took a box in the small theatre attached to Dessin's, he just as often spent his evenings in the hotel garden. There, in the summerhouse where hotel guests were served tea, Brummell began to write his memoirs.

14

MALE AND FEMALE COSTUME AND OTHER WORKS

1821–9

When we have made our love and gamed our gaming
Drest, voted, shone, and, maybe, something more
With dandies dined, heard Senators declaiming
There's little left but to be bored and bore . . .
                    Don Juan, Canto 15, xviii

Less than a year after Brummell had first fled to France a rumour spread that he was preparing to publish memoirs. Thomas Moore recorded in his diary that John Murray, Byron's publishers, was offering Brummell '£5000 for The Memoirs'. He added that he had heard 'that the Regent had sent Brummell £6000 to suppress!' Scrope Davies also heard that Murray 'really had some idea of going to Calais to treat with Brummell' and the Duke of Rutland was told that Brummell intended to 'set everything at defiance [and] disclose to the world every anecdote he has heard, everything that has come to his knowledge in the intimacy of friendship. And those who have thrown him off he shall treat with utmost severity.' London society was alarmed and excited at the prospect in about equal measure, and the publishers envisaged, especially after the runaway success of Harriette Wilson's *Memoirs by Herself*, that Brummell's might sell very well indeed.

In Calais, Brummell started to hint at what he might be writing.

He was often to be seen in the summerhouse in Dessin's gardens working at his memoirs. Or he would flick through the pages of his manuscript at his lodgings telling visitors, 'Here is a chapter on Carlton House; here one on Mrs Fitzherbert and the Prince, this is devoted to Lady Hertford.' It was all deliberately tantalising. Leleux told his tenant that he thought he would be foolish to turn down any offers of money for it. He was already aware that Brummell was struggling financially:

I frequently asked him why he did not accept [terms for publication], to this he usually made some frivolous excuse, but on one occasion, when I pressed hard for his real reason, he said this: 'I [have now] promised the Duchess of York that I would not publish any notes of mine during the lifetime of [the Prince Regent] or his brothers; and I am under so many obligations to her, and have such deep respect for her generous and amiable conduct to me in our early friendship, and since, that I would rather go to gaol than forfeit my word. She is the only link that binds me in this matter.'

Whether Princess Frederica was acting entirely from her own motives is unclear: the regent himself was informed of Brummell's plans to publish, and if he did not respond directly, he might well have put pressure on Frederica to use her influence on her friend. Brummell was not involved in anything so unseemly as blackmail, but there is a clear implication in one letter he wrote to his old friend from the 10th Light Dragoons, Lord Petersham, that he wished the regent to feel his distress. Petersham had risen to be a lord of the bedchamber to the regent. The letter Brummell sent to him from Calais in 1818 is preserved not in the Stanhope Papers, however, but in the Royal Archives at Windsor, thus indicating that it was probably shown to the prince.

I have been almost constantly occupied in writing a sort of history of my own times [wrote Brummell], confining myself to private society life . . . it will be ready for publication early in the winter [1818–19] – You may premise I have not inclined to the flattering side of representations in the many portraits that form my cabinet . . . Of <u>one</u>

personage who professed to be my earliest friend and patron I have endeavoured to speak with as much becoming deference to his public situation as candour and the nature of my review would allow . . . I have depicted what had come immediately under my own cognisance and forth it will go to the world with all its own faults as well as those of others upon its shoulders for I cannot starve from a punctilious principle of unrequited feeling even towards the highest among the Lord's anointed.

He then added just before his signature: 'You need not make this a secret.' The implication was clear: he wanted the regent to hear what he intended to do, from someone well placed to tell him – one of his lords of the bedchamber and a friend, from happier days, to both Brummell and the prince. Brummell begged to point out also that he 'never intentionally offended [the prince]' and was aware of the censure he risked from his former friends. 'I have not written to please their palates,' he went on, 'but to provide for my own. I have recorded nothing but the truth in my descriptions, and if the cap chafes their temples [if the cap fits?] let them remember their own desertion and abuse of me the moment misfortune had compelled me to seek refuge in another country.'

The prince might have considered paying Brummell off, as Thomas Moore had heard. But in the end he found a more expedient resource in his sister-in-law, Princess Frederica. Brummell had not issued a direct threat, and the indirect response was more courtly and, as it turned out, entirely efficient. Indeed, it seems likely Brummell neither wished to publish, nor to put direct pressure on his former friend to pay for his memoirs' suppression. Things went a roundabout route as Brummell might have intended. Frederica and the prince had been on friendly terms for nearly thirty years. Her letters to him are embroidered with some of the same grandiloquent playfulness she uses to Brummell, though they are a good deal less flirtatious. The prince had Frederica write to Brummell urgently supplicating him not to publish – and to destroy what he had written.

It is of deep regret to historians of the period that Brummell agreed. Beyond overcoming his financial embarrassment, he might simply have wanted an acknowledgement of his worth and of his former position. To be recognised had always been important to Brummell, and flaunting the possibility of memoirs may have been as tempting to him as to sell them.

Why Princess Frederica, among all others, should have been so anxious to suppress his writing, and be so beneficent towards him in his exile, exhibits an appealing loyalty to both Brummell and the prince. Allied with this was an interest in her own and the Royal Family's reputations.

She would have been keen to spare herself and the tarnished Grand Old Duke of York from any further embarrassment after the sex-and-sale-of-commissions scandal that had forced his resignation from the army. Moreover Frederica, as Princess Royal of Prussia in her own right, would instinctively have sought to protect the reputation of the Crown and the person of the regent, himself no stranger to scandal and embarrassment. Petersham's letter made it clear that the prince was more likely to find himself the butt of Brummell's ire or ironic humour than the bluff Duke of York in any impending memoirs.

And then there was the issue of inheritance: Princess Frederica had failed in her singular duty to provide an heir to the Hanoverian dynasty, and this ancient regret pressed more painfully after the death of Princess Charlotte in 1817. The old business of a Hanoverian heir was one on which Brummell's memoirs might have been expected to throw an ugly light. Brummell was in contact in his exile with the intended husband of Mrs Fitzherbert's 'niece' Minney Seymour. It is possible that Princess Frederica, along with the entire legitimate royal house, was alarmed at the prospect of someone as well placed as Brummell speculating anew on the marriage between Mrs Fitzherbert and the regent. More recent research has also thrown up compelling evidence that there was a large number of prospective 'heirs' from this illegal union, including Minney, all born in the years when Brummell had shared close friendship with the prince, the Yorks and Mrs Fitzherbert.

Above all this, Princess Frederica was motivated by genuine affection. She had loved Brummell, as a friend and quite possibly much more than that, and had a continuing desire to keep him from the ignominy of selling royal secrets. She gave Brummell money, tucked discreetly inside the handmade items that she made for Brummell and sent to France. 'A purse, a card-case, a note keeper; the work of her own fair hand' arrived for Brummell from Oatlands, and a glass-topped box framing a particularly fine piece of her own embroidery depicting two love-birds drinking out of the same vase. She had an armchair expensively covered with green velvet and decorated with some of her own needle-point, then shipped to France. It was delivered to Brummell in Calais, and was one of the few possessions he never gave up.

In return he began work on an appliqué collage screen to send to her. It became inordinately elaborate, the product of many idle hours, but also a coded commentary in pictures on his mind's new obsessions. Captain Jesse traced it via Brummell's valet, Sélègue, who had taken it – in part-payment for unpaid wages – to a pawnbroker's in Boulogne. Jesse found it there, and left a detailed description.

It was five and a half feet high, but once unfolded was nearly twelve feet long, divided into six two-foot panels. Quite a fashionable item at the time, this '*paravent*, or in vulgar English, a folding screen', as Brummell put it, he decorated with collage appliqué from images cut out of periodicals and prints, many of them sent from London by friends. This fashion for 'pasticcio' had begun with the eighteenth-century print rooms of English country houses, in which cartoons, etchings and classical archi-tecture were used to decorate walls and express their owner's interests and education. Brummell's screen was more in the tradition of later Victorian scrapbooks, and was instructive of his taste and interests in exile. It spoke also of his essential idleness.

He collected prints and etchings to cut out and stick on, but also drew a number of portraits of animals, birds and flowers. He wrote to friends in England to send 'scraps of allegories . . .

Cupids, in Medallions . . . flowers too and butterflies (forgive me) <u>as large as life in colours</u>'. Jesse had to admit the overall effect was confusing and overworked, but the individual panels told stories, or mocked individuals in ways Frederica would understand. The screen could be 'read' as much as admired, as a series of epistles, in collage.

A bust of Napoleon formed the central image of the first panel, superimposed on the neck of Chouni – the famous elephant who starred in the 1810 pantomime at Covent Garden but went berserk and had to be shot by a detachment of Guards. Such was Brummell's comment on the exiled emperor. The edges of each little pasted-on icon, Jesse wrote, were over-embroidered by Brummell with tiny flowers and fruits cut from other publications 'with as much nicety as a semptress [sic] would bestow on the hem of a *chemise d'homme*'.

On another panel a Trumpet of Fame was superimposed over a Russian eagle (for the Tsar), and Brummell cut out Dighton's caricatures of West End characters and pasted them elsewhere on the screen. These included strident caricatures of Prince Esterhazy, the Dukes of Argyll and Devonshire, Kangaroo Cooke, Thomas Raikes, the Marquess of Worcester, the Lords Manners, Alvanley and Westmoreland, Golden Ball Hughes, Poodle Byng, 'An Illustrious Consort', sometimes taken to be Julia Johnstone, and Mr Kemble, the actor, as Charles Surface, the young lead in *The School for Scandal*. It was a comprehensive illustration of the key figures in Brummell's London life. He collected prints of other famous friends when they were to hand: Sheridan, Fox, Nelson, Edmund Kean the actor – celebrities Frederica would know or recognise also – and begged specific others from his English correspondents: 'Wellington after Hoppner, half length of Lord Eldon in mezzotint, the small whole length of the Regent after Cosway, the latter I believe is rather scarce . . . having been executed in His R.Hss youth some thirty and seven years ago (don't tell him) you will know what I mean, it is in a Vandyke costume'. He surrounded these well-known figures, as commentary, with cut-out cupids, satyrs, bacchantes and shepherdesses as he deemed appropriate.

On other panels there were more classical than contemporary allusions: 'Telemachus relating his adventures to Calypso. Phaeton driving his car, Time his chariot.' On another. 'A French dragoon at bivouac preparing a fowl for the camp kettle; a *réligieuse* at her devotions, a minuet at a French fair, a gentleman and a shepherdess whose dog has seized the skirt of her dress and with an anxious look is endeavouring to detach her from her admirer' and so on. It must have taken Brummell months.

On the last panel, he pasted one of the many reproductions of Lord Byron, whose fame was fast eclipsing his own. He stuck a cut-out of a wasp on his throat. Jesse noted also a picture of a poor boy outside a grand house on a 'wretched night' singing the 'insinuating line: 'I've lost my way, ma'am; do pray let me in.'

This plea for sympathy from his royal supporter, if such it was, was never heard. Neither did she have a chance to decipher this elaborately coded artwork, which seems to bear strong testimony to Brummell's restive imagination. The screen was never quite completed and never sent to Oatlands because, in August 1820, Brummell received word that Frederica had died.

On the back of a note from the princess that Brummell had kept he scribbled that her death was met with the 'deep regret of all the world'. This was certainly an exaggeration, but the personal blow – they had been very close for more than fifteen years – was pressed home by a more urgent problem. She had been his primary financial support and her death put him into a still more perilous position.

He might have flirted again with publishing the memoirs. There is a theory that he came back to London, incognito, to negotiate with the publisher John Murray, or with Harriette Wilson's Joseph Stockdale, but this is based on a note in the weighing book at Berry Brothers. According to this much-thumbed almanac, Brummell came in for one last time on 26 July 1822. He weighed ten stone thirteen pounds in his boots. If it was him, he was a shadow of his former self (this is at odds with Harriette Wilson's description of his 'increased embonpoint', but a symptom of secondary syphilis can be fluctuating weight). It

seems scarcely credible that he should have been in London, least
of all in the heart of St James's where he owed money to dozens of
tradesmen, including, most likely, Berry Brothers themselves.
Why would he choose to announce his presence in this way?
Either he did it as one more reckless gamble – perhaps when he
was on the point of getting into a coach back to Dover, to cock a
snook at London one more time – or the entry is a red-herring,
perhaps the work of a dandy-prankster refusing to buy wine
unless Berry Brothers put him in their records as Brummell.

What is certain, however, is that by the early 1820s Brummell
was sinking fast in both spirits and finances. He had pinned some
hopes, it would seem, on the succession to the throne of the prince
regent, which finally took place on the death of George III in 1820.
Although he had held the reins of monarchy since 1811, it was
widely assumed that George IV's accession would mark a change
in a wide range of policies and attitudes. It did not. And,
specifically, it did not lead to any softening on the part of the
new King towards his estranged friend in Calais. Brummell
acknowledged his compromised hopes in a letter he wrote to
Raikes:

He is at length king! Will his past resentments still attach themselves to
his crown? An indulgent amnesty of former peccadilloes should be the
primary grace influencing newly throned sovereignty; at least towards
those who were once distinguished by his more intimate protection.
From my experience, however, of the personage in question, I must
doubt any favourable relaxation of those stubborn prejudices which
have during so may years operated to the total exclusion of one his
élèves from the royal notice; that unfortunate, I need not particularize.

You ask me how I am doing in Calais? Miserably! I am exposed
every hour to all the turmoil and jeopardy that attended my latter days
in England. I bear up as well as I can: and when the patience and mercy
of my claimants are exhausted, I shall submit without resistance to
bread and water and straw. I cannot decamp a second time.

Lord Sefton reported that he had received a letter from
Brummell complaining that he was 'lying on straw and grinning

through the bars of a gaol; eating bran bread, my good fellow, eating bran bread'. This was comic hyperbole: Brummell was not lying on straw. Lord Alvanley and Lord Petersham visited him in the autumn of 1820. They were accompanied by the travel writer Charles Macfarlane, *en route* to Italy, and they all dined together, with Brummell, at Dessin's. Macfarlane gives a vivid impression of him, still surrounded by his old friends, making the most of his reduced circumstances, trading off old stories and managing, almost, to hide his

sadness and despondency . . . [Alvanley and Petersham] were pupils and almost idolators of Brummell. They invited him to dinner, but he was engaged, if I remember right, with Scrope Davies, who had taken refuge in the dull old French town. However, he came in towards the small hours, and sat until long after sunrise. There was a terrible change in other things besides the financial ones; but still he was an elegant, striking man, and became very amusing and rather animated, though he drank but moderately. At times, however, I thought I saw a look of sadness and despondency. There was reason for it. At this moment he was cruelly embarrassed. [His stories] were all told with admirable humour, and most of them with good nature. I could understand a good deal of the secret of Brummell's extraordinary success and influence in the highest society. He was a vast deal more than a mere dandy; he had wit as well as humour and drollery, and the most perfect coolness and self-possession.

They touched on the subject of George IV, and Macfarlane noted no bitterness in Brummell's tone on the subject of his one-time friend:

On the contrary, he related several clever and two or three kind things of [King George IV], and gave him credit for a great deal of natural ability and esprit. He confirmed what Raikes and others have said of the Prince's extraordinary powers of mimicry. 'If his lot had fallen that way' [Brummell] said 'he would have been the best comic actor in Europe.' Brummell confessed to the story of [Who's your fat friend?] and his threat . . . to go down to Windsor and make the old [King

George III] fashionable [in place of the regent] but he emphatically denied the other common tale, '*George ring the bell!*'

'I knew the Prince too well,' said he, 'ever to take any kind of liberty with him! Drunk or sober, he would have resented it, with a vengeance! His vindictive spirit [the prince's] was the worst part of him and he could be vindictive about trifles. Where he once took a spite, he never forgave.'

Brummell had reason to have this truth about the prince and his lost friendship uppermost in his mind. Macfarlane, like everyone in Calais, was aware that George IV was almost certain to visit the French coast in the near future *en route* to his ancestral lands and other throne as King of Hanover. 'If my observations were shrewd and correct,' wrote Macfarlane, 'I should say that at this period the Beau did not quite despair of a reconciliation, or some token of the Royal bounty.'

The following September, 1821, George IV arrived in Calais. The mayor declared a holiday and, according to Macfarlane, Brummell accompanied him – the mayor was his wine merchant and also a friend – to the landing jetty that protruded from the city walls. Here they were due to meet the royal barge. 'I was told that many of the English purposely made room for [Brummell], sharing his hope and expectation that His Majesty would at least recognize him with a gracious smile, which might have the effect of tranquilizing some of his Calais creditors.' But Macfarlane related 'that the King, who almost touched him as he passed up the pier, must have seen him; [but] turned his Royal head another way, and that Brummell turned as pale as a ghost'.

'Falstaff,' remarked Macfarlane in literary vein, 'was not so sad when turned off by "sweet Prince Hal".'

The encounter was hardly less dramatic in the version told by Leleux, the landlord. He said that Brummell had missed the arrival of the King's boat as he was out walking his dog on the ramparts. As the King and the French ambassador were making their way across the Place d'Armes to the rue Royale and Dessin's Hotel, Monsieur Leleux was an eyewitness to Brummell's plight:

I was standing at my shop door and saw Mr Brummell trying to make his way across the street to my house, but the crowd was so great that he could not succeed, and he was therefore obliged to remain on the opposite side. Of course all hats were taken off as the carriage approached, and when it was close to the hotel door, I heard the King say in a loud voice: 'Good God, Brummell!'

The latter, who was uncovered at the time, now crossed over [the rue Royale] as pale as death, entered the house by [his] private door and retired to his room without addressing me.

Though differing slightly in geography, both stories paint Brummell as profoundly shocked by the encounter – or, rather, the missed encounter. He certainly appears to have been taken off guard, as were his friends in Calais. They had assumed that the central figure in all Brummell's anecdotes would do more for his old friend. However, the discomfort, for both parties, was far from over.

A 'sumptuous dinner' was given at Dessin's, within earshot of Brummell's lodgings, to which he was not invited. He lent his valet, Sélègue, to the hotel, as he spoke English and Brummell had trained him in the ways of English servants. He was to make a punch for the royal party. Brummell even remembered to send a bottle of maraschino, the King's favourite liqueur on which they had got drunk on the day of the royal wedding in 1796. He later claimed it was his best brandy: a thirty-year-old bottle. Still no invitation arrived. Later that evening the King found himself out of snuff, and asked someone near him, the mayor (or consul, according to Jesse) if he might borrow some. Word was sent to Brummell, who dispatched some of his own mix, 'with all my heart', while remembering not to include his best snuff-box, 'for if the King saw it I should never have it again'.

By the time the snuff arrived at Dessin's the royal party had moved on to the adjacent theatre, which had organised an evening's musical entertainment, and the King was reported as saying to the person who offered him the snuff-box: 'Why sir, there is only one person I know who can mix snuff in this way; where did you get this?'

To which the answer came: 'It is some of Mr Brummell's, Your Majesty.'

'And here,' Jesse records, 'the conversation closed.'

The next morning, despite all this, Brummell wrote his name in the visitors' book of the hotel – the equivalent of leaving his card – as further evidence that, from his point of view, the time had come for a reconciliation. If the King was made aware of it – it seems probable that he was not – he ignored it.

Brummell received other members of the royal retinue in his rooms at Leleux's, and Jesse reported that several tried to convince Brummell that he should ask for an audience with the King, either immediately or on the royal party's return from Hanover. Brummell pointed out that there had been no sign from the King thus far that such an overture would be favourably met and that he had done more than etiquette demanded of him already.

The King and his large retinue resumed their places in their carriages ready to depart. The King sat opposite Sir Arthur Cassel, who had commanded the yacht that had brought them from England. As they pulled away from Dessin's, the King looked out of the window, according to Sir Arthur, and said, 'I leave Calais, and have not seen Brummell.' But he did not ask to stop, nor make plans to see him on his return via Calais in the months to come.

Although this sad missed opportunity was marked by many as the beginning of the end for Brummell, Brummell at first took it all in good part. He claimed, initially, that the King's comments in the coach, which were reported back to him almost immediately, expressed regret that they had not met, and this proved that a reconciliation might still be possible. Yet when the King returned from Hanover a month later his carriage drove straight to the landing-stage without stopping in Calais at all.

～

In a quite uncharacteristic fit of practicality, Brummell gave up on being rescued by the King from his penury and put his energies back into writing. As well as the potential financial benefit, it seems likely he needed a different validation, a new idea of self-worth if he was to accept he was never again to be the prince's favourite or society's darling. The subject he chose to write about was the one dearest to his heart – once his friends and gossip had been put beyond the limit of his pen by his refusal to countenance the idea of selling his memoirs: fashion.

Male and Female Costume – a history and aesthetic study of Greek, Roman and British costume – became a work of exacting and slow pastiche, rather akin to the screen he had made for Princess Frederica. But unlike the screen, by 1822, *Male and Female Costume* was completed. *If* Brummell visited London in 1822, it might as easily have been in an attempt to sell his manuscript to a publisher. Not only did he use his time through 1821–2 to rediscover a schoolboy love of ancient civilisation – a third of the ensuing work was dedicated to the fashions of antiquity – he also decided his work should be illustrated, and indicated to his unnamed publisher the pictures that would be needed and how they should be coloured. He included a colour-diagram for the purpose. He cut out reproductions of classical dress from the works he used for consultation – ordered from Paris – and delicately shaded these with watercolours as text illustrations.

The work he produced is a detailed and at times amusing account, utterly of its moment. In his preface Brummell wrote that 'we [in Britain] have long imitated Grecian costume . . . with regular and steady approaches to the refined and elegant taste of antiquity'. From his small foreign outpost, he aimed straight at the London market. He tried to align fashion with the spirit of the time and of his native land, placing Britain as a natural imperial successor to Greece and Rome, and opining that modern London fashions were one of the highest expressions of neo-classicism. His opening advertisement, however, gave insight to less lofty ideals. He wrote that *Male and Female Costume, Grecian and*

Roman Costume, British Costume from the Roman Invasion until 1822 was intended to be the first edition in a new periodical on the subject of metropolitan fashion. This urbane fashion gazette was to be issued, eccentrically perhaps, from Calais.

'The Athenians,' he began, 'to whom we owe whatever we know of the fine arts, ranked Costume as one of these. However varied its details may be, its principles are as fixed, and its means of producing effects, its power of expression, as definite, as those of the other arts.' Brummell was schooled as a neo-classicist and his thesis on fashion was typical of the age. Rules of line and shape, simplicity and 'truth of judgement' shaped and codified taste. 'Did any men,' he asked rhetorically, 'ever look like Greeks and Romans? They were the handsomest, the noblest, the most unaffected, and the best dressing; in short, the most *gentlemanly* people that ever were or will be.' His thoughts on the culture of the ancients are now debatable, but were widely accepted at the time.

On the subject of 'modern' dress he wrote, of course, from direct experience. He demolished those who criticised the fashionable and fashion-conscious as 'paltry sophists', pointing out quite reasonably that 'there is quite as much vanity and coxcombry in slovenliness as there is in the most extravagant opposite'. Perhaps he was tilting gently at the cult of Byronic disarray when he went on to use as an example of this vanity of un-dress 'the minor poet who goes into company with a dirty neckcloth and straggling locks . . . and anticipates the question "Who *is* that?"' He was already aware that 'dandy' had come to mean something altogether more romantically distressed than anything he had seen fit to wear in St James's.

He traced with cool objectivity his own effect on the line of trousers: 'The reader will observe that breeches were extended into pantaloons; pantaloons were next widened into trowsers [*sic*] and we gradually assumed that dress of the limbs which distinguished our Gothic ancestors and the contiguous tribes before they left the shores of the Euxine . . . at once appropriate and beautiful.'

Only on trousers and whiskers had his aesthetic moved on slightly from the 1790s. By the 1820s, Brummell believed in looser-fitting trousers and in growing beards. He even went on to argue that the fall of the Greek and Roman empires was foreshadowed, in fashion terms, when men took to the 'effeminate' business of shaving, and was effected by 'Bearded Goths'. A lifetime of razor-rash and what Harriette Wilson described as a morning spent 'forever shaving' led him to rage at all 'those who emasculate themselves and who think themselves prettified by a painful and ridiculous imitation of the smoother face of women!' It is an unlikely image: the grizzled Brummell. He never did grow a beard or moustache. To judge by the various attributable miniatures of him he appears to have had luxuriant sideburns at different stages, but never a beard. Perhaps he was influenced by the vagaries of fashion more than he liked to admit: by the 1820s moustaches were commonplace and extravagant sideburns ubiquitous. But Brummell never gave up his elaborate shaving regime. As his syphilis advanced, he might have been incapable of contemplating living without it. His facial, head and body hair would have grown in unsightly patches – if it grew at all.

Brummell was at his most eloquent and scientific in *Male and Female Costume* on the subject of colour. Because the aesthetic he espoused segued smoothly into the dark sobriety of Victorian male fashions, and the dawning of what has been termed more recently the age of Men in Black, it is assumed he had little knowledge of or interest in colour. *Male and Female Costume* refutes this: his strict adherence to a limited palette of colours was based on sound colour principles that he attempted to define. His ideas were meant to be applicable to the more colourful wardrobe of women, but it was based on a predominance-of-one-colour ideology that was immediately recognisable as Brummell's, and as applicably masculine. It is worth quoting at length, as it has striking parallels with the systems of complexion colour-matching and colour-scheming that are used to this day in the fashion industry:

1. In the composition of colours for dress, there ought to be one predominating colour to which the rest should be subordinate.

2. To the predominating colour the subordinate ones should bear a relation, similar to that between the fundamental or the keynote [in music] and the series of sounds constituting a musical composition. And as, in a piece of music, there is a relation between the successive sounds or notes, so in dress the subordinate colours should be in harmony with each other.

   The power of perceiving this relation of colours constitutes the faculty called *taste* in colouring.

3. As painters –

   > Permit not two conspicuous lights to shine
   > With rival radiance in the same design

   so in dress, one half of the body should never be distinguished by one colour, and the other by another. Whatever divides the attention, diminishes the beauty of the object; and though each part, taken separately, may appear beautiful, yet as a whole the effect is destroyed. Were each particular limb differently coloured, the effect would be ridiculous. It is in this way . . . that mountebanks are dressed, and it never fails to produce the effect that is intended by it, to excite the mirth and ridicule of the common people.

4. The variety of colours which may be introduced in dress, depends on the expression of the predominating colour.

   Delicate colours require to be supported and enlivened, and, therefore, are best relieved by contrasts; but the contrast should not be so strong as to equal the colour it is intended to relieve, for it then becomes opposition, which should always be avoided. Contrast, skilfully managed, gives force and lustre to the colour relieved, while opposition destroys its effect.

5. In the composition of the subordinate colours, there is a maxim of Du Fresnoy's which applies as well to the arrangement of colours in dress as in painting:

   > Forbid two hostile colours close to meet
   > And win with middle tints their union sweet.

6. The choice of the predominating colour will be indicated by the situation, the age, the form and the complexion of the wearer.

Brummell then went on to explain, with the help of a colour diagram familiar to any painter, the principles of 'opposite colours' but from this deduced the most flattering colours for different complexions. However, few would now take up his suggestion of bright red clothes for women of ruddy complexion 'that by contrasting . . . a comparative fairness may be produced', but he understood portraiture and clothes well enough to know that 'neutral colours of depth will suit broken complexions'.

On women's fashions generally he was opinionated but less passionate than on men's, but he admitted that 'the taste of British women seems to have been at all times infinitely better than that of men'. He approved of veils, which 'at once heightens the beholder's interest, and . . . gives it the smoothness and polish which are essential to a high degree of beauty', and suggested that 'hats turned up before give a pert . . . sometimes witty air'. But he expended more ink on excoriation than advice, reserving particularly withering disdain for the high hairstyles worn by his mother's generation, 'generally formed of horsehair and something like a porters-knot' and the 'Cork-Rump' made of 'several large pieces of cork . . . in order that with this protuberance of this additional rump their waist may seem the smaller and more delicate'. Brummell preferred the natural look and feel.

Male and Female Costume is a work without the easy humour of Brummell's recorded speech and letters and is undeniably pedantic, despite the occasional arresting aphorism. Nevertheless it would doubtless have sold in London simply by virtue of having his name on the frontispiece, particularly as the subject matter was so pertinent to his fame. It seems probable that he could not find a publisher who would meet his terms or that, having completed it, possibly in the frenzy of a syphilitic 'manic' phase, he put it aside when the 'blue devils' returned. It came to light in the early twentieth century, and received a limited-edition publication in New York.

～

The death of the Duke of York in 1826 was a further blow to Brummell's prospects of financial redemption. Because he had been heir to the throne since the death of George IV's daughter Princess Charlotte in 1817 there had been reasonable prospects of advancement for Brummell in what had seemed the likely event of Frederick ascending the throne. On this assumption creditors had even extended money to the duke. He planned to demolish Oatlands and rebuild it with an eighty-two-foot ballroom, all financed on credit. Across the Channel, Brummell had encouraged his bankers in the same belief; even if George IV would not appoint him to some lucrative consulate, Frederick the First certainly would. It was not to be.

Lord William Lennox visited Brummell shortly after the news of York's death and found him in low spirits. Lennox was accompanied by Adolphus FitzClarence, an illegitimate son of the Duke of Clarence (later William IV). Both FitzClarence and Lennox were in the travelling retinue of the Duchess of Gloucester. When the duchess decided to press on to Hanover, the two younger men decided to stay put and enjoy the regal rooms at Dessin's that had been booked in advance. Lennox later wrote that 'my companion and myself found that dinner had been ordered for eight persons and there were only [we] two left to partake of it. We . . . at once sent for Brummell to make up a third'. He arrived looking

pale and emaciated; his still well-fitted clothes were what is usually termed 'seedy'; his boots were not so brilliant as they used to be when he lounged up Bond Street in the days of the fashionable promenade; his hat, though carefully brushed, showed symptoms of decay, and the only remnants of dandyism left were the well-brushed hair, the snow-white linen, and an unexceptional tie . . . At first the ex-king of fashion was dull, but after a few glasses of champagne he revived and kept us alive until a late hour, telling us anecdotes of his past career – his misunderstanding with the Prince Regent, his support for Mrs Fitzherbert.

There was a slight upturn in Brummell's mood and prospects in August 1827. George Canning, the prime minister, died and a cabinet reshuffle put Lord Dudley into the Foreign Office and

Lord Goderich into No. 10. Dudley had known Brummell, from Harriette Wilson's Cyprians' parties and boxes at the opera, and Lord Alvanley persuaded the Duke of Wellington to lobby him on Brummell's behalf. Even so, nothing happened. Two years later Lord Dudley told Charles Greville, clerk to the Privy Council, why. At first Dudley had 'objected [to lobbying the King for a consulate for Brummell] and at last owned that he was afraid the King [George IV] would not like it' and when he finally did approach him, Brummell's fat friend was as mercurial and petty as ever, 'abusing Brummell – said he was a damned fellow and had behaved very ill to him – the old story, always himself, *moi moi moi*'.

Even so, after the King had 'let out his tether of abuse', approval was apparently extracted. By late 1827, Mrs Fitzherbert was writing to her adopted daughter that 'George Brummell is to be made Consul at Calais. The King has given his consent.' Unfortunately, the Goderich government collapsed, Dudley lost his post, and the King's reluctant commands were left undone.

Once again, Brummell was left languishing and unclear about his financial future. His letters to England became increasingly anxious. He had managed to juggle his finances, paying the small shopkeepers whose services were vital, promising late payments to Leleux, and telling his bankers that all would be well. But it came to a head in the summer of 1828. As time went by the prospect of a consulship receded. But Brummell had treated every positive sign of attaining such a post as an excuse for immediate lavish expenditure. His larger creditors came to push much harder for repayment. Brummell was again forced to beg his English friends for help.

The young man he chose in 1828 as emissary for his round of pleas was well placed in London for the task. Lieutenant Colonel the Honourable George Dawson was the younger son of an Irish peer, Lord Portarlington. However, he had bagged one of the great prizes on the Regency marriage market, the adopted 'daughter' of Mrs Fitzherbert, Minney Seymour, more than commonly good-looking and with investments worth over

£40,000. Minney Seymour may also have been in possession of an uncommonly valuable secret: that she was the daughter, one of several children, born to Mrs Fitzherbert and the prince regent. If this was the case, it was probably a secret known also to George Brummell.

Mrs Fitzherbert had strongly disapproved of the match between Minney and Dawson, for while he had returned from Waterloo a hero – two horses had been shot from under him – he had few prospects, a reputation as a rake and, according to his prospective mother-in-law, had been spoiled as a child. In an attempt to separate the two, Mrs Fitzherbert had removed her daughter to the continent, and asked the Duke of York to have Dawson sent far away on military business. Through their travels, both Minney and Dawson came to know Brummell, probably through Alvanley who was frequently in Paris and Calais and was instrumental in keeping the lovers in touch. Dawson had even mentioned favourably Brummell's attractive Calais apartments. Fortunately for the lovers, a solution straight out of a Jane Austen novel was duly arranged, whereby Dawson's standing was artificially raised by an old aunt, who gave him her estate in Dorset on condition he change his name to Dawson-Damer, and Minney straightway did the same.

He was beholden to his adopted mother-in-law in matters financial and social, so it was canny that Brummell should write to him when he needed a favour. Dawson-Damer was a young man-about-town, but one with plenty of good will to earn in the royal circles he had joined. It may also, subtly, have reminded the well placed and well connected that George Brummell, too, had once been well placed and was still party to damaging secrets.

Calais, July 20, 1828

To Lieut Col the Hon George Dawson
c/o Mrs Fitzherbert, Tilney Street, Park Lane, London

My Dear Dawson,
Will you so far extend your usual kindness as to endeavour to be of *instant* service to me. It is not to yourself particularly that I

take liberty to address myself, for you must be very much changed, if you have any money at command; but to three or four of those former friends who you may think willing to stretch a point in my favour at the moment. I am in a serious scrape from my utter inability to provide for a rascally bill which had been long due . . . – the amount is £73.

Would you so essentially oblige me as to endeavour to gather together a few amiable Samaritans who might so kindly bear me and my actual difficulties in remembrance as to advance £25 each to satisfy this urgent demand? One hundred would relieve me and give me a few pounds over to scramble on with. It would make me very happy for the present . . .

I am, as you may have heard, expecting employment [a consular post] through the interference of that best of friends, [the Duke of] Wellington, but before such expectation may be realised I am sadly alarmed lest some overwhelming disaster should fall upon me.

Ever sincerely yrs

George Brummell

Mrs Fitzherbert was clearly meant to learn of Brummell's distress. He could not, for form's sake, directly approach a lady, but she was known to be wealthy, had also suffered from the inconstancy of George IV, and still had influence. The 'overwhelming disaster' Brummell spoke of was the threat of being rendered homeless if Leveux, his banker, refused him further credit and Leleux, his landlord, demanded his rent arrears. Brummell had some letter of encouragement back from Dawson, to which he immediately responded:

Calais August 12 1828

My Dear Dawson,

Do not condemn me for a troublesome beast . . . I am beset and reduced to expedients to bear up beyond endurance and almost beyond hope. A very little might enable me to purchase delay from this infernal persecution which frightens me out of the few wits that are left to me . . . You had the kindness to tell me you

could do something for me – upon my soul, I am ashamed to be
driven to recall such an assurance to you, but I am put to the
worst extremities, and I know not which way to turn to save
myself.

Dawson wrote back with excuses for his and everyone else's
delay. He pleaded illness and being bedridden. Brummell's
friends, he claimed, continued to be away from London. He
advised Brummell to continue pushing for any consular appointment, and to try to smooth the exit of the incumbent in Calais,
Captain Marshall, by keeping his ear to the ground for appointments elsewhere. Alvanley, meanwhile, sent him fifty pounds via
Drummond's, the bankers, so Brummell, yet again, was rescued at
the last minute.

He was in far better fettle when he was in contact with Thomas
Raikes, teasing him about clothes and demanding keener attention to detail with the requests Raikes was forwarding to their
tailor in London:

> Rue Royale, Calais
> I am persuaded you had no hand in the mutilation of the muslin
> that was sent to me. No, I said, he never could in cold blood have
> been guilty of this outrage. The fault then rests with that vandal
> Chapman, who, in the attempt to exculpate himself, has added a
> lie to the previous offence, for, according to all the rules of
> geometry, two triangles will form a square, to the end of the
> world, and of equal triangular proportions are the kerchiefs in
> question. The intention you profess of sending me some square
> assures me you are in good humour.

He continued:

> I heard of you the other day in a waistcoat that does you
> indisputable credit, spick and span from Paris, a broad stripe,
> salmon colour and cramoise. Keep it up, my dear fellow, and
> don't let them laugh you into a relapse so Gothic as that of your
> former English simplicity.

About this time Brummell found himself visited by Harriette Wilson, more resident in Paris than in London after the publication of her scandalous memoirs. Later she claimed she had bumped into Berkeley Craven in Leleux's bookstore, who had insisted she come upstairs to see Brummell. 'We found Brummell shaving . . . he is always shaving! He wore a linen robe de chambre. One gets tired of silks and satins,' she wrote cattily, 'after a long residence on the continent.' It was in fact a very hot day. Brummell had read her memoirs and had not been impressed. He 'shook his head, cap and all, at me,' Harriette wrote, 'and called my memoirs vile and infamous, I was *au désespoir*,' she continued sarcastically, 'and resolved to bring an end to them.'

She returned to London greatly offended that Brummell should abuse her, and continued her vitriol in the next instalment of the memoirs:

I am censured by very high authorities! Mr George Brummell of the parish of Calais, a naturalised Frenchman, declared, to me, not three days ago, that my book was infamous, abominable, shocking!! And at the last exclamation, he turned up his eyes to suit his looks to his language. 'What has the truly amiable woman the Duchess of Beaufort done, pray?' asked the great man of Calais. 'Abused me most shockingly to begin with, in letters addressed to her son,' I replied.

'And I? What have I done?' retorted the beau, whose self, was and will be ever, uppermost.

'Very little for the state, I believe, at least until you took your French leave of it. There indeed, your services are appreciated by unanimous consent; excepting only one or two who would gladly have detained you for the purpose of gratifying their private revenge, for having been taken in by you.'

'You are the most infamous woman in the world,' said Mr George Brummell.

'Amen,' responded the Hon Berkeley Craven, who was equally abusive, at being left out of [my] Memoirs as was Mr Brummell for having figured in [them.]

Of course I mean what I say: nothing more nor less than that

Brummell's very low birth placed him at the bottom of the list of fashionables. Oh! But someone told me the other day that he has grown a very good man, in Calais, lives quiet and puts up for the consulship in which case we must let him alone.

And so she did.

A picture of Brummell as he entered his fifty-first year is provided by the travel writer Major Chambre, who stayed in Calais in 1829 on the first leg of a continental tour.

I was naturally desirous of becoming acquainted with [Brummell], of whom I had heard so much in London Society. The day following my arrival I waited on him in his lodgings, leading off the Grande Place to Dessin's Hotel. The common and received idea of him in England was of a consummate dandy. I found him, on the contrary, a quiet, gentlemanlike man, without pretension, apparently about fifty years of age, and exceedingly agreeable. He was in his usual morning costume, dressing gown and gold-lace cap, which he invariably wore in the earlier part of the day.

He received me very graciously, and with a great deal of cordiality. The letter [of introduction] I presented to him was from one of his old London companions; and he had no sooner read it, than he begged I would dine with him whenever I was disengaged, as he always had sufficient for a friend in the portions sent in from the hotel close by [Dessin's]. I very often availed myself of this invitation; and on these occasions he spoke much of his past life, and the varied scenes he had witnessed during his residence abroad.

Chambre stayed in Calais longer than he had intended, simply to enjoy the company and stories of his new friend, Beau Brummell, and these provided him with a whole chapter of his subsequent travelogue. Brummell told him about the prince regent, about the visit to Calais when he 'quite forgot his kingly bearing' and declined to acknowledge Brummell. He told Chambre the story of his lucky sixpence and how to prepare best snuff: 'moistened with cold green tea'. He also told stories at the expense of the local burghers of Calais, including how he charmed people into inviting him to dinner and found ways to recycle the small gifts of pâté he brought as a gift to his hosts. Less amusing, as the weeks wore on, was Chambre's realisation that Brummell was in dire straits financially and that his delaying tactics were working less and less well:

Whenever any one of my creditors calls upon me [explained Brummell], I commence an amusing conversation, and tell him anecdotes that I think will interest him. This has hitherto succeeded very well, for I divert their attention from the subject that brings them to me. We shake hands, and part on good terms; but my stock in trade is exhausted, and I am now completely used up. I have nothing left to tell them, and what to do I know not.

Evidently Chambre was won over by Brummell's candour, and offered some small practical assistance, as he saw it, without realising that Brummell's financial incontinence was all but incurable. He suggested selling some of Brummell's collection of antiques. He had noticed in their evenings together that Brummell not only had a fine collection of furniture, but also many less practical items that he had accumulated over the years in exile, as gifts or as small purchases for himself: 'curious snuffboxes, articles of *vertu*'. Brummell 'jumped at the idea.' Chambre, true to his word, spoke to an auctioneer friend of his back in London – the son of William Crockford, the club-owner – who duly decided it was worth his while to come over to Calais. He gave Brummell a good price for a large part of his collection and shipped it back to England. Brummell had bought wisely and with taste over the years. It was a good time to be buying in France: much had come on to the market in the years after Napoleon's fall. At auction one tea-set owned by Brummell went for two hundred guineas, and a pair of vases for three hundred pounds; Brummell's Sèvres was described as 'the finest and purest ever imported into England'.

In January 1829 another visitor called in on the fast fading Brummell, the German Prince Puckler-Müskau:

I cannot judge whether long residence in Calais added to increasing years have rendered the dress of the former King of Fashion less classical, for I found him at his second toilette, in a flowered chintz dressing gown, velvet night cap with gold tassel, and Turkish slippers, shaving, and rubbing the remains of his teeth with his favourite red root. The furniture of the rooms was elegant enough, part of it might even be called rich, though faded; and I cannot deny that the whole man seems to me to correspond with it. Though depressed by his present situation, he exhibited a considerable fund of good humour and good nature . . . [He] took occasion to convince me that he was perfectly well informed as to all that was passing in the English world of fashion as well as of politics: '*Je suis au courant de tout*,' [he said]. '*Mais à quoi cela me sert-il? on me laisse mourir de faim ici. J'éspère pourtant que mon ancien ami le Duc de Wellington enverra un beau jour le consul d'ici en Chine, et qu'ensuite il me nommera à sa place. Alors je suis sauvé . . .*' And surely the English nation ought in justice to do something for the man who invented starched cravats!

In September 1829 Brummell had a note from Sir Robert Wilson, who was due in Calais. Wilson had been a friend to Queen Caroline (the unloved consort who had died soon after her attempt to be crowned in Westminster Abbey in 1821). A career soldier, he had been dismissed without reason from the army by George IV, though it was widely believed it was because he had sided with the late Queen. He, like Brummell, had expectations based on the likely accession to the throne of the Duke of Clarence, now in line to inherit since the death of the Duke of York. He and Brummell had much to discuss, and Brummell scribbled him a note inviting him to visit, sending it to catch up with Wilson *en route* from London:

Sir Robert Wilson, London/Dover
Calais 11 Sep 1829

My dear Wilson
Most happy shall I be to shake you once more by the hand and I am delighted to hear that the contemptible prohibition against

your *passe-partout* in these dominions is at an end. I am still vegetating, for I will not call it living, with the fat weeds that sleep within the stagnant ditches that surround this place. My dependence is placed upon the good offices of one <u>great man</u> who, as he had always extended every kindness towards me, will not neglect any favourable opportunity to be of service to me.
Ever truly yrs
George Brummell

But still Wellington seemed unable to elicit a definite answer from the ailing George IV, even though Dudley had already gained acceptance in principle for Brummell to receive a consul-ship. It seemed as if the obese old King – though half crazed on laudanum and looking like 'a featherbed' – would go on for ever.

It was a tough winter. Visitors were less frequent, creditors more pressing. Still Brummell remained, erratically, buoyant. In the spring, Charles Greville found himself stuck in Calais for the afternoon, between the arrival of *Rob Roy*, the new steam packet, and the departure of his coach for Paris. He spent the time with Brummell. 'Just as gay as ever. I found him in his old lodging, dressing; some pretty pieces of old furniture in the room, an entire Toilet of Silver and a large green Macaw perched on the back of a tattered silk chair with faded gilding, full of gaiety, impudence and misery.'

The old chair was the gift from Princess Frederica. The bird was the ageing Hobhouse. The silver shaving set was Brummell's pride and joy: one of the few important things he had not sold on to Crockford's. Greville took the trouble to write immediately to the Duke of Wellington, insisting Brummell have some immediate placement to a consulate. Finally, it was done. Brummell received notification that he would receive a position.

It was generally assumed that Brummell achieved his long-held ambition of a consulship only on the accession of the Duke of Clarence to the throne in 1830, and that the enmity that George IV had held against his former friend lasted to the end. But this was not quite the case.

At a little before three a.m. on 26 June 1830, George IV died
and his brother, with no heirs but ten illegitimate FitzClarences by
the actress Mrs Jordan, moved out of Chesterfield Street and
became King William IV. But the papers appointing Brummell as
His Britannic Majesty's Consul – to the vacant post of a small but
important coastal town, Caen in lower Normandy – were already
signed. George IV had relented as one of his dying acts.

Brummell was appointed before 20 March 1830 – probably as a
result of Greville's letter to Wellington, now lost. He did not take
up his post in Caen, however, until 25 September. This should not
be interpreted, as it was at the time, as evidence that he was only
appointed after the accession of William IV. It was because his
creditors in Calais, who had finally seen Brummell's ship come in,
would not let him go.

Principal among them were his banker, Leveux, and his valet,
Sélègue. Jesse took down details from the records he found in
France. As even Brummell's meals at Dessin's Hotel had been paid
for on account by Leveux, it makes for a comprehensive overview
of his living expenses in exile. He could hardly be said to have
learned much about economy after thirteen years 'vegetating':

Leveux's Bill	Francs
To his valet, François Sélègue, for house expenses and etcs	6162
Bill at Dessin's for dinners	3488
Lefevre, hatter	54
Lamotte, Pion, } tailors	373
Baudron, Samson, } chemists	176
Lafond Bressell, Bonvarlet, Lemoine, } upholsterers	75
Parque Waillier, draper	309
Ducastel, decorator of ceilings	24
Desjardins, Boissard, } jewellers	35

Fasquel, bootmaker	150
Piedfort, perruquier [wigmaker and restorer]	8
Washerwoman	100
Fille de chambre	50
Isaac Pecquet, banker	500

Cr: 0   Dr: 11,504

The linen, washing and even wig-maintenance bills are under-standable. But Brummell was also still spending a fair amount on clothes: the tailors' and draper's bills together total 682 francs. The greatest claim on him was from the long-suffering Sélègue, who was substantially out of pocket. It shows a touching loyalty, or an insider's confidence in Brummell's future prospects, that Sélègue should work for nothing for so long, and actually support his master out of his own pocket. He did not, however, opt to follow Brummell when he left Calais, but set up a hotel in Boulogne, then prospered greatly as the man who had been trained in service by Beau Brummell. The large chemist's bill Jesse tried to explain away as a consequence of Brummell's excessive use of cold cream, due to 'the extravagant character of his ordinary habits in dress'. The truth, of course, was that Brummell needed regular doses of expensive mercury pills and ointments to keep his syphilis at bay.

Only the so-called heavy metals of the day, mercury, bismuth and arsenic, were thought able to attack the spirochetes that caused syphilis deep in the tissue. There was empirical evidence that this could work and, in fact, early-nineteenth-century doctors under-stood much of what was going on with the progress of syphilis. Their drastic therapies, up to a point, were effective. Brummell seems to have been on a regime of old-fashioned *unguentum saracenium*, an ancient mercury ointment that was rubbed into the skin and genitals. This was used in conjunction with sweet mercury or calomel and white precipitate (mercuric nitrate) usually in blue pills called *Hydrargyrum cuim creta*, made of mercury and chalk. It was rendered palatable by the addition of rose-water and liquorice, which also hid the halitosis associated with mercury treatment.

The ointments were generally preferred to the pills and used in the dormant stage of the disease, now referred to as 'secondary syphilis'. This was because oral intake of mercury, even in conjunction with chalk, almost invariably caused diarrhoea.

The therapy – whether as pill or ointment – was taken to the point of salivation, in other words until the mouth began to moisten excessively. This was unsightly, but within the precepts of a time that understood health in terms of 'humours' and approved sweating-out a sickness. One pill, four times a day, was sufficient to clear up a secondary chancre. Ironically, Brummell's own regiment had been subjected to medical experiments during the Peninsular Campaign of 1808–14 to improve the treatment of syphilis. It was noted that the Portuguese seemed to recover from the rampant syphilitic infections within the armies of the time much more quickly than the British, but without mercury treatment. Further experiments were performed on infected Coldstream Guards, and published in 1817. But in a backwater like Calais, Brummell would have been stuck on mercury, as indeed were the majority of syphilitics well into the nineteenth century.

The money owed to Leveux and to Sélègue amounted to over a thousand pounds at the exchange rate of the day. Jesse claimed Brummell owed twelve thousand francs and had a further twelve-thousand-franc overdraft. He had already spent the money he had made from Crockford's auctioneers in servicing his previous debts. Brummell sold more of his 'Fine Old Furniture', but this brought in only five hundred pounds – half of what he needed.

On 20 March, therefore (which proves he already had the expectation of the consular appointment *before* the old King died), he signed over power of attorney and, as before with the Manners brothers, he sold his future to refinance his past:

Know all Men by These Present that I, George Bryan Brummell, have made ordained and constituted and appointed and do hereby make ordain constitute and appoint Lewis Hertslet and James Hertslet both of the Foreign Office Westminster Esquires my true and lawful Attornies and Attorney jointly or severally for me and in my name to ask demand and receive of and from the Teller of the Exchequer all Sums of Money that now are or hereafter may become due and payable to me at the said Exchequer on any account whatsoever.

The monies due to him by the Foreign Office for his services as British consul in Caen – £400 a year – were to be paid over to the Hertslet brothers, who in turn had arranged with Leveux to pay £320 a year to the Calais bank to redeem Brummell's debts. It is unclear when this arrangement was to end. It seems likely that Brummell had been forced to enter into another annuity arrangement where his debt would cost him proportionately vast amounts as the years went by. More to the point, in the short term, he would be obliged to put up in Caen on an income of eighty pounds a year – the sort of money he would once have spent on a coat.

Nevertheless, and remarkably, Brummell saw the appointment in Caen as the rescue he had longed for. He could turn over a new leaf, leave behind the tedium of Calais, establish himself in a town known for its elegant streets and educated inhabitants. And, for the first time in decades, he was briefly out of debt.

He responded with blithe amusement to his friend Marshall, the British consul, after a request to contribute to a new Anglican church for the English residents in Calais and an invitation to dinner with a passing bishop:

My Dear Marshall
You must excuse me not having the pleasure to dine with you and the Trustees of the Church establishment this day. I do not feel myself sufficiently in spirit to meet a bishop, or in pocket to encounter the plate after dinner; moreover I should be a fish out of water in such a convocation.
Truly Yours,
GB

[P.S.]
Really I am very sorry that you did not call last week, for it was only yesterday that I became a Catholic. But never mind, put my name down for a hundred francs.

Even once he was released from Calais, and had made his farewells to Leleux and Leveux, Captain Marshall and Sélègue, he did not proceed straight to his appointment. Instead he decided to visit his old friend Lord Stuart de Rothsay at the British Embassy on the rue Faubourg St-Honoré. He had spent thirteen years in France but had not had a passport, or the opportunity, to go to Paris.

He did not even have to pay for his journey. Captain Marshall arranged for him to travel with a King's Messenger carrying diplomatic papers. Brummell slept all the way to Paris. The King's Messenger later avowed that the celebrated Mr Brummell 'snored very much like a gentleman'.

15

HIS BRITANNIC
MAJESTY'S CONSUL

1830-2

During those years that I have vegetated upon the barren moor of my later life, I have sedulously avoided running my crazy head into what may be termed inconsequent distractions [but] now, in spite of all my theoretical circumspection . . . all considerate reason has . . . utterly abandoned me and I find myself over head and ears, heart and soul, in love with you. I cannot for the life of me, help telling you so. I shall put myself into a strait waistcoat, and be chained to the bed-post.

Consul Brummell, Caen, 1831

Brummell spent a week in Paris. It was like old times. He stayed at the palatial British Embassy on the rue Fauboug St-Honoré as a guest of Lord Stuart de Rothsay, and his host took advantage of having a celebrated house guest and invited a series of the great and not so good of Parisian society. The dazzlingly duplicitous Charles Maurice Talleyrand – Prince de Benevento, thanks to Napoleon, but no longer using the title – was a fellow guest on several nights. So, too, was Talleyrand's friend Beau Montrond. Brummell also sat next to the Princess Bagration, the notorious *bel ange nu*, a celebrated Parisian hostess, gourmet and *grande horizontale*. The kitchens of the British Embassy must have been put into something of a spin over these events, as

23. Princess Frederica of Prussia, Duchess of York. Twelve years his senior, 'Princess Fred' and Brummell formed a passionate and loyal friendship.

24. Georgiana, Duchess of Devonshire, the 'Most Envied Woman of the Day'. Forty-three years old when she met the seventeen-year-old Brummell, she later gave him several love poems.

25. 'I was never what you call handsome, but brilliant.' Lady Hester Stanhope, Downing Street hostess, traveller and eccentric. She called Brummell 'an exceedingly clever man.'

26. Elizabeth Howard, Duchess of Rutland. Their relationship cooled after Brummell publicly teased her about her dress-sense.

27. Covent Garden, the foyer to the private boxes. The courtesans took boxes by the season to advertise themselves.

28. Admission was by subscription token, or recognition by a box-keeper: an opera box for the season could cost over a thousand guineas. Seats could also be bought on the night – Brummell sent his valet Robinson to bag seats, so he could arrive fashionably late.

29. The King's Theatre on the Haymarket was larger and grander than La Scala in Milan. 'The lighting is better adapted for being seen than for watching . . . The Haut Ton seemed to assemble only to see and be seen.'

30. 'Julia and I are very old friends you know.' Julia Johnstone was one of the most famous courtesans of the age, one the Three Graces whose affairs and parties captivated Regency London.

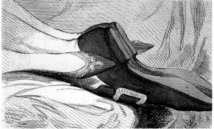

31. Fashionable Contrasts, or the Duchess's little Shoe yielding to the Magnitude of the Duke's Foot. Princess Frederica set a fashion for small, tight shoes.

32. Brummell's friend Harriette Wilson, another of the Three Graces and the century's most infamous courtesan after the publication of her memoirs. Her lovers were given the opportunity to buy their way out of being mentioned, leading the Duke of Wellington, it was said, to tell Harriette to 'publish and be damned'.

33. The Cyprians' Ball at the Argyle Rooms. The Regency Cyprians (courtesans) were sufficiently wealthy and confident to throw lavish parties. Harriette Wilson is on the far right, standing. Amy, the third of the Three Graces, is sitting below the cello. Julia, famed for her dancing, is likely to be on the dance-floor. No respectable woman could attend.

34. A high-class brothel in St James's – the last stop on a dandy's progress through the West End.

35. Roseolas – the rash that signifies the onset of secondary syphilis, depicted in a contemporary French medical textbook. Brummell's habit in later life of bathing in milk is explained by his syphilitic infection.

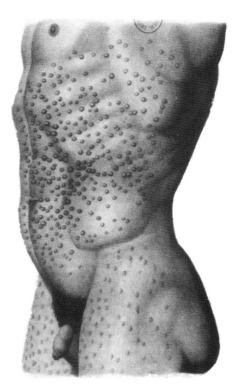

36. An advertisement from Brummell's time in France. There was a huge demand for discreet home remedies.

37. Caen, Normandy. The house of Madame Guerin de Saint-Ursin and her daughter Aimable on the rue des Carmes where Brummell lived from 1830 to 1832.

38. The Hôtel d'Angleterre, rue St Jean, Caen, where Brummell lived (on the top floor) from 1832 to 1839.

39. The Broken ~~Beau~~ Bow!
Brummell drew this for Aimable.
Cupid claws at his own flesh while
gazing pensively at his broken bow
and arrow. 'The ridiculous words [of
the title] were written in a moment of
haste,' Brummell said, 'not to be seen
by others.'

The broken Beau Bow!

40. Brummell in Caen outside
Armstrong's shop.

*Keen blows the wind, and piercing is
the cold
My pins are weak, and I am growing
old
[...] Alas! Alas! Which wind and rain
do beat
That great Beau Brummell should so
walk the street!*

very sincerely Yours
George Brummell.

41. Brummell, aged sixty. The
mercury treatments prescribed for
syphilis robbed him of his teeth
as well as all his hair, so he wore a
wig. Penury forced him to wear a
cheap black cravat.

42. and 43. The asylum of Bon Sauveur outside Caen where Brummell was admitted in 1839, suffering from 'general paralysis of the insane' (tertiary syphilis) and where he died in 1840. The room as it was when he died (*above*). The derelict pavilion of the asylum as it is today (*below*).

Talleyrand and Princess Bagration were two of the city's most famous gourmets.

Brummell ate very well, and he sang for his supper. He entertained the ambassador's guests to tales of life with the British regent and the mock-horrors of the bourgeois captivity from which he had just been released. If it was a shock to his increasingly fragile system to be dining with the richest gourmets in France, and in a Faubourg St-Honoré palace, when only a few months previously he had narrowly escaped bankruptcy, he took it all in his stride. On his first morning in Paris he strolled along the rue de la Paix. It was one of the capital's more fashionable new streets. He left an order at Dabert's, the jeweller, for a snuff-box in celebration of his freedom. It was to be gold and enamel and was to cost 2500 francs. He had no way of paying for it, but that had never hindered him in the past.

Eventually Brummell had to drag himself away from Paris. On 25 September 1830 he left the British Embassy in a carriage and four – most likely paid for by Lord de Rothsay as a last act of official beneficence – and travelled through the day to Caen.

It was late by the time the carriage wheels hit the hard cobbles of the old Pont de Vaucelles. The bridge over the river Orne marked the city boundary. The carriage drove up the slightly kinked rue St Jean and past the distinctly kinked tower of the church of St Jean – most of central Caen was built on a marshy island and several of the larger buildings leaned precipitously. It then spun into the courtyard of the old Hôtel de la Victoire, just by the castle gates. Brummell jumped out and beckoned to the first person he saw, who happened to be the hotel's cook. He addressed him, in English, with words remembered from his days in St James's: 'The best rooms, the best dinner,' he said, 'and the best Lafitte.'

Almost immediately he wrote to Lord Aberdeen, his employer at the Foreign Office, to announce his arrival and apologise lest the impression be received in London that he had neglected his duties to enjoy the high life in Paris:

My Lord

I have this day entered upon my duties as Consul. I will avail myself of this opportunity most humbly to request your Lordship's indulgent consideration upon the subject of my having taken the Liberty to absent myself so long from my post. After a residence of more than fourteen years at Calais, I had unavoidably involved myself in difficulties which it was not in my power to surmount at the instant. By making every sacrifice remaining to me I have been at length enabled to leave that place with credit to myself, and in such an honourable manner as, I feel persuaded, Your Lordship would approve.

For Brummell, Caen in 1830 presented a very different prospect than Calais had. Although less of a thoroughfare or port, it still had its fair share of travellers, boarding ships to set sail down the Orne and out to sea. It had a long-standing connection with England, from Norman times: its university had been founded by the same medieval English king who had founded Brummell's old school, Eton. Caen even looked a little English. Its houses were built of soft cream sandstone and its Norman and Perpendicular churches would not have looked out of place in the Cotswolds. There was also a long-established English-speaking community and Caen had been a stronghold of French Protestantism since the seventeenth century. So far as British consular positions were concerned, Caen was a welcoming port.

The main residential district was on an island, formed from a curve in the river Orne, the quayside itself, and a canal that separated the secular city from the many ecclesiastical and educational establishments to the west. Off the rue St Jean – which ran up the centre of this district from the river to the castle – were a great number of pretty streets lined with double-fronted four-storey townhouses. The British consulate was on one of these small streets, the rue des Carmes, named after a long-defunct Carmelite convent. There was a literary salon nearby on the rue de l'Engannerie, and along the rue St Jean there were as many elegant shops as one might expect in an affluent provincial town: Mullet the bootmaker, Mansel, who sold French and English books, Cayoc, a *patissier*, and Magron, a *marchand de nouveautés*. They all did well out of Brummell's love of shopping.

Brummell did not stay long at the Hôtel de la Victoire. He dubbed it the 'worst hotel in Europe', but the truth was that they had almost certainly heard of his reputation, and asked for payment in advance, in cash. He moved out after a week.

He found lodgings on the rue des Carmes, a few doors nearer the rue St Jean than the British consulate, right at the centre of Caen. He liked it so much he signed a twelve-month lease on his rooms for 1200 francs a year. From there, a few weeks later, he wrote to his friend Marshall in Calais:

October 25th 1830
rue des Carmes, Caen
My Dear Marshall,
You would certainly before this have heard *de mes nouvelles*, had I not been occupied and put out of my usual passive way of existence by endeavouring to settle myself in this place. After passing a week in Paris en route – I wish by the bye, I had not seen it for Stuart [Lord de Rothsay] and several of my friends have [ruined] me for at least a year to come – I arrived at my destination, and underwent all the horrors, and all the more horrible cheating of one of the worst hotels, I am confident, in Europe; though they tell me it is the best here. During seven days I gnawed on bones upon unwashed dowlas in this charnel-house – what a difference, after Stuart, [Prince] Talleyrand, [Princess] Bagration, and [Beau] Montrond! . . . Good fortune at length led my steps to an admirable lodging, half a house, the property of a most cleanly, devout old lady . . . excellently furnished with a delightful garden, two Angola cats, and a parrot that I have already thrown into apoplectic fits with sugar. From the letters [of introduction] which I brought with me from Paris . . . without a sixpence in my pocket, I am become a great man here. They dine and fête me liberally, and I have already been elected a member of their Société or club [the Salon Littéraire]

. . . All well-educated, well-mannered and well-conditioned people; no superannuated imbecile clodhoppers . . . Tomorrow I dine at a grand to-do given by the Préfet and Monsieur de Pommeraye the député, and I am preparing a neat little extempore which I shall let off upon success to the commerce of the countries being toasted. The English residents here are very respectable persons; they keep large and hospitable mansions. . . The two leading *Amphytrions de nos compatriots* established in Caen are Messrs. Villiers and Burton, two very good men of independent fortune, with numerous families. . . . The French of the best class mingle much in this society, and there is always a fiddle for the amusement of the young ladies. I am doing all that I can to make all parties satisfied with me. I condole with the outs, and agree with the ins; as to my own nation, I have upon all who are worthy of such a compliment. I shake hands and gossip with the fathers and mothers, and pat all their dirty-nosed children upon the head, and tell them that they are beautiful. What can I do more with my scanty means?

I am perfectly contented with my *Chancellor* Haytner, who is well versed in his business, and from my investigation, I believe to be an honourable adjoint. Prostrate my remembrances at the feet of Mrs Marshall, and of all your family. Scribble me what is going on in *your little fishing-town* of Calais, for I shall always bear an interest towards it; and if there is nothing better to record, tell me whether it makes fine or bad weather.

Very truly yours

George Brummell

Brummell's 'Chancellor' was the vice consul, Benjamin Haytner, a naval lieutenant on half-pay and a married man with six children and every reason to accept Brummell's offer that he stay on in his post and run the consulate. His 'cleanly devout' landlady was Madame Aimable-Angle Gueron de St-Ursain, a well-connected widow. She had one daughter, also called Aimable, who was just sixteen and '*une jolie blonde*' when Brummell became their lodger.

No. 47 rue des Carmes no longer stands, but there are photo-

graphs of it in the Caen archives and Jesse provides a description
of the interior as he had, characteristically, insisted on a tour. It
was a large, solid house opening straight on to the busy little
street. There was a walled garden at the back, facing on to the
gardens ef the rue de l'Engannerie. A kitchen and two large rooms
were on the ground floor; there were two large rooms and one
small one on the first floor, and the same again above that.
Madame de St-Ursain, her daughter, and the cook, Marie God-
ard, and maid, Marie Vantier, lived at the top. Brummell had two
rooms on the first floor, and one for his new valet, Isidore
Lébaudy, who replaced Sélègue. It was a crowded household
and, for Brummell, notably feminine. Even the cats, as he pointed
out and whom he befriended, were female.

The business of the consulate, on the corner of rue des Carmes
and the quayside, was minimal and conducted largely by Haytner.
There were British ships coming and going, cargoes of iron and
coal for the new foundry over the river, and imports from British
colonial possessions in the West Indies: coffee, sugar and spices.
Brummell was occasionally asked for his signature on official
documents – one remains in the Caen archive – but his intention
was to fulfil some less-defined diplomatic role as an exemplar of
British manners.

To begin with the people of Caen took to him rather well. There
had been excited expectation before his (delayed) arrival, and his
letters of introduction from Paris to the gentry of the town impressed all. Not only had he been, by repute, an intimate of the past
and present kings of England, he was also on friendly terms with
Count Molé and the Corsican minister of war General Sebastiani.
Both these dinner guests at the British Embassy had furnished
Brummell with introductions. So, although he lodged in somewhat
bourgeois conditions on the rue des Carmes, he had invitations from
the Marquise de Séran, 'a genuine marquise of the *ancien régime*',
who lived at No. 42 rue des Carmes, and from Pommeraye, the local
deputy who had ridden as escort to King Charles X.

The 'dirty-nosed children' of the British community whose
heads he felt obliged to pat were numerous indeed. The archives

of the Protestant church list sixty-five British families in residence
in Caen in 1830. There were also Irish. The Bennett family on the
rue de Vaucelles had seven children, the Darceys on the rue de
l'Engannerie had ten, Mrs Fitzgerald on the rue Singer had seven,
as did the Mackesons and the Shaws. The Misses Wheatcroft,
Eleanor and Mary, ran an English school on the rue des Quais.
Near Brummell in the Île St Jean were George Villiers, on the rue
St Louis, and Colonel Francis Burton, who lived in the rue
Guilbert, just parallel to the rue des Carmes. With both these
families – the Villiers seem to have had mainly young daughters –
Brummell became very friendly. Burton sounded out Brummell
about his attitude to the Masons: there was a lodge in Caen,
which Brummell would eventually join.

Several wealthy British lived outside the old city walls in a
street of large new houses called the rue des Chanoines, including
William Cooke, a gentleman of private means, and William Cox,
a retired colonel. There were also two doctors who administered
to the British community, a Dr James Woodman and a Dr John
Kelly. It was Kelly whom Brummell took aside, in the way a
gentleman did, to explain, as the Prince of Wales had once termed
it, about 'his old business'.

On his perambulations, introducing himself to the British and
the natives of Caen, Brummell also walked into the bay-
windowed shop of Charles Armstrong, an English grocer and
supplier of goods to the British community. It was at No. 133 rue
St Jean, between the leaning tower of the parish church and the
turning for the rue des Carmes. Armstrong became Brummell's
counsel and support, and ultimately his most loyal friend. To
begin with, however, it seems likely Brummell went in to enquire
after the availability of snuff.

The rhythms of his life followed their familiar course, but
Brummell was more settled, and definitely happier, than he had
been in Calais. He ordered new clothes, walked daily on the Cours
Cafarelli – a promenade of trees on the far side of the quay – and he
attended the Salon Littéraire on the rue de l'Engannerie. He even
went to the inauguration of a Caen Philharmonic in the little theatre

on the Champ de Foire. He fell in with the 'Legitimist' or 'Carlist' set, who opposed the new regime of Louis-Philippe, the Bourbon prince who had seized the throne from Charles X in the July Revolution of 1828. But his politics, as ever, were social rather than heartfelt: he refused to fly the union flag outside his residence on Louis-Philippe's official birthday, for fear of offending his Carlist landlady Madame de St-Ursain. But he and Haytner flew it outside the British consulate to keep in with the authorities.

Elements of his old behaviour returned: his caustic wit and unappealing interest in censuring as well as praising. One member of the local community, noted as 'Mrs G' by Jesse, who was almost certainly Mrs Giraud '*marchande de cosmétiques*', made the mistake of pressing her attentions rather publicly upon Brummell. As he was walking back over the wooden bridge from the Cours Cafarelli she shouted from her balcony, in the presence of others, 'Now won't you come up and take tea?' to which Brummell replied, as if he were still the toast of White's window, 'Madam, you *take* medicine, you *take* a walk, *you take* a liberty, but you *drink* tea.' Others of his compatriots, whose charity he would eventually solicit, he cruelly dismissed as 'deplorable . . . how can such people be received?' and the local French who sought to be hospitable were also dismissed if they failed to meet his exacting standards. One family, without the aristocratic pretensions of his neighbour the marquise, ventured to invite him to dinner. They ordered salmon from Rouen and ortolans – then as now a delicacy of hen's-tooth rarity – believing Brummell to be a gastronome. They later heard what he had said when he was asked about this epicurean to-do in his honour: 'Don't ask me [about it],' he said. 'The poor man! He did his best.'

Stories of Brummell's snobbery began to circulate around Caen, and especially within the British community. But one British visitor noted with surprise that even those who were the butt of his humour were unoffended. In fact he found 'like the generality of the world [the British in Caen were] always ready to laugh at . . . vulgarities and infirmities [even in themselves] and remained on excellent terms with [Brummell] so long as he retained the power of amusing them'. Brummell refound his element in Caen, adding to the gaiety of life in the small and insular community, and especially, it would seem, among its women. To judge by some of his – largely undated – letters, he amused himself by acting as both purveyor and creator of gossip:

My Dear Mrs [Burton]
You desired me to divulge the *dénouement* of the recent *entretien* with Mademoiselle – I will endeavour to recollect it in all its pristine purity. La Donzella had been asking me who figured at Mrs B[ennett]'s late hop. My answer was that there was not any one particularly *frappante*; that the only novelty I had remarked was a duenna in the family of Mr . . . To my amazement and discomfiture she *naïvement* asked me, 'Would you not prefer being married to the governess [Miss Wheatcroft] you have been praising than to the bottle in bed?' . . . I abruptly responded: 'The lady in question might indeed prove a preferable substitute for the innocent bottle, but I have too good an opinion of her to suppose she would entertain such warming-pan ideas.'

He signed himself 'Yours blushingly' before adding,

'PS Dr [Kelly] who *à l'instant* is feeling my left pulse, is anxious to be asked to your soirée this evening. I send you a sonnet upon Miss [the lady who teased him] of whose *propriété* I have my doubts:

Mes Adieux à Moggy
Fair Moggy, fair Moggy, the morning falls foggy
And your tears, like the rain, may soon piteously pelt;
Yet my hopes still denote, that at sight of my note,
Your reason, like butter in sunshine will melt.

'Tis unkind to deceive, in my candour believe
All the perfumes of Araby will not now plight us
Shed your skin, like the snake, and perhaps for your sake
More refreshing amitié may enfin unite us.

Brummell was indeed his old self in some key respects. He was flirtatious, gossipy and sometimes cruel, happy and amused to find himself the centre of an admiring crowd again, but with a new reason to keep his distance: he felt himself socially above them all. He made friends, notably among the wives of the British professionals who had settled in Caen.

With these [Jesse wrote, having himself attended some of the same soirées] his reserve gave way, he not only conversed with them freely on topics connected with his earlier days, laughing most heartily at the folly of those who had permitted him to exercise such an absolute influence over the fashionable world . . . to the few, both French and English, to whom he was really partial, particularly those of the *beau sexe*, he was most agreeable, and like many . . . he much preferred the society of young persons.

The young person he came to spend most time with, and with whom he became increasingly intimate, was Aimable, his landlady's teenage daughter.

Mademoiselle Aimable de St-Ursain was in her late teens when Brummell arrived in Caen, but she was mature for her age. Her mother, who had aristocratic pretensions and connections, for all she was a landlady, had high hopes for her daughter's future. For reasons of social advancement, both within Caen or with a view to travel, Madame de St-Ursain wanted her daughter to learn English. She asked Brummell if he would consent to be her tutor. Aimable already spoke Italian. Brummell accepted, possibly with a view to a future reduction in rent. Aimable and Brummell had lessons together, but also, happily, they wrote, sometimes several times a day, as a way to improve her written English. Many of these letters came into Jesse's hands via 'a relative of the lady' and it soon became apparent why Aimable had kept her famous tutor's letters. Swiftly, hopelessly – and certainly dangerously – Brummell had fallen in love. Aimable was seventeen. He was fifty-three.

November 1831
My Dear Miss Aimable,
During the present week I have led a most idle and unprofitable life; never in bed before the moon has retired, and in consequence

unable to open my jaded eyes till the morning has almost vanished. I am angry with myself, now that this dissipation is passed, because it has made me inattentive to our correspondence in English. I shall certainly turn over a new leaf, and amend the evil course of these late hours, if only in deference to my promise to improve you in the knowledge of my uncouth native dialect . . . Prosecute your studies with the same amiable attention and emulation that you have already evinced, and you will soon be omniscient. I am half asleep; my ideas are as dense and foggy as the morning; and one might write as well with Ourika's paw [the cat] as with the pen with which I am labouring.

Brummell had set out to tutor Aimable in the style and with the vocabulary of his own courtly education. But she was apparently undaunted. There is a necessary intimacy of teacher and pupil, especially if they are working together in the same house, and the letters are only one part of what must have been a rapid progression towards an unusually close friendship. To begin with, Brummell took his role as purveyor of recondite vocabulary quite seriously, but the letters soon began to touch also on his emotions.

Thursday Evening
It is in vain I had promised myself a quiet evening at home, I am really [obliged] to attend a stupid soirée and without being guilty of a palpable untruth, it is impossible for me to send an excuse. I am compelled, then, to defer the pleasure of writing to you, more diffusely, and more academically, till tomorrow morning. Good night, and happy dreams be with you.

He signed himself, 'Always yours'.
Having penned his evening epistle, Brummell would then call for Marie, the maid, and have her take the note upstairs to Aimable's bedroom. Most of the early letters are playful and lighthearted. Occasionally the correspondence concerned the books that Brummell had set as texts. Just as often, he wrote about the household's many cats:

Dear Miss Aimable,

You have recently made such a rapid progress in the English language and in the writing of it, that I do not think a partial relaxation from your daily task would be detrimental to this branch of your instruction . . .

To improve the head, it is not necessary to neglect the natural dictates of the heart, and I will beg to observe that for many days and nights there has not been any fresh straw in the basket bed of the two cats, Ourika and her *élève* Angolina . . . I cannot resist their mewing supplications, though I have latterly taken care to close their door, for fear their aide-de-camp, Tigre, might also get in and *hous-piller* [abuse] Jacko's cage. I would rather preserve my feelings of humanity and tenderness for these mute domestic creatures, than acquire all the languages in the world! Yours out of temper!
GB

At other times Brummell was more the pedagogue, and played his role, as learned English gentleman, to the hilt:

To Miss Aimable,
rue des Carmes.
2nd December 1831.
I have been engaged during the last four days with letters upon business; irksome, indeed to indite, but which admitted of no delay. So, mistaken Miss Aimable, do not unjustly reproach me with negligence or forgetfulness.

You are certainly severe, but incorrect, in your conjecture that the destruction by lightning of the tower at Harfleur was a judgment of Providence against the English heretics who built it . . . Would it not be less partial to your own countrymen, and more morally probable, to suppose that this summary infliction from above against the innocent tower, indicated the wrath of Heaven against those modern, insidious, Jesuitical, and intolerant Catholic priests, whose pernicious influence and profane buffoonery exasperated the whole nation, and effected the downfall of the unfortunate Bourbon dynasty?

But enough of religion; my fire is extinguished, because I have paid more attention to you and my best plume than to the tongs, and I am freezing. The best faith, I believe, in this weather, is that of the poor Laplander, who adores the sun alone, when he sees it.

By Christmas 1831, he wrote, fleetingly, of his growing affection, and also indulged in some seasonal self-pity.

Christmas Eve, 1831
My Very Dear Miss Aimable,
All the plagues of Egypt, in the shape of visitors, have obtruded themselves upon me this morning, on purpose, I believe, to interrupt my transcribing verses, or otherwise communing in manuscript with you; it is not, then, my fault, though I dare say you will accuse me of idleness, that I am compelled to be brief in writing to you; but you have promised to take a lesson with me to-morrow morning, Christmas Day! What a period of rejoicing and fête, according to the customs of my native country, this used to be to me, some years since, while now, of 'joys that are past how painful the remembrance'!

I am out of humour with myself this morning, and more so with those troublesome people that break in upon my domestic tranquillity: I have not, indeed, much to enliven me; but with all my cares and vexations, you are always a consolation to me.

By early January 1832, he was confiding to Aimable some of his innermost anxieties. He confessed to terrible headaches – a sign, unknown to both of them, of his advancing syphilis – and to his worsening depression.

Tuesday
The moment I had begun to write to you yesterday morning, one of my usual time-destroying friends came in, and extended his visit and his idle confabulations till it was too late in the day to pursue my letter. I am this instant out of bed, though I am half asleep, knocked up, and tormented with the headach [*sic*] and I really feel myself incapable of inditing [*sic*] two rational connected sentences to you . . . I commune with my inveterate morning companions, the blue devils – and be assured, my very

dear Miss Aimable, that one of the most prominent vexations of these evil spirits is, the compunction of having neglected my promised duty to write to you: I believe I am falling into second childhood, for I am incompetent to do anything but to ruminate over the broken toys of my past days.

Unfortunately, Aimable's replies to his heartfelt missives have not survived. The potential dramatic charge, however, of their arrival in her bedroom – from a celebrity, however faded – is unlikely to have been missed by a restive, clever teenager. Brummell, in a middle-age advanced by ill-health, had found a sort of perfection in Aimable. She was pretty, according to his letters, young, impressionable, and eager to learn from him. But this was only part of the novel passion that moved him. Doubtless her attention and her evident response to his epistolary wooing was flattering, but she was also, a little too late in his life, the perfectly placed intimate for Brummell: at one remove from him. She was a physical presence in his life, but also a young woman to whom he was obliged to *write*. He had found a way to re-create his image of himself as the *arbiter elegantarium*, the man who stood at the side of Almack's to judge the dancers. He had found a lover, with a bedroom floor for ever between them. The enforced, exquisite distance seems to have been part of the drama of the start of their unconsummated love affair.

A further romantic frisson involved her age: perhaps Brummell recognised in a precocious, attractive and ambitious seventeen-year-old something he remembered of himself. It is a common-place tinged with ridiculousness and tragedy that we often feel ourselves to be younger than we are, or at heart for ever some half-remembered younger age. Brummell had been catapulted into a world of glamour and wealth as a result of the vitality of his personality when he was in his late teens. It is not unreasonable to suppose it was the age he felt himself to be, despite the obvious decline in his fortunes and physical well-being. It is not unreasonable therefore to see in his love affair with Aimable, despite its hopelessness in practical terms, a heartfelt revisiting of his own youth, when he, like she, faced an exciting future.

The letters continued through the spring of 1832, and presumably they spent time together at other pursuits. Brummell discussed art with her; she shared his love of sketching, and they continued to read novels as subjects for improving conversations.

Caen, like many French towns, was all but deserted in the summer. The more affluent residents, and many who would scarcely have thought of themselves as even bourgeois, decamped to the beaches a few miles north of the city. Traditionally this had been done to avoid the malodorous city in the full heat of August. But the fashion for sea-bathing encouraged by Britain's regent had caught on in France, and the coast north of Caen, from Luc-sur-Mer all the way east to a village called Deauville, was filled in the summer with Caenaises and even Parisians taking the sea air and swimming.

Jesse noted that Luc-sur-Mer smelt of herrings and would not be worth considering a resort anywhere else in the world, but the beach was and is low, wide and sandy, and the little houses, then as now, opened straight on to the promenade. Brummell could not afford to stay in Colignon's principal hotel, otherwise known as L'Orient. Luckily de Chazot, one of his Carlist friends, sometimes invited him to his summer-house at Delivrande, a short distance inland from Luc. As well as the attractions of sea air and oysters, Luc was also the summer residence of Aimable. But when Aimable joined her mother and extended family at the tiny seaside resort of Luc-sur-Mer early in the summer of 1832, Brummell remained in Caen. He found himself suddenly at a loss without her company. When Aimable sent him a new novel he wrote back, declaring his love:

> Tuesday, July
> Millions of thanks to you for [the novel] *Ayesha*. I have not quite finished with her; for I cannot now read, nor write, nor do anything in a methodical way; therefore I return her to you, with every expression of admiration at your mutual excellences; with *Ayesha*, indeed, I have only made a transitory acquaintance – *you* I know already by heart.

Why, in the name of common prudence and my own tranquillity, could I not have been contented to restrict my knowledge of you to the worldly etiquette of taking off my hat to you when we casually met? During those years that I have vegetated upon the barren moor of my later life, I have sedulously avoided running my crazy head into what may be termed, inconsequent distractions; and now, in spite of all my theoretical circumspection and security, I find myself over head and ears, heart and soul, in love with you. I cannot for the life of me help telling you so; but, as all considerate reason has not at times utterly abandoned me, I shall put myself into a strait waistcoat, and be chained to the bed-post.

But you would laugh clandestinely at me in your bustled sleeve, for there is nothing more ridiculous than a person in my desperate state; and I should only have to 'bay at the moon' with my solitary plaints, and exasperate you, and the winds and the waves, with my vain jeremiads. For the future, I shall haunt you with sentimental elegies upon mourning paper, with a death's head crucified upon bones, by way of an appropriate vignette

What am I to do for a diurnal matinal correspondent and afternoon gossip, now that you are 'over the hills and far away'? I am almost inclined to think that your sensibilities are as marbrées as your snowy complexion; still I shall ever be immutably yours in this world, and if our most devoted wishes and memories are allowed in the next, mine will still remain inviolable towards you.

How Aimable responded to this letter is unknown. She seems to have been remarkably cool and self-possessed, which may have been part of her attraction for Brummell, whose letters soon returned to their earlier vein. But it seems likely she did not tell Madame de St-Ursain what was going on. They continued to discuss books and the seaside, almost as if nothing had been said of Brummell's feelings.

> Saturday evening, August
> My existence here has become perfectly dreary, insipid, and unprofitable: scarcely I see anyone, speak to anyone . . . My only excursions from my cell are to the Cafarelli . . . I detect myself frequently looking back, in the fancy of seeing you . . . coming over the bridge; but no such happiness awaits me . . . But enough of these fantastic vapours of the brain. [Here enclosed a copy of *The Butterfly's Funeral* dedicated to Georgiana, Duchess of Devonshire.] I could go on writing all night but my perverse lamp is getting sleepy and closing its eyes. It will leave me in the dark, as you did, by the abrupt and ungenerous termination of your last amiable note to me. Good night, good night; unfading welfare and happiness be constantly with you, and may you dream of butterflies. Eternally yours, GB

Eventually Aimable responded in some way Brummell found pleasing. He had always been mortified at the idea of offending anyone accidentally (deliberately was another matter). Having declared his love, he seems to have spent as much emotional energy pulling back again for fear of losing the friendship he would have known could never be more than that.

> À Mlle Aimable
> Luc-sur-Mer
> Tuesday evening.
> May the recording angel, who registers above the amiable feelings and thoughts of mortals, preserve you for having written that last note to me! It has at once extricated me from the very abyss . . . and has restored me to peace and equanimity. After reading it, I sought another wander into the Cafarelli, and returned home to my solitary room.

Through the summer letters of 1832 (and into 1833) Brummell expressed a more appropriately avuncular affection for Aimable. Theirs was an intimacy that continued, but never quite with the intensity of passion he at first allowed. He inspired her, with his album, to create one of her own, to which he contributed both verse and sketches. It occupied a great deal of their correspondence.

À Mademoiselle Aimable
Luc-sur-Mer
Monday morning
Allow me to present you with a sketch; it is in a sadly unfinished state but it will at least prove to you that I can sometimes keep my promise, and *travailler* for your album . . . the sketch is from memory: it is a resemblance of a very amiable person who is now no more, of Georgiana, Lady Worcester.

And on another occasion:

Monday.
I am ashamed to send you so unworthy a sketch of a beautiful woman; it is the rough outline from a portrait by Sir Joshua Reynolds of Georgiana, Duchess of Devonshire; the miniature, which afterwards was finished, was given to Lady Harriet Cavendish, now Lady Granville.

You shall have others as I go on, unwillingly digging in old green boxes: in the meantime I send you some lines of Lady Granville's, which I am sure you will admire.

At the same time that the middle-aged British consul was sending sketches and love-letters to his landlady's daughter, a separate drama was unfolding. All the while, a young army officer on leave from India was recording Brummell's sayings and doings, largely unaware at the time of the love-affair but sensing the separate issues of Brummell's crumbling physicality and finances. The army officer was William Jesse who would go on to write extensively on Brummell. He was only twenty-five at the time.

He and Brummell met first at one of Mrs Burton's soirées on the rue des Chanoines. Jesse immediately recognised Brummell from descriptions he had read of him, as far away as India. 'I felt he could be no other than the exiled Beau.' He was struck by his elegance, of dress and manner, and his eyes followed him round the room as he made a series of bows and smiled acknowledgements to the company.

His dress on the evening in question consisted of a blue coat with a velvet collar, and the consular button, a buff waistcoat, black trowsers and boots . . . the only articles of jewellery that I observed about him were a plain ring, and a massive chain of Venetian ducat gold, which served as a guard to his watch. Only two links of it were to be seen. The ring was dug up on the Field of the Cloth of Gold by a labourer, who sold it to Brummell when he was in Calais.

Jesse and Brummell were introduced, and came to be on friendly terms relatively quickly, as had happened with Major Chambre when he was passing through Calais. Brummell was often lonely, and happy to be visited at his lodgings. His elaborate dressing and exfoliating regime is recorded by Jesse, along with details of his daywear and manner. He wrote that Brummell still took elaborate pains in shaving and rubbed himself all over with a pig-bristle brush till he shone like a 'scarlet fever' victim. He was able to record all this as he watched the ageing dandy through a half-open door as they carried on their conversation. The skin regime was almost certainly an attempt on Brummell's part to keep the more obvious symptoms of his syphilis at bay. He was likely to have worked out, by 1832, a fairly reliable regime of mercury ointment 'inunction' that would immediately depress the rashes and secondary chancres that must have been developing by this stage of the disease.

Brummell had finally taken to using an umbrella, made of brown silk. The handle was a head of George IV: 'It was not flattering,' noted Jesse, 'and perhaps the more prized by Brummell on that account.' His dress otherwise had barely altered in thirty years. He was slightly stooped, a sign of the slow attack on his spine of the syphilis, and the 'creeping, snail-like' gait Jesse describes is further evidence that *tabes dorsalis*, the syphilitic attack on the spinal nerves, was taking hold. This in itself would be a sufficiently striking contrast with the man attempting to woo an eighteen-year-old, but Jesse also makes it clear that Brummell was not only totally bald but forced to be inordinately careful of his expensive wig. He was no longer able to doff his hat to ladies in the street for fear of dislodging it. He was a sorry sight.

The other issue impinging on Brummell's romantic frame of mind was his finances. Within less than a year of his arrival in Caen, he had been forced to write to his banker back in Calais. He wrote in French:

> À Monsieur Jacques Leveux,
> Banquier, Calais
> I scarcely expected [when I left Calais] to find myself once more reduced to the extremity of having recourse to your kindness . . . This situation has finally become most threatening . . . at the moment my honour is at stake, my reputation and all my present and future interests since I have reason to fear that the total lack of means to provide for the official expenditure which is daily demanded of me by my consular office and the ignominy of being continually harried for the small debts that I have necessarily contracted in this town, may shortly be the cause of my losing my place here.

This was a clever argument to Leveux in Calais, because the Calais debts could never be recouped if Brummell lost his job in Caen. By the same token, Leveux knew that Brummell's professional outgoings were negligible: it was the cost of being Beau Brummell that was forcing him back towards bankruptcy.

> I therefore beg you to consider the difficulties of my situation in your own interests, which I vow are more sacred to me than my own.
>
> *Je suis, mon cher Monsieur*
> *Votre tres-fidèle et obeisant serviteur*

Leveux did not respond. Brummell wrote again a month later 'pushed to the last extremity . . . I have only the shirt on my back left', and Leveux relented and cashed a cheque for him in order that he might pay his most pressing new debts in Caen. He must have known that Brummell could not survive on the small portion of his consular salary that reached him. Like everyone else, the Calais banker had been impressed into believing that Brummell's rich London friends would continue to bail him out, and they did – but the money took longer to arrive, the amounts became smaller and Brummell's debts continued to rise. The London friends, meanwhile, were surprised to find their long-standing generosity was still to be called upon. They had assumed that Brummell's appointment was the end of his, and their, worries.

Brummell wrote to his old acquaintance from Harriette Wilson's parties, Lord Palmerston, now at the Foreign Office, to request a brief leave. He needed to make a rendezvous in Le Havre with an attorney. Seemingly this was with regard to his ancient annuities, or monies that had been arranged for him by Princess Frederica. Either that, or he was finally in negotiation to sell his memoirs. Whatever it was, it required a meeting at a mid-point between London and Caen as the mysterious stranger 'cannot be away from London for more than five days' (the round trip to Caen took more than a week). In requesting a few days' absence, Brummell took the opportunity of addressing Palmerston on his own future prospects. He still had his eye on the more lucrative consulship at Calais, or a post in Italy, ideally at Leghorn, as the Tuscan port of Livorno was then known. 'I will take the liberty of availing myself of this occasion in most humbly soliciting Your Lordship's consideration of me, should a vacancy occur in the Consular establishments of any of the other Ports of [France], and particularly that of Calais.' To strengthen his case for promotion, Brummell next took a big political gamble. He decided to tell Palmerston that the Caen consulship should be abolished:

I may represent to Your Lordship that which might be prejudicial to my own individual interest, but, with every zealous anxiety to make myself of use in preserving Your Lordship's protection and the only means which enable me to exist, I will beg unreservedly to state the almost total inutility of the appointment of a Consul at this place, and that the situation might be abolished altogether without any probable detriment to His Majesty's Service.

Brummell was granted his few days' leave – unnecessarily as it turned out, as his attorney could not get away – and there was no immediate response to his bold suggestions. But in time there would be.

Meanwhile, Aimable and her family returned for the summer to Luc-sur-Mer, and Brummell hinted to her that he thought he would win a consulate elsewhere on the continent:

Mademoiselle Aimable
Luc-sur-Mer
Thursday evening.
It would be trespassing too much upon your indulgence to retain your album any longer. I restore it to you . . . I have obtained some new magnifying glasses, and have been striving to make two drawings for you. I have accomplished all the preliminary outlines, and to proceed, I am only awaiting my colours, which Mrs B[urton] (devil take her carelessness) has decamped to the country. I am, however, concerned to perceive, that I cannot draw and finish as I used to do; my vision seems to grow opaque, and indiscriminating (I need not tell you this) my head is scarcely ever exempt from some disquietude or other; and my hand, from a sort of nervousness, which incessantly visits me, trembles like the rushes that shade the 'Grave of the Butterfly' . . .

It has lately been intimated to me, that I must be prepared to leave Caen; this is from the Government in England; how soon, I know not. I am ignorant also of my destination – that will depend upon, and be dictated by, those in power, who have still the kind consideration to think of me and my broken fortunes. For years, I have cherished the wish to go to Italy; and, if what I have solicited in my answer should be accorded to me, I shall take up my wallet and my staff, and seek the auspicious heaven of that country and climate. This is no fairy dream!

À Mademoiselle [Aimable]
Luc-sur-Mer.
Tuesday Evening.
My colours are redeemed, and without any further intermission
you shall be obeyed, and I will prosecute *mon travail* for you. In
the meantime, to demonstrate to you that I have not been idle
and forgetful of you, I prelude my humble oblations at your
shrine, and your shrine alone, by a precipitate sketch, which is
out of my usual way of drawing, as it is a landscape, but which,
between ourselves, is not so bad a beginning.

I am afraid I wrote some sad nonsense to you on Saturday
night. I had been in pain during the day, and had recourse to that
deranging drug, at least for the senses, laudanum – I know all my
failings when I come into the possession of my intellects again.

Occasionally Brummell found ways to join his young friends at
the seaside, usually staying with the Count de Chazot and his
younger countess. She recalled one summer day when Brummell
joined 'Mme de St Ursain, M. de Ste Marie, Henry de Vauquelin,
M. De Valmont et M. du Pille' in a landau out to Luc. The French
all wanted to picnic on the beach but Brummell fought the idea –
he seems always to have disliked sand. The countess claimed he
relented when he saw the food: 'Pâté d'allouettes au foie gras du
boeuf en gêlée, un dindonneau farci aux truffes, des gâteaux, des
fraises, des cerises, des fameuses bouteilles de Luc-Saluces et de
Château Eyquemet du Champagne.' Brummell was proved right,
however: the strawberries were ruined by sand in a gust of wind,
so the party went instead to the Café de Grand Orient. Brummell
appears on this occasion to have returned to Caen, where he was
anxiously awaiting news from Palmerston about a new consulship.

À Mademoiselle [Aimable]
Luc-sur-Mer.
Saturday, July 20th.
Why had you not the amiable recollection to write me two
words, to say you had received the books I sent you Tuesday? Do

so in considerate amity to me tomorrow. I am very forlorn and miserable here – abandoned by everyone whose presence was in some measure satisfactory to me – I start at my own shadow. I must put an end to this, or I shall expire upon my own solitary lucubrations. There is nothing left to liberate me from this state of mental dissolution but going down to Luc, and once more seeing and shaking hands with you all. That, I am persuaded, would do me more good than any other earthly regimen, and contribute to enable me to linger on in this world for perhaps another year.

As he waited for news, Brummell began to lean on the locals financially, rather than rely solely on his friends back in England, and in particular on George Armstrong, the grocer. Armstrong was known and trusted by the whole British community and did far more for them than dispense tea and snuff. He sold tickets for the steam packet, he was a wine merchant, lodgings agent, and, in the absence of anyone better qualified for the posts, he acted as American vice consul and minor banker, in so far as he cashed cheques. It was in this last capacity that he came to play a central role in Brummell's life in Caen. The English wrote cheques to him for Brummell, and he provided money. Eventually he extended credit to Consul Brummell.

Dear Armstrong,
I have been reduced to so low an ebb during the last three weeks, by delay, and not receiving promised remittances from England, that it is impossible for me to hold up my head, or to exist in my actual state for a day longer. For ten days I have actually not had five francs in my possession, and I have not the means of procuring either wood or peat, for my scanty fire, or of getting my things from the washerwoman. A trifling advance would arrange these difficulties, and give me further time, but I know not who to apply to in this place.

You have as yet been a good friend to me, and may have sufficient confidence in me, and inclination to extend some additional timely service to me. What I have already assured you I now repeat, with every honourable intention and feeling; you will not repent your kindness.

I have not anything to offer you by way of security, excepting my signature, if it is not my small stock of plate, for which I paid six hundred francs, and my watch and chain, worth as much more: to these you are welcome, only do not let me be exposed to the most utter distress and want, from my temporary inability to command a few miserable francs. I am not going out, and if you can spare five minutes in the course of the morning, you will oblige me by coming down here: these matters are better arranged in person than by writing.

Brummell could arrange credit for most of the necessities of life; he had a lifetime's experience of living in that way. But servants required wages, and he had not found, in Isidore, as compliant a manservant as Sélègue had been in Calais. He was forced again to go to Armstrong:

À Monsieur Armstrong.
Rue St Jean.
That [damned] ungrateful brute, Isidore, persecutes me at every instant: the fellow says he is going to Paris on Thursday, and will not depart without being paid, in money or by bill, and I believe him capable of employing a *huissier* [bailiff].

I am wretchedly bedevilled, and out of spirits, and hate going out of the house.

Things became worse fairly rapidly. Word got out, almost certainly from Isidore, that the consul was struggling to meet his obligations. Other creditors pressed Brummell for payment, and he could think of no one other than Armstrong to turn to for ready money. He wanted to sell or pawn some of this possessions but was afraid of causing more alarm in town if he was seen doing so.

I am positively pressed for two hundred and eighty francs, at the moment, that is, before four o'clock today, or I shall be exposed to the utmost disgrace. The things, that is, the plate, are in the closet in my room, and you may have them by sending any confidential person for them; but I do not like to <u>trust</u> my servant with them, as it may be known, or he may be seen with them in the street. It is the urgency of the moment that I am anxious to weather; small difficulties often extend to irreparable destruction of character; such is my situation at this instant.

Then Brummell received a letter from England bearing diplomatic seals. He must have thought he had been saved again at the eleventh hour. His letter to Palmerston had been taken seriously, much more seriously than he could have thought – but not in the way he wanted. He was not offered a consulate in Italy or elsewhere in France. In March 1832, he found that Palmerston had taken his advice and was abolishing the post of consul at Caen. He did not offer Brummell any other post in its place.

March 21 1832

Sir,

His Majesty's Government having had under their consideration the present Consular Establishment of the country with a view to effect therein every practicable reduction, they have come to the conclusion that the Post of British Consul at Caen may be abolished without prejudice to the public service.

In acquainting you with the determination of His Majesty's Govt. to abolish the office of Consul at Caen, I have the satisfaction to express to you my approval of your conduct during the period in which you have executed the Duties of that Office.

Your Consular Functions being at an end, your Salary will cease on the 31 May – and you are at liberty to quit Caen as soon after the receipt of this Despatch as may suit your convenience.

Brummell was out of a job, and immediately deeply out of favour with his various creditors. It should not have been known that he was due to leave, but, with impressive selflessness, one of his first thoughts when he had read Palmerston's letter had been for Haytner, the vice consul, and his six children. Brummell wrote to the Foreign Office, recommending Haytner's 'assiduity, skill and accuracy', and suggesting he at least be retained. Haytner's wife, ungraciously but with understandable annoyance at Brummell for the original letter he had written, let the cat out of the bag. Within hours all Caen had heard that Brummell had been dismissed as consul. His creditors came straight to get their money.

Bailiffs arrived at the door of No. 47, early in May 1832, and Brummell was forced to hide in Madame de St-Ursain's bedroom (bailiffs were forbidden to enter a lady's bedroom under French law). The full force of the civil law had been set on him by Longuet, the restaurateur on the rue St Jean: Brummell owed him 1200 francs for meals and wine. Such was Brummell's social popularity in Caen, however, among those to whom he did not owe money, that a delegation of regular Longuet diners was got up to persuade the restaurateur to cease persecuting the now ex-consul, and, briefly, he staved off the bailiffs.

He wrote frantically to Armstrong: 'Send me seventy-five francs to pay my washerwoman: I cannot get a shirt from her, and she is really starving on my account. I have not actually money to pay my physician, or for my letters to and from England.'

It was touching that, on the verge of bankruptcy yet again, Brummell was worrying about the washerwoman 'starving on my account'. Meanwhile his health was suffering under the strain. His body needed all its defences as well as the chemical toxins to slow down the attack of the syphilis, and emotional strain would be followed by a new attack. Armstrong, possibly under guidance from Dr Kelly, was persuaded to let Brummell's friends in London know that things were again reaching an impasse. Many already knew Armstrong's name and his sound reputation. They also knew he cared for Brummell.

I really think [wrote one of Brummell's London contacts, possibly Dawson-Damer] that a personal interview with Mr Armstrong with [your friends here] would do more good than letters. The difficulty of doing so would be great, but all that I can do to insure [his introduction to] them I will. I don't know how to get at the Duke of Wellington or Willoughby. I will write to George Anson and his brother Litchfield, Bagot, Alvanley, and many others that may occur to me, who I may think can be of any use; and amongst them, by the way, old Allen, who I assure you, spoke of you the other day in the kindest manner . . . Worcester I fear is still in the country, otherwise I am sure he would have been more ready to exert himself than any one.

Armstrong agreed to visit London on Brummell's behalf. While he was gone, Brummell busied himself trying to retrieve expenses from the Foreign Office, and simultaneously lobbying them to reinstate Haytner as vice consul. Haytner also wrote to Palmerston, saying he was willing to work for nothing if he could retain the fees he collected (he was in a position to know that they could amount to more than a Foreign Office stipend anyway). He estimated this income to be forty pounds per annum, but explained that he had a 'large family of very young children' to support. By 1832 the Haytners had had their seventh child.

Both Haytner and Brummell were successful with their small requests: Haytner, for an unpaid post, and Brummell for 286 francs against a journey inland he had been forced to make as consul:

As it has pleased His Majesty's Government that my functions as Consul resident in this place should cease I will take the liberty to represent to you that the insignificant sum [286 francs] is now of the utmost importance to me. It would be intrusive if not absurd in me to talk of past services in the narrow situation I have held here, yet I am sensible that some trifling approbation might be extended to me for having reduced the charges and defrayments . . . attached to it by nearly one half during the period I have officiated in comparison with previous years.

This last plea fell on deaf ears and he received nothing more from the British government.

He was fifty-four, broke and beset by the manifold ailments of secondary syphilis. He ached constantly, and the pain woke him at night. He suffered headaches and acute sensitivity to heat and cold. All this he alluded to in his letters, but he was also suffering most likely from the intestinal ailments associated with the disease. Then on a particularly drab and cold evening, late in the summer of 1832, he suffered a new sort of attack. Aimable kept the letter he had been writing to her when he collapsed:

Oh this uncomfortable weather! I am freezing *au coin de mon feu*, and my ideas are as much congealed as my limbs. You must not, then, in common compassion, expect either amusement or instruction from a *malheureux* in my torpid state. There are moments too when I am subject to that sort of overwhelming depression of spirits that makes me incapable of any thing but to brood over my own grievances, fancied or intrinsic, it does not signify.

I cannot shake off its gloomy influence. I should like to retire to my bed, and, if it was possible, to sleep till the spring, or till nature would beneficially animate my dejected thoughts as she regenerates the leaves and flowers and the earth. I am at the instant subdued by chillness and blue devils, and feel as if I was in my grave, forsaken and forgotten by all those who were once so dear to me. *Le plus grand des malheurs est celui de ne tenir à rien, et d'etre isolé.** I am sick of the world and of existence.

> Whate'er they promised or profess'd
> In disappointment ends;
> In short, there's nothing I detest
> So much as all my friends.

You must perceive, that is, if you have the patience to read these vague saturnine jeremiads, that . . .

At this point Brummell's pen fell from his hand, and he slumped in his chair.

Someone heard the noise, went to check on him, and found him paralysed down his right side, unable to speak.

Dr Kelly was sent for. He administered leeches and blisters, but would have known that the paralysis was the worst possible sign: the syphilis was attacking Brummell's brain. Tabetic neuro-

---

* The greatest unhappiness is to be held to no one and to be alone.

syphilis arose from a treponemal attack on the substance of the spinal cord: a progressive wasting away that was characterised by sudden crises of intense pain, incoordination, peculiar sensations, loss of reflexes, and sudden, violent functional disturbances. Sudden paralysis was a classic symptom. Its effects were identical to those of a stroke except that recovery was relatively swift. Brummell carried on having intense headaches for several days but he recovered control of his facial muscles and regained his speech.

Perhaps it was the half-finished letter that gave the game away for Brummell and Aimable. Perhaps Madame de St-Ursain had guessed all along that something more than a teacher–pupil relationship had developed between them. But within days of the attack, Brummell had left no. 47 rue des Carmes. He made a relatively swift recovery from this first attack of paralysis, 'and those excruciating spasms', but it signalled for him the desperate hopelessness of his infatuation. It was a distressing time for everyone. Brummell had been intended to further Aimable's entrée into society – in Caen, Paris, maybe even London – but Madame de St-Ursain had not counted on him falling in love with her daughter, and she was not pleased. He owed her rent. The rooms were no longer necessary or affordable without the consular position. He left without saying goodbye – he later said he would willingly have done so 'but I was in tears'.

16

HOTEL
D'ANGLETERRE

1832–5

My papers are the only things I possess to which I attach
particular value, they are of no use to any one else, but to me
they are treasure.

George Brummell, on his arrest

The Hôtel d'Angleterre was on the east side of the busy rue St
Jean between the rue de la Poste and the rue de l'Engannerie. It
was yards from Caen's Salon Littéraire and only a few minutes'
walk from Madame de St-Ursain's on the rue des Carmes. Brummell took a set of rooms on the third floor, facing the street. There
were other long-term residents: a Mrs Emma Harris and her five
children, and Mr and Mrs George Morton with their two. At that
time a hotel in France would not have expected guests to move on
swiftly, and offered competitive rates compared to private rented
apartments and lodgings. Hoteliers like Monsieur and Madame
Fichet at the Angleterre made their money instead from their
restaurant, and guests were expected to eat in at the *table d'hôte*.
Brummell had full bed and board for sixty pounds a year, which
marked quite a saving on his outgoings at Madame de St-Ursain's,
not that he had been up to date with his rent there.

Although Brummell's health continued to be an anxiety, there
was soon good news from England and from Armstrong. He had

collected money in London from Alvanley, Worcester (Meyler had clearly been wrong all along in thinking Brummell had offended Worcester), Lord Pembroke, Charles Standish and Lord Burlington, among others. There was enough money to pay off Brummell's Caen debts – Longuet, the restaurateur, in particular – and the promise of regular contributions to support Brummell in his ailing retirement, to the tune of £120 a year. He continued his flirtation with Aimable by letter at the safer distance of one or two streets:

> Yesterday morning, I was subdued almost to insanity, but your note in the evening restored me to peace and equanimity, and, as if I had been redeemed from earthly purgatory, placed me in heaven. Thank you, thank you, dearest of beings; how can I retribute all this benevolent open-heartedness, this delightful proof and avowal of my not being indifferent to you? My heart's deepest affections for you . . . are rooted in my very soul and existence; they will never deviate; they will never die away.

Evidently Brummell had begun to deliver the letters to the rue des Carmes in person:

> By the dim light that was remaining I perceived something in white at your *porte-cochère*. It was evident that I was recognised, and the figure advanced with your *billet* . . . I lacerated the letter with impatience, and then the light of love and joy, and the refreshing breath of evening stole through the open window over my entranced senses.
>
> I have known few that could equal, none that could excel you; yet they possessed not your charms of countenance, your form, your heart, in my estimation. Certainly they did not possess that unaffected and fervent homage, which in my constant memory – in my heart's blood – and in my devoted soul I bear to you.

Brummell's 'blue devils', his sudden depressions, were often upon him, along with more physical pains associated with his illness. These were sometimes so severe that he prayed they 'would put an end to my sufferings in this world'. But on his good days, he felt, as he always had, that he could perform some service to the world if he could amuse it, and he continued to wave to other walkers on the Cours Cafarelli and to write letters to Aimable that were remarkable for their blithe disregard of his illness and his situation in life.

Madame de St-Ursain had other plans for her daughter than that she should languish in Caen with an ageing London dandy. Aimable was twenty in 1834, and her mother thought her firm command of English, along with the connections she could forge via her illustrious tutor, warranted a trip to England. It seems possible that this idea was first placed in her mind and Aimable's by Brummell. It certainly grew under his tutelage, as well it might, when their letters, and presumably conversations, were so taken up with English literature, history and the attractions of London. Brummell grafted on to Aimable his own metropolitan conceit that Caen was essentially a backwater from which people left for adventure. It was inevitable that she would go.

As a parting gift, he gave her his entire album, filled with verses by him and Sheridan, Georgiana, Duchess of Devonshire, and Charles James Fox. She had seen it often before, and used its contents for study. He sent it to her, with this letter:

> You are going away. It is a melancholy reflection for me that this is probably the last time I shall ever again write to you. Some day, perhaps, ere long, you will read more of me, with the rest of the world who may give themselves the trouble.
>
> Our acquaintance has been destined to a limited probation; but had it been for years I could not better estimate all your many amiable perfections, or more sensibly deplore your absence. If I can, at any time or under any circumstances, be of the remotest service to you, either in England or elsewhere, I will humbly request you to remember that the same zealous interest toward you which has always influenced me will remain undiminished to the end of my life.

As Aimable and her mother made final preparations to go, Brummell decided he could be of more practical benefit to his *protégée*: he would introduce her into London society:

Caen, March 1834.

Enclosed I send you letters, if you should wish to have recourse to them during your sejour [in England] I have taken the liberty to mention in them the name of [Alvanley?]. The persons to whom they are addressed are two of my oldest friends, high in their office at Court: and I will be responsible, that through their mediation you will be favourably received in the quarter to which they will present you.

In the progress of time you will visit London, and I have already told [my London friends] of the gratification I should derive from being the humble means of introducing you to some of those exalted female coryphées who still control what is termed the fashionable world . . . In this remote place I am apparently sequestered and estranged from those with whom my former life was intimately connected; but I am neither forgotten nor neglected by them. Should you enter into society, let it be confined to the best part; and to the best alone would I venture to recommend you . . .

My nerves are too much shattered, and my rheumatism too inveterate, to enable me to call and take leave. I mourn your departure, and cannot more truly represent the defected thoughts that at the instant press upon me, than by those beautiful lines of Petrarch

> O giorno, o ora, o ultimo momento
> O stelle congiurate a impoverirme!
> O fido sguardo e che vole' tu dirme
> Partend' io per non esser main contento?

Addio, amico per sempre carissima – mia intanto deplorata!*

In early 1834 Haytner, who had worked as vice consul, left Caen. He had tried to increase his salary from forty to a hundred

---

* 'This day, this hour, this last moment, / The stars that have sworn to impoverish me, / This faithful glance, and this thing you wish to tell me: / In learning it, will I ever be happy? / Farewell, always the dearest of friends – I will miss you for ever.' Petrarch

pounds but been refused, so with a mixture of pique and expediency (he had by now eight children) he decided to emigrate to the wide-open spaces of Canada. Charles Armstrong, the grocer and honorary American vice consul, applied to replace him, and asked for Brummell's support. Brummell pitched himself into campaigning, writing letters to Palmerston and Alvanley and hosting a testimonial dinner at the Hôtel d'Angleterre at which guests put their name to the application to be sent to Le Havre (the local consulate after the abolition of the Caen office) and to London.

Meanwhile Brummell wrote to Aimable who was staying outside London. She was not altogether impressed with English society and the company of Brummell's contacts:

To Miss [Aimable]
—— Park, Sussex
April 1834
For more than a month I have not heard a word from you; it is a disheartening lesson experience has long since taught me, that memories left to themselves, in absence soon fade away.

Exclusive discussions upon animals, agriculture, and politics, are sorry aliments for your 'elegant sensibilities'!

There certainly exist *de nos compatriots* of my nearer acquaintance who are gifted with the happy tact to make themselves agreeable without descending to the abominations of which you complain . . . You used to amuse yourself with a cursory meander in the romances of the day. Read Trevelyan if you have not; it is well written. It drives me into a brain fever even to think of it!

Aimable missed one aspect of Brummell's physical deterioration by her continued absence in England: by the mid 1830s, eating in public was becoming a trial for him. The *Lancet*, the medical journal, described at the time the

visible effect on the mucous membrane of the mouth and gums [after mercury treatment] attended with an unpleasant metallic taste, particularly in the morning; the saliva becomes secreted in greater quantity than usual, and is altered in quality, presenting a ropy consistence; and the breath has a particularly offensive odour.

Brummell's continuing recourse to mercury was leading to problems. Near the end of April 1834, he went down as he did every day for dinner in the hotel restaurant. It started, as meals perforce did in France in the 1830s, with soup. As he raised the spoon to his mouth, he had the sudden sensation of the most ghastly over-salivation, exactly the social embarrassment feared by any syphilitic on a mercury regime. He took the napkin to his mouth, as he must have done many times in the past, but realised as he returned it to his lap that it was not over-salivation this time, but soup that had been running down his chin. He stood up, the napkin shielding his mouth, and retired to the empty salon where there was a mirror.

One side of his face was pulled upwards in an unmoving rictus, like half of a masquerade mask. He had suffered another neuro-syphilitic stroke. He went up to his room and sent for Dr Kelly.

This time his recovery was slower. Dr Kelly almost certainly increased the dosage of mercury, and might have added the more fashionable arsenic and iodide treatments that were now being alternated with mercury cures. Potassium iodides made from burned fresh sponge and seaweed were taken in suspension or as pills, and had proved successful in Paris and Dublin as alternative or complementary additions to the traditional mercury cures. Dr Kelly must have been beginning to realise that Brummell was going to need increasingly expensive treatment, and was unlikely to be able to meet his bills. Although there was both ignorance and anxiety among patients and doctors on the issue of neurological disorders, the most pressing concern with syphilitics tended to be an abatement of the gross physical signifiers: the chancres, rashes, tumours and mouth ulcers. If these could be treated, and generally they could, it was wrongly believed that the disease would progress more slowly to the central nervous system. By 1834, Armstrong must also have been aware of Brummell's illness, if only as his medicines were such a regular item of his expenditure.

Jesse's descriptions of Brummell's skin regime suggests he was forced to apply mercury as ointment. This would have had its own unpleasant effects, in the medical language of the time: inunctions caused 'scattered inflammatory oozing, crusted and infiltrated patches and plaques of wide distribution . . . Purpuric manifestations are occasionally seen and a follicular popular eruption is recognised.' Brummell dressed as carefully as he always had, but with a slightly differing motive as the years went by: he needed to cover painful and unsightly blemishes. He continued to lose teeth and hair, and was plagued by chest pains, a symptom of the neurosyphilis, quite possibly a syphilitic tumour on his lungs. His eyesight was failing, and he misread colours as a result of the iritis that accompanied the syphilis. To add to his torments, Dr Kelly was a firm believer in cupping and blistering, the favoured method of the age for drawing evil humours, especially from the head. The last vestige of his hair, at the nape of his neck, was shaved at Kelly's insistence, to provide a new site for blistering.

'I am unwell,' Brummell confessed laconically. 'I flattered myself that I was progressing towards my ancient regular health; and now those who look after me professionally will insist upon it that my lungs are seriously affected, and pester me with all the alarming hyperbole of their vocation, upon my malady. They are weaving a shroud about me; still, I trust I shall escape.'

Within a few weeks he attempted to go down to the hotel restaurant for dinner, only to have to return to his room. Perhaps he was still struggling with his mouth muscles, but more likely – as it seems he was asked to leave by Monsieur Fichet, the hotel owner – he was over-salivating to a distressing degree and fellow diners, whether or not they recognised the symptom, would have been understandably upset. He improved, mercury dosage was regulated at a new level, and finally he was well enough by the summer of 1834 to accept an invitation to Luc-sur-Mer.

While Brummell recuperated by the sea, probably at de Chazot's house in Delivrande, Armstrong was again in London. In part he was on official business as vice consul, but he travelled with a letter from Brummell to Alvanley and also a copy of Brummell's Caen accounts, to demonstrate to his friends his reduced circumstances:

[August] 1834
My Dear Alvanley,
I have examined Armstrong's account of expenditure and receipts for me during the last twelve months, and I find it in every respect accurate and just. I have delivered to him the . . . Bank of England notes; but alas! My dear fellow, this will provide but in a very trifling degree for the liquidation of that I owe for my humble support during the last year [he owed six months' board and lodging to Fichet at the Hôtel d'Angleterre and was overdrawn with Armstrong by nearly two thousand francs]. I am suffering from a most severe and apparently fixed rheumatism in my leg, and I am in dread lest I should be compelled to have recourse to crutches for the rest of the ill-starred days.

My old friend, King Allen, promised, at least so it was represented to me, to send to me some habiliments for my body, denuded like a new-born infant – and what a Beau I once was!

Alvanley said he would send a cheque, and was true to his word, enclosing a note to Armstrong: 'I beg that you will protect and assist poor Brummell, and rely on my making it good to you.'

The money trickled in – enough to support Brummell but not to service his debt to Leveux's bank in Calais. He chose to ignore the issue. By the winter of 1834–5 he seemed largely recovered from his second stroke. He re-entered the Caen winter season of dinner and musical soirées at which he had become a fixture, and some of his easy good-humour resurfaced. On one occasion he was playing cards with an elderly spinster who was staying in town, possibly a relative of one of the British families, and when she laid down a card opposite Brummell, in the game écarte, and said, correctly, 'I propose,' Brummell responded, 'Yes, dearest.' The lady, a Miss Pawlter, either was 'or pretended to be' very angry at this impertinence. Brummell spent the next morning penning a mock-apologetic ditty:

To Miss Pawlter

I called you 'dearest,' dire offence!
'Twas only said in jest,
For 'dearest' in its common sense
Means her one loves the best.

But jealous of your virgin fame
And squeamish in a crowd,
With prim reproach, you scoff'd the name
Because 'twas said aloud.

Good night! But since a thoughtless joke
An idle fib, could fret you
Believe me, if the truth I spoke,
You'd curse the hour I met you.

He seemed resigned to a sedate but lonely old age, relieved only by the minimal diversions of the pretty little town he now knew as home.

Then on 4 May 1835, just after dawn, the Hôtel d'Angleterre was surrounded by *gens d'armes* and entered by a *juge-de-paix*. The justice had a warrant, issued by Leveux, the banker in Calais, for the arrest of George Brummell, debtor. A 'jack booted gentleman' entered room twenty-nine while Brummell was still asleep, woke him, and issued him with the writ for fifteen thousand francs. Brummell was informed he could either pay, or go immediately to prison.

Leveux was entirely within his rights to issue the writ. It followed years of prevarication by Brummell over the Calais debt, and specifically his inability to carry on paying over the £320 per annum from his consular salary, which had ceased in 1832. But Leveux was also moved to action by the knowledge that Brummell still had rich friends – friends who might make good the debt in the dramatic circumstances orchestrated on 5 May, with all the clatter and brouhaha that the local police could muster. Brummell was ordered to dress, and his request to do so in private was refused. He was told, indeed, to get a move on and that he was 'under the necessity of dressing in a hurry'.

Monsieur Fichet, meanwhile, had despatched one of the hotel workers, possibly his son Hippolyte, to acquaint Armstrong with what was happening.

By now all of the other guests were awake, and doubtless much of the immediate area too. The hotel had been surrounded, quite unnecessarily, but to prevent escape of the intended prisoner, by enough *gens d'armes* for the locals to comment they had never seen a debtor 'so handsomely arrested'. Brummell nervously entrusted his papers to Madame Fichet.

He was bundled into the waiting *fiacre* [hackney-coach] which clattered through the gathering market crowds of the rue St Jean, attracted by the drama of a big arrest, and by news of an ice-ship, newly arrived from Norway. The *fiacre* drove at speed past the exhibition of flowers at the Pavilion, and left on the rue St Pierre to the Place Fontette.

Just in front of the old Protestant cemetery of the city, in the area known as the Quartier St Martin, was the Place Fontette, with its forbidding courthouse and more forbidding gaol: La Prison Royale. It took only ten minutes to get there from the hotel. Brummell was taken through the courthouse and locked into a stone room, with three other new felons. Probably they were the others listed as arrested that week: Gaudron, Farine and Jean Besnard, all charged with vagabondage. There were three truckle beds only, all of them already occupied. Brummell stood in a corner by the door, until a gaoler brought in a chair.

17

PRISON

1835–9

In Prison 5 May 1835
I still breathe, though I am not of the living – the state of utter
abstraction in which I have been during the last thirty hours yet
clouds my every sense.

'I have just received your note,' Brummell wrote to Mrs Burton,
the wife of his rich Caen friend, Francis Burton, who had
been made instantly aware of his arrest. 'May heaven bless you all
for your good devotedness in remembering me at such a moment.
I have been the victim of a villain, who had closed upon me,
without giving me the remotest intimation of his designs. I am
perfectly innocent of any thing bearing the least dishonourable
construction in this *malheureuse affaire*; and if I was not deser-
ving of the interest you express as well as [show] towards me, I
would not demand it. I will write to you when I *can*.'

In truth Brummell had been given every intimation of what was
likely to happen. One day, he must have been aware, Leveux
would press for repayment. But Brummell had never treated debts
seriously, nor learned to fit his expenditure to his income. His life
had been punctuated by sudden deluges of money rather than
anything approximating a steady income. His inheritance, his
winnings from cards and dice, the kindness of his benefactors set
him on a pattern of overly optimistic financial management.

There had never been in his world a concept of money earned or saved, or ever any reason to assume that tomorrow might not bring good fortune as equally as bad.

He could also justify his actions to himself, in relation to Leveux, as those of a gentleman. He had made over his consular salary to his banker in all good faith at the time. If he had subsequently lost the post on which the deal was predicated, and through a selfless act of impartial advice to an ungrateful government, he was not to be blamed for being unable to service the debt.

Leveux, on the other hand, was simply acting in the best interests of his bank.

Brummell gave himself up to utter self-pity in the traumatic first days of imprisonment and 'sobbed like a child'. He 'threw himself into the arms' of his first sympathetic visitor, saying, 'I am surrounded by the greatest villains . . . imagine a position more wretched than mine.' Less sympathetic to the modern ear was what he added next: he complained bitterly about the poor quality of the food and then added that he had been 'put with all the *common* people'.

Brummell's French and English friends in Caen were unsurprised by his attitude and by what had happened. But if they could not do much to alleviate his debt, they could at least help with his last two concerns: the food and his immediate company. Debtors' prison, in France as in England, was a legal limbo of dubious practical benefit. It precluded the guilty from making amends for their crime, but it persuaded, in the case of Brummell, his friends to make amends on his behalf. Brummell was able to have visitors and to have his own food sent in. He was also moved, at the suggestion of his influential Caen friends and a note from Dr Kelly, to a semi-private sleeping space. He did not have his own room, so much as the end of a corridor, no wider than his bed. He slept there on a straw mattress, but during the day he was allowed to spend time with the gaol's most illustrious prisoner, Charles Godefroi.

The Prison Royale had many political detainees. The government of the 'revolutionary' Orléans Prince Louis-Philippe, the so-called 'July Monarchy', proved litigious and oppressive. Godefroi was the editor of the *Ami de la Verité*, a Legitimist – i.e. anti-Louis-Philippe – newspaper. It came out in Caen on every Sunday, Wednesday and Friday, and was doing well; in 1835, it started publishing in tabloid form. Yellowing copies of its later editions are kept in the city's municipal archives. With its innocuous advertisements for local lodgings and musical events – and for live swans, 'applications should be made in person to the office' – it seems at first glance an unlikely basis for the political imprisonment of its editor. But it also ran a column of news on press freedom called '*Liberté de la Presse*', which had led to Godefroi's arrest. *L'Ami de la Verité* loyally printed, week by week, the number of days Godefroi had been in prison. It struggled on, in the end for several years, without him. From his prison cell, as if to goad his political enemies, Godefroi mounted a running campaign of letters to his and others' papers, so much that Brummell worried he would 'probably prolong his detention here [by] ten years'.

But Godefroi had the largest room in the prison, the *chambre des prisonniers civils*, with what was considered one of the finer views: over the old Protestant cemetery, but also over the yard in which the women prisoners exercised. On the negative side, it was next door to the cell reserved for condemned men, and those awaiting deportation or sentences of hard labour. There was a communicating fireplace with a grille. It was to the accompaniment of 'lawless and riotous neighbours', and surrounded by the desperate grafitti of previous prisoners, that Brummell and Godefroi spent their days, telling each other stories and talking politics. Even in early summer, Brummell suffered from the cold and huddled by the large open fire, near the grille that separated him from the condemned. A feature of his declining health was persistent bone pain, which could be alleviated to some extent by heat, but he seemed to be losing any accurate sense of temperature, yet another symptom of the syphilis.

To begin with he held out hope that his friends in Caen would arrange for him to be sent to the hospital in the Abbaye des

Dames. He wrote optimistically to Mrs Burton on the Sunday after his arrest:

11 May [1835] In Prison. The kindness of every human being within the sphere of this town has by degrees restored me to equanimity. How shall I be able to repay you for this benevolence? . . . I am I believe this evening to be transferred from my present den of thieves to the towers of Matilda and to the sainted arms of *les Soeurs de Charité*. There I shall again breathe fresh air and be comparatively at peace. I cannot describe to you what I have suffered here.

Though he worried that the anxiety of his experience might make him 'relapse into my recent imbecilities', he ended the letter with a typical piece of Brummell whimsy: worrying about using a prison wafer instead of wax to seal his letter. 'You will perceive the extremities to which I am reduced – I am about to seal to you with a wafer! Do not even whisper this indecorum, for perhaps I may again frequent the world.'

He did not frequent the world nearly as soon as he wished, and he did not transfer to the hospital. Leveux wanted him kept in the gaol until the debt was paid, and the money could only realistically come from England. The banker instructed his lawyer to fight any attempt by Brummell for a transfer or release.

Armstrong, therefore, as well as planning a visit to London on Brummell's behalf also contracted the Hôtel d'Angleterre to send his meals to him in prison and make sure that the medical supplies arrived when they should. With both pharmacy and hotel bills still awaiting payment, the slow response from both businesses was perhaps understandable. Within the week, Brummell was complaining:

In Prison, Saturday
Dear Armstrong,
Henri de St Marie told me yesterday you had sent me a bottle of *Esprit de Savon* – I have never received it. If it has been left to Bassy, the chemist, to send, of course I shall never see it; should it

have been remitted for conveyance to the hotel, equal negligence will attend its destiny. In spite of all my friends have said to them in expostulation of the shameful pitifulness of the morsel they send to me by way of dinner, they get daily more meagre and miserable, and it is really not sufficient for the poor cat that keeps me company, neither does it arrive before half past six *malgré* your orders to them. I cannot help telling you what was the banquet yesterday despatched to me:

One solitary chop, about the size of an écu, enveloped in a quire of greasy paper, and the skeleton of a pigeon, a bird I could never fancy. I must not omit to mention the accompaniment of *half* a dozen potatoes. Such was my meal of yesterday evening, after a fast of twelve hours. It is not, I am certain, the fault of the son, but the *ladrerie* of the *père et mère*, with which I have been so long acquainted . . . I have not seen a soul today. I have no news, and I am in the very slough of despondency.

Armstrong talked to the Fichets and the chef at the Hôtel d'Angleterre, with some success, and Brummell was writing back within days to arrange for the safekeeping of his things at the hotel. But it was evident that there would be no quick release, and Brummell's thoughts turned to how he would maintain his strict regime of cleanliness and skin treatments in prison:

In Prison, Monday
My Dear Armstrong, Many thanks for your unremitting kindness in improving the quality of my humble repast. To your good offices, I had yesterday the satisfaction of being indebted for a sufficient, though homely, dinner . . . You will much oblige me by sending to me today, three towels for my toilette, and the same number every six days, for I cannot procure even a clout to rub myself down in this nauseous place. You will not, I am sure, forget, either, that every three days it is incumbent on me to pay for the necessities of breakfast, *eau-de-vie*, candles, etc – while you are here or during your absence. I will beg you carefully to take charge of everything I left behind me at the hotel, particularly two boxes: the one mahogany with brass ribs, and G. B. on

a plate at the top – the other with a glass on the top, covering worked birds drinking out of a vase; it was the labour and gift of the late Duchess of York, and I have a reverence for it – the latter had a leather case, which is either in the cupboard of the armoire out of the sitting room, or in the other recess where you will find my trunks etc etc. Pray send me what remains in the drawers of my bedroom – there are some waistcoats, drawers, pantaloons, etc, and in the upper *tiroir*, sundry trifling things which I forgot, but which I may have occasion for. The clock, vases, brown candlesticks, and in short everything in the room, is my own, not omitting the old green velvet armchair [also a gift from Princess Frederica].

Enclosed I deliver to you a list of every debt which I owe in the country of France, you will have the goodness to add your own just and excellent claims upon me, and those due to the hotel . . . Beyond these, so help Heaven, I have not an existing debt, whether in my handwriting or by oral promise in this country. Young B[urton] is waiting below to carry my letter; therefore I can only add, my dear Armstrong, how very sincerely I am yours.

Brummell was indeed deeply in Armstrong's debt. Without him, he might well have lost all his possessions at the hotel, but by listing them, and all his debts, Brummell was securing his immediate future and the possibility of presenting an overall sum in London that might guarantee his freedom. His anxiety and bitterness showed through nonetheless, and as his weeks in prison turned into months Armstrong had to face more and more of Brummell's unwarranted imperiousness.

In Prison, June.
My Dear Armstrong,
You would not, I am sensible, like to be imposed upon yourself, nor that I should be famished with hunger in a prison. I am ignorant both of the name and of the residence of the *traiteur*, or rather *traitor*, whom you have employed to purvey my daily meal; he has indeed but one merit and that is his punctuality at five o'clock. You shall judge yourself of his liberality, and I will

neither exaggerate nor extenuate in my report. Yesterday's portion was the following: half of the skeleton of a pigeon, which I firmly believe was the *moitié* of a crow, buried in rancid butter, and the solitary wing of an unfed *poulet* without even the consolatory addenda of its *cuisse* – half a dozen potatoes, and, by way of excuse for dessert, half a score of unripe cherries, accompanied with one pitiful biscuit, that looked like a bad halfpenny – this is the positive total of my dinner's calendar.

Twice I have beseeched you to send me three towels, and to repeat that number every six days. I have been reduced, for the last eight-and-forty hours to rub myself down with my dirty shirts, and that resource is now at an end, for they are gone to the washerwoman.

Amend these indispensable wants before you leave town <u>this</u> evening. I am also in want of some old waistcoats and pantaloons, which were in the drawers of the bureau in my bedroom, at the Hôtel d'Angleterre. There was also a pair of patched boots in the closet of the sitting room; and in the armoire a small glass bottle of Macouba snuff – will you have the goodness to transmit them to me?

Pray tell my friends that I am very fond of strawberries when they are in full season, and that they always do me good. In the schedule of my debts in Caen, which I wrote to you, I omitted to make the observation, that I was utterly in rags, and without the means of procuring better raiment. Goodbye; I would give half the remainder of my days to go down to the seaside with you this evening.

Armstrong dealt with the requests, and held his frustration with Brummell for later. Godefroi, too, benefited from Armstrong's attentions and was impressed with his new neighbour's attempts to maintain standards in prison. It is thanks to Godefroi, and Jesse's trouble in interviewing him a decade later, that we learn Brummell arranged to have his large wash-basin brought to the prison, and a daily delivery of twelve to fifteen litres of clean water with – to the astonishment of all – two litres of milk. With this, to equal astonishment on Godefroi's part, Brummell 'actually washed and shaved himself every day, and made a complete ablution of *every part of his body*'. Godefroi likewise noted Brummell's use of a 'dressing case full of vials of medicines and ointments', which doubtless included Dr Kelly's preparations against syphilitic eruptions. The use of milk, dismissed by Jesse as 'an absurd caprice', was almost certainly to counterbalance the toxic effect of the mercury ointments and soothe Brummell's skin.

To carry all this water and milk and to run small errands for Brummell, another prisoner, Paul Lépine, was contracted to act as valet, for a few *sous* a day, paid by Armstrong. Lépine was a former army drummer, recently returned from Africa, who was serving three months for a 'civil' offence.

At seven each morning Brummell was woken by a prison guard, who unlocked the end of the passage where he slept and rattled a 'bouquet of keys' in his face. The latrines in the prison were public and open air. They were in the far corners of the prison yards, Brummell's being in the distant apex of the Cours des Civils beyond the Cours du Geôlier. It was, he said, a particular horror to have to use it – he had once insisted, after all, on travelling with his own commode – and there was no door. The other prisoners sensed his 'bashfulness' and offered him cat-calls and hisses, before he scurried back to the *chambre des prisonniers civils* he shared with Godefroi.

As the spring of 1835 moved towards summer, there was still no sign of any money from England. Armstrong, still unable to leave his vice consular post in Caen, organised a whip-round of the local inhabitants. But this was always likely to prove inadequate. The ambassador in Paris – by then Lord Granville Leveson Gower, the son-in-law of Georgiana, Duchess of Devonshire – heard of Brummell's plight and opened a fund to help. His wife, Lady Granville, who had traded sonnets and sketches with Brummell in happier times, appealed to her brother, the Duke of Devonshire, who evidently responded positively, as her next letter makes clear: 'A thousand thanks for poor Mr Brummell. There never was such an act of charity. I am in good heart about the subscription.' But the Paris subscription fund did not amount to the £800 that Armstrong had calculated was needed to cover Brummell's Caen and Calais debts, and secure his release from prison.

Brummell wrote constantly to his various benefactors in Caen, especially Mrs Burton.

> Most earnestly I thank you for your amiable billet. Seldom I forget kindnesses; but my grateful remembrance of yours will survive to the end of my destined days . . . a consolation to me in these hours of wretchedness.
>
> Last night my dreams were violently disturbed by the abrupt entrance of all the *corps de garde* of the prison, who were on the alert in consequence of a rapid fire that was blazing without the walls, but within thirty yards of my cell, and were obliged to pass through it, in order to be ready for the approach of the flames, or the attempted escape of the *détenus*. I threw on my cloak and followed them. It was dreadful, being upon a timber-merchant's premises, but magnificent. I remained at a loophole gazing on the destruction till past two, when it subsided.

The tedium of prison life was relieved briefly by this fire, which lit up the local area and provided headlines for the *Ami de la Verité* for weeks to come. Brummell's life began to turn inwards, to the damp walls of the room he shared with Godefroi, and the cramped locked corridor where he slept. There were mice there, and a spider he spent a good deal of time studying. He befriended the prison's black cat, Minette, to whom he fed those parts of the meal from the Hôtel d'Angleterre he found unpalatable. The weeks dragged on. Brummell was losing faith in his supposed well-placed friends in London. It was pressed home to him in Caen prison that some of his truest friends were the local burghers, who could not help with his finances but offered him every other form of comfort. Mrs Burton and Mrs Villiers were particularly assiduous in their care and contact:

À Madame [Burton]
Rue [Guilbert]
In Prison, Sunday

You must believe me when I tell you that my senses have not been in an adequate state of composure to attempt manuscript: I should probably have written stark-staring bombast, in the essay to express my thanks for all your persevering kindness.

On the evening of this sacred day it was my authorized custom to sit around your fire, and endeavour to requite my welcome by making you laugh at my nonsense.

I try to dissipate the sinister troop of blue devils that haunt me . . . What, in the name of all my faults or in common justice from the remembrance of those many friends with whom my better years were passed, have I done to deserve this purgatory?

Of all those I have recently known in this part of the world, I can only speak with unqualified praise; – their attentions and good feeling toward me surpasses almost example in my recollection.

Brummell also found his mind and energies were taken up with the petty dramas of the prison, so very far removed from the high-society figures upon whom he relied still for support and, ultimately, his freedom.

À Madame [Burton]

During the principal part of this morning, I have been reduced to the forbidding study of the human face not divine but demoniac which Infests the *cour* beneath my window. Groups of these wretches, condemned of Heaven and of earth, attracted by the sun, have been sauntering in their chains within ten paces of me; and, for want of more palatable resource, I sat contemplating their hideous physiognomies, till I was recalled . . . by one of them exclaiming, '*Qu'est-ce qu'il regarde donc, ce scélérat de milord?*' This I soon perceived was addressed to my innocent self; and I retired from my reflections, and '*ma loge grille*', amply convinced that all I had read or heard of the atrocities of this *trempe* of malefactors was realized to my view.

I have nothing auspicious, in respect to my unfortunate

interests, to impart. A <u>month</u> tomorrow I have been <u>here</u>, in tribulation, in suspense and, at length, nearly in broken-heartedness; no news has, as yet, arrived to me from England.

His appetite appeared to grow in inverse proportion to his depression, and the ladies of Caen whose parties he had enlivened took to sending him presents of food, knowing they could do little of more practical benefit. 'Wine, punch, jellies, pâtés, and various other delicacies' were daily delivered at the *guichets* – the turnstiles – and taken by Lépine to Brummell. He wrote regular thank-you notes, from Godefroi's desk. This one appears to be to Mrs Burton.

In Prison, Wednesday
You are always good and amiable, but you will be the best of beings if you will have the kindness to renew your benefaction *en forme de gâteau*. I can assure you, it is my principal nourishment, for the *mesquin* repast they usually send me from the hotel would not be adequate to sustain even a demoiselle lost in love.

He read constantly during the day with Godefroi – there was insufficient light to read where he slept and his eyesight was failing. He even began a conversation with Godefroi about Byron, whose *Life* he had been sent, only to fall away into a sad reflection when he admitted 'this poet, this great man, he used to be my friend'. (Byron had been dead for a decade.) But still, no news came from England.

Armstrong's delay in going to London to seek help is explained in Foreign Office correspondence. It was several weeks before he could gain leave of absence to begin his journey.

You are aware [wrote George Boyd to John Bidwell at the Foreign Office on 11 June 1835] that poor Brummell, formerly Consul at Caen, is now a prisoner in the Common Gaol of that town at the suit of Person of the name of Le Veux [*sic*], a Merchant of Calais. Mr Armstrong, the Vice Consul at Caen, has kindly offered to proceed to Calais for the purpose of effecting some arrangement with this Le Veux for his liberation, and from thence coming to this country to communicate the result of his endeavour to Brummell's friends here. Mr Armstrong however is unable to put his kind intentions into execution without leave of absence from the Foreign Office, which if you can procure for him you will greatly oblige me and so enact a kindness to an unfortunate Individual.

Armstrong was able eventually to leave Caen on 7 July, two months after Brummell's arrest. He travelled via Calais, where he met with Leveux to ascertain the exact terms on which he would consent to Brummell's release, which, under French law, lay in his gift. Armed with this intelligence he proceeded to London.

Many of Brummell's Caen friends were leaving town for their summer residences at Luc-sur-Mer, which left Brummell with more time to write, but less to thank them for. His letters began to reflect not just the routine of prison life but a growing empathy with his fellow prisoners.

In Prison, July
You will soon be as well acquainted with our Newgate Calendar here as myself. I send you *L'Ami de la Vérité*, because it contains the account of a triple murder of the most horrible description, committed by a wretch who has just been surrendered by the *gens d'armes* to this last receptacle of his living days. He is rather a decent-looking reprobate, and I could not discriminate, by his countenance or manner, the least trace of compunction or shame. He seems so quiet and insouciant of his enormous delinquency, that I shall seek an early occasion to make him confess the whole detail of the circumstances attending his crime; for I understand he is very accessible upon the subject, and is even proud of relating them. God of heaven, what creatures bearing human faces and forms surround me!

But the misfortunes of others did not distract him for long from the pain of his own. Godefroi claimed he often found Brummell in tears in the months they were together. It was only Armstrong's eventual departure in early July 1835 that afforded Brummell some grounds for his natural optimism to break through. He was able to contemplate the possibility of release. Rumours began to spread in the prison that Brummell would get out within weeks.

Throughout July Brummell gave himself over to preparations for a dinner. It was to be held in gaol and paid for by a newly arrived prisoner, Baron de Bresnily. Bresnily was known to Brummell already, and had been sentenced to five days' imprisonment for shouting, '*Vive Henri V*', at a supporter of King Louis-Philippe. Henry V was the Legitimist claimant. Bresnily decided to celebrate his 'political martyrdom' and simultaneously Brummell's likely imminent release by paying for a lavish meal. It was to be served to Bresnily, Godefroi, Brummell and a few others, arranged by Brummell and paid for by the baron. Brummell 'seemed to recover the elasticity of spirits he must have possessed in his youth', said Godefroi, 'and the originality of his character came forth in such bright relief that I could easily comprehend why he had been so celebrated, and his society so much sought after'.

Brummell seems to have been gripped by one of the 'manic' phases that characterised his later life. He trained three felons as waiters. He contacted Longuet's restaurant with the order for the meal, to be sent into the prison, despite their previous contretemps about unpaid bills. Longuet's provided mushrooms and truffles, lobsters and glacé fruits. The *chambre des prisonniers civils* was transformed for the evening into a simulacrum of Watier's dining room, with Brummell taking special care of the wines – Chambertin and Lafitte. Another prisoner offered his best Andaye Cognac for the '*chasse*'. Unfortunately when the Cognac was sent to be uncorked, it had disappeared, the bottle discovered later, empty, next to a snoring drunken prison guard. Otherwise, the evening was counted a huge success and Bresnily and Godefroi recalled, years later, their good fortune in spending such a night with Brummell.

Armstrong returned with good news. He had secured the £800, and a promise of more. Although Thomas Raikes had feared that such a sum could not be raised 'after the endless applications that have been made by [Brummell] to his old friends since he left

England', Armstrong set about his task 'as a man of business . . . unembarrassed by any feelings of delicacy'. This direct and brutally honest approach worked. Lord Alvanley and Worcester naturally subscribed more money. But so, too, did the King, William IV, who was approached by General Upton and Sir Herbert Taylor after Armstrong had come knocking. General Upton had been the lover of Amy Dubochet, Harriette Wilson's sister, when they had all danced together at the Argyle Rooms. The Duke of Devonshire, Lord Sefton, General Grosvenor, Colonel Howard, Colonel Dawson-Damer, Mr Greville, Mr Chester and Mr Standish, former dandies to a man, all contributed. Lord Palmerston, once a member of the circle himself, was presented with a draft of a letter that would give official compensation from the government to Brummell for loss of the consulship:

> July 1835
> My Lords,
> On a Revision of the Consular Establishment in the early part of the year 1832, I found that the British Consulate at Caen in Normandy might be abolished without prejudice to the Service; and that the salary of £400 a year, assigned to that Post, might be saved to the Publick [sic].
>
> This reduction was accordingly carried into effect and Consul Brummell's salary ceased on the 31st May 1832. Subsequently to that Period I have received various representations [via Lord Alvanley and Charles Armstrong among others] from Mr Brummell stating the pecuniary difficulties into which he was plunged by the suddenness of the abolition of his consulship – the stopping of his Salary; and requesting that some sort of pecuniary assistance might be granted to enable him to effect his Release from Prison.

Palmerston deleted 'to enable him to effect his Release from Prison' and wrote instead simply 'him.' It was the gentlemanly thing to do.

Mr Brummell's case appearing to be one of great hardship, I venture to recommend to your Lordship's favourable consideration the grant of a Gratuity, equal to Half a year's salary [i.e. £200] as Compensation to Mr Brummell on the Abolition of his Office as HM's Consul at Caen, which he had held upwards of two years.

Palmerston changed the last words to 'nearly three', then initialled the draft to be written up and submitted. Armstrong was able to add the £200 to his fund, paid by the Treasury.

On the morning of 21 July 1835, Monsieur Youf, an attorney who worked in the courthouse next door, entered the room Brummell shared with Godefroi and Bresnily each day, and notified Brummell that Leveux's debt had been cleared and that he was free to go. Brummell took the news calmly, showing not 'the slightest surprise or joy, or indeed any emotion whatever'. He spent the afternoon packing his few things and at five o'clock walked out on to the *terrasse* of the prison overlooking the Place Fontette, a free man. Godefroi had said goodbye to him back in the *chambre des prisonniers civils*, Lépine showed him to the *guichets*. Despite his complaints about the food sent to prison by the Hôtel d'Angleterre, he nevertheless returned to room twenty-nine, the third-floor suite. His bill had been paid, and Armstrong had pointed out to Monsieur Fichet the potentially beneficial attraction to English tourists of the hotel's celebrated guest.

Brummell immediately changed for dinner. There was a large soirée that evening at General Corbet's home, and he decided to make an entrance back into Caen society with as much panache as he could muster. Because his release had been so sudden, his appearance made a distinct impact. He strode to the centre of Corbet's salon as all the company stood and applauded. With 'an air of nonchalance', such as he might have adopted in his King's Theatre box, he thanked the company for their good wishes and said, 'Today is the happiest day of my life; because I have been released from prison,' then added, 'and because we have salmon for dinner.'

In Caen as in London it was felt that after Brummell's prison experience he was never quite the same again. If they had not realised it already, his London friends now accepted that they would have to support him for the rest of his life, and only hoped he would find ways to economise. The British community in Caen, and the many French with whom Brummell socialised, were more aware of his continuing physical deterioration, and that imprisonment seemed to have 'shaken his intellect'. The reappraisal of Brummell's image in contemporaries' minds was compounded by a sketch he had made that was shown around Caen, much to Brummell's embarrassment. It was one of the many sentimental drawings he sent with letters to friends, Aimable in particular. It depicted Cupid, a frequent motif in Brummell's artwork, having apparently discarded a broken arrow. Brummell titled it 'The broken ~~Beau~~ Bow!'

Though it may have been given to Ellen Villiers, it seems more likely that the recipient again was Aimable – as it was offered to 'your album' in the letter that accompanied it. Brummell was mortified that others were allowed to see it. Fresh from the dishonour of prison, he did not want to be an object of pity, and the piece may have had more particular meaning. The 'ridiculous words [of the title] were written in a moment of haste,' he said, 'and with no other idea than being laughed at by <u>you</u> . . . not to be seen by others'. But the 'ridiculous' title was only part of the embarrassment: the picture held other meanings. It is a finely and delicately wrought piece by an accomplished copyist (Jesse even used it as a frontispiece to his chronicle of Brummell's life and letters). So it can be no accident that Cupid's hands are drawn as claws. The mythic messenger of desire claws at his own soft chest flesh while gazing pensively at his broken bow and arrow. Aimable had every right to feel a little shocked and embarrassed.

The gift of the Broken Beau sketch and the letters that accompanied it are among the last Brummell seems to have written to Aimable. Her extended family had largely left Caen, and it seemed likely that her life would take her elsewhere too. Brummell gave her more sketches for her collection – as the last of the many gifts he had bestowed on her.

À Mademoiselle [Aimable]
Rue [des Carmes]
Saturday

You are, I dare say, anxious for your album, and I am mutilating its pages in attempting to draw and write upon them. I know not how it is, but I cannot design upon leaves that are bound.

I have not . . . impressed . . . anything that would gratify you . . . I have no drawings left in my possession – they have all been given away, perhaps to thankless persons . . . The only one left is a half-finished crayon, which I began some years ago, as a model for another, which I accomplished afterwards in colours; it is the late poor Duchess of Rutland; we were great friends in those days you must know, and so, indeed, we remained till her death, ten years since. Pray have a respect for her, and protect her, now she is no more.

Brummell was fifty-seven, but looked much older. He had been bald for years, and may well have lost his eyebrows to the syphilitic alopecia. Another drawing of the period, most likely by Jesse himself and signed by Brummell, shows him as an old man, with tidy top hat but shaggy overcoat. He appears to be toothless. He had begun to shuffle when he was out walking. At first this was taken as a sign of his fastidiousness: an attempt to avoid the dirt of the street as he had so few clothes and a restricted laundry budget. He instructed friends to walk a few paces away from him, to avoid splashes. But the condition grew worse, and the man who had once had the 'best figure in England' began to stoop.

Tabes dorsalis was the term given to the wasting damage to the nerves in the spinal cord caused by syphilis. It took many years from the initial syphilitic infection to reach the spinal nerves, and even then the effect was slow. There was a slight loss of position sense and progressive inability to co-ordinate bodily movements; almost invariably it affected gait. The sense of having unusual sensations haunted tabetics. Stiffness of gait progressed to a wide-based stumbling, zigzag pattern of walking, sometimes with the dragging of a foot. Symptoms also included joint pains that could only be alleviated with heat, and incorrect perception of temperature changes. Brummell, who had spent his prison months huddled up to Godefroi's fire claiming he was cold, now had syphilis attacking the nerves of his lower limbs and back.

In 1836 a Cambridge undergraduate happened to be staying at the Hôtel d'Angleterre, where Brummell was pointed out to him in the dining room. He could not believe what he was being told. 'The very quiet, very refined elderly gentleman to whom some of the guests and all of the servants of the house seemed to pay unusual attention' was the great Beau Brummell. He looked, wrote the student, 'poor indeed'.

After the first few months out of prison his old spending habits began to creep back. He had agreed with Armstrong and his English benefactors to adhere to strict economy, and 'brought himself down to one complete change of linen [only]' per day. But he still ordered fresh primrose-yellow kid gloves regularly, expensive macassar oil for his wig, and shoe-blacking.

À Monsieur Armstrong,
133 Rue St Jean.
November 1836.
Mullet, the bootmaker, has this instant been with me, in an insolent manner, and says that as you have refused positively to pay his account, or the principal part of it, for *vernis* [shoe polish] he shall proceed against me for the amount of this debt, without it is settled the present day. Send me the money on my own account, and let me instantly settle it. I have, so help me Heaven, not four francs in my possession, and it will utterly destroy me to see a bailiff enter my room, or assault me in the street.

I will enter into any promise with you upon the subject of this damned polish that you may demand, if you will instantly enable me to pay this scoundrel.

Armstrong paid for the expensive boot-blacking, but was increasingly sharp with Brummell and stern about his finances. A month later, Brummell wrote again:

Do not any more be out of temper with me. I do not deserve it from you; I have never trespassed upon the rules of economy which you dictated to me, excepting in one instance, and that has been that damned execrable blacking. I have now relinquished it for ever!

You must not be again exasperated with me, when I make solicitations of your most friendly assistance for you shall not have reason for it; and at this moment, I am not ashamed to tell you candidly that I have not two *sous* remaining of the twenty francs you had the goodness to send me.

Armstrong began to insist on the most severe economy. He made it known around Caen that he would pay bills on Brummell's behalf only if he had agreed to the expenditure in the first place. He limited Brummell's linen and laundry expenses, and after this it was said that 'a great change took place in his personal appearance': Brummell ceased to wear his trademark white cravat. In mourning for his lost fortune and fashionability, he took to wearing black. Though much commented on in Caen, this was in truth Brummell's acceptance that fashion had moved on. Black stocks and cravats were eminently practical – especially, it was said, for snuff-takers – and the pre-formed black stock had become accepted city-wear throughout Europe and America by the middle of the century.

The rest of his wardrobe was deteriorating, and it gave Brummell as much pain as it aroused comment from those who saw him. He appealed to Armstrong on this point, but was met with practical, rather than dandy solutions. When Armstrong sent him a new winter dressing-gown not made of shawl, as was considered gentlemanly, but of towelling cotton, Brummell threw it from his third-floor window at the Hôtel d'Angleterre. It nearly caused an accident on the rue St Jean.

Armstrong, the Burtons, the Marquise de Séran all noted his continuing deterioration. At first it was small things. He repeated himself. He would tell anecdotes everyone knew already 'drawling with prolixity'. He frequently forgot who he was speaking to,

which sometimes caused embarrassment though equally sometimes led to comedy. While he was still on the side of confusion
that is called eccentricity, he was happily suffered by his Caen
hosts. He told the anxious mother of a teenage girl not to worry
about her daughter as she was 'too plain for anyone to run off
with her'. He commented loudly, and in unflattering terms, about
the menu at a dinner party, thinking he was at the *table d'hôte* of
the hotel. The hostess burst into tears, but the guests thought it
was funny. He was asked not to attend the philharmonic as he
moved his jaw constantly, and not in time to the music. Mrs
Burton was asked why she continued to invite 'the old driveller'.
'He is never in our way,' she explained, 'and though it is true he is
no longer the amusing character he used to be, I like to see him
take his seat before my fire.' But the invitations around town,
inevitably, dried up.

In July 1837 General Corbet asked him for dinner, but only
because Brummell's old friend Tom Moore was in town, along
with his grown son. 'The poor Beau's head's gone,' wrote Moore,
'and his whole looks so changed that I never should have
recognised him. Got wandering in his conversation more than
once at dinner.'

He went out less, and his social contact narrowed, which
accelerated his mental deterioration. Without the necessity to
dress, he would sometimes stay all day in the hotel in his dressing-
gown. And when his trousers needed mending, he was forced to
stay indoors, as by 1837 he had only one pair. The tailor, to whom
Brummell had given much business when he first came as consul,
took in his clothes and 'mended them for nothing'. 'I was
ashamed,' the tailor explained in French to Jesse, 'to see so
famous and distinguished a man, who had created a place for
himself in history, in so unhappy a state.' It was slightly easier for
Brummell in winter. His long fur-topped overcoat had survived
well and covered everything else, and in this, he could more easily
venture out.

Like his old friend George IV he took more and more to the
sweet comfort of maraschino brandy, a luxury, of course, denied

him by Armstrong. He begged it anyway from Madame Magdelaine who kept the café on the rue St Jean opposite the Hôtel
d'Angleterre. She gave him every day at two p.m. a single glass of
maraschino, and a *biscuit de Rheims* to dip into it. Brummell
would sit watching the traffic over the Pont Vaucelles and waving
to strangers with a little movement of his fingers 'like Charles X'.
Monsieur Magdelaine eventually noticed what was going on, and
asked Brummell to pay up. He was forced to pawn some of the
valuables Armstrong had saved for him: his vases and his gold
watch. But Brummell's maraschino habit kept up, and Magdelaine ended up with Brummell's gold ring, his gold watch chain
and his last silver snuff-box.

Brummell was again a sight on the streets as he had been in
Mayfair, stared at and pointed out, but for all the wrong reasons.
An English schoolboy on holiday in the town wrote a cruel ditty
that somehow found its way into Jesse's collection:

> Keen blows the wind, and piercing is the cold,
> My pins are weak, and I am growing old.
> Around my shoulders this worn cloak I spread,
> With an umbrella to protect my head,
> Which once had wit enough to astound the world,
> But now, possess nought but wig well-curled.
> Alas! Alas! Which wind and rain do beat,
> That great Beau Brummell should so walk the street!

In the winter of 1837–8, the Hôtel d'Angleterre had a mystery
visitor: a lady 'of a certain age', who seemed to come from
nowhere, 'without equipage, servant or luggage'. She asked to
speak to the owner. Monsieur Fichet did not recognise her, but
realised from her dress and manner that 'she had moved in the
highest circles'. She asked if it were possible that she could see Mr
Brummell, but without his seeing her. Fichet answered that this
was easily arranged, as Mr Brummell would pass at five o'clock
on his way down from his room to dinner. 'You will distinctly see
him,' he added, 'for he always has a [candle] in his hand.'

All this took place exactly as Fichet had explained to the

woman it would. When he saw her, a little later, still in the shadows where she had hidden to watch Brummell, 'he found her in tears and much affected'.

Jesse speculates that she might have been Lady Jersey or even Princess Bagration. They both passed through northern France that winter, but neither was especially familiar with Brummell. Whoever she was, she was deeply affected by the change in Brummell, or by the reflected thought of her own mortality. It seems more likely it was someone from much further back, one of the débutantes, perhaps, to whom he made mock proposals in the earliest years of the nineteenth century.

Brummell continued to solicit better care and attention from Armstrong, which meant, in effect, more money. Armstrong said he could not continue to act on Brummell's behalf if Brummell kept up his habit of also writing direct appeals to London. It became an issue of control as much as money.

It is, I can assure you, with the greatest reluctance I am compelled to solicit occasional assistance from you [he wrote to Armstrong in early 1837], but I told you the truth yesterday, when I represented the abject condition of my linen to you. I have not a single shirt that will hang to my back, nor are my socks and drawers in a better state . . . After the experience I have met with in this place, I have a horror of contracting new debts; and yet, during the last two months, I have not possessed five francs for the most indispensable purposes. I am in ignorance as to those who, through your mediation, have befriended me on the other side of the water, nor do I know precisely the amount of their contributions. Therefore am unable to write to them my thanks for what they have done, or to make them acquainted with my continued destitute situation – the belly, indeed, is filled, but the hand is empty, and the back and limbs unprovided for.

I have not heard from any one of them, excepting as you know, from my sister; and I could almost suppose she was laughing, when she says she hoped that I 'have everything comfortable about me'. Surely, my dear Armstrong, I had better immediately write to her, to Alvanley, and to others: they may imagine I am living in comfort, if not at ease, and the positive reverse is the case; and I see it cannot last long with me.

It was the one reference in thirty years to any contact between Brummell and his sister Maria Blackshaw. It seems likely she had been informed that he was increasingly confused, as well as physically unwell.

Elsewhere in France, Brummell's old friend Scrope Davies had been worrying about his own deteriorating condition. He knew from his doctor that his depression was likely to be 'a precursor of . . . [syphilitic] derangement'. 'Lethargic days and sleepless nights,' he wrote, 'have reduced me to a state of nervous irritability . . . At present I must visit nobody and strictly follow the advice which [my doctor] gave me . . . Of all uncertainties, the uncertain continuance of reason is the most dreadful.'

Similarly Brummell, while arranging practicalities with Armstrong, was intermittently aware that something was terribly wrong. In public he continued to blame prison, which he likened to a 'knock on the head'. In the semi-privacy of the hotel, he must have been aware that his mind was deteriorating. He was behaving very strangely. His confusion was inconsistent and alternated with extreme mania, when he would order staff around, and frantically obsess about his clothes. Then he would realise, quite suddenly, where he was and what was going on: that he was not in Mayfair, and no longer a dandy.

Tabes dorsalis had been the precursor with Brummell to something more alarming and psychologically bizarre. Just before the onset of full-blown tertiary syphilis and the dementia that attends it, something exotic was observed to happen to the mind:

Right before madness [writes one authority on the disease] the syphilitic was often rewarded in a kind of Faustian bargain for enduring the pain and despair, by episodes of creative euphoria; electrified, joyous energy . . . dazzling and almost mystical insights . . . mood shifts become more extreme as euphoria, electric excitement, bursts of creative energy, and grandiose self-reflections alternate with severe, often suicidal depression. Delusions of grandeur, paranoia, exaltation, irritability, rages and irrational, antisocial behaviour define the progress to insanity. The patient may suddenly begin to . . . imagine owning vast riches. A calm person becomes emotional, a neat person sloppy . . . Here the condition is often misdiagnosed as paranoid persecutory psychosis or schizophrenia.

For all these reasons, the detailed descriptions of Brummell's last months at the Hôtel d'Angleterre, given to Jesse and d'Aurevilly by the hotel staff, can be read now as textbook examples of incipient general paresis: syphilitic dementia.

While instruction was still clear and possible and Brummell appeared to be in command of his faculties, he began to hold soirées at the Hôtel d'Angleterre. At first Fichet and his staff were bemused, as they knew his social circle had shrunk, but they accepted orders for candles and flowers for Brummell's room. 'On these gala evenings,' Jesse was informed by hotel staff, 'some strange fancy would seize him.' He would rearrange the furniture and even set out a whist-table.

Suddenly, and as if divided into two, he announced in a loud voice the Prince of Wales, then Lady Conyngham, then Lord Yarmouth, then all the high personages of England for whom he had been the living law; and imagining them to appear as he announced them, and changing his voice, he went to the doors to receive them: the open double doors of the empty salon through which, alas, no one was to pass on this or any other evening. And he saluted these chimeras of his imagination, offered his arm to the women of this company of phantoms he had called up and who would certainly not have cared to leave their tombs for one instant to attend the fallen Dandy's rout.

Later Brummell trained the Fichet family to announce these phantom guests for him. They were, naturally enough, appalled but fascinated. Fichet would announce carriages at ten, and so end the macabre pantomime. On other occasions, the party ended earlier, when Brummell realised that his mind and memory had played a cruel trick on him. The contrast between nostalgic fantasy and present reality would reduce him to tears: 'Finally, when the room was full of these ghosts and when all the company had arrived from the other world, reason suddenly re-asserted itself, and the unhappy creature perceived his illusion and madness. And then he would fall stricken into one of the solitary chairs, and would be discovered weeping.'

The Fichets coped with the phantom galas. So long as Brummell's declining mental health stayed within the bounds they thought acceptable, his life could continue at the hotel, and on balance they were remarkably accommodating. But then Brummell had a series of falls that meant he required constant supervision. These seem to have taken place very late in 1837. He collapsed once in the street, on his way back from the chemist, and once in his room. At first an old woman was posted to keep an eye on him in room twenty-nine, but Brummell took an immense dislike to her – even in his confusion – and she was replaced by a former army corporal called François, who was strict with him 'but kindly'.

Jesse was told by François that, by the summer of 1838, 'Brummell's imbecility was complete.' He sat obsessively combing his wig, he raged incoherently at times, and at others was quiet for hours at a time. He destroyed a great number of letters and effects 'from royal personages' and billets '[enclosing] silken tresses'. He had a raging appetite, but was refused a place at the *table d'hôte* in the hotel's restaurant as he was considered 'injurious to himself' and in a 'deplorable state of person'.

Another mystery visitor came to view him, someone known to Armstrong and involved with the continuing monies from England. It was either Lord Sefton or Lord Alvanley. Whichever old friend it was, he did not want to be seen by Brummell for fear of upsetting him, but had Fichet detain him on the staircase, as he had done for the mystery woman visitor the year before.

'*Avez-vous entendu les nouvelles?*' asked Fichet of Brummell, to keep him loitering in view of the hidden English visitor.

'*Non,*' said Brummell.

'*George Quatre est mort!*'

(He had been dead eight years.)

'*Ah*,' said Brummell, '*est-il vrai?*'

Late in the summer of 1838 Brummell became doubly incontinent, the effect of the advanced tabetic attack on his spinal nerves. He was aware of what was happening, and tried to blame the mess, and the smell in his room, on the hotel's dog, a pointer called Stop. In October, the Fichets told Armstrong they could not cope any longer. In November, Armstrong wrote to London, probably to Alvanley:

> I have deferred writing for some time, hoping to be able to inform you that I had succeeded in getting Mr Brummell into one of the public institutions, but I am sorry to say that I have failed; I have also tried to get him into a private house; but no one will undertake the charge of him in his present state: in fact, it would be totally impossible for me to describe the dreadful situation he is in. For the last two months I have been obliged to pay a person to be with him night and day, and still we cannot keep him clean; he now lies upon a straw mattress, which is changed every day. They will not keep him at the hotel, and what to do I know not: I should think that some of his old friends in England would be able to get him into some hospital, where he could be taken care of for the rest of his days. I beg and entreat of you to get something done for him, for it is quite out of the question that he can remain where he is. The clergyman and physician here can bear testimony to the melancholy state of idiocy he is in.

Still nothing happened through the Christmas season of 1838–9. François seems to have left the employ of the hotel, and Brummell, other than occasional visits from the Anglican curate, was left lying on a soiled straw mattress in the corner of room twenty-nine. 'His linen,' Jesse was informed, 'was changed once a month.'

~

In January 1839 Armstrong and Fichet came together to room twenty-nine. They found Brummell sitting in his dressing-gown, with his wig on his lap. Rather than tending it with oil, as was his usual obsession, he had worked up a lather in a shaving bowl, and was painting the foam on to it.

'*Bonjour, Monsieur!*' said Fichet.

'*Laissez moi tranquille!*' replied Brummell.

Jesse continues his record of the scene, from Fichet's memory of it, in English: 'But I have ordered a carriage for you to take a drive with me. You promised that you would go, and the carriage is now at the door.'

Brummell said he was not well and did not wish to go.

Armstrong and Fichet then said what a lovely day it was for a ride. Brummell still refused. Fichet lost his temper, grabbed the wig, which had fixed Brummell's attention, and threw it across the room. The scene degenerated into a brawl. Armstrong and Fichet, possibly with the help of Fichet's son and others, bundled Brummell down the three flights to the rue St Jean. 'He kicked and fought as violently as his swollen legs and reduced strength would permit; screaming and shouting at the top of his voice, "You are taking me to prison – I have done nothing.'" And then, according to Fichet, 'a shriek followed that was heard at the end of the court'.

Within minutes of being in the carriage, somewhere at the top of the rue St Jean where it turns into the rue St Pierre, Brummell suddenly calmed. He saw an acquaintance he recognised, but explained to Armstrong, 'I did not bow to him, for I am not fit to be seen in such a dishabille as this.'

His mood changed just as swiftly as the large iron doors of Bon Sauveur asylum shut behind him, and he 'wept bitterly, muttering, "A prison, a prison,"' but a nun took him by the hand and somewhere his old courtly manners came to his rescue: '*Vous êtes bien une jolie femme*', he said, and she led him into his new room.

18

ASYLUM

1839–40

It's like being bound hand and foot in the bottom of a deep dark well. Fear. White moss in the mouth. Sweet thick hair falls to the floor, gleaming patches of scalp in the candlelight. Salve: mercury mixed with rosewater, honey, liquorice, conserve of rose petals, lard. I rub it everywhere . . . I smell like fried potato . . . Tongue like an ox . . . Saliva gushes like a river, teeth rattle, and rot, penis the colour of slate.

Portrait of a nineteenth-century syphilitic

Babylon in all its desolation is a sight not so awful as that of the human mind in ruins. It is a firmament without a sun, a temple without a God. I have survived most of my friends; Heaven forbid I should survive myself . . . The dead are less to be deplored than the insane.

Scrope Davies to Thomas Raikes

The Abbé Jamet had been receiving lunatics into the former Capuchin convent at Bon Sauveur since 1818. He was considered fashionably progressive in his treatments of the insane, and Bon Sauveur was expanding to meet the growing demand in early-nineteenth-century France for secular treatments for the disabled and the mentally ill.

Founded originally in 1723 at St Lô by an aristocratic nun called Anne Leroy and intended for deranged and fallen women, the convent had been suppressed during the Revolution and not refounded until 1804. In 1806 it had again begun to admit patients: fifteen women. They were to be cared for by twenty-one Sisters of Charity, some lay workers and Abbé Pierre-François Jamet. From 1820, the new Bon Sauveur accepted men.

Abbé Jamet had an amateur interest in the new sciences of the mind and body, and in hydrotherapy. He was also considered a 'financial gymnast' and secured for the convent an eighteen-hectare site on the outskirts of Caen, surrounding the original Capuchin convent, which happened to have a tributary of the Orne river flowing through it. Bon Sauveur, with its sympathetic regime and modish water therapies, attracted patients from all over Normandy and even beyond. It specialised in the treatment of the deaf and dumb, as well as all those who were, in the terminology of the time, classed *aliené*: 'deranged'.

The early nineteenth century saw a rapid expansion in the institutionalisation of mental illness, as well as discussion, both medical and political, on the right means of housing and defining the 'insane'. Post-revolutionary governments, especially Napoleon's, had sought a rationalisation and modernisation of France's mental institutions. Bon Sauveur was soon being held up as an example of church–state co-operation and the application of modern science to the atavistic anxieties surrounding the insane. In the radical *Loi Sur Les Alienés* of 1838, the asylum was mentioned by name. It was under the terms of this relatively new legislation that 'Georges Brummell' was entered at the asylum, against his will, on 17 January 1839. The signatures of the presiding doctor, Edouard Vastel, as well as Brummell's own doctor, John Kelly, secured the detention. Under the new law, no priest or politician had this right, but men of science did. Doctors Vastel and Kelly attested that Brummell's 'corporal infirmity and mental affliction' rendered him incapable of fending for himself, and this was sufficient to make sure he would never again see beyond the high walls of Bon Sauveur asylum.

By modern standards the huge site was bleakly institutional, but to a town like Caen – which only a generation before had kept lunatics in dungeons, and fed them with scraps thrown down by passers-by – Bon Sauveur looked paradisiacal. It was dominated by a cathedral-like chapel and fifty-foot bell-tower, and many of the elegant pavilions had four storeys. The windows, however, were all barred.

Bon Sauveur had continued over the years to take in 'fallen' women – often pregnant unmarried girls – as well as the blind, deaf, disabled and disturbed, and together they tended vegetable and flower-beds. When Brummell entered, there were between six and seven hundred inmates. Bon Saveur had grown, in the twenty years it had been accepting both sexes, to be the third largest asylum in France. But there was still only one doctor. According to Brummell's surviving medical records – kept in the institution that operates as an asylum to this day – he was seen once every two months by Dr Vastel.

The Sisters of Charity who ran Bon Sauveur had a reputation for kindliness. The grounds were enormous and the scale of the new site, which the Mother Superior had described in 1818 as 'salubrious and well aired', had encouraged an ambitious building programme. Bon Sauveur boasted that none of its inmates were in dormitories, but 'each madman has his own cell . . . [being] quieter and cleaner in isolated rooms'. Bourienne, previously Napoleon's secretary, had found benign sanctuary at Bon Sauveur in the closing years of his life and Destouches, who inspired Barbey d'Aurevilly's most famous novel, *Le Chevalier des Touches*, was also incarcerated there.

All classes were represented at the asylum but on the whole they did not mix. The sexes were separated, and so, too, were broad classes of inmates, defined socially as well as medically; those considered '*tranquilles*' were separated from the '*semi-tranquilles*' and '*épileptiques*' from '*les malpropres, les gâteux et les agités*' – the unclean, depraved and disturbed. Because of Brummell's incontinence and erratic behaviour, Armstrong had feared he would be placed with the common incurables in the notorious *cachets* and *cabanons* or chained cells. But a little extra money, as well as Brummell's local celebrity, found him a room of his own, with a view – one of the finest in the asylum. Brummell was unaware that the locked chamber in which he was placed – just off the gardens in the Pavilion Saint Joseph – was the one in which Bourienne had died a few years before. Here he was attended almost constantly, and remained, mainly, calm.

Surprisingly, quite a lot is known about the daily routine for inmates. An unusual statement of intent written at the asylum has survived from just before the law of 1838, which gives an indication of the regime Brummell faced at Bon Sauveur. Though some items are missing, it is stated that the means of treatment should be ordered accordingly:

1. A total 'rupture' from normality and the acceptance of the necessity of obedience . . . is the first means of treatment . . . isolation is one way.
2. [missing]
3. Warm baths, not daily except to begin with, but always frequent – the head being refreshed with light showering, constitutes the principal and greatest means of treatment, with very rare exceptions.
4. Manual occupations like gardening, the care of the [Bon Sauveur] farm, laundry, help given to the wardens, can be of very great aid in the treatment of the working classes.
5. Walking and carriage riding, excursions to the countryside, billiards and music will replace manual work for those of our inmates whose social position or infirmity makes such exercise unsalutary.
6. [missing]
7. [missing]
8. We have no special medication for the treatment of insanity. The drug we use most often however is valerian water [a sedative] which despite its unpleasant odour is quite happily accepted by our inmates.
9. Moral care; kindness and distraction; the example of a religious and regulated life.

Brummell was in no physical state to join the flower-bed digging detachments, but in any case his class precluded this: Armstrong had made it clear in signing him over to the Bon

Sauveur authorities that 'Brummell, Georges, célibataire' was 'ex Consul de Sa Majesté Britannique'.

Life in the asylum was run with strict discipline. Even in 1839, it was, in theory, controlled by the doctor, Edouard Vastel, who was not answerable to Abbé Jamet or the Mother Superior and it was under his supervision that the nuns and lay workers structured the daily lives of inmates.

Brummell was woken each day at five thirty. He was allowed an extra half-hour in bed through the winter of 1839–40. One of the Sisters of Charity would check his bed linen in case it had been soiled during the night, and then he would be encouraged, with the help of a nun, to make his own bed.

He had the right to a weekly shave by the asylum barber, but had brought his dressing case with him: Armstrong knew what was important to Brummell even in his confusion.

A half-hour after the inmates were woken, breakfast was served in one of the large refectories – there was one for each social class. It was considered important to get them out of their rooms and in this time the lay staff had the unpleasant task of emptying chamber-pots and commodes.

A prayer was 'said in full voice' before each meal – a return to school for Brummell – and the nuns served café au lait and bread.

At seven there was mass, but it was not obligatory, and it is highly unlikely Brummell attended.

The only palliative Bon Sauveur could offer syphilitics was water treatment. Recent studies at the Hôpital des Vénériens in Paris under Dr Philip Ricord had recommended frequent alkaline and mercurial baths for cases like Brummell's. These involved adding to a 'tubful of warm water . . . two pounds of glue . . . two pounds of subcarbonate of potash and half an ounce of corrosive sublimate'. He also recommended turpentine, lead plaster, lavender oil, hyssop and wormwood, followed by bathing.

Dr Vastel at Bon Sauveur recognised in Brummell the symptoms of meningeal syphilis, which presented with headaches, nausea, vomiting, cranial nerve palsies and seizures, as well as personality changes and memory loss. Brummell's was a classic case. Meningovascular syphilis, specifically, from which Brummell was clearly suffering, begins with headaches, insomnia and psychological abnormalities. Facial strokes are a key signifier. The catalogue of symptoms explained to Vastel by Dr Kelly would have alerted him to this diagnosis in Brummell, and for this reason – there was no test possible – he recorded after his examination on 2 February 1839 that Brummell was suffering 'dementia and general paralysis'. He was not paralysed in the physical sense: the term was used to express the wider effect of the syphilis attacking the meninges, the membranous wrappings about the brain and spinal cord. General paralysis, or general paresis, the terms used interchangeably at this time in France as in England, was believed – correctly, as it turned out – to be the final stage of a syphilitic infection. Once the disease attacked the central nervous system, the mercury therapies were regarded as ineffectual. There was no cure, and Vastel would have known that the signs of infection in the brain meant that Brummell's decline would be fast and devastating, both physically and psychologically.

The insane gentlefolk were expected to sit in the ornamental gardens and sew or sketch. Brummell had little ability left to do either. His iritis was well advanced now, and it is unlikely that he could distinguish colours at all. Some would even have been painful to him.

Though he did not work in the fields of Bon Sauveur, he benefited from their produce. One feature of Bon Sauveur was that the food was plentiful. Again, there are records of what was consumed per inmate – over 180 grams of meat a day, or the equivalent amount of fish on Fridays and Saturdays. They were also entitled to six decilitres of bouillon 'de bonne qualité et convenablement assaisonné'. The amount of cider recorded as consumed is noteworthy: 1.5 litres per inmate per day, with the manual labourers on rations of over three litres daily. The cider was brewed in lead vats, and many of the inmates were already on valerian sedatives. Small wonder, then, that the 'folles, incensés et *alienés'* of Bon Sauveur were considered so compliant: they were lulled with alcohol, sedatives, and, unknown to patients, staff or doctor, were being slowly poisoned with lead.

At one o'clock each day many of the inmates returned from the fields to help in the kitchens. Work stopped at five, or six in the summer. Everyone, including gentry like Brummell, had to be in bed by eight, supervised by a nun or guard, who then locked all the doors and windows. The Mother Superior checked the entire asylum nightly around eight thirty.

On Wednesday, nails and hair were inspected. On Saturdays clean linen appeared. Every other Saturday, letters were collected and distributed; they were censored coming in and out. But Brummell was far beyond writing or reading.

He was wheeled up and down the gravelled walkways of the gardens in an 'easy chair'. The nuns and staff whom Jesse interviewed gave the best possible impression of Brummell's mood and his time in the asylum, as well they might, and said he was rarely left alone. When he was visited by a Caen friend – possibly Mr or Mrs Burton – he claimed that 'this excellent nurse of mine [one of the nuns] is so kind to me that she refuses me nothing; I have all I wish to eat and such a large fire; I was never so comfortable in my life'.

On the whole and for many of the inmates, including Brummell, Bon Sauveur offered balm to tortured minds and bodies. But the asylum archives make it evident that not everyone was compliant all the time, and it is unlikely, given the advanced state of his dementia, that Brummell was always the 'docile patient' the nuns later spoke of.

Jesse and d'Aurevilly both allude to degradations so awful that even mention of them would be unpalatable, and it is likely that both writers knew of the advanced state of Brummell's syphilis in Bon Sauveur, and the more extreme remedial treatments he suffered.

Bon Sauveur straitjacketed three per cent of its inmates at any given time, and had force-feeding implements for those no longer able or willing to partake of its famously nutritious soups. It also had a row of isolation cells, '*cabanons*', which were the first mentioned item on the statute of remedies for the non-compliant. These were reserved for the 'violent, mutinous, chronically deranged and those who used profane invective or were sexually exhibitionist'. They were much used at night, though it was barely possible to lie down. There was straw on the floor and an open latrine hole in one corner.

As the disease took its final hold on Brummell's brain and body the symptoms became increasingly distressing. Syphilitics who survived well into the tertiary phase, as Brummell did, suffered facial paralysis and quivering, as well as loss of bladder and bowel control. Their teeth fell out, if they had not already, and their nails. Eventually Brummell's tongue would have swollen, turned black and cracked, as would have his genitals, and this was accompanied almost invariably in male cases by large testicular tumours and scrotal ulcers. All the mucous membranes of Brummell's body would then have ulcerated: his throat, tonsils, gums and nostrils. Doctors spoke of the particular smell associated with tertiary syphilis: a sweet smell of decay, not unlike the mercury and rosewater ointments that had previously held the disease at bay, or like 'fried potatoes'. The bones ached unremittingly, which was often misattributed as rheumatism, as it was with Brummell. At night the deep bone pains were excruciating. The brain itself shrank away from the insides of the skull and granulated. 'Gummy tumours' developed in the legs and large unbleeding buboes – or swollen glands – opened spontaneously on the limbs. Sufferers of advanced tertiary syphilis like Brummell could survive many months like this, with the syphilitic pallida well advanced in the brain and flowering as weeping thymus ulcers in every sensitive part of the body.

The indignities and horrors of which Jesse and d'Aurevilly spoke were the final stages of tertiary syphilis, when Brummell, alternately raving and quivering like a lost soul, and most likely covered in sores, was hosed down in a *cabanon* when the staff could no longer bear to touch him. Sufferers like Brummell remained intermittently conscious: their confusion alternated with recurrent patches of complete lucidity, clarity and an awareness of their pain and what was happening to them, which was, in a sense, the cruellest thing of all.

The summer and autumn of 1839 passed with some less bad days in the midst of these horrors. There were moments of relative calm. Brummell was visited by some of his Caen friends, though he did not recognise them. Just once he realised who Fichet was and immediately ordered a place at dinner for that evening – '*Table d'hôte toujours à cinq heures? Très bien, très bien, je descendrai.*' His condition stabilised a little during the winter but he declined steeply through the early months of 1840. Dr Vastel noted that he was 'sinking further and further'. Armstrong and the Burtons visited and, in his professional capacity, the Anglican pastor. Jesse does not name him, but the local records make it clear that this was the Reverend Martin Rollin. Brummell seems not to have attended the 'Temple Protestant' in Caen, but Rollin had taken to visiting him in the final months he spent at the Hôtel d'Angleterre, finding that Brummell, like the character in *Granby*, 'thought religion was a good thing, and ought to be kept up, and that, like cheap soup, it was excellent for the poor'. Rollin was unsympathetic to Brummell's plight, and frustrated in his attempts to persuade Brummell to repent for past sins:

Mr Brummell was in an imbecile state . . . incapable of remembering any occurrence five minutes together; but occasionally recalling some anecdote of days long since passed. Mr Brummell appeared quite incapable of conversing on religious subjects. I failed in every attempt to lead his mind – if he can be said to have retained any power of mind – to their consideration. I never, in all the course of my attendance upon the sick, aged and dying, came in contact with so painful an exhibition of human vanity and apparent ignorance, and thoughtlessness, of and respecting a future state; for I have before visited persons whose mental powers were equally shattered, but still it was possible to touch some chord connected with religion . . . with him there was some response, when sounded on worldly subjects; none on religious –

until a few hours before he died, when in reply to my repeated entreaties that he would try and pray, he said, 'I do try,' but he added something which made me doubt whether he understood me.

The dying man was granted almost permanent supervision. The epilepsy-like seizures had become more frequent. When they came, he needed restraint. He shook almost constantly.

On Monday, 30 March 1840, the weather changed suddenly for the better: it had rained almost daily since January, but the sun shone, and Brummell was taken out into the garden. Just after the hour when he should have been sleeping, the nun in attendance noticed something in his manner she had not seen before:

The debility having become extreme [she told Jesse], I observed him assume an appearance of intense anxiety and fear, and he fixed his eyes upon me, with an expression of entreaty, raising his hands towards me, as he lay in the bed, and as though asking for assistance (*ayant l'air d'implorer que je vienne à son secours*) but saying nothing. Upon this, I requested him to repeat after me the *acte de contrition* of the Roman ritual, as in our prayer books. He immediately consented, and repeated after me in an earnest manner (*un air pénétré*) that form of prayer. He then became more composed, and laid down his head on one side; but this tranquillity was interrupted, about an hour after, by his turning himself over, and uttering a cry, at the same time appearing to be in pain; he soon, however, turned himself back, with his face laid on the pillow towards the wall, so as to be hidden from us who were on the side. After this he never moved, dying imperceptibly.

It was a quarter past nine in the evening.

~

The records of the Protestant cemetery in Caen do not relate who paid for Brummell to be buried. His funeral and the small plot, two square metres only, conceded to his body in perpetuity, cost a hundred francs. The space allowed only six feet in length, which was inadequate for Brummell and may have been the reason an extra fifty francs was paid without the usual guarantee of having a stone tended for twenty years. It is likely, but unproved, that

Armstrong and the local lodge of Masons put up the money for the coffin and cemetery plot. The local undertaker had frequent requests for lead coffins to repatriate bodies to England, but this was not suggested for Brummell. Armstrong went to record Brummell's death at the Hôtel de Ville, as both friend and vice consul, but did not go to the burial, which, it is related, was attended only by Rollin. As the body passed by without mourners, a girl on the rue St Pierre asked: *'Qui est-ce?'*

'Un pauvre fou,' replied her mother. *'Un certain Brummell.'*

Epilogue

The old idea of Manhood has grown obsolete, and the new is
still invisible to us, and we grope after it in the darkness, one
clutching this phantom, another that: Byronism, even Brum-
mellism, each has its day.

Thomas Carlyle, *Characteristics*, 1831

I sometimes think that there are only two areas of any importance in the world's history. The first is the appearance of a
new medium of art, and the second is the appearance of a new
personality for art also . . . [Dorian Gray's] personality has
suggested to me an entirely new manner in art, an entirely new
mode in style. I see things differently, I think of them differently
. . . He is all my art to me now!

Oscar Wilde, *The Picture of Dorian Gray*, 1891

On 18 May 1844 *Punch* magazine ran a page advertisement
for donations towards a commemorative statue.

Punch has received exclusive intelligence of a subscription which is
now quietly growing at White's, at Brookes's and other clubs for the
purpose of erecting a statue to the memory of GEORGE BRYAN
BRUMMELL, the man who invented starched neckcloths . . . Brummell's neckcloths, the trophies of his life, are, it will be seen, [to be]
chastely grouped behind him. Trafalgar Square has very rightly been
selected as the place for this erection.

It was a joke, a political satire, only partly at Brummell's
expense for *Punch* advocated erecting the statue next to one of
the late King, George IV. 'Many and deep must be the reflections suggested by the two statues – George the Beau, by

464

force of his genius, made himself master of a Prince . . . George the Beau had wit, George the King only malice,' and so on. In England Brummell's fame was at first wedded to George IV's and his reputation in some quarters was accordingly sullied. George Brummell, despite being more obviously 'at the heart of a galaxy of talent, charm and high spirits' than the late King, was, like him, depicted as the antithesis of early-Victorian sobriety, and much that was written about the late King was initially applied also to Brummell. 'It was his misfortune to reign at an epoch when the middle class was emerging into power,' wrote one courtier of George IV, but he could equally have been pronouncing about Brummell's 'reign' in London society; 'his activities were immediately misrepresented by a class to which "taste" and "art" were apt to be synonymous with waste and with licentiousness.'

In the immediate aftermath of Brummell's death he was barely mentioned at all. *The Times* did not recognise his demise as news, and no one paid for a death notice to grace the society columns. His friends wrote to let each other know, but the wider world had assumed, for some years, that he was dead already. Thomas Raikes thought it was 'a happy release for [Brummell] but when I call to mind his gay career and success in London,' he wrote, 'a wretched end like his suggests an awful lesson'. The diarist Joseph Farington noted, in similarly sententious tones, 'I have seen the rise of the Father [William Brummell] and the fall of the Son [who] enjoyed for a time but dissipated what had been acquired for Him.' It seemed concluded in the most symmetrical of fashions, as in the best morality tales: 'The pavilion at Bon Sauveur took payment for Brighton Pavilion. Between these two [lay] his career.' No statue was erected in Trafalgar Square of Brummell or, indeed, of George IV. Brummell's fame, however, refused to die. Instead it increased over the years, in the retelling of anecdotes, in the referencing of his style and manner, and as a result of one highly influential essay. 'Like the great actor,' d'Aurevilly wrote, 'Brummell left nothing but a name mysteriously sparkling in all the memoirs of the time.' In truth, Brummell left a great deal more.

~

First, there was simply the fashion. By 1815, men had largely abandoned the demandingly tight pantaloons Brummell had made famous, but his stirruped trousers were ubiquitous. By 1830, the frock coat had almost entirely replaced the tailcoat with which Brummell was familiar, and it was increasingly common as the century progressed for coats and trousers to match directly, rather than merely co-ordinate, but they were made according to the principles of tailoring Brummell would have recognised from Schweitzer's. His starched neckcloths evolved in two ways. On one side they became stiff collars, made separately from the shirt and performing on their own the uncomfortable but flattering purpose of wrapping the neck in an unyielding cylinder of white, just as Brummell had intended. On the other, the necktie itself, still white on the most formal occasions, was used to mark an outfit as complete and, as with Brummell, lightly adorn the upper chest. But it lengthened too, especially in the absence of a waistcoat, in a manner usually understood as phallic. Many details changed, and the classic men's fashion of today, or even of Edwardian England, might seem a world away from Brummell's Hessians and pantaloons, yet in principle things remained the same. Through the nineteenth century a structured, sculptural style for men developed out of Brummell's look, in monochrome and military fabrics. It became the uniform for modern man: the urban style of Men in Black. The governing shape of men's attire remained the classical body, and the reputation of Savile Row's tailors grew in accordance with their abilities to remould a figure into the more idealised form made fashionable by Brummell. Like Georgian architecture, neo-classical tailoring has achieved longevity in its fusion of function, form and fashion; of simple craft principles and antique ideals.

The influence of Brummell thus modernised menswear, at first in London's West End and then throughout the Western world. An expansionist empire closely allied with the textile industry doubtless played its part in this, but the style Brummell made famous had universal appeal. Men looked powerful, serious and of singular, unified intent, in marked contrast to the fashions for Victorian women. There had been seriousness and sobriety of colour in men's fashions before, but the Brummell aesthetic, as it related to clothes, matched well the nineteenth-century male concerns: respectability, homogeneity and Mammon. These same factors led to its easy adoption in America, where it lent structure and appeal to a new fashion concept: ready-to-wear.

Though approximations of Brummell's attire are now only seen at formal weddings, and the black-and-white uniform of Almack's has been corralled into white-tie and then black-tie evening wear, the silhouette he made fashionable remains. Tailoring, in terms of the paddings, sculptings and basic trouser/jacket/collar vocabulary of Western dress continues to dominate men's and women's formal wear, and Brummell's colour rules still govern men's informal attire.

What might have surprised Brummell has been the extent to which his style has been democratised. In this there are two related lineages of his fashion legacy: the dandy as fashion maverick and the dandyism that adhered to his strictures on dress and the fine details of Savile Row.

Dandyism influenced the aesthetic movement of the late nineteenth century. Dandies like Oscar Wilde were of that mark of *outré* dresser that in their keenness for John Bull to turn his head in the street took to wearing buttonholes of coloured carnations. But even *outré* men's styles have repeatedly referenced the structured, flattering elements of Brummell's neo-classical tailoring, and this can be seen in the Edwardian (later 'Teddy') styles, both of the actual Edwardian era and then again after the Second World War when South London youngsters copied Mayfair dandyism to distinctly proletarian ends. Savile Row had made a conscious attempt after the war to reclaim leadership in men's fashions and relaunched fine tailoring and dandyism as a masculine version of Dior's New Look. It was copied and enjoyed by more than they had intended, in an era of mass-produced suits and mass-media images of the sort of 'cool' they chose to project. It was exaggerated in the Teddy Boy look, just as the American zoot suit took essential dandy forms and made them cartoon. Moss Bros even advertised itself in the 1950s with the ghosts of past dandies, Brummell primarily, loitering outside their Covent Garden headquarters.

In the sartorial style of Noël Coward, Cecil Beaton and F. Scott Fitzgerald, an urbane dandyism continued that Brummell would have recognised. The close-detail insignia of Savile Row have endured, remarkably unchanged, and the well-made suit remains one standard by which the well-made man judges and is judged. But the real power of Brummell's genius – or the genius of the style he made famous – is the ubiquity of its elements beyond the close confines of the two-thousand-pound suit. They are resilient constants in every supposed revolution from the New Look of the 1950s to the New Romantics of the 1980s to the New Men of the 1990s and the recurrent patrician styles of American menswear, as created by Ralph Lauren, Tommy Hilfiger and Tom Ford. In New York or Hong Kong, at every gathering of world leaders, businessmen, lawyers or doctors, not to mention actors on red carpets, the basic forms of Brummell's look are delineated. As one fashion historian wrote, 'It is possible to make the case that masculine formal dress of today is directly [Brummell's] responsibility.' The colours of Eton's Montem polemen, which happened also to be quasi-militaristic – blue, black, white – the cloths and trouser lines of early-nineteenth-century Hussar regiments, the tailoring skills of a nascent West End shopping economy and an artistic cult that drew on ancient ideals with distinctly corporeal attractions met in Brummell's look and endured. Much later, aspects of the sculptural and the monochrome were added to women's fashion, largely through the person of a later Parisian dandy, Coco Chanel, but that story is French, and more properly d'Aurevilly's.

～

The second legacy of Brummell's unique career in English society is less clearly delineated and less physical but may be the more pervasive effect of a life unusually lived. 'Nothing succeeds in London like insolence,' wrote Chateaubriand, a little after Brummell's heyday, and it seems the pose of supposedly effortless superiority, elegance or 'cool' was admired and copied in Brummell's wake, a style and manner that have also endured. The dandy-gent was a trope in fiction even before Brummell's death, sufficient for him to tease Jesse that he had evidently been reading *Pelham*. The manner – the poise, deft wit and an air of languorous indifference – became a signifier of the gentleman, just as clearly as his clothes. And it is this manner, as much as the well-cut suit, that has remained as a recognisable type in English fiction, in English life and in the wider sphere of masculine aspiration.

Brummell was not an aristocrat, yet he lorded it over the richest and most class-bound capital in the world: it was a stage trick in part based on his performed masculinity. His masquerade of superiority was noted by contemporaries and admired. The role had obvious uses and appeal: anyone could do it. Thus Brummell, the snob and social-climber, is also the son of the French Revolution: a man whose style made it possible for Everyman to act like a prince, and for a regent to relish the title First Gentleman of Europe. For some, therefore, dandyism marked the death of kings, and the dawn of modern concepts of self. But if the combination of emotional reticence, dry humour and condescension became emblematic of British masculinity – *sangfroid* as the revolutionary French dubbed it – it had appeal in other places beyond England and France and other times than the Age of Elegance. The through-line is perhaps best told in fictive terms. Bulwer Lytton wrote in the preface to the second edition of his influential 1828 novel *Pelham, The Adventures of a Gentleman*,

I have drawn for the Hero of my work . . . a personal combination of antithesis – a fop and a philosopher, a voluptuary and a moralist – a trifler in appearances but rather one to whom trifles are instructive . . . accustomed to draw sage conclusions from the follies he adopts, and while professing himself a votary of pleasure, desirous in reality to become a disciple of Wisdom.

It was a reasonable working definition of Brummell's dandyism, but the character he goes on to describe forms the model for recognisable heroes of British fiction ever since, from his time to our own. Indifference, emotional detachment and a superior wit developed into a recognisable suit in themselves: the desiderata of modern heroism, and a model to be aspired to in drama as in life. *Pelham* was used as a guidebook, both for future literary heroes (Bulwer Lytton and Disraeli even corresponded on the subject) but also in real life. The fashionable novel grew out of it. The discussion of gentlemanly behaviour in the novels of Dickens, Trollope or Gaskell would have been impossible without it.

Bulwer Lytton never had a bigger success, although in the 1830s he published *Paul Clifford*, a novel in the style of *The Beggar's Opera*, which brought a further twist to the story of the literary dandy: the dandy as criminal. Dickens took up the theme, as did Wilde and Edgar Allen Poe, and the idea fed directly into Raffles: the gentleman thief. Benjamin Disraeli also wrote a novel inspired by Brummell's dandyism. It was called *Vivian Grey* and presented a subtly different dandy form: the dandy scoundrel. He was a male Becky Sharp: a manipulator and adventurer, able and willing to use the carapace of dandyism to climb in society – 'The world's my oyster,' he declared, 'which with my sword I'll open.' Brummell found that his visitors in Calais and Caen had read about dandyism in novels like *Vivian Grey*, and others that made much of the dandy as (misunderstood) hero. But as the century progressed, elements of Brummell's style – a slightly more austere and masculine dandihood – were subsumed into the mainstream. From Sydney Carton in *A Tale of Two Cities* to Sherlock Holmes or Richard Hannay, the dandy pose and elements of Brummell's sartorial style became signifiers of complex, intriguing and heroic modern masculinity. In this regard, the emotionally reticent, self-created heroes of the American West, in fact and fiction, have also been described as dandies, men in the tradition of Brummell.

~

Brummell's legacy had two primary sites: England and France. This had little to do with his exile in Calais and Caen, as dandyism in France was restricted to Paris, whose fashionable environs did not include the northern ports. Where Londoners had the *Bon Ton*, Paris had, symmetrically, *le High Life*, and dandies became the new aristocrats of a more democratic age. Perhaps, then, it is not surprising that the immediate successor to Brummell was French, although the scene of his sartorial conquest was London. Count Alfred d'Orsay, born in 1801 to parents connected with the Napoleonic and the Bourbon aristocracy, left for England aged twenty. He might have encountered Brummell in Calais *en route*. At only twenty-one, he 'made himself the centre of a court of fashionables [in London] who imitated him . . . everybody who prided themselves on elegance, swore only by him; he had picked up,' it was said, 'the sceptre of Brummell.' That same year he met the Irish Countess Blessington, whose creamy décolletage now adorns the Wallace Collection. She, d'Orsay and her husband set up in a *ménage à trois*, the more scandalous as d'Orsay later married one of Blessington's daughters and was made heir to the vast Blessington fortune. His was, then, a dandyism more charged with cupidity than Brummell's, but as a London celebrity his trajectory was markedly similar. According to one recent biographer, d'Orsay was a bisexual chancer who played cat-and-mouse with the popular press, living up to an image of being a dandy. London of the 1820s and 1830s was certainly a harsher environment, in press terms, than had been the case for Brummell, and new magazines like *Age*, the *Satirist* and later *Punch* would catalogue d'Orsay's supposed deviance as well as what he wore, with much more attention to detail than had been so for Brummell with *Bon Ton Magazine*. But if the dandy image became even more widely disseminated as a result of d'Orsay, it also became more allied with sexual danger than had previously been the case. In d'Orsay, dandyism seemed to find a new anti-hero, someone much more aligned with what passed later as the full-blown Victorian cad. In marrying his mistress's virginal sixteen-year-old step-daughter, d'Orsay scandalised society. It did not become apparent until much later that he was probably also the lover of the bride's father.

D'Orsay's name, like Brummell's, became linked in reality and the public imagination with Byron's. The Blessington–d'Orsay ménage travelled to Genoa in 1823, and spent sufficient time in the company of Byron for Lady Blessington to write a volume of memoirs on the subject. Byron described d'Orsay as *Cupid déchaîné* (Cupid let loose), which was more accurate than perhaps he intended. The sense of the dandy as sexually other, androgynous perhaps, predatory or deviant often, was fixed in the popular imagination by Byron and d'Orsay. Byron, who had known Brummell sufficiently well to contribute intimate poems to his Album and to joke that Brummell was to be admired over Napoleon or even himself, was in thrall to d'Orsay. Around the three men – Brummell, Byron and d'Orsay – a new image of masculinity was defined, which took both the dandy pose (indifferent, removed) and the dandy style of dress (serious, sculptural) and gave flesh to the newly defined heroes of nineteenth-century fiction. The three also conformed to a powerful new idea of the rebel-artist, someone who broke rules while appearing to create them. Thus d'Orsay's sexual adventuring and press manipulation and Byron's disregard for societal and political norms can be seen as extensions of Brummell's capriciousness, originality and self-destructiveness. But d'Orsay came to symbolise a turning-point in the perception of the dandy, for where the fashionable novels of the early century had struggled over the issue of the difference between a dandy and a gentleman, d'Orsay, who lived off his mistress, her husband and their daughter, made it clear that he was one and not the other.

~

The third strand to be explored in the legacy of Brummell takes us exclusively to the land of his death. The intellectual and artistic content of dandyism – some have even called it a spiritual position – was argued first and most strongly in France. D'Aurevilly's *On Dandyism and George Brummell* (1844) had a profound and lasting impact on French intellectual life. In itself, though opalescent in its small perfection, this essay would not have had such impact had it not been taken up and used in different ways by various artists and writers in nineteenth-century Paris. Honoré de Balzac read d'Aurevilly, and found in the essay confirmation of his own ideas about Brummell and dandyism already published in the magazine *La Mode* in the 1830s. He had created a fictional interview with Brummell in '*Traité de la Vie Élégante*', written in instalments for the magazine, imagining the two of them (Balzac and Brummell) discussing dandyism in exile. Balzac was one of the first to take up the theme of Brummell as another fallen emperor, as important in his way as the exiled Napoleon in St Helena. But Balzac's essay chimed directly with d'Aurevilly's interest in Brummell. 'We owe to Brummell the demonstration [of] how much elegant life is tied to the perfection of all human society,' Balzac wrote. Brummell's life as an icon of French philosophy had begun.

Balzac, like d'Aurevilly, found a romantic disavowal of industrial society in the rarefied cult of dandyism. It was a theme developed mainly in France. The primary text in this philosophical dandyism came in 1863 and was directly inspired by d'Aurevilly and Brummell: Charles Baudelaire's *Le Peintre de la vie moderne*. Dandies, Baudelaire argued, spoke of a society on the point of huge change. For d'Aurevilly, dandyism had been a specifically English, and specifically Regency, florescence born of the '*ennui*' and 'satiety' of the world's first industrial nation. For Baudelaire, dandyism appeared 'in all periods of transition, when democracy is not yet all powerful and aristocracy is only just beginning to totter and fall. In the disorder of these times, certain men who are socially, politically and financially ill at ease, but are rich in native energy, may conceive the idea of establishing a new kind of aristocracy.' 'The word dandy', according to Baudelaire, 'implies a quintessence of character and a subtle understanding of the entire moral mechanism of *this world*.' Baudelaire was the first writer to recognise the prescience of the dandy: holding the dying culture and a new one in congruence, not just enjoying the liminal but defining it. It was quite some proposition to base on a man like Brummell, whose dandy set, Byron claimed, were avowedly anti-intellectual. But it is as a 'type' or as an intellectual

473

position that Brummell's dandyism has had a further life beyond manner, humour or dress sense. Baudelaire found a 'quality of opposition and revolt' in the dandy and thereby a universal relevance. It was this aesthetic philosophy of dandyism that inspired Oscar Wilde and later Max Beerbohm, who even titled one of his key essays 'In Defence of Cosmetics', in imitation of Baudelaire. It lent moral authority and philosophical weight to a position that had seemed at the time as evanescent as the butterfly about which Brummell versified.

It is unclear if Oscar Wilde first came to know Brummell through d'Aurevilly. It is just as likely that he appreciated him as a London character, and a 'type' from the fiction of the day and the writings and artistic philosophy of his Oxford tutor, W. Pater. Wilde's and Brummell's style and lives came to have uncanny parallels. Outsiders both, they came to the attention of London society by virtue of a theatrical presence and their light-comedic rhetoric. Wilde was first quoted as an undergraduate, already a collector of *objets d'art* like Brummell, saying, 'I find it harder every day to live up to my blue china,' a sentiment worthy of Brummell and entirely in his rhetorical style. Wilde's paradoxical whimsy allowed him to escape the obligations of regular conversation by pronouncing witticisms from imaginary Olympian heights, just as Brummell had done even as an Eton schoolboy. Wilde was also meticulous about his appearance, and used the new modes of photographic reproduction to promulgate an image for the press to flesh out his wit. 'Dandy of dress, dandy of speech, dandy of manner, dandy of wit, dandy even of ideas and intellect', as Micheál mac Liammóir described him, Oscar Wilde reestablished the unified completeness of the dandy: person and lifestyle as one construct, missing since Beau Brummell. Unsurprisingly, therefore, Brummell and Wilde have almost become fused in the popular imagination, their lives reflected also in the parallel, tragic third acts: in penury and in France.

Wilde's most personal testament to the style created by Brummell is in *The Picture of Dorian Gray*, understood almost from the start as a discourse on dandyism. Dorian's life is his art, for all that he remains ignorant of it. He becomes a picture in an attic, and a physical image of spiritual decay. His cankerous appearance has been discussed in relation to Wilde's own syphilitic condition, and although Wilde cannot have known of Brummell's infection it is tempting to speculate that he re-created in Gray's story a paradigm that he knew from those of the Beau. Wilde wrote of the characters in *Dorian Gray*: 'Basil is what I think I am: Lord Henry what the world thinks me: Dorian what I would like to be – in other ages, perhaps.' It is not too far-fetched to suggest that Dorian was his picture of himself as Brummell.

Wilde's dandyism segues into a truly modern sensibility of celebrity and mass-media stardom. He had a career, like Brummell's, of public celebrity some time before his great dramatic and literary successes. He cultivated what is now often recognised as a homosexual sensibility, but was considered in his own time as dandy or aesthetic. It was in America, tellingly, that Wilde launched his dandy-celebrity self. His 1882 tour of the United States instructed him on the new ways of using a constructed persona to personal advantage: he launched, on the back of a fame based on little more than Brummell's at the time, an Oscar Wilde soap, a clothing range and even an 'Oscar Wilde Waltz'. To Degas, after America Wilde seemed to have 'the look of an amateur playing Lord Byron in a suburban theatre'. But the mass-marketing of dandyism was set in motion, stalled only by Wilde's disgrace and flight, like Brummell's, to France.

Wilde's dandyism affected and infuriated by turns his friend the painter James McNeill Whistler, who is another link in the Franco-Anglo-American axis of the dandy aesthetic in the later nineteenth century as he also became fascinated with the person of Brummell through the d'Aurevilly essay. Through Whistler, the philosophy had a personal and social link to the many influential men with whom he mixed in Paris: Monet, Manet and Proust – the latter used Brummell's dandyism as one of his models for Charles Swann. On the one hand, Whistler's dandyism is evidenced in his 'contrived simplicity of design', in life and in his art. On the other he found in d'Aurevilly's Brummell an icon of modernist art: 'a work of art in himself'. Like Baudelaire before him, who had claimed that having read d'Aurevilly there was nothing else to write, Whistler was mesmerised not so much by the person of Brummell as by the image d'Aurevilly painted of him: a paradox of puritanism and vanity, fashion and profundity.

Dandyism was not restricted to the countries Brummell had lived in. In St Petersburg Pushkin read d'Aurevilly and *Pelham*, and used the latter's duelling, dandified hero as the model for his own behaviour and dress, and in his most famous creation, Eugene Onegin, who 'at least three hours peruses/His figure in the looking glass'. The Brummell original, thus metamorphosed through two literary variations, became a type in Russian literature and life: the insider-outsider, the artist whose greatest attachment to life comes through his distance from it. Nineteenth-century Russia understood painfully the connection between artifice and art, just as Onegin struggled with his position as a dandified European Russian. To be a Russian aristocrat was to be a performer and a poseur, speaking in a 'foreign' language (French) and acting on the stage-set of St Petersburg. The dandy's commentary on this, his cool disregard for human comfort, and willingness to risk everything for very little in the arch art of duelling, sat comfortably with Russian nihilism. In St Petersburg in particular dandyism thrived. Brummell's ghost is immediately recognisable in the salon Onegin enters where there are

> No lasting truths or dissertations –
> And no one's ears were shocked a bit
> By all the flow of lively wit.

It was through Pushkin, and specifically through translating *Onegin*, that Vladmir Nabokov came to dandyism and Brummell. Nabokov's chief literary passion was Pushkin – he once said, 'I shall only be remembered by *Lolita* and my work on *Eugene Onegin*,' and in 1964 he published a translation of the Russian verse classic, with an extended commentary on dandyism. For Nabokov, Brummell was the obvious and complete model for Onegin. He went on to use elements of dandyism in *Pale Fire*, and even, in terms of the *ennui* and the misogyny, in the character of the *Lolita* anti-hero Humbert Humbert.

Brummell's dandyism appeared again in the twentieth century, in the person of Max Beerbohm: cartoonist, wit and actor. 'The dandy,' Beerbohm wrote, 'presents himself to the nation every time he sallies from his front door.' He took particular pains before he arrived in the United States in 1895: in his self-penned 'press release', he described himself as 'the modern Beau Brummell', offering to make an event of his *toilette* and boasting that he had 'sixty-eight pairs of trousers, seventy boots . . . and four hundred and sixty-nine different cravats.'

Between 1893 and 1896 Beerbohm published essays on dandyism in Oxford, London and Chicago, later collected together in the works as *Dandies and Dandies*. It was an unexpected follow-up to his semi-satirical 'In Defence of Cosmetics', but it posited Brummell's style as the ideal for modern man, 'quiet, reasonable, plastic, economical, scrupulous'. He writes of the 'symmetry, austerity, subtlety, and sombre restraint of the ideal dandy, chastened of all flamboyance.' In this, he kicked the regency aesthetic of Brummell into something that was written about as post-modernism; he wanted, according to one friend, 'to live and die in the mirror'. This same philosophy allowed him to turn Thomas Carlyle's *Sartor Resartus* on its head – rescuing the term 'dandiacal' (also dandaical) from the taint of mania because Beerbohm *approved* of being 'heroically consecrated' to clothes. Similarly, he wrote of George IV's excesses – gastronomic, financial, amatory – as key signifiers in a life heroically self-penned as 'a poem in the praise of Pleasure'. For Beerbohm, Brummell was an heroic decadent, the natural grandfather to Oscar Wilde and the aesthetic movement. For him dressing up was the very essence of 'free will' at work, 'the liberty of all expression'. But he also had a fellow dandy's appreciation of the character of Brummell, with whom he supposed himself to share a particular sensitivity and what would now be called a damaged or damaging childhood. 'Dandyism,' Beerbohm wrote, 'is ever the outcome of a carefully cultivated temperament . . . Mr Brummell did most steadfastly maintain [his] attitude. Like the single-minded artist that he was, he turned full and square towards his art and looked life straight in the face out of the corners of his eyes.'

In 1929 Virginia Woolf also turned to Beau Brummell as an unexpected subject in a discussion on modernism. 'Some curious combination of wit, of taste, of insolence, of independence,' she wrote, had propelled Brummell to the forefront of his era, but had also caught her imagination as speaking across the century since his death to her own. 'He floated buoyantly and gaily and without apparent effort to the top of whatever society he found.' And if it 'were too heavy handed to call [it] a philosophy of life', it was a style worth understanding, 'so skilful, so adroit' that the ideas of Brummell's life 'slip into the mind and stay there when more important [things] were forgotten'. Woolf had evidently read d'Aurevilly but also Jesse's *Life* and was struck by the image of Brummell in decline as much as by the style that defined his ascendancy. For her he was a symbol of the decadence of the modern world, but also a figure to whom she related, as Byron had, 'with a mingled emotion of respect and jealousy'. For an intellectual, the person who has lived out a philosophy, however tragically, is the object of awe and jealousy.

In the light of its reverberations down the decades in Western thought and letters, d'Aurevilly's essay looks astonishingly prescient. Brummell emerges as a grandfather to the aesthetic movement of the later nineteenth century and an inspirational figure in the birth of the modern age. His symbolic significance was given further life in the mid-twentieth century by Albert Camus, who picked up on these themes in his 1951 *Homme Revolté* (*The Rebel*) with a good deal of antipathy for Brummell and the person of the dandy. Camus was fascinated but repelled by dandyism, rather as Thomas Carlyle had been a century before. The dandy was a theatrical construct for Camus, utterly reliant on the response from the same audience he affected to despise. Yet he also saw in Brummell a proto-revolutionary and a vital role model for more modern rebels: 'Between the days of the eighteenth-century eccentric and the adventurers of the twentieth century, [the dandies] are already fighting, however ostentatiously, for freedom.' As a result of Camus, dandyism and Brummell have influenced a wide range of mid-twentienth-century discourses on masculinity and rebellion, from the dandy Alex in *A Clockwork Orange*, the sardonic and alienated Angry Young Men who graced the theatre of the 1960s and the radical New Men of 1950s French and American cinema – emblematically Marlon Brando in *The Wild One*.

In twentieth-century fashion, Brummell's dandyism moved on in unexpected ways. During a seventy-year career in France, Coco Chanel transformed the way women dress throughout the modern world, but with reference to an unexpected source: a London dandy who had been dead for a century. In key respects Coco Chanel was a dandy herself. She was a woman of the theatre, and later of film, designing costumes that helped publicise her look almost as Brummell had exhibited himself in his theatre box. She had a love of the English country look, while eschewing actual hunting and shooting, as had Brummell. Her tweeds and working-fabrics look was called the '*miserabilisme de luxe*'. She marketed her own style, as clothes, obviously, but in perfume and jewellery too, as a whole narrative style of new womanhood. She encouraged women to tan, for instance, just as Brummell had helped render unfashionable the pallid wigs of the *ancien régime*. Her style was delivered to women via the persons of Chanel-shaped models and later iterated in the form of Twiggy. One fashion historian notes that 'what Brummell's aesthetic claimed for men in the nineteenth century had won over [in Chanel] the feminine universe . . . Flamboyant display was eclipsed in favour of the democratic aesthetic of purity, restraint, and comfort.' Another asserts that Chanel's 'image was founded on the Beau Brummell principle that clothes while they are being worn must seem not to matter at all'. But her debt to Brummell did not end there: like him, she broke through class boundaries, consorted with royalty, and created a cult of self that owed its form to aristocratic and unreachable glamour but was then disseminated to Everywoman. 'Her work and her legacy prove that dandyism never died, it only evolved, merging with modern fashion to enter the twentieth century – the era of mass culture, media celebrity, and, of course, cheap designer knock-offs.'

For Susan Sontag, the modern projection of dandyism is simple: it is camp. This is not to say that the early-nineteenth-century dandies were camp, or even epicene. As we have seen, many were recognised and lauded for their projections of classical masculinity, Brummell in particular. 'Camp', however, takes a position in relation to society and culture that is both critical and often humorous, but rarely engaged. 'Detachment is the prerogative of the élite,' Sontag wrote (in 1964), 'and as the dandy is the nineteenth century's surrogate for the aristocrat in matters of culture, so Camp is the modern dandyism. Camp is the answer to the problem: how to be a dandy in an age of mass culture.' Camp has been subsumed into mainstream culture in the West in a telling way since Sontag related it to dandyism, becoming the constant quotation marks of modern critical discourse and, 'like', modern conversation. Its pervasiveness has also allowed Brummell to be misread as a camp icon, and for that matter a gay icon, as a 'Regency Quentin Crisp', which, whatever their similarities of wit or otherness, are a long way from the Brummell who lived and breathed in Regency England.

Given the artifice, the theatricality and the tragic arc of Brummell's life it was perhaps inevitable that his story should also have an afterlife as drama. Brummell first appeared as a fictional character on stage in *Beau Brummell, the King of Calais*, which opened at the Royal Lyceum Theatre in the West End on 11 April 1859. It was based on Jesse's newly reprinted *Life* and featured Isidore the valet as one of the leads, but carefully changed the names of Brummell's friends, some of whom were still alive. By the 1870s Brummell's name was of sufficiently popular celebrity to warrant a music-hall song, 'The Bond Street Beau', featuring the refrain 'I am a Bond Street Beau', to be sung aloud by the entire theatre. The greatest theatrical heights were scaled in

1908 by a play called *Beau Brummel* [*sic*] by Clyde Fitch, which ran in New York and London. It was later turned into a silent movie, starring John Barrymore, who had played the role on stage, and Mary Astor, but by the time it was released, in 1924, there had already been five silent versions of Brummell's story. Its pathos and obvious physical glamour made it particularly suitable for the silent treatment, but often film publicity piggy-backed on the success of theatre plays and Fitch's play was considered a gem of its period. The *dramatis personae* featured Princess Frederica, Lady Hester Stanhope and Alvanley, but intriguingly Mary Astor played 'Lady Margery Alvanley' and, more bizarre still, Barrymore was the Byronic hybrid 'Gordon Byron Beau Brummel'. In Paris, meanwhile, there was an operetta *Brummell*, text and lyrics by Georges Thenon and Robert Dieudonné. This was first performed at the Théâtre Folies-Wagram in 1931. There were two further Brummell musicals in the 1930s, in London: *Beau Brummell* (Savoy Theatre, 1933) and *By Appointment* (New Theatre, 1934). For many people today the image of Beau Brummell is fixed from a half-remembered film glimpsed as a TV matinée: the 1954 Hollywood film *Beau Brummell* starring Stewart Granger, Elizabeth Taylor and Peter Ustinov. Written in part by *How Green Was My Valley* author Richard Llewellyn and Karl Tunberg, it was based, like the Barrymore film, on the Clyde Fitch play. More recently, Brummell was back on a West End stage in Ron Hutchinson's 2001 *Brummell*, again set in the Beau's exile and featuring Isidore not only as a co-star but as the only co-star.

The name Beau Brummell lives on in unexpected ways: the Beau Brummells were a five-piece group formed in northern California who had a hit, 'Laugh, Laugh', in 1964. Rosemary Stevens, a Briton transplanted to the United States, like some of the Beau Brummells band members, has written a series of successful detective novels set in Regency London with Brummell as dandy sleuth. He also appears in several Georgette Heyer novels. As a marketing tool or cultural reference, his name is bandied frequently and internationally, in the lyrics of Billy Joel and in *Annie*, the musical, from Beau Brummell American leather-wear, specialising in wallets, to British Beau Brummell school blazers, from a French aftershave to a downtown New York menswear store.

In 2002, a statue was erected in London's West End at the instigation of the Bond Street department store owner Christopher Fenwick. 'Beau Brummell is an icon, quite simply. Everyone knows the name. His is the spirit of this glamorous part of town.' He was supported by the shops and clubs of the parish of St James's. Originally intended for Bond Street, it was eventually placed at the bottom of Piccadilly Arcade where it joins Jermyn Street, appropriately just opposite the site of the Brummell family lodging-house.

The currency of Brummell's name and the ability of dandyism to inspire debate and creativity begs the inevitable question: who are the modern-day Brummells? Men – and increasingly women, despite Baudelaire's wild assertion that women were the opposite of dandies – have laid claim to be latter-day dandies. For many, the spirit of dandyism has moved away from clothing and fashion, now that we all have access to an unlimited dressing-up box: 'To inoculate contemporary clothing with a bit of dandyism, via Fashion, was fatally to destroy dandyism itself . . . It is in fact Fashion that killed Dandyism,' wrote Roland Barthes. Rather, dandies are to be found in other media. D'Aurevilly translator George Walden in his *Who's a Dandy?* suggested Brummell's tradition was flourishing in the modern British art scene, and posited Damian Hirst, Jarvis Cocker and Tracey Emin as dandified modern icons, while describing Brummell as 'a cross between Versace and the late Alan Clark'. Once you start looking, dandies seem to be everywhere, in fashion, of course, but as much in the Brummellian understated chic of Paul Smith as in the theatricality of Vivienne Westwood or John Galliano. In the cultural landscape outside fashion, the dandy philosophy has been used to describe the works of artists and writers as wide-ranging as Diaghilev, Valentino, the Sitwells, Tom Wolfe, Martin Amis, Andy Warhol, Steven Berkoff and Madonna. An aesthetic so broad and slippery in definition that it can encompass such a list almost ceases to have a meaning. The paradoxes inherent in dandyism are what give it its scintillating interest, but means it is used or misused in slipshod cultural criticism: hardly the sort of thing the man himself could have desired.

~

George Brummell's was a fractured personality, rebuilt in masquerade in the mirror of other people's expectations of him. In this he was indeed the empty vessel decried by Thomas Carlyle or Albert Camus, but Brummell had true originality of spirit and it is this that has allowed him to hold a pre-eminent place in what became a cultural as well as a fashion phenomenon. He was an icon of the Regency period not just because of the projections upon his person by subsequent writers or even by the many who knew only the public construct of his persona. He had a force within him for change, for rethinking what it was to be a gentleman, an Englishman, a man. He was an utter original. It is in this questioning of those aspects that most informed who he was that Brummell's life achieves its extra, exhilarating dimension.

Though his end must not define his life, the Dorian Gray disintegration of his physical and sartorial self, understood through the nineteenth century as *emblematic* of a syphilitic decay, and only now acknowledged as precisely that, gave immense symbolic power to the image of the Beau. He had not so much *done* something as *been* something: he symbolised a style and a period, and lit up – by a personality variously remembered – a crucial era in the history of his city, his culture and his sex. Dandyism as masquerade, as performed personality and constructed and commodified persona, is the clear antecedent to modern celebrity: the movie star and pop icon. Dandyism, the position of 'entertaining antithetical propositions simultaneously', has enormous comic mileage, realised most keenly in the comedic works of Oscar Wilde, but has also proved a tantalising idea in more wide-ranging modern thought. Both the early British social dandyism that had its greatest star in Beau

Brummell, and the later French philosophical dandyism that used him as its martyr, announced and promulgated the self-created modern man who made an effect, brought about a 'happening'. Once he departs the eighteenth and early nineteenth century, George Bryan Brummell's dandyism moves inevitably into our understanding of the modern media star, and the star's ability to reflect ourselves.

Acknowledgements

This biography was mainly written in the Rare Books Room of the British Library, and in the London Library in St James's Square – yards from Brummell's family home, his clubs and several shops he knew and frequented. I am enormously grateful for all the friendly assistance of the staff in both libraries, especially in the Rare Books and Manuscripts Rooms at the British Library, and to the London Library for trusting me with the long-term loan of a great number of first-edition memoirs written by Brummell's contemporaries. I would also wish to thank the staff of the Royal Archive at Windsor Castle, especially Allison Derrett, and of the Museum of London Archive, the Wellcome Institute, the Westminster City Archive, the National Portrait Gallery, the Guildhall Library, the London Metropolitan Archives, the New York Public Library and the Bibliothèque Nationale in Paris. Of the many small and private archives relevant to Brummell's life I am particularly grateful for the assistance of Rob Petre at Oriel College, Oxford, Tony Trowles at the Westminster Abbey Library, Penny Hatfield at the Eton College Library, J. R. Webster at the Muniments Room Archive, Belvoir Castle, and Charles Noble and Hannah Obee at Chatsworth House, Derbyshire. Madame Geneviève Mouchel and Madame Dordron at the Archives Municipales de Caen were particularly kind and informative, and at the archives of the Hôpital Psychiatrique Départementale du Bon Saveur de Caen my researches were met with the dedicated interest of Professor Pierre Morel, who not only uncovered and guarded Brummell's medical records but also took the trouble to explain them to me, give me an 'insider's' tour of the asylum buildings, and shared his insights into the Bon Sauveur regime in Brummell's day and the psychological aspects of syphilis and its treatment. Without him this story would have been greatly impoverished.

～

For permissions to consult and quote manuscripts in the Royal Archive I wish to acknowledge the gracious permission of Her Majesty Queen Elizabeth II, and with regard to other private collections, the kind permissions, access and help given by His Grace the Duke of Rutland, His Grace the Duke of Devonshire, Her Grace the Dowager Duchess of Devonshire, the Provost and Fellows of Eton College, the Dean of Westminster Abbey and the Provost and Fellows of Oriel College, Oxford. All efforts have been made to ask relevant permissions, but I apologise here if anyone has been missed: full amends will be made wherever possible.

～

I have worked in the shadow of many writers on this project. There have been several previous biographies of George Brummell and I am particularly indebted to the research provided by Hubert Cole, and by Kathleen Campbell in the 1930s – an insider at the Foreign Office – in tracing Brummell's consular correspondence and Brummell family documents, and also to Maurice-Charles Renard, Jacques de Langlade and to Lewis Melville for their further insights into Brummell's time in France and with regard to Brummell's own writing. The monumental work of Captain Jesse, *A Life of George Bryan Brummell*, is the main source for any writing on Brummell. Any subsequent work on Brummell is in his debt and shadow. However, I should acknowledge also the inspiration of Jules Barbey d'Aurevilly's essay on Brummell, which I first read in the vibrant translation provided by George Walden, as well as key secondary texts that have allowed me fast access to the detail in the wide panorama of Brummell's life: the works of Ellen Moers, Roy Porter, Frances Wilson, Deborah Hayden, Christopher Breward and Anne Hollander, to name but a few, have all informed the style and substance of this book. I hope they would approve. Of those who have read early drafts of the text, and added greatly with suggestions based on their deep knowledge of the period, I would like to thank Paula Byrne, Julie Peakman, Steven Parissien, Sarah Parker, Stephen Calloway and Victoria Kortes Papp, who also provided many insights into Brummell's possible mental state in her other capacity as a practising psychoanalyst. My editors Rupert Lancaster at Hodder & Stoughton, London, and Leslie Meredith at Simon & Schuster, New York, have taught me the pleasure of being edited: I would like to acknowledge here my profound gratitude for their skill, support, patience and friendship. And special thanks are due to my dandy agent, Ivan Mulcahy, who first encouraged me to pursue the elusive figure of George Brummell.

I have endeavoured, wherever possible, to walk in the footsteps of Brummell, so must thank many people for physical guidance: first, those at Donnington Grove, Berkshire, James Gladstone, Chio Gladstone and Brita Elmes, and also Karen Hutt of Donnington Grove Country Club; at No. 4, Chesterfield Street, Mayfair, and Chatsworth, Her Grace the Dowager Duchess of Devonshire, Helen Marchant and especially Iris Armitage, and at Oatlands Park, Susan E. Barber and Karam Dhala; at Hampton Court Palace, Sarah Parker, Mark Meltonville and Richard Fitch; in St James's Street, Simon Berry, Carol Tyrrell and Julian Stevens, of Berry Brothers & Rudd Wine Merchants, and Anthony Lejeune at White's Club, and Mrs Sheila Markham, Miss Elizabeth Goodman and Mr Graham Snell at Brooks's Club; on Charing Cross Road, the staff of the Snuff Shop and especially James Clapham; on Jermyn Street, Christopher Fenwick and the Jermyn Street Association, John Gaze of the Carlton Club, Richard Briers and Lucy Briers have all guided me towards important information. At St Margaret's, Westminster, and St James's Church, Piccadilly, I would like to thank the staff and clergy and especially Mr Wai Tsang, and at St-Martin-in-the-Fields, Mrs Sheila Fletcher. I would also like to thank Sir Martin and Lady Nourse of Dullingham House, and especially Gay and Martin Slater of Stradishall Manor, Newmarket.

In France, I was greatly assisted by the staff of the Archives Municipales de Calais, and Calais Syndicat d'Initiative, and in Caen by Direction Régionale des Affaires Culturelles de Basse-Normandie, and CH du BS Centre Hôpitalier Specialisé du Bon Sauveur – now housed in some of the asylum pavilions Brummell would have known. The staff of the Archives Départementale du Calvados, also at Caen, and the Caen Memorial were particularly welcoming, and my thanks are due especially to Madame Denise Vogt of the Temple Église Reformée de France in Caen for her help in tracing the church and cemetery archives via the Société d'Histoire du Protestantisme en Normandie. At Luc-sur-Mer, Monsieur Lamy Pascal and the owners of Le Grand Orient on rue Charcot were very helpful, and my thanks and acknowledgement for support also to Brittany Ferries, Ross Williams at Brighter PR, Andrew Bamford at Les Fontaines, Barbery, Calvados and Valentina Harris at Le Touvent.

~

I have been guided towards the manifold pleasures of fashion, clothing, fabric and decorative arts by Stephen Calloway at the Victoria and Albert Museum and Christopher Breward, and at the Bath Museum of Costume by Elly Summers. I am particularly indebted to Juliet Brightmore at Hodder for her keen eye, and to Edwina Ehrman, curator of Dress, Textiles and Decorative Arts at the Museum of London Collections, and Oriole Cullen, her assistant curator, for their generosity with time, advice, and in allowing me to see and touch fabrics and clothes of the period. In terms of an education in the ongoing legacy of Brummell, I would like to thank Gieves & Hawkes, Hugh Holland, Lara Mingay and John McCabe at Kilgours, Savile Row, and also Campbell Carey and Michael Smith, the last bespoke breeches maker in London. Brian Lewis and Paul Laverty of the military tailors Meyer & Mortimer Ltd, 6 Sackville Street – direct descendants of Brummell's own tailors, Jonathan Meyers – were also very helpful, as was Janet Taylor at Brummell's hatters, James Lock and Company of St James's Street. Tom Ford, Oswald Boeteng, Dan Crowe and Lauren Goldstein have all offered ideas, advice and enthusiasm. Thanks are due to Joanna Morgan, Gabriella Ingram and Charlotte Sewell for their help in tracing the tailors and costumiers Alan Selzer, Clare Christie and Tony Angel. And the late Chris Prins at Cosprop Costumiers in London, whose intimate knowledge of Regency undergarments and details of nineteenth-century men's tailoring was probably unsurpassed, lent his usual good humour, taste and eye for detail to this project, as well as allowing me to try on original early-nineteenth-century menswear from the Cosprop collection. You are greatly missed.

~

On the subject of the Georgian underworld, syphilis, its treatment and history, I am enormously in the debt of Julie Peakman at the Wellcome Trust, Natasha McEnroe of Dr Johnson's House and to Hallie Rubenhold and Jonathan Meades. My thanks also to Simon Chaplin at the Hunterian Institute and family members in the medical and scientific worlds: Mr Andrew Kelly, Professor Donald Kelly and Dr Kate Gurney.

For their thoughts on dandyism, I am indebted to George and Sarah Walden, Philip Hoare, Ron Hutchinson and Caroline Hunt, and on Russian dandyism in general and Pushkin in particular I am grateful for the advice and translations of Tobin Auber in St Petersburg. On the subject of Brummell in opera and drama, I am grateful to Patrick O'Connell of BBC Radio 3. With regards to Brummell's time in the 10th Light Dragoons I am grateful for the help and advice of Richard Adlington, military historian, Major Tim Guthrie-Harrison and the staff of the National Army Museum.

For help with translations I am grateful for the kind assistance of Boe Paschall and Zacharias Rogkotis, language and classics lecturers at Davies, Laing and Dick College, London, and my brother David Kelly. I have borrowed frequently from the translations of Captain Jesse, Kathleen Campbell and d'Aurevilly's various adapters, but especially George Walden and D. B. Wyndham Lewis.

~

On a more personal note, I would like to thank Joe Guthrie-Harrison, Isabel Pollen and Hugo Wilkinson for technical assistance and special thanks are due to Hazel Orme, whose skill in close-detail copy-editing is both fearsome and inspiring. Heartfelt thanks are also due to those many friends and family members who have extended hospitality, or, vitally, donated their time in helping out with childcare. First among them must be my mother and father, but also Mo Guthrie-Harrison, Andrew and Kate Kelly, Brigit and Jerry Gurney, Andrew and Blanche Sibbald, Lindsay Clay and Matthew White, Neneh Jalloh and Dawn Mayne. For hospitality and help in the early months of this project and for their subsequent detective work towards finding Brummell's *Male and Female Costume*, I would like to thank Arthur and Ellen Wagner in New York and also Simon Green, Jason Morell, Deborah Shaw, Peter Tear, Elysabeth Kleinhans and all the staff at 59e59 Theatre in Manhattan. And for invaluable and friendly counsel in the British Library tea rooms and elsewhere I would like to thank my friends Mark Ashurst, Philip Hoare, Ingrid Waasenaar, Kate Chisholm and, as always, Erica Wagner.

Lastly, but loudly, I owe thanks beyond measure for the forbearance, inspiration and patient interest shown over many months by Claire, who, like my son Oscar, has simultaneously suffered my absences for months of late nights in libraries. I owe you both many bath-times.

Picture Acknowledgements

Private Collections: 2, 3, 15, 16, 22, 38, 42. The Royal Collection © 2005, Her Majesty Queen Elizabeth II: 23 portrait miniature by Richard Cosway.

Bibliography

Manuscripts

ROYAL ARCHIVES
RA GEO/29210–29427 (Accounts, 1783–1830; Wardrobe, Swords, Spurs, Regimental Colours)
RA GEO/29428–29643 (Accounts, 1783–1830; Wardrobe, Swords, Spurs, Regimental Colours)
RA GEO/22219–20 (Letter from G.B. Brummell to Lord Petersham)
RA GEO/44527–44558 (Letters of the Duchess of York to Prince Regent and Duchess of Cambridge)
RA GEO/Add 50/98–105 (Letters of the Duchess of York to Charles Culling Smith)

BRITISH MUSEUM
Scrope Davies Papers – MSS Loan 70
Whitefoord Papers – Add MSS 36 595 No. 295, No. 305
Sir Robert Wilson Select English Letters – Add MSS 30 115
Add MSS 41335 380m – Masonic Initiation Certificate
L'An de la V L 58 32 le 19ème jour du 2ème mois (19 February 1832)
Add MSS 36 593, 38233, 38307

NATIONAL ARCHIVES (PUBLIC RECORDS OFFICE, KEW)
FO 27/419, 435, 453, 455, 491, 493, 510
PRO 30/29/417 Prob 11/958, 1242

LONDON METROPOLITAN ARCHIVES
Brooks's and White's Betting Books
Memorials of Brooks's MDCCLXIV–MCM 2 April 1799.
White's Betting Book 1743–1878. 1811

WESTMINSTER ABBEY ARCHIVE
St Margaret's, Westminster: baptismal, marriage and burial records

WESTMINSTER CITY ARCHIVES
Baptismal, marriage and burial records, St James's Piccadilly and St-Martin-in-the-
  Fields
Rate Books: Bond Street, Piccadilly, Bury Street
Account Ledgers: Fribourg and Treyer

BELVOIR CASTLE MUNIMENTS ROOM
Letter from G. B. Brummell to Lords Charles and Robert Manners, 1816
Annuities, Lords Charles and Robert Manners

BERRY BROS & RUDD, ST JAMES'S STREET, LONDON
weighing books

JAMES LOCK & CO, HATTERS, ST JAMES'S STREET,
LONDON
Ledgers, 1798–1815

MEYER & MORTIMER, TAILORS, SACKVILLE STREET,
LONDON
Ledger, 1809–17
Waterloo tailor's notebook

BODLEIAN LIBRARY
North Family MSS

ETON COLLEGE ARCHIVES
Musae Etonenses, Nugae Etonenses
School Lists, Montem Lists, Boarding House Appendices
On the Montem, composed by Herbertus Stockhore, 1793
Eton College Register 1753–90
Preces Quotidianae in usum Scholae Collegii Regalis apud Etonam, Eton College
  Daily Prayer Book, 1793
*Etoniana Ancient and Modern, Being the Notes of the History and Traditions of
  Eton College* republished from *Blackwood's Magazine* with additions, 1865

ORIEL COLLEGE, OXFORD
Archives, 1768–1809, Easter Term, 1794 [ref. S II K 14]
Buttery Books, 1793–95

ARCHIVES DE L'HÔPITAL PSYCHIATRIQUE DU BON SAUVEUR, CAEN.

Admissions and Inmates: *G. B. Brummell, ex Consul de Sa Majesté Britannique*, 1839–40

ARCHIVES DÉPARTEMENTALES DU CALVADOS

M 220 Nomination d'un Consul Étranger, 1830
Archives du Cimetière Protestant
Register of Concessions
MSS 80F44 – Archives Départementales du Calvados

ARCHIVES MUNICIPALES DE CAEN

Plan de l'Hôtel d'Angleterre, Troisième Etage, 79–81 rue St Jean, Caen, Calvados, avant guerre 1939–45
Plan Général au rez de chaussée de Prisons Royales de la Ville de Caen, 1788. Archives Municipales du Calvados

Costume Collections

The Museum of London, Collection of Dress and Textiles
The National Museum of Costume, Bath
The Victoria and Albert Museum
Cosprop Costumiers, London

Contemporary Periodicals

Alfred and Westminster Evening Gazette
Annual Register
Bon Ton Magazine, or Microscope of Fashion and Folly
Covent Garden Journal
Crim-Con Gazette
Fraser's Magazine
Gentleman's Magazine
Harris's Lists of the Ladies of Covent Garden
Journal de la Normandie
Lady's Magazine
L'Ami de la Verité, Caen
Lancet
Monthly Magazine
Morning Chronicle

Morning Post
Public Advertiser
Punch
Ramblers' Magazine
Revue de Paris
Spectator
St James's Chronicle
Tatler
The Times

Other Primary Material

MEMOIRS, DIARIES AND LETTERS

Anon., *Picture of London for 1805 Being a Correct Guide to All the Curiosities, Amusements, Exhibitions, Public Establishments, and Remarkable Objects In and Near London with a Collection of Appropriate Tables*, London, 1805

Aspinall, A. (ed.), *Correspondence of King George IV, 1812–1830*, Cambridge, Cambridge University Press, 1938

Aspinall, A. (ed.), *Correspondence of George, Prince of Wales, 1770–1812*, London, Cassell, 1963

Bentley, Richard (ed.), *Anecdotes of the Upper Ten Thousand: their legends and their lives* (by Grantley F. Berkeley), 2 vols, London, 1867

Bickley, Francis (ed.), *The Glenbervie Journals*, Constable, London, 1928

Brownlow, Lady Emma Sophia, *The Eve of Victorianism, Reminiscences of the Years 1802–34*, London, 1840

Butler, E. M. (ed.), *A Regency Visitor; The English Tour of Prince Pückler-Muskau described in his letters 1826–1828*, trans. Sarah Austen, London, Collins, 1957

Cave, Kathryn, Garlick, Kenneth and Macintyre, Augus (eds), *The Diary of Joseph Farington (the years 1793–1821)*, New York, Yale University Press, 1998

Chambre, Major, *Recollections of West End Life with Sketches of Society in Paris, India Etc.*, 2 vols, London, 1858

Chateaubriand, François-René, *Mémoires d'Outre-Tombe*, Paris, Flammation, 1950

Creasy, Edward Shepherd, *Memoirs of Eminent Etonians: with notices of the early history of Eton College*, London, 1850

Croker, John Wilson, *The Correspondence and Diaries of the late Rt Hon. John Wilson Croker*, 3 vols, London, John Murray, 1884

d'Aurevilly, Jules Barbey, *Du Dandysme et de George Brummel* [sic], 3ème édition, Paris, 1876

d'Aurevilly, Jules Barbey, *Du Dandysme et de George Brummel* [sic], trans. D. B. Wyndham Lewis, *The Anatomy of Dandyism*, London, 1928

d'Aurevilly, Jules Barbey, *Du Dandysme et de George Brummell*, 1844, trans. George Walden, *Who's a Dandy?*, Gibson Square Books, London, 2002

Dowden, Wilfred (ed.), *The Letters of Thomas Moore*, 2 vols, Clarendon Press, Oxford, 1964

Edgcumbe, Richard (Earl Edgcumbe), *Musical Reminiscences of an Old Amateur Chiefly respecting Italian Opera in England, 1773–1823*, London, 1827

Edgcumbe, Richard (ed.), *The Diary of Frances, Lady Shelley 1787–1817*, London, 1912

Foster, V. (ed.), *The Two Duchesses: Family Correspondence of Georgiana, Duchess of Devonshire and Elizabeth, Duchess of Devonshire*, Bath, 1898

Fraser, William Augustus, *Words on Wellington*, London, 1889

Goede, C. A. G., *A Stranger in England; or, Travels in Great Britain*, London, 1807

Graham, Peter W. (ed.), *Letters of John Cam Hobhouse to Lord Byron, 'Byron's Bulldog'*, Columbus, Ohio State University Press, 1966

Greville, Charles, *The Greville Memoirs*, 3 vols, London, 1875

Grenville, Richard Plantagenet Temple Nugent Brydges Chandos, *Memoirs of the Court of George IV . . . From original family documents*, 2 vols, London, 1859

Gronow, Captain Rees-Howell, *Reminiscences of Captain Gronow Formerly of the Grenadier Guards and M.P. for Stafford being Anecdotes of the Camp, The Court and The Clubs at the close of the last war with France, related by Himself*, 1st edition, London, 1862; 2nd edition, London, 1863

Gronow, Captain Rees-Howell, *Captain Gronow's Last Recollections being the Fourth and Final Series of his Reminiscences and Anecdotes*, London, 1866

Hairby, James, *Rambles in Normandy*, London, 1846

Harris, James, *Diaries and Correspondence of James Harris, First Lord Malmesbury*, London, 1844

Hillard, G. S. (ed.), *Life, Letters, and Journals of George Ticknor*, Boston, 1876

Hobhouse, John Cam, *The Substance of Some Letters Written from Paris during the Last Reign of the Emperor Napoleon and addressed principally to The Rt Hon Lord Byron*, London, 1817

Hobhouse, John Cam, *Recollections of a Long Life, In Five Volumes*, London, 1865

Hook, Theodore, *Sayings and Doings*, second series: *The Sutherlands, The Man of Many Friends, Doubts and Fears, Passion and Principle*, London, 1825

Jerrold, Walter (ed.), *Bon-Mots of Samuel Foote and Theodore Hook*, London, 1894

Jesse, Captain William, *A Life of George Brummell, Esq., Commonly Known as Beau Brummell*, 2 vols, London, 1844; with additions and illustrations, 1854, 1886; new edition, London, Navarre Society, 1927

Johnson, Samuel, *Prefaces, Biographical and Critical, to the Works of the English Poets*, London, 1781

Johnstone, Julia, *Confessions of Julia Johnstone, written by herself in contradiction to the fables of Harriette Wilson*, London, 1825

Khan, Mizra Abul Hassan, *A Persian at the Court of King George IV, 1809–10, The Journal of Mizra Abul Hassan Khan*, trans. M. M. Cloake, London, 1988

Lennox, William Pitt (Lord), *The Story of My Life*, 3 vols, London, 1857

Lennox, William Pitt (Lord), *Fifty Years' Biographical Reminiscences*, 2 vols, London, 1863

Lennox, William Pitt (Lord), *The Adventures of a Man of Family*, 3 vols, London, 1864

Lennox, William Pitt (Lord), *My Recollections from 1806 to 1873*, 2 vols, London, 1874

Lennox, William Pitt (Lord), *Celebrities I Have Known, with Episodes, Political, Social, Sporting and Theatrical*, first series, 2 vols, London, 1876; second series, 2 vols, London, 1877

Leveson Gower, Sir G. (ed.), *Hary-O: the Letters of Lady Harriet Cavendish, 1796–1809*, London, John Murray, 1940

Lieven, Dorothea, *The Private letters of Princess Lieven to Prince Metternich 1820–1826*, London, 1937

Macdonald, John, *Memoirs of an 18th Century Footman*, London, Century, 1985

Macnamara, Ulysses, *The British Army: Condition at the Close of the Eighteenth Century, Compared with its Present State and Prospects*, London, 1839

MacQueen, John (ed.), *The Court of England under George IV: The Diary of a Lady-in-Waiting* [Lady Charlotte Bury], London, 1896

Meryon, Dr C. L. (ed.), *Memoirs of Lady Hester Stanhope, as related by Herself to her Physician, Comprising her opinions and Anecdotes of Some of the Most Remarkable Persons of her Time*, 3 vols, London, 1845

Moore, Thomas (ed.), Byron (George G.), 6th Baron, *The Works of Lord Byron; with his Letters and Journals*, London, John Murray, 1832–3

Moreland, Olivia, *The Charms of Dandyism, or, living in style. By Olivia Moreland, chief of the female dandies, and edited by Captain Ashe*, 3 vols, London, 1819

Owenson, Sydney (Lady Morgan), *La France; par Lady Morgan. Par l'auteur de Quinze Jours et de Six Mois à Londres*, trans. P. A. Lebrun des Charmettes, Paris, 1817

Owenson, Sydney (Lady Morgan), *The Book of the Boudoir*, London, 1829

Priestley, J. B. (ed.), *Tom Moore's Diary*, Cambridge, Cambridge University Press 1925

Pückler-Muskau, Prince, *Die Ruckkehr. Vom Verfasser der Briefe eines Verstorbenen*, Berlin, 1846

Raikes, Thomas, *France since 1830*, 2 vols, London, 1841

Raikes, Thomas, *A Portion of his Journal from 1831–1847*, vols I–IV, London, 1856

Raikes, Thomas, *Reminiscences of Social and Political Life in London and Paris*, London, 1856

Reynolds, F., *The Life and Times of Frederic Reynolds*, vol. 1, London, 1826

Smyth, William, *Memoir of Mr Sheridan*, Leeds, 1840

Stoddard, R. H. (ed.), 'Recollections of Thomas Raikes' in *Personal Reminiscences*, New York, Armstrong & Company, 1875

Tattershall, John F. (ed.), *Reminiscences of a Literary Life, Charles Macfarlane 1799–1858, Author and Traveller*, from two quarto manuscript volumes, London, 1917

Vermont, de (Marquis), *London and Paris, or Comparative Sketches*, London, 1823

Walpole, Horace, and Wright, John (ed.), *Letters*, London, 1840–46

Watkins, John, *A Biographical Memoir of His Late Royal Highness, Frederick, Duke of York and Albany*, London, 1827

Wilson, Harriette, *Memoirs of Harriette Wilson, Written by herself in Eight Volumes*, London, Peter Davies, 1929

FASHION

Anon., *Dandymania, Just published Price One Shilling. Embellished with a coloured likeness of a well-known Dandy*, London, 1819

Anon., *Essay Philosophical and Medical Concerning Modern Clothing*, London, 1792

Anon., *Indispensable Requisites for Dandies of Both Sexes, by A Lady*, Dublin, 1820

Anon., *Necklothitania or Tietania, Being an Essay on Starchers, by One of the Cloth*, London, 1818

Anon., *Taylor's Complete Guide*, London, 1796

Anon., *The Art of Tying the Cravat*, London, 1829

Anon., *The Tailor's Masterpiece*, London, c. 1829

Anon., *The Whole Art of Dress, by a Cavalry Officer*, London, 1830

Brummell, George Bryan, *Male and Female Costume, Grecian and Roman Costume, British Costume from the Roman Invasion until 1822 and the Principles of Costume applied to the Improved Dress of the Present Day (1822)*, New York, Doubleday, Doran & Company, 1932

Carlyle, Thomas, *Sartor Resartus (Fraser's, Magazine 1833–4)*, London; Canongate Classics, 2002

Compaing, C., and de Vere, Louis, *The Tailor's Guide*, London, 1856

de Vere, Louis, *The Handbook of Practical Cutting*, London, 1866

Le Blanc, H., *The History of the Cravat*, London, c. 1825

Le Blanc, H., *The Art of Tying the Cravat Demonstrated in Sixteen Lessons including Thirty Two Different Styles forming a Pocket Manual*, London, 1828

Le Blanc, H., *The Art of Tying the Cravat, Preceded by a History of the Cravat*, London, 1829

SEX AND SYPHILIS

Adams, Joseph, *Observations on morbid poisons, phagedœna, and cancer: containing a comparative view of the theories of Dr. Swediaur, John Hunter, Messrs. Foot, Moore, and Bell, on the laws of the venereal virus*, London, 1795

Bacot, John, *A Treatise on Syphilis; in which the history, symptoms, and method of treating every form of that disease, are fully considered*, London, Longman, Rees, Orme, Brown, and Green, 1829

Beaney, James George, *Constitutional syphilis: being a practical illustration of the disease in its secondary and tertiary phases*, 3rd edition, Melbourne, 1878

Davies, David, Hunter, R., and Manchee, T. J., *An essay on mercury; wherein are presented formulae for some preparations of this metal . . . Being the result of long experience and diligent observation*, London and Bristol, 1820

Drysdale, Charles R., MD, *On the Treatment of Syphilis and Other Diseases without Mercury being a collection of evidence to prove that mercury is a cause of disease, not a remedy*, Royal College of Physicians, London, 1863

Lagneau, L. V., *Exposé des diverses methods de traiter la Maladie Vénérienne*, Paris, 1803

Marten, Dr John, *A Treatise of all the Degrees and Symptoms of the Venereal Disease*, London, 1704

Parker, Langston, *The modern treatment of syphilitic diseases, both primary and secondary. Comprising an account of the new remedies, with numerous formulae for their preparation, and mode of administration*, London, 1839

Plenck, Joseph James, *A new and easy method of giving mercury, to those affected with the venereal disease* [also known as *Methodus nova et facilis argentum vivum aegris venerea labe infectis exhibendi.*], trans. William Saunders, Edinburgh, 1772

Ricord, Philip, *Illustrations of Syphilitic Disease with the addition of a History of Syphilis*, trans. Thomas Betton, MD, Philadelphia, 1851

Swediaur, F., MD, *Practical Observations on Venereal Complaints, To which were added an Account of the New Venereal Disease which has lately appeared in Canada*, 3rd edition, Edinburgh, 1788

Swediaur, F., *Traité complet sur les symptomes, les effets, la nature et le traitement des maladies syphilitiques*, 4th edition, Paris, 1801

Wallace, William, *A treatise of the venereal disease and its varieties*, London, Renshaw, 1838

Welbank, Richard, *Practical commentaries on the present knowledge and treatment of syphilis: with coloured illustrations of some ordinary forms of that disease*, London, Longman, Hurst, Rees, Orme, Browne and Green, 1825

MISCELLANEOUS

Anon., *An Address to Her Royal Highness the Dutchess [sic] of York Against the Use of Sugar*, London, 1792

Anon., *Don John or Don Juan Unmasked being a key to the mystery attending that remarkable publication*, 3rd edition, London, 1819

Anon., *Picture of London for 1805 Being a Correct Guide to All the Curiosities, Amusements, Exhibitions, Public Establishments, and Remarkable Objects In and Near London with a Collection of Appropriate Tables*, London, 1805

Anon., *The British Code of Duel; A reference to The Laws of Honour and the Character of Gentlemen, An appendix in which is strictly examined the case between the Tenth Hussars and Mr Battier; Cpt Calla'n, Mr Finch, &c noted*, London, 1824

Barrow, William, *An Essay on Education*, 2 vols, London, 1802

Byron, George Gordon (Lord), *Don Juan*, London, 1819

Carlyle, Thomas, *Sartor Resartus, Fraser's Magazine*, London, 1833–4

Coghlan, Francis, *A Guide to France, or, Travellers, Their Own Commissioners, explaining every form and expense from London to Paris*, London, 1829

Goldsmith, Oliver, *The Citizen of the World*, London, 1837

Knox, Vicesimus, *Liberal Education*, Dublin, 1781

Luttrell, Henry, *Advice to Julia, A Letter in Rhyme*, London, 1820

Luttrell, Henry, *Letters to Julia in Rhyme to which are added Lines Written at Ampthill-Park*, London, 1822

McGann, Jerome J. (ed.), *Lord Byron: The Complete Poetical Works*, 7 vols, Oxford, Clarendon Press, 1980

Moncrieff, William Thomas, *Tom and Jerry; or, Life in London; an operatic extravaganza, in three acts and in prose, with songs*, 2nd edition, London, 1828

Moore, John, *View of Society and Manners in Italy*, 2nd edition, 2 vols, London, 1781

Pyne, W. H., *The Royal Residences of England; Windsor Castle, Hampton Court, St James's Palace, Carlton House, Buckingham House*, vol. II, London, 1819

Roque, J., *An Accurate Survey of Speen Manor . . . belonging to the Duke of Chandos, 1730s–1740s* (Newbury Museum), Map of Berkshire, 1761

Temple, Lancelot, *A Short Ramble Through Some Parts of Italy and France*, London, 1751

Secondary Material

Adams, James Eli, *Dandies and Desert Saints; Styles of Victorian Masculinity*, Ithaca, Cornell University Press, 1995

Adburgham, Alison, *Shopping in Style: London from the Restoration to Edwardian Elegance*, London, Thames & Hudson, 1979

Adburgham, Alison, *Silver Fork Society: Fashionable Life and Literature 1814–1840*, London, Constable, 1983

Allen, Peter Lewis, *The Wages of Sin: Sex and Disease, Past and Present*, Chicago, University of Chicago Press, 2000

Anon., *A Most Humoursome and Laughable Description of those Modern Would-be Ring-tail Cocked-up Dandies, etc.*, Belfast, c. 1820

Anon., *Etoniana Ancient and Modern being notes of the history and traditions of Eton College*, London, William Blackwood & Sons, 1865

Anon., *La Vie Caennaise du Consulat au Second Empire racontée par un bourgeois et un homme du peuple*, Caen, 1927

Arnold, Dana (ed.), 'Lecture 6. Scandal and Society by Lindsay Boynton' in *Squanderous and Lavish Profusion, George IV and his Image and Patronage of the Arts*, London, Georgian Group, 1995

Ashley-Cooper, F. S., *Eton and Harrow at the Wicket*, London, 1922

Auty, Susan G., *The Comic Spirit of Eighteenth-century Novels*, London, Kennikat Press, 1975

Bank, Alfred (ed.), *The Drama: Its History, Literature and Influence on Civilisation*, vol. 15, London, 1906

Barrow, William, *An Essay on Education*, 2 vols, London, 1802

Barthes, Roland, *Le Dandysme et la Mode*, Paris, Editions du Seuil, 1971

Baudelaire, Charles, *The Painter of Modern Life and Other Essays*, trans. and ed. J. Mayne, London, Phaidon Press, 1963

Beaney, James George, *Constitutional Syphilis; being a practical illustration of the disease in its secondary and tertiary phases*, Melbourne, F. F. Ballière, 1878

Becker, S. William, and Obermayer, Maximilian E., *Modern Dermatology and Syphilology*, London, J. B. Lippincott, 1943

Beerbohm, Max, *Dandies and Dandies*, 1896, in S. C. Roberts (ed.), *The Incomparable Max*, London, Heinemann, 1962

Berthe, Léon-Noël, Bougard, Pierre, Canlier, Danielle, Decelle, Jean-Michel, and Jessenne, Jean-Pierre, *Villes et Villages du Pas-de-Calais en 1790, Vol. II, Districts de Béthune, de Boulogne et de Calais*, Arras, Mémoires de la Commission Départementale d'Histoire et d'Archéologie du Pas-de-Calais, 1992

Blanch, Lesley (ed.), *Harriette Wilson's Memoirs: The Greatest Courtesan of her Age*, London, Phoenix, 2003

Borde, Christian, *Calais et la Mer, 1814–1914*, Paris, Presses Universitaires du Septentrion, 1997

Boulenger, Jacques, *Sous Louis-Philippe; Les Dandys*, Paris, Libraires Paul Ollendorff, 1907

Bourne, Ursula, *Snuff*, Princes Risborough, Shire Publications, 1990

Boutet de Monvel, Roger, *George Brummell et George IV*, Paris, 1906

Boutet de Monvel, Roger, *Beau Brummell and His Times*, London, 1908

Brereton, Austin, *A Walk down Bond Street. The centenary souvenir of the house of Ashton and Mitchell, 1820–1920*, London, Selwyn & Blount, 1920

Breward, Christopher, *Fashioning London: Clothing and the Modern Metropolis*, London, Berg, 2004

Brewer, John, *The Pleasures of the Imagination: English Culture in the Eighteenth Century*, HarperCollins, London, 1997

Brooks, Stewart M., *The VD Story*, New York, Littlefield, Adams & Co., 1973

Bruce, A. P. C., *The Purchase System in the British Army, 1660–1871*, London, Royal Historical Society, 1980

Bryant, Julius, *Kenwood, The Iveagh Bequest*, London and New Haven, Yale University Press, 2003

Budd, Michael Anton, *The Sculpture Machine; Physical Culture and Body Politics in the Age of Empire*, New York, New York University Press, 1997

Burford, E. J., *Royal St James's, Being a Story of Kings, Clubmen and Courtesans*, London, Robert Hale, 1988

Burford, E. J., *Wits, Wenches and Wantons: London's Low Life: Covent Garden in the Eighteenth Century*, London, Robert Hale, 1990

Burford, E. J., and Wotton, Joy, *Private Vices, Public Virtues: Bawdry in London*, London, Robert Hale, 1995

Burnett, T. A. J., *The Rise and Fall of a Regency Dandy: the Life and Times of Scrope Berdmore Davies*, London, John Murray, 1981

Byrne, Paula, *Jane Austen and the Theatre*, London, Hambledon, 2002

Byrne, Paula, *Perdita; The Life of Mary Robinson*, London, Harper Collins, 2005

Calloway, Stephen, and Colvin, David, *The Exquisite Life of Oscar Wilde*, London, Orion Books, 1997

Campbell, Kathleen, *Beau Brummell*, London, Hammond, Hammond & Co., 1948

Camus, A., *L'Homme Revolté*, trans. Anthony Bower, *The Dandy's Rebellion*, London, Penguin, 2000

Carassus, Emilien (ed.), *Le Dandysme et la Mode*, Paris, A. Colin, 1971

Card, Tim, *Eton Established: a history from 1440 to 1860*, London, John Murray, 2001

Carman, W., *British Military Uniforms*, Feltham, Spring Books, 1968

Castronovo, David, *The English Gentleman: Images and Ideals in Literature and Society*, New York, Ungar, 1987

Chancellor, E. Beresford, *The Memorials of St James's Street Together with the Annals of Almack's*, London, Grant Richards, 1922

Chandos, John, *Boys Together: English public schools 1800–1864*, London, Hutchinson, 1984

Chenoune, Faid, *The History of Men's Fashion*, trans. Deke Dusinberre, Paris, Flammarion, 1993

Clark, Andrew (ed.), *The Colleges of Oxford: their history and traditions. XXI chapters contributed by members of the colleges*, London, 1891

Coblence, Françoise, *Le Dandysme: obligation d'incertitude*, Paris, PUF, 1988

Cochrane, Alexander Dundas Ross, *In the Days of the Dandies*, London, W. Blackwood & Sons, 1890

Cohen, Michèle, 'The Construction of the Gentleman', in Gobel, Walter, Schabio, Saskia, and Windisch, Martin (eds), *Engendering Images of Man in the Long Eighteenth Century*, Trier, Wissenschaftlicher Verlag, 1987

Cohen, Michèle, *Fashioning Masculinity: National Identity and Language in the Eighteenth Century*, London, Routledge, 1996

Cole, Hubert, *Beau Brummell*, London, Granada, 1976

Colson, Percy, *White's 1693–1950*, London, Heinemann, 1951

Connelly, Willard, *The Reign of Beau Brummell*, London, Cassell, 1940

Connelly, Willard, *Count d'Orsay; the Dandy of Dandies*, London, 1952

Craft, Christopher, *Another Kind of Love: Male Homosexual Desire in English Discourse*, Los Angeles, University of California Press, 1994

Cumming, Valerie, 'Pantomime and Pageantry: the Coronation of George IV', in Fox, Celina (ed.), *London – World City*, London and New Haven, Yale University Press and Museum of London, 1992

Daudet, Alphonse, *In the Land of Pain*, trans. and ed. Julian Barnes, Jonathan Cape, London, 2002

d'Aurevilly, Jules Barbey, *Oeuvres Complètes: Le Rideau cramsoisi*, Paris, Gallimard, 1970

David, Saul, *The Prince of Pleasure: The Prince of Wales and the Making of the Regency*, London, Little, Brown, 1998

Day, Roger W., *Decline to Glory: A Reassessment of the Life and Times of Lady Hester Stanhope*, Salzburg University Studies in English Literature Romantic Reassessment, Salzburg and Portland, Oregon, International Specialised Book Services, 1997

de Balzac, Honoré, *'Traité de la vie Elegante'*, *Oeuvres Complètes*, vol. 2, 1830–35, Paris, Louis Conard, 1938

de Contades, G., *'La Fin d'un dandy. George Brummell à Caen'*, in *Bulletin de la Société des antiquaries de Normandie*, Caen, 1954

de Langlade, Jacques, *Brummel ou le Prince des Dandys*, Paris, Presse de la Renaissance, 1984

Delbourg-Delphis, Marylène, *Masculin singulier; le dandyisme et son histoire*, Paris, Hachette, 1985

Deschamps, Colette, *Sur les pas de Brummell à Caen*, Caen, 1996

Donelan, Charles, 'Romanticism and Male Fantasy in Byron's Don Juan', in *A Marketable Vice*, London, Macmillan, 2000

Dumont, E., *La vie caennasie du Consulat au Second Empire*, Caen, Jouan & Bigot, 1929

Ellmann, Richard, *Oscar Wilde*, London, Penguin, 1987

Evans, Mark (ed.), *Princes as Patrons, The Art Collections of the Princes of Wales*, London, Merrell Holberton, National Museums and the Royal Collection 1998

Feldman, Jessica R., *Gender on the Divide: The Dandy in Modernist Literature*, Ithaca, Cornell University Press, 1989

Felstiner, John, and Gollancz, Victor, *The Art of Lies: Max Beerbohm's Parody and Caricature*, London, Gollancz, 1973

Feschott, Jacques, *Sur la tombe de Brummell*, Caen, Société d'Impression de Basse-Normandie, 1932

Figes, Orlando, *Natasha's Dance: A Cultural History of Russia*, London, Allen Lane, 2002

Fillin-Yeh, Susan (ed.), *Dandies: Fashion and Finesse in Art and Culture*, New York, New York University Press, 2001

Fitzmaurice, Edmund George Petty, *Life of William, Earl of Shelburne, afterwards first Marquess of Lansdowne. With extracts from his papers and correspondence,* London, 1875

Foord-Kelcey, Jim and Philippa, *Mrs Fitzherbert and Sons*, Sussex, The Book Guild, 1991

Foreman, Amanda, *Georgiana, Duchess of Devonshire*, London, HarperCollins, 1999

Foulkes, Nick, *The Last of the Dandies, A life of Count Alfred d'Orsay: Passion and Celebrity in the Nineteenth Century*, London, Little, Brown, 2003

Fox, Wilfrid S., *Syphilis and Its Treatment: with special reference to syphilis of the skin*, London, H. K. Lewis, 1920

Franzero, Carlo Maria, *The Life and Times of Beau Brummell*, London, Alvin Redman, 1958

Fraser, Flora, *The Unruly Queen*, London, Macmillan, 1996

Garelick, Rhonda K., *Rising Star, Dandyism, Gender and Performance in the Fin de Siècle*, Princeton, Princeton University Press, 1998

Gathorne-Hardy, Jonathan, *The Public School Phenomenon 697–1977*, London, Hodder & Stoughton, 1977

George, Laura, 'Byron, Brummell and the Fashionable Figure', *Byron Journal*, London, The Byron Society, 1996

Girault, Jean-Marie, *Mon été 44; Les ruins de l'adolescence*, Caen, Editions du Mémorial de Caen, 2004

Gloag, John Edwards, *Georgian Grace. A social history of design 1660–1830*, London, Adam & Charles Black, 1956

Gordon, A. G., *Diagnosis of Oscar Wilde*, Lancet, vol. 357, no. 9263, 14 April 2001

Grant, R. C., *The Brighton Garrisons, 1793–1900*, Worthing, CPO Print, 1997

Hague, William, *William Pitt the Younger*, London, HarperCollins, 2004

Halstead, Ivor, *Bond Street*, Falmouth, Barcliff Advertising & Publishing, 1952

Hamel, Frank, *Lady Hester Lucy Stanhope: a new light on her life and love affairs*, Cassell, London, 1913

Harper, Charles G., *The Brighton Road: old times and new on a classic highway*, London, Chatto & Windus, 1892

Harvey, A., *Sex in Georgian England: Attitudes and Prejudices from the 1720s to the 1820s*, London, Duckworth, 1994

Harvey, John, *Men in Black*, London, Reaktion Books, 1997

Hayden, Deborah, *Pox. Genius, Madness and the Mysteries of Syphilis*, New York, Basic Books, 2003

Hazlitt, William, *The Complete Works of William Hazlitt*, London, J. M. Dent, 1932

Hetenyi, G., 'The terminal illness of Franz Schubert and the treatment of syphilis in Vienna in the eighteen hundred and twenties', *Canadian Bulletin of Medical History*, vol. 3, pp 51–65, 1986

Hibbert, Christopher, *George IV*, London, Penguin, 1972

Hickman, Katie, *Courtesans*, London, Harper Perennial, 2003

Hobhouse, Christopher, *Fox*, London, Constable, 1934

Holland, Vyvyan, Holland, Merlin, and Hart-Davis, Rupert (eds), *Complete Letters of Oscar Wilde*, London, Henry Holt, 2000

Hollander, Anne, *Sex and Suits*, New York, Knopf, 1994

Horne, Alistair, *The Age of Napoleon*, London, Modern Library Edition, 2004

Houlding, J. A., *Fit for Service: The Training of the British Army 1715–1795*, Oxford, Clarendon Press, 1981

Howells, Bernard (ed.), *Baudelaire: Individualism, Dandyism and the Philosophy of History*, Oxford, Oxford University Press, 1996

Jenkin, H. C. Fleeming, *Mrs Siddons as Lady Macbeth and as Queen Katherine*, New York, Dramatic Museum of Columbia University, 1915

Jerrold, Clare, *The Beaux and the Dandies: Nash, Brummell, and D'Orsay, with their courts*, London, 1910

Jones, Christopher, *No. 10 Downing Street: the story of a house*, London, BBC Book, 1985

Jump, John D. (ed.), *Byron, A Symposium*, London, Macmillan, 1975

Kempf, Roger, *Sur le Dandysme, Vie de George Brummell, Balzac, Baudelaire, Barbey d'Aurevilly*, Paris, Union Générale d'Éditions, 1971

Kosofsky-Sedgwick, Eve, *Between Men: English Literature and Male Homosocial Desire*, New York, Columbia University Press, 1985

Langley Moore, Doris, 'Byronic Dress', *Costume, the Journal of the Costume Society*, London, V&A Society, 1971

Langley Moore, Doris, *Lord Byron: Accounts Rendered*, London, John Murray, 1974

Law, Ernest, *The History of Hampton Court Palace*, London, 1897

Lejeune, Anthony, *White's, The First Three Hundred Years*, London, A. & C. Black, 1993

Levillain, Henriette, *L'Esprit Dandy de Brummell à Baudelaire*, Paris, Librairie José Corti, 1991

MacCarthy, Fiona, *Byron, Life and Legend*, London, Faber, 2002

McDowell, Colin, *The Man of Fashion: Peacock Males and Perfect Gentlemen*, London, Thames & Hudson, 1997

MacKie, Erin Skye, *Market à la Mode: Fashion Commodity and Gender in 'The Tatler' and 'The Spectator'*, Baltimore and London, John Hopkins University Press, 1997

mac Liammóir, Micheál, *The Importance of Being Oscar*, Dublin, Dolmen Press, 1963

Mannings, D., and Postle, M., *Sir Joshua Reynolds. A Complete Catalogue of His Paintings*, London, 2000

Marchand, Leslie A., *Byron, A Portrait*, London, The Cresset Library, 1970.

Maxwell-Lyte, H. C., KCB, *A History of Eton College, 1440–1884*, London, Macmillan & Co., 1899, 4th edition 1911.

Melville, Lewis, *The Beaux of the Regency*, London, Hutchinson, 1908

Melville, Lewis, *Beau Brummell, His Life and Letters*, London, 1924

Melvin, John, *Eton Observed: an Architectural Guide to the Buildings of Eton*, Burford, Wysdom, 1998

Millar, Oliver, *Later Georgian Pictures*, London, Phaidon, 1969

Miltoun, Francis, *Rambles in Normandy*, London, Duckworth, 1909

Moers, Ellen, *The Dandy. From Brummell to Beerbohm*, London, Secker & Warburg, 1960

Mollo, John, *The Prince's Dolls*, London, Leo Cooper, 1997

Morel, P., and Quetel, C., *Du Bon Sauveur au CHS: Deux Siècles et Demi de Psychiatre Caennaise*, Paris, Éditions du Luy, 1992

Muir, Edward, and Ruggiero, Guido, *Sex and Gender in Historical Perspective*, trans. Margaret A. Gallucci with Mary M. Gallucci and Carole C. Gallucci, Baltimore, Johns Hopkins University Press, 1990

Munson, James, *Maria Fitzherbert: The Secret Wife of George IV*, London, Constable, 2001

Murray, Venetia, *High Society in the Regency Period*, London, Penguin, 1998

Northcoate, James, *Conversations with James Northcoate, RA, with James Ward on art and artists*, ed. E. Fletcher, London, 1901

Ollard, Richard, *An English Education: A Perspective of Eton*, London, Collins, 1982

Oman, C., *Wellington's Army, 1809–14*, London, Edward Arnold, 1912

Oriel, J. D., *The Scars of Venus, A History of Venereology*, London, Springer-Verlag, 1994

O'Toole, Fintan, *A Traitor's Kiss: The Life of Richard Brinsley Sheridan*, London, Granta, 1997

Page, Frederick (ed.), *Byron, Complete Poetical Works*, Oxford, Oxford University Press, 1970

Parissien, Steven, *George IV, The Grand Entertainment*, London, John Murray, 2001

Peakman, Julie, *Lascivious Bodies, A Sexual History of the 18th Century*, London, Atlantic Books, 2004

Perry, Gill, and Rossington, Michael (eds), *Femininity and Masculinity in Eighteenth Century Art and Culture*, London, Manchester University Press, 1994

Pevsner, Nicolaus, *The Buildings of England: Berkshire*, London, Penguin 1966

Pine, Richard, *The Dandy and the Herald: Manners, Mind and Morals from Brummell to Durrell*, London, Macmillan Press, 1988

Poole, Stanley Lane, *The Life of the Right Hon. Stratford Canning, Viscount Stratford de Redcliffe*, London, Longmans, 1888

Porter, Roy, *Mind-Forg'd Manacles: A History of Madness in England from the Restoration to the Regency*, London, Athlone Press, 1987

Porter, Roy, *Edward Gibbon, Making History*, London, Weidenfeld and Nicolson, 1988

Porter, Roy, *Flesh in the Age of Reason*, London, Penguin, 2003

Porter, Roy, *London, A Social History*, London, Hamish Hamilton, 1994

Price, Curtis, Milhous, Judith, and Hume, Robert D., *Italian Opera in Late Eighteenth-century London*, Oxford, Clarendon Press, 1995

Pushkin, Alexander, *Eugene Onegin*, trans. J. Falen, Oxford, Oxford University Press, 1995

Quennell, Peter, *The Singular Preference, Portraits and Essays*, Washington, Kennikat Press, 1953

Quennell, Peter (ed.), *Genius in the Drawing Room, the Literary Salon in the Nineteenth Century*, London, Weidenfeld & Nicolson, 1980

Quetel, Claude, *History of Syphilis*, trans. Judith Braddock and Brian Pike, London, Polity Press, 1990

Rappaport, Erika Diane, *Shopping for Pleasure: Women in the Making of London's West End*, Princeton, Princeton University Press, *c.* 2000

Renard, Maurice Charles, *Brummell et son ombre, Caen, 1830–1840*, Paris, 1944

Ribiero, Aileen, *The Art of Dress: Fashion in England and France 1750–1820*, New Haven, Yale University Press, 1995

Roe, Frederic Gordon, *The Georgian Child*, London, Phoenix, 1961

Rogers, Samuel, *Recollections of the Table Talk of Samuel Rogers To Which is Added Porsoniana*, London, 1856

Ross, C. J., *Old Bond Street As a Centre of Fashion 1686–1906; A Souvenir of the inauguration of the Business of J & G Ross, 32 Old Bond Street*, London, 1906

Sampson, Geraldine, *The Uncrowned Queen: the story of Maria Fitzherbert*, Brighton, 1971

Schoene-Harwood, Berthold, *Writing Men: Literary Masculinities from Frankenstein to the New Man*, Edinburgh, Edinburgh University Press, 2000

Shiroff, Homai J., *The Eighteenth Century Novel: The Idea of the Gentleman*, London, Edward Arnold, 1978

Simon, Chanoine G. A., *Le Bon Sauveur de Caen*, Caen, Ozanne, 1955

Sitwell, Edith, *The English Eccentrics*, London, Faber, 1933

Société historique du 6e Arrondissement (eds), *Splendeurs et Misères du Dandysme*, Paris, Mairie du 6ème Arrondissement de Paris, 1986

Sontag, Susan, *Susan Sontag Reader*, New York, Farrar, Straus Giroux, 1982

Stokes, John H., Beerman, Herman, and Ingraham Jr, Norman R., *Modern Clinical Syphilology; diagnosis, treatment, case study*, 3rd edition, London, W. B. Saunders, 1944

Stone, Lawrence, *The Family, Sex and Marriage in England, 1500–1800*, London, Penguin, 1977

Tannahill, Reay, *Regency England*, London, Folio Society, 1964

Tenenbaum, Samuel, *The Incredible Beau Brummell*, London and New York, Thomas Yoseloff, 1967

Thackeray, William Makepeace, *The Four Georges*, London, Smith Elder, 1879

Timbs, John, *Clubs and Club Life in London from the Seventeenth Century to the Present Times*, London, 1872

Tweedie, Ethel, *Hyde Park, Its History*, London, Besant, 1930

Vance, Norman, *The Sinews of the Spirit, The Ideal of Christian Manliness in Victorian Literature and Religious Thought*, Cambridge, Cambridge University Press, 1985

Vincent, Leon H., *Dandies and Men of Letters*, London, Duckworth, 1914

Wagner, Peter, *Eros Revived; Erotica of the Enlightenment in England and America*, London, Secker & Warburg, 1988

Wahrman, Dror, *The Making of the Modern Self: Identity and Culture in Eighteenth Century England*, Yale, Yale University Press, 2004

Walden, Sarah, *Whistler and His Mother: Secrets of an American Masterpiece*, London, Gibson Square Books, 2003

Walker, Richard, *The Savile Row Story*, London, Prion, 1988

Wardroper, John, *The Caricatures of George Cruikshank*, London, Gordon Fraser, 1977

Waugh, Nora, *The Cut of Men's Clothes, 1600–1900*, New York, Theatre Arts Books, 1964

Werner, Alex, *London Bodies: The Changing Shape of Londoners*, London, Museum of London, 1998

Wharton, Grace and Philip, *The Wits and Beaux of Society*, London, 1860

Wheatley, H., *A Short History of Bond Street Old and New . . . Also lists of the inhabitants in 1811, 1840 and 1911*, London; Fine Arts Society, 1911

White, Chris (ed.) *Nineteenth Century Writings on Homosexuality, A Sourcebook*, London, Routledge, 1999

Whitwell, J. R., *Syphilis in Earlier Days*, London, H. K. Lewis, 1940

Williams, Andrew P. (ed.), *The Image of Manhood in Early Modern Literature; Viewing the Male*, London, Greenwood Press, 1999

Wilson, A. N., *London: A Short History*, London, Weidenfeld & Nicolson, 2004

Wilson, Frances, *The Courtesan's Revenge: Harriette Wilson, the Woman who blackmailed the King*, London, Faber, 2003

Woodfield, Ian, *Opera and Drama in Eighteenth Century London: The King's Theatre, Garrick and the Business of Performance*, Cambridge, Cambridge University Press, 2001

Woolf, Virginia, *Beau Brummell*, New York, Rimington & Hooper, 1930

Worster-Drought, C., *Neurosyphilis: syphilis of the nervous system*, London, John Bale, 1940

Ziegler, Philip, and Seward, David (eds), *Brooks's: A Social History*, London, Constable, 1991

Novels and Plays

NOVELS
Humphry Clinker, Tobias Smollett, 1771
Evelina, Fanny Burney, 1778
Cecilia, or Memoirs of an Heiress, Fanny Burney 1782
Belinda, Maria Edgeworth, 1801
A Winter in London, T. S. Surr, 1806
Tales of Fashionable Life, Maria Edgeworth, 1809–1812
Sense and Sensibility, Jane Austen, 1811
Pride and Prejudice, Jane Austen, 1813
Patronage, Maria Edgeworth, 1814
Mansfield Park, Jane Austen, 1814
Beppo in London, A Metropolitan Story
   (satire on Byron's *Beppo*), Anon., 1819
The Charms of Dandyism or Living in Style, Olivia Moreland, 1820
The English Spy by Bernard Blackmantle (Charles Westmacott), 1825
Granby, T. H. Lister, 1826
Vivian Gray, Benjamin Disraeli, 1826
Pelham, The Adventures of a Gentleman, Lord E. Bulwer Lytton, 1828
The Exclusives, Lady Charlotte Campbell Bury, 1830
Arlington, A Novel, T. H. Lister, 1832
Godolphin, E. Bulwer Lytton, 1833
Cecil, or the Adventures of a Coxcomb, Catherine Gore, 1841

Plays

The School for Scandal, R. B. Sheridan
The Rivals, R. B. Sheridan
The Heir-at-Law, George Coleman the Younger
The Clandestine Marriage, George Coleman the Elder
Love, Law and Physic, James Kenny
The Poor Gentleman, George Coleman the Younger
A Cure for the Heartache, Thomas Moreton
The Wags of Windsor, George Coleman the Younger
Life in London: The true history of Tom and Jerry, Pierce Egan
A Busy Day, Fanny Burney
Love and Fashion, Fanny Burney
The Modern Theatre, a Collection of Successful Modern Plays, as Acted at the
   Theatre Royal, London, 10 vols., London 1811
Beau Brummell, [sic] *A Play in 4 Acts*, Clyde Fitch, New York, 1908
The Beau, Ron Hutchinson, 2001

Notes on Sources

Full publishing details of the items cited or quoted are provided in the bibliography. Translations are the author's own unless otherwise stated. The rare 1844 first edition of Captain Jesse's *A Life of George Bryan Brummell, Esq.* has been cited whenever possible. Some letters and some of Jesse's own interpolations are quoted from the 1854, 1886 and from the 1927 Navarre Society editions, and the references alter accordingly. The following abbreviations are used in the notes:

ADCC   Archives Départementales du Calvados, Caen
AMC   Archives Municipales de Caen
BL   British Library
DNB   *Dictionary of National Biography*
MLCC   Museum of London Costume Collection
OED   *Oxford English Dictionary*
PRO   National Archives (Kew), Public Records Office
RA   Royal Archives, Windsor Castle

p. vi 'Much more than the cult of': Camus, A., *L'Homme Révolté*; 'Bien plus que le culte de l'individu, le romantisme inaugure le culte du personage.'

AUTHOR'S NOTE
p. ix 'Similarly, the various marquesses': *Burke's Peerage, Baronetage and Knightage*, 107th edition, London, 2003, p. lxxxi.

PROLOGUE
p. xi 'Nothing was lacking. Lustres, candelabra': J. B. d'Aurevilly, trans. D. B. Wyndham Lewis, *The Anatomy of Dandyism*, p. 60n.
p. xii 'Room twenty-nine was at the top': AMC, *Extrait du Plan de l'Hôtel d'Angleterre, Troisième Étage*. The front rooms of the hotel were nos 29–33 in a plan that may post-date Brummell's era at the hotel: it is possible, therefore, that the room numbers had changed over the years. However, room 29 was, in effect, the

only suite of two rooms on the third floor, which tallies with Kathleen Campbell's description from the later 1930s before the hotel was destroyed. 'They still show the room with pride. It seems painfully small and dark, and the tiny dressing room will hold no more than a chest of drawers', K. Campbell, *Beau Brummell*, p. 172.

p. xiii 'Babylon in all its desolation': T. Raikes, *A Portion of his Journal from 1831–1847*, vol. II, pp. 113ff. Letter from Scrope Davies, Monday 25 May 1835: Davies appears to be writing about his own impending symptoms of tertiary syphilis, as diagnosed by Sir George Tuthill.

p. xiv 'Fichet blew out the candles': Details of Brummell's last soirée are taken from a note in d'Aurevilly's *Du Dandysme* as well as from Jesse's *Life*. D'Aurevilly appears to be deploying an anecdote he collected in Caen from the staff of the Hôtel d'Angleterre that he had intended for use in a biography of Brummell; the note spills over three pages of the text. D'Aurevilly, trans. D. B. Wyndham Lewis, *The Anatomy of Dandyism*, pp. 59–61n; Jesse, *A Life of George Brummell, Esq.*, 1927, vol. II, pp. 244–5.

Introduction: Dandy, Dando, Dandum

p. 1 'Dandi, Dando, Dandum': the Dandy Motto (meaningless cod Latin), from *The Dandy Crest*, Cruikshank cartoon, *c.* 1815.

p. 1 'If John Bull turns around': H. Wilson, *Memoirs of Harriette Wilson*, 1831, vol. I, p. 100.

p. 2 'on the Scottish borders': *OED*, seventeenth century, 'Jack-a-dandy'. Diminutive form in Scotland of 'Andrew'. Possible relation to French *dandin*, but considered unlikely.

p. 4 'gentlemen would communicate with one another': C. McDowell, *The Man of Fashion: Peacock Males and Perfect Gentlemen*, p. 45.

p. 5 'To put modern man into white shirt': R. Hutchinson, *Beau Brummell* (Haymarket Theatre, London, 2000, dir. Caroline Hunt). Brummell: 'There was some antique genius who put the Roman into a toga – some Caledonian prankster the Scotsman in his kilt – I, Brummell, put the modern man into pants, dark coat, white shirt and clean linen. I dare say that will be sufficient to secure my fame.'

p. 5 'in the Chanel sense': A. Hollander, *Sex and Suits*, p. 135 and pp. 165ff for further discussion of the impact of Brummell's style of sculpted tailoring on women's fashion, as compared to men's.

p. 5 'he did not have a different': J. B. d'Aurevilly, trans. D. B. Wyndham Lewis, *The Anatomy of Dandyism*, p. 8n.

p. 6 'Even had he wished to marshal': S. Johnson, *Prefaces, Biographical and Critical, to the Works of the English Poets*, pp. 27ff.

p. 6 'What Brummell actually *did*': V. Woolf, *Beau Brummell*, pp. 1–7.

p. 8 'This man possessed such a powerful': J. B. d'Aurevilly, trans. G. Walden, *Who's a Dandy?*, p. 39.

p. 8 'One of the dandy's main characteristics': *ibid.*, p. 40.

p. 9 'If the world is so silly': D. Castronovo, *The English Gentleman*, p. 98.

p. 9 'If three things sum up': J. B. d'Aurevilly, trans. G. Walden, *Who's a Dandy?*, pp. 15–16.

p. 9 'But long before our time . . . *in his person*': d'Aurevilly, trans. D. B. Wyndham Lewis, *The Anatomy of Dandyism*, p. 32 (my italics).

p. 9 'cold, heartless and satirical': H. Wilson, *Memoirs*, 1831, vol. 1, p. 100.

p. 10 'the most admired man': W. Jesse, *A Life of George Brummell Esq.*, 1844, vol. 1, pp. 141ff.

p. 12 'First amongst the fresh': F. Wilson, *The Courtesan's Revenge*, L. Blanch (ed), *Harriette Wilson's Memoirs*; K. Hickman, *Courtesans*; J. Peakman, *Lascivious Bodies*.

p. 13 'experienced venereal specialists at the time': in France it was understood to be passed on between men. See Chapter 11.

p. 16 'satellite to the great': Lord William Pitt Lennox, *Celebrities I Have Known*, vol. II, pp. 92–4.

p. 16 'long list of ruin': T. Raikes, 'Recollections of Thomas Raikes' in R. H. Stoddard (ed.), *Personal Reminiscences*, p. 278.

p. 17 'His writing and army careers': W. Jesse, *Caravan Journeys and Wanderings in Persia, Afghanistan, Turkistan and Beloochistan*, London, 1856 (original manuscript in French); W. Jesse, *History of the Afghans*, London, 1858; W. Jesse, *Plan of Sevastopol*, London, 1839.

p. 17 'More than a third of the 1844': L. Melville, *Beau Brummell*, p. xi. The original letters were in the possession of Mr J. Preston Beecher, vice consul in Le Havre in the 1920s. Brummell's *Male and Female Costume*, dated 1822, was owned by Messrs E. Parsons and Sons, 43 Brompton Road, London, in the 1920s, but sold and published in New York in the 1930s.

p. 18 'It forms the foundation': G. Brummell, *Male and Female Costume*. 'In the fall of 1924 I bought an old manuscript, Male and Female Costume . . . It was listed as an original, unpublished manuscript by G. B. Brummell. It is bound in two volumes and dated 1822': Eleanor Parker in the preface to the 1931 edition. Lewis Melville had noted the existence of the Treatise and been allowed access to it by Messrs E. Parsons for his *Beau Brummell*.

p. 18 'a dish of scandal . . . so hot': W. Jesse, *A Life*, 1886, pp. x–xi.

p. 19 'the model for dandyhood': E. Moers, *The Dandy*, p. 253.

p. 21 'that Frivolity could show': J. B. d'Aurevilly, trans. G. Walden, *Who's a Dandy?*, p. 95.

Part I: Ascendancy, 1778–99

1: BLESSED ARE THE PLACEMAKERS, 1778–86

p. 27 'Blessed are the placemakers': Matthew 5:9 'Blessed are the peacemakers for they shall be called the children of God': misprint from the Geneva Bible, known as a result in the eighteenth century as the 'Whig Bible'.

p. 27 'Walk in gentlemen': R. B. Sheridan, *The School for Scandal*.

p. 27 'Here lies the body': The tablet was legible as late as the 1960s, but is no longer known: it is likely to be one of those worn-down in the area now used for markets and a coffee shop. It may have been moved from its original location after the substantial bomb damage suffered by St James's Church and churchyard in the Second World War.

p. 27 'When the small family vault': Westminster City Archives, microfilm no. 281, 1816, St James's, Piccadilly. '*Benjamin Brummell of Frith Street, buried 1 March 1816 aged 72 years.*'

p. 28 'But he was to find a final': The vaults of St Martin-in-the-Fields where William and Mary Brummell, George's parents, were buried, were already considered dangerously overcrowded with corpses by the mid-eighteenth century. An ordinance of the churchwarden insisted on burial in expensive lead-lined coffins from 1754. All of the bodies were removed in the early twentieth century to be reburied in mass graves in Kent. The crypt is now a coffee shop and shelter for the homeless.

p. 28 'Its population was estimated': Anon., *Picture of London for 1805 Being a Correct Guide to All the Curiosities*, London, 1805, pp. 20–1.

p. 28 'In the road itself, chaise after chaise': Georg Christoph Lichtenberg, German philosopher, writing to a friend in Göttingen, 1775, in R. Porter, *London, A Social History*, p. 145.

p. 30 'Sweet Lavender', 'Cherries Ripe': E. Tweedie, *Hyde Park*, p. 27.

p. 30 'pernicious [by] breathing the streams': T. Smollett, *Humphry Clinker*.

p. 30 'London, or Lonnon': S. Rogers, *Recollections of the Table Talk of Samuel Rogers*, p. 252.

p. 30 'swarm up to London': T. Smollett, *Humphry Clinker*, p. 104.

p. 31 'All provided shelter': J. Macdonald, *Memoirs of an 18th Century Footman*, p. 236. 'Beau' Macdonald, a Scottish footman, was teased for using a silk umbrella in the rain in London: 'If it rained, I wore my fine silk umbrella, then the people would call after me, 'What Frenchman, why do you not get a coach!'

p. 32 'On both sides tall houses': Georg Christopher Lichtenberg, in R. Porter, *London*, p. 145.

p. 33 'immigrant German family': Bruml or Brüml is a name of Czech-German or possibly Bohemian origin, often anglicised to Brummell in the case of nineteenth-century migration to America. The name in the context of eighteenth-century London could just as easily have been a variant of Bramhall or Bramwell, names originating in the north-west of England, concentrated in Cheshire.

p. 35 'I hate your St James's': V. Murray, *High Society in the Regency Period*, p. 91; 'Je desteste votre St James's Street: on n'y voit que des hommes!'

p. 35 'It may have been that the windows': F. Burney, *A Busy Day*, Act 1, Cleveland and Eliza: 'Though nominally an hotel this is in fact a notorious gaming house.' 'Let me hasten from it instantly.' Hern Books, London, adapted for the modern stage by Alan Coveney, premièred, Lyric Theatre, Shaftesbury Avenue, June 2000.

p. 36 'There were two chandlers': Mason's Yard is now the site of the extension annexe of the London Library. Fortnum & Mason is directly north on Piccadilly.

p. 36 *Harris's List of Cyprians*: appeared annually from the late eighteenth and into the nineteenth century. A sort of sexual *Guide Michelin*, it was commonly known as *Harris's List*.

p. 37 'When the courtesan, Harriette Wilson': J. Johnstone, *Confessions of Julia Johnstone*, p. 25.

p. 38 'He had even penned election songs': *DNB*, 1992, Charles Jenkinson (1727–1808).

p. 40 'and in a review': *DNB*.

p. 41 'He may have had accommodation': There have been regular redevelopments of the Treasury-owned buildings around what is now No. 10 Downing Street but was then No. 5, and sometimes referred to as a house in Downing Square. The only direct reference to the Brummells' residence in Downing Street is in a letter of 1780 in which Brummell is described as living 'in the same street'. It is therefore possible that he lived with his wife in one of the houses on the other side of the street, now the back of the Foreign and Commonwealth Office.

p. 42 'The "awkward" house proved': W. Hague, *William Pitt the Younger*, p. 103.

p. 42 'Dr Johnson lobbied': E. Law, *The History of Hampton Court Palace*, vol. 3, pp. 308ff.

p. 43 'Marry his mistress,' F. Bickley (ed.), *The Glenbervie Journals*, vol. 1, p. 122

p. 43 'Maria, William and George Bryan Brummell': Westminster Abbey Archives, St Margaret's Register, Baptisms, 1769–86, July 1778. '2. *George Bryan Brummell S of Wm Esqr by Mary born June 7*'.

p. 43 'She was called Mary': The first name of Mrs Brummell, mother of George Bryan, is often given as Jane. This error seems to have been an early misattribution of the grandmother's name to the mother, or reference to the later frame on the Dance painting, which is wrongly labelled 'Jane Brummell'. The baptismal records for both William and George Bryan are unequivocal: her name was Mary.

p. 44 'a footman to Mr Pelham': BL Add 36 595 no. 305, Whitefoord Papers, vol. IV. Letter of correction to 'your record of Mr Brummell, Ld Norths secretary' from 'Veritas' to Mr Woodfall.

p. 44 'I was myself the channel': Ross Mackay, treasurer and paymaster of the Ordnance in 1763, recorded in a conversation in 1790 at Lord Bessborough's by Sir William Wraxall, in H. Cole, *Beau Brummell*, p. 18.

p. 45 'if you can be of any use': ibid., p. 17.

p. 45 'that there was a hole a foot deep': H. Walpole and J. Wright (ed.), *Letters*, vol. IX, p. 420.

p. 46 'for he is active': H. Cole, *Beau Brummell*, p. 35.

p. 47 'with no particular attention to personal hygiene': C. Hobhouse, *Fox*, pp. 8ff.

p. 48 'in habits of intimacy': W. Jesse, *A Life of George Bryan Brummell Esq.*, 1844, vol. 1, p. 27.

p. 48 'No. 10 or No. 11 Downing Street': BL Add Manuscripts 41335 380m. The records of the Brummell boys' baptisms, kept at Westminster Abbey but from the register of St Margaret's, Westminster, give no place of birth. The records do not contain reference to Maria, or to the Brummell parents' wedding. Although, by 1786, the Brummells seem to have had an address on Abingdon Street, Westminster, they are referred to as living on Downing Street at late as 1780. The likelihood therefore remains that George was born in Downing Street, not Abingdon Street as is sometimes stated. On his certificate of admission to the Masonic Lodge in Caen, his place of birth is cited as 'Witchall, cité de Westminster' (Whitehall).

p. 48 'He was christened, by family tradition': Westminster Abbey Archives, St Margaret's Register, 1769–86, '*February 1777, 27, William Brummell, S of William, by Mary born Janry 30*'.

p. 50 'moral rigorism': R. Porter, *Flesh in the Age of Reason*, p. 278.

p. 51 'The deaths in childhood rise': Westminster City Archives, Register of Burials, St Margaret's, Westminster, St Martin-in-the-Fields, St James's, Piccadilly, 1780–1816.

p. 51 'Only if you survived': A. Werner, *London Bodies, The Changing Shape of Londoners*, p. 90.

p. 51 'Nearly 15 per cent of London children': ibid., p. 91.

p. 51 'It was said that each morning': ibid., p. 86.

p. 51 'always enveloped in a cloud': C. Goede, *A Stranger in England*, p. 81.

p. 53 'grand rackets there': E. Fletcher (ed.), *Conversations with James Northcoate, RA*, p. 78.

p. 53 'Their mother visited the studio on 22 March': D. Mannings, and M. Postle, *Sir Joshua Reynolds. A Complete Catalogue of His Paintings*, Cat. 269.

p. 53 'These two paintings': J. Bryan, *Kenwood*, Cats. 48 and 83.

p. 54 'Mary Robinson, known to history': P. Byrne, *Perdita*, pp. 184ff.

p. 54 '*Ainsi va le Monde*': ibid., p. 183.

p. 56 'a weak, stupid, fat-headed mule': BL Add MSS 36 595 No. 295, Whitefoord Papers, vol. IV.

p. 56 'fixed as the Hanover succession': W. Dowden (ed.), *The Journal of Thomas Moore*, vol. 2, p. 642.

p. 56 'the argument became so heated': F. O'Toole, *A Traitor's Kiss*, p. 171; C. Hobhouse, *Fox*, p. 119.

p. 57 'built only twenty years before': N. Pevsner, *The Buildings of England*, pp. 128–9; *Country Life*, 124 (18 September 1958), pp. 588–91 (25 September 1958), pp. 654–7, (2 October 1958), pp. 714–17. The house may have been built as early as 1759, but a date of 1763 seems more likely.

p. 57 'The house looks a little': Mr James Gladstone, the grandson of Mrs Daisy Fellowes, the last private owner of the house, knew Donnington Grove first at exactly the same age as Brummell, and describes living there as decidedly 'gloomthy' in the winter, despite his grandmother's successes in refurnishing Donnington Grove with a glamorous collection of antiques suitable to the period of the house.

p. 58 'Donnington Grove . . . is built': *Gentleman's Magazine*, December 1772.

p. 58 'Church Speen and Chieveley': J. Roque, *An Accurate Survey of Speen Manor . . . belonging to the Duke of Chandos.*

p. 58 'realigning the old Bagnor and Lambourn': *History of Newbury*, 1839, p. 171.

p. 59 'Chippendale Gothic': N. Pevsner, *The Buildings of England*, pp. 128–9.

p. 59 'applause and laughter': F. Reynolds, *The Life and Times of Frederic Reynolds*, vol. 1, p. 110.

p. 59 'dressed herself in the costume': W. Jesse, *A Life*, 1844, vol. 1, p. 28.

p. 60 'wit and humour': W. Smyth, *Memoir of Mr Sheridan*, p. 65.

p. 60 'There was shooting and riding': Recent archaeological digs as a result of the Newbury bypass (A34) and for English Heritage have uncovered a wealth of musket shot from the period, but also livery buttons predating their mass production in the later nineteenth century. Archaeological reports held at Donnington Grove, pp. 9 and 11. English Heritage, Register of Parks and Gardens, PG1516 30/11/1986.

p. 60 'Donnington Priory, had children of the same age': It was also the childhood home of Thomas Hughes, author of *Tom Brown's Schooldays.*

p. 60 'There were only eight principal bedrooms': Mrs Brita Elmes, who still lives on the estate, recalls the private parties held there by her relative, Mrs Daisy Fellowes. Despite additions of many servants' rooms since Brummell's time, house-parties rarely numbered more than a dozen.

p. 61 'Captain Blackshaw of a local family': George Blackshaw of the Rifle Brigade was painted by Sir Thomas Lawrence (1769–1830) sometime before 1806. Honolulu Academy of Arts.

p. 61 'Maria's move from London': Maria seems to have been unwilling, as much as unable, to contribute to the collections made to help her brother in his later penury, although she wrote to him. See Chapter 16. Her two daughters married well although, tellingly, abroad: such was the scandal their uncle had brought upon the family. Mary Blackshaw became Baroness de Maltzhan and Fanny Blackshaw Countess Linowska.

p. 61 'the flint hermitage by the weir': Inappropriately for a 'hermitage', the flint folly at Donnington is close to the busy small bridge by which visitors arrive. News from London, if the boys were playing at the hermitage, might be delivered there before guests reached the house.

2: THESE ARE NOT CHILDISH THINGS: ETON, 1786–93

p. 63 'These are not childish': M. Campbell, *Lord Dismiss Us*, Heinemann, 1968, after the first letter of Paul of Tarsus to the school at Corinth (13:11): 'When I was a child, I spake as a child, I understood as a child, I thought as a child: but when I became a man, I put away childish things.'

p. 63 'Three times a year': The pub is listed as both on Bishopsgate and Lad Lane. The name is a corruption of the swan with two nicks, the nicking of birds' necks being the signifier of ownership.

p. 64 'beer and pork griskings': BL MSS Loan 70, vol. 1, Scrope Davies Eton Accounts; lean loin of pork, sold with potatoes or loaves 'buttered at a shilling' at the Christopher Inn.

p. 64 'Temple Bar': This arch over the Strand marked the westernmost point of City authority. It was demolished in the late nineteenth century to ease traffic congestion.

p. 65 'Spence's tooth powder': BL MSS Loan 70, vol. 1, Scrope Davies Eton Accounts.

p. 65 'The masters had it shut down': The freehold of the land on which it stood was swapped with the Crown for lands Eton owned – including Primrose Hill.

p. 66 'Of the boys in Brummell's year': Eton College Archive, Eton College Lists, 1792.

p. 66 'Both he and Fox': ibid., *Musae Etonenses*, vol. 1, 1759–1810.

p. 67 'Lags of the school': youngest boys.

p. 67 'We went straight to our Dame's house': H. C. Maxwell-Lyte, *A History of Eton College*, 1911, p. xx.

p. 67 'Instead monies to individual masters': BL MSS Loan 70, vol. 1, Scrope Davies Eton Accounts. Mrs Harrington's bill to Xmas 1796: '2 guineas 2 shillings to Dr Heath and 4 guineas to tutor, Mr Keate.'

p. 68 'Brothers often slept together': Eton College Archive, Occupation of Boarding Houses, Appendix 1.

p. 69 'The only younger boy, marked as Mr King': Eton College Archive, R. A. Austen-Leigh (ed.), *Eton College Register, 1753–1790*, Eton College, 1921.

p. 69 '*Deus pro sua infinia*': *Preces Quotidianae in usum Scholae Collegii Regalis apud Etonam*; trans. author, with Zacharias Rogkotis.

p. 70 'in consequence of a violent cold': Eton College Archive, R. A. Austen-Leigh, *Register*, p. 313.

p. 70 'What is your name and surname?': Eton College Archive, trans. author, with Zacharias Rogkotis.

p. 71 'A 1766 document': H. C. Maxwell-Lyte, *A History of Eton College*, 1911, pp. 294ff. The original 1766 document was then in the possession of Mr L. Vernon Harcourt who acquired it from the Rev. C. C. James, formerly Assistant Master of Eton.

p. 72 '*The Whole Duty of Man*': Samuel Pufendorf's *The Whole Duty of Man according to the Law of Nature* was first published in Latin in 1673. It is unclear whether the Eton boys heard it in its original Latin form, or, as is more likely, in one of its several English translations, but its centrality in the Eton syllabus should not be taken as a sign of radical or anti-clerical leanings. It was frequently cited by preachers.

p. 72 'I give thee most humble': *Preces Quotidianae in usum Scholae Collegii Regalis apud Etonam*.

p. 73 'George was taught French': Mark Anthony Porny (Antoine Pyron du Martre) later went on to found a school for the poor of Eton, and the primary school there still bears his name.

p. 73 'If either found an apt pupil': H. Wilson, *Memoirs of Harriette Wilson*, 1831, vol. 4, p. 208.

p. 73 'Mr John Robert Cozens': John Robert's father, Alexander Cozens, had taught drawing at Eton. Alexander was the natural son of Peter the Great of Russia and a woman from Deptford whom the Tsar had kept as his mistress when in England learning ship-building. Alexander Cozens had some impact on the course of watercolour painting in Britain, as well as tutoring generations of Eton schoolboys. His son, also an artist and drawing-master, declined into madness after 1794.

p. 73 'are supposed to read': H. C. Maxwell-Lyte, *A History of Eton College*, 1911, pp. 294ff.

p. 75 'When the novelist Fanny Burney': Frances Burney, 1752–1840, later Madame d'Arblay; Second Keeper of the Robes to Queen Charlotte, 1786–91.

p. 75 'George became familiar with': Eton College Archive, *In usum scholae Etonensis*. All four plays were issued, with notes, by Thomas Morell and John King.

p. 76 '*Out of the Frying Pan and Into the Fire*': Wren Library, Trinity College, Cambridge.

p. 76 'Otiosus': trans. author, with Zacharias Rogkotis.

p. 77 'If the boys are not able': H. C. Maxwell-Lyte, *A History of Eton College*, 1911, pp. 294ff.

p. 78 'begetting some Scrooples': Lord Byron to Douglas Kinaird, 3 February 1817, T. A. J. Burnett, *The Rise and Fall of a Regency Dandy*, p. 37.

p. 79 'Both Scrope and George': BL MSS Loan 70, vol. 1.

p. 79 'This term's accounts': As today, in the eighteenth century there were three terms to the Eton academic year.

p. 79 'In total that term Scrope': BL MSS Loan 70, vol 1. At the same time, his tutor and the headmaster put in for two guineas, two shillings, and four guineas respectively, a bargain compared to his couture expenses.

p. 80 'knee breeches and stockings': F. G. Roe, *The Georgian Child*, p. 51.

p. 80 'more than common care': W. Jesse, *A Life of George Bryan Brummell Esq.*, 1844, vol. 1, pp. 31–2; vol II, p. 382.

p. 80 'They came top of the list': P. Wagner, *Eros Revived*, pp. 140ff.

p. 81 'An unusual series of documents': Eton College Archive, *Nugae Etonenses*, 1767.

p. 81 'When I went to Eton': *Etoniana Ancient and Modern*, p. 93.

p. 81 '"Cocky" Keate': Dr John Keate, later headmaster, famous for floggings.

p. 81 'little autocrat'. R. Gronow, *Captain Gronow's Last Recollections*, 1866, pp. 53–5

p. 81 'scarce observed a boy': E. Fitzmaurice, *Life of Shelburne*, vol. 1, p. 72.

p. 82 'Boys will stand flogging', *Etoniana Ancient and Modern*, p. 97.

p. 83 '*le vice anglais*': J. Peakman, *Lascivious Bodies*, pp. 240ff.

p. 84 'A boatman cad who had found himself': W. Jesse, *A Life*, vol. 1, pp. 32–3.

p. 84 'My dear fellows, don't': ibid., p. 32.

p. 84 'I was appointed to fag . . . heels in the air': H. C. Maxwell-Lyte, *A History of Eton College*, 1911, pp. 453ff.

p. 85 'Dear Papa, Eton is a very bad place': T. Card, *Eton Established*, Morley Saunders to his father, 1767, p. 102.

p. 85 'Whatever might be the success in after life': S. Poole, *The Life of Stratford Canning*, vol. 1, p. 16.

p. 86 'he was never flogged': W. Jesse, *A Life*, 1844, vol. II, pp. 380ff. (writing to Captain Jesse, but too late for the first volume and therefore included as an appendix to the second).

p. 86 'All these three most happy years': ibid., vol. 1, p. 35.

p. 86 'Dr Goodall': Dr Joseph Goodall, headmaster 1802–9, succeeded Dr Heath.

p. 87 'scoring 0 out and 12 runs': F. Ashley-Cooper, *Eton and Harrow at the Wicket* p. 18. (Ashley-Cooper is further convinced that Brummell became an early member of the MCC but no records survive before 1833.)

p. 87 'I knew Brummell at Eton': W. Jesse, *A Life*, 1844, vol II, p. 382.

p. 88 'roughed about among boys': Maria Edgeworth, in N. Vance, *The Sinews of the Spirit*, p. 11.

p. 88 'whether some miscarriages': V. Knox, *Liberal Education*, p. 354.

p. 88 'from hardy sports': speech by the Chancellor of Cambridge University, 1811, in M. Cohen, 'The Construction of the Gentleman', in Gobel, Schabio and Windisch, *Engendering Images of Man in the Long Eighteenth Century*, p. 226.

p. 89 'Cricket, Fives, Shirking Walls': H. C. Maxwell-Lyte, *A History of Eton College*, 1911, p. 318.

p. 91 'Certainly there was a widening gap': L. Stone, *The Family, Sex and Marriage in England, 1500–1800*, p. 320.

p. 92 'This book expanded exponentially': P. Wagner, *Eros Revived*, p. 17.

p. 92 'lassitude, epilepsy, convulsions': L. Stone, *The Family, Sex and Marriage*, p. 321.

p. 92 'O do away, as the Night': *Preces Quotidianae in usum Scholae Collegii Regalis apud Etonam*. It should be allowed that 'ejaculation' was rarely used in the eighteenth century in its current sense, but the 'transgressions . . . in the night . . . and youthful lusts' make evident the concerns of the prayer-writer.

p. 93 'each will have a bed to himself': L. Stone, *The Family, Sex and Marriage*, p. 322.

p. 93 'Despite the easy tolerance': The only widely accepted study of teenage sexual practice as it relates to masturbation is, of course, from a much later period, but worth noting nonetheless: *The Kinsey Report* more or less denied the possibility of the sublimation of sexuality in adolescence, and found that 95 per cent of boys were sexually active, in terms of masturbation, by their fifteenth birthday.

p. 93 'The literature suggests, for adolescents': J. Peakman, *Lascivious Bodies*, pp. 159ff. This is less the case with the scandals at St Dunstan's School, Stepney, Wadham College and Dulwich College earlier in the century where attempted 'sodomy' by masters upon pupils and students led to a series of court cases. However, what would now be described as sexual abuse stands outside the arena of tolerance in London's *demi-monde*, or among teenage boys at school.

p. 94 'Those very boys': J. Gathorne-Hardy, *The Public School Phenomenon 697–1977*, pp. 172ff.

p. 94 'to assume him a closet homosexual': S. David, *The Prince of Pleasure*, pp. 283–4. David was the first writer to state this emphatically, citing Brummell's flirtatiousness with both sexes and failure to marry.

p. 94 'at the very least "metrosexual" ': S. Parissien, *George IV*, p. 113. Parissien describes Brummell as a 'bitchy queen', and has further noted that in his extensive knowledge of George IV he is unaware of any other close relationship between the prince and a younger man.

p. 94 'Isn't it really rather dangerous': R. Ollard, *A Perspective of Eton*, p. 125, quoting William Johnson Cory, 1860s Eton master, who was himself accused of a homosexual affair.

p. 94 'Our sons should be Spartans': W. Barrow, *An Essay on Education*, vol. 2, pp. 164–5.

p. 95 'The inbuilt forces that made for this last tendency': R. Ollard, p. 123.

p. 96 'The "Captain of Montem", a "blooming youth" ': Eton College Archive, 'On the Montem', in *A New Copy of Verses*, composed by Herbertus Stockhore, 1793. This poem places George Brummell at the 1793 Montem, as it states Harris as the captain:

> *Next the Capt Harris, a blooming youth, I'm told*

The Montem Lists, also in the Eton College Archive, clearly have Brummell as a musician poleman in the same Montem that Harris is captain, even though this Montem is assigned the date, in pencil, 1790.

p. 96 ' "Captain Dyson" spent £205': Eton College Archives, Montem Lists.

p. 97 'Captain Harris netted £1000': ibid.

p. 97 'a triennial event': ibid. Brummell is recorded in the Montem Lists of 1787, 1790 and 1793.

p. 98 'Eton uniform': There was no school uniform at Eton until much later in the nineteenth century. The black uniform in use today is often said to have originated as mourning for George III, but there is no record of this being true.

p. 98 'This first time I saw him': W. Jesse, *A Life*, 1844, vol. II, p. 382.

p. 99 'Social historians have argued': E. Kosofsky-Sedgwick, *Between Men*, pp. 1–5 and pp. 83ff.

p. 99 'The Younger Brother's Claim': G. Brummell, in L. Melville, *Beau Brummell*, pp. 142–3.

p. 101 ' "George," said I, "What's the matter?" ': W. Jesse, *A Life*, 1854, vol. 1, p. 27.

3: THE WORLD IS VERY UNCHARITABLE, 1793–4

p. 102 '[A young man] may commit an hundred': J. Johnstone, *Confessions of Julia Johnstone*, pp. 52–3.

p. 102 'Julia Johnstone, née Storer': The name 'Mrs Johnstone' was taken by Julia in her later life with Colonel Cotton. She was never married and there was never a Mr Johnstone.

p. 103 'What a fortune is my mother's!': J. Johnstone, *Confessions*, p. 10.

p. 104 'I was handed out of the carriage': ibid., p. 12.

p. 104 'Julia, like George, first saw the modish uniform': The barracks at Hampton Court Palace, on the approach to the main gate from Hampton Bridge, remain the oldest continuously inhabited barracks in the country.

p. 105 'The Brummell family had moved from Suite XVII': Suite XVII was given to Thomas Tickell, brother-in-law of R. B. Sheridan; he either fell or jumped from it in 1793.

p. 105 'Each grace-and-favour apartment found a way to improvise': The original Tudor kitchens have recently been restored and are used again as kitchens. The Georgian kitchens, built away from the palace at the end of the Tennis Court Lane, remain a separate residence.

p. 106 'He is an old flame of mine': H. Wilson, *Memoirs of Harriette Wilson*, vol. 1, p. 86.

p. 106 'a little Eau de Portugal': ibid., p. 103. Like eau-de-Cologne, eau-de-Portugal was a light aftershave.

p. 107 'For never handsome gypsy drew in': H. Luttrell, *Advice to Julia*, p. 2.

p. 108 'I never had the honour to refuse': J. Johnstone, *Confessions*, p. 64.

p. 108 'Julia and I are very old friends': H. Wilson, *Memoirs*, vol. 1, p. 227.

p. 109 '*To Julia*. Since you will needs my heart possess': Thomas Sheridan, in Jesse, *A Life*, and L. Melville, *Beau Brummell*, pp. 295–6.

p. 109 'Unhappy child of indiscretion': This poem, written in Brummell's hand in his Album, is also attributed to Georgiana, Duchess of Devonshire. The sexes reversed in the fourth stanza, she sent the poem as a comment on her illegitimate child (born in 1792) at a later date. Of Brummell and Georgiana, who was the originator and who the copyist is a matter for conjecture. Attributed to Georgiana, Duchess of Devonshire: A. Foreman, *Georgiana*, p. 267; to Brummell, W. Jesse, *A Life of George Bryan Brummell Esq.*, 1844, vol. 1, pp 190–1.

p. 110 'A hussar's cap and feather': J. Johnstone, *Confessions*, p. 11.

p. 110 'In early March 1793': Westminster City Archives, St Martin-in-the-Fields, Register of Burials, vol. 115, March 1793.

p. 111 'a year and a day exactly': ibid., March 1794.

p. 112 'The jewels of a metropolitan beauty': The diamonds were handed down through the family, and a set of necklace and earrings, almost certainly once Mary (Richardson) Brummell's and then Maria Blackshaw's, was sold at Sotheby's in June 1998. *Sotheby's Important Jewels*, 18 June 1998, p. 158.

p. 113 'The will, however, makes no mention': H. Cole, *Beau Brummell*, p. 227.

p. 114 'In May 1794, after the Easter holidays': Oriel College Archives, 1768–1809, S II K 14, Easter Term 1794. 'William Brummell. Mr White, 6 Lincolns Inn, Commoner, May 27. George Brummell. Commoner. May 27.' These two entries are consecutive in the register, which may explain why there are no contact details for parents or guardians in George's entry.

p. 114 'his contemporary, the Marquess of Worcester': A. Clark (ed.), *The Colleges of Oxford*, p. 120. 'Henry, Fourth Duke of Beaufort [previously Marquess of Worcester] founded four exhibitions [scholarships] for the counties of Gloucester, Monmouth and Glamorgan.'

p. 114 'I spent fourteen months at Magdalen': R. Porter, *Edward Gibbon, Making History*, p. 35.

p. 114 'the discipline of the university': J. Harris, *Diaries and Correspondence of James Harris, First Lord Malmesbury*, vol. 1, p. ix.

p. 115 'consumed a considerable quantity of midnight oil': T. H. Lister, *Granby*, vol. I, pp. 108ff.

p. 115 'was more celebrated, however, for his systematic': ibid., pp. 106–8.

p. 115 'appeared on the screen': The screens that separate the hall from the kitchens in many Oxford and Cambridge colleges were and remain the site of noticeboards for official and unofficial 'publications'.

p. 115 'turned a tame jackdaw, with a pair of bands': Like modern English barristers' bands, the sign of academic standing, as worn by Oxford undergraduates and academics.

p. 116 'two men of — Hall': St Edward's Hall was considered socially inferior.

p. 116 'consummate tuft hunter': Social climber. Titled Oxbridge undergraduates wore a modified academic gown and a mortar-board with a gold tassel, known as a 'tuft'. D. Langley Moore 'Byronic Dress', in *Costume*, V&A Society, 1971, no. 5, p. 3.

p. 116 'George was at Oriel through the Easter term': Oriel College Archive, Buttery Book 1793–4. Both William and George are recorded from 23 May–4 July; neither is recorded in the weeks covering the vacation. Buttery Book for 1794–5: William is recorded from 17 October–12 December 1794. A space was left for George's account from 17 October–7 November, but no entries were made. In the following term William's entry for 23 January 1795 is blank, and there is no record of any Brummell for or after 30 January.

p. 117 '*The Angry Child*': *The Times*, 21 and 22 May 1816. Christie's advertisement for the sale of Brummell's possessions: '. . . and in fine condition, the much-admired original drawing, *The Angry Child*, and others by Holmes, Christal, Dewindt and Stephanoff . . .'

p. 117 'Go—! Triumph securely – the treacherous vow': J. McGann, *Lord Byron: The Complete Poetical Works*, vol. 3, p. 393. Once thought to be addressed to Lady Frances Wedderburn Webster by Byron, critical opinion now favours Lady Caroline Lamb as the 'woman once fallen'. 'There is one MS copy in Texas (MS T) . . . It was first published by Captain Jesse in his *Life of Beau Brummell* 1886 [*sic* – actually 1844] from an album in which Brummell had copied it. It was published again by H. M. Combe Martin, *Notes of Queries*, January 1967, 26, from a manuscript owned by him in the hand of Lady Anne Hardy (MS H) who copied it from a MS . . . The supposition made in MS H that the poem was addressed to Lady Frances Wedderburn Webster is not correct . . . The poem was actually written in Sept 1812 and its subject is Lady

Caroline Lamb with whom Byron was at that time breaking off relations.' Captain Jesse was correct in stating in 1844 that this poem had not been published anywhere else. Jesse, *A Life*, London, 1844, vol. 1, p. 307.

4: THE PRINCE'S OWN 1794-9

p. 119 'You all no doubt have heard': *The Hussars, a New Song, attributed to a Field Officer of The Marines the Accompaniment for the Piano Forte by the Band of the Tenth*, London, *c.* 1825.

p. 120 'every kind of uniform': W. Thackeray, *The Four Georges*, p. 92.

p. 120 'a bottle green and claret-coloured': *Bon Ton Magazine*, August 1791.

p. 121 'Bastille of Whalebone': MLCC A27042. Donated by A. T. Barber in 1924. The prince's waist expanded eventually to over fifty inches (125 centimetres).

p. 121 'the compleat uniforms, accoutrements': A. Aspinall (ed.), *The Correspondence of King George IV, 1812–1830*, vol. 4, p. 298.

p. 121 'My husband understands how a shoe': V. Cumming, 'Pantomime and Pageantry', in C. Fox (ed.), *London*, p. 40.

p. 122 'I have no option but to lead': Aspinall (ed.), *Correspondence of George IV*, vol. 3, pp. 38 and 47.

p. 123 'cornetcy – the first rank of commissioned officer': The rank was abolished in 1871, but until then it was a cornet who held the regimental banner.

p. 123 'soon as he began to mix in society': R. Gronow, *Captain Gronow's Last Recollections*, p. 59.

p. 124 'acquitted himself to the Prince's satisfaction': W. Jesse, *A Life of George Bryan Brummell Esq.* 1844, p. 40.

p. 124 'He . . . displayed there all that the Prince of Wales': J. B. d'Aurevilly, trans. D. B. Wyndham Lewis, *The Anatomy of Dandyism*, p. 21.

p. 125 'Sir John Macpherson, a close associate': A. Aspinall (ed.), *The Correspondence of George Prince of Wales, 1770–1812*, vol. 2, p. 24. 'PS 20 July I am now with our friend Mr Brommell [*sic*] at Donington [*sic*] Grove near Newbury on my way to Bath.' Sir John Macpherson to Captain J. W. Payne, Letter 463.

p. 125 'to buy a cornetcy in the 10th Light Dragoons': A. P. C. Bruce, *The Purchase System in the British Army, 1660–1871*, p. 41ff. The money was held by the Government against an officer's good behaviour. The purchase system of ranks in the British Army was not abolished until 1871. The prices were first fixed and published in 1720. By 1854 the average entry commission – cornet or ensign – stood at over £1000.

p. 125 'It would coast him £735': C. Oman, *Wellington's Army, 1809–1814*, pp. 198–201, 'General Regulations for the Army, 12 August 1811'. The prices were later changed, but had been standard for many years.

p. 125 '"Tarleton" helmet"': P. Byrne, *Perdita*, p. 180. Tarleton and Mary Robinson were lovers. They met in Joshua Reynolds's studio on the same day that Mary Robinson met three-year-old George Brummell.

p. 126 'They made all the prince's uniforms': RA GEO/29408, 29410, 29417, 29419. The prince bought 10th Light Dragoons outfits from Schweitzer and Davidson in the 1790s and into the 1800s, but switched his allegiance to Jonathan Meyers, possibly at Brummell's instigation, and even occasionally ordered uniforms from John Weston, RA GEO/29431.

p. 126 'single uniform bill of £399 7s. 6d.': W. Carman, *British Military Uniforms*, p. 121.

p. 126 'and the prince's uniforms . . . over £344 each': RA GEO/29457, J. Meyer 1807: complete Hussar uniform.

p. 127 'It was the most expensive part': RA/GEO 29337, Schweitzer and Davidson accounts, 1803.

p. 127 'Extra superfine blue cloth Polony': RA GEO/29408, J. Meyer.

p. 128 'the White Horse cellar': C. Harper, *The Brighton Road*, p. 4. The site is now occupied by the Ritz Hotel.

p. 128 'Only four passengers could ride inside': ibid., pp. 4 and 23ff.

p. 130 'I need not, I trust, add . . . composed of Men of Fashion': J. Mollo, *The Prince's Dolls*, p. 16.

p. 130 'The officers of those days': U. Macnamara, *The British Army*, pp. 38ff.

p. 131 'The reputation of being . . . left the table': ibid.

p. 131 'the life and soul of the mess': W. Jesse, *A Life*, 1886, vol. 1, p. 39.

p. 131 'powers of mimicry were so extraordinary': C. Hibbert, *George IV*, p. 63.

p. 131 'all more or less distinguished': G. and P. Wharton, in L. Melville, *Beau Brummell*, p. 32.

p. 132 'Tik nuttis': H. Wilson, *Memoirs of Harriette Wilson*, 1929, p. 331. 'Take notice! The word "draw" is only a caution! At the word "swords" you draws them out, taking a firm and positive grip on the hilt. At the same time, throwing the sheath smartly backwards, thus: "DRAW SWORDS!"'

p. 132 'to teach their Subalterns their duty': J. Houlding, *Fit for Service: The Training of the British Army 1715–1795*, pp. 272ff.

p. 133 'Whose horse is that?': Slade MSS. Notes on the life and career of Sir John Slade, compiled by his son Wyndham Slade, *c.* 1916 (Col. Mitford Slade, 1972).

p. 134 'a transparent painting of His Royal Highness's': *Public Advertiser*, July 1794.

p. 135 'No, Your Highness, for alas, His Grace': J. Munson, *Maria Fitzherbert*, p. 253.

p. 136 'If, as seems most probable, he contracted a venereal disease': *Lancet*, 1846, vol. I, p. 703; vol II, p. 369. The *Lancet* claimed that 25 per cent of military recruits were already infected with venereal disease, but that a full third of the Merchant Navy was infected, causing particular concern to garrisons in close contact with ports and sea traffic.

p. 136 'are the fertile hotbeds': G. Dartnell, 'On the Prevalence and Severity of Syphilis in the British Army', *British Medical Journal*, 28 April 1860.

p. 137 'This marriage was illegal': The 1772 Royal Marriages Act forbade marriage by members of the Royal Family, under the age of twenty-six, without the consent of the King and Privy Council, and marriages to Roman Catholics were illegal for the House of Hanover after the 1701 Act of Settlement.

p. 137 'treated as a queen': J. Croker, *The Correspondence and Diaries of the late John Wilson Croker*, p. 125.

p. 137 'She also attended with them the race meetings': J. Munson, *Maria Fitzherbert*, p. 253.

p. 138 'To complicate matters, Mrs Fitzherbert': J. and P. Foord-Kelcey, *Mrs Fitzherbert and Sons*, pp. 48ff.

p. 138 'In a scurrilous rating of the attributes': 'Countess of Jersey Beauty: 11, Figure: 6, Elegance: 1, Wit: 2, Sense: 0, Grace: 11, Expression: 12, Sensibility: 5, Principles: 0' scored out of 20. 'Scale of the Bon Ton', in *Morning Post*, July 1776.

p. 138 'In London society she was known as "Lucretia" ': R. Edgcumbe (ed.), *The Diary of Frances, Lady Shelley 1787–1817*, p. 37.

p. 139 'in which she was to have an important situation': recollections of Lord Stourton, in J. Munson, *Maria Fitzherbert*, p. 259.

p. 139 'the union between this fashionable pair': *Bon Ton Magazine*, July 1794, p. 194.

p. 140 'indelicate manners, indifferent character': Wellington to Lady Salisbury, F. Fraser, *The Unruly Queen*, p. 43.

p. 141 'Does the prince always behave like this': Harris, *Correspondence of First Lord Malmesbury*, vol. 3, p. 218.

p. 141 'whose virtues no less': *Bon Ton Magazine*, April 1795, p. 39.

p. 142 'passed the greatest part of his bridal night': Lady Charlotte Bury, in S. David, *Prince of Pleasures*, p. 168; Thackeray, *Four Georges*, p. 111; Fraser, *The Unruly Queen*, p. 62.

p. 142 'constantly drunk, sleeping': Caroline, Princess of Wales, as reported by Lord Minto; A. Aspinall (ed.), *Correspondence of George Prince of Wales*, vol. 2, p. 460.

p. 144 'On returning, they found that the two officers': R. Grant, *The Brighton Garrisons, 1793–1900*, p. 15.

p. 145 'The scene was considered so exceptional': ibid., pp. 17ff.

p. 145 'the square thing'; 'Just the thing': His catchphrase, according to Harriette Wilson.

p. 146 'keep up his expensive uniform and horse appointments': A. Bruce, *Purchase System in the British Army*, p. 73.

p. 146 'gave them an interest in the country': William Wyndham, in ibid., p. 88.

p. 147 'The fact is, Your Royal Highness': W. Jesse, *A Life*, 1844, vol. 1, p. 46. Jesse includes the note: ' "This conversation about Manchester" observes Brummell's friend Jack Robinson, "is utterly unworthy of him and impossible; he was incapable of it." All I [Jesse] can say is that Brummell told this anecdote to my friend Wells and other persons at Caen. But it is possible his [true] reason for leaving the 10th was that the expense exceeded his means, and that he wanted the money with which he purchased his commissions.'

p. 148 'Hussar dress – outlandish, outrageous': J. Mollo, *The Prince's Dolls*, p. 33.

p. 148 'One of his brother officers': W. Jesse, *A Life*, 1844, vol. 1, p. 46.

p. 149 'The future George IV': J. B. d'Aurevilly, trans. D. B. Wyndham Lewis, *The Anatomy of Dandyism*, p. 21.

p. 149 'violent intimacy': T. Raikes, *Reminiscences*, p. 270.

p. 149 'Indeed, one biographer of the prince regent': S. David, *Prince of Pleasures*, pp. 283–4. 'The obvious inference is that Brummell was homosexual. He certainly enjoyed displaying his naked body to morning callers (including the Prince).'

p. 150 'He was liberal, friendly . . . always living': Raikes, *Reminiscences*, p. 278.

Part II: 'A Day in the High Life', 1799–1816

p. 151 'I will attempt to sketch the day': C. Goede, *A Stranger in England*, vol. 1, pp. 88–9.

5: DANDIACAL BODY

p. 157 'A Dandy is heroically consecrated': T. Carlyle, *Sartor Resartus*, p. 279.

p. 157 'Amongst the curious freaks of fortune': R. Gronow, *Reminiscences of Captain Gronow*, 1862, p. 56.

p. 157 '£20,000 . . . a middle figure of £30,000': W. Jesse, *A Life of George Bryan Brummell Esq.*, 1844, vol. 1, p. 51; Jesse claimed that the money had 'accumulated during his minority [and] amounted to thirty thousand pounds'.

p. 157 'His brother William': William Brummell married Miss Anne Daniell, daughter of James Daniell of the East India Company, in 1800.

p. 158 'The house he moved into in 1799': For an examination of Number 4 Chesterfield Street before major renovations in 2004–5 I am indebted to Her Grace the Dowager Duchess of Devonshire, and also Mrs Iris Armitage and Strutt & Parker Estate Agents. The house belonged to Anthony Eden until 1952, then to the 11th Duke of Devonshire until it was sold in 2004.

p. 158 '(since demolished)': Devonshire House was pulled down in 1925. The site was redeveloped but includes the current north entrance of Green Park Underground station.

p. 158 'enclose[d] more intelligence': George Selwyn, quoted in R. Tannahill, *Regency England*, p. 36.

p. 159 'a fine Arab stallion named Stiletto': 'Stiletto': a short dagger considered in eighteenth century a Moorish weapon (OED). ie probably an Arab stallion. See Lady Hester Stanhope to George Bryan Brummell, Chapter 7.

p. 160 'Make it two hundred guineas': £150 a year was a reasonable but not exorbitant wage for a valet: the Royal Archives show that many of the Royal Household's valets earned less, although they had substantial perks on pitch-and-platter days (anniversaries of royal events). R. Gronow, *Reminiscences*, 1862, p. 222.

p. 160 'the best works of the best authors': ibid., p. 62.

p. 160 'Amongst the books were some good historical works': W. Jesse, *A Life*, 1844, vol. 1, p. 348.

p. 161 'a bet that he would be married': 'Mr Brummell bets Mr Osborne twenty guineas that (Mr B) is married before him (Mr O)': 'Paid' is recorded against Brummell's name. White's Betting Record, 1798–1800, White's Club, St James's Street (London Metropolitan Archives).

p. 161 'and every part of his body': This last observation is from Caen gaol, so may relate to Brummell's regime to keep the symptoms of his syphilis at bay – but he bathed religiously from an early age. W. Jesse, *A Life*, 1844, vol. II, p. 203

p. 161 'trinkets or gew-gaws': W. Pitt Lennox, in L. Melville, *Beau Brummell*, p. 46.

p. 162 'He exfoliated his body all over': Both the exfoliation and the milk regime may have been added to Brummell's elaborate toilette only after he had suffered an initial skin outbreak associated with his syphilis. W. Jesse, *A Life*, 1844, vol. II, p. 60.

p. 162 'Kings by birth were shaved by others': S. Rogers, *Recollections*, p. 274.

p. 162 'The Dandiacal Body bought cakes': BL MSS Loan 70, vol. 4, Spike 3, 200.

p. 162 'One modern barber': Geo. Trumper, Jermyn Street and Mayfair.

p. 163 'was the first who revived and improved': W. Jesse, *A Life*, 1844, vol. 1, p. 61.

p. 163 'test their fitness for use': ibid.

p. 163 'The collars on Brummell's shirts': MLCC 77.97, 2 1052.

p. 163 'The first *coup d'archet*': W. Jesse, *A Life*, 1844, vol. 1, p. 60.

p. 163 'The [neckcloth] oft bespeaks the man': *Necklothitania*, 1818, p. 3.

p. 164 'More tellingly, the arrangement of No. 4 Chesterfield Street': There was a small servants' staircase behind the main grand staircase in an area now utilised by a dumb waiter and a series of cupboards and wardrobes.

p. 165 'My neckcloth, of course forms my principal care': L. Melville, *Beau Brummell*, p. 47.

p. 165 'Lord Byron was an assiduous disciple': D. Langley Moore, 'Byronic Dress', in *Costume*, pp. 1–4.

p. 165 'As a sample of the necessities': E. M. Butler (ed.), *A Regency Visitor*, p. 215.

p. 166 'half a nail': A 'nail' was two and a quarter inches, or a sixteenth of a yard. Its use denoted an expensive, often embroidered, fabric.

p. 166 'finest Irish muslin or cambric': MLCC 77.97 and 2 1052: shirts made for George IV, some dating from his regency or before. The shirts have pleated fine Irish muslin over the chest.

p. 166 'Lord Byron also required six nightcaps': D. Langley Moore, *Lord Byron, Accounts Rendered*, p. 485.

p. 166 'Thomas Jefferson . . . Thomas Coutts': MLCC and Monticello Collection, University of Virginia, Charlottesville, VA, USA.

p. 167 'once irredeemably sweat-stained': MLCC 77.97 and 2 1052. One white waistcoat belonging to the regent from 1817 also has underarm crescents: 38.294/4.3 and 2.

p. 167 'Even so, it was an expensive business': BL MSS Loan 70, vols 3 and 4, tailor bills: 111 and 245.

p. 167 'It can hardly be imagined how political events': *Necklothitania*, p. 4.

p. 168 'The character of the classical body': C. Char, in G. Perry and M. Rossington (eds), *Femininity and Masculinity in Eighteenth Century Art and Culture*, p. 154.

p. 168 'He was tall, well made': T. Raikes, *Reminiscences*, p. 277.

p. 168 'He was about the same height': W. Jesse, *A Life*, 1844, vol. I, p. 52.

p. 168 'the Apollo Belvedere': Named after its location, the Belvedere Courtyard (now part of the Pio-Clementine Museum at the Vatican), the statue was placed there by Pope Julius II in 1503. It is seven feet (over two metres) tall but appears of perfect proportion and 'lifesize'. *Vatican Museum Guide*, 2002.

p. 169 'hero in wool': A. Hollander, *Sex and Suits*, p. 88.

p. 170 'He has shot his arrow': J. Moore, *View of Society and Manners in Italy*, vol. 1, pp. 501–2.

p. 170 'His is indeed a strong expression': ibid.

p. 170 'If I was a woman': L. Temple, *A Short Ramble Through Some Parts of Italy and France*, pp. 34–5.

p. 171 'Dressed form became an abstraction of nude form': A. Hollander, *Sex and Suits*, p. 89.

p. 172 'I have heard sensible people say that a man': L. Temple, *A Short Ramble*, p. 36.

p. 173 'Thanks to the descriptions of Brummell': if it is taken as a principle that the Apollo Belvedere might also fit contemporary models of ideal proportion.

p. 173 'After four years of almost constant riding': Berry Brothers' Great Scales Ledger, no. 3 St James's Street, London. George Brummell Esq.: 38 entries from 23 January 1798 to 6 July 1815. His brother William is also recorded, but only twice. William was not as large as George, weighing only nine stone nine (135 pounds or 63 kilograms) in his shoes in 1812.

p. 173 'Boots like these in a private collection': Cosprop, Rochester Mews, London. Hessian boots, made from an original pair. Size 9. 2 lbs precisely.

p. 173 'the currently accepted scale of ideal weight': height/weight tables, G. G. Harrison, *Annals of Internal Medicine*, 1985, no. 103, pp. 489–94.

p. 173 'a full six inches taller than the average': Average height for males in late-eighteenth-century London was around five foot six (or 168 cm – Brummell stood around 183 cm.) A. Werner, *London Bodies*, p. 86.

p. 174 'having well-fashioned the character of a gentleman': H. Wilson, *Memoirs*, 1825, vol. 1, p. 101.

p. 174 'Surviving examples': MLCC. Silk jersey breeches, A9243, 1800; buff leather breeches, A 15048, 1805; coats: 53.101/23 1810, 33.119 1800, A 9244 (Sir Gilbert Heathcoat) 1795.

p. 175 'designed to fit a body trained': C. Breward, *Fashioning London*, p. 23.

p. 175 'Evening breeches, by contrast': MLCC. Black silk-jersey evening or court knee breeches, belonging to Sir Gilbert Heathcoat, A9243.

p. 176 'The prince became a devotee': G. Cruikshank, *His Most Gracious Majesty King George IV*, British Museum Prints and Drawings.

p. 177 'Keep your mind free from all violent affections': E. Bulwer Lytton, *Pelham*, pp. 115–17.

p. 177 'The Father of Modern Costume': Max Beerbohm, in E. Moers, *The Dandy*, p. 33.

p. 178 'the man who is rich and idle': C. Baudelaire, *The Painter of Modern Life and Other Essays*, pp. 26–7.

p. 179 'I give it to you not for taking me': R. Gronow, *Reminiscences of Captain Gronow*, 1862, p. 227.

p. 179 'his growing repertoire of impersonations': ibid., p. 197.

p. 179 'I had more than a touch of dandyism', L. Marchand, *Byron, A Portrait*, p. 146.

p. 180 'far back in his Eton days': E. Chancellor, *The Memorials of St James's Street Together with the Annals of Almack's*, p. 251.

p. 180 'Ah, Byng – a family vehicle': Jesse, *A Life*, 1844, vol. 1, p. 117.

p. 180 'Brummell set the fashion, Ball Hughes': W. Pitt Lennox, *Celebrities I Have Known*, p. 101.

p. 181 'Je wouldrai si je couldrai': Melville, *The Beaux of the Regency*, vol, 2, pp. 74–7.

p. 181 'The manners of the Dandies': T. Raikes, *Reminiscences*, p. 278.

p. 182 'By early in the nineteenth century': RA GEO/29388, John Weston accounts, 1805: 2 dozen white waistcoats £43 4–.

p. 182 'buff and black pantaloons': RA GEO/29392, Schweitzer and Davidson accounts, 1805: '6 buff cassimere waistcoats, 9 pair of breeches in drab or white nankin [*sic*] . . . cassimere stays, 2 pairs white stocking pantaloons. Repairing and new silk pockets to a pair of muslin trowsers [*sic*] 2 pairs Callico trowsers [*sic*] with silk lining.'

p. 182 'relining and repairing . . . off-white pantaloons': RA GEO/29398, 29399, 29402, 29405, 29406. Nearly all the tailors' bills include some mending and altering, but this increases markedly after 1800.

p. 182 'The physiognomy of both sexes': C. A. G. Goede, *A Stranger in England*, vol. II, pp. 84ff.

p. 183 'that bright morning': M. Beerbohm, *Dandies and Dandies*, in S. C. Roberts (ed.), *The Incomparable Max*, pp. 12–13.

p. 183 'He was envied and admired': Lady Hester Stanhope, in W. Jesse, *A Life*, 1844, vol. 1, p. 143.

p. 183 'She saw, therefore, with surprise': T. Lister, *Granby*, vol. I, pp. 88ff.

p. 184 'struck by the misapplication of this title': Rev. G. Crabbe, in Jesse, *A Life*, 1844, vol. 1, p. 68.

p. 184 'similar to that of every other gentleman': ibid., vol. 1, p. 46.

6: SIC ITUR AD ASTRA: BESPEAKING THE WEST END

p. 186 'Turning the corner of a lane': T. Carlyle, *Sartor Resartus*, p. 297.

p. 186 'the umbrella being a novelty': J. Macdonald, *Memoirs of an 18th Century Footman*, p. 236.

p. 187 'And single-handedly he began the decimation': R. Grant, *Ghost Riders: Travels with American Nomads*, London, 2003, pp. 112ff. 'Brummell popularised a new style of beaver felt hat, which spread from London to Paris, Vienna, St Petersburg, New York, and all over the civilised world, which decimated beaver populations in Europe and raised the price of beaver pelts, and so enabled the Rocky Mountain fur trade.'

p. 187 'Not only might it bring the Prince of Wales': Approximately £35,000 in today's money. RA GEO/29331–29347.

p. 188 'boxing match tickets': BL MSS Loan 70, vol. 2/26.

p. 188 'gridlocked by the press of carriages': This was one of the main practical reasons for the construction of Regent Street.

p. 188 'At one [o'clock] the streets begin': C. A. G. Goede, *A Stranger in England*, pp. 76–8.

p. 189 'He died worth £120,000': H. Cole, *Beau Brummell*, p. 80.

p. 189 'Anything from coaches to country estates': H. Wheatley, *Bond Street Old and New*, London, 1911, pp. 29ff.

p. 190 'The real embalmed head of Oliver Cromwell': *Morning Chronicle*, 18 March 1799. Cromwell's body was disinterred after the Restoration in 1661, and his head was impaled on a spike until at least 1684. The head on display at Mead's in 1799 seems to have had valid provenance, having been bought by James Cox for his private museum and sold on to the Hughes brothers of Bond Street in the 1790s for £230. It was finally buried at Sidney Sussex College, Cambridge, Cromwell's college, in 1960.

p. 190 'dazzled my eyes': Marquis de Vermont, *London and Paris, or, Comparative Sketches*, pp. 20–1.

p. 190 'toothpick between his teeth': G. Coleman the Younger, *The Heir-at-Law*, Act II.

p. 190 'Glasshouse Street': Glasshouse Street, west of Regent Street, is now Vigo Street and Burlington Gardens.

p. 190 'Mr Sheridan had set up home there': The house is now the headquarters of the couturier Hardy Amies. An internal window is preserved on the central staircase, from which Sheridan would spy approaching visitors and claim to be out if they were creditors.

p. 191 'The Prince wears superfine': 'Sir John . . . a good-humoured baronet and brother Etonian . . .' related this story to Jesse: W. Jesse, *A Life*, 1844, vol. 1, p. 48.

p. 191 'a-shopping': N. Waugh, *The Cut of Men's Clothes, 1600–1900*, p. 117.

p. 192 'it was a gentleman's world': Savile Row tailor Tom Gilby, in R. Walker, *The Savile Row Story*, p. 65.

p. 192 'The first, Schweitzer and Davidson': Savile Row, before the creation of

Regent Street in the early nineteenth century, had more the feel of one of Soho's small alleyways. It was a dead end until, with the redevelopment of the area, Regent Street cut through to the east.

p. 192 'He bought his hats on St James's Street': Westminster City Archives, rate books, Fribourg and Treyer ledgers, Lock's Hatters, St James's Street, ledgers.

p. 193 '[This] tailor was of course a foreigner': T. Hook, *Sayings and Doings*, 2nd series: *The Sutherlands, The Man of Many Friends, Doubts and Fears, Passion and Principle*, p. 194.

p. 193 'a small fortune invested': A. Adburgham, *Silver Fork Society*, p. 130.

p. 193 '£100,000': ibid., p. 131. Stultz the tailor was rumoured to have retired on this sum.

p. 194 'When he stopped to be measured': T. Surr, *A Winter in London*, vol. II, pp. 82–3.

p. 194 'Soft domette': a soft plain cloth in which the warp is cotton and the weft wool.

p. 194 'lappet-cloth': or lappet-hair, now called 'lapthair' on Savile Row. Modern lapthair is still made with horsehair but also synthetic fibres that allow it to bend in only one direction. It is unclear if this effect was possible in the early nineteenth century.

p. 194 'baiste', 'baisters', 'baiste fittings' remain a commonplace of Savile Row bespoke suit-making, but the term is unknown to the OED, although *baisters* and *baisting* are acknowledged as early nineteenth-century terms in buttonhole making and finishing.

p. 194 'Pockets were relegated': MLCC 33.119.

p. 195 'you might almost say the body thought': W. Jesse, *A Life*, 1844, vol. 1, p. 70.

p. 195 'The shape of the coat': W. Pitt Lennox, *Fifty Years' Biographical Reminiscences*, vol. I, p. 74.

p. 195 'Though the cut is fuller': MLCC. Coat made by John Weston, Old Bond Street, 1803.

p. 196 'Good morning Sir; happy to see you': E. Bulwer Lytton, *Pelham*, p. 113–14.

p. 197 'forty-two and a half inches from nape': *c*. 73 inch = total height. Seven eighths of 73 = *c*. 64, two thirds of 64 = *c*. 42 and a half.

p. 199 'the Prince of Wales once took seventeen': RA 29250, RA 29384–8. Schweitzer and Davidson accounts.

p. 199 'It is but of little consequence': Anon., *Taylor's Complete Guide*, p. 7.

p. 199 'The art sublime, ineffable': H. Luttrell, *Advice to Julia*, p. 47.

p. 200 'pantaloons': pantaloons, originally 'connected breeches and stockings in the same stuff', took their name from the Italian Commedia del'Arte character, Pantalone. Modern American usage of 'pants' may have descended from this, or via the French '*pantalon*'. Trousers were initially taken to mean wide-cut trousers in imitation of naval, military and boys' wear, but by the early nineteenth century the terms were becoming interchangeable.

p. 201 'I found my very constant and steady admirer': H. Wilson, *Memoirs of Harriette Wilson*, 1831, vol. 1, p. 223.

p. 202 'Those leather breeches are not bad': ibid., vol. II, p. 273.

p. 202 'Recent fashion theorists': A. Ribiero, *The Art of Dress*, pp. 105ff.

p. 202 'immodest and unflattering to the figure': M. Khan, *A Persian at the Court of King George IV, 1809–10, The Journal of Mizra Abul Hassan Khan*, p. 137.

p. 203 'extremely handsome and very fit': Anon., *Essay Philosophical and Medical Concerning Modern Clothing*, p. 45. A French doctor, L. J. Clairian, meanwhile opined that trousers (pantaloons) that were too tight would be prejudicial to men's health, but that conversely complete lack of support could be harmful: *Recherches et considérations médicales sur les vêtements des hommes, 1803*.

p. 203 'one could always tell what a young man': F. Chenoune, *The History of Men's Fashion*, 1993, p. 30.

p. 204 'ruthlessly starched': MLCC 38.294/4 and 38.294/3, waistcoats, *c.* 1815.

p. 205 'You can tell a Stultz coat anywhere': E. Bulwer Lytton, *Pelham*, in A. Adburgham, *Shopping in Style*, p. 129.

p. 205 'scorned to share his fame with his tailor': T. H. Lister, *Granby*, vol. 1, p. 108.

p. 206 'ride in ladies' gloves, particularly, he said': H. Wilson, *Memoirs*, 1831, vol. 1, p. 100.

p. 206 'Dandy Lawyers, Dandy Parsons, Dandy Physicians': Jackey Dandy, *Dandymania*, 1819; Frontispiece advertisement in Anon., *Beppo in London, A Metropolitan Story*, 1819.

p. 206 'the nameless grace of polished ease': T. Lister, *Granby*, vol. 1, p. 109.

p. 207 'It is folly that is the making of me': George Brummell to Lady Hester Stanhope, in W. Jesse, *A Life*, vol. 1, 1844, p. 148.

p. 207 'Eccentricity [is the] fruit of English soil': J. B. d'Aurevilly, trans. D. B. Wyndham Lewis, *The Anatomy of Dandyism*, p. 10.

p. 207 'Dandyism . . . is the force of English originality': ibid., p. 3.

p. 208 'Lock's, Brummell's hatters': Lock's Hatters, St James's Street. Sales Ledger, 1808': Friday 9th December 1808, Mr Brummell paid Mr Lock . . . 2 Round hats.' The wording on the ledger 'Paid Mr Lock' strongly suggests that James Lock II served Brummell.

7: A RIDE ON ROTTEN ROW

p. 211 'According to Lord Byron': In 1820 Scrope Davies had also fled England deep in debt. Byron wrote to Hobhouse: 'So Scrope is gone – down-diddled . . . gone to Bruges where he will get tipsy with Dutch beer and shoot himself the first foggy morning. Brummell at Calais . . . Buonaparte in St Helena, I in Ravenna; only think! so many great men! There has been nothing like this since Themistocles at Magnesia and Marius at Carthage.' L. Marchand, *Byron, A Portrait*, p. 322.

p. 211 'lost in vapour': Byron, *Don Juan*, Canto 1, ccxviii.

p. 211 'That congregated mass of folly': T. H. Lister, *Arlington*, p. 224.

p. 212 'curious freaks of fortune': R. Gronow, *Reminiscences of Captain Gronow*, 1862, p. 56.

p. 212 'always pronounced the name of Brummell': Byron, in V. Woolf, *Beau Brummell*, p. 8. The conflation of these two pronouncements by Byron into 'The three greatest men of the age are myself, Napoleon and Brummell, but the greatest of these is Brummell' (misquoting Corinthians 'and the greatest of these is love/charity) can first be traced to Jesse who began his seminal work on Brummell, 'I will now enter upon the life of him who Lord Byron said was one of the three great men of the nineteenth century, placing himself third, Napoleon second, and Brummell first', W. Jesse, *A Life of George Bryan Brummell Esq.*, 1844, vol. 1, p. 15; and d'Aurevilly, who wrote that 'Byron quipped that he would rather be Brummell than Napoleon', d'Aurevilly, trans. G. Walden, *What's a Dandy?*, p. 85. The parody of Corinthians dates from the play *Beau Brummel [sic], A Play in 4 Acts*, by Clyde Fitch, John Lane and Co, New York 1908.

p. 213 'almost as often as each session of Parliament': Chateaubriand, *Mémoires d'Outre-Tombe*, vol. III, p. 210.

p. 213 'The Society of the Ton': Lady C. Bury, *The Exclusives*, London, 1830, p. 17.

p. 213 'See how the universal throng': Luttrell, *Advice to Julia*, pp. 21, 25, 41.

p. 213 'In the afternoon, especially in good weather': Henry VIII had originally appropriated the land for hunting after the dissolution of the monasteries.

p. 213 'Rotten Row': 'Rotten Row' is thought to be a corruption of *Route de Roi*, and may be the original King's Road, west from the capital.

p. 214 'Where the fashionable fair': Byron, *Don Juan*, Canto II, lxv.

p. 214 'In the art of cutting': T. Lister, *Granby*, vol. 1, p. 108.

p. 214 'Have you ever endured so poor a summer': R. Gronow, *Reminiscences*, 1863, p. 72.

p. 215 'None view it awestruck or surprised': H. Luttrell, *Advice to Julia*, p. 41.

p. 215 '"Robinson," he said, turning to his valet': W. Jesse, *A Life*, 1844, vol. 1, p. 118.

p. 215 'Apsley Gate': Hyde Park Corner.

p. 215 'Is there a more gay and graceful': Disraeli, in E. Moers, *The Dandy*, p. 65.

p. 216 'In those days . . . of rank and of fashion': R. Gronow, *Reminiscences*, 1863, p. 73.

p. 216 'Never was there such a man': T. Raikes, *Reminiscences*, pp. 268–9.

p. 217 'His face was rather long': W. Jesse, *A Life*, 1844, vol. 1, p. 54.

p. 217 '[Brummell] had great powers of entertainment': T. Lister, *Granby*, vol. 1, pp. 108–12.

p. 220 'I was never what you call handsome': Dr C. L. Meryon (ed.), *Memoirs of Lady Hester Stanhope*, vol. II, p. 19.

p. 220 'For God's sake take [them] off': ibid., vol. II, p. 18.

p. 220 'She was excellent at mimicry': ibid., pp. 18–20.

p. 220 'black and green velvet ornamented', *Lady's Magazine*, 1806, vol. XXXVI, p. 30.

p. 221 'The Arabs have never looked upon me'; Pückler-Muskau, *Die Ruckkehr*, Berlin, 1846, vol. II, p. 250.

p. 221 'to Walmer': Walmer Castle in Kent, official residence of her uncle, Mr Pitt, the Prime Minister, as Warden of the Cinque Ports.

p. 221 'your friend Capel': Hon. Sir Thomas Bladen Capel, KCB, youngest son of the 4th Earl of Essex. Signal lieutenant on Nelson's ship *Vanguard* at battle of the Nile in 1798; in command of the *Phoebe* in the Mediterranean when he met Lady Hester at Naples. He, like Brummell, was a member of White's Club, but rarely in London.

p. 221 'Lord Althorp': Courtesy title of the heir to the Earl Spencer. Nephew of Georgiana, Duchess of Devonshire, and friend of Brummell through the Devonshire House set.

p. 221 'Admiral of the White': i.e. of White's Club, St James's Street.

p. 221 'a rival of yours . . . William Hill': William Noel Hill, later Lord Berwick, and ambassador to the Court of Turin.

p. 223 'Her conversation was more than ordinarily eloquent': W. Jesse, *A Life*, 1844, vol. 1, p. 141.

p. 224 'Ah, my dear lady Hester, who indeed': ibid., pp. 141ff.

p. 225 'Little G' (Georgiana)': Lady Georgiana Cavendish (1783–1858) married the brother of Brummell's other great love, Elizabeth, Duchess of Rutland, George Howard, 6th Earl of Carlisle.

p. 226 'I've Known all the Blessings of Sight': by Georgiana, Duchess of Devonshire in Brummell's Album, in L. Melville, *Beau Brummell*, pp. 277ff.

p. 227 'These additional stanzas': V. Foster (ed.), *The Two Duchesses: Family Correspondence of Georgiana, Duchess of Devonshire and Elizabeth, Duchess of Devonshire*, p. 131.

p. 228 'generous natures': Letter from G. B. Brummell 'To a Lady', in L. Melville, *Beau Brummell*, p. 144.

p. 228 'Here in the bower of beauty': by Georgiana, Duchess of Devonshire, in Brummell's Album, in ibid., pp. 278ff.

p. 229 'My cherished hope, my fondest dream': W. Jesse, *A Life*, 1844, vol. 1, p. 181.

p. 229 'O'er her white breast he spread his purple wing': by Georgiana, Duchess of Devonshire, in Brummell's Album, in L. Melville, *Beau Brummell*, pp. 278ff.

p. 230 'It is related of [Brummell] that he came': W. Jesse, *A Life*, 1844, vol. 1, p. 125. It is impossible to attribute this anecdote precisely to any one occasion or affair: the 1844 version refers to an earl and 'your countess', some later versions have 'noble friend' and 'your duchess'. It seems likely, given Brummell's known relationships with three duchesses – Devonshire, York and Rutland – and no noted countesses that Jesse deliberately obfuscated by changing the title. If it is a countess, the most likely candidate is the Countess of Bessborough, Georgiana's sister.

p. 231 *The Butterfly's Ball*: *The Butterfly's Ball and the Grasshopper's Feast*, by W. Roscoe for his children, was set to music by order of George III and Queen Charlotte for Princess Mary, later Duchess of Gloucester. W. Jesse, *A Life*, 1844, vol. 1, p. 241.

p. 231 *The Butterfly's Funeral*: ibid., pp. 240ff.

p. 232 'John Wallis, went on to sell more': ibid., p. 240.

p. 232 'Mr Brummell keeps us waiting rather than wishing for him': Se fait plutot attendre que desirer.

p. 234 'the twenty-one-year-old Duke of Rutland': John Henry Manners (1778–1857), 5th Duke of Rutland.

p. 234 'Lady Elizabeth Howard . . . married': 22 April 1799. *Burke's Peerage*, 107th Edition, vol. III, 'Manners'.

p. 235 'Brummell, meanwhile, sketched from life': In 1844 this painting was in Jesse's possession but has subsequently been lost; Jesse, *A Life*, 1844, vol II, p. 95.

p. 235 'James Wyatt, would eventually inspire': James was the brother of Jeffrey Wyatt (later Wyattville). Both brothers worked on Windsor Castle and Great Park.

p. 235 'He wrote from Oatlands Park, Surrey, in August 1813': The year is established not in MS but by the date of birth of the Marquess of Granby. The original is kept in the Muniments Room (archive) at Belvoir Castle and is reproduced from Campbell, *Beau Brummell*, p. 113, by permission of His Grace the Duke of Rutland.

p. 235 'As to young Granby': The eldest son of the Duke of Rutland holds the courtesy title Marquess of Granby.

p. 236 'easily consoles herself for the loss of a [dandy] lover': E. Bulwer Lytton, *Pelham*, p. 75.

p. 236 'Ah there she is! . . . that I mayn't see it': W. Jesse, *A Life*, 1844, vol. 1, pp. 90ff. 'All this, however, My Lady [D. of Rutland] seems to have forgotten now, and all was graciousness', J. B. Priestley (ed.), *Tom Moore's Diary*, p. 468.

p. 237 'Princess Frederica Charlotte Ulrica Catherine': Princess Frederica, Duchess of York, born 7 May 1767, eldest daughter of King William II of Prussia, married HRH Prince Frederick, Duke of York and Albany and Bishop of Osnabruck, Berlin, 29 September 1791 in Berlin. Died, Oatlands Park, Surrey, 6 August 1820.

p. 237 'Frederique': RA GEO/44527–44558, letters of the Duchess of York to Prince Regent and Duchess of Cambridge.

p. 238 'The Duchess was very partial': R. H. Stoddard (ed.), *Personal Reminiscences*, pp. 270–1.

p. 238 'The Duchess resides entirely at Oatlands': *Bon Ton Magazine*, April 1793.

p. 238 'I have several times stayed at Oatlands': S. Rogers, *Recollections*, pp. 164–5.

p. 239 'Their elaborate mausoleums': Oatlands Park, much altered, is now a country-house hotel, conference centre and golf club.

p. 239 'Mein Gott, dey are so dependent': Matthew 'Monk' Lewis, in L. Melville, *Beau Brummell*, p. 151.

p. 239 'she pays her tradesmen's bills': *Bon Ton Magazine*, August 1792, p. 234.

p. 239 'These were enclosed with her trademark pink': RA GEO/44527–44558, letters of the Duchess of York to Prince Regent and Duchess of Cambridge. RA GEO/44558 deep pink. RA GEO/Add 50/103, Duchess of York to Charles Culling Smith.

p. 239 'It has been mentioned': Anon., *An Address to Her Royal Highness the Dutchess [sic] of York Against the Use of Sugar, Nihil humani a me alienum puto*, p. 10.

p. 240 'inspired a fashion for tiny tight shoes': The Duchess's feet were a subject of great curiosity after her husband ordered shoes for his bride-to-be. See illustrations.

p. 240 'a very superior mind', T. Raikes, in W. Jesse, *A Life*, 1844, vol. II, p. 2.

p. 240 'the most unvarying steadfast affection': Letter from George IV to the Duke of York on the occasion of the death of his wife, 1825, in C. Hibbert, *George IV*, p. 711.

p. 241 'I will never forget the tender moments': Duchess of York to G. Brummell, in L. Melville, *Beau Brummell*, p. 83.

p. 241 'they once bought a lottery ticket together': W. Jesse, *A Life*, 1927, vol. 1, p. 219.

p. 241 'Please accept my most sincere thanks': ibid., pp. 220–1.

p. 241 'It was one of the more expensive items': RA GEO/Add 50/99–100.

p. 242 'Yet, who see him in rounds': Manuscript poem in Brummell's Album quoted in full in Jesse, 1844, vol. 1, pp. 285ff, written by Lord Erskine (1750–1823), Lord Chancellor, 'melancholy in private but always vivacious in company'.

8: THE DANDY CLUBS

p. 244 'White's and Brooks's . . . in 1799': *Memorials of Brooks's MDCCLXIV–MCM*, 'Mr Brummell. Proposer and Seconder Mr Fawkener. Date of Election 2 April 1799'.

p. 244 'To be admitted a member of that body': W. Fraser, *Words on Wellington*, p. 202.

p. 245 'The Rules also stipulated that': After 1813 membership rose to 500.

p. 245 'a little later a bay window was added': in 1811.

p. 245 'mustered in force': R. Gronow, *Reminiscences, of Captain Gronow*, 1863, p. 46.

p. 245 'an ordinary frequenter of White's: C. Gore, *Sketches of English Character*, in E. Moers, *The Dandy*, p. 43.

p. 246 'The conversation upon the topics': W. Pitt Lennox, *Celebrities I Have Known*, vol. 1, p. 295.

p. 246 ' "My dear fellow," said Brummell': Grantley Berkeley, in L. Melville, *Beau Brummell*, pp. 40ff.

p. 247 'Damn the fellows . . . they're upstarts': Colonel Sebright, in A. Lejeune, *White's, The First Three Hundred Years*, p. 89.

p. 247 'Shot from yon Heavenly Bow': H. Luttrell, *Advice to Julia*, p. 163.

p. 247 'White's Window would not permit it': W. Fraser, *Words on Wellington*, pp. 202–3.

p. 248 'the most famous political club': Trevelyan, in P. Ziegler and D. Seward (eds), *Brooks's*, p. 27.

p. 248 'Whig Party at Dinner': ibid., p. 42.

p. 248 'the Whigs kept the best company': recorded by John Cam Hobhouse, from a conversation between Brummell, Scrope Davies and himself in Calais, July 1817, in T. A. J. Burnett, *Rise and Fall of a Regency Dandy*, p. 145.

p. 249 'having won only £12,000': P. Ziegler and D. Seward, *Brooks's*, p. 26.

p. 249 'broiled blade-bone of mutton': E. Chancellor, *The Memorials of St James's Street Together with the Annals of Almack's*, p. 155.

p. 249 'practically on first-name terms': S. Rogers, *Recollections*, p. 194.

p. 250 'Mr Brummell bets Mr Irby': London Metropolitan Archives, White's Betting Book, 1743–1878, 1811: 'Mr Brummell bets Mr Blackford thirty guineas to twenty-five that Mr William Jones beats Mr Darston for the County of Gloucester now contesting between them, February 1811.'

p. 251 'The dinner to be always upon the Table': A. Lejeune, *White's*, p. 52.

p. 252 'costing as many pounds as there were guests': P. Colson, *White's 1693–1950*, p. 71.

p. 252 'cold meats, oysters etc': J. Timbs, *Clubs and Club Life in London from the Seventeenth Century to the Present Times*, p. 96, quoting White's Rules, 1797.

p. 252 'cold fowl, fruit, bisquits [*sic*]': C. Ray, *Table Talk*, in P. Ziegler and D. Seward, *Brooks's*, p. 166.

p. 252 'One of the earliest uses of the word': OED, Gibbon's *Journal*, 24 November 1762.

p. 253 'the eternal joints, or beef-steaks': R. Gronow, *Reminiscences*, 1863, p. 79.

p. 253 'Labourie's dinners': C. Ray, *Table Talk*, in P. Ziegler and D. Seward, *Brooks's*, p. 165.

p. 254 'the dinners were so recherché': T. Raikes, in L. Melville, *Beau Brummell*, p. 70.

p. 254 'Watier's': The spelling of Watier's, like Brooks's, varies in the period: Wattier's, Brook's, Brookes's, etc. The modern spelling is Brooks's. Watier's Club no longer exists, but the favoured spelling stuck with the chef's name and one *t*.

p. 255 'reduced to a state after dinner': R. Gronow, *Reminiscences*, 1863, p. 47.

p. 255 'Brummell bought snuff for the prince as early as 1799': Fribourg and Treyer ledgers, Westminster City Archives.

p. 256 'White's accounts concur': P. Colson, *White's*, p. 95.

p. 256 'Brummell bought Martinique': Fribourg and Treyer ledgers, Westminster City Archives. The last of Fribourg and Treyer's own blend of Macouba can still be bought at the Snuff Shop, G. Smith's, on Charing Cross Road.

p. 256 'Sniff . . . with precision, with both nostrils': U. Bourne, *Snuff*, p. 7.

p. 257 'My Lord! Allow me to observe': H. Cole, *Beau Brummell*, p. 93.

p. 257 'The hogshead was duly opened': W. Jesse, *A Life*, 1844, vol. 1, p. 102.

9: THEATRE ROYAL

p. 261 'Not a nod, not a curtsy': O. Goldsmith, *The Citizen of the World*, vol. 1, p. 83.

p. 261 'Many a beau turned his head': H. Wilson, *Memoirs of Harriette Wilson* 1831, vol. 3, p. 76, and vol. 1, p. 100.

p. 261 'Fred Bentinck': Younger son of the immensely wealthy Duke of Portland, Lord Fred Bentinck was an inner member of the dandy circle and frequenter of Harriette Wilson's; 'Lord Fred,' Harriette wrote, 'always makes me merry.'

p. 261 'Lord Fife': James Duff, 4th Earl of Fife (1776–1857). Had a long-standing affair with London's prima ballerina La Mercandotti, who became the toast of the town aged only fifteen; he lost her to the *nouveau riche* dandy Golden Ball Hughes – the subject of a ditty at Fife's expense:

> *The fair damsel is gone and no wonder at all*
> *That bred to the dance she has gone to the Ball.*

p. 261 'the Duc de Berri': Charles Ferdinand de Bourbon, Duc de Berri (1778–1820). A French prince of the blood, son of the Comte d'Artois, later Charles X of France, he spent many years in London during the First Empire. He fought against Napoleon and entered Paris in 1814 with the Victorious Allies. A famous womaniser, his few legitimate children all predeceased him, but one posthumous child (the duc was assassinated at the Paris opera in 1820) became Henry V of France.

p. 261 'the King's Theatre': The four previous theatres on the site of today's Her Majesty's Theatre, Haymarket, included the King's Theatre, or Italian Opera House, known to Brummell. It became widely known as Her Majesty's after the accession of Queen Victoria in 1837 so that is the term used by Gronow, writing in the 1860s; it had originally been the Queen's Theatre, or Her Majesty's, in the days of Queen Anne (1704, as designed by Sir John Vanbrugh). Today's Theatre Royal, Haymarket, is opposite, and dates from 1821. It is the oldest West End theatre still in use. The Little Theatre stood on the same side of Haymarket, slightly nearer to Piccadilly Circus.

p. 262 'Between them, by the beginning of the nineteenth century': F. O'Toole, *A Traitor's Kiss*, p. 114.

p. 262 'my friend Sherry': W. Jesse, *A Life of George Bryan Brummell Esq.*, 1844, vol. 1, p. 246.

p. 262 'grander than La Scala': E. Burford, *Royal St James's*, p. 238.

p. 262 'it was suggested a Persian': Montesquieu, in F. O'Toole, *A Traitor's Kiss*, p. 116.

p. 262 'to furnish out a part of the entertainment': O. Goldsmith, *The Citizen of the World*, p. 75.

p. 262 'to assemble only to see and be seen': C. A. G. Goede, *A Stranger in England*, vol. II, pp. 106ff.

p. 263 'Mrs Siddons performed the Thane's wife': H. Jenkin, *Mrs Siddons as Lady Macbeth and as Queen Katherine*, p. 9. She may have played the role even longer, as there were benefit nights at Covent Garden in which she played excerpts from her most famous roles up until 1819.

p. 263 'The nobility seldom arrive': C. Goede, *A Stranger in England*, vol. II, pp. 106ff.

p. 263 'As for the First [Act]': B. Blackmantle, *The English Spy*, London, 1825.

p. 264 'One particularly popular late-night show': *Gentleman's Magazine*, May 1816.

p. 264 'Sheridan for one employed': F. O'Toole, *A Traitor's Kiss*, p. 119.

p. 265 'the King's Theatre auditorium': In 1799 the interior of the Opera House (King's Theatre) was remodelled by Marinari, the principal scenery-painter at Drury Lane. Jane Austen writes sympathetically to her sister when she is unable to see inside (D. Le Faye, ed., *Jane Austen's Letters*, Oxford, 1995, p. 71); see also P. Byrne, *Jane Austen and the Theatre*, London and New York, 2002, pp. 61–2.

p. 265 'The ensuing riot': A. Bank (ed.), *The Drama: Its History, Literature and Influence on Civilisation*, vol. 15, pp. 101–2.

p. 265 'This was probably an exaggeration': MLCC A9243. Silk jersey breeches; either court or formal evening wear, *c.* 1810.

p. 265 'The theatre was not ticketed': W. Pitt Lennox, *My Recollections from 1806 to 1873*, p. 226.

p. 266 'The Duke of Bedford, for instance': ibid., p. 222.

p. 266 'I make it a rule never to lend my box': Duke of Bedford to G. Brummell, in W. Jesse, *A Life*, 1844, vol. 1, p. 84.

p. 266 'all fitted up with crimson velvet': Jane Austen to Cassandra Austen, in P. Byrne, *Jane Austen and the Theatre*, p. 51.

p. 266 'in front of every box': E. M. Butler (ed.), *A Regency Visitor*, p. 178.

p. 266 'ran up three times to the opera': H. Wilson, *Memoirs*, 1929, p. 206.

p. 267 'seated in the box nearest the stage': E. Bulwer Lytton, *Pelham*, p. 162.

p. 267 'one half come to prosecute their debaucheries': J. Brewer, *The Pleasures of the Imagination*, p. 348.

p. 267 'The celebrated beau, George Brummell': H. Wilson, *Memoirs*, 1831, vol. 3, p. 76.

p. 268 'when the performance had concluded': ibid., vol. I, p. 100.

p. 268 'happy was she in whose opera box': T. Raikes, *Reminiscences*, p. 268.

p. 268 'were meant for no more than six': W. Pitt Lennox, *My Recollections*, p. 226.

p. 270 '[his flexibility of feature]': W. Jesse, *A Life*, 1844, vol. 1, p. 54.

p. 270 'Lady Catherine de Burgh': J. Austen, *Pride and Prejudice*, 1811, and F. Burney, *A Busy Day*, 1801, respectively.

p. 271 'I now observed a very corpulent gentleman': H. Wilson, *Memoirs*, 1831, vol. 3, pp. 181ff.

p. 272 'Brummell came out, talking eagerly to some friends': T. Raikes, *Reminiscences*, pp. 267ff.

p. 273 'Opera boxes could cost from a hundred': F. Wilson, *The Courtesan's Revenge*, p. 67.

p. 273 'The opera may be called the exclusive property': C. A. G. Goede, *A Stranger in England*, vol. II, pp. 106ff.

p. 273 'Let the theatre be got up upon the same': 'Dramatic Taste', *Fraser's Magazine*, February 1830.

p. 273 'in full court dress': R. Gronow, *Reminiscences of Captain Gronow*, 1863, p. 49.

p. 273 'stamped with aristocratic elegance': ibid., p. 49.

p. 274 'circular vestibule, almost lined': F. Wilson, *The Courtesan's Revenge*, p. 68.

p. 274 'Sketches from the Round Room': ibid., p. 68.

p. 274 'Not only was she rapturously applauded': R. Edgcumbe, *Musical Reminiscences of an Old Amateur Chiefly respecting Italian Opera in England, 1773–1823*, p. 96.

p. 274 'introduced to the London stage': ibid., p. 102.

p. 275 'cold, heartless and satirical': H. Wilson, *Memoirs*, 1831, vol. 1, p. 100.

p. 276 'From under Holland's Ionic columns': The columns now grace the portico of the National Gallery on the north side of Trafalgar Square. Other smaller internal fixtures of the house were salvaged for use at Buckingham Palace.

p. 276 'see over the gates': W. Jesse, *A Life*, 1844, vol. I, p. 271.

p. 276 'Big Ben Caunt': Big Ben Caunt, born Newstead, Nottinghamshire (1814), champion of All England 1841–5. The famous bell and its clock tower may equally have been nicknamed Big Ben after Sir Benjamin Hall, the commissioner of works appointed to rebuild the Palace of Westminster after the fire of 1834. Nevertheless, the earliest record of the nickname in common use, beyond the portals of Carlton House, is its attachment to Ben Caunt the boxer.

p. 277 'For larger banquets, this opened out': W. H. Pyne, *The Royal Residences of England*, vol. II (Carlton House).

p. 278 'Mr Brummell, the place for your box': R. Gronow, *Captain Gronow's Last Recollections*, p. 57.

p. 278 'It was this more than anything else': ibid., pp. 57ff.

p. 279 'Neither have I resentments': W. Jesse, *A Life*, 1844, vol. I, p. 273.

p. 279 'in a superfine passion': 'Superfine' was one of the matte broadcloths used for men's coats that Brummell had brought into high fashion.

p. 279 'Three thousand guests were invited': M. Evans (ed.), *Princes as Patrons*, p. 109.

p. 280 'Nothing was ever half so magnificent': W. Dowden (ed.), *The Letters of Thomas Moore*, Vol. 1, pp. 152–3.

10: SEVENTH HEAVEN OF THE FASHIONABLE WORLD

p. 281 'happy was the young lady': W. Pitt Lennox, *Celebrities I Have Known*, vol. 1, p. 318.

p. 282 'most magnificent suite of rooms': E. Chancellor, *The Memorials of St James's Street Together with the Annals of Almack's*, p. 197.

p. 282 'solemn proclamation': R. Gronow, *Reminiscences of Captain Gronow*, 1863, p. 44.

p. 282 'silk stockings, thin shoes, and white': Major Chambre, *Recollections of West End Life*, vol. I, p. 241.

p. 282 'Into this sanctum sanctorum': Lady Clementia Davies, in E. Chancellor, *Memorials*, p. 210.

p. 283 'not more than half a dozen': R. Gronow, *Reminiscences*, 1863, pp. 43ff.

p. 283 'All on that magic List depends': H. Luttrell, *Advice to Julia*, pp. 10 and 60.

p. 283 'Lady Louisa Lennox': *Burke's Peerage*, vols I and II; 'Lady Louisa Lennox d. 1843. Dau. Duke of Richmond and Gordon, Duc d'Aubigny etc of Goodwood Park.' Captain Jesse is evasive about the lady in question, and he could equally be referring to one of the other Lady Louisas in the extended Lennox family at the time, or even Lady Louisa, daughter of the Duke of Beaufort, who were all presented at Court in the early nineteenth century.

p. 284 'He is now speaking to Lord': W. Jesse, *A Life*, 1844, vol. I, pp. 99–100.

p. 284 'this is no fiction': ibid., vol. I, p. 100.

p. 284 'No lady or gentleman's name': Major Chambre, *Recollections*, vol. II, pp. 261–2.

p. 285 'Though the Almack's ballroom was over ninety feet': E. Chancellor, *Memorials*, p. 198.

p. 285 'the upper end, on a raised seat': W. Pitt Lennox, *Fifty Years' Biographical Reminiscences*, vol. I, p. 32.

p. 285 'There shall be no ostentation': E. Bulwer Lytton, *Godolphin*, vol. I, p. 127.

p. 285 'A ballroom is nothing': ibid., vol. I, p. 82.

p. 285 'You, who know Almack's': E. Moers, *The Dandy*, p. 45.

p. 286 'such that hereafter no one': G. S. Hillard (ed.), *Life, Letters and Journals of George Ticknor*, vol. I, pp. 296–7.

p. 286 'No event ever produced so great a sensation': T. Raikes, in A. Adburgham, *Shopping in Style*, p. 8.

p. 287 'Despite all her talents and attractions': R. Gronow, *Captain Gronow's Last Recollections*, p. 120.

p. 287 'He shall not be so pretty than you': H. Cole, *Beau Brummell*, pp. 107–8, quoting variously Lord Byron, Lord Alvanley and Captain Gronow.

p. 288 '£800 on candles': P. Colson, *White's*, pp. 68–9.

p. 288 'illuminations and fireworks': Lady Emma Sophia Brownlow, *The Eve of Victorianism*, p. 54.

p. 289 'no repose either of body or mind': J. C. Hobhouse, *Recollections*, vol. 1, p. 73.

p. 289 'five in the afternoon as, by so doing': H. Wilson, *Memoirs of Harriette Wilson*, 1831, vol. 4, p. 159.

p. 289 'They were unmasked. No one else': ibid., vol. 4, p. 160.

p. 290 'How easy is [their] only rule!': H. Luttrell, *Advice to Julia*, p. 83.

p. 290 'pharoah': this is the older spelling, from the original French cards that had a picture of an Egyptian pharaoh in place of the king.

p. 290 'I never saw such a transition': A. Lejeune, *White's*, pp. 83–4.

p. 291 'It was five o'clock one summer's morning': T. Raikes, *Reminiscences*, p. 272.

p. 291 'Mr Brummell, if you wish to put an end': Lejeune, *White's*, p. 94.

p. 292 'Tom Sheridan was never in the habit': T. Raikes, *Journals*, vol. III, pp. 85–6.

p. 292 'The life which Brummell led at last': T. Raikes, *Journals*, vol. II, p. 210.

p. 293 'I have a notion': T. Moore, *Lord Byron, Letters and Journals*, vol. IX, *Detached Thoughts*, No. 33.

p. 293 'the true impulse in obstinate incorrigible gamesters': T. de Quincy, *The English Opium Eater*, vol. I, p. 173.

p. 294 'emanating from the leading ladies': W. Pitt Lennox, *My Recollections from 1806 to 1873*, vol. II, p. 228.

11: NO MORE A-ROVING SO LATE INTO THE NIGHT

p. 296 'So, we'll go no more a-roving': G. G. Byron, *Complete Poetical Works*, 1970, p. 101.

p. 296 'In Society, stay as long as you need', J. B. d'Aurevilly, trans. G. Walden, *What's a Dandy?*, p. 103.

p. 296 'Dates make ladies nervous': H. Wilson, *Harriette Wilson's Memoirs of Herself and Others*, 1929, p. 26.

p. 297 'advice on sex to professional courtesans': H. Wilson, *Memoirs of Harriette Wilson*, 1831, vol. 5, p. 334.

p. 297 'Mrs Philip's Warehouse': Wellcome Institute, Images Collection L0022456. Advertisement for Mrs Philip's Warehouse on Half Moon Street: 'Seven doors up from The Strand, on the left'.

   None in our wares e're found a flaw/Self-preservation's nature's law . . .

p. 297 'that he suffered for many years from syphilis': Dr Edouard Vastel and John Kelly, MD, served the Caen asylum and the British community in Caen respectively in the 1830s. They attended Brummell, signed the medical certificates and attested to cause of death, recorded and kept in the Bon Sauveur asylum, Caen, where Brummell died. Professor Pierre Morel, former director of l'Hôpital Psychiatrique Départementale du Bon Sauveur, Caen, has copies of the original medical files kept at Bon Sauveur, which record the 'general paralysis of the insane' [*démence et paralysie générale*]', i.e. tertiary syphilis, from which Brummell died in 1840. The originals are in disputed ownership between the asylum and the Archives Départementales du Calvados, also at Caen.

p. 297 '15 per cent of the population': D. Hayden, *Pox*, pp. 44ff.

p. 298 'overstated manliness' . . . 'unambiguous masculinity': D. Wahrman, *The Making of the Modern Self*, pp. 62–4.

p. 298 'The organ of love in his cranium': W. Jesse, *A Life*, 1844, vol. 1, p. 126.

p. 299 'there is a splendid [new] pox in town': Théophile Gautier, in C. Quetel, *History of Syphilis*, pp. 118ff.

p. 299 'Francis I': King of France (1494–1547). Not only did his reign see the arrival of syphilis in France, from the Americas, but his incessant warring helped spread the disease across European borders. He was also famously a sufferer himself; one nineteenth-century hagiographical reference noted '*l'abus des plaisirs lui avait causé des apostumes* [Self-indulgent pleasure-seeking had caused him physical corruption]', *Nouvelle Biographie Universelle*, Paris, 1861, p. 530.

p. 300 'mincing': E. Tweedie, *Hyde Park*, p. 69.

p. 300 'bitchy queen': S. Parissien, *George IV*, p. 113.

p. 300 'a monstrous sin against nature': J. Peakman, *Lascivious Bodies*, p. 148.

p. 300 'silken tresses and delicate': W. Jesse, *A Life*, 1844, vol. II, p. 267.

p. 301 'With such success, such command': J. B. d'Aurevilly, trans. G. Walden, *What's a Dandy?*, p. 103.

p. 301 'Dear Miss ————': Jesse leaves the name blank in the newspaper and gossip-sheet tradition of the time.

p. 301 'When I wrote to you a century ago': W. Jesse, *A Life*, 1844, vol. I, p. 130. The letter is also quoted in L. Melville, *Beau Brummell*, pp. 145–6, and wrongly attributed to Brummell's time in Calais. Jesse's is the earlier and more authoritative voice, and the opening line assumes a change of century and places the letter in 1800.

p. 302 'frenical': OED, Frenzical, fransical (*obs*); wildly enthusiastic

p. 303 'He never attained any degree of intimacy': W. Jesse, *A Life*, 1844, vol. 1, pp. 124–5.

p. 303 'The most favourable opportunity': ibid., pp. 125–6.

p. 304 'eleemosynary': of or pertaining to almshouses and alms-giving, OED.

p. 305 'that unaffected and fervent homage': W. Jesse, *A Life*, 1844, vol. 1, p. 132.

p. 305 'If a gentleman detract from another': *The British Code of Duel, A reference to The Laws of Honour and the Character of Gentlemen* p. 14.

p. 306 'You have taken a load off my mind': W. Jesse, *A Life*, 1844, vol. 1, pp. 298ff.

p. 307 'Vow not at all, but if thou must': First published in W. Jesse, *A Life*, 1844, vol. 1, p. 288. J. McGann (ed.), *Lord Byron: The Complete Poetical Works*, vol. III, pp. 458–9: 'Commentary Note 230: MS A copy in an unknown hand [possibly Brummell's] with "Byron" written at end (MS T location: Texas). Uncollected. First published in Capt Jesse's *Life of George Brummell* (1844) 1, p. 288 from a copy in Brummell's (now lost) album book of verses; MS T printed in *Pratt* 128 where a date of 1806 is conjectured . . . In 1812 Byron had sent at least one stanza of "To [Lady Caroline Lamb]" to Lady Melbourne, and it is probable that Brummell had both poems from her, though Byron could have given them to Brummell himself (Byron's close acquaintance with Brummell in fact began only a few weeks after his 25 April letter to Lady Melbourne; see BLJ, iv, 117).'

p. 307 'A Woman's Hair': ibid., pp. 6–7.

p. 307 'The letters Brummell had in his possession': W. Jesse, *A Life*, 1886, Preface, p. xvi.

p. 308 'from the tender to the devastatingly dismissive': J. D. Jump, (ed.), *Byron, A Symposium*, p. 113.

p. 308 'He abounds in sublime': Anon., *Don John or Don Juan Unmasked*, p. 8.

p. 309 'There had been no such thing as a "homosexual"': The terms homosexual, bisexual and heterosexual all post-date Brummell, but that is not to say there was no sense of a homosexual community in London in the eighteenth and nineteenth centuries; it has been argued that some men saw themselves as part of a 'sodomitical group'. See J. Peakman, *Lascivious Bodies*; C. Craft, *Another Kind of Love*; C. White (ed.), *Nineteenth Century Writings on Homosexuality*.

p. 310 'The existence of this club': *The Times*, 13 July 1810.

p. 310 'They were put in the stocks': ibid., 28 September 1810.

p. 310 'of sodomies and bestialities': F. Swediaur, *Practical Observations on Venereal Complaints*, p. 314.

p. 310 'after a voyage of four months': ibid., p. 4.

p. 310 'It is worth noting that later in the nineteenth century': P. Ricord, *Illustrations of Syphilitic Disease*, p. 262.

p. 310 'any Friction or rubbing of the Yard': J. Marten, *A Treatise of all the Degrees and Symptoms of the Venereal Disease*, p. 68.

p. 310 'one Man's conversing with, or having Carnal use': J. Peakman, *Lascivious Bodies*, pp. 21–3.

p. 310 'Syphilitic husbands': Ricord, *Illustrations of Syphilitic Disease*, p. 264. 'The husband of this lady [she had anal syphilitic chancres] had chancres himself and had communicated them to her prepostera venere [via anal sex]. He supposed that connection in this way prevented contagion. Unfortunately the event did not justify his preconceived ideas.'

p. 310 'to have, when the original is dust': Byron, *Don Juan*, London, 1819, Canto 1, ccxviii.

p. 310 'His was the most famous image': There are two colour miniatures, neither of absolutely certain attribution. One was owned by the late Major Daniell, OBE, the other came on to the market in the late twentieth century, sold at auction at Bonham's, London. National Portrait Gallery Records, London, G. B. Brummell.

p. 312 'in his zeal for cold chicken': H. Wilson, *Memoirs*, 1831, vol. 1, p. 103.

p. 312 'In the supper room': B. Blackmantle, *The English Spy*, vol. II, pp. 61ff. The Mysteries of Cytherea = sex.

p. 313 'I vote for cutting all the grocers': H. Wilson, *Memoirs*, 1831, vol. 1, p. 108.

p. 313 'Palmerston': Henry John Temple, 3rd Viscount Palmerston (1784–1865). MP from 1806, and at the War Office from 1809 where he 'held his post for nearly twenty years, til 1828', so Brummell was wrong in his conjecture that he would not 'keep his place' unless he meant that Palmerston was likely to rise in the political world, which indeed he did. He was secretary of state for foreign affairs from 1830 to 1841, for which reason he had further contact with Brummell in his later work for the Foreign Office. He became prime minister, aged seventy, in 1854. In his youth he was described as 'a man of fashion, a sportsman, a bit of a dandy, a light of Almack's' (*DNB*) and Gronow wrote of him at 'the mazy waltz . . . describing an infinite number of circles with the Princess de Lieven', all of which explains his presence at one of the Three Graces' louche parties.

p. 314 'Marquess of Lorne': Courtesy title of the eldest son of the Duke of Argyll. Harriette's predilection for young men in line to inherit dukedoms speaks less of snobbery than financial acumen: she, like the money-lenders, knew that the expectations of the eldest son were great, while his current wealth might be circumscribed. She sought, and gained, annuities in these situations, which were meant to keep her in old age. It was the Duke of Beaufort's reneging on this, in effect, that later drove her to publish 'and be damned'.

p. 314 'To Argyll House': H. Wilson, *Memoirs*, 1831, vol. 1, pp. 108ff.

p. 314 'My reflections were interrupted': ibid., p. 181.

p. 314 'The man does not want you to pass': ibid., vol. 5, p. 334.

p. 315 'conceal passion and reveal it': J. B. d'Aurevilly, trans. G. Walden, *What's a Dandy?*, p. 104.

p. 315 'a woman can hardly be expected': W. Jesse, *A Life*, 1844, vol. 1, p. 299.

p. 315 'making strong love': H. Wilson, *Memoirs*, 1831, vol. I, p. 220.

p. 315 'the majestic pox!' 2 March 1877. Guy de Maupassant was twenty-seven. His euphoric response to a diagnosis of syphilis was in the context of a history of sexual athleticism. However, the sexual fever of the early syphilitic is widely recorded. C. Quetel, *History of Syphilis*, p. 128.

p. 316 'Protestant nunnery': *The Meretriciad*, in E. Burford, *Royal St James's*, p. 220.

p. 316 'administered Absolution in the most desperate cases': *Town and Country Magazine*, in ibid., pp. 220–1.

p. 317 'purl rods' . . . 'tipping the velvet': ibid., pp. 210–11, illustration. Copyright © Trustees of the British Museum.

p. 317 'the many noted Houses': ibid., p. 197.

p. 318 'she knew the value of repeated First Editions': E. Burford, *Private Vices, Public Virtues*, pp. 150–1.

p. 318 'many West End madams sold condoms': E. Burford, *Royal St James's*, pp. 219–29.

p. 318 'a prize for which the young and gay': B. Blackmantle, *The English Spy*, vol. II, p. 42.

p. 319 'taste, luxury, debauchery and vice': J. Peakman, *Lascivious Bodies*, pp. 106ff – private papers of Sir Francis Dashwood.

p. 319 'all spotless virgins': E. Burford, *Royal St James's*, p. 228.

p. 320 'sexual relation that has been described as homosocial': E. Kosofsky-Sedgwick, *Between Men*, pp. 1ff.

p. 321 'It was a strange thing to see a man': E. Bulwer Lytton, *Pelham*, p. 150.

12: PLAY . . . HAS BEEN THE RUIN OF US ALL

p. 325 'Play . . . has been the ruin of all': H. Wilson, *Memoirs of Harriette Wilson*, 1831, vol. 4, pp. 207ff.

p. 326 'presumed heirs to the dukedom': Until the birth of the Marquess of Granby in 1813 – fourteen years after the Rutlands' marriage – his younger brothers had been the duke's heirs.

p. 326 'Covenant between George Bryan Brummell': Belvoir Castle Muniments Room, MSS, in Campbell, pp. 118–19 and reproduced by permission of His Grace the Duke of Rutland.

p. 326 'to the death of the last of the two rakes': In signing joint annuities it was expected, in the place of modern life insurance cover, that each co-lender would bequeath assets to the others to cover the continuing debt.

p. 327 'exhausted the other two': J. C. Hobhouse, *Recollections*, vol. 1, pp. 86–7.

p. 328 'the dandykiller': H. Wilson, *Memoirs*, 1831, vol. 4, p. 196.

p. 328 'Meyler sat with his friend the Duchess of Beaufort': L. Blanch (ed.), *Harriette Wilson's Memoirs*, 2003, p. 313.

p. 329 'Brummell sat, laughing, with Harriette': At this time Harriette had a box at the opera, bought by her lover the Marquess of Worcester, in which Brummell was a regular: Meyler, meanwhile, was a guest often in the Beauforts' box, directly opposite.

p. 329 'His countenance is so peculiarly voluptuous': H. Wilson, *Harriette Wilson's Memoirs*, 2003, p. 314.

p. 329 'a very tyrant': F. Wilson, *The Courtesan's Revenge*, pp. 138–40.

p. 330 'The story was this . . . that particular time': H. Wilson, *Memoirs*, 1831, vol. 4, pp. 192ff.

p. 331 'Fribourg and Treyer': Final entries, Brummell account: 15 April 1816 and 17 December 1818. Total of £14. 8s. 0d. It seems likely that this latter date was when the account was wound up, and the purchase of a 2.5 lb jar of Martinique relates to the earlier date. Fribourg and Treyer ledgers, 1816, 1817, 1818, Westminster City Archive.

p. 331 'My Dear Scrope': R. Gronow, *Reminiscences of Captain Gronow*, 1863, p. 211.

p. 332 '*La Cosa Rara*': (now more usually *Una Cosa Rara*) by Vicente Martin, 1776. Often cited as the first occasion at which a waltz was heard on stage.

p. 332 '*Love, Law and Physic*': *The Times*, 16–20 May. *La Cosa Rara* was advertised as Mr Braham's benefit night for Thursday 16 May – 'Tickets and boxes sold at The King's Theatre and from No 3, Tavistock Square'. The second performance is listed as Saturday 18 May. There was no opera playing at the King's on the night Brummell left London, Friday 17 May. *Love, Law and Physic*, a Farce in Two Acts by James Kenny, played at Covent Garden. The lead role, Flexible, required of its actor 'a ready assurance, a glib tongue and strong powers of mimicry'.

p. 333 'It was Solomans's Judgement': Solomans's were Jewish money-lenders. E. Chancellor, *The Memorials of St James's*, p. 248.

Part III: A Man of Fashion, Gone to the Continent, 1816–40

13: ROI DE CALAIS, 1816–21

p. 335 A Catalogue of A very choice': Frontispiece of Christie's Sale Catalogue, No. 13 Chapel Street, Park Lane, 22 and 23 May 1816, reproduced in W. Jesse, *A Life of George Bryan Brummell Esq.*, 1844, vol. 1, pp. 275–6 and also in *The Times*, 21 and 22 May 1816, which carried an advertisement with the same wording as the catalogue title page, but with the painting titled *The Refractory School Boy* referred to by its other name, *The Angry Child*, in the catalogue itself.

p. 340 'most often in the notorious King's Bench prison': W. Pitt Lennox, *My Recollections from 1806 to 1873*, vol. II, pp 3–4.

p. 340 'An Englishman was beyond English law': F. Coghlan, *A Guide to France, or, Travellers, Their Own Commissioners*, p. 5.

p. 340 'commodious baths': ibid., p. 16.

p. 340 '*L' Auberge des rois*': C. Borde, *Calais et la Mer 1814–1914*, pp. 36ff.

p. 340 'Dear Lords Charles and Robert': Belvoir Castle MSS, Muniments Room, G. B. Brummell to Lords C. and R. Manners, 18 May 1816.

p. 342 'What a long list of ruin': R. H. Stoddard (ed.), *Personal Reminiscences*, p. 278.

p. 342 'Brummell's private debts are very considerable': *The Diary of a Diplomatist*, 21 and 24 May 1816, entries reprinted in *Monthly Magazine*, November 1846.

p. 343 'Mr Brummell has decamped to the confusion': Sir Robert Peel, chief secretary for Ireland, to Lord Whitworth, 20 May 1816.

p. 343 'Rare old Sève [*sic*] Porcelain, Buhl', *The Times*, 21 and 22 May 1816.

p. 344 'This snuffbox was intended for': W. Jesse, *A Life*, 1844, vol. 1, pp. 348–50.

p. 344 'how Brummell had changed since we saw him at Brighton': F. Bickley (ed.), *The Glenbervie Journals*, Lord Glenbervie to his son Frederick, MP for Banbury. He exaggerates the number of years since Brummell was in the 10th Light Dragoons by five years: Brummell left in 1798; Lord Glenbervie was writing in 1816. Vol. II, pp. 193–4.

p. 344 'The hotel . . . was frequented by none but': F. Coghlan, *A Guide to France*, p. 16.

p. 345 'three guineas extra': ibid., p. 11.

p. 345 'Listed as a joiner': L.-N. Berthe, P. Bougard, D. Canlier *et al* (eds), *Villes et Villages du Pas-de-Calais en 1790*, pp. 502–3. 1790 '*Questionnaire*' '*Leleu . . . menuisier.*' Garde Nationale, formed 21 August 1789; 545 names, p. 502.

p. 346 'between London and Paris': T. Raikes, *Reminiscences*, p. 275; also, Pückler-Muskau quotes Brummell as describing himself as '*le ci-devant jeune homme qui passe sa vie entre Paris et Londres*', in L. Melville, *Beau Brummell*, p. 165.

p. 346 'Next he papered': W. Jesse, *A Life*, 1844, vol. 1, p. 350.

p. 346 'a large cabinet with brass wire doors': ibid.

p. 347 'The quayside was rebuilt': C. Borde, *Calais et la Mer 1814–1914*, p. 37; 442 crossings between mid-October and mid-November 1818.

p. 347 'The Dukes of Wellington, Richmond, Beaufort': W. Jesse, *A Life*, 1844, vol. 1, p. 109.

p. 347 'pays the former patriarch': Prince Pückler-Muskau, in L. Melville, *Beau Brummell*, p. 165.

p. 347 '2lb of Façon de Paris': K. Campbell, *Beau Brummell*, p. 126.

p. 347 'Mr Brummell is the happiest of men': ibid., p. 133.

p. 348 'I have heard all about your late tricks': H. Wilson, *Memoirs of Harriette Wilson*, 1831, vol. 4, pp. 207ff.

p. 349 'nature itself' . . . 'at a little distance': R. H. Stoddard (ed.), *Personal Reminiscences*, p. 274. Raikes dated the letter as 22 May 1816, only two days after Brummell's arrival, which seems dubious given Brummell's obvious familiarity with Calais.

p. 349 'As to the alteration in my looks': ibid., pp. 272–4.

p. 349 'It was wrongly assumed at the time': D. Hayden, *Pox*, pp. 58ff.

p. 350 'and expressed surprise that he had never learned to speak': '*que c'etoit aussi etonnat qu'heureux qu'il n'eut jamais appris à parler François en Angleterre [sic]*', H. Wilson, *Memoirs*, vol. 4, pp. 207ff.

p. 350 'I would have kept him for nothing': W. Jesse, *A Life*, 1844, vol. I, p. 344.

p. 350 'We used to call him *le roi de Calais*': ibid., vol II, pp. 13–14.

p. 350 'running schoolboy joke about their bad French': 'Prostrate my remembrances at the feet of Mrs Marshall and all your family . . . tell me whether it *makes* fine or bad weather', letter, G. Brummell to Captain Marshall, W. Jesse, *A Life*, 1844, vol. II, p. 37.

p. 351 'surprised to find the sudden': R. H. Stoddard (ed.), *Personal Reminiscences*, pp. 272–3.

p. 351 'I dine at five, and my evening': ibid., pp. 272–4.

p. 351 '*Ah, voilà Monsieur Brummell*': W. Jesse, *A Life*, 1844, vol. 1, p. 337.

p. 352 'I could hardly believe my eyes': Hobhouse visited Brummell in July 1817 in the company of Scrope Davies. T. A. J. Burnett, *The Rise and Fall of a Regency Dandy*, p. 121.

p. 352 'Brummell, in great distress standing at her side': W. Jesse, *A Life*, 1844, vol. 1, p. 363.

p. 352 'Like a true cynic': ibid., p. 364.

14: MALE AND FEMALE COSTUME AND OTHER WORKS, 1821–9

p. 354 '£5000 for The Memoirs . . . going to Calais to treat with Brummell': J. B. Priestley (ed.), *Tom Moore's Diary*, p. 19.

p. 354 'set everything at defiance': L. Melville, *Beau Brummell*, p. 140.

p. 354 '*Memoirs by Herself*': 1825, but rumoured for some years beforehand.

p. 355 'I promised the Duchess': T. Raikes, *Journals*, vol. I, pp. 146ff.

p. 355 'I have been almost constantly occupied . . .': RA/GEO 22219–20. Letter from G. Brummell to Lord Petersham, Calais, 18 October 1818.

p. 357 'all born in the years when Brummell had shared': J. and P. Foord-Kelcey, *Mrs Fitzherbert and Sons*, pp. 48ff, pp. 72–3 and 112ff.

p. 358 'A purse, a card-case, a note keeper': W. Jesse, *A Life*, 1844, vol. 1, p. 108.

p. 358 '*paravent*, or in vulgar English, a folding screen': RA/GEO 22219–20. Letter from G. Brummell to Lord Petersham, Calais, 18 October 1818.

p. 358 'scraps of allegories . . . Cupids': ibid.

p. 359 'with as much nicety': W. Jesse, *A Life*, 1844, vol. 1, p. 355.

p. 359 'These included strident caricatures': Museum of London, Prints Collection, 245.13, *West End Characters*.

p. 359 'Wellington after Hoppner, half length': RA/GEO 22219–20. Letter from G. Brummell to Lord Petersham, Calais, 18 October 1818.

p. 360 'I've lost my way, ma'am': W. Jesse, *A Life*, 1844, vol. 1, pp. 359ff.

p. 360 'deep regret of all the world': ibid., vol. II, p. 6. Back of 'The Petition for a Newfoundland Dog', given to the Duchess of York in 1815 and passed on to Brummell (the petition, not the dog).

p. 360 'He weighed ten stone thirteen pounds': Berry Brothers' Weighing Books, 'George Brummell, Esq 1822. July 26 10, 13 Boots'.

p. 361 'He is at length king!': R. H. Stoddard (ed.), *Personal Reminiscences*, p. 274.

p. 361 'bread and water and straw': i.e., French debtors' prison.

p. 361 'lying on straw and grinning through': H. Cole, *Beau Brummell*, p. 138.

p. 362 'sadness and despondency': J. F. Tattershall, *Reminiscences of a Literary Life, Charles Macfarlane*, pp. 269ff. Macfarlane was *en route* to 'southern Italy', probably Naples. He wrote a series of travel books on Italy: *Popular Customs and Recollections of Southern Italy* (1846), *Sicily* (1849) and *Glance at Revolutionary Italy* (1849). It was almost certainly the first of these that was the subject of his travel and research in 1820.

p. 363 'King of Hanover': According to Salic Law, the Hanoverian throne could not pass to a woman so in 1837, with the accession of Queen Victoria, it was alienated from the British Crown.

p. 363 'If my observations were shrewd': J. Tattershall (ed.), *Reminiscences*, p. 270.

p. 363 'Falstaff was not so sad'; ibid.

p. 364 'I was standing at my shop door': W. Jesse, *A Life*, 1844, vol. II, pp 7–8.

p. 364 'He later claimed it was his best brandy': Major Chambre, *Recollections of West End Life*, p. 285.

p. 365 'And here the conversation closed': W. Jesse, *A Life*, 1844, vol. II, pp. 10–11.

p. 366 '*Male and Female Costume*': *Male and Female Costume, Grecian and Roman Costume, British Costume from the Roman Invasion until 1822* was lost for many years. It came on the market first in 1856, and was owned in the early 1920s by Messrs E. Parsons and Sons, antiquarian booksellers on London's Brompton Road. An enterprising New Yorker, Eleanor Parker, bought it from Bretano's Antiquarian

Books in Manhattan, who, presumably, had it from Parsons. It was published in America in 1932 and reissued in 1972.

p. 367 'Did any men ever look like Greeks': G. Brummell, *Male and Female Costume*, p. 123.

p. 367 'there is quite as much vanity': ibid., p. 122.

p. 367 'the minor poet who goes into company': ibid.

p. 367 'The reader will observe': ibid., p. 127.

p. 368 'those who emasculate themselves': ibid., p. 129.

p. 368 'His facial, head and body hair': P. Ricord, *Illustrations of Syphilitic Disease*.

p. 368 'the age of Men in Black': J. Harvey, *Men in Black*,

p. 368 '1. In the composition': G. Brummell, *Male and Female Costume*, pp. 313ff.

p. 370 'that by contrasting . . . a comparitive fairness': ibid., p. 315.

p. 370 'the taste of British women': ibid., p. 133.

p. 370 'at once heightens the beholder's interest': ibid., pp. 311–12.

p. 370 'generally formed of horsehair': ibid., p. 296.

p. 371 'my companion and myself found that dinner': W. Pitt Lennox, *Celebrities I Have Known*, vol. 1, p. 298.

p. 371 'pale and emaciated; his still well-fitting': ibid., pp. 298ff.

p. 388 'abusing Brummell – said he was a damned fellow': Charles Greville, *Letters*, in H. Cole, *Beau Brummell*, p. 155.

p. 372 'investments worth over £40,000': O. Munson, *Maria Fitzherbert*, p. 339.

p. 372 'one of several children': J. and P. Foord-Kelcey, *Mrs Fitzherbert and Sons*, pp. 48ff and 72–3.

p. 372 'according to his prospective mother-in-law': Bodleian Library, North Family MSS d 30 and 31: letter, Mrs Fitzherbert to Lady Guildford, not dated but *c.* 24 July 1822.

p. 372 'To Lieut Col the Hon George Dawson': MSS owned by Earl Fortescue in 1924, in L. Melville, *Beau Brummell*, p. 167.

p. 372 'Calais August 12 1828': ibid., p. 168.

p. 375 'Rue Royale, Calais. I am persuaded': ibid., pp. 154–5.

p. 376 'I am censured by very high authorities!': H. Wilson, *Memoirs of Harriette Wilson*, 1825, vol. 7, pp. 321–9.

p. 377 'I was naturally desirous': Major Chambre, *Recollections*, vol. 1, pp. 282–3.

p. 377 'The letter [of introduction]': Very likely from Lord Alvanley whom Major Chambre knew in London.

p. 377 'moistened with cold green tea': Major Chambre, *Recollections*, vol. 1, p. 286.

p. 378 'Whenever any one of my creditor calls upon me': ibid., p. 292.

p. 378 'curious snuff-boxes, articles': ibid., pp. 292–3.

p. 378 'At auction one tea-set': Cole, *Beau Brummell*, p. 161.

p. 479 I cannot judge whether long residence': Prince Pückler-Muskau, in W. Jesse, *A Life*, 1844, vol. II, pp. 17–19, 'I am up to date about everything [said Brummell]. But what use is it to me? They've left me to starve here. I am hoping however that my old friend the Duke of Wellington will one fine day send the current consul here to China, and will then nominate me to replace him. Then I will be saved!'

p. 379 'Sir Robert Wilson, London/Dover': BL MSS Whitefoord Papers, vol. IV, British Museum, Add 36 595; Sir Robert Wilson, Select English Letters, BL Add 30 115.

p. 380 '*great man*': the Duke of Wellington, who directly raised the matter of a consulship with George IV.

p. 380 'Just as gay as ever': C. Greville, *Memoirs*, vol. 1, pp. 282–3.

p. 381 'Leveux's Bill': W. Jesse, *A Life*, 1844, vol. II, pp. 24ff.

p. 383 'One pill, four times a day': J. Oriel, *The Scars of Venus*, p. 83.

p. 383 'Further experiments were performed on infected Coldstream': T. Rose, *Observations on the treatment of syphilis with an account of several cases of that disease in which a cure was effected without mercury*, 1817, Med-Chir. Trans 8:550.

p. 383 'as were the majority of syphilitics well into': J. Oriel, *The Scars of Venus*, pp. 81ff.

p. 384 'My Dear Marshall': L. Melville, *Beau Brummell.*, pp. 159ff.

p. 384 'in spirit to meet a bishop': Dr Michael Henry Thornhill Luscombe, later chaplain to the British Embassy in Paris and Bishop of the Episcopalian Church. He came to later fame as the cleric who officiated at W. M. Thackeray's wedding in Paris in April 1836.

p. 385 'The King's Messenger later avowed': W. Jesse, *A Life*, 1844, vol. II, p. 28.

15: HIS BRITANNIC MAJESTY'S CONSUL, 1830–2

p. 387 'It was to be gold and enamel': W. Jesse, *A Life of George Bryan Brummell Esq.*, 1844, vol. II, p. 30.

p. 387 'The best rooms, the best dinner': ibid.

p. 388 'My Lord, I have this day': G. Brummell to Lord Aberdeen, Foreign Office Records, in H. Cole, *Beau Brummell*, p. 166.

p. 388 'founded by the same medieval english king': King Henry VI.

p. 389 'October 25th 1830, rue de Carmes': W. Jesse, *A Life*, 1844, vol. II, pp. 33ff.

p. 390 '*Amphytrions de nos compatriots*': Amphytrion, a gourmet and food-lover; from the eponymous hero of the Molière comedy but very current in Brummell's France as a term for fine hosts with superior tables, after the success of the *Manuel des Amphytrions*, a guide to gastronomy and the best places to eat in Paris.

p. 391 'The "dirty-nosed children" of the British community': Appendix: British Community in Caen, Protestant Church Records; M. Renard, *Brummell et son ombre*, pp. 248ff.

p. 392 'the Villiers seem to have had mainly young daughters': The Villiers' daughter, Ellen, was believed by some later writers to be the recipient of some of Brummell's love letters. Although the family did move away, which would account for Brummell's letters on partings, and Ellen most likely made trips to England, Aimable still seems the more likely recipient of the most impassioned ones. Several of Brummell's letters to 'Madame' may be to Mrs Villiers.

p. 392 'about his attitude to the Masons': BL Add MSS 41335 380m: Masonic Initiation Certificate, Caen Lodge, L'An de la V L 58 32 le 19ème jour du 2 ème mois (19 February 1832) George Bryan Brummell. Signed by Burton.

p. 393 '*marchande de cosmétiques*': Appendix: British Community in Caen from Protestant Church Records; P. Renard, *Brummell et son ombre*, p. 249.

p. 393 'Madam, you *take* medicine, you *take* a walk': W. Jesse, *A Life*, 1844, vol. II, p. 50.

p. 393 'Don't ask me [about it]': ibid., p. 51.

p. 393 'like the generality of the world': ibid., p. 52.

p. 393 'My Dear Mrs [Burton]': Jesse does not name the married lady to whom Brummell wrote, but the scale of the soirée and their clear intimacy make it most likely that he addressed the wife of his fellow mason, Colonel Francis Burton; W. Jesse, *A Life*, 1844, vol. II, pp. 52–4. Melville places it in Calais, but the reference to Corbet as well as Jesse's positioning of the letter puts it in Caen in the early 1830s.

p. 394 '*Mes Adieux*': W. Jesse, *A Life*, 1844, vol. II, p. 54.

p. 395 'With these his reserve gave way': ibid., pp. 55–6.

p. 395 'November 1831': ibid., pp. 67–9.

p. 396 'Thursday Evening. It is vain I had promised': ibid., p. 69.

p. 397 'Dear Miss Aimable, You have recently made': L. Melville, *Beau Brummell*, p. 152.

p. 397 'To Miss Aimable, rue des Carmes, 2nd December 1832': W. Jesse, *A Life*, 1927, vol. II, pp. 90–1.

p. 398 'Christmas Eve, 1831': ibid., pp. 69–70.

p. 398 'Tuesday. The moment I had begun': W. Jesse, *A Life*, 1844, vol. II, pp. 70–1.

p. 400 'Tuesday, July. Millions of thanks': ibid., pp. 122–5.

p. 400 '*Ayesha*': *The Maid of Kars*, a novel by James Justinian Morier, 1832.

p. 402 'Saturday evening, August': W. Jesse, *A Life*, 1927, vol. II, pp. 98–9. Jesse dates this letter as August 1833 but a letter to Aimable that he places as 1832 mentions the same poem that Brummell first enclosed with this one.

p. 402 'Luc-Sur-Mer, Tuesday evening': ibid., pp. 104–5.

p. 403 'Luc-Sur-Mer, Monday morning': ibid., pp. 117–8.

p. 403 'Monday, I am ashamed to send you': ibid., pp. 70–1.

p. 404 'His dress on the evening in question': W. Jesse, *A Life*, 1844, vol. II, pp. 76–7.

p. 404 'and perhaps the more prized by Brummell': ibid., p. 81.

p. 405 'I scarcely expected to find myself': ibid., pp. 59–60.

p. 405 'I therefore beg you to consider': ibid., pp. 60–1.

p. 406 'I may represent to Your Lordship': G. Brummell to Viscount Palmerston, 19 May 1831, Foreign Officer Papers, National Archives; H. Cole, *Beau Brummell*, p. 174.

p. 407 'Thursday evening. It would be trespassing': W. Jesse, *A Life*, 1927, vol. II, pp. 118–21.

p. 408 'À Mademoiselle, Luc-Sur-Mer': ibid., pp. 125–6.

p. 408 'Mme de St Ursain, M. de Ste Marie': Working from the journals of the Countess de Chazot, whose husband was a friend of Brummell, Marcel Madelaine, writing in *Liberté*, 29 July 1988, relates details of a picnic attended by Brummell. Archives Municipales de Caen,

p. 408 'À Mademoiselle, Luc-Sur-Mer, Saturday, July 20th': W. Jesse, *A Life*, 1927, vol. II, pp. 127–8.

p. 409 'Dear Armstrong, I have been reduced': ibid., pp. 48–9.

p. 410 'À Monsieur Armstrong': ibid., p. 49.

p. 410 'I am positively pressed': ibid., p. 50.

p. 411 'March 21 1832. Sir': PRO Foreign Office Papers. H. Cole, *Beau Brummell*, p. 182.

p. 412 'Send me seventy-five francs to pay': W. Jesse, *A Life*, 1844, vol. II, p. 107.

p. 412 'I really think that a personal interview': ibid., pp. 107–8.

p. 413 'As it has pleased His Majesty's Government': PRO Foreign Office Papers. H. Cole, *Beau Brummell*, p. 186.

p. 414 'Oh this uncomfortable weather!' W. Jesse, *A Life*, 1844, vol. II, p. 109–10.

p. 414 'Whate'er they promised or profess'd': ibid., p. 110 and note: 'These words are General Fitzpatrick's.'

p. 414 'Tabetic neurosyphilis . . . Sudden paralysis was a classic symptom': S. M. Brooks, *The VD Story*, pp. 34ff.

p. 415 'and those excruciating spasms': W. Jesse, *A Life*, 1844, vol. II, p. 111.

16: HÔTEL D'ANGLETERRE, 1832–5

p. 416 'My papers are the only things': W. Jesse, *A Life of George Bryan Brummell Esq.*, 1844, vol. II, pp. 182–4.

p. 417 'Yesterday morning': L. Melville, *Beau Brummell*, pp. 146–7. In his collection of the Jesse letters and others, Melville places this in Calais. If so, Brummell had a series of passionate epistolary flirtations with women, married and unmarried, from the earliest days of his time in France. It bears such marked similarity with his terms of address to Aimable that I believe it dates from just after his departure from Madame de St-Ursain's.

p. 417 'would put an end to my sufferings in this world': W. Jesse, *A Life*, 1844, vol. II, p. 111.

p. 418 'As a parting gift, he gave her his entire Album': Cole is of the opinion that the recipient of Brummell's later letters was not Aimable de St-Ursain but Ellen Villiers, daughter of one of the English families. Jesse does distinguish between the earlier and later letters, but there is much to link them: Jesse introduces the recipient of the later letters as 'Brummell's favourite correspondent' and she clearly has French, English and Italian, like Aimable. Jesse was trying to protect the reputation of Mademoiselle St-Ursain, whose family he knew.

p. 418 'You are going away': W. Jesse, *A Life*, 1927, vol. II, p. 133.

p. 419 'Caen, March 1834': ibid., pp. 135–7. Petrarch trans. Boe Paschall and author's own.

p. 420 'To Miss [Aimable]': ibid., pp. 137–9.

p. 420 'visible effect on the mucous membrane': *Lancet*, vol. 336, 7 March 1840, p. 787.

p. 421 'in Paris and Dublin as alternative or complementary': J. Oriel, *The Scars of Venus*, pp. 87ff.

p. 422 'scattered inflammatory oozing': C. Drysdale, *On the Treatment of Syphilis and Other Diseases* and evidence from after the Peninsular Wars quoted in J. Stokes et al. (eds), *Modern Clinical Syphilology*, p. 217.

p. 422 'The last vestige of his hair': W. Jesse, *A Life*, 1844, vol. II, p. 153.

p. 422 'I am unwell': ibid., p. 156.

p. 423 '[August] 1834. My Dear Alvanley': ibid., pp. 168–9.

p. 425 'By now all of the other guests were awake': ibid., pp. 182–4.

p. 425 'exhibition of flowers': *L'Ami de la Verité*, 27 April 1835, Archives Municipales de Caen.

p. 425 'all charged with vagabondage': ibid., 8 May 1835, Archives Municipales de Caen.

17: PRISON, 1835–9

p. 426 'I still breathe, though I am not of the living': W. Jesse, *A Life of George Bryan Brummell Esq.*, 1927, vol. II, p. 142.

p. 427 'put with all the *common* people': Jesse, *A Life*, 1844, vol. II, p. 186.

p. 428 'applications should be made in person': *L'Ami de la Verité*, 17 April 1835, Archives Municipales de Caen.

p. 428 'It struggled on . . . for several years, without him': *Ami de la Verité*, Archives Municipales de Caen. Godefroi was released in 1839. He accompanied Jesse on a tour of the prison in 1843. The prison was demolished in 1906 to make way for an exit road from the Place Fontette.

p. 428 'probably prolong his detention': W. Jesse, *A Life*, 1927, vol. II, p. 164.

p. 428 'There was a communicating fireplace': *Plan Général au rez de chaussée de Prisons Royales de la Ville de Caen*, ADCC.

p. 429 '11 May [1835]': Jesse, *A Life*, 1927, vol. II, p. 149.

p. 429 'towers of Matilda': The Abbaye des Dames was founded by Queen Matilda, consort of King William I.

p. 429 'You will perceive the extremities': Jesse, *A Life*, 1844, vol. II, pp. 194–5.

p. 429 'In Prison, Saturday. Dear Armstrong': Jesse, *A Life*, 1927, vol. II, p. 151.

p. 430 'In Prison, Monday. My Dear Armstrong': ibid., pp. 152–4.

p. 431 'In prison, June. My Dear Armstrong, You would not': ibid., pp. 174–5.

p. 433 'actually washed and shaved': ibid., vol. II, p. 156 (my italics).

p. 433 '*chambre des prisonniers civils*': *Plan Général au rez de chaussée de Prisons Royales de la Ville de Caen*, ADCC.

p. 434 'Most earnestly I thank you for amiable billet': Jesse, *A Life*, 1927, vol. II, pp. 57–9.

p. 435 'À Madame [Burton]': ibid., pp. 160–61.

p. 435 'À Madame [Burton], During the principal part': ibid., pp. 167–8.

p. 436 'In Prison, Wednesday. You are always': ibid., pp. 162–3.

p. 436 'this poet, this great man': ibid., p. 167, *'ce poète, ce grand homme, fut mon ami'*.

p. 436 'You are aware that poor Brummell': PRO. Foreign Office Papers. H. Cole, *Beau Brummell*, pp. 211–12.

p. 437 'In Prison, July. You will soon be as well acquainted': W. Jesse, *A Life*, 1927, vol. II, pp. 199–200.

p. 438 'and the originality of his character': W. Jesse, *A Life*, 1844, vol. II, p. 251.

p. 438 'Longuet's provided mushrooms, and truffles': ibid., p. 252.

p. 439 'as a man of business': ibid., pp. 256–7.

p. 439 'July 1835. My Lords': Draft letter, 27 July 1835. (This money followed that which secured Brummell's immediate release.) Foreign Office MSS, in H. Cole, *Beau Brummell*, pp. 213–214.

p. 440 'the slightest surprise or joy': W. Jesse, *A Life*, 1844, vol. II, p. 263.

p. 440 'an air of nonchalance': ibid., p. 264.

p. 441 'shaken his intellect': ibid., p. 303.

p. 441 'ridiculous words [of the title]': ibid., p. 288.

p. 442 'You are, I dare say, anxious for your album': W. Jesse, *A Life*, 1927, vol. II, pp. 213–14.

p. 442 *Tabes dorsalis* . . . nerves of his lower limbs and back': D. Hayden, *Pox*, p. 58.

p. 443 'brought himself down to one': W. Jesse, *A Life*, 1844, vol. II, p. 296.

p. 443 'Mullet, the bootmaker, has this instant': W. Jesse, *A Life*, 1927, vol. II, p. 228.

p. 444 'Do not any more be out of temper': ibid., p. 229.

p. 444 'a great change . . . in his personal appearance': W. Jesse, *A Life*, 1844, vol. II, p. 300.

p. 444 'When Armstrong sent him a new winter': ibid., vol. II, p. 303.

p. 444 'drawling with prolixity': W. Jesse, *A Life*, 1844, vol. II, p. 304.

p. 445 *Letters* cited in Bibliog. Also *Tom Moore's Diary*, ed. J. B. Priestley 'The poor Beau's head's gone': W. Dowden (ed.), *The Journal of Thomas Moore*, Vol. 5, pp. 1892–3; diary entry, July 1837.

p. 445 'I was ashamed to see so famous and distinguished': 'J'avais honte de voir un homme si celebre et si distinguée et qui s'etait crée une place dans l'histoire dans un état si malheureux.' W. Jesse, *A Life*, 1844, vol. II, p. 308.

p. 446 'Keen blows the wind, and piercing is the cold': ibid., p. 312.

p. 446 'In the winter of 1837–8': ibid., p. 314.

p. 447 'It is, I can assure you': W. Jesse, *A Life*, 1927, vol. II, pp. 232–3.

p. 448 'a precursor of': Letter from Scrope Davies, Monday, 25 May 1835; T. Raikes, *A Portion of his Journal from 1831–1847*, vol. II, pp. 113ff.

p. 448 'Right before madness': D. Haydn, *Pox*, p. 56.

p. 449 'Suddenly, and as if divided into two': J. B. d'Aurevilly, trans. D. B. Wyndham Lewis, *The Anatomy of Dandyism*, pp. 59–61.

p. 450 'Finally, when the room was full': ibid.

p. 450 'but kindly': W. Jesse, *A Life*, 1844, vol. II, pp. 319–20.

p. 450 'from royal personages': ibid., p. 322.

p. 450 *'Avez-vous entendu les nouvelles?'*: ibid., p. 325.

p. 451 'I have deferred writing for some time': W. Jesse, *A Life*, 1927, vol. II, pp. 251–2.

p. 451 'His linen . . . was changed once a month': W. Jesse, *A Life*, 1844, vol. II, p. 331.

p. 451 'In January 1839': Jesse claimed Brummell was not moved to Bon Sauveur until May, but the asylum records place his date of entry as 17 January and his first proper examination by Dr Vastel as 2 February. Archives de l'Hôpital Psychiatrique du Bon Sauveur, Caen, January 1839.

p. 452 ' *"Bonjour, Monsieur!"* said Fichet': W. Jesse, *A Life*, 1844, vol. II, pp. 346ff.

18: ASYLUM, 1839–40.

p. 453 'It's like being bound hand and foot': D. Haydn, *Pox*, pp. xiff.

p. 453 'Babylon in all its desolation': T. Raikes, *A Portion of his Journal*, vol. II, pp. 113ff. Letter from Scrope Davies, Monday, 25 May 1835. Davies appears to be writing about his own impending symptoms of tertiary syphilis, as diagnosed by Sir George Tuthill. He is advised 'on such occasions [as an outbreak, to] avoid all possible excitement, or the consequences must be most lamentable'.

p. 454 'corporal infirmity and mental affliction': AMC, Medical Records, G. Brummell, Hôpital du Bon Sauveur, Caen. Entered 17 January 1839. Signed by John Kelly, MD, 24 January 1839, countersigned by Edouard Vastel, 18 January 1839 and 1 February 1839.

p. 455 'salubrious and well aired': P. Morel and C. Quetel, *Du Bon Sauveur au CHS*, p. 26.

p. 455 'each madman has his own cell': ibid. p. 26. 'Mère Supérieure en 1818, 'chaque insense à sa cellule . . . ils sont plus tranquilles et plus sainement dans des chambres isolée.'

p. 456 '1. A total "rupture" from normality': ibid., pp. 48–9.

p. 457 *'Brummell, Georges, célibataire'*: AMC MSS, 'Age et domicile du malade, Brummell, Georges. 17 Janvier 1839', Archive de l'Hôpital Psychiatrique du Bon Sauveur.

p. 457 'A half hour after the inmates were woken': P. Morel and C. Quetel, *Du Bon Sauveur*, pp. 55–6.

p. 457 'tubful of warm water': P. Ricord, *Illustrations of Syphilitic Disease*, pp. 71–3.

p. 458 'general paresis, the terms used interchangeably': Alexander Morison of Bethlem Hospital (Bedlam) gave a good description of general paresis in 1840 and observed that Esquirol (1814 and 1838) and Palmeil (1826) had previously termed the condition 'general paralysis of the insane'. 'The possible relation of syphilis to general paresis was commented upon by Esmarch and Jesser as early as 1857, while Kjelberg of Uppsala in 1863 expressed the definitive opinion that syphilitic infection was invariably the cause of general paresis or general paralysis. Not until 1913 were Moore and Noguchi able to demonstrate the presence of Spirochaete pallida in the brains of general paretics.' C. Worster-Drought, *Neurosyphilis*, p. 118.

p. 458 *'folles, incensés et alienés'*: P. Morel and C. Quetel, *Du Bon Sauveur*, p. 57.

p. 459 'this excellent nurse of mine': W. Jesse, *A Life*, 1927, vol. II, p. 266.

p. 460 'violent, mutinous, chronically deranged': P. Morel and C. Quetel, *Du Bon Sauveur*, p. 60.

p. 460 'All the mucous membranes of Brummell's body': J. Beaney, *Constitutional Syphilis . . . in its Secondary and Tertiary Phases*.

p. 460 'Gummy tumours': P. Ricord, *Illustrations of Syphilitic Disease*, pp. 327ff.

p. 460 'unbleeding buboes': J. Bacot, *A Treatise on Syphilis*, pp. 223ff.

p. 461 *'Table d'hôte toujours'*: W. Jesse, *A Life*, 1844, vol. II, p. 348.

p. 461 'sinking further and further': AMC, Archives du Bon Sauveur, G. Brummell, 1839–40. 'Le malade s'affaisse de plus en plus, fevrier 1840, idem mars – il est mort le 30 mars 1840.'

p. 461 'but the local records': ADCC, MSS 80F7.

p. 461 'Mr Brummell was in an imbecile state': W. Jesse, *A Life*, 1844, vol. II, pp. 349–50.

p. 462 'it had rained almost daily since January': *The Times*, 5 April 1840, reporting the newly arrived French papers.

p. 462 *'ayant l'air d'implorer'*: Jesse uses her original French in his report.

p. 462 'an extra fifty francs was paid': ADCC, 80F44, no. 49 in the cemetery Register of Concessions.

p. 463 *'Qui est-ce?'*: 'Les Dix Ans de la vie caennais du "dandy" ', *Caen Hebdo*, 21 April 1971, quoting local story.

19: EPILOGUE

p. 464 'I sometimes think that there are': O. Wilde, *The Picture of Dorian Gray*, in *The Complete Works of Oscar Wilde*, pp. 9–10.

p. 464 *'Punch* has received exclusive': *Punch*, 18 May 1844, in C. Jerrold, *The Beaux and the Dandies*, p. 273.

p. 465 'at the heart of a galaxy of talent': O. Millar, *Later Georgian Pictures*, vol. 1, p. xxviii.

p. 465 'his activities were immediately misrepresented': H. Clifford Smith, 'Buckingham Palace', in *Country Life*, 1931, p. 34.

p. 465 'I have seen the rise of the Father': K. Cave, K. Garlick and A. Macintyre (eds), *The Diary of Joseph Farington*, vol. XV, p. 5179.

p. 465 'The pavilion at Bon Sauveur': J. B. d'Aurevilly, trans. D. B. Wyndham Lewis, *The Anatomy of Dandyism*, p. 61.

p. 468 'It is possible to make the case': C. McDowell, *The Man of Fashion*, p. 59.

p. 469 'the dawn of modern concepts of self': D. Wahrman, *The Making of the Modern Self*.

p. 469 'I have drawn for the Hero of my work': E. Bulwer Lytton, *Pelham*, p. vi.

p. 470 'Bulwer Lytton and Disraeli': R. K. Garelick, *Rising Star*, p. 6.

p. 471 'the sceptre of Brummell': J. Boulenger, *Sous Louis-Philippe*, p. 48.

p. 471 'According to one recent biographer': N. Foulkes, *The Last of the Dandies*.

p. 471 'the lover of the bride's father': For a full discussion of d'Orsay's sexuality, see ibid., p. 105.

p. 472 'Byron described d'Orsay': P. Quennell (ed.), *Genius in the Drawing Room*, p. 720.

p. 473 'We owe to Brummell the demonstration': H. de Balzac, 'Traité de la vie Élégante', *Oeuvres Complètes*, vol. 2,

p. 473 'in all periods of transition': C. Baudelaire, *Le Peintre de la vie moderne in Art in Paris, 1845–1862*, pp. 27–8.

p. 474 'I find it harder every day to live up to': O. Wilde, in S. Calloway and D. Colvin, *The Exquisite Life of Oscar Wilde*, p. 19.

p. 474 'Dandy of dress, dandy of speech': M. mac Liammóir, *The Importance of Being Oscar*, p. 22.

p. 475 'Basil is what I think I am': V. Holland, M. Holland and R. Hart-Davies (eds), *Complete Letters of Oscar Wilde*, p. 352.

p. 475 'the look of an amateur playing Lord Byron': Calloway and Colvin, *Exquisite Life*, p. 37.

p. 476 'a work of art in himself': S. Walden, *Whistler and His Mother*, p. 159.

p. 476 'at least three hours peruses': A. Pushkin, *Eugene Onegin*, p. 15.

p. 476 'No lasting truths', ibid.

p. 477 'Humbert Humbert': J. Feldman, 'Nabokov's Dandy', in *Gender on the Divide*, chapter 7.

p. 277 'presents himself to the nation': J. Felstiner and V. Gollancz, *The Art of Lies*, p. 17.

p. 477 'sixty-eight pairs of trousers': ibid., pp. 17–18.

p. 477 'symmetry, austerity, subtlety': Felstiner and Gollancz, *The Art of Lies*, p. 18.

p. 477 'to live and die in the mirror': 'Il doit vivre et mourir devant un miroir', 1892, applying Baudelaire's aphorism to Beerbohm, ibid., p. 19.

p. 477 'the liberty of all expression': ibid., pp. 21–2.

p. 477 'Dandyism is ever the outcome': M. Beerbohm, *Dandies and Dandies, p.* 6.

p. 478 'In 1929 Virginia Woolf': V. Woolf, *Beau Brummell* pp. 5–8.

p. 478 'Between the days of the eighteenth-century': A. Camus, *L'Homme Revolté*, trans. Anthony Bower, *The Dandy's Rebellion*, p. 49.

p. 479 'image was founded on the Beau Brummell principle': R. Garelick, quoting Anne Hollander in *Dandies: Fashion and Finesse in Art and Culture*, ed. Susan Fillin-Yeh, p. 53.

p. 480 'Her work and her legacy': ibid., pp. 53ff.

p. 480 'and as the dandy is the nineteenth century's': S. Sontag, *Susan Sontag Reader*, pp. 105–19.

p. 480 'Regency Quentin Crisp': Garelick, *Dandies: Fashion and Finesse*, pp. 272–3.

p. 480 'I am a Bond Street Beau': Frank W. Green, music by Alfred Lee, from *Lee Vocal Music*, British Library Music Collection.

p. 482 'In 2002, a statue': by Czech sculptor Irena Sedlecka.

p. 482 'To inoculate contemporary clothing': R. Barthes, *Le Dandysme et la Mode*, pp. 312–15.

p. 482 'a cross between Versace and the late': G. Walden, *London Evening Standard*, 11 June 2001.

p. 483 'Dandyism, the position of "entertaining antithetical" ': *Twiggy and Trotsky or What the Soviet Dandy will be Wearing This Five Year Plan*, by Allen Svede, in S. Fillin-Yeh (ed.), *Dandies: Fashion and Finesse in Art and Culture*, p. 243.

Appendix: Chapter-title Illustrations

The chapter-title illustrations and the explanations below are taken from *Necklothitania or Tietania, Being an Essay on Starchers by One of the Cloth*, printed for J. J. Stockdale, 41 Pall Mall, London, in 1818 and the slightly later *The Art of Tying the Cravat* by H. Le Blanc.

Prologue, Introduction, Chapters 1 and 2: The Art of Putting on the Cravat; The Gordian Knot

In the first place the cravat for this tie must be of ample size and properly starched, ironed and folded. It will then be necessary to meditate deeply and seriously on the five following directions:

1. When you have decided on the cravat, it must be placed on the back of the neck, and the ends left hanging.
2. You must take the point K, pass it on the inside of point Z and raise it.
3. You lower the point K on the tie, now half-formed O.
4. Then, without leaving the point K, you bend it inside and draw it between the point Z which you repass to the left, Y; in the tie now formed, Y, O, you thus accomplish the formation of the desired knot.
5. And last, after having tightened the knot, and flattened it with the thumb and fore-finger, or more properly with the iron, you lower the points K, Z, cross them, and place a pin at the point of junction H, and at once solve the problem of the Gordian Knot. He who is perfectly conversant with the theory and practice of this tie, may truly boast that he possesses the key to all the others, which are, in fact, derived from this alone. A Cravat that has once been worn in this way, can only be used afterwards *en négligée*, as it will be so much tumbled by the intricate arrangement.

Chapter 3: Mathematical Tie

There are three creases in the Mathematical or Triangular Tie. On coming down from under each ear, till it meets the bow of the neck-cloth, and a third, in an horizontal direction, stretching from one of the side indentures to the other. The colour best suited to it, is that called *couleur de la cuisse d'une nymphe emue* [trembling nymph's thigh].

Chapter 4: Tie Collier de Cheval

This style greatly resembles the Oriental, from which it is evidently derived. It has been greatly admired by the fair sex, who have praised it to their husbands, their lovers, and even to their relations, and have thus promoted its adoption by every means in their power. The ends are fastened at the back of the neck, or are concealed in the folds; a whalebone stiffener is requisite, but starch is unnecessary.

Chapter 5: Oriental Tie

The Oriental Tie (not City dandies but owes its appellation to the Gentlemen of the East India College) is made with very stiff and rigid cloth so that there cannot be the least danger of its yielding or bending to the exertions and sudden twists of the head and neck. Care should be taken, that not a single indenture or crease should be visible in this tie: it must present a round, smooth and even surface – the least deviation from this rule will prevent its being so named.

This neck-cloth ought not to be attempted, unless full confidence and reliance can be placed in its stiffness. It must not be made with coloured neck-cloths but of the brilliant white.

Chapter 6: Sentimental Tie

The name alone of this cravat is sufficient to explain that it is not alike suitable to all faces. Be assured that if your physiognomy does not inspire sensations of love and passion, and you should adopt the *Cravat Sentimentale* . . . It is for the juvenile only, and they should be something boyish in the general appearance of the wearer. It may be worn from the age of seventeen to twenty-seven; but after that age it cannot. It is more fashionable in the country than in town. Cambric is generally preferred.

Chapter 7: Horse Collar Tie

The Horse Collar has become, from some unaccountable reason, very universal. I can only attribute it to the inability of its wearers to make any other. It is certainly the worst and most vulgar, and I should not have given it a place in these pages, were it not for the purpose of cautioning my readers, from ever wearing it. It has the appearance of a great half-moon, or horse-collar. I sincerely hope it will soon be dropped entirely – *nam super omnes vitandum est.*

Chapter 8: Tie à l'Américaine or à la Washington

The shape of the *Cravate à l'Américaine* is extremely pretty and easily formed, provided the handkerchief is well starched. When it is correctly formed it presents the appearance of a column destined to support a Corinthian capital. This style has many admirers here, and also among our friends the fashionable of New York, who pride themselves on its name, which they call 'Independence'; this title may, to a certain point, be disputed, as the neck is fixed in a kind of vice, which entirely prohibits any very free movements. It requires a whalebone stiffener, and is commenced in the same way as the Gordian Knot, the ends are brought in front and lowered and fastened to the shirt bosom, like the *Cravat en Cascade.*

Chapter 9: Maharatta Tie

The Maharatta, or Nabob Tie, is very cool, as it is always made with fine muslin neck-cloths. It is first placed on the back of the neck, the ends are then brought forward, and joined as a chain-link, the remainder is then turned back, and fastened behind. Its colour: *Eau d'Ispahan.*

Chapter 10: Ball Room Tie

The Ball Room Tie when well put on, is quite delicious. It unites the qualities of the Mathematical and Irish, having two collateral dents and two horizontal ones, the one above as in the former, the other below as in the latter. It has no knot, but is fastened as the Napoleon. This should never of course be made with colours, but with the purest and most brilliant *blanc d'innocence virginale.*

Chapter 11: Trone d'Amour Tie

So called for its resemblance to the Seat of Love. The trone d'amour is the most austere after the Oriental Tie – it must be extremely well stiffened with starch. It is formed by one single horizontal dent in the middle. Colour: *Yeux de fille en extase*.

Chapter 12: The Gordian Knot

Or *Noeud Gordien* – see Chapters 1 and 2.

Chapter 13: Osbaldstone Tie

This neck-cloth is first laid on the back of the neck, the ends are then brought forward, and tied in a large knot, the breadth of which must be at least four inches, and two inches deep. This tie is very well adapted for summer; because instead of going round the neck twice, it confines itself to once. The best colour is ethereal azure.

Chapter 14: Irish Tie

This cravat very closely resembles the Mathematical, and differs only in the arrangement of the ends, which in the Irish are joined in the front and twine round each other – each end is then brought back to the side it comes from, and is fastened at the back of the neck. A whalebone stiffener is necessary.

Chapter 15: Hunting Tie

The Hunting or Diana Tie (not that I suppose Diana ever did wear a Tie) is formed by two collateral dents on each side, and meeting in the middle, without any horizontal ones. It is generally accompanied by a crossing of the ends, as in the Ball Room and Napoleon.

Chapter 16: *Tie en Coquille*

The tie of this cravat should resemble a shell; it is very pleasing, and easily formed; it consists of a double or triple knot, and the ends are fastened at the back of the neck. It does not require starch.

Chapter 17: *Napoleon Tie*

I have heard it said that Napoleon wore one of this sort on his return from Elba, and on board the *Northumberland*. It is first laid on the back of the neck, the ends being brought forwards and crossed, without tying, and then fastened to the braces or carried under the arms and tied on the back. It has a very pretty appearance, giving the wearer a languishingly amorous look. The violet colour, and *la couleur des lèvres d'amour* are the best suited for it.

Chapter 18: *Tie à la Talma*

This style is worn in mourning only. It is placed on the neck in the same way as the Byron.

Chapter 19: *Epilogue: Tie à la Byron*

As Lord Byron differed so widely from the world in general, we can hardly expect to find in the cravat worn by the prince of poets any of that *élégance recherchée* which generally characterizes an Englishman of rank. It is universally allowed that the least constraint of the body has a corresponding effect on the mind, and it must, therefore, be admitted that to a certain extent a tight cravat will cramp the imagination, and, as it were, suffocate the thoughts. That Lord Byron feared this effect is proved from his submitting to the inconveniences of a cravat, only when accommodating himself to the *beinséances* of society, and in every other portrait where he is painted in the ardour of composition, his neck is always free from the trammels of the neck-cloth. The cravat which bears his name differs widely from most others – this difference consists in the manner in which it is first placed on the neck. It is commenced at the back of the neck – the ends are then brought in front under the chin, and fastened in a large bow, or rosette, at least six inches in length and four in circumference. The fashion is extremely comfortable in summer, and during long journeys, as it forms but one turn round the neck, which is thus left comparatively free.

Neck-cloths should always (except those worn in the evening, and even then they may be worn, if the ribs or cheques are not too visible) be made of ribbed or chequed materials, as it makes far better ties than when the stuff is plain. Muslin makes beautiful ties, especially for evenings.

Independently of all these numerous advantages – what an apparent superiority does not a starcher give to a man? It gives him a look of *hauteur* and greatness, which can scarcely be acquired otherwise. This is produced solely by the austere rigidity of the cravat, which so far from yielding to the natural motions of the head, forms a strong support to the cheeks. It pushes them up, and gives a rotundity of appearance on the whole face thereby unquestionably giving a man the air of being puffed up with pride, vanity, and conceit (very necessary, nay, indispensable qualifications for a man of fashion) and appearing as quite towering over the rest of mankind.

Index